Third Edition

FORENSIC SCIENCE
the basics

Third Edition

FORENSIC SCIENCE
the basics

Jay A. Siegel
Emeritus Professor of Forensic Science
Michigan State University
East Lansing, Michigan, USA

Kathy Mirakovits
Portage Northern High School
Portage, Michigan, USA

CRC Press
Taylor & Francis Group
Boca Raton London New York

CRC Press is an imprint of the
Taylor & Francis Group, an **informa** business

CRC Press
Taylor & Francis Group
6000 Broken Sound Parkway NW, Suite 300
Boca Raton, FL 33487-2742

© 2016 by Taylor & Francis Group, LLC
CRC Press is an imprint of Taylor & Francis Group, an Informa business

No claim to original U.S. Government works

Printed and bound in India by Replika Press Pvt. Ltd.

Printed on acid-free paper
Version Date: 20150818

International Standard Book Number-13: 978-1-4822-2333-0 (Hardback)

Visit the Taylor & Francis Web site at
http://www.taylorandfrancis.com

and the CRC Press Web site at
http://www.crcpress.com

Dedication

To Ben and Tommy, my grandsons and my beacons of hope and love for the future.

Jay A. Siegel

To Aaron and Lindsay, my grown-up children, who have given me the desire to be the best role model I can be. I am so proud of all you do and hope you echo the same about me. You have given me hope and joy for a bright tomorrow.

Kathy Mirakovits

Contents

PART II: Tools of the Trade

PART IV: Forensic Biology

PART VI: Legal Aspects of Forensic Science

Preface

Since the second edition of *Forensic Science: The Basics* was published in 2010, there have been a number of noteworthy developments in the field that make this third edition even more compelling. First and foremost, the National Academy of Sciences released a highly anticipated and thought-provoking report on the status of forensic science, "Strengthening Forensic Science in the United States: A Path Forward." Although the report came out in the fall of 2009, its discussions and recommendations continue to reverberate throughout the fields of forensic science as well as the criminal and civil justice systems, the courts, the U.S. Congress, and many of the states. The report praises some aspects of forensic science and is highly critical of others. It makes far-reaching recommendations that have not, at this writing, been implemented. The report has spawned Congressional hearings and legislation. A White House science subcommittee studied the recommendations and possible solutions for more than two years. Currently, a new National Commission on Forensic Science is seeking solutions and implementations of the recommendations and is looking more broadly at the needs of the field.

One of the recommendations of this report calls for increased efforts in the education of the next generation of forensic scientists. The recommendation highlights the need for more highly trained scientists, teachers, and researchers. This ups the ante for high-quality text and reference books that begin the process of educating students in the basic principles of forensic science. The third edition of *Forensic Science: The Basics* builds upon the quality educational values of the second edition to meet these needs.

Like the successful first and second editions of this book, the third edition adheres to the authors' basic philosophy about teaching forensic science: build upon students' knowledge of the natural and physical sciences and introduce them to the applications of science to the justice system. The book takes students through the basic concepts of what makes forensic science a unique blend of criminal justice and science, introducing them to crime scene investigation and the criminal justice system from the crime to the court. It still contains basic foundations in the tools of forensic science, including separation sciences, spectroscopy, and microscopy. Then, this foundation is used to teach students how to apply scientific concepts and methods to analyze evidence. The areas of forensic biology and chemistry are covered in detail as well as the pattern evidence types such as fingerprints, firearms and tool marks, and questioned documents.

Although the basic structure and philosophy of forensic science is maintained in the third edition, there are major changes and especially additions to the lineup. First, in recognition of the importance of the Academy of Sciences report, we provide basic information about the report itself in Chapter 1—Introduction, and then we discuss its implications for the analysis of certain types of evidence and presentation of forensic evidence in court. We have also added three new chapters to the third edition. The new Chapter 7—Detector Dogs as Forensic Tools—is unique to introductory textbooks in forensics. It discusses how dogs are trained and used to discover fire residues, explosives, drugs, and even human remains. Some case studies will illustrate the increasingly important role that dogs play in investigations. This chapter was guest authored by Sue M. Stejskal, a human remains detection (HRD) dog trainer and handler. Sue has many credentials. She is a board-certified toxicologist, licensed veterinary technician, and a special deputy and HRD dog handler with the St. Joseph County (Michigan) Sheriff's Department. With more than 25 years of educational and professional experience, Stejskal has, for the past 10 years, participated in land and water searches throughout Michigan and the central Midwest. She is founder and executive director of Recover K9, a nonprofit organization that provides support for much of her service and educational work. Stejskal is a member of the scientific working group on Dog and Orthogonal Detector Guidelines (SWGDOG). Stejskal's work in toxicology and pathology and her experience as a dog handler led to the development of practical forensic science training for law enforcement dog handlers, detectives, and crime scene technicians. She provides this training for police agencies throughout the country. Sue is the author of the CRC Press book, *Death, Decomposition, and Detector Dogs: From Science to Scene*, 2013.

We have also added a chapter on the rapidly developing use of computers and other electronic devices in both the commission of crimes and their solutions. Chapter 8—Digital Evidence—takes students through the basics of digital devices and their role in crime investigations. Another important area of forensic investigations is engineering. Two of the major areas of engineering sciences, traffic accident reconstruction and failure analysis, are discussed in the new Chapter 9—Forensic Engineering. The authors thank another contributor, Christopher A. Puckett, manager of the accident reconstruction unit at Digits, LLC. Chris has over 20 years of experience in law enforcement with the New York State Police prior to working in the private sector. His contributions to the accident reconstruction section of Chapter 9 are greatly appreciated. All of the existing chapters are still in the book and have been brought up to date. The section of Chapter 1 on forensic science education has been expanded to include the accreditation of college and university education programs. We have also added a section on the role of human factors, especially bias in the analysis and presentation of evidence in Chapter 24—Legal Aspects.

One of the most exciting developments in the evolution of *Forensic Science: The Basics* is our treatment of laboratory exercises. In the second edition, we added some laboratory exercises to the chapters themselves and then supplemented the book with a set of more involved experiments. With the third edition, we have taken a new approach. Much of the laboratory materials have been removed from the textbook and incorporated into a new laboratory manual written by Kathy Mirakovits and Gina Londino. Kathy is one of the authors of *Forensic Science: The Basics* and a long-time, innovative high-school forensic science teacher. Gina is a lecturer in forensic science at Indiana University–Purdue University Indianapolis. She teaches basic lecture and laboratory courses in forensic science as well as forensic microscopy. The book can be used by itself or in conjunction with *Forensic Science: The Basics*. It will be comprehensive in nature, with exercises in many of the areas covered by this book as well as lists of materials and how to obtain them. It will stress on exercises that do not require expensive instrumentation or laboratory equipment. Look for it when you decide to adopt *Forensic Science: The Basics*.

The authors have designed this book to meet and exceed your wants and needs in teaching an introductory class in forensic science. The book is comprehensive enough to be used in a one or two introductory course in forensic science. Each chapter is complete and stands on its own, and they can be used in any order that is comfortable to the teacher. We hope you will enjoy using the book and that your students will see it as a primary resource. Please feel free to contact us with suggestions, comments, and questions.

Authors

Jay A. Siegel holds a PhD in analytical chemistry from the George Washington University, Washington, DC and received its Distinguished Faculty Scholar award in 2009. He worked as a forensic chemist with the Virginia Bureau of Forensic Sciences for three years, analyzing illicit drugs, fire residues, paints, and fibers. He then spent 25 years as professor and director of the Forensic Science Program in the School of Criminal Justice at Michigan State University. In 2003, he went to Indiana University–Purdue University Indianapolis (IUPUI) as founder and director of the Forensic and Investigative Sciences Program in the School of Science. In 2008, he was named the chair of the Department of Chemistry and Chemical Biology. He retired from IUPUI in 2012. Dr. Siegel is the coeditor of *Forensic Science Policy & Management: An International Journal*, the coauthor of *Fundamentals of Forensic Science*, the coeditor of *Encyclopedia of Forensic Sciences, 2nd Edition* (Elsevier), and the author of *Forensic Science: A Beginner's Guide*. He has testified over 200 times in federal and military courts in seven states. He was named distinguished fellow of the American Academy of Forensic Sciences in 2009.

Kathy Mirakovits teaches forensic science and physics at Portage Northern High School in Portage, Michigan, and physics at Kalamazoo Valley Community College in Kalamazoo, Michigan. She holds an MS in science education from Western Michigan University, a bachelor's degree in science education from Miami University, and has completed over 15 graduate hours in forensic science. She has taught general science, physical science, chemistry, biology, earth science, and physics at the high school and two-year college level for a total of 25 years. Additionally, Kathy conducts workshops across the United States for teachers who wish to learn the application of forensic science in a school curriculum. Information on those workshops can be found at her website: www.forensicscience-ed.com. She has developed numerous forensic science educational products for a national science supplier and has led workshops at the National Science Teachers Association (NSTA) in forensic science.

Kathy has served as president of the Michigan Chapter of the American Association of Physics Teachers (AAPT) and as a curriculum writer for the Michigan Department of Education. Currently, Kathy is the high school director for the Michigan Science Teachers Association. She has received the RadioShack Science Teaching Award and is a state finalist for the Presidential Award for Excellence in Math and Science Teaching (PAEMST).

Contributors

Susan Stejskal, LVT, PhD, DABT, is a board-certified toxicologist, licensed veterinary technician, and Special Deputy/Human Remains Detection (HRD) dog handler with the St. Joseph County Sheriff's Department (Michigan). With more than 30 years of educational and professional experience, she has, for the past 15 years, participated in land and water searches throughout Michigan and the central Midwest. Stejskal is founder and executive director of Recover K9, a nonprofit organization that provides support for much of her service and educational work. Dr. Stejskal's work in toxicology and pathology and her experience as a dog handler led to the development of practical forensic science training programs for law enforcement dog handlers, detectives, and crime scene technicians. She provides this training for police agencies throughout the country.

Christopher A. Puckett, is manager of the Accident Reconstruction Unit with Digits LLC, Buffalo, New York (www.digitsllc.com). During his 20-year law enforcement career as an investigator with the New York State Police, Puckett found himself investigating crime scenes and motor vehicle collisions. He has provided collision reconstruction services for numerous agencies and the private sector. Puckett provided investigation and reconstruction of hundreds of motor vehicle collisions involving property damage, physical injury, and death. These investigations include the use of applicable theories in collision reconstruction and the fulfillment of reporting requirements as stipulated by the New York State Police.

PART I

Forensic Science and Investigation

1
Introduction to Forensic Science

Learning Objectives

1. To be able to define forensic science and describe its various areas
2. To be able to describe the major events in the history of forensic science and relate them to modern day practice
3. To be able to describe the duties of a forensic scientist
4. To be able to describe the organization of federal, state, and local forensic science laboratories
5. To be able to diagram and describe the flow of evidence through a crime laboratory
6. To be able to describe the qualifications for becoming a forensic scientist
7. To be able to get information on careers in forensic science

Chapter 1
Introduction to Forensic Science

Chapter Outline

Mini Glossary

Behavioral forensic sciences: Applications of psychology and psychiatry to criminal matters including competency, interrogation, and crime scene reconstruction.

Computer forensics: Applications of computer science to criminal and civil offenses including the use of computers to commit crimes and the use of computers to help solve crimes.

Criminalistics: Analysis of physical evidence generated by a crime scene. Also, the pattern science areas of forensic evidence including fingerprints, firearms, and questioned documents.

Forensic anthropology: Analysis of skeletal remains recovered from crime scenes for the purposes of developing a biological profile and identification of the remains.

Forensic engineering: Application of engineering principles in forensic cases including failure analysis and traffic accident reconstruction.

Forensic entomology: Study of insect activity and cadavers assist in the determination of time of death (postmortem interval) and for other forensic purposes.

Forensic odontology: Synonymous with forensic dentistry. Analysis of dentition for the purposes of human identification and injuries. Also, analysis of bite marks.

Forensic pathology: Determination of the cause and manner of death in cases of unattended or suspicious death.

Forensic science: Application of science to matters involving the public or applications of science to legal matters.

Forensic scientist: A scientist who analyzes evidence generated by criminal or civil offenses and who can offer expert testimony concerning the evidence in court of law.

Lay witness: A witness to a crime who testifies what she saw or heard. Lay witnesses do not normally give opinions. They are contrasted with expert witnesses who do have to render opinions at times.

Acronyms

AAFS: American Academy of Forensic Sciences
ATF: Bureau of Alcohol, Tobacco, Firearms and Explosives
CSI: Crime scene investigation or investigator
DEA: Drug Enforcement Administration
FBI: Federal Bureau of Investigation
FEPAC: Forensic Science Education Program Accreditation Commission
FSS: Forensic Science Service (United Kingdom)
FWS: U.S. Fish and Wildlife Service
IRS: Internal Revenue Service
NAS: National Academy of Sciences
USPS: U.S. Postal Service
USSS: United States Secret Service

Introduction

Forensic science, forensic computing, forensic art, forensic accounting, forensic psychology. Forensic is the buzzword of the twenty-first century. It seems like there is forensic everything. More than 150 colleges and universities in the United States and more than 300 in the United Kingdom now offer some type of forensic science degree program. Movies, books, and TV shows that are about forensic science abound. Everyone is familiar with the site of a white robed scientist peering into a microscope or staring at a computer screen and uttering some dramatic statement about evidence from a crime; the hair came from the victim, the DNA matches the suspect, the white powder is cocaine. At this writing, the TV show *CSI* is still going strong. Why the sudden popularity? After all, forensic science has been practiced in one form or another for over 5000 years. An important reason is that recent serious cases have occurred in the United States and elsewhere where forensic science has played a major role. Jon Benet Ramsey, OJ Simpson, Theodore Bundy, and the Green River Killer have all exploded onto the headlines in recent years and forensic science has played an important part of all of them. People all over the world are fascinated by crime, its investigation, and its solution. People enjoy using clues to solve puzzles and problems. They are concerned with violent crime and want to do something about it. All of this feeds into the popularity of forensic science. The major impact of this field seems to have been on women. Today, more than 80% of all students in forensic science education programs in the United Sates are women, and this trend seems to be the same in other countries such as Australia and England. In some ways, the booming interest in forensic science is not a new phenomenon. For more than a century, people have been fascinated by the exploits of Sherlock Holmes, the clever detective penned by Arthur Conan Doyle. In just the past few years, there have been several movies and TV series about the great detective. As far back as the early days of TV and the movies, there have been shows about crime, policing, lawyers, and criminals. In recent years, the focus has shifted to forensic science. Although some people decry CSI and the other shows about forensic science, the fact is that they have raised the public conscience about science and its role in crime solving. Forensic science provides a unique way of teaching students the principles of science as well as problem solving, critical thinking, oral and written skills, and the role of bias in the practice of science.

Is the portrayal of forensic science and scientists in the media accurate? What do forensic scientists really do? How is forensic science presented in court and what effect does it have on juries as they deliberate the fate of the accused? This is what this book is all about. You will learn about the various branches of forensic science, how crime labs are organized, how evidence is collected and analyzed, and how scientific testimony is presented in court.

What Is Forensic Science?

In the ancient Roman Empire, the Senate used to conduct its meetings in a public place called the *forum*. Anyone who wanted to could listen to the great debates of the day and watch government in action. The key here is that the forum was a place where everyone could come and observe. The term forum is Latin for public and forensic is derived from that term. "Forensic science" implies, then, something about science and public. In the broadest sense then, forensic science can be defined as the methods of science applied to public matters. By this definition, forensic science does not necessarily have to do with crime; however, the term has evolved in modern times to mean the application of science to court or criminal matters. Most forensic scientists work in the criminal area of the justice system, although civil cases are an important component of forensic science. In this book, focus will be on the applications of science to criminal matters.

Depth and Breadth of Forensic Science

If forensic science means science applied to criminal and civil law, one may wonder which of the sciences are forensic sciences? The answer may surprise you. Any science can be a forensic science if it has some application to justice. Think about how many different areas of science could potentially be brought to bear on solving crimes. Many medical, physical, and biological sciences have forensic applications, as do math, business practices, sociology, and psychology. The list is nearly endless. The most common areas of science that have forensic applications are described later. This will give you an idea of the "big tent" that is forensic science.

Forensic Science v. Crime Scene Investigation

There is a good deal of confusion about the relationship between forensic science and crime scene investigation/investigators (CSI). Part of this may be due to TV shows such as *CSI*, which blur the distinctions between them by depicting the same people who collect evidence from a crime scene as the ones who analyze the evidence in the crime lab. In reality, these are different functions, but with some overlap. CSIs are usually, but not always, police officers who are trained and then assigned to the crime scene unit. They learn how to recognize evidence, protect it from contamination, collect it properly, thoroughly document its location and condition, and maintain a chain of custody to help authenticate the evidence when it gets to court. Some CSIs have a science background but many do not. Some CSIs are also trained in some procedures that could be considered forensic science because they involve preliminary (or complete) analysis of some types of evidence. Examples include preliminary analysis of suspected illicit drugs (so-called "field tests"), collection and analysis of fingerprints, and documentation and analysis of bloodstain patterns. To the extent that they analyze this evidence and reach scientific conclusions and then testify in court as experts, these investigators would be considered to be forensic scientists and this part of their job would be forensic science. This type of activity among CSIs is relatively rare but still common enough to bear mention. Under normal circumstances, the job of CSIs stops when the evidence is delivered to the laboratory where the actual work of the forensic scientist begins. Most people in the forensic science field do not consider crime scene investigation activities to be part of forensic science in spite of the fact that many crime scene units are administratively within the crime lab structure and that increasingly forensic scientists are going to some crime scenes to help with investigations.

Criminalistics

The term criminalistics was first coined by Paul Kirk, considered by many to be the father of forensic science in the United States. In some quarters, criminalistics is synonymous with forensic science and the two terms are often used interchangeably. In California, forensic scientists are often officially called criminalists. The term can be used to describe the comparative forensic sciences such as fingerprints, questioned documents, firearms, and tool marks. Most commonly, however, criminalistics refers to the myriad of types of physical evidence generated by crime scenes. This includes illicit drugs, blood and DNA, fire and explosive residues, hairs and fibers, glass and soil particles, paints and plastics, fingerprints, bullets, and much more.

A Bit of History: Paul Kirk

Paul Leland Kirk was a chemist and forensic scientist. He held a PhD in biochemistry from the University of California at Berkeley. He started his career at Berkeley in the biochemistry department and became interested in forensic science when authorities asked him to examine evidence from a rape case. Because of his interest and experience in microscopy, he was asked to head up the new Berkeley criminology program in 1937. He subsequently worked as a microscopist on the Manhattan Project where he helped isolate fissionable material for making bombs. In 1946, he returned to Berkeley and headed up the technical criminology major and served as head of the criminalistics department. Kirk is best known professionally for his work in the Sam Sheppard murder case. In this case, Dr. Sam Sheppard was falsely accused of murdering his wife. He escaped from custody and helped the police find the "one armed" man who committed the crime. This case was the basis for *The Fugitive* book, TV show, and movie. Kirk examined bloodstain patterns from the scene and his subsequent report and testimony at the second trial helped free Sheppard. Today, Kirk's legacy lives on in the Paul Kirk award, the highest award given by the "Criminalistics" section of the American Academy of Forensic Sciences.

Pathology

When some people think of forensic science, they envision dead bodies and autopsies. Some people got this idea originally from watching the TV show *Quincy*. The part of forensic science that is concerned with determining how and why people die is called forensic pathology. The forensic pathologist is a medical doctor who first specialized in pathology and then in forensic pathology. Forensic pathologists determine the cause and manner of death in cases where someone dies under suspicious or other circumstances as prescribed by state law. Many forensic pathologists work for state or local medical examiners or coroners. These are appointed or elected officials who must decide when a medicolegal autopsy (an autopsy in a case of suspicious death or homicide) is needed and they must sign death certificates that indicate the cause and manner of death. Medical examiners and coroners do not usually perform the autopsies themselves. They employ forensic pathologists to do this. Forensic pathology is discussed in detail in Chapter 13. If you would like to learn more about medicolegal autopsies, check out http://www.nlm.nih.gov/exhibition/visibleproofs/education/medical/index.html.

Anthropology

A Bit of History: An Early Case in Forensic Anthropology

In 1849, a Boston physician, Dr. George Parkman was murdered. The suspect in the case was John Webster, a professor of chemistry at Harvard, who was in considerable debt to Dr. Parkman. The *modus operandi* of the crime was that Professor Webster incinerated Dr. Parkman. When investigators searched through the ashes, they found some remains of skull and some badly damaged remains of dentures. The prosecution retained several experts in osteology and physiology who examined the bone fragments. They determined that they belonged to a white male, about 50–60 years of age, about 6 ft tall. Dr. Parkman was 60 years old and 5 ft 11 in. tall. In addition, experts matched the dentures to Dr. Parkman (Berryman, 13 *Crime Lab Digest*, 1986).

Forensic anthropologists work with skeletal remains. They identify bones as being human or animal. If animal, they determine the species. If human, they determine from what part of the body the bone originated. If they have the right bones, gender can be determined. Sometimes, age can be approximated and racial characteristics determined, and even socio-economic status may be estimated. If there is an injury to a skeleton or major bones, the anthropologist can help determine the cause of the injury or even death. Forensic anthropologists do other things besides identifying bones. They also work closely with skulls. It is possible to literally build a face onto a skull using clay and wooden or plastic pegs of various sizes. Using charts that give average tissue depth figures for various parts of a face, an anthropologist constructs a face and then makes judgments as to eye, nose, and mouth characteristics. Facial reconstruction can be useful in helping to identify a missing person from the face built up on the recovered skull. It is also possible for a forensic anthropologist to superimpose a skull onto a picture of a face to see if they are one and the same person. This is not usually definitive but can be quite helpful in establishing the identity of a skull. The process of building a face on a skull and the process of superimposition of skulls and faces is now done nearly exclusively by computer, a much faster and more accurate process. Forensic anthropology is discussed in detail in Chapter 14.

Odontology

Odontology is a synonym for dentistry. You may be curious about how a dentist could be a forensic scientist. Actually, there are several applications of dentistry to forensic science. A few years ago in Pennsylvania, a burglar broke into a house and ransacked it for valuables while the owners were on vacation. During his foray, he got hungry and rooted through the refrigerator for something to eat. He found a hunk of Swiss cheese and took a bite. Later he was arrested, trying to fence (sell on the black market) the stolen merchandise. When the police investigated the home looking for clues that would tie him to the scene, they found the cheese. A forensic dentist made a cast of the bite mark in the cheese and matched it to an impression of the burglar's teeth.

The most famous case where bite marks were crucial evidence involved Theodore Bundy. He was suspected of killing more than 30 young women in his career as a serial killer. He operated first in Washington, Utah, and Colorado, and then moved to Florida. During his last homicide, he bit his victim on her buttock after strangling her. A forensic dentist was able to match Bundy's teeth to this bite mark. He was executed in Florida for this murder in 1993.

Key Figures in Forensic Science: Ted Bundy

Ted Bundy was born in 1946 in Vermont in a home for unwed mothers. His father's identity was not conclusively determined. He was raised by his grandparents. He later moved to Washington State where he went to high school. Before he graduated from high school, he was a thief and shoplifter. In high school and early in college, he was quite introverted and had poor social skills. After graduation from high school, he went to the University of Washington and ultimately earned a degree in psychology. By all accounts, he was an honors student and well liked by his teachers. He subsequently began law school there but dropped out.

Some experts including those who knew Bundy believe that he started his killing spree during his early teens. At one point, he told is attorney that he attempted his first kidnapping when he was in college. The earliest murders that could conclusively be attributed to him occurred when he was 27. He started a string of brutal killings of young, white women in Washington and Oregon, and then Utah and Colorado. He was caught in Colorado but escaped twice from jail and fled to Florida where he resumed his rampage after more than 2 years. His last murders took place in Tallahassee at a sorority house. It was these murders for which he was tried and ultimately executed. Some of the crucial evidence in these murders was a bite mark that he left on the buttock of one of his victims. At his trial, a forensic odontologist testified that he matched the bite mark to a cast made of Bundy's teeth. Several jurors told the media after the trial that this was the crucial piece of evidence against Bundy. This was the first instance in the United States where bite marks had been used as evidence in this fashion. It should be noted that, as Bundy's execution date neared, he tried to buy time or get his sentence commuted to life in prison by offering to tell families where the bodies of some of his victims were in exchange for their writing letters to the judge asking for clemency. Not one family agreed to this, and he was electrocuted in January of 1989.

Forensic odontologists can also be very helpful in identifying the remains of victims of mass disasters such as airplane crashes. Sometimes, bodies are so badly burned or dismembered the only way to identify the remains is by using dental records. Postmortem dental records are taken and matched to x-rays taken before death.

Finally, forensic dentists may play a role in child or other abuse cases. A forensic dentist can often tell if facial injuries received by a person were the result of falling down a flight of stairs or if they were due to blunt force injury such as striking the person with a fist or other object. Forensic odontology is covered in more detail in Chapter 14.

Engineering

Forensic engineers can be valuable in cases where something has gone wrong with a mechanical or structural entity or in cases of automobile crashes. A few years ago, a balcony collapsed in the lobby of a Hyatt hotel in Kansas City. Many people were on the balcony at the time watching a rock concert going on in the lobby, several stories below. Questions arose about why the balcony collapsed. Forensic engineers were called in to examine the structural remains of the balcony and the concrete that fell. They concluded that the construction of the balcony was faulty and contributed to its failure. Failure analysis is one of the major contributions that forensic engineers make to the justice system. Figure 1.1 shows the damage to the Hyatt hotel in Kansas City after the walkway collapse. When the World Trade Center buildings in New York City were destroyed by airplane crashes, forensic engineers were called in to investigate the disaster. The buildings were constructed to withstand such an impact, and the engineers were asked to determine why the structure failed.

The majority of the work of forensic engineers is in the investigation of traffic crashes. Accident reconstruction is used to determine speeds, directions of impact, and who was driving the vehicle at the time of the crash. Insurance companies and police departments use forensic engineers quite extensively in traffic incident investigation. Forensic engineering is covered in more detail in Chapter 9.

Entomology

When a person dies and the body is exposed to the elements, who gets there first? Not witnesses or detectives—it is flies, more specifically a species commonly called the blow fly. During the bombing of the Murrah Federal Building in Oklahoma City, bodies were buried in the tons of rubble from the collapsed building.

Figure 1.1 Wreckage of the collapsed Hyatt Regency Hotel in Kansas City. (Associated Press file photo. With permission.)

Investigators literally followed the flies into the rubble and were able to locate some bodies this way. Female blow flies and other insects lay their eggs in decaying flesh. Different insects do this at different times. Other insects such as beetles and wasps will attack and feed off the insects and the eggs. Depending upon temperature and other environmental factors, this parade of visitors takes place at surprisingly consistent time intervals. By inspecting the corpse, forensic entomologists can give a pretty good estimate of the time since death whether the body has been there for many hours or several days.

In addition to the postmortem interval, there is other information that can be gained from studying insects feeding on a corpse. If a person has been poisoned, the flies and other insects will ingest some of the poison. A toxicologist can capture some of these critters, chop them up, and extract the poison and identify it. There are also cases where a person took cocaine and then died. Some of the maggots became abnormally large in size owing to their ingestion of the cocaine. Forensic entomology is covered in detail in Chapter 15.

Behavioral Forensic Sciences

Forensic psychiatry and psychology have been long contributors to the forensic sciences. As long as there has been crime, people have wrestled with the concept of responsibility. Our laws and those of most other countries have long had provisions for how people are treated who commit crimes and have diminished capacity. If a person is truly insane, can she be held responsible for committing a crime? Although the definitions vary as to what constitutes responsibility, insanity, etc., it falls to forensic psychiatrists and psychologists to examine defendants and render expert opinions to courts. There are real differences between psychiatrists and psychologists. Psychiatry is a medical specialty attained by medical doctors. Psychology is a behavioral science that does not involve medical training. Both have a role to play in determining responsibility for committing crimes.

Forensic psychologists play other roles in the criminal justice system. Some crime investigations include a component of psychological crime reconstruction.

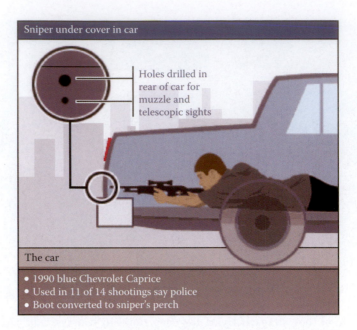

Figure 1.2 A drawing of a car outfitted so that a sniper can fire a weapon out of the back without being detected. This is similar to the setup used by the DC snipers.

Serial killers and others who commit multiple crimes develop habits and traits that show up time after time as they commit crimes. Discovering and understanding these patterns can help lead investigators to the right suspect. Specially trained forensic psychologists can examine a series of crime scenes and develop some theories about the type of person who committed the crimes. It must be noted that this is much more art than science and can be fraught with uncertainties. A case in point is the Washington, DC, snipers case of October 2002. Forensic psychologists and criminal investigators initially determined that the killer was a young, white male. As it turned out, the killers were two black males. Such attempts to determine a profile of a serial killer can be very difficult even if there are many incidents to draw upon for data. Figure 1.2 is a drawing of the car that the killers used when killing their victims.

Psychological profiling has also been used in other criminal and civil areas. For example, the Transportation Security Administration (TSA) uses forensic psychologists to create profiles of what a likely airplane hijacker might look like or behave like so security checkpoint officials can subject people who meet the profile to additional screening. This has been going on for many years in one form or another. The Department of Homeland Security has a similar program for border guards to help spot potential terrorists.

There are other types of behavioral forensic scientists. Some study interrogation and investigation techniques such as polygraph instruments to determine their accuracy and usefulness in criminal and civil investigations. Others do research in developing new areas of interrogation and deception detection.

Digital Evidence

This area is sometimes called digital forensics as well as by other descriptors. Computers and other electronic devices such as cell phones have become very important in crime today, both as instruments of crime and in helping to solve crime. Many criminals and criminal enterprises conduct much of their business and keep their business records on computers. Sometimes, these records are highly encrypted. When caught, criminals often try to erase or physically destroy the data to avoid it being used against them. Computer forensic scientists and engineers study ways to recover data even from smashed hard disk drives. They also learn how to handle a computer found at a crime scene, especially one that is turned on. Computers are also used to steal identities from people as well as merchandize from companies. They can be used to disrupt entire networks and hack into otherwise secure, private websites. Computers can also be used to help solve crimes. They can track people, store incriminating data that can be used against criminals, and help test and improve computer security. Digital forensics is one of the fastest growing areas of forensic science and will continue to grow in the future. Digital evidence is covered in more detail in Chapter 8.

History and Development of Forensic Science

When did people actually start doing forensic science? When was science first applied to answering questions about crimes or civil issues? Some baby boomers remember the *Quincy* TV show as the first time they saw forensic science in action. Twenty- and thirty-somethings think of the OJ Simpson case as the beginning of the use of science to solve real crimes. Today, many people think of *CSI* as the birth of forensic science. In reality, some aspects of forensic science have been at least recognized for centuries. An excellent outline of the history of forensic science in the form of a timeline has been published by Norah Rudin and Keith Inman and can be found on the web at http://www.forensicdna.com/Timeline020702.pdf. This organizes the history of forensic science by time. The earliest milestones in all areas are covered first and then gradually brought up to date. In this chapter, data from the timeline referenced earlier will be used to illustrate the history of forensic science highlighting three important examples: fingerprints, crime laboratories, and blood analysis.

As in many other fields of knowledge, the Chinese were the first to discover the value of forensic science in identification. They were the first to use fingerprints to identify the owner of objects such as pottery, but, of course, had no formal classification process. In later centuries, a number of scientists, such as Marcello Malphighi, noted the presence of fingerprints and that they had interesting characteristics, but did not make any connection to personal identification. The first person to recognize that fingerprints could be classified into types (nine major kinds) was John Purkinji, a professor of anatomy. In 1880, a Scottish physician, Henry Faulds published an article in the journal *Nature* that suggested that the uniqueness of fingerprints could be used to identify someone. This was quickly followed in the 1890s by Frances Galton, who published the first book on fingerprints, Juan Vucetich, who developed a fingerprint classification system that is still used today in South America and Sir Edward Henry, who developed the fingerprint classification system that has been adopted in the United States and Europe.

The development of a forensic science infrastructure including crime labs is much more recent but quite interesting. For example, the first detective force was developed in France, *The Sûreté of Paris* in 1810 by Eugene Vidocq. In 1905, President Teddy Roosevelt established the Federal Bureau of Investigation (FBI), but the FBI lab was not established until 1932. The first crime laboratory was established in France in 1910 by Edmund Locard, a professor of forensic medicine. He later espoused his famous *Locard Exchange Principle*, which will be discussed in Chapter 3.

In the United States, the first crime laboratory was established by August Vollmer, chief of police in Los Angeles. The first journal devoted to forensic science was begun by Calvin Goddard and his staff in 1930 at the newly formed Scientific Crime Detection Laboratory on the campus of Northwestern University. The journal was called *American Journal of Police Science*. It was later changed to the *Journal of Criminal Law, Criminology and Police Science*. In 1937, Paul Kirk established the first university-based forensic science program at the University of California at Berkeley. It was called *Technical Criminology*. Dr. Kirk is generally considered to be the father of modern forensic science in the United States. In 1950, the American Academy of Forensic Science was founded in Chicago. The American Academy of Forensic Sciences (AAFS) is the largest forensic science society in the world and has members from many different countries. The Academy began publication of the *Journal of Forensic Sciences*, the professional journal of forensic science, shortly after AAFS was founded.

The realization that blood and body fluids had the potential for being important evidence in criminal investigation is an old idea. Bloody palm prints were used as evidence more than 1000 years ago in Rome. In 1853, Ludwig Teichmann developed the first of a number of crystalline tests still used today in the characterization of blood. His test detected the presence of hemoglobin. The German scientist, Schönbein, developed the first presumptive test for blood. It takes advantage of the ability of hydrogen peroxide to react with hemoglobin. This was in 1863. In 1900, Karl Landsteiner made the major breakthroughs in the analysis of blood when he determined that there are actually four types of human blood. This became the basis for the ABO blood typing system and set the stage for all further work in serology. Landsteiner won the Nobel Prize for his work in 1930. Max Richter took Landsteiner's results and adapted them to blood stains, such as those found in crime scenes. Fifteen years later, Leone Lattes, a professor in Italy, developed a test to determine blood type in the ABO system and wrote a book about how to type dried stains. There were a number of advances over the next 30 years, culminating in the work of Sir Alec Jeffries of the University of Leicester. In 1984, Jeffries used a technique called *DNA Fingerprinting* to solve a double murder case in England, the first case solved by DNA analysis. The year before, Kary Mullis developed the *polymerase chain reaction* (PCR), which is the basis for all DNA typing in forensic cases today. He also won the Nobel Prize for his work.

What Is a Forensic Scientist?

Since practically any science can be a forensic science at times, many scientists can be forensic scientists. It is partially a matter of what they do in their jobs but also a matter of training and education. Forensic pathologists, for example, are educated as physicians and then trained as pathologists. After that, they can get specialized training in the forensic aspects of pathology and become certified as a forensic pathologist. This assures that they will have the proper education, training, and licensure to practice their pathology on medicolegal cases. There is, however, a critical shortage of certified forensic pathologists in the United States and many medicolegal autopsies are performed by pathologists who have no forensic training. Are they forensic pathologists by virtue of their performing forensic autopsies? Most pathologists would agree that they are not. The situation is somewhat different for forensic anthropologists, odontologists, and entomologists. There are a few forensic anthropology degrees but essentially none in odontology or entomology. There are certifications for all three that result in a designation as forensic anthropologist, odontologist, or entomologist. The fact is, however, that most of what would be considered forensic cases in these areas are performed by noncertified but professional scientists. With increased attention being paid to these forensic sciences, questions of who should be performing forensic analysis becomes more important.

The majority of forensic scientists work in crime laboratories on the local, state, or national level. Most forensic science laboratories are associated with law enforcement agencies; for example, Detroit Police Department Crime Lab, Indiana State Police Forensic Lab, FBI Lab. Although early in their history most of these laboratories were staffed by enlisted officers, special agents, and the like, today, increasing numbers are civilians and have no police duties. One of the reasons for this is that, as forensic science has become more sophisticated and rigorous, it has been harder to find scientifically trained police officers. The other reason for this is that police departments want to put more officers on the street and are transferring analysts out of the lab to law enforcement duty.

In a crime laboratory, forensic scientists have two major duties; to analyze evidence and to testify in court. Forensic science laboratories behave in a reactive role. When a crime is committed, the crime scene unit collects the evidence and turns it over to the police investigators (sometimes detectives) who then bring it to the crime lab. In some cases, the crime scene investigation unit may turn it directly over to the lab. The lab scientists then analyze the evidence. They generally do not have much input into what evidence is collected, although there may be occasions where a forensic scientist asks the police to collect additional items of evidence for comparison or further analysis. In recent years, there has been an increasing trend toward having forensic scientists attend at least some crime scenes. For example, the Michigan State Police Forensic Science Division forms teams of forensic scientists that are called upon to help process serious crime scenes such as those in which there is a dead body. These scientists work along with the police CSI team to help process the scene and collect evidence.

The other major duty of forensic scientists is to testify in court. In the U.S. criminal justice system, there are basically two types of witnesses that testify in court, lay and expert witnesses. A lay witness is someone who is not an expert but has something to contribute to help the judge or jury determine the guilt or innocence of the accused. This person may have been an eyewitness to a crime, a victim or someone who knows something about the suspect or the crime. Such witnesses are supposed to testify only to what they have perceived with their five senses; touch, taste, smell, sight, or hearing. They are not to give their opinions. It is the jury's job to make conclusions about the evidence presented to them, not the witness. For example, if a witness offers testimony that the driver of a car involved in a traffic accident was drunk, that conclusion would not be permitted in court. Being "drunk" in the motor vehicle code sense requires an expert finding of sufficient alcohol in the driver's body exceeding the legal limit.

The other type of witness in a court is an *expert witness*. This is a person who has knowledge and/or skills, derived from education and/or experience, that qualifies him or her to take a set of facts and reach conclusions not attainable by the average person (the judge or jury). Most people think of experts as being PhD scientists or doctors and although many of them are, other experts may derive their expertise from experience rather than formal education. For example, suppose that a man is driving down a mountainous road when his car's brakes fail. He crashes his car and dies. The police investigator would want to know why the brakes failed. Were they old and in need of repair? Were they installed improperly by a mechanic? Were they tampered with so that they would fail purposefully? Each of these explanations would call for a different response by the justice system. If someone were put on trial for killing the driver, it would not be prudent to have the jury go to the garage where the wrecked car was stored and have the jurors inspect the brakes to see what caused them to fail. Most jurors would not have the knowledge to inspect the brakes (the facts) and draw conclusions (the opinions) about how they failed. An expert brake mechanic should be called upon to inspect the brakes and determine the cause of their failure. This individual can give testimony as an expert about the failure of the brakes.

Whether a trial is by jury or judge, it is the judge's responsibility to decide if expert testimony is needed and who is qualified to offer it. Even if a forensic scientist has testified hundreds of times, he or she must be requalified as an expert for every trial. It is important that the expert explain complex scientific or technical principles in a language that a jury can understand. Forensic scientists must be equally competent in the trial part and the scientific part of their jobs. The legal aspects of forensic science are covered in more detail in Chapter 24.

So You Want to be a Forensic Scientist

So now you know what forensic scientists do and where they work, but what does it take to be one? This depends upon what type of forensic scientist you want to be and what type of work you want to do. Becoming a forensic scientist requires both education and training. We shall discuss a few of the more common areas of forensic study. Table 1.1 is a chart that summarizes selected forensic science careers, optimal education, and job markets.

Crime laboratory forensic scientist—The entry-level requirements for forensic scientists who work in the traditional areas of forensic science in a forensic science laboratory vary with the particular discipline. Forensic chemists analyze chemical evidence such as drugs, fibers, paints, explosives, fire residues, etc. They would be expected to have a strong background in chemistry and related sciences as well as microscopy. Forensic biologists are responsible for the analysis of blood, other body fluids and, particularly, DNA. They should have a strong background in the biological sciences including molecular biology, genetics, and population statistics, as well as chemistry and biochemistry. For those forensic scientists who analyze pattern evidence such as fingerprints, firearms, and tool marks and questioned documents, educational requirements are somewhat less specific. Methods of analysis of these types of evidence have evolved over the years to include chemical, microscopic, and even biological tests, and it is advisable that those who specialize in pattern evidence have some background in the natural and physical sciences and statistics.

Until the middle of the twentieth century, most people who would work in the natural or physical science areas of a forensic science laboratory pursued a bachelors of science degree in one of the chemical or biological sciences. Starting in the 1940s, some institutions began to offer forensic science classes of a general nature that students could take as electives. Later, some classes in specific areas such as questioned documents or firearms began to show up. Then, a few universities began to offer entire degrees in forensic science. These started as largely criminal justice programs with science, forensic science, and law classes included. Often, an internship in a forensic science laboratory was also available. As the twentieth century wore on, forensic science became ever more popular, fueled by the rise of movies, books, and TV shows that glamorized the field. Many universities and colleges offered forensic science degrees that ranged from very rigorous curricula

TABLE 1.1
Types of Careers and Best Educational Preparation for Various Areas of Forensic Science

Career	Job Description	Optimal Education	Job Market
Crime lab forensic scientist	Analyze scientific evidence Testify in court	At least a BS degree in science MS degree preferred	Robust but spotty More than 1900 new forensic scientist needed
Forensic pathologist	Determine cause and manner of death in suspicious or unattended deaths	BS or BA degree +4 year-medical school degree + 3–4-year residency in pathology + 1–2-year residency in forensic pathology	Excellent. There is a nationwide, critical
Forensic anthropologist	Excavate crime scenes and analyze skeletal remains	PhD in physical or forensic anthropology	Most forensic anthropologists teach at colleges and do forensic anthropology on the side. Job market is small
Forensic odontologist	Analyze bite marks, facial injuries, and identify human remains from dental work	BS or BA degree +4 years of dental school. No residencies in forensic dentistry	Few people make a living strictly on forensic dentistry. Most have conventional dental practices and do forensic work on the side. Job market is small
Forensic engineer	Reconstruct vehicle accidents, structural failure analysis, explosion analysis, electrical systems	PhD in engineering, lots of experience	Most forensic engineers are in private practice. Need for experienced engineers is pretty large
Computer forensic scientist	Determine role of computers in crime Reconstruct media devices and computers Track down criminals who hack into sites and steal identities	Experience is most important consideration. Bachelor's degree in relevant field is desirable	Some are in private practice. Many work for colleges as teachers/researchers and do forensic work on the side

dominated by chemistry, biology, and math coursework, to those that were little more than criminal justice with an internship thrown in. Presently, there are more than 100 forensic science degree programs in the United States and more than 300 in the United Kingdom! This situation put a great burden on students who wanted to become forensic scientists and their academic advisors. With all of these forensic science degrees, how is one to decide which ones are rigorous and relevant enough to arm one with the credentials needed to work in a forensic science laboratory?

In the early part of the twenty-first century, the AAFS and the American Society of Crime Laboratory Directors (ASCLD) teamed up to create an accreditation process whereby colleges and universities could qualify for accredited status for their forensic science programs. The process started with the creation of a Technical Working Group on Forensic Science Education (TWGED), made up of more than 40 scientists and practitioners. They developed a set of curricular mandates and requirements that must be met for a program to be accredited. This, in turn, led to the formation of a Forensic Science Education Accreditation Commission (FEPAC), which contained five forensic science educators, five ASCLD members, and one public member. They took the recommendations from TWGED and created an accreditation process for BS and MS degrees in forensic science. To become accredited by FEPAC, a forensic science degree program must meet rigorous curricular, infrastructure, and staffing requirements. Emphasis is placed on courses in the natural, biological, physical and mathematical sciences, forensic science, law, and criminal justice. Internships or other similar experiences are required. At the graduate level, a research experience is also required. Currently, approximately 30 BS and MS degree programs are accredited. A student who attends one of these programs is assured of a rigorous, science-based degree that will qualify them for employment in virtually every forensic science laboratory in the United States.

Information about FEPAC and its accreditation program as well as the educational requirements for accreditation and a current list of accredited degree programs can be found at the website of the AAFS; www.aafs.org.

- *Forensic pathologist*: To become a forensic pathologist, you first need to graduate from college with an excellent academic record. Then, you must graduate from medical school, requiring another 4 years. After medical school, you complete a residency in pathology that takes an additional 4 years. Finally, an additional residency in forensic pathology is recommended in order to become certified. This takes another year to complete.
- *Forensic anthropologist*: Few crime labs can afford to hire a forensic anthropologist full time. If you have another area of specialization such as trace evidence or DNA typing, you could get hired by a crime lab and then do anthropology cases as they come up. Another way of getting into the field is to obtain a PhD in physical or forensic anthropology and teach and do research at a university and then local crime labs would come to you for your services as needed.
- *Forensic odontologist*: This is similar to the route for a forensic pathologist except that you would complete dental school instead of medical school. There are few (if any) residencies in forensic odontology; therefore, you would have to work with police departments on an as-needed basis.
- *Forensic engineer*: This career requires education in engineering and the more the better. Usually, PhDs are in demand for forensic engineering. Most forensic engineers have their own private companies that are hired by prosecutors or defendants.

- *Computer forensic scientist*: There are few education programs that turn out computer forensic scientists. People who work in this area invariably have a strong interest and educational background in computer science and engineering. Their designation as computer forensic scientists arises from the types of cases that they work on or the type of research and teaching that they do.
- *Related careers*: Not everyone wants to be a forensic scientist in a laboratory. Some people decide that they want to work in a career that makes use of their strong science background and perhaps a forensic science education. There are a large number of related careers that one could consider. If you decide to be a lawyer, a science background can be very handy in the field of patent law. Many patents require practice and skill in reading and digesting sometimes complicated journal articles and books. These particular skills are highly developed in a science education. Environmental forensic science is becoming a major area of environmental science. Scientists work for environmental analytical laboratories determining pollution levels in air, water, and soil and can help companies comply with environmental laws or, conversely, help government agencies track down and prosecute polluters. The pharmaceutical industry is very interested in people with a strong analytical chemistry background. Many forensic science educational programs teach the chemistry and analysis of illicit drugs; information that can be valuable in a career in pharmaceutical chemistry. The insurance industry is also interested in employing scientists including those with a forensic science background. They do investigations of fires, explosions, traffic accidents, stolen automobiles, and other property incidents to help determine if a crime was committed or a covered loss occurred.

For More Information on Careers in Forensic Science

The websites of any of the federal agencies listed in the section on the organization of Federal forensic science labs will provide information about how one joins that organization as a forensic scientist. In addition, one can check the website of the state or local law enforcement agency where crime labs are housed for information about obtaining employment.

General job and career information in forensic science can be found at the AAFS; www.aafs.org. The Academy is the major national organization for forensic scientists. There is a section on their website with job openings in the field. They also have written information on careers in forensic science.

Information about careers in particular areas of forensic science can be found on the websites of their association or society. A few of the more common ones are

- AAFS: www.aafs.org
- National Association of Medical Examiners: www.thename.org/
- Society of Forensic Toxicologists: www.soft-tox.org/
- American Society of Questioned Document Examiners: www.asqde.org/
- American Board of Forensic Anthropology: www.csuchico.edu/anth/ABFA/
- Forensic Entomology: www.forensic-entomology.com/
- Association of Firearm and Tool Mark Examiners: www.afte.org/index_forum.php
- American Society of Forensic Odontology: www.forensicdentistryonline.org/new_asfo/newasfo.htm

The United States Forensic Science System

There are approximately 400 forensic science laboratories in the United States. Most of them are public labs supported by a unit of federal, state, or local government. Others are private labs. A laboratory may be full service, running tests in all of the major areas of forensic science. Others may conduct only the most common examinations of evidence such as drugs, firearms, and fingerprints. The federal government and all 50 state governments administer some form of laboratory system or network.

Federal Forensic Science Laboratories

Most people are familiar with the FBI laboratory, and many people think that it is the only crime lab that is run by the U.S. government. The fact is that there are many federal laboratories, and they are located within several cabinet departments. Figure 1.3 is a diagram of how the federal forensic science labs are arranged.

The Justice Department

Most of the federal crime labs are located within the Department of Justice. They are under the administrative control of the Attorney General of the United States.

The FBI Laboratory

The FBI (www.fbi.gov/) has its laboratory in Quantico Virginia. It is supported by the Forensic Science Research and Training Center (FSRTC), also located in Quantico. The FBI lab is one of the best-known and most prestigious forensic science laboratories in the world. The FBI lab supports the law enforcement and antiterrorism

Figure 1.3 An organizational chart of the major federal forensic science laboratories.

Figure 1.4 The FBI Training Center and Research Laboratories, Quantico, Virginia.

missions of the FBI by analyzing evidence generated by these activities. The FBI lab also processes evidence sent in by state and local law enforcement agencies or crime labs. Personnel from the FBI lab will also travel to foreign countries to help indigenous law enforcement agents solve crimes against U.S. citizens and those with global implications. Figure 1.4 is the FBI Training Center and Research Laboratory in Quantico, Virginia.

The Drug Enforcement Administration (DEA)

The DEA (www.usdoj.gov/dea/) has a network of regional laboratories located in Washington, DC, Miami, Chicago, Dallas, San Francisco, and New York. They are supported by the Special Testing and Research Lab in Virginia. The DEA analyzes illicit drugs seized by DEA agents and by task forces made up of state or local drug agents working with the DEA. They also work with foreign countries to help eradicate illicit drugs or help prevent their importation into the United States. The DEA shares training facilities with the FBI in Quantico, Virginia.

The Department of the Treasury

Most people are surprised to find that the Department of the Treasury has crime labs, but in fact they have several. These labs have definite areas of responsibility.

The Bureau of Alcohol, Tobacco, Firearms and Explosives (BATF)

The BATF (www.atf.treas.gov) has a number of missions that are supported by a network of its three laboratories located in Beltsville, Maryland, Atlanta, and San Francisco. As the name of the agency suggests, agents of the BATF are in charge of making sure that all alcohol produced in or imported into the United States has the proper tax stamp indicating that the correct taxes have been paid. This is a revenue function that explains why the agency used to be in the Department of the Treasury. Likewise, the BATF has similar functions in the tobacco industry to ensure that the proper taxes have been paid on cigarettes and that contraband tobacco products such as Cuban cigars are not imported illegally. The firearms mission is a bit different. The Bureau is charged with making sure that illegal firearms are not produced, imported, or exported and that the proper taxes and duties are paid on them. In addition to the areas mentioned earlier, the BATF labs have some of the world's leading experts in fire and explosive analysis and they work with law enforcement agencies all over the world. The labs also have expertise in trace evidence, fingerprints, and questioned documents.

The Secret Service

When most people think of the Secret Service (www.ustreas.gov/usss/index.shtml), they picture serious, dark-suited people guarding the President of the United States and other domestic and international VIPs. Certainly, the protective function is the most visible part of the Service, but not the only one. The Secret Service maintains a laboratory in Washington, DC, that has several functions. It supports the protective services of the agency by continuously developing methods that counter attempts to harm the people that the Service is guarding. In addition, the agency is charged with preventing attempts at counterfeiting money and credit cards. This explains why the agency is in the Department of the Treasury. As one would expect, there are leading experts in counterfeiting and questioned documents as well as trace evidence employed in the Secret Service lab.

The Internal Revenue Service (IRS)

No discussion of the Department of the Treasury would be complete without mention of the IRS (www.irs.gov/). The IRS is charged with making sure that everyone pays their fair share of taxes according to the law, and there are many IRS agents who do that job. They are supported by a laboratory in Chicago, whose major expertise lies in the area of questioned documents. This lab has experts in handwriting, typewriting, and printers, inks, and papers. In addition to their analytical work, they carry out numerous training activities for other agencies.

The Department of the Interior

Wait, doesn't the Department of the Interior (www.lb.fws.gov/) take care of the National Parks and National Forests and the environment? What do they need with a crime lab? Doesn't the FBI have jurisdiction in the parks and forests? Well, yes and no. The FBI lab has a lot of experts but none in wildlife biology and animal body parts. So, in 1987, the United States Fish and Wildlife Service established the world's first and only laboratory that specializes in wildlife forensic science in Ashland, Oregon. This lab supports the enforcement activities of the Fish and Wildlife agents who patrol the National Parks and Forests to help prevent poaching and hunting of endangered species. The lab also supports such efforts worldwide.

The United States Postal Service

The United States Postal Service (www.usps.com/postalinspectors/crimelab.htm) has an investigative arm that swings into action when someone uses the mail to commit a crime. Such crimes can include fraud, extortion, mailing anthrax, or another dangerous substance to a government official, illegal gambling, or other shady activities such as pyramid schemes, etc. The United States Postal Service Laboratory in

Washington, DC, supports these investigative activities. The emphasis here is on document analysis but other areas of forensic science are also represented. These include trace evidence and fingerprints. The Postal Service is a quasi-governmental agency, meaning that it is private but is also government subsidized.

State and Local Forensic Science Systems

Each of the 50 states in the United States has a public crime lab system. The types and numbers of laboratories depend upon the size and population of the state. For example, Montana has one laboratory that serves the entire state, whereas California has more than 50 public laboratories that operate at all levels of government. Every state has at least one, publicly funded forensic science laboratory. Governmental units that administer crime labs include the state police, state highway patrol, and attorney general's office. Some states have a consolidated laboratory division, which may also include health department, toxicology and agricultural laboratories, and state medical examiner or coroner. For example, the Michigan State Police have seven regional laboratories throughout the state. The headquarters lab in Lansing is considered to be full service. It has all of the forensic science services needed in the state including toxicology and behavioral forensic sciences. The other six labs have the services that are in the most demand locally such as drug analysis, trace evidence, firearms, and fingerprints. In addition to state-run laboratories, most states have some locally controlled facilities. In Maryland, some of the larger counties have laboratories attached to the county police. In California, the county sheriff in many large counties such as Los Angeles has an associated crime lab. Many large cities also have their own crime labs, usually within the city police department. These include New York City and Los Angeles.

Private Forensic Science Laboratories

Besides the federal, state, and local forensic science crime labs, there are numerous private laboratories and their number is increasing. These range from one person "niche" laboratories where one type of forensic science analysis is done, to nationwide networks of labs that may do several types of analysis. Many of the one-person labs have been started by forensic scientists who have retired from a public laboratory. They continue to ply their trade using prior contacts and word of mouth or print advertising to build a client base. In the criminal arena, they usually work for defendants. The prosecutor has the use of the local or state public laboratory and in most cases, the defendant cannot have access to the public facilities unless a judge specifically orders it. The private labs perform a service to the criminal justice system by providing resources for defendants of crimes. A few private laboratories operate in the public arena. For example, the Northern Illinois Police Crime Laboratory is a private laboratory that contracts its services to the northeastern areas of Illinois between Chicago and the Wisconsin border near Milwaukee. Another example is Bode Laboratories, which has a nationwide network of private DNA labs that provide paternity testing services to public and private clients. Bode performs the majority of noncriminal paternity cases in the United States each year. One area where private labs seem to prosper is forensic engineering. Most professional forensic engineers are privately employed. They may work for the prosecutor, the plaintiff, or the defendant. Some are connected with colleges or universities and work as consultants on the side.

Other Forensic Science Systems

There is no standard organizational structure for a forensic science laboratory system. Each country has a system that best meets its needs. Organizational decisions are based on historical precedent, population and its distribution, resources available, and levels and patterns of crime.

The United Kingdom

England and Wales used to have a public laboratory system, The Forensic Science Service (FSS). More than 20 years ago, the FSS changed to a "pay as you go" system. However, in recent years it has been losing lots of money and was finally abolished about 5 years ago. Now, forensic science services are delivered mostly by private laboratories.

Australia

In a country the size of the United States but with 10% of the population, where most people live on the coast, one would expect a different type of forensic science system. Each of the seven states in Australia supports some type of laboratory. These range from single, full service laboratories such as the Victoria Police Science Centre near Melbourne, to the fragmented system in New South Wales, which has separate laboratories for firearms and fingerprints and for drugs and for chemical evidence. There is also a laboratory within the Australian Federal Police in Canberra.

Columbia

A large South American country, Columbia's judicial system has undergone major changes in recent years. These include development of a forensic science laboratory system. There are four regional laboratories. Three are part of the federal Law Enforcement system that includes the Prosecutor General and the National Police. The fourth lab is a medical lab that supports the national medical examiner system.

The Organization of Forensic Science Laboratories

If you were to look at the inside of a forensic science laboratory, it would, at first glance, look like any other analytical laboratory. There are lots of instruments, glassware, implements, and scientists in white lab coats and safety glasses. Like most laboratories, forensic science labs are secure facilities that allow only very limited, escorted access to the public. But if you look a little deeper into a forensic science lab, you would see some things that you would not find in other types of scientific labs. Many crime labs have few windows because windows are less secure. On the other hand, questioned document examiners like to have windows in their sections because they like to have natural light for document examination. The common sections of a crime lab are listed later. Figure 1.5 is a chart that shows the major sections of a typical crime lab.

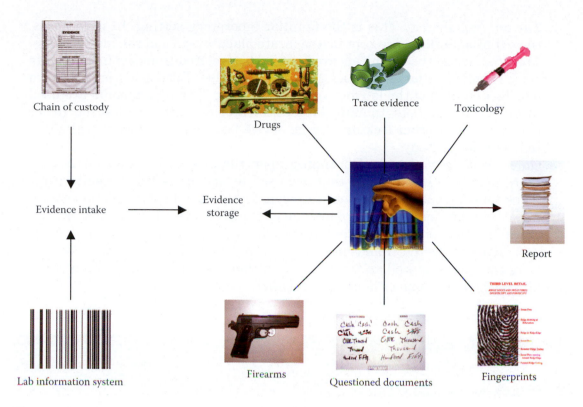

Figure 1.5 Various sections of a typical forensic science laboratory.

In order for physical evidence to be admissible in a court for a trial, it must be authenticated. That is, there must be proof that the evidence seized at the crime scene is the same evidence that is now being introduced into court. There must be a document that records who was in custody of the evidence at all times. The evidence must be kept in a secure container such that any attempt to breach the seal would be evident. When the evidence container is opened the person opening, it must reseal it with initials, date, and time. All of these procedures and the custody record collectively make up the chain of custody. An improper chain of custody can be grounds to render evidence inadmissible.

Once impounded, the evidence will be put in a locked storage room. At some point, the evidence will be assigned to one or more scientists for processing. Some items of evidence require more than one type of analysis and decisions will have to be made about which section analyzes it first. One of the important considerations here is to make sure that one test done on the evidence does not ruin it for another test. For example, suppose a gun is submitted for evidence and the gun may have the suspect's fingerprints on it along with some blood spots. The gun will have to be test fired so a known bullet can be recovered for comparison. The blood will have to be removed and tested for DNA. The fingerprints will have to be carefully lifted and compared with the suspect's prints. The order in which these tests are done is important. When a decision is made, the evidence is turned over to the scientist, who uses the bar code to log possession of the evidence.

1. *The intake section*: This is at the front of the lab. There will usually be an intake officer who will log in the evidence to the *laboratory information system* (LIMS). Typically, a bar code will be affixed to all of the pieces of evidence. Each item will have its own, unique identification number.

2. *The analysis area(s)*: This is the familiar laboratory setting. In most cases, the scientists' offices are kept in a separate place away from the instruments. The area where the chemicals are kept is also isolated from the instruments since chemicals and electronics are not compatible. Each scientist will have a dedicated area of the lab for evidence handling. The instruments are used by all of the scientists. In many larger laboratories, each scientist has his or her own safe or other locking storage device for keeping evidence while it is in his or her custody.

3. *Other sections of the lab*: Depending upon the size and nature of the lab, there may be other sections that are used by scientists from time to time. Some labs have a garage where cars can be kept for inspection and searching. Many firearms sections have huge, stainless steel tanks that are full of water. These are used to test-fire weapons for comparison with bullets or cartridges recovered from crime scenes. Some large labs have collections of seized weapons as well as ammunition. If there is a polygraph section of the lab, there will be one or more interrogation rooms.

Examination of the Forensic Sciences by Outside Organizations

Over the past few decades, there have been many studies of the status of forensic science or some of its major areas of study. Several of the more important studies have been conducted by committees of the National Academy of Sciences (NAS), an arm of the National Research Council. The NAS traces its beginnings to around 1865, when it was formed by President Abraham Lincoln as a means of providing the Congress with scientific advice and expertise. The Congress provides the NAS with funds to create study committees in many scientific areas. In 2006, the forensic science community (representatives of most of the major forensic science organizations in the United States) approached the Congress with a request to form a committee to study the needs of forensic science in the twenty-first century and to make recommendations for improvement. A 17-member committee was formed by the NAS. The Committee was made up of forensic scientists, other scientists, legal and other scholars, and members of the judicial system in the United States. Over a period of more than 2 years, the Committee met eight times, partly in open session and partly closed to the public. In 2009, the Committee issued a report; "Strengthening Forensic Science in the United States: A Path Forward." This report contained 13 recommendations for improvement in the forensic sciences. In the more than 5 years since the report came out, there has been a great deal of discussion in the forensic science and criminal justice communities as well as the public at large. Many of the recommendations, if implemented, would have major impact on forensic science and some of its most important fields. At this writing, none have been officially implemented but the Congress has held several hearings on the report and several pieces of potential legislation have been introduced into both houses of the Congress. Since the NAS report came out, a White House science and technology committee was formed to further study the issues that were raised by the NAS report, and most recently, a new National Commission on Forensic Science has been created by the Departments of Justice and Commerce (the National Institute of Standards and Technology).

The 13 recommendations are listed, *verbatim*, below. In Chapter 3, those that are specifically concerned with the issues of the status of various types of evidence and their admissibility will be discussed. These will be reinforced in other chapters of this book that are impacted by the recommendations. Copies of the report are available at various sites on the Web.

Recommendation 1

To promote the development of forensic science into a mature field of multidisciplinary research and practice, founded on the systematic collection and analysis of relevant data, Congress should establish and appropriate funds for an independent federal entity, the National Institute of Forensic Science (NIFS). NIFS should have a full-time administrator and an advisory board with expertise in research and education, the forensic science disciplines, physical and life sciences, forensic pathology, engineering, information technology, measurements and standards, testing and evaluation, law, national security, and public policy. NIFS should focus on

1. Establishing and enforcing best practices for forensic science professionals and laboratories
2. Establishing standards for the mandatory accreditation of forensic science laboratories and the mandatory certification of forensic scientists and medical examiners/forensic pathologists—and identifying the entity/entities that will develop and implement accreditation and certification
3. Promoting scholarly, competitive peer-reviewed research and technical development in the forensic science disciplines and forensic medicine
4. Developing a strategy to improve forensic science research and educational programs, including forensic pathology
5. Establishing a strategy, based on accurate data on the forensic science community, for the efficient allocation of available funds to give strong support to forensic methodologies and practices in addition to DNA analysis
6. Funding state and local forensic science agencies, independent research projects, and educational programs as recommended in this report, with conditions that aim to advance the credibility and reliability of the forensic science disciplines
7. Overseeing education standards and the accreditation of forensic science programs in colleges and universities
8. Developing programs to improve understanding of the forensic science disciplines and their limitations within legal systems
9. Assessing the development and introduction of new technologies in forensic investigations, including a comparison of new technologies with former ones

Recommendation 2

The NIFS, after reviewing established standards such as ISO 17025, and in consultation with its advisory board, should establish standard terminology to be used in reporting on and testifying about the results of forensic science investigations. Similarly, it should establish model laboratory reports for different forensic science disciplines and specify the minimum information that should be included. As part of the accreditation and certification processes, laboratories and forensic scientists should be required to utilize model laboratory reports when summarizing the results of their analyses.

Recommendation 3

Research is needed to address issues of accuracy, reliability, and validity in the forensic science disciplines. The NIFS should competitively fund peer-reviewed research in the following areas:

1. Studies establishing the scientific bases demonstrating the validity of forensic methods.
2. The development and establishment of quantifiable measures of the reliability and accuracy of forensic analyses. Studies of the reliability and accuracy of forensic techniques should reflect actual practice on realistic case scenarios, averaged across a representative sample of forensic scientists and laboratories. Studies also should establish the limits of reliability and accuracy that analytic methods can be expected to achieve as the conditions of forensic evidence vary. The research by which measures of reliability and accuracy are determined should be peer reviewed and published in respected scientific journals.
3. The development of quantifiable measures of uncertainty in the conclusions of forensic analyses.
4. Automated techniques capable of enhancing forensic technologies.

Recommendation 4

To improve the scientific bases of forensic science examinations and to maximize independence from or autonomy within the law enforcement community, Congress should authorize and appropriate incentive funds to the NIFS for allocation to state and local jurisdictions for the purpose of removing all public forensic laboratories and facilities from the administrative control of law enforcement agencies or prosecutors' offices.

Recommendation 5

The NIFS should encourage research programs on human observer bias and sources of human error in forensic examinations. Such programs might include studies to determine the effects of contextual bias in forensic practice (e.g., studies to determine whether and to what extent the results of forensic analyses are influenced by knowledge regarding the background of the suspect and the investigator's theory of the case). In addition, research on sources of human error should be closely linked with research conducted to quantify and characterize the amount of error. Based on the results of these studies, and in consultation with its advisory board, the NIFS should develop standard operating procedures (that will lay the foundation for model protocols) to minimize, to the greatest extent reasonably possible, potential bias and sources of human error in forensic practice. These standard operating procedures should apply to all forensic analyses that may be used in litigation.

Recommendation 6

To facilitate the work of the NIFS, Congress should authorize and appropriate funds to NIFS to work with the National Institute of Standards and Technology (NIST), in conjunction with government laboratories, universities, and private laboratories, and in consultation with Scientific Working Groups, to develop tools for advancing measurement, validation, reliability, information sharing, and proficiency testing in forensic science and to establish protocols for forensic examinations, methods, and practices. Standards should reflect best practices and serve as accreditation tools for laboratories and as guides for the education, training, and certification of professionals. Upon completion of its work, the NIST and its partners should report findings and recommendations to NIFS for further dissemination and implementation.

Recommendation 7

Laboratory accreditation and individual certification of forensic science professionals should be mandatory, and all forensic science professionals should have access to a certification process. In determining appropriate standards for accreditation and certification, the NIFS should take into account established and recognized international standards, such as those published by the International Organization for Standardization (ISO). No person (public or private) should be allowed to practice in a forensic science discipline or testify as a forensic science professional without certification. Certification requirements should include, at a minimum, written examinations, supervised practice, proficiency testing, continuing education, recertification procedures, adherence to a code of ethics, and effective disciplinary procedures. All laboratories and facilities (public or private) should be accredited, and all forensic science professionals should be certified, when eligible, within a time period established by NIFS.

Recommendation 8

Forensic laboratories should establish routine quality assurance and quality control procedures to ensure the accuracy of forensic analyses and the work of forensic practitioners. Quality control procedures should be designed to identify mistakes, fraud, and bias; confirm the continued validity and reliability of standard operating procedures and protocols; ensure that best practices are being followed; and correct procedures and protocols that are found to need improvement.

Recommendation 9

The NIFS, in consultation with its advisory board, should establish a national code of ethics for all forensic science disciplines and encourage individual societies to incorporate this national code as part of their professional code of ethics. Additionally, the NIFS should explore mechanisms of enforcement for those forensic scientists who commit serious ethical violations. Such a code could be enforced through a certification process for forensic scientists.

Recommendation 10

To attract students in the physical and life sciences to pursue graduate studies in multidisciplinary fields critical to forensic science practice, Congress should authorize and appropriate funds to the NIFS to work with appropriate organizations and educational institutions to improve and develop graduate education programs designed to cut across organizational, programmatic, and disciplinary boundaries. To make these programs appealing to potential students, they must include attractive scholarship and fellowship offerings. Emphasis should be placed on developing and improving research methods and methodologies applicable to forensic science practice and on funding research programs to attract research universities and students in fields relevant to forensic science. The NIFS should also support law school administrators and judicial education organizations in establishing continuing legal education programs for law students, practitioners, and judges.

Recommendation 11

To improve medicolegal death investigation:

1. Congress should authorize and appropriate incentive funds to the NIFS for allocation to states and jurisdictions to establish medical examiner systems, with the goal of replacing and eventually eliminating existing coroner systems. Funds are needed to build regional medical examiner offices, secure necessary equipment, improve administration, and ensure the education, training, and staffing of medical examiner offices. Funding could also be used to help current medical examiner systems modernize their facilities to meet current Centers for Disease Control and Prevention–recommended autopsy safety requirements.
2. Congress should appropriate resources to the National Institutes of Health (NIH) and NIFS, jointly, to support research, education, and training in forensic pathology. NIH, with NIFS participation, or NIFS in collaboration with content experts, should establish a study section to establish goals, to review and evaluate proposals in these areas, and to allocate funding for collaborative research to be conducted by medical examiner offices and medical universities. In addition, funding, in the form of medical student loan forgiveness and/or fellowship support should be made available to pathology residents who choose forensic pathology as their specialty.
3. NIFS, in collaboration with NIH, the National Association of Medical Examiners, the American Board of Medicolegal Death Investigators, and other appropriate professional organizations, should establish a Scientific Working Group (SWG) for forensic pathology and medicolegal death investigation. The SWG should develop and promote standards for best practices, administration, staffing, education, training, and continuing education for competent death scene investigation and postmortem examinations. Best practices should include the utilization of new technologies such as laboratory testing for the molecular basis of diseases and the implementation of specialized imaging techniques.
4. All medical examiner offices should be accredited pursuant to NIFS-endorsed standards within a timeframe to be established by NIFS.
5. All federal funding should be restricted to accredited offices that meet NIFS-endorsed standards or that demonstrate significant and measurable progress in achieving accreditation within prescribed deadlines.
6. All medicolegal autopsies should be performed or supervised by a board certified forensic pathologist. This requirement should take effect within a timeframe to be established by NIFS, following consultation with governing state institutions.

Recommendation 12

Congress should authorize and appropriate funds for the NIFS to launch a new broad-based effort to achieve nationwide fingerprint data interoperability. To that end, NIFS should convene a task force comprising relevant experts from the National Institute of Standards and Technology and the major law enforcement agencies (including representatives from the local, state, federal, and, perhaps, international levels) and industry, as appropriate, to develop

1. Standards for representing and communicating image and minutiae data among Automated Fingerprint Identification Systems. Common data standards would facilitate the sharing of fingerprint data among law enforcement

agencies at the local, state, federal, and even international levels, which could result in more solved crimes, fewer wrongful identifications, and greater efficiency with respect to fingerprint searches.

2. Baseline standards—to be used with computer algorithms—to map, record, and recognize features in fingerprint images, and a research agenda for the continued improvement, refinement, and characterization of the accuracy of these algorithms (including quantification of error rates).

Recommendation 13

Congress should provide funding to the NIFS to prepare, in conjunction with the Centers for Disease Control and Prevention and the FBI, forensic scientists and CSIs for their potential roles in managing and analyzing evidence from events that affect homeland security, so that maximum evidentiary value is preserved from these unusual circumstances and the safety of these personnel is guarded. This preparation also should include planning and preparedness (to include exercises) for the interoperability of local forensic personnel with federal counterterrorism organizations.

Summary

Forensic science is the application of scientific methods to solving crimes. Any science can be a forensic science if it has an application to the criminal justice system. The largest area of forensic science is criminalistics, which includes the physical evidence that commonly occurs at crime scenes. There are about 400 crime labs in the United States. Several departments in the Federal Government have forensic science labs. These include Justice, Treasury and Interior. Each state has its own forensic science laboratory system. These include labs run by state or local government.

Forensic scientists analyze evidence and testify in court as expert witnesses. They may also go to some crime scenes where especially serious or notorious crimes have been committed. Crime laboratories must be secure so that evidence can be protected. There are many types of labs but they all have an intake section, an analysis section, and a storage location for evidence.

Test Yourself

Multiple Choice

1. Which of the following Federal Departments does *not* have a forensic science lab?
   a. Interior
   b. Justice
   c. Commerce
   d. Treasury
   e. All of these have forensic science labs
2. Which of the following is generally *not* considered to be a forensic science?
   a. Chemistry
   b. Biology
   c. Anthropology
   d. Odontology
   e. Sociology

3. California has about ____% of the crime labs in the United States
   a. 10
   b. 50
   c. 25
   d. 12
   e. 1
4. Which of the following is *not* part of forensic anthropology?
   a. Matching teeth to a bitemark
   b. Identification of skeletal remains
   c. Building a face on a skull
   d. Superimposition of the picture of a face onto a skull
   e. Determining the gender of a skeleton
5. DNA typing is part of
   a. Forensic pathology
   b. Criminalistics
   c. Odontology
   d. Engineering
   e. Criminal investigation
6. If a forensic science laboratory uses a barcode system as part of its evidence identification, the barcode would be affixed to the evidence when
   a. The evidence is about to be analyzed
   b. When the final report is written
   c. As soon as the evidence is accepted by the lab
   d. When the evidence is put in central storage
   e. When the evidence is returned to the submitting officer
7. Which of the following is *not* a forensic application of science?
   a. Identification of human remains through dental x-rays
   b. Verifying the composition of an aspirin tablet before it leaves the factory
   c. Identification of a bag of tablets taken from a car when the driver is stopped for erratic driving
   d. Determination of why a ferris wheel crashed at an amusement park when three people were killed
8. From the time you graduate from high school until you are certified as a forensic pathologist takes about ____ years.
   a. 4
   b. 8
   c. 12
   d. 13
   e. 16
9. Go to the AAFS (www.aafs.org) and look up "Daubert Tracker." This service permits a site visitor to
   a. Tracks Dauberts
   b. Keeps the forensic scientist up to date on some legal aspects of scientific evidence
   c. Determine when the annual Academy meeting is
   d. Keep track of new types of scientific evidence
   e. Tracks dues payments to the Academy
10. On the website for the Society of Forensic Toxicology (www.soft-tox.org), the definition of forensic toxicology includes all of the following *except*
    a. Postmortem forensic toxicology
    b. Analysis of suspected drug powders

   c. Forensic urine testing

   d. Analysis of blood and body fluids for human performance altering drugs

   e. All of these are included in the definition of forensic toxicology

Match Each of the Following Terms with Its Definition

11. Determines cause and manner of death_____	a. Anthropology
12. Identifies people from their teeth_____	b. Pathology
13. Reconstructs hard disc drives_____	c. Entomology
14. Analyzes bone fragments_____	d. Computer forensics
15. Determines role of insects in investigations_____	e. Engineer
16. Determines how a bridge collapsed_____	f. Odontologist

Fill in the Blanks

17. The _____ is the United Kingdom national forensic science system.

18. Mail fraud is investigated by the _____.

19. The federal laboratory whose responsibility is the investigation and analysis of illicit drugs is the _____.

20. The two major duties of a forensic scientist in a crime lab are _____ and _____.

21. The national "umbrella" organization for forensic science in the United States is the _____.

22. When evidence is brought into a crime laboratory it is delivered to the _____ section.

Short Essays

23. What makes a science "forensic"? Give an example of dentistry (odontology) that is forensic and one that is not? Do the same thing for engineering?

24. An increasing trend in crime scene investigation is to have forensic scientists from a crime lab go to some crime scenes and help the CSIs with searching the scene for evidence. What advantages and disadvantages would there be to this practice?

25. Since 1992, the national forensic science system in the United Kingdom now operates on a fee per service basis; everyone, police and defendants alike, are charged for forensic analysis, whereas in the United States, crime labs are generally run be a unit of government and they are for the use of police and prosecutors only. Defendants have no access to public crime lab facilities. What are the advantages and disadvantages of each system? Why do you think that the United Kingdom changed over to fee for service model?

Further Reading

James, S. H. and J. J. Nordby (eds.). (2003). *Forensic Science: An Introduction to Scientific and Investigative Techniques*. CRC Press, Boca Raton, FL.

National Research Council. (2009). *Strengthening Forensic Science in the United States: A Path Forward*. National Research Council, Washington, DC.

Siegel, J. and P. Sauko (eds.). (2011). *Encyclopedia of Forensic Sciences*, vols. 1–4, 2nd edn. Academic Press, London, U.K.

Thorwald, J. (1964). *The Century of the Detective*. Harcourt, Brace & World, New York.

On the Web

How does a forensic anthropologist analyze bone fragments? http://www.anthro4n6.net/forensics/.

Learn all about forensic entomology including some real cases: http://research.missouri.edu/entomology/.

Take an online tour of a real crime lab: http://www.ok.gov/osbi/Forensic_Laboratory/Virtual_Tour/index.html.

You can learn a lot about forensic science and solve a virtual crime at: http://www.virtualmuseum.ca/Exhibitions/Myst/en/game/entry/index.phtml.

2

Crime Scene Investigation

Learning Objectives

1. To be able to describe the characteristics of a crime scene
2. To be able to list the steps in the investigation of a crime scene
3. To be able to list the steps in the collection of evidence
4. To be able to define the chain of custody and describe its elements
5. To be able to list and describe the ways of searching a crime scene
6. To be able to list and describe the ways of documenting a crime scene
7. To be able to complete a rough draft and final sketch of a mock crime scene

Chapter 2
Crime Scene Investigation

Chapter Outline

Mini Glossary

Authentication: Documenting who has possession of crime-related evidence from the point of collection to its appearance in a court of law.

Chain of custody: A physical log for a single piece of evidence that documents who had possession of the evidence and when the evidence was in his or her possession. It is a flowchart of the movement of evidence from collection to processing at the crime lab to presentation in court.

***Corpus delicti*:** The Latin translation is "body of crime." *Corpus delicti* means that it must be proven that a crime has occurred before an individual can be convicted of committing a crime. For example: A death must be ruled a homicide before anyone can be tried for murder or a fire must be ruled as an arson in order for a person to be tried for setting the fire.

CSI: The acronym for Crime Scene Investigation or Crime Scene Investigator.

Documentation: Recording in detail the conditions when the crime occurred.

Druggist's fold (or evidence fold): Small pieces of evidence are packaged in druggist folds (papers) to ensure that they are not lost. They are sometimes also referred to as "evidence folds." The folded paper is then placed in standard evidence packaging.

Exemplars: These are baseline, known evidence such as fingerprints, DNA, hair, or voiceprints collected from suspects or victims in order to compare with evidence taken from a crime scene. Exemplars are sometimes referred to as "knowns" or "controls."

First responder: The initial police officer at the crime scene is regarded as the first responder.

***Modus Operandi* (MO):** The Latin translation means "mode of operation." This refers to the style or method that a criminal uses when committing a crime. For repeat offenders, an MO may assist investigators in locating the suspect due to his or her characteristic way of committing the crime.

***Postmortem* Interval (PMI):** *Postmortem* interval is the length of time from discovery of a dead body to the time the victim died.

Probative: A piece of evidence that tends to prove or disprove a fact or assertion.

Protocol: In criminal investigations, protocol is an established, detailed plan or procedure that must be implemented for evidence to be valid.

Search methods: Evidence may be located using a systematic approach to survey the site. These methods employ spiral, grid, line, or zone techniques.

Sting operation: Law enforcement agents stage a scenario whereby criminals are encouraged to commit crimes that they would probably have committed anyway.

Tamper-evident packaging: Specific types of containers or packages for crime scene evidence that have seals that can only be opened by tearing or cutting, thereby giving proof of access.

Acronyms

BATF: Bureau of Alcohol, Tobacco and Firearms
CSI: Crime scene investigation or crime scene investigator
MO: Modus Operandi
PMI: Postmortem Interval

Introduction

A crime has been committed. It was a recent event, but it happened in the past, therefore a crime scene can be thought of as a piece of history. Like all historical places, the crime scene has a story to tell. Anthropologists and archaeologists investigate places where ancient civilizations once lived. They look for evidence of who lived there and how they lived. Perhaps they will find clues as to the fate of the citizens. Historians examine the site of a Civil War battlefield to learn many things, like how the battle was fought, how many people fought and died, what they wore, and what armaments they used. Crime scene investigators carefully and systematically sift through a crime scene to learn how and when the crime was committed, who committed it and why, and perhaps what items may have been removed from the scene. All of these historical scenes—the ancient village, the hundred-year-old battlefield, and yesterday's homicide scene—contain evidence that, if properly collected, analyzed, and interpreted, tells the story behind the events that took place.

Crime Scene as Recent History

It is useful to think of a crime scene as history because it has much in common with older historical sites. The proper methods of conducting an archaeological dig and reconstruction of a battle are similar to the methods that should be used to successfully search a crime scene. Some areas of similarity are as follows:

Timing: A historical scene changes all the time, especially if it is outdoors. For ancient ruins, this may not be too important in the short run. A couple of weeks of delay in searching a ten-thousand-year-old village will probably have little consequence. For crimes that occurred only a few hours or days ago, however, *time may be of the essence*. For example, if a burglary is not discovered and solved within an hour after it occurs, research has shown that it probably never will be. The trail gets cold really quickly.

Plan of attack: There must be a plan for *systematically searching the site* that ensures that no stone is left unturned without needlessly covering the same area again and again.

Safety issues: *Safety of the scene searchers* must be considered. Hazards at the ancient remains of a city are going to be different from those at a modern crime scene, although the flooring in a house that had major fire damage may be just as unstable as the ancient ruins of a building.

Appropriate personnel: Only *highly qualified, trained personnel should conduct the search* of the site.

Controlling the scene: *Contamination must be minimized* by permitting access to the site to as few people as possible. Additionally, those persons at the scene may be asked to give elimination samples if necessary to compare with collected evidence. For example, CSI team members may be asked for samples of their DNA.

Documentation: Every instance of searching an historical site further changes it. Evidence is found and then is moved or removed. Gathering evidence is a vital part of learning the story of the site. Once it changes, it will never be the same again. This is an important concept in searching a crime scene. The *crime scene must be documented thoroughly* so that a record can be made of its condition when the crime occurred. This includes labeling the location of each piece of evidence when it is discovered. Ultimately, the evidence will be useful in establishing that a crime has actually occurred and someone must be prosecuted for it, a process called *corpus delicti*.

One major difference in the documentation of a crime scene from that of historical sites is that there must be a *chain of custody* for each piece of evidence that is removed from the scene. The chain of custody begins when the evidence is discovered.

In the remainder of this chapter, the crime scene investigation process will be detailed. Evidence collection procedures described are the recognition of evidence, documentation of evidence, collection of evidence, and the delivery of evidence to the laboratory for analysis.

Crime Scene Investigation Process

A number of procedures take place at a crime scene. Some procedures are always followed, while others depend on the nature of the scene and the circumstances surrounding the crime. Figure 2.1 shows the overall process that takes place during a crime scene investigation.

Crime Occurs and Is Discovered

There are three ways that crimes are discovered:

1. A witness sees a crime in progress and reports it to the police.
2. The victim of a crime reports it to the police.
3. The police discover a crime in progress.

In the first case, someone witnesses a crime in progress. An example of this is when someone is walking down the street at night and sees someone leaving a dark electronics store with arms full of merchandize. Another example is when someone hears what sounds like a gunshot at a next door neighbor's house and runs over to investigate, only to find the owner dead or injured. No one else seems to be around.

In an example of a crime being reported by a victim, the owner of a small business arrives at work one morning and finds that the safe has been opened and money stolen. The owner calls the police to report the robbery and the crime scene investigation begins.

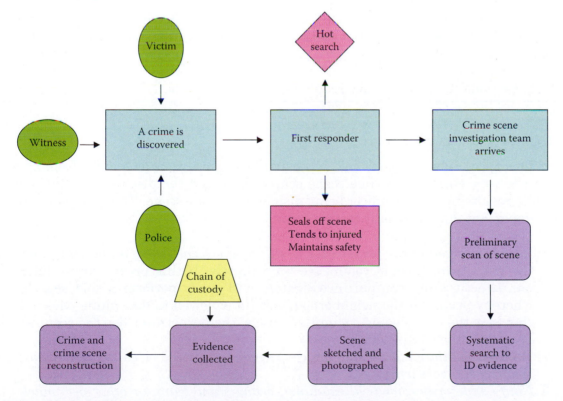

Figure 2.1 This diagram shows the steps in a typical crime scene investigation.

A situation where a police officer discovers a crime in progress is when an officer stops a speeding car and finds a hoard of illegal weapons in the back seat. Police may also "discover" a crime by staging a *sting operation*. These are situations where law enforcement agents set up a scenario whereby criminals are encouraged to commit crimes that they would probably have done anyway.

Example of a Sting Operation

A sting operation is set up by the local police and/or federal agents as a type of proactive law enforcement. One of the earliest examples of a sting operations occurred in Washington, DC, in the 1960s. This was a joint FBI and Washington, DC Police Department operation to combat major theft rings operating in the city. The agents and police set up a storefront operation and put the word out on the street that the store was a well-financed "fencing" operation (a fence is someone who buys stolen merchandise and resells it at a profit). Further, the word was that this operation was being run by "organized crime" (the Mafia). Anyone who had something of value to sell would get top dollar with no questions asked.

The "store" was rigged with a one-way mirror so that the police could videotape the "sales" through the glass without being detected. All the crooks could see was a mirror. To make sure that each seller would look at the camera, a picture of a bikini-clad model was prominently posted.

The sting operation was supposed to last a month and had a budget of several thousand dollars. It was so wildly successful that the operation ran out of money in a week and had captured more than two hundred transactions on tape. Included in the haul were stacks of stolen Social Security checks and typewriters (no computers back then) from government buildings.

In order to avoid having to track down all of the crooks and arrest them, the "owners" advertised a big party at the end of the operation. Virtually all of the participants were invited and were promised a chance to meet the "Godfather." What they got were handcuffs and a trip to jail. Faced with a videotape of their "transactions" every one of the scofflaws pled guilty to theft.

First Officer at the Crime Scene

Archaeological digs and battlefield reconstructions involve large teams of searchers from the very start. In a crime scene search, however, the discovery of the crime usually results in a police officer being dispatched to the scene. This officer has several important duties, usually in this order:

1. *Ascertain whether the perpetrator is still at the scene*: If so, a hot search for the perpetrator should commence immediately. If this proves futile, later on, detectives or criminal investigators will likely perform a cold search, whereby people in the neighborhood are interviewed to determine whether they saw the crime being committed or saw the perpetrator flee the scene or observed other suspicious events.
2. *Tend to the injured*: If an ambulance is needed, it should be called right away. Waiting can cost lives.
3. *Notify supervisors, medical examiner, crime scene team, or other personnel*: It will take time for requested personnel to arrive at the location. Once the team has arrived, the investigation process can commence.

4. *Secure consent or a warrant to search the scene*: Unless there is an emergency situation, such as threats to someone's life or safety, destruction or removal of evidence, or possible escape of the perpetrator, the officer should obtain the right to enter a crime scene. According to the Fourth Amendment of the United States Constitution, in order for the crime scene search to be constitutional, "consent must be given voluntarily by a person reasonably believed by law enforcement officers to have lawful access and control over the premises. In most cases, this will be the person who called police to the scene." If consent is not possible, a warrant or judicial order authorizing a search must be obtained.

5. *Secure the scene*: Contamination of the scene must be minimized. The number of people who have access to the scene must be limited and the entry and exit paths of these personnel should be determined. Initially, it is advantageous to make the scene perimeter large to prevent loss of any pertinent evidence. For example, if a crime occurred in a home, consider the entry and exit of the perpetrator as important and secure the outside of the home, too. Footprints and tire tracks are just as important as the physical evidence found inside a residence. If a body is found in the woods, the potential scene can be quite large and isolating it can be difficult.

6. *Avoid walking through the scene and searching for evidence*: Remember that any contact with a crime scene alters it forever. Searches of even localized crime scenes must be done by professionals who have formulated a search plan. In some cases, what appears to be the scene of the crime may not be. The site may have been set up to look like a crime scene so as to divert attention from the real scene.

7. *Note any obvious safety hazards*: Strange smells could be gas or potentially dangerous chemicals that may pose a fire or poison hazard. Structures may be weakened or rigged to kill or maim. Electrical wires may be exposed. The job of the first officer at the scene is not to remediate these hazards but to protect others from them and to warn personnel who subsequently come to the scene. The 1991 Universal Studios movie, *Backdraft* had a scene that illustrates the situation where a crime scene is rigged to cause harm to investigators. A fire was set in a building that was then completely sealed up. When the oxygen became depleted and could no longer support flames, the fire began to smolder. When the fire department arrived and broke in to the building, the onrush of oxygen into the building caused the fire to explode into flame. Firemen were killed and injured. This also happens in real-life fires and may occur naturally as a fire proceeds.

Protocol at the Crime Scene

The examination of a crime scene must follow the *protocol* established for the crime scene investigative unit. Protocol is a detailed plan or procedure established by law enforcement that must be implemented for evidence to be valid and admissible in a court of law. Following protocol insures that all crime scenes will be investigated in the same manner by using established guidelines. Following procedural guidelines becomes important when police officers and crime scene investigators must testify in court regarding the validity of evidence.

As soon as possible after the crime scene has been discovered and protected, the *crime scene investigation* (CSI) *unit* will arrive. If there is a deceased individual at the scene, someone from the medical examiner's or coroner's office will take charge of processing the body. This person will normally be a forensic pathologist who certifies that the person is dead and makes a preliminary determination of the *postmortem interval* (PMI) or the time since death. This topic will be covered in more detail in the chapter on forensic pathology. If there is a body at the scene, some police departments dispatch a death scene CSI squad to process and remove the body from the scene. This processing includes photographing the body, making sure all trace evidence is protected and gathered, and transporting the body to the medical examiner's or coroner's laboratory.

Once any victim(s) has been cared for, the crime scene unit, usually made up of specially trained police officers, takes charge of the crime scene. Each member of the team has a defined role, such as sketching the scene, photographing the scene, searching the scene for evidence or documenting the collection of evidence. Fingerprint and blood spatter technicians may also be called to the scene if needed.

Preliminary Scene Examination

The first duty of the CSI unit is to conduct a preliminary examination of the scene. This is done for a number of reasons. Safety hazards can be promptly addressed and remediated. The boundaries of the crime scene must be ascertained. This may be a simple process if the crime clearly occurred in one room of a house (keeping in mind that routes of entry and escape can be very important sources of evidence). If the crime is outdoors, then fixing the boundaries of the scene can be very difficult. The area where the crime was committed may only be the primary crime scene. Perpetrators often carry evidence away from the scene and there may be one or more secondary locations where important evidence may be found.

Additionally, if preliminary examination of the scene has some aspects similar to other recent crimes in an area, the investigators may look at the *modus operandi* or MO of the crime. *Modus operandi* is the pattern or method of operation that a criminal repeatedly uses during an illegal act. A repetitive MO could imply the work of a single criminal in more than one crime.

Systematic Search of the Crime Scene

After the preliminary examination of the scene has been made, systematic documentation and searching begins. This is a meticulous process carried out to minimize alteration of the scene, which can happen if personnel are not careful when conducting their investigation. Photographing the scene is carried out as early as possible. Although regular film photography is still used in crime scene investigations, the recent trend has been to use digital photography because digital photographs can be seen immediately. In addition, digital pictures are easily incorporated into computerized crime records and reports. It is also common for the crime scene team to use videotape or digital movies to complete a walk-through of the scene. This is very effective for the jury in order to get an overall sense of the scene. It is important, however, for the audio of the tape to be silenced so that no comments are inadvertently shared that could influence a jury.

One of the first decisions to be made is the search pattern that will be used at the crime scene. There are four basic types of *search methods* that can be used, depending on the type of crime scene. For example, if the entire crime scene is one room of a house, a search may begin at one end of the room and proceed in a *spiral* fashion toward the center or may be a back-and-forth (*line*) pattern across the room. If the scene includes several rooms, each one is searched systematically using a *zone* method. If the scene is outdoors in a large area, it may be necessary to divide the scene into *grids* and then search each grid. Examples of each method are shown in Figure 2.2.

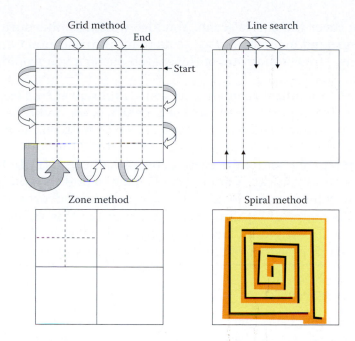

Figure 2.2 Four general methods used to systematically search a crime scene.

Sometimes, unusual tactics are used to search a crime scene such as those described in the 1984 shooting of police officer Yvonne Fletcher at the Libyan Embassy in London, England. It is seldom necessary to devote the large amounts of investigative resources that were used in this case, but the crime was very serious and had major political implications at the time. Also, the police had lost one of their own and they were eager to find the evidence that would bring the killer(s) to justice. This case illustrates that sometimes unusual methods are needed to effectively search a crime scene.

Yvonne Fletcher

On April 27, 1984, an 11-day siege ended at the Libyan Embassy in London. The siege was the result of the shooting of a London police officer, Yvonne Fletcher, on April 17. Witnesses saw smoke and flame from a first floor window of the Embassy right before the officer fell. When she was loaded onto a gurney and taken to the hospital, a slug that had hit her fell out of her body and onto the ground. The slug was missing when the forensic pathologist did the *postmortem* examination. It was very important to find the slug so it could be compared to the weapon if found. The area in question was a large courtyard in front of the embassy. More than fifty police officers gathered in the courtyard and then crawled shoulder to shoulder on their hands and knees all the way across the courtyard in search of the slug. It was found and later matched to the suspect weapon.

Something for You to Do

Go into the largest room in your house (this may be the garage). Ask someone in your family to plant a piece of "evidence" in the room. This could be a small object that could be evidence in a real crime. It could be hair, fiber, or paint chips, or other trace evidence. You should figure out how you would search this scene to make sure you cover the entire scene. You also want to make sure you do not go over the same ground more than once so as to minimize contact and contamination of the scene. Draw a diagram of the search pattern you would use to search this scene.

Now go into the smallest room in your house and repeat this exercise. Next go outdoors to your front yard or backyard or a nearby park and repeat the exercise again. Did you decide to use the same type of search pattern in each case? Why? In which case(s) would you try and get help in searching the scene? After you have developed a strategy for searching each scene, pick one and try to find the object.

See if your strategy works. You may not be able to find the object, especially if you do not know what you are looking for or you may inadvertently step on it or track extraneous material into the scene and mistake this for evidence. This is what crime scene investigators face every day in their work. Crime scene investigation is a difficult process even for experienced investigators.

Recording the Crime Scene

Historically, there have been two basic methods of documenting a crime scene and recording its condition and the locations of all of the evidence. The first was making a sketch of the crime scene, while the second was using photography to document a scene. Each method enhanced the effectiveness of the other.

The crime scene sketch was done by first making a freehand sketch and then taking measurements of the positions of various objects with reference to at least two fixed positions in the scene. Later on, this sketch would be translated into a scale drawing of the scene. The second method was by still photography (35 mm) using regular film. Many pictures would be taken under various light conditions and at various distances and angles in the hope that some would properly record the scene. Measuring instruments, such as small rulers, would be put in photographs where size perspective was important, as with shoeprints and tire treads. Without a scale to show size for such evidence, it would be difficult to admit such evidence into court as demonstrative evidence. Figure 2.3 shows a picture of a shoeprint. Note the ruler in the picture.

Today, the situation is different but some of the old practices are still used. Hand-drawn crime scene sketches, as shown in Figure 2.4, are still used and measurements

Figure 2.3 A shoeprint in soil with a ruler. The ruler is used to show the size of the shoeprint. (From Bodziak, W.T., *Footwear Impression Evidence*, 2nd edn., Taylor & Francis, New York, 2000. With permission.)

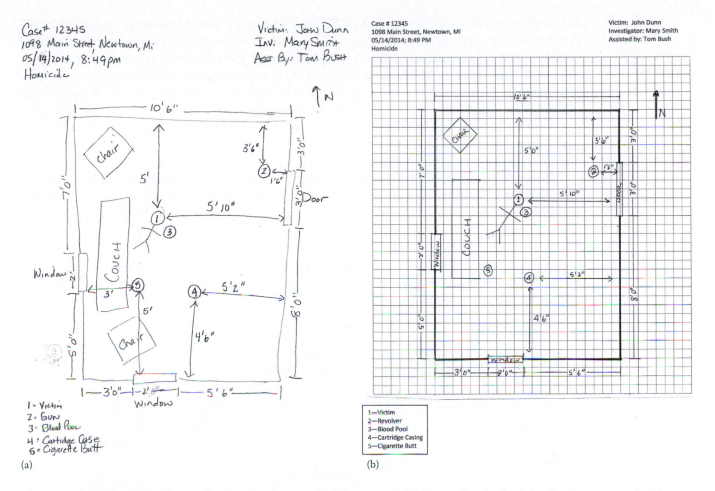

Case# 12345
1098 Main Street, Newtown, Mi
05/14/2014, 8:49pm
Homicide

Victim: John Dunn
Inv: Mary Smith
Ass By: Tom Bush

Case # 12345
1098 Main Street, Newtown, MI
05/14/2014; 8:49 PM
Homicide

Victim: John Dunn
Investigator: Mary Smith
Assisted by: Tom Bush

1 = Victim
2 = Gun
3 = Blood Pool
4 = Cartidge Case
5 = Cigarette Butt

1—Victim
2—Revolver
3—Blood Pool
4—Cartridge Casing
5—Cigarette Butt

(a)

(b)

Figure 2.4 (a) Example of a rough sketch—done at the crime scene. (b) Example of a final draft crime scene sketch.

taken, but the scale drawings are often rendered on a computer that has specialized crime scene reconstruction software.

Sometimes, scale models of crime scenes are made from cardboard, wood, plaster, and the like. An extreme example of modeling is performed at the Federal Bureau of Alcohol, Tobacco, and Firearms (BATF) at its fire research laboratory near Beltsville, MD. In cases where a fire has occurred in an apartment or house, a construction crew builds an exact model of the structure to scale and then recreates the fire conditions as precisely as possible so the progress and damage caused by the fire can be studied. The BATF laboratory employs professional builders to construct the structures that are then sacrificed to research. The fires are carried out in a huge building equipped with exhaust fans and filters that prevent particulates and harmful gases from escaping.

Today, crime scenes are often videotaped. A crime scene investigator will walk the crime scene with a video camera and take footage from all angles. This can take the place of some of the still photography, but will not replace the crime scene sketch. There is even one company, 3rd Tech, that makes an automatic video system. A camera is set up in a room and it takes thousands of frames of the scene in a 360° arc that, when reconstructed, provides unprecedented details about the locations of objects and perspectives at the scene.

The 35 mm cameras are still used at crime scenes to photograph individual objects, but this method of taking photos is rapidly being replaced by digital photography.

Advantages to digital photography of crime scenes include the ability to easily incorporate pictures into reports and the ability to examine a photo right after it has been taken so the photographer will know right away if the picture is useable. Digital photographs can also be *enhanced* or touched up using computer software such as Adobe Photoshop®. This is not the same as *altering* digital photos, which would be called into question in a court of law. The forensic photographer must inform the court which photos were enhanced and what was done to enhance them. Enhancement is used only to make the original photo clearer for presentation to the jury, and must never be used to change the photographic evidence or alter it.

Photographs are taken in an organized manner. First, the entire scene is photographed from each corner of the structure, room or object. Then the item of interest is photographed from a distance, mid-range, and then close-up with and without a scale in the picture. Figure 2.5 shows outside and interior room photography. Figure 2.6 illustrates photography of a victim.

Additionally, it is useful to photograph any bystanders at the crime scene. These photographs can aid in identifying witnesses or in some cases the actual perpetrator, as criminals sometimes like to watch the police process crime scenes.

Distance shot of residence, walkway to entrance, front door entrance

Living room views from all four corners.

Figure 2.5 Crime scene photography. Outside photographs should document the entire residence, the path to the residence, and the entrance. Similar shots should be made of the rear of the home. Each room should be photographed entirely and as seen from all four corners.

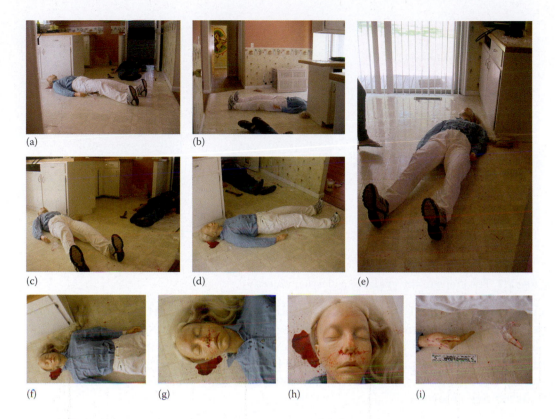

Figure 2.6 Crime scene photography. The female victim is photographed at various locations in the room (a–e). Then close-up shots are captured of her injuries and potentially important evidence (f–i).

Collection of Evidence

There is an old saying in crime labs: "You cannot make chicken salad out of chicken feathers." This is a reminder that the results of the scientific analysis of evidence from a crime scene are only as good as the evidence brought to the lab. If evidence is contaminated or degraded or the wrong evidence is collected, the evidence will be of limited or no value. The collection, preservation, and packaging of evidence are crucial to a successful criminal investigation. Under ideal circumstances, crime scene investigation would be done by the forensic scientists who analyze the evidence because they know best how to recognize, collect, preserve, and package it.

Unfortunately, caseloads being what they are, forensic scientists cannot afford the time it would take to process all crime scenes. The trend today, however, is to have a forensic scientist team respond to homicides and other serious crimes and they work with the crime scene investigators to process the scene. They form a team of experts whose areas of expertise might be important to the investigation. This would include DNA analysts, serologists (who are experts in locating and collecting small blood stains or other body fluids and who can process blood spatter patterns), and trace evidence scientists (who are adept at recognizing which trace evidence is important and how to properly collect it). Other specialists may be called in from time to time. For example, one or more forensic drug chemists are usually called on to help investigate scenes of clandestine drug activity such as a methamphetamine lab operation. These scenes can be very dangerous because of flammable chemicals and a lack of safety concerns by the homeowner. Clandestine laboratories are discussed in greater detail in the chapter on illicit drugs. When forensic scientist crime scene teams are sent to help local crime scene investigators process complex scenes,

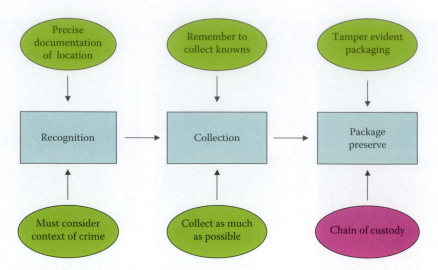

Figure 2.7 The steps in the evidence collection process.

there is an agreement in place that establishes when the lab team is sent out and how the chain of command at the crime scene will be determined.

Three major steps in the process of evidence collection are recognition, collection, and packaging/preservation. Each has other considerations that are important for the other steps. Figure 2.7 shows how these steps and their associated processes are related.

Recognition of Evidence

An object at a crime scene must be recognized as evidence before it can be collected. When you did the exercise of searching a room in your house or outdoors for evidence, you had the advantage of knowing what is supposed to be in these rooms. It is easier to recognize something that is out of place or does not belong to that place. That advantage is lost at a crime scene. The crime scene investigators do not know what objects belong to that particular location and therefore they do not know what objects may have been left there by the perpetrator. So how do investigators know what *is* evidence and what *is not*? This takes a thorough knowledge of what is likely to be present at the scene of a given type of crime. Homicides, burglaries, sexual assaults, and other types of crimes usually contain characteristic types of evidence that the crime scene investigator would hope or expect to find. For a homicide, this might be a weapon, blood, fiber, and hair, and fingerprints. For a burglary, one might expect to find tools, glass, soil, and perhaps fingerprints. For a rape scene, investigation often turns up hair, fiber, and body fluid such as semen. This does not mean, of course, that these are the only items that will be present. These are guidelines that investigators use to start their search. The context of the crime, the type of crime, and the type of scene are very important in providing clues to what evidence should be present. If the crime looks similar to another recent one, investigators might be watchful for evidence that would suggest the same MO (*modus operandi*) and therefore the same perpetrator.

In general, there is no such thing as too much evidence. If an investigator has doubts about whether an object is significant, it should be collected and sent to the lab. As the investigation proceeds and the scene is reconstructed, it will be easier to determine whether the material is actually evidence. Once the crime scene unit is finished with the scene and it is released to the owners, it will not be possible to return and collect more evidence. For example, suppose an investigator comes upon fibers at a scene and neglects to collect them. Later on, it is determined that these fibers are important evidence, but the owners have taken possession of the premises and have vacuumed the carpets. The evidence is lost forever.

Once evidence is located but before it is collected, its exact location must be recorded. This may be done by photography and/or measurements with respect to a fixed object. This is necessary so that when reconstruction of the crime scene is done, the location of the evidence will be known. After it is moved and taken to the lab, evidence cannot be relocated at the scene. Besides the location of the evidence, other information must be recorded for chain of custody purposes. This will be discussed in more detail in the "Packaging and Preserving" section.

Collection

How much evidence should be collected? The short answer is: as much as possible. At clandestine drug laboratories, everything that could have any remote connection with the manufacturing operation is collected. In the case of illicit drug seizures, all of the drugs are collected, even if tons are involved. The forensic science laboratory will sort out the issue of sampling for analysis purposes later. In many cases involving trace evidence, the lack of sample may limit the tests that the scientists can do. In addition, the rules of evidence in the United States require that the defendant be given a fair chance to perform tests on the evidence. If it can be shown that there was more evidence available that was not collected or the government crime lab used all that was collected, the defense attorney may be able to have the evidence excluded from the trial on the grounds that the defense did not have an opportunity to analyze the evidence with its own expert.

Another important consideration in the collection of evidence is the issue of comparison samples, or "knowns." Knowns are also referred to as *exemplars*. Exemplars are baseline, known evidence such as fingerprints, DNA, hair, or voiceprints collected from suspects or victims for comparison with evidence taken from a crime scene. (The concept of known versus unknown evidence is further discussed in the next chapter.) With many types of evidence, the *probative* value or significance in the case can be greatly enhanced if it can be compared with and linked to a known material or object. Fingerprints found on an object have little meaning unless they can be compared to the exemplar fingerprints of a suspect and then shown to have originated from that person. Known evidence may be found at the crime scene or may be taken later from a suspect or another location linked to the primary crime scene. Known evidence (or exemplars) may link a suspect to the crime or may serve as elimination samples—samples that clear an individual from involvement in the crime.

A Really Big Case

In 1985, the U.S. Coast Guard seized a private boat that was racing up the Atlantic Coast near Virginia. The boat was boarded and 8.5 tons (17,000 lb) of suspected marijuana was found. This was taken to the Drug Enforcement Administration (DEA) lab in Washington, DC, where it was identified as marijuana. Then it was transported to the Baltimore garbage incinerator where it was to be destroyed. The defense attorney in the case wanted the evidence analyzed by his own expert prior to its destruction. The expert (one of the authors of this book) went to the incinerator and found hundreds of bales of marijuana, each weighing hundreds of pounds. He took representative core samples from each bale. A DEA chemist followed behind and also took a sample from each bale. After each bale was sampled, it was incinerated. The resulting total sample weighed approximately 5 lb. This raises the issue of representative sampling of large exhibits of drugs. This topic is covered in the chapter on illicit drugs.

Packaging and Preserving Evidence

Once the evidence has been located and collected, it must be properly packaged. This may not seem too important at first glance, but it can be critical to a case. There are physical, scientific, and legal requirements that determine how evidence should be packaged, and today appropriate packaging is available for all types of evidence.

Attention to detail and following proper protocol are vital when collecting evidence. Only one type of item can be collected per container or package. Crime scene personnel must change their gloves and tools after each item is collected to avoid contamination. These procedural guidelines make collection and preservation a long, tedious process, but they are essential for the proper preservation of evidence.

Chain of custody: Rules of evidence in federal and every state court in the United States require that all evidence be *authenticated*. Authentication requires:

1. A record of *who is in possession* of the evidence from the time it is collected at the crime scene until the time it is delivered to court. This detailed record is called the *chain of custody*.
2. The evidence must also be *uniquely identified* (e.g., using a bar code) in such a way so that it cannot be confused with any other piece of evidence and so that it can be shown that the evidence being used in court is the same evidence that was taken from the crime scene.
3. The evidence must also be *packaged* in *tamper-evident packaging*. This is both a document and a process that insures the integrity of the evidence. If the chain of custody has a substantial break—one that would seriously call into question the quality or integrity of the evidence—the evidence may be ruled inadmissible in court.

At one time, certain evidence from sexual assault cases was frequently challenged on chain of custody grounds. In cases of sexual assault, the victim is taken to a hospital (or often now to a SANE clinic—sexual assault nurse examiner). The victim's clothing is removed pursuant to an examination by a nurse or doctor. In years past, the clothes might be left in an examining room or elsewhere in the clinic that was not secure from the public. This clothing could potentially be the source of critical evidence of the identity of the perpetrator, especially in these days of DNA typing. Since no one was in possession and in charge of the evidence, the chain of custody might have been seriously damaged and evidence from these clothes might not have been admissible. Today, most hospitals and clinics have doctors and nurses who are trained in the collection and preservation of evidence from the victim. Crime labs or SANE clinics now supply doctors and nurses with "rape kits"—evidence kits that contain packaging for various types of evidence such as hair, vaginal swabs, individual articles of clothing, and so on. The packaging is suitable for the criminal justice system and the chain of custody.

Figure 2.8 shows a typical journey of evidence from crime scene to court with chain of custody considerations along the way. Note how many times the evidence changes hands during its journey. This is why it is so important to maintain a record of who is in possession of the evidence at any given time.

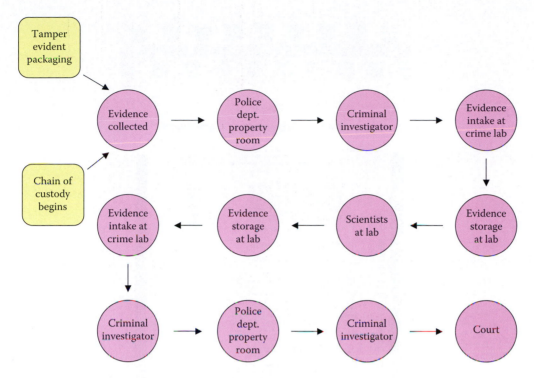

Figure 2.8 The flow of evidence from crime scene to court.

Two of the most important elements of the chain of custody are tamper-evident packaging and the custody form. Tamper-evident packaging is just that. Once the package is sealed, no one can open it without leaving evidence that the package was opened. It must be cut or torn to get inside. This is sometimes erroneously called "tamper-proof" packaging, but there is no such thing. Any package can be opened using whatever force is necessary. In addition, there must be a form, sometimes incorporated in the package itself that has space for whoever has custody of the evidence to sign and date the form. Every time the evidence changes hands, the donor and receiver sign and date the form. This form is kept with the evidence at all times. Figure 2.9 is an example of a chain of custody form.

An alternative to the tamper-evident container is tamper-evident tape. This can be applied to any bag, box, or pouch. It is very sticky and shreds when removed. Also, some of the glue from the tape is left behind on the package. Figure 2.10 shows one type of evidence tape.

Preserving Evidence

In addition to being tamper-evident, packaging for evidence must also be designed to preserve the evidence to the maximum extent possible. From the time evidence is collected, it may be weeks or months until scientists at the crime lab are able to analyze it (many labs have several months of case backlogs). Different types of evidence require unique packaging to preserve it. Some of the more common evidence types that need special packaging are the following:

Living plants (marijuana) must be packaged in "breathable" containers such as paper bags. If the plants are packaged in airtight containers, they will rot and may become useless.

Biological evidence (wet blood or body fluids) should be allowed to dry or, if packaged wet, the container must be breathable. Blood can also be packaged

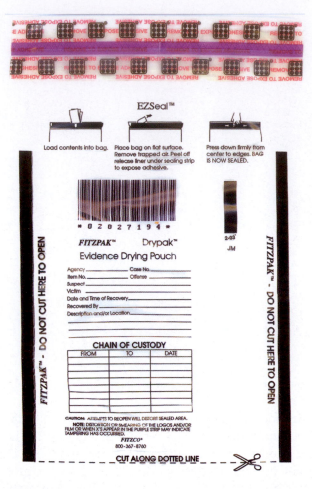

Figure 2.9 Tamper-evident packaging.

Figure 2.10 Tamper-proof evidence tape.

in a glass or plastic culture tube that contains a preservative, usually ethyl-enediamene tetraacetic acid (EDTA).

Wet paint should be allowed to dry or packaged in breathable container.

Trace evidence (hair, fiber, small paint chips, or glass) should be placed in an envelope or plastic baggie sealed on all sides. It is not recommended to use tape to hold this evidence (commonly called a "tape lift"). The glue in the tape can interfere with the chemical analysis of the evidence and the evidence may be difficult to remove from the tape. Evidence can be put in a *druggist's fold* (also called an *evidence fold*) and then put into a tamper-evident envelope. A druggist fold is a piece of paper folded in such a way as to keep the evidence from leaking or falling out.

Small amounts of powder should be put in paper with a druggist's fold and then an envelope or baggie.

Fire residue must be put in an airtight container. Unused paint cans are best. If fire residue is put in breathable containers, the accelerant will evaporate.

As a side note, *fingerprints* are typically the last evidence taken at the scene due to possible contamination of fingerprint dust with other crime scene evidence.

Reconstruction

Remember that a crime scene is a slice of recent history. It has a story to tell and the evidence at the scene helps tell the story. Each piece of evidence contributes to the story. Once the evidence has been collected, analyzed, and compared to known evidence, the criminal investigators, often with the help of forensic scientists, attempt to reconstruct the crime, including the identities of the victim(s) and the perpetrator(s) and the sequence of events that took place leading to the crime. The focus here is, of course, to link the suspect(s) to the crime through evidence and build a case that will stand up in court and convince a judge or jury of the guilt of the suspect beyond any reasonable doubt. Many types of evidence and circumstances go into building such a case, but one of the major foci must be the place where the crime occurred and the evidence that always accompanies the commission of any crime.

Summary

A crime scene is a place where a recent historical event—a crime—has taken place. As such, it has a story to tell about the events leading up to the crime, the crime itself, and the immediate aftermath including the escape of the perpetrator from the scene. Like scenes of ancient history, crime scenes contain clues or evidence that help tell the story of the crime. This evidence must be recognized, carefully collected and preserved, and delivered to a crime laboratory for analysis.

The basic steps in crime scene investigation include

Discovery of the crime
First officer responds
Crime scene protocol
Preliminary scene examination
Systematic search
Documentation
Evidence collection and preservation
Reconstructing the crime

This process must meet legal requirements, including the chain of custody, in order for the evidence to be admissible in court.

Test Yourself

Multiple Choice

1. A crime scene does *not* have which of the following in common with historical events:
   a. Highly trained persons should be involved in the investigation
   b. A systematic plan must always be followed
   c. The safety of the searchers is important
   d. Care should be taken to avoid contamination
   e. Documentation of items collected is optional
2. The purpose of documenting the chain of custody of evidence is
   a. To make sure it gets to the correct scientist in the lab
   b. To keep the evidence from falling out and getting lost
   c. To make sure that the evidence is admissible in court
   d. To keep it from getting stolen
   e. To be able to identify the type of evidence
3. Which of the following is *not* a duty of the first responder to a crime scene?
   a. Tend to injured people
   b. Transport a dead body to the morgue
   c. Seal off the crime scene
   d. Notify crime scene investigators
   e. Perform a hot search
4. Search methods of a scene include which of the following:
   a. Grid, line, zone, and aerial
   b. Grid, line, zone, and spiral
   c. Line, zone, aerial, and spiral
   d. Zone, spiral, sweep, and line
   e. Aerial, sweep, line, and zone
5. Photographs of a crime scene should be taken
   a. From a distance, mid-range, and close-up with and without a scale
   b. From a distance, mid-range, and close-up with a scale
   c. From a distance and close-up with and without a scale
   d. From four views at a distance and close-up
   e. Only from mid-range and close-up

True or False

6. All crime scene searches can be done by the grid method.
7. A cold search takes place long after the crime has occurred and assumes that the perpetrator has left the area.
8. An emergency medical technician (EMT) goes to a death scene to certify the death and make preliminary determinations as to the PMI.
9. A situation in which a police department sets up a scenario where people can commit crimes if they choose is called a reconstruction.
10. A druggist fold is used to package trace evidence.
11. Hand-drawn sketches of crime scenes are no longer done because of computer crime scene software.
12. All crime scenes are searched using the same type of search pattern.

Short Essay

13. List at least three roles that crime scene investigators can play at a crime scene.
14. Research and describe the difference between a primary crime scene and a secondary crime scene.
15. List three types of evidence that should be placed in "breathable" containers and explain why it is important to use these types of containers.

Matching

16. Chain of custody	a. The police officer who responded to a 911 call
17. *Corpus delicti*	b. The methods of a suspect when committing a crime
18. Exemplar	c. The length of time from death to discovery of a body
19. First responder	d. A staged event to cause a suspect to commit a crime
20. *Modus operandi*	e. The log of evidence from crime scene to court
21. PMI	f. Evidence used for comparison, a known sample
22. Probative	g. Containers for evidence that seal and prevent altering
23. Protocol	h. Evidence that can prove or disprove
24. Sting operation	i. Deems it necessary to prove a crime occurred
25. Tamper-evident	j. Detailed plan or procedure followed in an investigation packaging

Further Reading

Bodziak, W. T. (2000). *Footwear Impression Evidence*, 2nd edn. Taylor & Francis, New York.
Fisher, B. A. J. (2004). *Techniques of Crime Scene Investigation*, 7th edn. CRC Press, Boca Raton, FL.
Grant, S. (2005). *CSI: Crime Scene Investigation: Secret Identity*. IDW Publishing, New York.
Wecht, C. H. (2004). *Crime Scene Investigation*. Reader's Digest, New York.

On the Web

http://science.howstuffworks.com/csi.htm.
www.crime-scene-investigator.net.
www.mycriminaljustice.com.
www.feinc.net/cs-inv-p.htm.
www.ncjrs.gov/pdffiles1/nij/178280.pdf.
www.crimeandclues.com/crimescene.htm.
www.atf.treas.gov/labs/frl/index.htm.

4

Separating Complex Mixtures

Learning Objectives

1. To be able to explain the concept of pH
2. To be able to recognize polar and nonpolar substances and distinguish between them
3. To be able to explain how a liquid extraction of an acid or basic drug is carried out
4. To be able to define and characterize the different types of chromatography
5. To be able to explain the basic principles of gas chromatography
6. To be able to explain the basic principles of high-performance liquid chromatography
7. To be able to explain the basic principles of thin-layer chromatography
8. To be able to explain the basic principles of electrophoresis

Chapter 4
Separating Complex Mixtures

Mini Glossary

Adsorption: A process whereby a solid in solution or liquid is attracted to the surface of a finely divided solid such as charcoal.

Analyte: The mixture of substances that are to be analyzed or separated.

Chromatography: A family of separation techniques based upon the attraction of components of an analyte by a stationary or mobile phase.

Electrophoresis: A type of chromatography where the mobile phase is an electric current. It is capable of separating substances which are very similar in structure, such as fragments of DNA.

Elution: After an analyte component is captured by a stationary phase in chromatography, it can be washed off with a suitable solvent. This process is called elution.

Gas chromatography: A type of chromatography where the stationary phase is a solid and the mobile phase is a gas.

High-performance liquid chromatography: A type of chromatography where the mobile phase is a liquid or liquid solution and the stationary phase is a solid or viscous liquid in a column. The analyte is dissolved and then mixed with the mobile phase and then pumped through the stationary phase.

Immiscible: A condition whereby two liquids will not mix or dissolve in one another. Examples include water and gasoline.

Ionic: Made up of ions, which are molecules that have extra electrons (negative ions) or are deficient in electrons (positive ions).

Liquid–liquid extraction: A type of extraction process where the analyte is dissolved in a liquid and then extracted with an immiscible liquid to remove one or more components.

Mobile phase: A liquid solution or gas that carries the analyte over or through the stationary phase in chromatography.

pH: The negative logarithm of the concentration of H^+ in an aqueous solution. A measure of the acidity of the solution.

Polarity: The property of molecules whereby they act like magnets with a positive and negative side. Nonpolar molecules are neutral, having neither a positive or negative side.

Pyrogram: A chromatographic chart of peaks representing fragments of a substance that has undergone pyrolysis.

Pyrolysis: Heating a substance to high temperatures in the absence of oxygen. Instead of burning, the substance decomposes into simpler fragments. Pyrolysis can be carried out with gas chromatography to analyze substances with high boiling points such as plastics, paints, and fibers.

Separatory funnel: A piece of glassware that is used to separate two immiscible liquids.

Solid-phase extraction: An extraction method whereby a finely divided solid is used to adsorb liquids or solids in solution

Stationary phase: A solid or viscous liquid that attracts various components of the analyte and separates them.

Thin-Layer Chromatography: A type of chromatography where the stationary phase is a solid that is coated onto the surface of a plastic or glass plate. The mobile phase is a liquid or solution that travels through the stationary phase by capillary action carrying the analyte.

Retention factor: In thin-layer chromatography, the retention factor is the ratio between the distance that a given analyte component traveled up the plate from the point where the analyte spots are made, to the distance that the mobile phase travels. An Rf is specific to a substance using a particular stationary phase and a particular mobile phase.

Resolution: The ability of a chromatographic system to separate and detect two closely related compounds.

Acronyms

GC: Gas chromatography; same as
GLC: Gas–liquid chromatography
HPLC: High-performance liquid chromatography
PyGC or PGC: Pyrolysis gas chromatography
TLC: Thin-layer chromatography

Introduction

Very few substances in our environment exist in a pure state. Air is a solution of many gases including oxygen, nitrogen, carbon dioxide, many pollutants, and other substances. Our drinking water contains many minerals, salts and unfortunately, pollutants. The same is true with forensic chemical evidence. In some cases, only one component of the mixture is important. An example of this would be a white powder that contains an illicit drug such as cocaine that has been mixed with other inert powders such as sugars. These are used to dilute the drug in order to maximize profit. In other cases, the entire mixture is the evidence. For example, gasoline is a common accelerant used to start fires. It contains over 300 separate substances. It is identified as gasoline by separating these substances from each other and examining the separated components. It is the only substance that has these particular hydrocarbons in unique proportions. There are many cases where forensic chemists are called upon to identify one or more components of a mixture. Often, it is necessary to separate the mixture into individual substances before identifying them. Sometimes, the evidence consists of many exhibits or large quantities of a single mixture. Other times the mixture occurs in only trace amounts in a particular case. Figure 4.1 shows various kinds of complex mixtures.

Many types of chemical evidence consist of mixtures. There are solid mixtures such as illicit drugs, paint chips containing pigment and polymers, or piles of rubble containing explosive residues. There are liquid/solid mixtures such as soil that contains liquid residues from an accelerant used in a fire. There are liquid mixtures such as gasoline or blood. Each of these different types of mixtures requires different methods of handling and analysis, including methods to separate the components of the mixtures. In some cases, we are interested in separating and perhaps identifying most or all the components of the mixture. In other cases, only one component of the mixture is of interest such as the drug in an illicit drug mixture or the explosive residue in a pile of rubble at the scene of an explosion. In this chapter, we will discuss various types of mixtures and how they are separated into individual components and how they analyzed. We will consider large quantities of mixtures and very small ones, and various combinations of solid and liquid mixtures.

Figure 4.1 Examples of complex mixtures. Milk is both a solution and suspension and is very complex. Soil is a mixture of organic and inorganic solids. Paint is also both a solution and suspension and is one of the most complex commercial products.

Physical Separation of Mixtures

A physical separation is used when one or more of the components of the mixture must be separated from the rest of the mixture and recovered. An example of this is the explosive residue in the pile of rubble mentioned earlier. Most of this debris is not evidence and thus not important to investigators. But the debris may contain particles of undetonated explosive and/or pieces of the bomb that contained the explosive, perhaps pieces of a timing device or some tape that held the bomb together. The best method for sifting through this rubble may be physically sorting using a low-power stereomicroscope. The stereomicroscope magnifies objects and allows them to be viewed in three dimensions. This is discussed in detail in Chapter 6. This can be a time-consuming, arduous task, and requires a skilled examiner who can identify particles of explosives and explosive devices.

Another example of a physical separation occurs in adulterated products. One of the authors had a case a few years ago where glass particles had been added to a package of salad mix. The product had to be hand searched to pick out the glass particles from the vegetables.

Sometimes, a single sieve or a set of nested sieves can be very useful for physically separating solid mixtures. If one is trying to find bullet fragments in a pile of sand, a sieve of the appropriate mesh to pass the sand through but trap the bullet fragments can be used. Sometimes, soil samples are profiled by separating the soil into particles of various sizes. A set of nested sieves, with each one having successively smaller mesh sizes, can be used. A soil sample is dried and weighed and then poured through the nest of sieves. Various size ranges of particles are trapped in each sieve. The percentage of each size range in the soil sample can then be calculated by weighing the contents of each sieve. Figure 4.2 shows a set of nested sieves.

Figure 4.2 A group of nested sieves. Each sieve has a finer mesh than the one above it. The sieves are put in a series and soil or other material is poured through it. After gentle shaking, the soil is distributed throughout the sieves by particle size.

Figure 4.12 A photograph of an HPLC instrument. These instruments are generally quite modular so that a variety of pumps can be mounted into the system. There is also room for several detectors mounted in series.

the very polar. The mobile phase is a liquid or a solution of two or more liquids. These can also vary in polarity from nonpolar to polar. This is an advantage over gas chromatography, where the mobile phase is always very nonpolar. With HPLC, a greater variety of substances can be separated. In addition, by incorporating two or more liquid pumps, the composition and polarity of the mobile phase can change on the fly during a run. This adds even more flexibility to the technique. HPLC is generally run at room temperature. The analyte must be soluble in the mobile phase. It is dissolved and then injected into an injector where it is mixed with the mobile phase, which is then pumped through the column containing the stationary phase. The detectors used in liquid chromatography are different than those used in GC, because they are detecting liquid solutions rather than vapor solutions; however, they work on the principle of converting a signal of the presence of an analyte component to an electric current. The output is a chart with each component of the analyte represented by a triangular peak as in GC. Thus these HPLC chromatograms can be used for quantitative analysis as with GC. Figure 4.12 is a photograph of an HPLC.

HPLC is widely used in forensic chemistry. It is useful for substances that cannot be heated without decomposing and for relatively nonvolatile liquids. Pyrolysis cannot be used but it is common now to incorporate a mass spectrometer as a detector for identification of the separated analyte components. Some of the types of evidence commonly analyzed by HPLC include, inks, dyes, pigments, drugs, alcohol in drunk driving cases, soil extracts, explosive residues, and some fire residues.

Thin-Layer Chromatography

GC and HPLC are similar in that they both employ a stationary phase housed in a hollow column, either coating the inside walls or filling the column with particles. These then require a sample delivery system (injector), a way to force the mobile phase through the stationary phase (pumps or pressure) and sophisticated detectors that permit the display of signals through a computer when an analyte component gets through the stationary phase. Although these types of chromatography are extremely versatile and sensitive, they are also expensive and, of necessity, can process only one sample at a time. One of the oldest chromatographic techniques was developed along different lines. Instead of a tubular column holding the stationary phase, certain types of paper could serve as the stationary phase. The analyte would then be dissolved in a small amount of solvent. Tiny spots of this analyte would be made at one end of the paper just above the bottom. The paper would then be dipped in the mobile phase, which would travel up the paper by a process known as *capillary action*, carrying the analyte with it. As the various components travel up the paper, they separate. This is called *paper chromatography*. It was developed nearly 100 years ago. Over time it has undergone major enhancements. The paper has been replaced by a glass or plastic plate onto which a thin coating of a pure solid is coated. This is the stationary phase. There are a wide variety of solids that can be used of varying polarity, adding versatility compared to just having to use paper. This type of chromatography is called *thin-layer chromatography*. It is widely used in forensic science laboratories for a variety of evidence. It is the most versatile type of chromatography because of the wide variety of stationary and mobile phases, its portability and low cost, and the ability to run more than one analyte at a time.

Running Thin-Layer Chromatography

Figure 4.13 shows a typical TLC apparatus and set up. The plastic or glass plate is usually the size of a microscope slide although sometimes much larger ones are

Figure 4.13 A thin-layer chromatography apparatus. The filter paper in the beaker is there to keep the atmosphere inside the container saturated with mobile phase. This can greatly improve the quality and reproducibility of the chromatogram.

used for preparative work. The stationary phase coatings are commonly pure, finely divided silica (sand) or alumina (aluminum oxide), or even any of several types of wax. The thickness of the coating can range from a few microns to 1 mm or more. The stationary phase is mixed with a binder that holds it onto the surface of the plate. The mobile phase is a liquid or liquid solution just as in HPLC. The solution can contain various concentrations of polar and/or nonpolar liquids that determine its overall polarity. The analyte can be a mixture of solids or liquids, although solids are generally used.

A small amount of the solid is dissolved in a suitable, volatile solvent such as methanol or chloroform. This can be done in a spot plate. A small capillary tube with an inside diameter of about 5 μg is dipped into the solvent which fills the tube. The end of the tube is then touched to the stationary phase about 1 cm above the bottom of the plate. This makes a small spot of analyte. It may be necessary to over-spot an analyte to make sure that enough has been loaded onto the plate. This is usually a matter of trial and error. If over-spotting is done, the spot is allowed to dry before over-spotting in order to avoid getting too large a spot. The goal is to make a spot that is as small as possible. It is possible to then load another analyte or standard next to the first one, leaving at least a couple of spot diameters between spots. Once the analytes have been loaded, the plate is placed into a chamber that contains mobile phase. The amount of mobile phase should not be so great as to cover the spots. Usually, a piece of filter paper is used to line the inside of the chamber to saturate the chamber with mobile phase vapor. This improves the chromatography. Once the plate comes in contact with the mobile phase, the liquid travels up the plate. As the mobile phase travels up through the stationary phase, it carries the analyte. Interactions of the analyte components with the stationary and mobile phases causes them to separate. When the mobile phase has reached the top of the plate, the plate is removed from the chamber and dried.

Detection of TLC Analyte Components   There are several ways of detecting the presence of analyte component spots on the plate. One common way is to pretreat the stationary phase with a fluorescent dye. When the plate is put under an ultraviolet light, the most common dye that is employed in TLC fluoresces with a green color. In those places where analyte spots are present, the green color is masked and a dark spot appears. Another way to visualize some materials is to take advantage of their fluorescence. Illuminating them with an ultraviolet light will cause them to fluoresce. The most versatile way of visualizing spots is by spraying them with a reagent that reacts with the analyte to form a colored product. Some of these spray reagents are specific for certain types of materials. Examples include *Fast Blue BB*, which colors the naturally occurring cannabinoids in marihuana red to orange depending upon which one(s) are present, and Ehrlich's reagent, which colors LSD and similar substances, purple. Other spray reagents are more general in their color reactions. *Greiss* reagents (a series of two) color all nitrate containing compounds bright red. Even more nonspecific is *Iodoplatinate* reagent, which adds iodine across carbon–carbon double bonds and turns the analyte brown. These and other sprays are not completely specific for a single substance. The advantage to using a fluorescent plate or taking advantage of the native fluorescence of an analyte component is that treating the spots with a spray reagent is destructive and the separated analyte component cannot be used for further analysis.

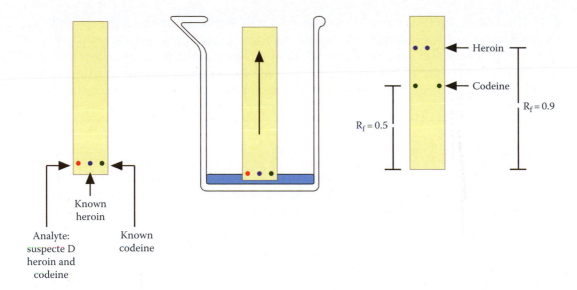

Figure 4.14 A TLC plate with Rfs of the various analyte components. (Courtesy of Meredith Haddon.)

Interpreting TLC Plates   When the spots have been visualized, the *retention factor*, Rf, is measured. The retention factor is the ratio between the distance that a given analyte component travels up the plate from the point where the analyte spots are made to the distance that the mobile phase travels. An Rf is specific to a substance using a particular stationary phase and a particular mobile phase. It is a good way of comparing results between laboratories if the same conditions are used. It is important to remember that the Rf of a substance is not unique. There may be many different substances that have the same Rf in a TLC experiment, so this technique, like other chromatographic methods, is not used for absolute identification. TLC is often used to give presumptive or tentative information about the presence of a substance. For example, if an unknown white powder has a spot with the same Rf as the spot from a known sample of morphine, it can be presumed that morphine is present, but this still must be confirmed by other tests. Figure 4.14 illustrates the use of Rfs to make tentative identifications.

Thin-layer chromatography is used on a wide variety of evidence types. These include drugs, inks and dyes, explosive residues, cosmetics such as lipsticks and nail polishes, and many other types. It is very quick, inexpensive, and versatile.

Something for You to Do

You can do some chromatography at home. It will be similar to thin-layer chromatography, and you will end up with a custom T-shirt. You can also practice your technique on large pieces of blotter paper.

Take a clean white T-shirt (or piece of blotter paper). Get some liquid inks like the kinds that are used in fountain pens or ink refills for ink jet printers. Get a couple of different colors. To get the best results, you may have to dilute the ink with water. Make sure that you put something like blotter paper between the front and back of the T-shirt so the ink does not bleed through. Using an eyedropper, drip ink onto the shirt. You can overspot the same place to make the spots bigger and darker. You can drop the ink from several feet up to make splatters. When the ink hits the shirt, it will spread out away from the drop point in all directions like waves in a pond after a stone is dropped into it. The various dyes that make up the colorants in the inks will separate as the inks spread out. Depending upon the complexity of the colorants, you may see several dyes in one ink. If you make several spots in different parts of the shirt, they will run together as they spread out, resulting in some interesting effects. While you are having fun designing your own clothes, remember that you are actually doing chromatography.

Electrophoresis

One of the few drawbacks of chromatography is that these techniques do not result in absolute identification of the separated substances in an analyte. The peaks in a gas chromatogram or liquid chromatogram and the spots in a thin-layer chromatogram are not unique to one particular substance. This is due to the concept of *resolution*. Resolution in chromatography is the ability of the technique to separate very similar substances. It frequently happens that two substances in an analyte are so similar that they won't separate and will show up as one peak or one spot. (Question: how do we know or find out if a peak or spot is really one substance?) We can usually design a chromatographic system that will separate common mixtures that occur as evidence such as drugs or fiber dyes, etc., but sometimes it is not possible to separate components of a mixture by conventional chromatographic methods. An important example is DNA. DNA is analyzed by isolating pieces or fragments that differ from person to person. These fragments may differ only slightly in length or composition and cannot be separated and displayed as separate units by conventional chromatography. In such cases, the technique of *electrophoresis* can be used. Electrophoresis is a form of chromatography; it is used to separate components of a mixture and display them as spots or peaks. One type of electrophoresis is similar to liquid chromatography. Another type is similar to TLC. In both cases, there are, however, important differences. The stationary phases are somewhat different although they are solid materials. The mobile phase is very different. It is an electric current! There are two major types of electrophoresis used in forensic science: *gel* and *capillary*. They are described below.

Gel Electrophoresis

Gel electrophoresis is somewhat like thin-layer chromatography, but there are important differences. The stationary phase in electrophoresis is a slab of a gelatin-like material, usually *agarose* or *polyacrylamide*. Instead of being a thin layer, the slab is several millimeters thick. The DNA fragment mixture is mixed with a bit of liquid and put in wells that are made at one end of the gel. The entire gel slab is then immersed in a buffer solution that maintains a constant pH. A strong electric current (hundreds or even thousands of volts) is then put across the gel with the negative pole on the side where the DNA has been deposited. The other side of the slab has the positive pole. The buffer imparts a slightly negative charge to the DNA. When the current is turned on, the DNA will flow toward the positive pole because of its negative charge. The moving electric current is actually the mobile phase in electrophoresis. The current carries the DNA fragments through the gel. After a couple of hours, the current is turned off. The DNA fragments will have separated. The principle of separation of DNA fragments by gel electrophoresis is essentially mass action. The lighter, smaller fragments travel faster and farther through the gel than the heavier, larger ones, so the fragments are separated. When the electrophoresis is finished, the DNA is stained with a fluorescent dye or treated with a radioactive material that will expose

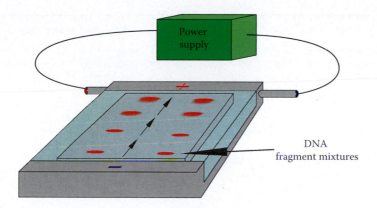

Figure 4.15 A gel electrophoresis apparatus. The power supply puts an electric charge onto the gel slab, positive on one side and negative on the other. The DNA fragments are loaded onto the negative side of the gel and they migrate towards the positive side, separating as they travel through the gel. (Courtesy of Meredith Haddon.)

an x-ray film to visualize the DNA fragments. For most DNA typing applications, gel electrophoresis has been supplanted by capillary electrophoresis because of its higher resolution and ability to determine the quantity of DNA present as well as the types. Figure 4.15 is a diagram of a gel electrophoresis apparatus.

Capillary Electrophoresis

A diagram of a capillary electrophoresis instrument is shown in Figure 4.16. Instead of a slab of gel, a very thin column containing a stationary phase, often polyacrylamide gel, and both ends are immersed in a buffer solution. An electric charge is put across the column. When the analyte, such as DNA fragments, are introduced into the column, they travel through and are detected by their fluorescence. As in gel electrophoresis, the mobile phase is an electric current. The advantages of the gel column over the gel slab is that it is very efficient at separating DNA fragments and it is much more sensitive. In some experiments, only a few nanograms of material are needed for separation. As with HPLC, the results of the analysis show a series of peaks, each of which represents a fragment of DNA. These peaks yield quantitative information as well as the size of each fragment. Figure 4.17 shows an *electropherogram* of a DNA sample. Note that this electropherogram shows peaks

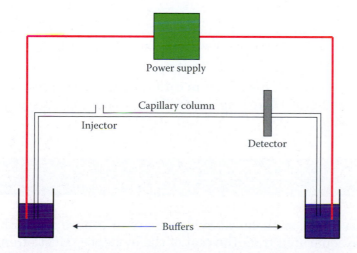

Figure 4.16 A capillary electrophoresis instrument. (Courtesy of Meredith Haddon.)

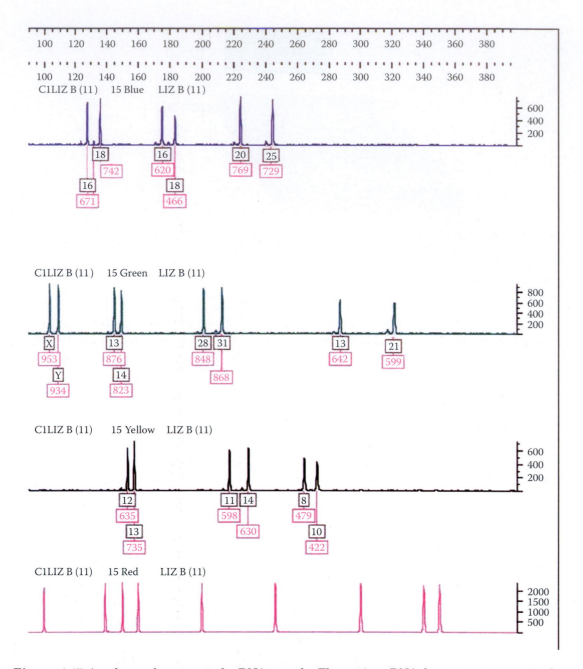

Figure 4.17 An electropherogram of a DNA sample. The various DNA fragments are put in three groups, each with its own fluorescent dye. Each fragment shows up as one or two peaks, depending upon inheritance from the mother and father.

in several different colors. This is due to different fluorescent dyes that are applied to different categories of DNA fragments. The purpose of this process is to make interpretation easier.

Summary

Because very few types of chemical evidence are in a pure state, the material(s) of interest must be separated from the rest of the evidence. Most often, physical separation of the analyte is not possible or practical because of the amount of material and the time it would take to effect a separation. As a result, chemical separations are usually used to separate the evidence from the unneeded substances. The type of chemical separation employed depends upon the nature and amount of material present. For large amounts of materials (grams or more), liquid or solid phase extractions can be used. For smaller amounts of material, one of several forms of chromatography are usually employed. If the analyte is stable at high temperatures and can be easily vaporized, then gas chromatography is most often employed. If not, then either high-performance liquid chromatography or thin-layer chromatography can be employed. For materials that are extremely similar such as DNA fragments, a variation of liquid chromatography called electrophoresis is used. The principle of separation in all types of chromatography is that different analyte components have a greater or lesser affinity for the stationary or mobile phase. An important characteristic of chromatography is resolution, the ability to separate two closely related substances.

Test Yourself

Multiple Choice

1. A solution whose pH is 9 has
   a. An H^+ concentration of 9
   b. An H^+ concentration of -9
   c. An H^+ concentration of 10^9
   d. An H^+ concentration of 10^{-9}
2. A polar compound
   a. Is insoluble in water
   b. Always has oxygen
   c. Has a positive side and a negative side
   d. Has a pH of less than 7
3. In gas chromatography, the mobile phase
   a. Is an inert gas
   b. Is a liquid solution
   c. Is always polar
   d. Is located in a column
4. A mixture of four basic drugs
   a. Cannot be separated
   b. Would show four peaks on a chromatogram
   c. Must be separated using a liquid extraction method
   d. Can only be separated using thin-layer chromatography
5. In HPLC,
   a. The mobile phase is a solid
   b. A coated microscope slide is the stationary phase
   c. The mobile phase moves through the stationary phase by gravity
   d. The mobile phase is a liquid solution or pure liquid
6. All types of chromatography
   a. Have a stationary phase and a mobile phase
   b. Have chromatograms with peaks on a chart
   c. Can be used to separate explosive residues from the debris of an explosion
   d. Have a liquid mobile phase

7. Gel electrophoresis
   a. Cannot separate DNA fragments
   b. Is similar to gas chromatography
   c. Has a very thin column for the stationary phase
   d. Uses an electric current as the mobile phase
8. The first experiments that led to the development of chromatography
   a. Used an inert gas as the stationary phase
   b. Showed that plant pigments could be separated and located by their color
   c. Used pumps to push the mobile phase through the column
   d. Were very much like today's thin-layer chromatography
9. One of the major differences between GC and HPLC is that
   a. GC has a liquid mobile phase
   b. GC uses columns to hold the mobile phase, whereas HPLC does not
   c. GC columns are heated, whereas HPLC columns are kept at room temperature
   d. HPLC always uses at least two liquids in its stationary phase
10. An ionic compound
    a. Is more likely to dissolve in a polar solvent such as water than a nonpolar solvent
    b. Always has a pH greater than 7
    c. Generates excess OH− when dissolved in water
    d. Cannot be separated from another ionic compound in a mixture

True-False

11. Chromatography techniques are used for separation and absolute identification of substances.
12. In order to be analyzed by gas chromatography, an analyte must be thermally stable up to about 300°C.
13. pH is a measure of the acidity of an aqueous solution.
14. Electrophoresis is similar to liquid chromatography except for the nature of the mobile phase.
15. In HPLC, the mobile phase is always a gas.
16. In thin-layer chromatography, the mobile phase is a liquid or solution.

Matching—Match Each Term with Its Definition

17. Retention time
18. Polarity
19. Adsorption
20. Electrophoresis
21. Thin-layer chromatography
22. Mobile phase

a. Carries the analyte through the stationary phase
b. Mobile phase is electric current
c. More than one sample can be separated at the same time
d. Time it takes a sample to move through stationary phase
e. Process where a solid grabs and holds an analyte
f. Property of a substance where it acts like a magnet

Short Essay

23. What is polarity? Give some examples of polar and nonpolar substances.
24. What is a mobile phase? What is its purpose in chromatography?
25. How is gel electrophoresis similar to thin-layer chromatography? How is it different?

Further Reading

Saferstein, R. (2002). Forensic applications of mass spectrometry, in *Forensic Science Handbook*, vol. 1, 2nd edn., R. Saferstein, ed. Prentice Hall, Upper Saddle River, NJ.

Staford, D. T. (1988). Forensic capillary gas chromatography, in *Forensic Science Handbook*, vol. 2, R. Saferstein, ed. Prentice Hall, Upper Saddle River, NJ.

Suzuki, E. M. (1993). Forensic applications of infrared spectroscopy, in *Forensic Science Handbook*, vol. 3, R. Saferstein, ed. Prentice Hall, Upper Saddle River, NJ.

On the Web

A brief outline to chromatography with some good illustrations: http://antoine.frostburg.edu/chem/senese/101/matter/chromatography.shtml.

Animations of gas chromatograpy and electrophoresis and how they work: http://www.shsu.edu/~chm_tgc/sounds/sound.html.

Good diagrams of gas chromatography and thin layer chromatography: http://antoine.frostburg.edu/chem/senese/101/matter/chromatography.shtml.

Videos of solid phase microextraction: http://www.sigmaaldrich.com/analytical-chromatography/video/spme-video.html.

YouTube video of a liquid-liquid extraction: http://www.youtube.com/watch?v=vcwfhDhLiQU.

5
Light and Matter

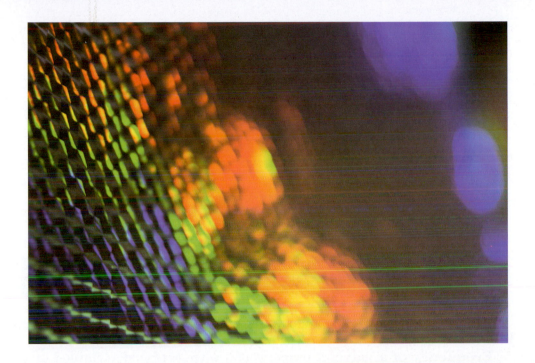

Learning Objectives

1. To be able to describe the wave nature of light
2. To be able to define and describe the properties of a wave: wavelength, frequency, period, and amplitude
3. To compute the wavelength and/or frequency of a wave using wave formulas
4. To be able to describe the particle nature (quantum nature) of the absorption of light
5. To be able to describe the major regions of the electromagnetic spectrum and their effects upon matter
6. To be able to describe the effect of UV/visible light on matter and the types of matter that absorb these types of light
7. To be able to describe the effect of infrared on matter and the types of matter that absorb these types of light
8. To be able to sketch and label a typical spectrophotometer
9. To be able to define mass spectrometry
10. To be able to sketch and label a diagram of a mass spectrometer
11. To be able to describe how substances are ionized and analyzed in mass spectrometry
12. To be able to define *parent peak* and *base peak*

Chapter 5
Light and Matter

Chapter Outline

Mini Glossary

Electromagnetic (EM) spectrum: A large range of wavelengths of radiation that can travel through a vacuum.

Frequency of a wave: A property of a wave that is determined by the number of complete cycles of the wave moving past a given point in a time interval (usually a second).

Infrared (IR) radiation: An invisible wave in the electromagnetic spectrum characterized by lower frequency and longer wavelength, and sensed as heat.

Longitudinal wave: A wave in which the individual particles move back and forth parallel to the direction of energy transfer.

Period of a wave: A property of a wave that indicates the time taken for one complete cycle of a wave.

Photon: A discrete bundle or quantum of electromagnetic energy in the form of light.

Transverse (sine) wave: A wave that oscillates perpendicular (at right angles) to the direction of energy transfer.

Ultraviolet (UV) radiation: An invisible wave in the electromagnetic spectrum characterized by higher frequency and shorter wavelength, falling between X-rays and visible light.

Visible light: Part of the electromagnetic spectrum that is discernable by the human eye.

Wavelength: A property of a wave determined by the linear distance between two successive identical parts of a wave.

Acronyms

EM: Electromagnetic
FTIR: Fourier transform infrared spectrophotometry
IR: Infrared
LDMS: Laser desorption mass spectrometry
MALDI: Matrix-assisted laser desorption/ionization
UV: Ultraviolet

Introduction

Some shirts are red while others are blue. Exposing food to microwaves cooks it quickly and silently. X-rays can see the interior of a human body. All of these events occur because of the interaction between *electromagnetic radiation* and the atoms and molecules that comprise all matter. Electromagnetic radiation is energy in the form of waves. Some electromagnetic radiation is very energetic, such as x-rays and gamma radiation while other types have relatively very little energy associated with them, such as microwaves and radio waves. Most forms of electromagnetic radiation are invisible to the human eye, whereas a small portion of the electromagnetic spectrum is manifested as *light energy*. Some of this light is visible to humans as color. This chapter will describe the effects of some of the forms of electromagnetic radiation on matter. As we will see, certain materials can be characterized and even identified by measuring the changes they undergo when exposed to certain types of electromagnetic radiation. This can be significant forensically as part of the process of identifying unknown samples taken at a crime scene as evidence.

Many people use the term "light" to mean all electromagnetic radiation, whereas others refer to light as only the electromagnetic radiation we can see. In this chapter, the two terms will be used interchangeably.

What Is Light?

Light is radiant energy that comes to earth via our sun. Visible light, that which we sense with our eyes, is only a small portion of the energy that travels through the vacuum of space to our planet. The sun's energy travels in the form of *electromagnetic waves*, which are fluctuations of electric and magnetic fields that transport energy from one location to another. See Figure 5.1. These waves are able to move through space as they do not need a medium (particles) transfer the energy.

Visible light exhibits what is called a "dual nature," meaning it can act as an electromagnetic wave and as a particle called a *photon*. Scientists make use of this dual nature in various instruments used in research and testing.

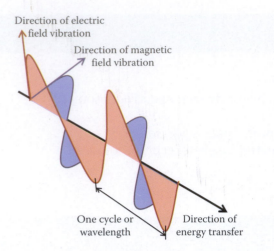

Direction of electric
field vibration

Direction of magnetic
field vibration

One cycle or
wavelength

Direction of
energy transfer

Figure 5.1 The magnetic and electric field orientation in an electromagnetic wave.

Light as a Wave: The Electromagnetic Spectrum

Other forms of electromagnetic radiation are not visible to the naked eye and include radio waves, television waves, microwaves, *infrared waves*, *ultraviolet waves*, x-rays, and gamma rays. All of these waves have one property in common; they all travel at the same speed, the speed of light. But they differ and are classified according to their wavelength and frequency.

The shortest wavelength waves that we normally encounter in our world are gamma rays. Because they have the shortest wavelength, they are the highest energy waves of those in the spectrum. We will examine this relationship later in the chapter. The longest wavelength waves are radio waves, which are lowest in energy. If the electromagnetic radiation is arranged in order of increasing wavelength (or decreasing frequency), it is known as the *electromagnetic (EM) spectrum*. This arrangement is shown in Figure 5.2.

Proceeding from left to right on the chart, the wavelengths go from longest to shortest and the frequencies from lowest to highest. The long wavelength radio waves have wavelengths that are in the range of 1–10 m long. TV waves are slightly shorter wavelengths. Because these two types of waves are long wavelength, low-frequency waves they contain very little energy and are not harmful to humans. The next shorter wavelength region belongs to microwave radiation. Energy beams with these wavelengths cause molecules to spin. Microwaves are used to cook foods by causing the water molecules in the food to rotate rapidly. These spinning water molecules come in contact with each other and generate heat by friction. The heat produced cooks the food.

One of the most important areas of the electromagnetic spectrum is the *infrared (IR) region*. Infrared radiation is invisible energy characterized by lower frequency and longer wavelength, and sensed as heat. Radiation in this region causes the bonds in molecules to vibrate as if the bonds were springs. Every type of bond in every molecule will vibrate and there are many ways that a bond can undergo vibrations. Because of this, infrared spectra are very complex and unique. This will be discussed in more detail later.

Radiation with higher frequencies than infrared are visible to the naked eye. This visible region is usually described by its wavelengths, which are measured

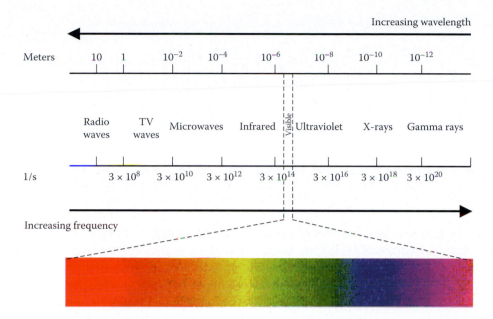

Figure 5.2 The electromagnetic (EM) spectrum. The visible region of light is a very narrow band between the infrared (IR) and the ultraviolet (UV) regions.

in nanometers. Visible light ranges from about 400 to 800 nm (10^{-9} m). Note in Figure 5.2 that visible light proceeds from red to violet as the frequency increases. This is why the region below the visible red light in frequency is called infrared. *Infra* means "below." The next higher frequencies comprise the *ultraviolet (UV)* region. The term *ultra* means "above." This region is above the frequency of visible violet light. Light in the visible and UV regions have outermost electrons that absorb energy and move to higher atomic levels or orbitals. When they drop back to their ground state orbitals, these electrons must release energy in the form of visible or ultraviolet light. Ultraviolet light possesses enough energy to damage living cells. UV energy causes sunburn and can cause skin cancer.

Light with shorter wavelengths such as x-rays and gamma (γ)-rays possess enough energy to severely damage living cells and can destroy them. Gamma rays are emitted by nuclear weapons in great quantities and are one reason why exposure to a nuclear explosion is usually fatal.

Properties of Waves

There are two types of wave motion, longitudinal and transverse. Both wave types transfer energy from one place to another by repeatable motion of energy or particles. Sound waves are *longitudinal waves* and need a medium for the transfer of sound energy. The molecules in the medium move back and forth, creating regions of high and low pressure. As the molecules compress and expand, they collide and transfer the energy parallel along the wave. The basic structure on a longitudinal wave is shown in Figure 5.3. Although these types of waves are not used in the instrumentation discussed in this chapter, it is important to realize how sound waves are different from the waves of the EM spectrum. Radio waves are *not* sound waves, but are part of the electromagnetic spectrum and therefore do not need a medium for travel.

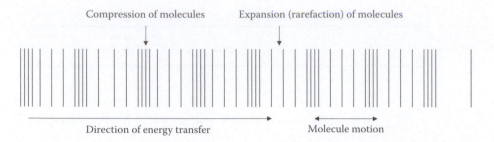

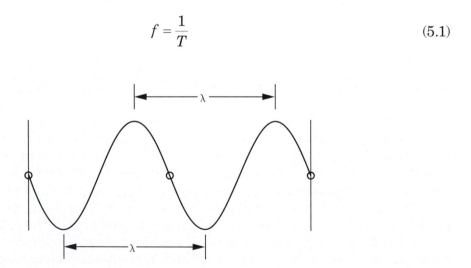

Figure 5.3 A longitudinal sound wave. The areas of high density of molecules are due to *compression* of the air and the areas of low density of molecules are due to *expansion* (called a *rarefaction*) of the air. The motion of the molecules is parallel to the direction of energy transfer.

Light as a wave can be described as electromagnetic energy that oscillates in cycles (refer to Figure 5.1). It can be described as a *transverse wave* or sine wave. A transverse wave is shown in Figure 5.4. It is *periodic*, meaning that it oscillates back and forth repeatedly. The direction of its oscillation is perpendicular to the direction of energy propagation. There are several ways that a transverse wave can be described. The *wavelength* (λ) is the distance between any two adjacent peaks or valleys of the waves. It is measured in units of length that vary with the type of wave. For example, radio waves are very long and are measured in meters. X-rays, on the other hand, are very short and are measured in micrometers (μm or 10^{-6} m), which are millionths of meters.

Another way of describing waves is by their *frequency* (*f*). The frequency of light is the number of cycles that pass a given point in 1 second. If you were standing on a street corner and could see and count the waves of red light being emitted by a traffic signal, the number of waves that pass you in 1 second (s) would be the frequency of that light. Frequency is measured in *Hertz* (Hz). One Hertz = one cycle per second. Its units are expressed as (1/s or /s).

The *period* (*T*) of a wave is a measure of time. It is the time taken for the wave to complete one cycle and is measured in seconds. Since both period and frequency have time in common, they are related to each other. The frequency (cycles/s) of a wave is the inverse of the period (s/cycle) of a wave. Equation 5.1 shows this relationship.

$$f = \frac{1}{T} \tag{5.1}$$

Figure 5.4 Light can be visualized as a series of transverse or sine waves. A given photon of light can be described in terms of its wavelength (λ), the distance between two adjacent peaks or valleys.

Additionally, frequency and wavelength are related to each other. They are also inversely proportional; as one gets larger, the other gets smaller. This is because the velocity of light is always the same (as it travels through air or a vacuum). The velocity of light (c) is approximately 3×10^8 m/s. If you are back at that street corner counting waves, you would notice that waves from the red stop light have longer wavelengths than waves emanating from the green light. Further, you would count fewer red waves passing you in 1 s than green ones because they are both traveling at the same speed. The relationship between the speed of light, its wavelength, and its frequency is expressed in Equation 5.2.

$$c = \lambda f \qquad (5.2)$$

where
    c is the speed of light in m/s
    λ is the wavelength in m
    f is the frequency in Hz or /s

Note that the speed of light must have the same length units as the wavelength because in order for any equation to be valid its units must be the same on both sides. This equation allows us to determine the wavelength of any beam of light if we know its frequency and *vice versa*.

Sample Problem

Suppose your favorite FM radio station is at 120 on the dial. We want to calculate the wavelength of this station. FM stations broadcast in the megahertz region of the electromagnetic spectrum. This station has a frequency of 120 MHz or 120×10^6 Hz (/s). Recall that the speed of light is 3×10^8 m/s.

Rearranging Equation 5.1 we get: $\lambda = c/f$
Since $c = 3 \times 10^8$ m/s and $f = 120 \times 10^6$/s
Substitute in the equation and solve:

$$\lambda = \frac{3 \times 10^8 \text{ m/s}}{120 \times 10^6 \text{ /s}} = 2.5 \text{ m}$$

The final wavelength is **2.5 m**. Radio waves are very long indeed!

On Your Own

Go back to that street corner and look at the green light. Suppose you could measure its wavelength and found it to be 500 nm. A nanometer is 10^{-9} m. How many green waves would pass you in 1 s? (*Answer*: 6×10^{14}/s)

Energy of Light: The Photon

In restaurants, freshly cooked food is often kept hot until served by placing it under an infrared lamp. Clearly this type of light is hot. It contains energy. In fact, all radiation contains energy. Early in the twentieth century, a man named Max Plank deduced that radiation is made up of discrete bundles of energy called quanta. He deduced that the amount of energy in these quanta is directly dependent on the frequency of vibration. From the work of Max Plank came the notion that light, a form of radiation, contains these bundles or quanta of energy, which we call *photons* of light.

The metric unit (SI unit) of energy is the joule (J). Another common unit of energy is the erg. The joule is a larger energy unit than the erg such that one joule is equal to 10^7 ergs. Equation 5.3 shows how frequency (f) and energy (E) are related.

$$E = hf \qquad (5.3)$$

In this equation, energy (E) is measured in joules (J) and frequency in 1/s. h is a constant of proportionality to get the units the same on both sides of the equation. It is called *Plank's constant* and its units are joules × seconds (J s). It has the value of 6.626×10^{-34} J s or 6.626×10^{-27} erg s.

Sample Problem

Now let us see how much energy the waves that carry your favorite FM station have.
Recall that the frequency is 120×10^6 Hz.
By substituting in Equation 5.3, we get

$$E = (6.626 \times 10^{-34} \text{ J s}) \times (120 \times 10^6/\text{s}) = 7.95 \times 10^{-26} \text{ J}$$

On Your Own

Calculate the energy of that beam of green light from the traffic light on the corner.

(*Answer*: 3.98×10^{-19} J)

Compare your value to the energy of the radio station. What does this tell you about how the frequency is related to energy?

If you have the wavelength of light instead of the frequency, substitute the wave equation (5.2) solved for frequency into Equation 5.3. The energy of the light can be calculated from the new Equation 5.4:

$$\text{Since } f = c/\lambda \quad E = hc/\lambda \qquad (5.4)$$

Interactions of Light Energy and Matter

Many types of electromagnetic radiation can affect materials. Forensic science is most interested in those interactions that help describe or identify particular substances that are encountered as evidence. These substances include drugs, explosives, fibers, paints, and others. The areas of the electromagnetic spectrum that are most important to forensic scientists are the infrared, the visible, and the ultraviolet regions. These will be discussed separately, but first it is necessary to learn how the interactions of light and matter are measured, recorded and displayed.

The types of interactions that matter undergoes when exposed to light depend upon the energy (and thus the frequency) of the light. The interactions with a

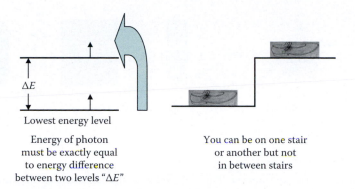

Lowest energy level

Energy of photon
must be exactly equal
to energy difference
between two levels "ΔE"

You can be on one stair
or another but not
in between stairs

Figure 5.5 Energy levels of electrons are quantized. An electron can only exist in a lower or higher energy state but not between them. A photon of light must have energy exactly equal to the difference in energy between two electronic states in order for it to be absorbed by the molecule and promote an electron to a higher state. This is analogous to a shoe being on one stair or another but it cannot be between the stairs.

particular substance are dependent upon its chemical structure. Different substances interact with certain wavelengths of light but not others.

Infrared, ultraviolet, and visible light interact with electrons and bonds in molecules. Normally, these electrons reside in their lowest energy state, which is closest to the nucleus of the atom. Electromagnetic radiation will cause the electrons and bonds to absorb energy and move to a higher energy level further from the atomic nucleus. The amount of energy absorbed by the radiated molecule is measured. Quantum mechanics dictates that the packet or *photon* of radiation must contain the exact energy needed to promote an electron or bond to a higher level. The molecule cannot absorb half of the frequency (or energy) and reject the rest. If a photon has 10^5 joules of energy, a substance cannot absorb 10^2 and reject the rest. Think of climbing a staircase. You can be on one stair or another stair, but you cannot be between the stairs. So it is with electrons. They can be on one level or another but not between the levels. This is shown graphically in Figure 5.5.

Spectrophotometer

Each material will absorb energy from some photons and not others. An instrument called a *spectrophotometer* is used to measure which frequencies (or wavelengths) of light are absorbed and how much. A simplified diagram of a spectrophotometer is shown in Figure 5.6.

The source emits light of all of the wavelengths in that region of the spectrum. Different types of sources are used for each type of light. For example, a *Nerntz Glower* emits light in the infrared region. A *xenon lamp* is used to obtain visible light and a *deuterium lamp* emits ultraviolet light.

The *monochromator* is usually a prism or grating. It has the property of *refracting* (bending) light waves. Shorter wavelength light is refracted to a greater degree than long wave light. In the visible range, violet light is bent more than red light. The ability of a monochromator to refract light enables it to separate the light from the source into individual wavelengths. The monochromator can be turned slowly so that different wavelengths are exposed to the sample over time. During the course of a run, all of the wavelengths will reach the sample eventually. The type of sample

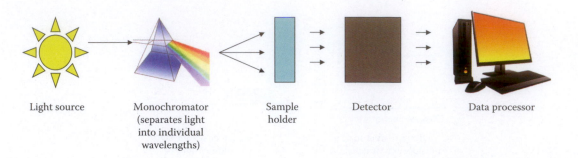

Light source   Monochromator   Sample   Detector   Data processor
                (separates light   holder
                into individual
                wavelengths)

Figure 5.6 A typical spectrophotometer. The light source will differ depending upon the type of light (e.g., infrared or visible) that is being studied. The monochromator separates the light into individual wavelengths using a prism. The detector design depends upon the type of light being analyzed. For example, a UV light detector would be a type of photocell.

holder used in a spectrophotometer depends upon what type of analysis is being performed. In some cases, liquids or solutions are best, in others, solids are used.

As the light passes through the sample, some of it will be absorbed, the rest transmitted. The light that is transmitted reaches the detector. The type of detector used depends upon the type of light being analyzed. For example, infrared light detectors are generally some type of *thermocouple*, a device that is able to convert heat into electricity. The more light that reaches the detector, the more electricity can be generated. For UV and visible light, a *photocell* is used. A photocell converts light to electricity and like the thermocouple, creates more electricity when it receives more light.

The monochromator and the detector are both controlled and monitored by a data processor, which is usually a computer. The data processor collects data about the wavelength of light and the response of the detector. It ultimately creates a plot of wavelength (or frequency) verses the amount of light transmitted or absorbed by the sample. This plot is called a *spectrum*.

Ultraviolet/Visible Spectrophotometry

One of the most important characteristics of evidence is its color. This is most useful in paints and fibers. For example, there are many red fibers and, although the human eye is a very good discriminator of color, it can be fooled. Scientific evidence analysis requires something more objective than a scientist's opinion that two fibers are the same color. There is also the problem of *metamerism*, the property of color where two objects may appear to be the same color in one type of light but different in another (see Figure 5.7).

In the end, the only objective means of determining the exact color of an object is to measure the amounts and wavelengths of visible light that it absorbs. This requires a visible spectrophotometer.

The absorbance of visible and ultraviolet light depends upon the outer shell or valence electrons; those that participate in the covalent chemical bonds that bind atoms together in molecules. As it turns out, not all molecules absorb light in the ultraviolet/visible region. Only those molecules that have bonds of low enough energy will be UV/visible active. The best UV/visible absorbers are molecules with *conjugated carbon-carbon (or nitrogen) double bonds*. These are double bonds that alternate with single bonds. Some examples are shown in Figure 5.8.

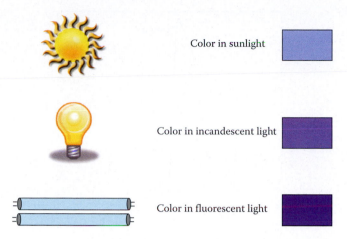

Figure 5.7 Metamerism is the effect that different light sources have on the color of an object. The hue of the color changes depending on the source of illumination.

Benzene   Naphthalene   1,3,5 Hexa triene

Figure 5.8 These substances are examples of molecules that readily absorb UV light.

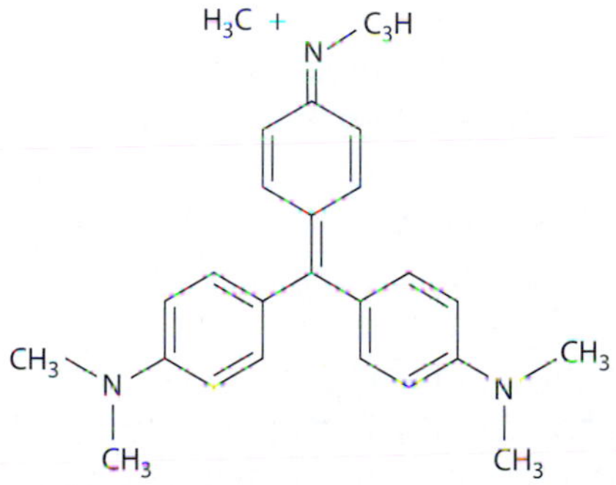

Figure 5.9 The structure of crystal violet.

The structure of crystal violet, a common blue dye found in ball point pen inks is shown in Figure 5.9. Note the large number of conjugated double bonds in this molecule. This explains its bright color. Most dyes and pigments are highly conjugated.

As mentioned previously, UV/visible spectra arise from the transition of valence electrons from a lower energy level to a higher one. In most molecules, spectra are relatively simple, with only one or two transitions. Because of the energy supplied by room temperature, the transitions tend to be very broad. The UV spectrum of heroin is shown in Figure 5.10. Note that there are two absorptions (peaks) that lie close to each other and are quite broad.

Sometimes, it is necessary or desirable to obtain the visible and/or UV spectrum of a microscopic sample such as a single fiber. In such a case, a UV/visible micro-spectrophotometer is used. This instrument is a combination of a microscope and a spectrophotometer. It is explained in detail in Chapter 6.

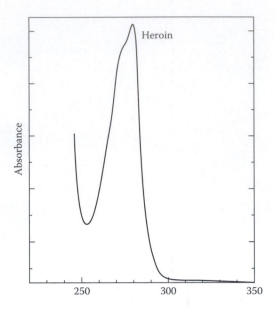

Figure 5.10 The ultraviolet spectrum of heroin.

Infrared Spectrophotometry

Every covalent chemical bond consists of one, two, or three pairs of electrons between two atoms. Each atom usually contributes half of the electrons in the bond. The best way to understand how infrared spectrophotometry occurs is to consider each bond as two weights connected by a spring. This is shown in Figure 5.11, where the red and green balls represent the two atoms and the spring represents the bond. Two weights connected by a spring are collectively called a *harmonic oscillator*. If the spring is stretched, it will vibrate back and forth at a constant frequency that depends upon the strength of the spring and the masses of the two weights. Any change, however slight, in the mass of either weight or the strength of the spring, will change the harmonic frequency. So it is with atoms that are joined by chemical bonds. Each bond will absorb just the right energy (quantized) to get the bond vibrating. Every type of bond connecting every type of atoms will have different frequencies of vibration. Not only that, but each bond can undergo several different types of

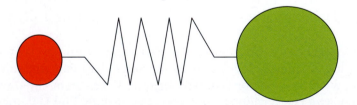

Figure 5.11 The absorption of infrared energy by a molecule can be visualized by considering a spring with weights at each end. In order to get the spring vibrating, energy of the exact magnitude must be available. The amount of energy depends upon the strength of the spring and the masses of the two weights. Likewise, the photon of infrared light that will be absorbed by a bond depends upon the strength of the bond and the masses of the atoms that are bonded.

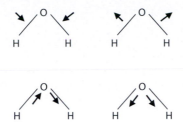

Figure 5.12 These are some of the vibrations that a water molecule can undergo. Some of these will show up as peaks in the infrared spectrum of water. Not all molecular vibrations are active in the infrared region.

vibrations, each one requiring a different energy photon of light. Figure 5.12 shows some of the vibrations of the water molecule.

The more bonds there are in a molecule, the more vibrations there are and the more complex will be the infrared spectrum. Even very similar molecules can have different infrared spectra. Figure 5.13 shows the structure of amphetamine and methamphetamine. Figure 5.14 shows their infrared spectra. Even though the molecules are very similar in structure, their infrared spectra can be easily differentiated.

Infrared spectra are so complex that each molecule has a unique spectrum. This means that infrared spectrophotometry can be used to unequivocally identify a pure substance.

Sometimes, it is necessary or desirable to obtain the infrared spectrum of a microscopic sample such as a single fiber, a bit of ink, or a small paint chip. In these cases, an IR microspectrophotometer can be used. This instrument is a combination of a microscope and in infrared spectrophotometer. It is explained in detail in Chapter 6.

These basic principles of the spectrophotometer apply to UV/visible and infrared instruments. Today's infrared spectrophotometers work on a somewhat different principle. Instead of the monochromator that selects which wavelengths of light reach the sample, the source light is sent instead to a *Michaelson Interferometer*. This apparatus converts the light beam containing all the wavelengths of infrared light into an *interferogram*, which is a set of all of the wavelengths of light formed into a pattern of added and subtracted intensities of light. The interferogram is then projected on to the sample that absorbs and transmits the light as usual. The interferogram is then turned back into individual wavelengths using a mathematical process called the *Fourier transform*. The wavelengths and absorptions are then plotted as usual. This type of infrared spectroscopy is called *Fourier transform infrared spectrophotometry* (FTIR).

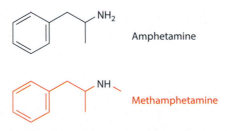

Figure 5.13 Structures of methamphetamine and amphetamine.

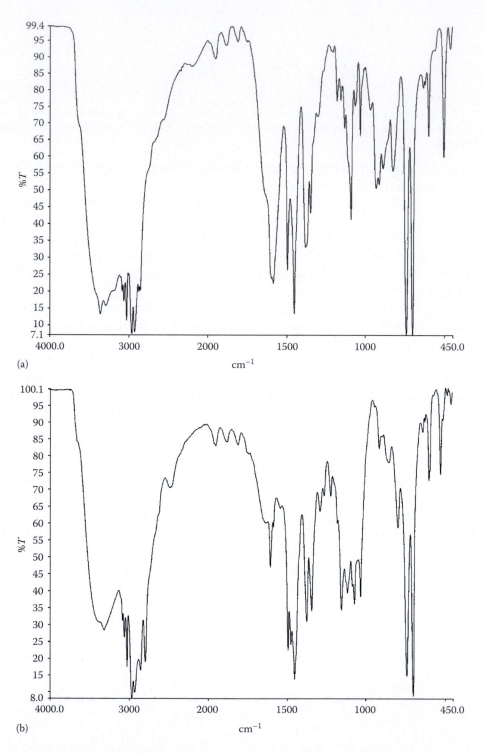

Figure 5.14 Infrared spectra of amphetamine (a) and methamphetamine (b). Even though the molecules are structurally similar, their infrared spectra can be used to differentiate them.

Mass Spectrometry

Up until now, we have been looking at the interactions of electromagnetic radiation and matter focusing on UV/visible and infrared light. Now, the focus will shift to another type of interaction. Instead of using light as a means of delivering energy to matter, a beam of high-speed electrons can be used. A pure chemical substance is converted to a vapor and introduced into an evacuated chamber and then bombarded with a beam of high-speed electrons. The energy of the electrons is absorbed by the substance. This causes the substance to lose an electron of its own and form a positive ion. In mass spectrometry, this is called the *molecular* (M^+) *ion*. In some cases, the molecule will lose 2 electrons and will then have a +2 charge, but this relatively rare. The M^+ ion is usually unstable and will decompose, producing *daughter ions*. These are fragments of the original molecule that are also positive ions. Depending upon their stability, the daughter ions may undergo further decomposition into smaller fragments. If a substance is subjected to bombardment with an electron beam under the same conditions each time, the number, amounts, and sizes of each fragment will be reproducible.

After the ionization step, the ions are accelerated down a tube and focused using magnets. This step separates the fragments by weight. A mass detector is used to arrange the fragments by increasing mass and displaying them as vertical lines from smallest mass to largest. A diagram of a mass spectrometer is shown in Figure 5.15. The mass spectrum of cocaine is shown in Figure 5.16. With few exceptions, the pattern of fragments and their relative amounts is unique to each substance so mass spectrometry can be used to identify a pure chemical compound.

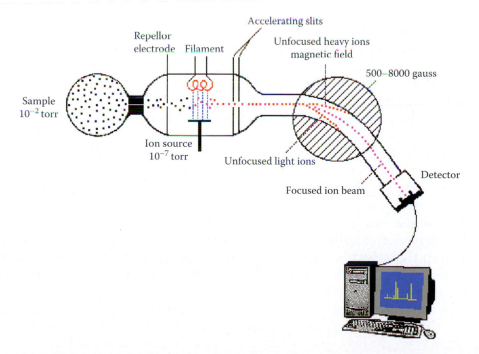

Figure 5.15 Diagram of a mass spectrometer. (Reprinted from William Reusch, http://www.cem. msu.edu/~reusch/VirtualText/Spectrpy/MassSpec/masspec1.htm. With permission.)

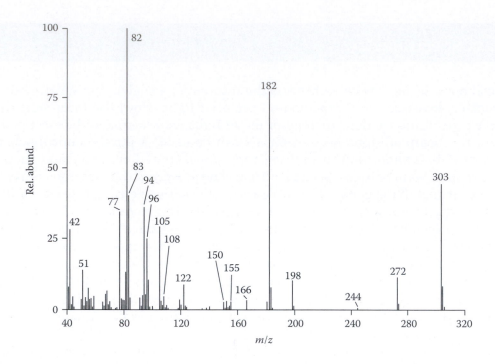

Figure 5.16 Mass spectrum of cocaine.

Strictly speaking, a mass spectrum does not show the masses of the fragments but the mass (*m*) divided by the charge of an electron (*e*) or *m/e*. This is because, as mentioned earlier, some molecules or fragments may lose two electrons. A fragment with a mass of 78 that has lost two electrons would show up at *m/e* 39 (78/2).

Certain ions have special significance in a mass spectrum. The ion that represents the original molecule without any fragmentation is called the *parent peak*. The mass of this ion is the molecular weight of the substance. Knowing the molecular weight can be very important in identifying unknown materials. The fragment that is most stable and has the highest abundance is called the *base peak*. In the mass spectrum of cocaine in Figure 5.16, the base peak of cocaine is 82 and the parent peak is at 303.

There are a large number of modifications of the basic mass spectrometer in use today. There are different types of sources, methods of ionization, sample chambers, and focusing systems. For example, instead of an electron beam as the source of energy, a variable energy laser beam can be used. The beam can be focused on the sample, which can be a solid or vapor. The laser ionizes the molecules in the sample but does not contain enough energy to cause fragmentation. The only ion that is seen in the mass spectrum is the parent peak, making it easy to determine the molecular weight of an unknown substance. This type of mass spectrometry is called laser desorption mass spectrometry (LDMS). Sometimes, it is difficult to transfer the energy from the laser directly to the sample, so the sample is embedded in a conducting matrix that accepts energy from the laser and transfers it to the sample. This type of mass spectrometry is called matrix-assisted laser desorption/ionization (MALDI). LDMS and MALDI have been used on a number of types of evidence, most recently on inks. LDMS spectra of ink on paper can be generated directly, without removing the ink first.

Summary

Light has the unique character of presenting as an electromagnetic wave or as a particle. Light waves are transverse waves consisting of oscillations of electric and magnetic fields that travel through space. Light as a particle is a packet of energy called a photon. Waves can be described by their frequency (the number of waves that pass by each second) or by wavelength, the distance between the same points on two, adjacent waves. The energy associated with a photon of light is dependent upon its frequency; the higher the frequency, the more energy. Light waves are arranged into the electromagnetic spectrum. Each region of the spectrum contains waves that have different effects upon matter.

The interactions of light and matter are measured using a spectrophotometer. This instrument consists of a light source, a monochromator that selects the wavelengths of light that reach the sample, the sample compartment, a detector for determining which wavelengths of light were transmitted through the sample and a data processor that collects information about the wavelengths of light and the amount of light absorbed and transmitted by the sample.

The areas of the electromagnetic spectrum that are of most interest to forensic scientists are the ultraviolet/visible range and the infrared range. When matter is exposed to UV/visible light, it promotes electrons to higher orbitals. These spectra tend to be broad with only one or two major peaks. Not all substances absorb UV/visible light. Organic compounds that have conjugated double bonds are the most active in this region. Visible light is a narrow region of the UV/visible spectrum whose wavelengths of light can be seen by the human eye as color.

The infrared region causes the bonds between atoms in all substances to vibrate. There are several different types of vibrations that can take place in a chemical bond. Infrared spectra are so complex that the spectrum for each chemical substance is unique.

Mass spectrometry uses a beam of electrons to interact with light. The electrons cause the substance to lose one or sometimes two of its own electrons, forming a positive ion. This ion may undergo degradation to smaller ions. The ions are separated and detected by the mass spectrometer and displayed as a series of peaks of increasing mass to charge ratio. The mass spectrum for a pure substance is reproducible and unique to that substance.

Test Yourself

Multiple Choice

1. The velocity of light in a vacuum or air is approximately
   a. 3×10^{10} m/s
   b. 3×10^{8} m/s
   c. 186,000 m/s
   d. 186,000 miles/min
2. The number of light waves that pass a point in 1 s is called its
   a. Frequency
   b. Wavelength
   c. Period
   d. Quantum

3. As the frequency of light increases
   a. Its energy increases
   b. Its wavelength increases
   c. Plank's constant increases
   d. Its energy decreases
4. Plank's constant
   a. Is a measure of the speed of light in frequency units
   b. Is a measure of wavelength
   c. Relates the energy of a photon of light to its frequency
   d. Varies with the medium that the light is passing through
5. The part of the spectrophotometer that selects the wavelength of light that reaches the sample is
   a. The Nernst glower
   b. The monochromator
   c. The photocell
   d. The thermocouple
6. If a spectrophotometer has a photocell detector and a xenon lamp source, it is a
   a. Mass spectrometer
   b. An infrared spectrophotometer
   c. A microwave instrument
   d. A UV/visible spectrophotometer
7. The type of spectrometry that measures the energy absorbed by molecules causing bond vibrations is
   a. UV/visible
   b. Infrared
   c. Mass
   d. X-ray
8. The type of spectrometry that uses electrons to bombard a sample is
   a. Scanning electron microscopy
   b. Mass spectrometry
   c. Infrared spectrophotometry
   d. Microwave spectrometry
9. The parent peak in a mass spectrum refers to
   a. A substance used to calibrate the instrument
   b. The most abundant ion
   c. An ion that has lost two electrons
   d. The molecular ion
10. The _____ spectrum is so complex it is considered to be unique
    a. Visible
    b. Ultraviolet
    c. Infrared
    d. Microwave
11. Light has a "dual nature," which means that it can act as both
    a. A transverse and longitudinal wave
    b. A wave and a particle
    c. A photon and a quanta
    d. An electric wave and a magnetic wave
12. The period of a wave is
    a. The number of waves passing a point in a second
    b. The number of waves passing a point in a meter

   c. The time it takes for one complete wave to pass a point
   d. The distance it takes for one complete wave to pass a point
13. A photon is
   a. An electromagnetic wave
   b. An object that splits light into its component colors
   c. The time for a complete wave
   d. A discrete packet of energy
14. As the wavelength of radiation increases, its energy
   a. Increases
   b. Decreases
   c. Stays the same
15. All forms of radiation in the electromagnetic spectrum have what in common?
   a. Wavelength
   b. Frequency
   c. Period
   d. Velocity

True-False

16. Light is an oscillating longitudinal wave.
17. Electrons can absorb electromagnetic energy in discrete packets called photons.
18. The period and frequency of a transverse wave are inversely related to each other.
19. Spectrophotometers are used to determine what frequencies of light are absorbed by a substance.
20. If a wave has a high frequency, it will also be high in energy content.

Short Answer

21. Explain what happens to the electrons in an atom when they absorb a photon of energy.
22. Sketch the basic structure of the spectrophotometer.
23. Determine the wavelength of the following transverse wave.

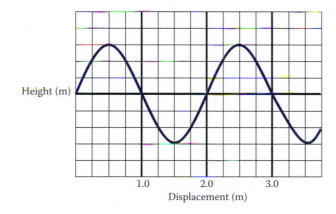

Problem Solving

24. a. Green light has a wavelength of 510 nm. What is the frequency of the light?
    b. One possible frequency of x-rays is 30×10^{15} Hz. What is the wavelength of this x-ray?

25. a. Calculate the energy content in each of the radiation sources in Problem 24.
    b. Another electromagnetic wave has an energy of 1.98×10^{-17} J, find the wavelength.
    c. What type of EM wave is this?

Further Reading

Humecki, H. J. (ed.). (1995). *Practical Guide to Infrared Microspectroscopy*. Marcel Dekker, New York.

Perkampus, H. H. and H. C. Grinter. (1992). *UV-Vis Spectroscopy and Its Applications (Springer Laboratory)*. Springer Verlag, New York.

Skoog, D. A., Holler, F. J., and T. A. Nieman. (1997). *Principles of Instrumental Analysis*, 5th edn. Brooks Cole, Belmont, CA.

Helpful Websites

For background on the dual nature of light: http://nobelprize.org/nobel_prizes/physics/articles/ekspong/index.html.

Infrared radiation: http://www.gemini.edu/public/infrared.html.

Plank's Constant and the Energy of a Photon: http://www.colorado.edu/physics/2000/quantumzone/photoelectric2.html.

Ultraviolet radiation: http://www.biospherical.com/nsf/student/page3.html.

6
Microscopy

Learning Objectives

1. To be able to describe the light path through a simple lens
2. To be able to define a compound microscope and describe the light path through it
3. To be able to name the parts of a compound microscope
4. To be able to describe how a comparison microscope is constructed
5. To be able describe how a stereo microscope is constructed
6. To be able to define plane polarized light
7. To be able to describe how a polarized light microscope works
8. To be able to describe how a scanning electron microscope works
9. To be able to define and describe energy-dispersive x-ray analysis

Chapter 6
Microscopy

Chapter Outline

Mini Glossary

Analyzer: A removable polarizer in a microscope that has a fixed plane of polarization.

Anisotropic: The property of matter whereby it reacts differently to light depending upon the direction the light strikes the specimen.

Backscattered electrons: Electrons form the primary beam that are reflected off the surface of a specimen in an electron microscope.

Binocular: A microscope with two ocular lenses.

Body (viewing) tube: The part of the compound microscope that holds the ocular and objective lenses.

Comparison bridge: A device in a comparison microscope that uses mirrors to focus light from two stages to oculars that are next to each other.

Comparison microscope: Two compound microscopes that are connected with a comparison bridge that enables the observer to view two objects at the same time, one with each eye.

Compound microscope: A microscope consisting of two convex lenses. The first magnifies the object creating a virtual image, and the second magnifies this image to yield a further magnified image. The total magnification is the produce of the magnification of each lens.

Condenser: A lens that focuses light from the illuminator to the specimen.

Depth of focus: A measure of how far inside the object the image will be in focus.

Diaphragm: A device in a microscope that eliminates extraneous light from the illuminator.

Electron microscopy: A type of high-resolution microscopy that uses a beam of electrons to magnify a specimen. The electron microscope is capable of magnifying an object more than 200,000 times.

Energy-dispersive x-ray analysis: Identification of a chemical element by the characteristic x-rays it emits when it is bombarded with a beam of electrons in an electron microscope.

Eyepiece (ocular): A convex lens placed at the top of the body tube of the microscope. The observer looks through the ocular at the object.

Field diaphragm: A device in a microscope that controls the intensity of light that reaches the specimen.

Field of view: The amount of a specimen that is in view at any one time.

Focal length: There are points on each side of a lens where an object would be in exact focus. The distance between these two points is the focal length of that lens.

Isotropic: The property of matter whereby it reacts the same way no matter what direction light that strikes it is coming from.

Microspectrophotometry: A combination of a microscope and a spectrophotometer that permits the analysis of microscopic specimens.

Monocular: A microscope with a single ocular lens.

Objective lens: The second lens, located at the bottom of the body tube, usually on a turret, which contains several lenses of varying magnification.

Polarized light: Light that passes through a special filter that allows only light in a single plane to pass through.

Reflected light microscopy: A type of microscopy where light is reflected off the surface of an opaque object and then passes through the lenses to the observer's eye.

Refraction: Bending and slowing of a light beam as it passes through a transparent medium. All transparent gases, liquids, and solids refract light.

Resolution: The ability of the human eye to see two closely spaced objects. It is the minimum distance between two objects that can still be seen as two distinct objects.

Scanning electron microscopy: A type of electron microscopy where electrons reflect off the surface of a specimen and are captured and magnify the specimen.

Secondary electrons: Electrons that are emitted by a specimen in an electron microscope when it is bombarded by a beam of primary electrons.

Simple magnifier: A device that employs a single convex lens to magnify an object.

Spectrophotometer: An instrument used to measure the interaction of light and matter.

Spectroscopy: The interaction of light and matter.

Stage: The platform upon which the specimen is viewed.

Stereo microscope: A microscope made with two objective lenses that focus in a slightly different place on the specimen so that the observer can see the specimen in three dimensions.

Transmission electron microscopy: A type of electron microscopy that uses thin sections of specimens that the electron beam can pass through.

Transmitted light microscopy: A type of microscopy where light passes through a transparent specimen to the observer's eye.

Trinocular: A microscope with two ocular lenses and a holder for a camera that can see what the observer sees under the microscope.

Virtual image: An image created by a convex lens on the other side of the lens from the observer. It is not a real image and a screen placed on that side of the lens will not show the image.

Working distance: The distance between the objective lens and the stage.

Acronyms

EDX: Energy-dispersive x-ray analysis
EM: Electron microscope
PLM: Polarized light microscope
SEM: Scanning electron microscopy
×: Times. The amount of magnification of an image. 10× = 10 times magnification.

Introduction

If there is such a thing as a universal instrument of science, it is the microscope, or perhaps "microscopes," because there are many different kinds. Microscopes are so versatile that they have become indispensible in all types of scientific and technical laboratories; medical, environmental, pharmaceutical, geological, and, of course, forensic science. Practically, every forensic science laboratory in the world has at least one, and usually several, microscope. Practically, all types of forensic evidence are analyzed by at least one type of microscope. The reasons for the popularity of microscopes in a crime laboratory are numerous:

1. Sample preparation is often minimal. Usually, the object of interest is placed under the microscope without preparation beyond using a microscope slide and cover slip. Sometimes, thin sections of a material may be prepared or the object may be immersed in a liquid of particular refractive index to improve viewing, but that is usually the extent of it.
2. Microscopes can be used for separation and identification. A material of interest such as suspected explosive residues may be mixed with debris such as that from an explosion. Individual particles of explosive can be picked out and physically separated and sometimes identified by their overall appearance and crystal structure.
3. In the majority of cases, microscopy is nondestructive. Little or no material is consumed during analysis by microscopy. This is very important in forensic science where the evidence often consists solely of a few particles of a material. If it is consumed during analysis, there is no way that reanalysis can take place or further work can be done on it. Microscopy is also very versatile. There are microscopes that magnify an object only a few times while the operator manipulates it in three-dimensional space, thus revealing important information about its surface characteristics. There are also microscopes that can magnify an object more than 200,000 times and, at the same time, determine its elemental composition. Some microscopes can magnify images while comparing two objects side by side and are equipped with

high-resolution cameras that can photograph what the operator sees. Lenses, filters, and polarizers permit viewing of an object under various light conditions, thus increasing the amount of information available about it.

4. Microscopes can be combined with other analytical instruments such as spectrophotometers (Chapter 5) to extend the instrument's capabilities. For example, an infrared microspectrophotometer can isolate and magnify a single fiber and then collect its infrared spectrum.

In this chapter, we will explore the roles that microscopy plays in forensic science. We will look at everything from a simple hand magnifier that magnifies an object 2 or 3 times to an electron microscope that is capable of magnifying an object more than 200,000 times. We will see how basic microscopes can be modified to compare two objects or illuminate them with polarized light or magnify an object in three dimensions.

Types of Microscopes

Microscopes are usually differentiated by the amount of useful magnification they can provide without distorting the appearance of an object. Several of the most useful microscopes in a forensic science laboratory are based upon the *compound microscope*. Most of this chapter will be devoted to the compound microscope and its modifications. Compound microscopes normally can be used to magnify an object from about 40 to 1000 times. Simple microscopes can be used to magnify an object approximately 4–20 times. At the other end of the scale, electron microscopy can magnify an object more than 200,000 times.

Forensic Microscopy

Because of the versatility of microscopes, one type or another is used on nearly every kind of scientific evidence. In some types of evidence or some cases where evidence is limited, most or all of the analysis is done by microscopy. In the hands of a skilled microscopist, many objects and materials can be completely identified by using a microscope and no other analysis is needed. In most situations, however, microscopy is teamed with other techniques of analysis. For example, a microscope may be used to perform preliminary screening or analysis to learn about the general features, size distribution, purity, color, or other characteristics of an object. Table 6.1 presents some of the common types of forensic evidence and the types of microscopes that are employed in their analysis. The last column indicates whether the microscope is the main tool for analysis or is used as part of a team of instruments or techniques.

Lens: How Objects Are Magnified

Simple Magnifiers

A lens is usually a circular curved object made of glass or another transparent material. Glass lenses are the highest quality. For most microscopes, the lenses are *convex*. They are wide in the middle and then taper around the edges. Convex lenses bend and focus light to a point on the other side of the lens. The bending of light by a lens is called *refraction*. A single lens can be used as a *simple magnifier*. If you take

TABLE 6.1
Common Types of Forensic Evidence and Types of Microscopes Employed in Their Analysis

Type of Evidence	Type(s) of Microscopes	Level of Use
Bullets and cartridges	Comparison	Principle
Drugs	Stereo, simple compound	Ancillary
Dust	Basic compound, polarizing	Principle
Fibers	Basic compound, polarizing, microspectrophotometer	Ancillary
Fingerprints	Magnifying glass	Principle
Glass	Basic compound	Principle
Hair	Basic compound	Principle
Paint	Basic compound, microspectrophotometer	Ancillary
Soil	Magnifying glass	Principle
Serology	Magnifying glass, basic compound	Principle
Tool marks	Magnifying glass, comparison	Principle
Gunshot residue	Scanning electron microscopy	Principle
Paint fragments, other microscopic particles	Scanning electron microscopy	Ancillary

a magnifying glass and focus it on an object, you see an enlarged view of the object. The light rays from the object to the eye form a *virtual image* further away from the lens. This is called a virtual image because it is not real. If you held a white screen up in the plane where the image would be, it would not show up on the screen. The formation of a virtual image by a simple convex lens is shown in Figure 6.1.

The size and shape of the lens determine the amount of magnification it can achieve. The main factor is the *focal length* of the lens. There are points on each side of a lens where an object would be in exact focus. The distance between these two points is the focal length of that lens. This is shown in Figure 6.2.

Another important characteristic of lens optics is *resolution*, the ability of the human eye to see two closely spaced objects. It is the minimum distance between two objects that can still be seen as two distinct objects. The human eye can distinguish two objects next to each other easily from a distance of about 80 cm. At this distance, two objects can be separated by about 20 mm. If we want to see more detail in an object with better resolution, we need to magnify the object. As magnification increases, the light passing through the lens must be increasingly refracted. In order to do this, the lens diameter must decrease. If we want to magnify an object

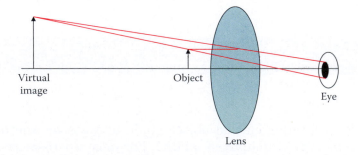

Figure 6.1 A simple convex lens. As light passes through the lens, it is refracted (bent) and forms virtual image on the other side of the lens that is magnified according to the size and degree of curvature of the lens.

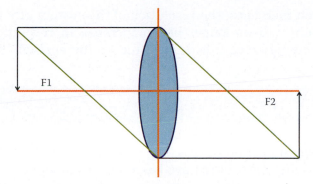

Figure 6.2 Focal length of a lens. The focal length of a lens is the distance between two in-focus images on either side of the lens.

100 times, we would need a simple lens of abut ½ in. in diameter. This limits the practical magnifications of simple hand lenses to about 15×.

Compound Magnifiers

As explained earlier, the geometry of a simple lens limits its magnification. It is often necessary or desirable to magnify an object 100 times or more. This can be accomplished by using a *compound magnifier*. This employs two simple lenses arranged in a line. The first lens magnifies the object as shown in Figure 6.1. The other lens is placed at the location of the virtual image produced by the first lens. The virtual image is magnified by the second lens producing a real image whose total magnification is the product of the magnification of each lens. Thus, if the first lens magnifies the object 10 times and the second lens magnifies it 20 times, the total magnification is 200 times. Figure 6.3 shows how two convex lenses magnify an object. The practical limits of magnification using compound lenses are about 1000×. With specialized lenses, it is possible to go even higher, but there are limits.

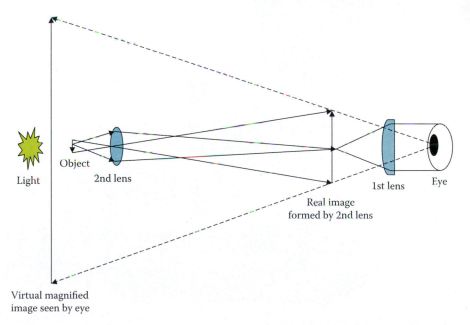

Figure 6.3 Compound lenses. Two convex lenses will magnify an object equal to the product of the magnification of each lens. The first lens magnifies the object, creating a virtual image. The second lens is placed so that magnifies this image, creating a real image.

As the magnification increases, the resolution of the system also increases. At some point, however, there will no longer be an increase in resolution with continued magnification. This *empty magnification* results in increasingly fuzzy images.

Compound Microscope

The design of a basic compound microscope has been remarkably stable since it was invented over 100 years ago. There have been improvements in virtually every part of the instrument so that even an inexpensive model can be suitable for many applications. A compound microscope basically consists of two convex lenses, a stage to mount the object, a system to project light through the lenses or reflect off the surface of the object being studied, and a system for focusing objects. Refer to Figure 6.4 as the various parts of a compound microscope are described in it.

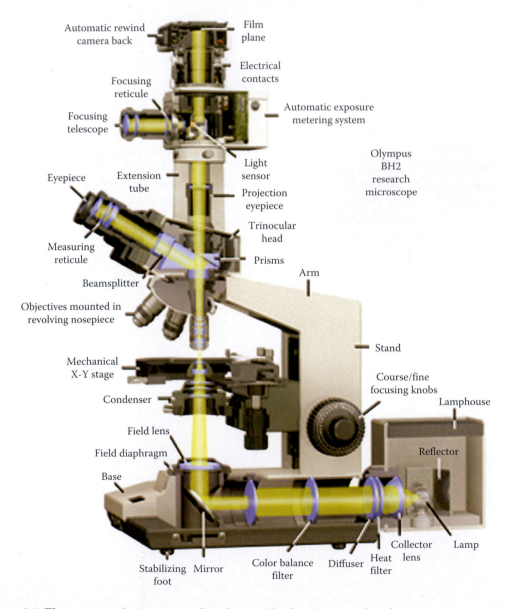

Figure 6.4 The compound microscope. See the text for descriptions of each part.

At the top of the microscope, you look through the first convex lens, the *eyepiece* or *ocular*. If there is one eyepiece, it is referred to as *monocular*. In many microscopes, there are two identical eyepieces, one for each eye; both show the same field of view. This is called a *binocular* eyepiece. Increasingly, microscopes are even *trinocular*; there are the two ocular lenses and a tube for a video camera that can project an image into a computer where it can be viewed, printed, and saved. Most ocular lenses have 5× or 10× magnification. In binocular instruments, one or both of the oculars may be focusable independently to compensate for differences in vision in each eye. Oculars can be outfitted with fine cross hair lines so that an object can be centered in the field of view. Sometimes, a measuring scale can be etched into an ocular. This can be used, along with a calibration slide, to accurately measure the size of an object. The ocular is at the top of the *viewing tube*. This tube contains both lenses.

Below the ocular, at the bottom of the viewing tube is the other convex lens, the *objective* lens (or just, objective), so called because of its proximity to the object. Most microscopes today have several objective lenses (e.g., 4×, 10×, 20×) mounted on a turret that can be turned, thus swinging a particular objective into place. Objective lenses have many special characteristics and may be chosen for particular applications. Their characteristics are etched into the body of the lens.

The *stage* of the microscope is a horizontal surface where the sample is mounted. It has a hole in the center where light emanating from the light source underneath the stage is passed through the sample. In some microscopes, the stage is circular and rotates 360°. In other microscopes, the stage is fixed. There may be special holders or clips for microscope slides on the stage. The object that is being viewed is mounted on the stage. Most often the object is put on a microscope slide and held there with a cover slip. Stages can be rotated or moved up and down or left and right to center the object in the field of view. There are two types of illumination systems. If the object is thin and transparent, then *transmitted light* microscopy is used. The light shines up from below the object, and the light source is located underneath the stage. Light passes through the hole in the stage onto the object. Between the light source and the stage, there is a *condenser*. This is a lens that focuses and condenses the light onto the object. It has its own *diaphragm* that is used to eliminate extraneous light. The microscope may also have a *field diaphragm* that controls the intensity of light that reaches the object. Some microscopes can magnify opaque objects such as bullets or cartridges. Light cannot pass through these objects so light sources mounted beneath the object will not be of much use. Instead, *reflected light microscopy* is used. In this microscope, the light source is external and is aimed at the object from the top or side. The light reflects off the surface of the object and then passes through the objective and ocular lenses. This concept will be discussed later in the section on comparison microscopes.

When viewing an object, the examiner must first decide how much of it should be in view at one time. This is the *field of view*. The field of view is inversely proportional to the magnification. A microscopist will usually mount an object at low-power magnification to survey as much of the object as possible. Then magnification can be increased to focus on one part of the object with a higher resolution. The *depth of focus* is a measure of how far inside the object the image will be in focus. This can be useful where a transparent object is heterogeneous and the analyst wants to be able to see the different parts in focus at the same time. Depth of focus increases as magnification decreases.

Every microscope has a focusing system. Focusing is accomplished in one of two ways. Either the viewing tube is raised or lowered or the stage is raised or lowered.

Two focusing knobs are used; one for coarse focus and the other for finer adjustments. Microscopes can also be outfitted with many accessories that help tailor it for particular applications. There may be light filters, interference filters, or, most importantly, polarizers that are mounted usually below and/or above the stage. Polarized light microscopy will be discussed later in this chapter.

Modifications of the Compound Microscope

The basic compound microscope is very versatile, offering a variety of magnifications, sample holders, and types of illumination and has achieved great popularity in forensic analysis. It is also a very flexible instrument. A number of modifications have been made to compound microscopes over the years to extend its capabilities. Some of these are quite simple, whereas others are major overhauls that can multiply the cost of the microscope several times over. In this section, we will discuss four major types of modifications of the basic compound microscope described earlier that extend its utility greatly, making it useful for most types of forensic evidence. These modifications include

- Comparison microscope
- Stereo microscope
- Polarized light microscope
- Microspectrophotometer

Comparison Microscope

Consider the following forensic situation: you have received two bullets (or two human hairs or two fibers) that you must compare microscopically. You have one compound microscope at your disposal, modified so it can use reflected light for the bullets as needed. How could you use this microscope to compare two similar objects to see if they have the same or different microscopic characteristics? In some cases, you could mount both objects on the same slide but then you cannot manipulate them separately and you cannot do this with large objects such as bullets. You could view one object at a time and try to remember or draw the characteristics you see but that would be far from useful. If you had a binocular or trinocular instrument, you could mount a camera and take pictures of each object and compare the pictures. Unfortunately, no picture has the resolution of the human eye and some data are bound to be lost. Clearly, the best solution to the problem would be to be able to see both objects under the microscope at the same time and be able to manipulate them independently and then photograph the comparison of the two objects. A compound microscope can be modified to accomplish this. Actually, this requires two compound microscopes. The result is a *comparison microscope*. These microscopes are universally employed in crime laboratories for the analysis of bullets and cartridges and widely used for the comparison of hairs, fibers, glass, tears, and fractures.

The comparison microscope consists of two compound microscopes that are connected with a comparison bridge. A picture of a typical comparison microscope is shown in Figure 6.5.

There are two separate microscope bodies each with its own stage and objective lenses. Some have transmitted light sources with all of the accompanying optics including condensers and field diaphragms. Others have external light sources on

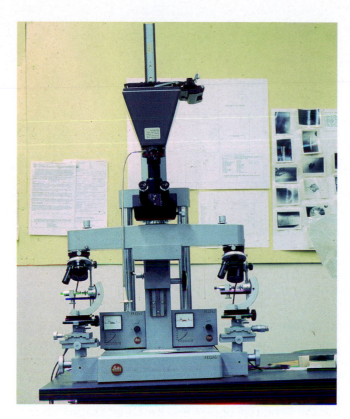

Figure 6.5 The comparison microscope. Specimens are mounted on each stage. The comparison bridge near the top directs each image to a separate ocular lens. Both specimens can be seen simultaneously, one with each eye.

each stage for reflected light microscopy. Some comparison microscopes have both transmitted and reflected light sources. Instead of oculars at the top of each microscope, the two viewing tubes are connected by a *comparison bridge* that culminates in a binocular or trinocular eyepiece. See Figure 6.6 for a photomicrograph of two cut wires.

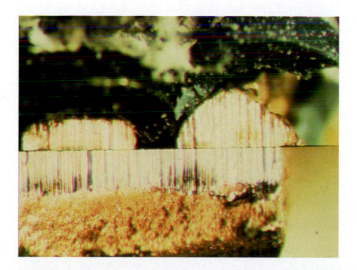

Figure 6.6 Comparison of two tool marks under a comparison microscope. The image at the bottom is a piece of metal cut by a large pair of wire cutters. The image at the top is two wires from a bundle of telephone cables that were alleged to have been cut by the wire cutters. The wire on the right is an excellent match from the wire cutters. The wire on the left is not line up correctly with the part of the metal that was cut by the same part of the wire cutter blade.

Figure 6.7 Photomicrograph of markings on the sides of two bullets fired from same weapon. Note the vertical line in the middle of the picture. This demarks the field of view seen by each eye. The markings on the two bullets can be easily compared this way.

The comparison bridge consists of a closed tube containing two sets of identical mirrors that direct the light from the objective lenses toward the center of the bridge. Additional mirrors then direct the light from each microscope up to a monocular eyepiece. The two eyepieces are mounted next to each other so that the examiner can look through them at the same time. The left eye sees the object on the left stage, and the right eye sees the object on the right stage. There is a line down the middle of the images from top to bottom that indicates how much of the combined image is from the left microscope and how much from the right. The comparison bridge mirrors can be manipulated so that only one of the two images is in view. Also, the two images can be overlaid one on top of the other. Virtually, all modern comparison microscopes have a camera mounted on the eyepiece to capture the compared images. Figure 6.7 shows a photomicrograph of the stria (horizontal markings on the surface of bullets made by the inside of the barrel) on two bullets under a comparison microscope.

In addition to the standard flat stage, many comparison microscopes have specialized sample holders for objects such as bullets and cartridges. A bullet holder is shown in Figure 6.8.

Figure 6.8 A bullet holder that fits on the stage of a comparison microscope. This type of holder permits manipulation of the bullet in all directions and, in addition, allows it to be rotated on its long axis. (Courtesy of Leeds Forensic Systems, Inc., Minneapolis, MN.)

Stereomicroscope

As we have seen so far, hand magnifiers are used on flat objects and can magnify them up to about 15×. Basic compound microscopes can magnify images over 1000 times but need transmitted light for high magnifications. Reflected light can be used on opaque objects at lower magnifications but only surface characteristics can be examined. Sometimes, a laboratory receives evidence that is three-dimensional in nature. It is necessary to magnify and view all sides of the evidence and be able to manipulate the evidence while viewing it. In such cases, only low magnification is required, usually 25× to 50×. For such applications, the stereomicroscope was developed. Stereomicroscopes are always binocular; these usually have several objective lenses of varying magnification and a long *working distance*, the space between the stage and the objective lens. In a stereomicroscope, the stage is below the objective lens, and in some models, there is no stage; the object is placed on the table. Working distances are often 6–12 in. Another important point: because of the optics involved, compound microscopes always invert the object but the stereoscope contains additional optics that orient the object as it is without the microscope, making manipulation easier.

A basic stereomicroscope is shown in Figure 6.9. Notice that there is no stage in this model. The illumination source is a ring of light surrounding the objective and pointing down toward the table surface.

The light path through the microscope is shown in Figure 6.10. The stereo microscope consists of two monocular, compound microscopes mounted side by side and aligned so that the objective lenses are slightly offset so that they view slightly different parts of the object, resulting in a three-dimensional appearance. Today, many stereomicroscopes have a trinocular head that permits the addition of a real-time digital video camera that allows the examiner to view the object on a computer screen. The image can then be manipulated and enhanced and photographed.

As you might expect, there are many applications of stereomicroscopy in forensic science. One common use is in the analysis of marihuana. The leaves and seeds of the plant have characteristic shapes and appearances. There are two different types of hairs on the top and bottom surfaces of the leaves. One of the major examinations of marihuana consists of viewing the various structures on

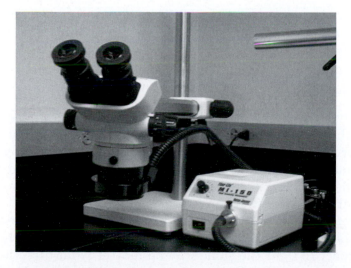

Figure 6.9 A stereo microscope. Note the absence of a stage. Specimens are mounted directly on the table. Light is supplied by a light ring below the objective lens.

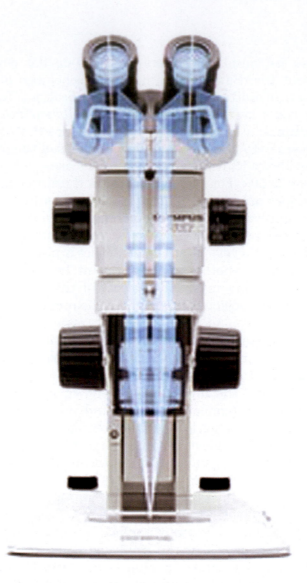

Figure 6.10 The light path through a stereo microscope. Note that the two light paths converge slightly away from each other, thus creating a three-dimensional image.

the leaves and the appearance of the seeds under the stereomicroscope at about 25× magnification. A photograph of marihuana leaves under a stereomicroscope is shown in Figure 6.11.

Polarized Light Microscope

With some relatively minor modifications, a compound microscope can have polarized light capabilities. This is one of the most powerful tools in the forensic science laboratory. Unfortunately, many, if not most, forensic scientists rely heavily on analytical instrumentation and do not take the time or effort needed to learn how to use this powerful tool. One can discover details about the structure of materials and their surface characteristics that can lead to identification.

With respect to optical properties, there are two types of materials. The first consists of substances such as gases, liquids, and some solids whose structure is such that they react to light the same way no matter what direction it comes from or how it strikes the material. Such materials are designated *isotropic*. The other type of material, which are mostly solids, reacts to light differently depending upon

Figure 6.11 Marihuana leaf material under a stereo microscope at 40× magnification.

its orientation and direction. These are designated *anisotropic*. Consider corduroy pants. The fabric has ribs that are aligned in one direction. The structure of many solids is such that they have a kind of alignment and they will react differently to light that is in the direction of the alignment than to light that is 90° away from the alignment. When light is emitted from a source, it travels in waves that can be aligned in any direction. A *polarizer* is a kind of light filter. It blocks out all light except that which is traveling in a single plane, the one aligned with the polarizer. This is called *polarized light*. This can be seen in Figure 6.12.

Anisotropic materials have a preferred directionality to their structure. Polarized light will have different optical effects on these substances depending upon how the light is aligned with the preferred direction. A PLM contains two polarizers.

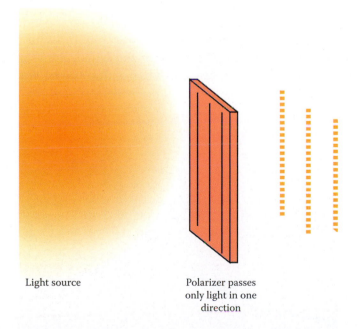

Light source   Polarizer passes
                                     only light in one
                                     direction

Figure 6.12 How light is polarized. Light normally travels in waves in all directions and planes. A polarizer is a filter that blocks out all light except that which is traveling in one particular plane. (Courtesy of Meredith Haddon.)

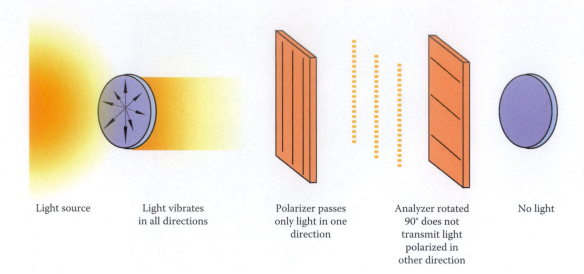

Light source | Light vibrates in all directions | Polarizer passes only light in one direction | Analyzer rotated 90° does not transmit light polarized in other direction | No light

Figure 6.13 Crossed polarizers. If the two polarizers are oriented 90° from each other, then no light will emerge from the second one. (Courtesy of Meredith Haddon.)

One, aptly called the polarizer, is located below the stage and is aligned east-west, so that the only light that gets through is aligned east-west. When it strikes the object on the stage, it will react in some way by showing a particular color. If the object is rotated, it will show a different color if it is anisotropic. The other polarizer is located above the stage. It is oriented north-south, the opposite of the orientation of the polarizer. It is called the analyzer. If east-west light from the polarizer tries to pass through the analyzer, none will get through. This is shown in Figure 6.13.

If an isotropic material is placed between the crossed polarizers, no light should emerge through the analyzer because the material does not affect the light at all. If, however, an anisotropic material is placed between the two polarizers, the material will slightly change the direction of the light so that some of it will get through the analyzer and the image of the material will be seen.

Figure 6.14 shows some white acrylic fibers that are exposed to polarized light. Because of their structure, many fibers are anisotropic and will show different colors depending upon the alignment of the polarized light. Some of the fibers in this figure appear blue while others are orange. This is due to the way they are aligned relative to the polarized light.

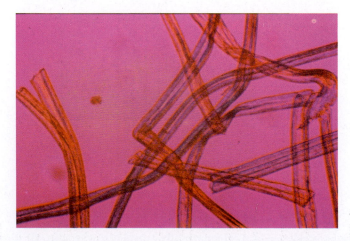

Figure 6.14 White acrylic fibers under polarized light. The orange and blue interference colors are due to the different interactions of the fibers owing to their orientation toward the polarized light.

Microspectrophotometry

As we have seen in the discussion of polarized light, it is clear that certain materials will react when exposed to some types of light. Light may be absorbed or reflected by the material. When a transparent material absorbs light, some of it may pass through, some may be scattered, and some may be affected to the extent that it changes wavelength. The behavior of light and its measurement when it interacts with matter is called *spectroscopy*, and the measuring instrument is called a *spectrophotometer*. This is discussed in detail in Chapter 5. It is pretty easy to measure the effects of matter on light when there is a relatively large quantity of matter. In forensic science, however, we often receive only very small amounts of material such as a single fiber or tiny paint chip. We would like to know the exact color of a fiber and whether two fibers are exactly the same color, for example, but conventional spectroscopy cannot be performed because of the small amount of material available. To solve this problem, forensic scientists employ a *microspectrophotometer*, a marriage between a microscope and a spectrophotometer. In microspectrophotometry, a sample such as a fiber is mounted under a microscope. After the light passes through the sample and the image is magnified, it is sent to the spectrophotometer for analysis. Any transparent object that can be suitably magnified by the microscope is a candidate for microspectrophotometry.

There are two types of microspectrophotometers. One type is essentially a microscope where the light source may be ultraviolet, visible, or infrared light. This passes through the sample that is mounted on the microscope stage. After passing through the lenses, the light is channeled to a detector, as it is in a conventional spectrophotometer. A picture of a UV-visible-near infrared microspectrophotometer is shown in Figure 6.15.

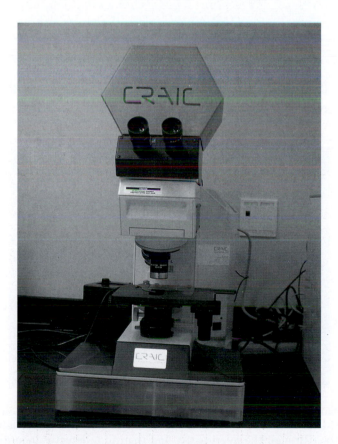

Figure 6.15 A microspectrophotometer. The large box on top of the microscope is the detector. Ultraviolet, visible, and near infrared light can be used as the light source.

The size of the light beam that reaches the sample can be controlled either manually through an iris diaphragm or electronically through a computer. The size of the spot of light is seen as a "cursor" under the microscope or on a computer screen. The light cursor can be moved around the object to obtain a spectrum of a particular part. In some cases, the amount of sample within the cursor is controlled by changing the objective lens to increase or decrease magnification. In other cases, the size and shape of the cursor can be controlled from the computer. It is necessary to properly adjust the cursor because a correct spectrum can only be obtained if all of the light that reaches the detector has passed through the object. No stray light should reach the detector. A picture of pieces of cosmetic glitter under the microscope in Figure 6.15 is shown in Figure 6.16.

The other type of microspectrophotometer is shown in Figure 6.17. This is essentially a conventional infrared spectrophotometer that has a microscope mounted as

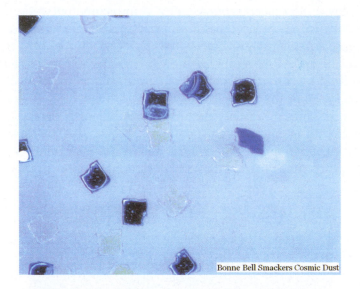

Figure 6.16 Cosmetic glitter particles under a microspectrophotometer.

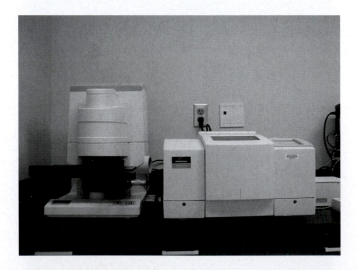

Figure 6.17 An infrared microspectrophotometer. The infrared spectrophotometer is on the right side of the picture. This is connected by a light pipe to the microscope on the left. The infrared light travels from the bench, through the microscope, and then to a detector mounted inside the microscope. There is no ocular lens. Instead, there is a video camera that captures the images and sends them to a computer. The stage is controlled by a "joy stick."

an accessory. Under the control of a computer, the light from the spectrophotometer can be redirected so that it passes through the microscope where it interacts with the object mounted on the stage. In the instrument pictured in Figure 6.17, there is no ocular on the microscope. There is instead a digital camera that is connected to the computer. The magnified object is shown on the computer screen. A mechanical "joystick" controls the movement of the stage.

Whether the microspectrophotometer is a modified microscope or a modified spectrophotometer is a matter of manufacturing choice. The same type of instrument (ultraviolet or infrared) can be configured either way.

Electron Microscopy

All of the compound microscopes discussed thus far suffer from the same limitation: they can achieve a maximum magnification of about 1000 power. At magnifications over about 400 power, the object and objective lens must usually be immersed in a special liquid to alter the refractive index so that the object can be clearly viewed. This magnification limitation is due to the need to increase the curvature and decrease the size of the lens so much that it causes distortion of the light above these values. There is also a limit to the amount of resolution that can be obtained from this optical system of magnification. In forensic science, however, there are many instances when it is necessary to magnify images higher than the maximum of a light microscope. An instrument that could accomplish this would have to use a magnification system other than light and lenses. The *electron microscope* uses electrons rather than light to magnify images. There are no lenses involved so distortion of light is not an issue. Magnifications exceeding 200,000 times are easily achievable. There are two types of electron microscope. If an image is made thin enough, then a beam of electrons can pass through a material and interact with it. This is called *transmission electron microscopy*. This type of electron microscopy is not commonly used in forensic science since most of the forensic applications require relatively thick particles that the electrons cannot pass through. The other type of electron microscopy is called *scanning electron microscopy* and the measuring instrument is called the scanning electron microscope (SEM). An SEM can magnify an image from about 50 to more than 200,000 times. A photograph of an SEM is shown in Figure 6.18. A simplified schematic of how an SEM works is shown in Figure 6.19. A tiny object is usually mounted on a metal stub and put in an evacuated sample compartment. In order to get proper interactions between the electron beam and the object, it must be able to conduct electricity. A coating of carbon or gold is usually applied to the object to facilitate this. A beam of electrons is aimed at the object. The object absorbs most of the electrons. Where the beam touches the object, it causes *secondary electrons* to be emitted from the chemical elements present in the object. In addition, some of the original electrons in the beam aimed at the object reflect off the surface. These are called *backscattered electrons*. Both secondary and backscattered electrons are captured, amplified, and aimed at a cathode ray tube (CRT), which is essentially a television tube. The inside of the screen of the tube contains phosphorescent materials that glow when struck with electrons. The primary electron beam is scanned across the object, and a magnified image of the object shows up on the CRT.

When the beam of electrons from the SEM source strikes the material that is being magnified, a great deal of energy is absorbed by the material. This causes

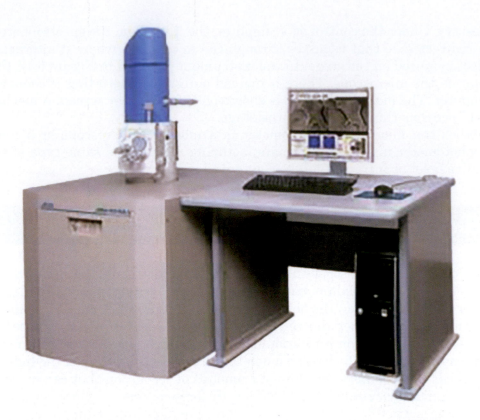

Figure 6.18 A scanning electron microscope.

the atoms that make up the material to be unstable and their nuclei to emit x-rays. Each chemical element has its own characteristics set of x-rays of particular frequencies. Some SEMs have the capability of measuring these x-rays. This technique is called *energy dispersive x-ray analysis* (EDX). An *x-ray analyzer* captures the x-rays and displays them by frequency and quantity. It will also assign element identities to each bundle of x-rays by their frequencies. For example, many samples of gunshot residue contain particles of the primer used to set off the propellant (see Chapter 12). Most common ammunition primers today contain barium, antimony, and lead. If gunshot residues are analyzed by SEM, they will emit x-rays whose frequencies are characteristic of these elements. The presence of these elements in spherical particles from suspected gunshot residue constitutes proof of the presence of a primer. Figure 6.20 shows the display from an x-ray analyzer of a suspected primer particle from gunshot residue. The presence of antimony, barium, and lead can clearly be seen.

SEM/EDX is one of the most versatile analytical methods in forensic science because it allows the microscopist to visualize and examine extremely small particles in three dimensions as well as determine the chemical composition of many materials.

An Unusual Case Involving SEM/EDX

One of the authors of this book was involved in a case where a homeowner was installing a gas water heater in his own home. He tried to get the pilot light to ignite using the automatic igniter built into the heater, but was unable to. He then lit a match to try and get the pilot light ignited, and this caused an explosion. A forensic engineer was brought in to examine the remains of the water heater. He noted that

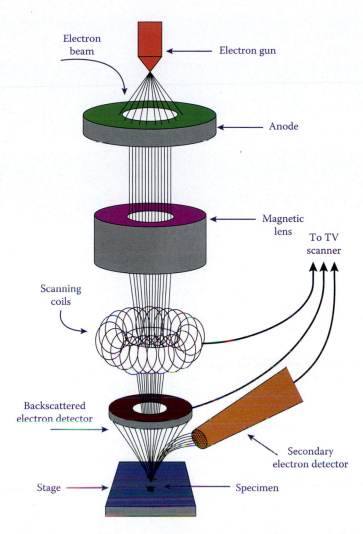

Electron beam

Electron gun

Anode

Magnetic lens

To TV scanner

Scanning coils

Backscattered electron detector

Secondary electron detector

Stage

Specimen

Figure 6.19 A simplified diagram of how an SEM operates. The electron gun produces electrons that are focused through a magnetic lens onto the specimen. Backscattered electrons are captured by a detector and sent to a cathode ray tube or computer screen where the object is visualized. Secondary electrons may also be captured and analyzed. (Courtesy of Josh Klesel, Material Sciences Unit, Iowa State University, Ames, IA.)

an orifice that was supposed to carry gas to the pilot light assembly was partially clogged. The attorneys involved in the case wanted to know what was blocking the orifice. It was thought that, rather than being a foreign material, the blockage was caused by improper machining or cleaning of the orifice during manufacture. The diameter of the orifice was approximately 20 μm, the approximate thickness of a human hair.

It was decided that the only hope of analyzing such a tiny particle would be to ream out the orifice with a fine wire while holding it over top of an SEM sample stub. This was accomplished; the particle landed on the stub and was held there by sticky tape. The particle was smaller than the size of a period (.) on this page. The stub was inserted into the SEM. The particle was clearly visible and EDX analysis indicated the presence of mostly zinc with some tin. The piece of metal that contained the orifice was made mostly of iron with some copper. Therefore, the blockage had to have come from the outside. It could not be a part of the metal left behind when the orifice was reamed out. The origin of the particle was never determined.

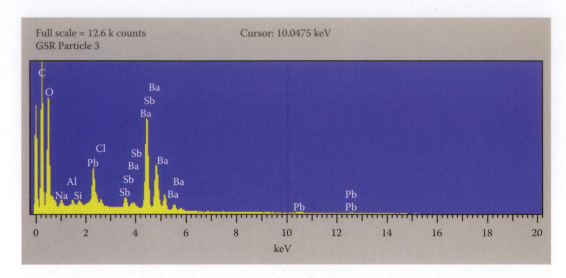

Full scale = 12.6 k counts   Cursor: 10.0475 keV
GSR Particle 3

Figure 6.20 The printout from an energy dispersive x-ray analyzer focused on a particle of suspected gunshot residue. Note the presence of barium, antimony, and lead, which are characteristic of gunshot residue.

Summary

Microscopy is the most powerful tool in the analytical arsenal of forensic science. Much of the evidence received in a crime laboratory consists of microscopic particles. Microscopy enables the forensic examiner to see this evidence, and in some cases, identify it without further analysis. Microscopes range from simple hand magnifiers to powerful electron microscopes. The simplest microscope is the convex lens. Two convex lenses constitute the optics of the compound microscope. The combined magnification of a multiple lens system is the product of the magnification of each lens. The compound microscope can be operated as a transmitted light system or a reflected light system. The major parts are the light source, condenser, and iris diaphragm to control the light. The object sits on a moveable stage. There are one or more objective lenses above the stage. They are at the bottom of the body tube. At the top is the ocular or eyepiece lens. Practically, all microscopes have a coarse and a fine focus. The practical limit of magnification of a lens is measured by its numerical aperture. A microscope can magnify an image more than 1000 times. Microscopes can operate in transmission or reflection mode. A transmission microscope is the most popular. It requires that the object being magnified be transparent and thin enough to allow sufficient light through. Reflecting microscopes shine light on the surface of an opaque object and magnify it. It is useful for evidence such as bullets and cartridges.

The comparison microscope consists of two compound microscopes connected by a comparison bridge so that the examiner can see two objects at the same time, one with each eye. This permits direct observation of the microscopic characteristics of the two objects. The stereo microscope is a low-power instrument that enables viewing of objects in three dimensions and allows the examiner to manipulate the object easily because of a long working distance. The polarizing light microscope has two polarizing filters that block out all light except that which propagates in a particular plane. This kind of light is useful for examining the characteristics of anisotropic substances, which behave differently depending upon how the light is aligned. Microspectrophotometers are a combination of a microscope and a spectrophotometer. These instruments allow the generation of ultraviolet, visible, or infrared spectra of a microscopic object whose size precludes analysis by conventional spectrophotometers. The SEM uses a beam of electrons to magnify an object. The beam strikes a sample causing it to emit secondary electrons that are captured, amplified, and displayed using a CRT. This enables magnifications of up to 200,000 times. At the same time, the elements in the object emit x-rays whose frequencies are characteristic of the elements in the object. EDX analysis displays the x-rays by frequency and determines which elements are present and in what relative concentrations.

Test Yourself

Multiple Choice

1. The ocular of a compound microscope has a magnification of 10 X and the objective has a magnification of 10×. The total magnification of the microscope is
   a. 10×
   b. 20×
   c. 100×
   d. 1000×
2. The objective lens of a compound microscope has an N.A. of 0.4. The maximum useful magnification of the microscope is
   a. 400×
   b. 1000×
   c. 10×
   d. There is not enough information given to calculate this
3. The part of the microscope that focuses the light on an object is the
   a. Iris diaphragm
   b. Coarse focus
   c. Condenser
   d. Body tube
4. The polarizing filter in a PLM that is located above the objective is called the
   a. Polarizer
   b. Analyzer
   c. Abbe condenser
   d. Iris
5. A substance that reacts the same to light polarized in any direction is
   a. An isotope
   b. Anisotropic
   c. Isotropic
   d. Divergent
6. The part of the comparison microscope that allows the examiner to view two objects simultaneously is called the
   a. Comparator
   b. Comparison bridge
   c. Spectroscope
   d. Stage

7. A stereo microscope can best be described as
   a. Two compound microscopes aligned so that they each see a slightly different part of an object
   b. Two compound microscopes aligned with a comparison bridge
   c. A compound microscope with two separate stages and one ocular
   d. A compound microscope with two eyepieces and a camera mount
8. In SEM, secondary electrons
   a. Strike the object releasing other electrons
   b. Strike the object and then reflect off the surface
   c. Are emitted when a beam of primary electrons strikes the object
   d. Are emitted by the nucleus of the various elements when the object is struck by a beam of x-rays
9. In microscopy, resolution is a measure of
   a. The ability of the lenses to separate two tiny details that are close together
   b. The total magnification power of the microscope
   c. The empty magnification of the microscope
   d. The ability of an electron microscope to determine the presence of a large number of elements

True-False

11. Empty magnification is magnification above the level where resolution is increased.
12. Two polarizers aligned 90° from each other will block out all light.
13. A stereo microscope consists of two complete compound microscopes connected by a comparison bridge.
14. A simple convex lens creates a magnified real image of an object.
15. A trinocular microscope has three objective lenses mounted on a turret.
16. An electron microscope uses secondary electrons to magnify an image.
17. Liquids and gases are usually isotropic

Matching—Match Each Term with Its Definition

18. Compound microscope
19. Electron microscope
20. Stereomicroscope
21. Comparison microscope
22. Simple hand magnifier
23. Polarizing microscope

a. Has a polarizer and an analyzer
b. Permits viewing of two objects at once
c. Consists of a single convex lens
d. Long working distance, three-dimensional
e. Basic 2 convex lens microscope
f. Magnify images more than 100,000 times

Short Essay

24. Show by diagram how a virtual image of an object is created by a convex lens.
25. Why is there a practical limitation of magnification by a compound microscope about 1600×? What causes this?
26. How does a comparison microscope work? What are its advantages over just using two compound microscopes?

Further Reading

DeForest, P. R. (2002). Foundations of forensic microscopy, in *Forensic Science Handbook*, vol. I, 2nd edn., R. Saferstein, ed. Prentice Hall, Englewood Cliffs, NJ.

McCrone, W. C. (1986). Forensic microscopy, in *Forensic Science*, 2nd edn., G. Davies, ed. American Chemical Society, Washington, DC.

Palenik, S. (1988). Microscopy and microchemistry of physical evidence, in *Forensic Science Handbook*, vol. 2, R. Saferstein, ed. Prentice Hall, Upper Saddle River NJ.

On the Web

An excellent resource for microscopy. Includes descriptions of various types of microscopy, virtual microscopy and even a museum of microscopy: http://micro.magnet.fsu.edu/primer/java/electronmicroscopy/magnify1/index.html.

Beautiful photomicrographs: http://education.denniskunkel.com/.

Free online journal: Microscopy & Analysis: http://www.microscopyebooks.com/.

Homepage of the Microscopy Society of America: http://www.microscopy.org/.

7
Detector Dogs as Forensic Tools

Susan Stejskal

Learning Objectives

At the end of this chapter, the reader should be able to

1. Understand the basics of the canine olfactory system and how it works
2. Understand the differences between the capacities of human and canine olfaction
3. Understand what trained dogs are capable of detecting
4. Understand the basic steps in training a detector dog
5. Understand the role of canines in forensic science and law enforcement

Chapter 7
Detector Dogs as Forensic Tools

Chapter Outline

Mini Glossary
Acronyms
Introduction
Scenarios
    Accelerant Detection
    Narcotics Detection
    Human Remains Detection
Forensic Tool: Canine Olfaction
    Know the Nose
    Anatomy
    Training the Tool
    Deploying the Tool
Back to the Cases
    Accelerant Detection
    Narcotics Detection
    Human Remains Detection
Utility in Forensics
Summary
Test Yourself
References
On the Web

Mini Glossary

Active alert: The trained response of a detector dog to indicate finding a target odor by barking, scratching, or digging.

Chemoreceptors: Specialized cells with receptors that combine with a specific chemical to send a nerve impulse to the brain.

Detector dog: Highly trained canines used to find specific target odors.

Olfactory bulb: The area of the brain involved in odor detection.

Olfactory receptors: The receptors in the olfactory system that interact with chemical stimuli.

Olfactory system: The body system that is responsible for the sense of smell.

Passive alert: The trained response of a detector dog to indicate finding a target odor by sitting or lying down.

Turbinates: A highly coiled pathway in the canine nose that helps warm, filter, and humidify inhaled air before it gets to the lungs.

Acronyms

ADD: accelerant detector dog
EDD: explosive detector dog
HRDD: human remains detector dog
NDD: narcotics detector dog
OR: olfactory receptors
ORC: olfactory receptor cells
OSAC: Organization of Scientific Area Committees
SWGDOG: Scientific Working Group of Dog and Orthogonal device Guidelines

Introduction

Dogs have lived with man for thousands of years helping by providing protection, hunting, and companionship (Figure 7.1).

Over time, dogs have become an integral part of everyday life, working alongside people helping them live richer, safer, and fuller lives. Working as service dogs or therapy dogs, they assist those with physical disabilities or those needing emotional or psychological support. Due to their keen sense of smell, the role of dogs has expanded over the past several years. One of those roles is the use of trained detector dogs as forensic tools to assist law enforcement.

Figure 7.1 Dogs are willing partners. (Photo courtesy of S.M. Stejskal.)

This chapter addresses how trained dogs can be used in detector work. Much of the information found in this chapter is based on the book *Death, Decomposition, and Detector Dogs: From Science to Scene*, published by CRC Press (Stejskal, 2013).

Scenarios

The following scenarios demonstrate how detector dogs can assist with potential criminal investigations.

Accelerant Detection

There has been another house fire in an area where there are many rental units (Figure 7.2).

The owner of the property is apparently in arrears on taxes for this property and several others. The fire inspector reports that the fire may not have started accidentally.

Narcotics Detection

A major delivery service has contacted the local police department with reports of multiple packages being delivered to a suspected drug house. They have just received another large box scheduled for delivery and so are waiting for direction on what to do next.

Human Remains Detection

A 32-year-old man disappeared about 18 months ago. It is suspected that his room-mate at that time killed him, but the local police department has not been able to locate the decedent. New information has just come in alerting the police to a possible location where the body may have been left. The area is state game land and has very large, heavily wooded areas with marshes and lakes.

Figure 7.2 Fully engulfed house fire. (Photo courtesy of R. Hetu.)

Figure 7.3 The tool! (Photo courtesy of S.M. Stejskal.)

Forensic Tool: Canine Olfaction

Know the Nose

Humans depend primarily on their sense of sight to get through their day. People watch body language and facial expressions of others to guide their social interactions; they read books and signs, watch television, and use computers to communicate. People depend on their eyes.

Dogs go through their days reacting to their environment through their sense of smell. Unlike humans, dogs are designed to use their nose (Figure 7.3).

Anatomy

In order to understand how dogs are able to use their noses so effectively, it is necessary to understand how the olfactory system is "built" and how it functions. Although the anatomy and physiology of olfaction is essentially the same in humans and dogs, there are major differences that make the dog nose much more sensitive. There are many books that provide information about the canine olfactory system (Helton, 2009; Horowitz, 2009; Pearsall and Verbruggen, 1982; Rebmann et al., 2000).

Simply, olfaction depends on odor getting through the nose to specialized cells that can send a message to the brain. This is described in the following.

Nostrils and Nasal Passage (Turbinates)

Odor is made up of chemicals carried with water vapor in air. Different odors are made up of different chemicals of varying amounts in air. Air carrying odor chemicals is inhaled through the nostrils (or nares) and into the nasal passage. Part of the passage includes the turbinates, a highly coiled pathway with extensive blood supply and cells that help warm, filter, and humidify the air before it gets to the lungs.

Olfactory Receptor Cells (ORC) and Olfactory Receptors (OR)

There are specific areas in the nasal turbinates where the olfactory receptor cells (ORCs) are located. These cells are very different from the other cells—they are bipolar nerve cells that have specialized cilia (hair-like projections) on one end of the cell. The end with the cilia is located in the nasal passage (Figure 7.4).

The other end of the ORC is the "nerve" that is capable of sending information to the brain (Figure 7.5).

The olfactory receptors (OR) are located on the cilia of the ORCs. These receptors are called chemoreceptors because they interact with chemicals. They work like

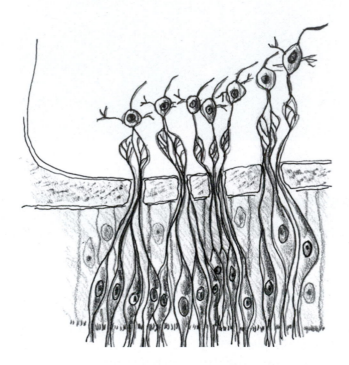

Figure 7.4 Close-up representation of the olfactory receptor cells with cilia (bottom) in the nasal passage and the neuronal interface (top). (Drawing courtesy of M.L. Fojtik.)

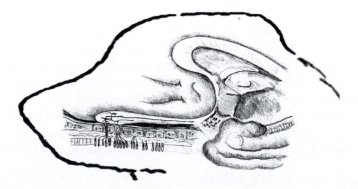

Figure 7.5 Representation of the canine olfactory system highlighting the olfactory receptor cells and the olfactory bulb. (Drawing courtesy of M.L. Fojtik.)

taste buds, which are also chemoreceptors. Simply, chemoreceptors work like a lock and key, where the chemical is the key and the receptor is the lock.

The human taste buds (sweet, sour, salty, and bitter) provide a nice example of how chemoreceptors work. If a person eats something sugary and sweet, the sugar molecules will pass by the sour, salty, and bitter taste buds. But when that sugar (key) hits the sweet receptor (lock) and fits, the lock is unlocked and a message is sent by nerves to the brain. The person knows he just ate something sweet!

Air containing many different types of chemicals is breathed in. As the air passes through the turbinates, each chemical (key) will potentially pass by millions of receptors (locks). If a chemical matches a receptor, like a key fitting in a lock, the receptor is activated and sends an electrical message via the olfactory nerves to the olfactory bulb in the brain.

Olfactory Nerve and Bulb

Each ORC can send electrical signals to the brain. Because there are millions of ORCs, each one "ties" in to make up the olfactory nerves (the left and right sides are wired separately). These "wires" feed into the olfactory bulb, the part of the brain that processes the incoming messages to determine what odor was detected. If that odor is something that has been encountered before (example: SKUNK!), then the brain processes it and determines what the odor is. Then a message may be sent from the brain giving directions to the rest of the body (RUN!).

Function of the Canine Olfactory System

Although training a detector dog will be covered in another section, it may help to understand how a dog may use its nose. For the canine, there is a big difference between breathing and sniffing. When a dog breathes through his nose, some of the inhaled air passes by and encounters the ORCs. When a dog breathes through his mouth, less of the air makes it into the nasal passage and the ORCs. But sniffing is different. Sniffing involves the intake of short, rapid bursts of air into the nose, and with this, forces the air into areas where ORCs are concentrated. Sniffing allows more air containing odor chemicals to reach the ORCs.

Interspecies Differences

There are many differences between the human and canine olfactory systems that explain the greater olfactory acuity seen in dogs. Some of those differences include:

1. *Capacity of air inhaled*: According to Pearsall and Verbruggen (1982), the German Shepherd Dog can breathe in five times more air than a human can. That is primarily due to the greater amount of coiling seen in the nasal turbinates, giving the dog more capacity and surface area. For example, the coiling and length of the dog turbinates is like a long garden hose (dog) compared to a short sprayer hose in the kitchen sink (human).
2. *Number of ORCs*: Because of the increased surface area of the turbinates in the dog, they have more room for far more ORCs than the human. Coren and Hodgson (2011) provided estimates of 5 million ORCs in the human compared to a range of 125–300 million in the dog. The area containing ORCs in the human is estimated to be about 1.6 in.^{2} compared to 26 in.^{2} in the dog (Kaldenbach, 1998).

Figure 7.6 Not all cameras or noses are the same! (Photo courtesy of S.M. Stejskal.)

3. *Types of ORs*: Research has shown that there are more than 1000 genes that control the ORs in the dog, likely creating many different types of chemoreceptors in the dog nose. These ORs are unique and each probably binds with a chemical with a specific size, shape, structure, and concentration (Lesniak et al., 2008). Genetic diversity among individual dogs and breeds probably results in lots of variation in their olfactory abilities (Tacher et al., 2005).

4. *Size of the olfactory bulb in the brain*: Because of the higher number of ORCs in the dog, the olfactory bulb is about 40 times larger than the olfactory bulb in the human (Correa, 2005). It is obvious that the dog requires more brain power to process all the incoming information. Additionally, differences in microscopic structure of the olfactory bulb have been reported in dogs of different ages, demonstrating that the olfactory system develops with age (Wei et al., 2008).

5. *Directionality*: Dogs have a unique nasal airflow pattern that occurs during sniffing—each nostril can get separate odor samples which, after being processed in the brain, allows a dog to localize the source of the odor (Craven et al., 2009). The human does not have this ability.

6. *Olfactory fatigue*: When a human smells an odor for the first time, it may seem very strong. But as time goes on, a person perceives that the strength of the odor decreases. This is actually due to an adaptive temporary inability to distinguish a particular odor after prolonged exposure. This response is called olfactory fatigue (NIH, 2014). Unlike the human, the canine olfactory system does not experience olfactory fatigue. As long as the odor is still present, the dog will smell it in each and every breath he takes and the concentration or strength is as strong as the breath before it. This provides the dog an opportunity to follow air containing odor that he is trained to locate.

In summary, the olfactory system of the dog allows it to smell a range of distinct and different odors with sensitivity far greater than that of the human. Because of these anatomical and physiological differences, a dog is able to detect a "higher resolution of scent." This results in the dog's scent picture being one of high resolution and detail and the human's of low quality and poor focus (Theby, 2010) (Figure 7.6).

Training the Tool

Due to the sensitivity of canine olfaction and the trainability of dogs, the use of detector dogs has greatly expanded through the last few decades. Dogs are used to locate the odor of narcotics, explosives, and accelerants. They are also used to detect things like bed bugs, agricultural pests, contraband, counterfeit drugs and money, as well as locating the odor of exotic or invasive species. Dogs are trained to assist people through their ability to detect medical conditions such as seizures, diabetes, cancer, etc. (Cornu et al., 2011; Gilden, 2008; Palosuo, 2011; Waggoner, 2001).

The training used to teach a dog to detect a substance is basically the same across the detector dog disciplines. It consists of three major parts: odor recognition, training a specific notification response behavior, and then linking those two behaviors together. This is a repetitive process that trains a dog to associate the target odor with a positive outcome (reward). The detector dog has to be able to perform this work, reliably and consistently, in a variety of places with different environmental conditions.

Initial Training: Odor Recognition

This most basic, yet essential, part is what makes a detector dog. Whether training the dog to locate a beehive with colony collapse (Johnson, 2009) or to detect cell phones in prison (Coren, 2011), the training starts the same way.

The training aids should be the target odors that a detector dog would find in a real-world setting. Odor recognition involves isolating the target odor and allowing the dog to smell it. When the dog smells it or shows interest in the target odor, he is rewarded. Rewards vary among dogs and trainers, but usually involve either food, toy, or praise. Each time the dog encounters the odor, he is fed, played with, or praised, with the reward being given at or near the odor source.

Trained Notification Response

The next step involves training some kind of behavior that the dog will perform when he encounters the target odor. The training of the notification response is done at the same time as odor recognition, but is done separately. Although the term used to describe how the dog will notify the handler that he has encountered the odor may vary, the term "response" will be used for this section. Most detector dogs will be trained to perform either an active or passive response. Examples of active responses are barking, finding, and then maybe bringing the handler to the source (re-find), or a scratch/dig. Passive responses are as the name indicates, usually a sit or down.

Pairing or Linking Behaviors

Once the dog has learned to recognize the target odor and perform the trained response as separate exercises, it is time to start linking the two together. Continuing with the same methods used to train odor recognition, once the dog demonstrates that he has located the target odor, the handler will cue (command) the dog to do its trained response. In the case of some detector dogs, this will require the command "sit" as the dog shows the interest in the source. In this case, until the dog sits, no reward is given. The cue may be given again and as soon as the dog sits, the reward is delivered. This is repeated over and over in different settings with the verbal cue dropped as the dog begins to perform the trained response on his own.

According to the Scientific Working Group on Detector dog and Orthogonal device Guidelines (SWGDOG, 2014), the term alert is defined as a "characteristic change in ongoing behavior in response to a trained odor, as interpreted by the handler. The components of the alert may include: change of behavior (COB), interest, and final response or indication." It is through repeated training and observation of the dog's behavior that the handler is able to identify and call the final response.

The dog uses a method called air scenting when looking for the target odor. SWGDOG describes this as "a technique used by the dog to locate a target odor. The dog searches for target odor on wind/air currents and attempts to identify/work on a scent cone to the source." Once locating even a whiff of target odor, the dog will show a very characteristic change in behavior, working toward higher and higher concentrations of the target odor. Then, if the concentration of the target odor is present in the air and enough of the ORs send messages to the brain, the detection threshold (concentration of chemical in the air) is met (Helton, 2009). After processing the incoming information, the brain will send a message to the rest of the dog to perform its trained response, alerting the handler that the odor has been located.

Training for Deployment

The next part is a never-ending training of the dog to get ready for operational use. This is the time when target odors are placed in real-life settings, with the team training inside buildings, outside in the woods, or locating odor from sources hidden in vehicles, packages, etc.

Training also includes working in different environmental conditions. These conditions (temperature, humidity, barometric pressure, wind speed and direction, etc.) provide a critical influence on if or how the target odor disperses. Explosive detector dogs (EDD) who work in an airport will face far different conditions that an HRD dog looking for odor from a cold case burial. It is important for the K9 team to train in conditions similar to ones in which they may be deployed.

Each additional target odor (e.g., adding bone, blood, etc., for HRD dog) requires more training, depending on where and how the dog will be deployed. The dog team will also work in areas where there are no training aids (negative or blank area search) or in areas where there are distracting odor sources. By expanding the locations, sites, and/or conditions the team may encounter in the real world, the dog team becomes prepared to work in a number of locations and environmental conditions.

Testing and Certifications

Following the initial training, the canine detector teams are frequently evaluated to determine how the team is performing and to address any training gaps that may arise. Proficiency assessments are commonly recommended and usually include working the dog team in an area where the handler (and dog) does not know the location of the training aid (blind area search).

Testing is usually done before a team is considered to be "mission ready" (Rebmann et al., 2000). This evaluation should not only consider whether the dog can indicate the scent source, but how the handler plans the search, how effectively the handler works the area, control of the dog, and whether the dog performs its trained alert appropriately.

Certification is an evaluation process. Although there are currently no national standards for certification among detector disciplines, there are a few states that have them. Many detector canine teams certify through national police canine associations that will hold periodic certification trials. Depending on the organization, dog teams are often certified annually.

Maintenance Training

This is the last phase of training; it is continuous in nature and never ends throughout the detector dog's career. This is training where the dog's "library" of odors may be expanded, working under more challenging conditions, and usually decreasing the dog's detection threshold. The dog team continues to undergo proficiency assessments and certifications until the team is retired.

Figure 7.7 Smoke provides a visual example of how odor may disperse from a source. (Photo courtesy of S.M. Stejskal.)

Role of the Handler

Often people think that the role of the handler is limited to bringing the detector dog to the scene and letting it do its work. Nothing could be further from the truth—the handler and dog make up the K9 team. The handler's job is to train the dog, keep training the dog, go through periodic proficiency assessments and certifications, maintain records, and keep the dog healthy and ready to work when needed. And then when called, the handler brings the dog to the search area, but must understand the conditions that can influence the dispersion and/or availability of odor before the dog is ever worked. The handler must work with the dog to ensure a successful outcome, whether it is locating the odor or not. In summary, a successful dog handler is a highly trained and skilled practitioner who can use the forensic tool (the dog) efficiently and accurately.

Deploying the Tool

It is very important that canine handlers understand how their dogs work and as important, what affects the availability of odor to their dog. A critical point to grasp is that the odor has to be available to the dog for it to locate it. Odors do not disperse uniformly from a source and instead, are highly affected by the movement of air which can cause "discontinuous and complex patterns" of odor. Environmental conditions may cause there to be areas of air with varying concentrations of chemicals mixed with air that contains either none of those chemicals or very low concentrations (Helton, 2009). Due to the characteristics of specific chemicals, odors may become trapped or pool in specific areas, providing an odor "sink" for detector dogs. One way to understand how odor may disperse is through the example of smoke from a fire (Figure 7.7).

Back to the Cases

Accelerant Detection

After the fire was out, the scenes cool, and the structure was deemed safe, a fire investigator went out on behalf of the insurance company. After a preliminary

Figure 7.8 Accelerant detector dog team at work. (Photo courtesy of R. Hetu.)

search of the structure, an accelerant detector dog (ADD) was requested in order to conduct a search for trace ignitable liquids. Prior to conducting a search of the structure, the handler was briefed by the fire investigator and was informed that the fire occurred a few weeks earlier.

The structure was a single story, wood sided, single family dwelling. The canine team conducted an exterior/interior search of the structure/fire debris (Figure 7.8).

The AD dog gave a trained final response for an ignitable liquid at three locations inside the house including a cloth bedding/sheet, papers, and a small section of carpet.

Following established procedures, the items were photographed, collected, and submitted for laboratory examination (NFPA, 2014). Each of the items tested positive for gasoline.

Narcotics Detection

The local police department deployed a NDD team. At the instruction of the handler, the suspicious parcel was placed among similar sized parcels with the K-9 team not knowing which parcel was suspect. The NDD team arrived at the location and conducted a sniff of the packages. The dog performed his trained response at the suspect package and based on that, a search warrant was obtained. Inside the package were two boxes with high heel, knee high leather boots, and two pounds of marijuana was discovered inside the boots (Figure 7.9).

Figure 7.9 Yield from search by narcotics detector dog. (Photo courtesy of R. Kerimian.)

Human Remains Detection

New information was received about the possible location for a 32-year-old man who disappeared about 18 months ago. Because the area is state game land, no warrant was required. Two certified HRD dogs were requested and independently were deployed in two separate areas. The first team deployed in a boat (Figure 7.10).

There was no change in behavior or alerts demonstrated by that dog. The second team was deployed to search an area in the state game land (Figure 7.11).

While working that area, the HRD dog located a decedent, believed to be the victim they were trying to locate.

Figure 7.10 Human remains detector dog working from a boat. (Photo courtesy of S.M. Stejskal.)

Figure 7.11 Human remains detector dog working in a field. (Photo courtesy of S.M. Stejskal.)

Utility in Forensics

The role that trained detector dogs bring to the criminal justice systems has been recognized in the public arena, and more importantly, in the courts (Ensminger, 2011). Because of this, there has been a move for over a decade to develop "best practices" for many aspects of detector dogs. *SWGDOG* was made up of a partnership of professionals from local, state, federal, and international agencies. The mission of SWGDOG was to develop consensus-based best practice documents to help improve the "consistency and performance of deployed teams in combination with detection devices to improve interdiction efforts as well as courtroom acceptance."

This effort continues today under the recently reorganized Organization of Scientific Area Committees (OSAC) Dogs and Sensors Subcommittee. OSAC is a part of the National Institute of Standards and Technology (NIST) whose mission is to strengthen forensic science in the United States (NIST, 2014).

Summary

Detector dogs have found a niche in many areas of forensic science. From accelerant to human remains detection, the sensitivity of the canine nose is an important tool that is used to aid investigations. By understanding canine behavior, it is possible to train dogs to locate and alert the handler of a target odor. The team is made up of the dog and handler. Handlers need to be aware of surroundings, hazards, and environmental conditions in order to efficiently and safely deploy their detector dogs.

Test Yourself

Multiple Choice

1. The olfactory system is responsible for the sense of
   a. Sight
   b. Smell
   c. Taste
   d. Hearing
2. Odor is carried through the air with the help of
   a. Oxygen
   b. Carbon dioxide
   c. Water vapor
   d. Carbon monoxide
3. The coiled pathways in the nose line with blood vessels are called
   a. Turbinates
   b. Tubules
   c. Olfactory bulbs
   d. Olfactory receptors

4. One of the following is NOT a function of the turbinates
   a. Warming the air
   b. Filtering the air
   c. Making the air moist
   d. Increasing the flow of the air
5. Olfactory receptor cells are a type of
   a. Nerve cell
   b. Brain cell
   c. Nasal cell
   d. Blood cell
6. The olfactory receptors are a type of
   a. Pressure receptor
   b. Chemoreceptor
   c. Baroreceptor
   d. Neuroreceptor
7. Dogs can breathe in more air than humans primarily due to
   a. Their noses are bigger
   b. Their nostrils are flared
   c. The turbinates are more coiled
   d. The lungs are bigger
8. The sense of smell is processed in what part of the brain?
   a. Frontal lobe
   b. Hippocampus
   c. Sensory bulb
   d. Olfactory bulb
9. Olfactory fatigue is defined as
   a. Decrease in perceived strength of smell due to lack of sleep
   b. Decrease in perceived strength of smell due to aging
   c. Decrease in perceived strength of smell due to prolonged exposure
   d. Decrease in perceived strength of smell due to infection
10. SWGDOG was formed to
    a. Keep a database of detector dog DNA
    b. Keep a database of detector dog handler contact information
    c. Develop and train K9 handlers
    d. Develops best practice guidelines for detector dog teams

True or False

11. Dogs and humans have equal scenting capabilities.
12. Odor is made up of chemicals carried on oil droplets in air.
13. The olfactory bulb is responsible for processing messages sent from the brain.
14. Turbinates are located in the brain.
15. Taste buds are a type of chemoreceptors.
16. Research shows that dogs and humans have similar capacity to establish odor directionality.
17. Passive final responses are the preferred type for explosive detector dogs.
18. Certified detector dogs are always able to locate what they are trained to find.

Short Answer

19. List four odors that dogs are regularly trained to detect.
20. List and describe three major steps in training a detector dog.

Matching

21. The part of the brain that responds to smell
22. The part of the cell that responds to chemical odor stimulation
23. Any cell that responds chemical stimulation
24. Canine response is barking or scratching
25. Canine response is sitting or lying down

a. Active alert
b. Chemoreceptor
c. Olfactory bulb
d. Olfactory receptor
e. Passive alert

References

Coren, S. (2011). Cell phone sniffing dogs: A new weapon against high tech crime. *Psychology Today*, December 18, 2011. Retrieved on November 14, 2014 from: https://psychologytoday.com/blog/canine-corner/201112/cell-phone-sniffingdogs-as.

Coren, S. and S. Hodgson. (2011). Understanding a dog's sense of smell. Retrieved on November 1, 2014 from: http://www.dummies.com/how-to/content/understanding-a-dogs-sense-of-smell.navId-323759.

Cornu, J., Cancel-Tassin, G., Ondet, V., Girardet, C., and O. Cussenot. (2011). Olfactory detection of prostate cancer by dogs sniffing urine: A step forward in early diagnosis. *European Urology* 59:197–201.

Correa, J. E. (2005). The dog's sense of smell. Alabama Cooperative Extension System—UNP-66. http://www.aces.edu (accessed January 12, 2011).

Craven, B. A., Paterson, E. G., and G. S. Settles. (2009). The fluid dynamics of canine olfaction: unique nasal airflow patterns as an explanation of macrosomia. *The Royal Society*. Retrieved on November 14, 2014 from: http://rsif.royalsocietypublishing.org/content/7/47/933.abstract.

Ensminger, J. J. and L. E. Papet. (2012). Chapter 19: Cadaver dogs, in *Police and Military Dogs: Criminal Detection, Forensic Evidence, and Judicial Admissability*. Ensminger, J. J., ed. CRC Press, Boca Raton FL.

Gilden, J. (2008). Trained dogs able to detect ovarian cancer's specific scent. *Medical News Today*, June 27, 2008. Retrieved on November 14, 2014 from: http://www.medicalnewstoday.com/printerfriendlynews.php?newsid=113085.

Helton, W. S. (2009). Chapter 5: Overview of scent detection work—Issues and opportunities, in *Canine Ergonomics: The Science of Working Dogs*. Helton, W. S., ed. CRC Press, Boca Raton, FL.

Horowitz, A. (2009). *Inside of a Dog: What Dogs See, Smell, and Know*. Scribner (A Division of Simon & Schuster), New York.

Johnson, J. (2009). Maryland dog sniffs out diseased bee colonies, *Washington Post*, March 5, 2009. Retrieved on November 1, 2014 from: 'washingtonpost.com'.

Kaldenbach, J. (1998). *K9 Scent Detection: My Favorite Judge Lives in a Kennel*. Detselig Enterprises Ltd., Calgary, Alerta, Canada.

Lesniak, A., Walczak, M., Jezierski, T., Sacharczuk, M., Gawkowski, M., and K. Jaszczak. (2008). Canine olfactory receptor gene polymorphism and its relation to odor detection performance by sniffer dogs. *Journal of Heredity* 99(5):518–527.

National Fire Protection Association (NFPA). (2014). NFPA 921: Guide for fire and explosion investigations. Retrieved on November 23, 2014 from http://www.nfpa.org.

National Institute of Health (NIH). (2004). Sense of smell. Retrieved on November 15, 2014 from http://www.tools.niehs.nih.gov.

National Institute of Standards and Technology (NIST). (2014). OSAC Committees. Retrieved on November 15, 2014 from http://www.NIST.gov/forensics/OSAC.

Palosuo, N. (2011). 'Viagradogs' sniff out fake medicines. *PfizerWorld*. Retrieved on April 18 2011 from http://world.pfizer.com/Pages?ViagradogsSniffsOutFakeMedicines.aspx?:Referrer=Newsletter.

Pearsall, M. D. and H. Verbruggen. (1985). *Scent: Training to Track, Search, and Rescue.* Alpine Publications, Loveland CO.

Rebmann, A., David, E., and M. Sorg. (2000). *Cadaver Dog Handbook: Forensic Training and Tactics for the Recovery of Human Remains.* CRC Press, Boca Raton, FL.

Stejskal, S. M. (2013). *Death, Decomposition, and Detector Dogs: From Science to Scene.* CRC Press, Boca Raton, FL.

SWGDOG. (2014). Scientific Working Group on detector dogs and orthogonal device guidelines. Retrieved on November 30, 2014 from: http://www.swgdog.org.

Tacher, S., Quignon, P., Rimbault, M., Dreano, S., Andre, C., and F. Galibert. (2005). Olfactory receptor sequence polymorphism within and between breeds of dogs. *Journal of Heredity* 96(7):812–816.

Theby, V. (2010). *Smellorama: Nose Games for Dogs.* Veloce Publishing Ltd., Dorchester, U.K.

Waggoner, L. P. (2001). Canine olfactory sensitivity and detection odor signatures for mines/UXO, testing support for Tuft's Medical School E-nose, and fate and effects team participation (MDA972-97-1-00026). Auburn University, Auburn, AL.

Wei, Q., Zhang, H., and B. Guo. (2008). Histological structure difference of dog's olfactory bulb between different age and sex. *Zoological Research* 29(5):537–545.

On the Web

National Institute of Standards and Technology: www.nist.gov/forensics/OSAC/sub-dogs.cfm.
Scientific Working Group on detector Dog and Orthogonal detector Guidelines: swgdog.org.

8

Digital Evidence, Computer Forensics, and Investigation*

* Various portions of the following chapters, from the following three books, were combined to comprise this chapter:
Welch, T., *Information Security Management Handbook*, 6th edn., Harold F. Tipton and Micki Krause (eds.), Section 10.2, Auerbach Publications.
Ciaramitaro, B., *Digital Forensics Explained*, G. Goglin (ed.), Chapter 9, Auerbach Publications.
Goglin, G. (ed.), *Digital Forensics Explained*, Chapter 5, Auerbach Publications.
Marcella, A., Jr. and D. Menendez (eds.), *Cyber Forensics: A Field Manual for Collecting, Examining, and Preserving Evidence of Computer Crimes*, 2nd edn., Chapters 4 and 12, Auerbach Publications.

Learning Objectives

1. To be able to define and describe cyber crime
2. To be able to define and describe computer crime
3. To be able to define and describe computer forensics
4. To be able to describe the various aspects of a computer crime investigation
5. To understand and describe the role of cell phones and other portable devices in computer crime
6. To be able to describe the reporting aspects of computer crime investigation

Chapter 8
Digital Evidence, Computer Forensics, and Investigation

Chapter Outline

Mini Glossary

Cyber crime: Any criminal act dealing with computers or other digital devices.

Computer crime: Any illegal act for which knowledge of computer technology is essential for its perpetration, investigation, or prosecution.

Computer forensics: The study of computer technology as it relates to the law.

Jurisdiction: The geographic area where the crime had been committed and any portion of the surrounding area over, or through which the suspect passed, is en route to, or going away from, the actual scene of the crime.

Acronyms

COTS: Commercial off-the-shelf
GLBA: Gramm–Leach–Bliley Act of 1999
HIPAA: Health Insurance Portability and Accountability Act of 1996

NET: No Electronic Theft Act of 1997
PDA: Personal digital assistant
SoX: Sarbanes–Oxley Act of 2002

Introduction

Computer, cell phone, and handheld technology has advanced exponentially over the last several years. The same technology that has allowed for the advancement and automation of many business processes, not to mention personal use, has also opened the door to many new forms of computer abuse. While some of these systems attacks merely use contemporary methods to commit older, more familiar types of crime, others involve the use of completely new forms of criminal activity that have evolved along with the technology.

New technology provides new opportunities for criminals and crimes both in the physical and virtual (digital) worlds. Police now monitor criminals' use of the Internet and computer technology to commit a wide range of financial crimes and crimes involving malicious destruction of others' property. This chapter will look at computer crime and investigations, the nature of digital evidence and computer forensics, and the emergence of social media as a tool for investigators. Throughout it, keep in mind that any device capable of recording and storing digital, audio, and video data may contain digital evidence relevant—and in some cases, essential—to a digital forensic investigation.

Challenges

Incidents of computer-related crime and fraud have increased dramatically over the past several decades. Despite this, there have been a limited number of prosecutions and even fewer convictions. This is due to both the nature of the crime and the limits of expertise and resources within the legal, law enforcement, and investigative community. Add to this the myriad phone and wireless handheld devices and the knowledge and skill an investigator needs to be able to handle and extract evidence is immense.

Cyber crime is typically described as any criminal act dealing with computers or computer networks. It is also called by other names (e-crime, computer crime, or Internet crime in different jurisdictions), which have roughly the equivalent meanings. Regardless of the definitions, the use of computers and the Internet in the commission of crimes requires investigators to apply cyber forensic techniques to extract data for those investigating, prosecuting, and passing the ultimate judgment on the offenders in such cases. Identity theft, a term almost unheard of 30 years ago, now makes up a large portion of the caseloads of police agencies and prosecutors throughout the world.

In reality, these identity theft cases present very little that is actually new in the realm of criminal behavior. However, the emergence of new technology requires the law enforcement community—from police and investigators to prosecutors to judges—to utilize different strategies and different tools in addressing the new ways today's criminals commit these traditional crimes. In addition to pornography, fraud, and identity theft, computers and the Internet allow malicious cyber-criminals to violate copyright protection, cause enormous damage to data and equipment, and to lure children—and even adults—into situations where they can be sexually and physically assaulted or exploited.

Computer crime investigation and computer forensics are also evolving sciences that are affected by many external factors: continued advancements in technology, societal issues, legal issues, etc. There are many gray areas that need to be sorted out and tested through the courts. Until then, cyber attackers and criminals will have a clear advantage and computer abuse will continue to increase.

Physical versus Virtual Crimes

When a detective responds to a homicide scene, one of the first things she or he does is to make sure that the area is protected from anyone who would change or remove the evidence. Yellow crime scene tape goes up. Patrol officers are posted to enforce the boundary. Nobody enters the area inside the tape without specific authority and, even then, careful notes are made detailing exactly when the person came under the tape and what the person did. These precautions are critical because at trial the prosecutor will need to establish that the evidence was not contaminated. There may be trace evidence like fibers or hairs that link the suspect to the killing. Blood and fingerprint evidence will be gathered. Without crime scene integrity, a jury cannot properly draw conclusions about the crime because neither the investigators nor the evidence will have credibility.

Computer crime evidence requires the same care and control; however, it exists in such a different form that the precautions connected with its discovery, storage, and retrieval are much different. The investigator is required to establish procedures or protocols that guarantee that evidence from data storage media is unchanged from the time of its seizure or discovery. The computer forensic investigator will need to put up the electronic equivalent of yellow crime scene tape to make sure that the data is not compromised.

This means that, at a minimum, forensic investigators must have adequate knowledge of computer hardware systems, computer forensics software, and the typical consumer software that will usually be seized. Additionally, investigators need a solid understanding of the requirements of the relevant constitutional law and evidentiary law. The legal knowledge enables them to conduct their investigations in a way that does not run afoul of suspects' rights—ensuring admissibility of evidence—and in a way that allows them to understand the procedural requirements of evidence seizure (e.g., how to legally obtain subscriber information from an Internet Service Provider (ISP)).

Computer Crime

According to the *American Heritage Dictionary,* a "crime" is any act committed or omitted in violation of the law. This is a problem for law enforcement when dealing with computer-related crime because some of today's computer-related crime has not violated any formal law. The laws in many states, as currently constituted, generally envision situations involving traditional types of criminal activity, such as burglary, larceny, fraud, etc. Unfortunately, the modern computer criminal, unless perpetrating crimes in the physical world, reveals the difficulties in applying older traditional laws to situations involving "computer-related crimes." While some federal laws have been passed, and some states work to amend their laws, some jurisdictions are still woefully behind. And the nature of cyber crime is such that crimes can often be perpetrated from across the world and, in many cases, anonymously.

In 1979, the United States Department of Justice established a definition for "computer crime," stating that "a computer crime is any illegal act for which knowledge of computer technology is essential for its perpetration, investigation, or prosecution." This definition is too broad and has since been further refined by new, or modified, state and federal criminal statutes.

Criminal Law

Criminal law falls under two main jurisdictions: Federal and State. Although there are many federal and state statutes that may be used against traditional criminal offenses, many cases fail to reach prosecution or fail to result in conviction. The reason is due large to gaps which exists in the Federal Criminal Code and the individual state criminal statutes.

Some new state laws have gone into effect over the last several years to keep abreast of the constant changes in the technological forum. Some of these issues, such as privacy, copyright infringement, and software ownership, are yet to be resolved; thus, we can expect many more changes to the current collection of laws. Some of the computer-related crimes, which are addressed by the new state and federal laws, are

- Unauthorized access
- Exceed authorized access
- Intellectual property theft or misuse of information
- Child Pornography
- Theft of services
- Forgery
- Property theft (i.e., computer hardware, chips, etc.)
- Invasion of privacy
- Denial of services
- Computer fraud
- Viruses
- Sabotage (data alteration or malicious destruction)
- Extortion
- Embezzlement
- Espionage
- Terrorism

Just as there has been legislation at the State level, there have also been federal policies affecting computing, and potential computer crime, passed into law:

Electronic Communications Privacy Act (1986)
Computer Security Act (1987)
Health Insurance Portability and Accountability Act (HIPAA) of 1996
Economic Espionage Act of 1996

National Information Infrastructure Protection Act (1996)
No Electronic Theft ("NET") Act of 1997
Wire Fraud Act (1997)
Digital Millennium Copyright Act (1998)
Children's Online Protection Act (1998)
Identity Theft and Assumption Deterrence Act (1998)
Gramm–Leach–Bliley Act (GLBA) of 1999
Local Law Enforcement Hate Crimes Prevention Act (2001)
Computer Fraud and Abuse Act (2001)
Sarbanes–Oxley Act of 2002 (SoX)
USA PATRIOT and Terrorism Prevention Reauthorization Act of 2005 (HR 3199)
Child Pornography Prevention Act (2005)

These laws and policies have been established, some in part and in varying degrees, to deal with computer and telecommunications abuses at the federal level.

Computer Crime Investigation

Computer crime investigation should start immediately following the report of any alleged criminal activity. At a minimum, the investigator must ascertain if a crime has occurred; and if so, he or she must identify the nature and extent of the abuse. It is important for the investigator to remember that the alleged attack or intrusion may not be a crime at all.

The preliminary investigation usually involves a review of the initial complaint, inspection of the alleged damage or abuse, witness interviews, and, finally, examination of the system and system logs. If during the preliminary investigation it is determined that some alleged criminal activity has occurred, the investigator must address the basic elements of the crime to ascertain the chances of successfully prosecuting a suspect either civilly or criminally.

If it is a physical crime and the computer or device in question is related to a physical crime, the same procedural measures to collect, preserve, and document the examination of the evidence must be ensured. Often, any investigation of suspect devices will be done in tandem with the police investigation.

Determine if Disclosure Is Required

If the crime or fraud occurs to a corporation or entity, it must be determined if a disclosure is required or warranted, due to laws or regulations. Disclosure may be required by law or regulation or may be required if the loss affects a corporation's financial statement. If an insurance claim is to be submitted, a police report is usually necessary. When making the decision to prosecute a case, the victim must clearly understand the overall objective.

Keep in mind that a civil trial and criminal trial can happen in parallel. Information obtained during the criminal trial can be used as part of the civil trial. The key is to know what you want to do at the outset, so all activity can be coordinated. Once probable cause has been identified, law enforcement officers have the ability to execute search warrants, subpoenas, and wire taps. The warrant process was formed in order to protect the rights of the people.

The Fourth Amendment to the Constitution of the United States established the following:

> The right of the people to be secure in their persons, houses, papers, and effects, against unreasonable searches and seizures, shall not be violated, and no Warrants shall issue, but upon probable cause, supported by oath or affirmation, and particularly describing the place to be searched, and the persons or things to be seized.

There are certain exceptions to this. The "exigent circumstances" doctrine allows for a warrantless seizure, by law enforcement, when the destruction of evidence is impending. In *United States v. David*, the court held that "When destruction of evidence is imminent, a warrantless seizure of that evidence is justified if there is probable cause to believe that the item seized constitutes evidence of criminal activity."

A major issue that affects a law enforcement investigation is jurisdiction. Jurisdiction is the geographic area where the crime had been committed and any portion of the surrounding area over, or through which the suspect passed, is en route to, or going away from, the actual scene of the crime. Any portion of this area adjacent to the actual scene over which the suspect, or the victim, might have passed, and where evidence might be found, is considered part of the crime scene. When a system is attacked or otherwise compromised remotely, where did the crime occur? Most courts submit that the crime scene is the victim's location. But what about "en route to"? Does this suggest that a crime scene may also encompass the telecommunications path used by the attacker? If so, and a theft occurred, is this interstate transport of stolen goods? There seem to be more questions than answers but only through cases being presented in court can precedence be set. It will take time for the answers to shake out.

The majority of law enforcement agencies have limited budgets and, as such, place an emphasis on problems related to violent crime and drugs. Also, with technology changing so rapidly, many law enforcement officers lack the technical training to adequately investigate an alleged intrusion.

The same problems hold true for the prosecution and the judiciary. To successfully prosecute a case, both the prosecutor and the judge must have a reasonable understanding of high-tech laws and the crime in question. This is not always the case. Additionally, many of the current laws are woefully inadequate. Even though an action may be morally and ethically wrong, it is still possible that no law is violated. Even when there is a law that has been violated, many of these laws remain untested and lack precedence. Because of this, many prosecutors are reluctant to prosecute high-tech crime cases.

Investigative Process

As with any type of criminal investigation, the goal of the investigation is to know who, what, when, where, why, and how.

Once the decision is made to further investigate a criminal incident, or a computer or device potentially involved in a criminal incident, the next course of action for the investigative team is to establish a detailed investigative plan, including the search and seizure plan. The plan should consist of an informal strategy that will be employed throughout the investigation, including the search and seizure:

- Identify any potential suspects
- Identify potential witnesses
- Identify whether a suspect is known or not

- Determine what type of system and/or device is to be seized
- Identify the Search and Seizure Team Members
- Obtain a Search Warrant (if required)
- Determine if there is risk of the suspect destroying evidence or causing greater losses

Identify the Type of System That Is to Be Seized

It is imperative to learn as much as possible about the target computer system(s) or device(s). If possible, obtain the configuration of the system, including the network environment (if any), hardware, and software. The following data should be acquired prior to the seizure:

- Is a security system in place on the system, If so, what kind? Are passwords used? Can a root password be obtained?
- Where is the system located? Will simultaneous raids be required?
- Obtain the required media supplies in advance of the operation
- What law has been violated? Discuss the elements of proof. These should be the focus of the search and seizure.
- What is your probable cause? Obtain a warrant if necessary.
- Determine if the analysis of the computer system will be conducted on site or back in the office or forensics lab.

Obtaining and Serving Search Warrants

If it is believed that the suspect has crucial evidence at his or her home or office, then a search warrant will be required to seize the evidence. If a search warrant is going to be needed, then it should be done as quickly as possible before evidence can be tampered with or otherwise destroyed. The investigator must establish that a crime has been committed and that the suspect is somehow involved in the criminal activity. He or she must also show why a search of the suspect's home or office is required. Prior to the execution of the plan, the investigative team should ascertain if the suspect, if known, is currently working on the system. If so, the team must be prepared to move swiftly, so that evidence is not destroyed. The investigator should determine if the computer is protected by any physical or logical access control systems and be prepared to respond to such systems. It should also be decided early on what will be done if the computer is on at the commencement of the seizure. The goal of this planning is to minimize any risk of evidence contamination or destruction.

Executing the Plan

The first step in executing the plan is to secure and control the scene. This includes securing the power, network servers, wireless, and telecommunications links. If the suspect is near the system, it may be necessary to physically remove the individual. This allows the investigative team to protect the evidence and continue with the investigation. Investigator should enter the area slowly so as not to disturb or destroy the evidence. They should evaluate the entire situation. In no other type of investigation can evidence be destroyed more quickly.

The investigator may wish to videotape the entire evidence collection process. There are two schools of thought on this. The first is that if you videotape the search and seizure, any mistakes can nullify the whole operation. The second school of thought is that if you videotape the evidence collection process, many of the claims by the defense can be silenced. In either case, an investigator must be careful what is said if the audio is turned on. The crime scene should be sketched and photographed before anything is touched. Sketches should be drawn to scale. Still photographs of critical pieces of evidence should then be taken. At a minimum, the following should be captured:

- Layout of desks and computers (include dimensions and measurements)
- Configuration of all the computers on the network
- Configuration of the suspect computer, including network connections, peripheral connections, internal and external components, and system backplane
- Suspect computer display
- Any additional relevant handheld and or phone devices (unless these items are the sole source of digital evidence)

Finally, phones, answering machines, desk calendars, day-timers, fax machines, pocket organizers, electronic watches, etc., are all sources of potential evidence. If the case warrants, seize and analyze all sources of data, both, electronic and manual. Document all activity in an Activity Log and, if necessary, secure the crime scene.

Wireless and Handheld Devices

To this point, we have referenced primarily computers, with some mention of handheld devices. The reality is that computing capabilities have expanded so broadly that desktops and laptops have given rise to tablets, PDAs, and multipurpose cell phones—all of which could be categorized as mini-computers. As such, all of these are devices in which criminal can perpetrate crimes and otherwise house valuable evidence (Figure 8.1).

Handheld devices are considered embedded systems; that is, systems that are designed primarily to do one thing. However, functionality has been expanded in mobile devices such as tablets and similar devices, so there is significant overlap

Figure 8.1 In addition to desktop and laptop computers, all such handheld and cell phone devices are capable of holding valuable evidence.

in capabilities between handhelds and mobile devices. Because of this, the following discussion will treat handheld and mobile devices as synonymous even though there may be some distinguishing characteristics between the two. Characteristics that complicate forensics include the active device nature of handhelds and mobile devices. Storage capacities have historically been relatively small, but with advances in cloud technology, local storage is not a limiting factor in terms of device functionality. The communication, remote connectivity, and ability for storage in the cloud all need to be taken into consideration in the processing of this physical evidence.

Understanding mobile forensics is an exercise in adaptability due to both the vast number of devices and the rapid rate of innovation. Between different brands, operating systems, connectivity to the cloud through carriers and various wireless connections, phones versus handhelds, and the increasing blurred distinctions between them, there are various dynamics for an investigator to consider.

Mobile devices often have the ability to be modified or wiped remotely. This is a security feature, but it also can be used to destroy evidence and make it unrecoverable in an investigation. One way of removing this threat is to utilize Faraday technology such as a Faraday bag or a Faraday cage. Faraday technology traces its roots to the nineteenth-century physicist Michael Faraday. He discovered that an electrical charge is carried on the exterior surface of a conductor, that is, the charge had no influence on anything contained within the conductor. By using this principle, a cell phone can be placed inside a Faraday device such as a Faraday cage or a Faraday bag and thus prevent the device from receiving cell signals and outside connectivity. Faraday bags are often sealed with Velcro and care must be taken to ensure that a proper seal is made in order to establish a signal shield.

An investigator should be aware that a powered on cellular device placed in a Faraday container might begin searching for service. This can drain battery life quickly. Placing the device in an airplane mode can help minimize the battery drain. Connecting the device to a charger by running a cable through an opening in the Faraday container can act like an antenna, which would establish signal connection and defeat the purpose of the Faraday container. It is possible to connect a self-contained trickle charger to the phone to help maintain battery life and place both the phone and the charger in the Faraday container.

One of the complexities with investigating mobile devices and cell phones is the variety of information sources and, often, figuring out how they fit together. Some of the sources of evidence in mobile devices are as follows:

- Provider/carrier
  - Pen link register—call detail, subscriber ID, equipment ID, and personal ID number/personal unlock key
- Phone
  - Calls, text messaging, and media (i.e., graphics, audio/video, and pictures)
- SIM card
  - Text messages, phone numbers (typically no graphics)
- Media card (graphics, audio/video, and pictures)

Typical provider information includes originating and terminating phone numbers, equipment ID, initiating and terminating towers, service type, service date/time, and length of service/call. An investigator should verify the information before submitting their report. An investigator must also have an understanding of how cell phones work.

Digital Cell Phone and Handheld Investigation

Of course, the first step to any forensic investigation is to make sure that you have the authority to initiate the investigation. Laws and rationale for an investigation vary, and ethical practices should always be a primary objective. What is legal and what is ethical are not always the same thing, and an investigator needs to consider both aspects carefully. Once this is answered, the investigator should plan the investigation.

The steps to investigate a cell phone incident have many similarities to computer investigations, but there are also some distinct differences. Cell phones are often passcode protected, so if a phone is active, it should remain in active state if there is any question about being able to gain access if the device were to be turned off. However, remote wiping is a concern, so the device should be placed in a Faraday bag to prevent wiping from occurring. Checking the device settings to make sure that it does not revert to protected mode is also a prudent precaution.

Cell phones often have media cards and SIM cards, which are additional sources of information. A common location for serial number and model information is on a sticker underneath the battery. Since maintaining power is often an issue, use of a search engine to find images of a phone is often a preferred way of determining model information. After the investigation is complete, the battery can be removed and the model information verified.

Tools of the Trade

There are numerous software tools to help investigators, some that are quite expensive and others that are actually freeware. Certain forensic tools for investigators attempt to support as many devices as possible. Other forensic tools focus on a targeted environment such as Apple iOS devices and those that use the Android OS. This specialization can allow the vendor to go deeper in its forensic analysis and provide more detailed analysis for investigators. Likewise, some tools target specific functions of wireless devices. For example, a forensic tool may be able to extract the address book entries, but not text messages. It is important to have multiple tools that have overlapping capabilities.

Although mobile forensic tools often generate a detailed report, documenting the device and circumstances around the device should still be done. Similar to forensically processing a computer, mobile device investigation is well served by using a form to document both the device and the investigation. The reason this is beneficial is that multiple tools may be used in a forensic examination, so keeping track of what types of analysis and which tools have been used can become difficult. Submitting a seizure form along with the seizure itself, can assist in documenting an investigation and reduce errors and omissions.

Introduction to Social Media

The transition from static Web pages and content online to more collaborative technology is what marked the beginning of Web 2.0. With the introduction of Web 2.0, Internet-based sites and tools—that are collectively known as social media—have led to an explosion of user-created content and collaboration.

Social media refers to Internet-based technology tools that allow individuals to communicate, collaborate, and establish a community with others. There are several categories of social media, each of which provides different information and functionality to its users. Here is a brief list of the most common social media tools and notable sites:

- Social Networking (e.g., Facebook, Google+).
- E-mail (e.g., Gmail, Yahoo! Mail).
- Blogs (short for Web logs, running log entries made by individuals or entities; blog search engines such as Technorati and Digg).
- Microblogs (e.g., Twitter; Twitter is the most recognizable player in this space).
- Event coordination (e.g., http://www.meetup.com). Members join groups they are interested in, unified by a common interest.
- Location identification (e.g., Foursquare). Utilizes Global Positioning Satellite (GPS) services to identify where users are.
- Multimedia sharing (e.g., Flickr and YouTube). Repositories for user-created multimedia content.
- Search. (Search Engines are a fundamental function for many users. Examples include Google, Bing, Yahoo!, and some countries have established their own specific search engines such as Baidu (http://www.baidu.com) in China.)
- Wikis (e.g. Wikipedia.com; created for the collaborative development of content by multiple users).
- Web conferencing (various vendors provide software with text chat, video conferencing, sharing of desktops, sharing of files, polling, and discussion sessions functionality).
- Virtual Worlds (e.g., Second Life and such games as World of Warcraft) are digital worlds created virtually using computer technologies.

Investigating Using Social Media

The most common element of all the social media sites and technologies described earlier is the massive amount of information posted, created, and linked to by individual users. These data collections provide forensic investigators with an invaluable resource useful in a variety of investigations and analyses (Figure 8.2). Let us

Figure 8.2 While social media has led to vast amounts of user-created content, collaboration, and online communities, it can also provide forensic investigators with an invaluable resource useful in a variety of investigations.

now examine the various social media tools with a focus on using them to conduct forensic investigations.

Forensic investigation involves looking for digital evidence and information in support of investigations conducted by the law enforcement personnel, military organizations, internal investigators, private investigators, and researchers. As you have learned so far in this chapter, forensic investigation involves two key elements: data and people.

When we consider forensic investigation of social media, we also rely on these two elements. How can we track the flow of data and information through social media sites and technologies? How can we track people, their roles and place in an organizational structure, and their knowledge and information through social media? There are some significant distinctions between traditional digital forensics and social media forensics that are important to highlight.

In a traditional case of digital forensics, one or more computer devices are examined for evidence or relevant information. The focus is primarily on a single medium, the computer. In addition, in traditional digital forensics, the focus is often on a single individual or small group of individuals.

In social media forensics, however, the focus is much broader. One or more persons of interest may post information in any number of social media sites, using any number of social media technologies. In addition, social media is often used to organize events, of which some may have nefarious or hostile intent. Social media forensic analysis, by its very nature, will also involve a degree of social network analysis in which organizational structures, key players, and linkages between them are examined and identified. When conducting a social media forensic examination, it is important that an investigator be much broader in the search for evidence or relevant information. Such social media investigations using social media forensics include street gangs, pornography rings, terrorist organizations, and white-collar crimes.

Investigative Reporting

The goal of the investigation is to identify all available facts related to the case. The investigative report should provide a detailed account of the incident, highlighting any discrepancies in witness statements. The report should be a well-organized document that contains a description of the incident, all witness statements, references to all evidentiary articles, pictures of the crime scene, drawings and schematics of the computer and the computer network (if applicable), and finally, a written description of the forensic analysis. The report should state final conclusions, based solely on the facts. It should not include the investigator's opinions, unless he or she is an expert. Keep in mind that all documentation related to the investigation is subject to discovery by the defense; so be careful about what is written down!

Computer Forensics

Computer forensics is the study of computer technology as it relates to the law. The objective of the forensic process is to learn as much about the suspect system as possible. This generally means analyzing the system using a variety of forensic tools and processes. Bear in mind that the examination of the suspect system may lead to other victims and other suspects. The actual forensic process will be different for each system analyzed as there are many tools available to the forensic analyst to assist in the collection, preservation, and analysis of computer-based evidence. Before analyzing any system, it is extremely important to protect the systems and disk drives from static electricity. The analyst should always use an anti-static or static-dissipative wristband and mat before conducting any forensic analysis.

There are a number of commercially available utilities that allow the analyst to quickly create a directory tree, list system files, identify hidden files, and to conduct keyword searches. The analyst should make notes during each step in the process, especially when restoring hidden or deleted files, or modifying the suspect system. The analyst should also note that what may have happened on the system may have resulted from error or incompetence rather than from a malicious user. It is a good idea to check for viruses to, first, note their existence, and secondly, to avoid potential contamination.

Since forensic analysis can be a laborious and time-consuming process, it is sometimes better to distribute the workload to other analysts and case agents. Since it would be too costly to have multiple forensic systems and to replicate the suspect data on multiple hard drives, it may be more effective to make copies of the hard disk contents that can be distributed and analyzed by different individuals. This is certainly more cost effective and will likely accelerate the analysis process.

Copying data should be structured in a way that will enhance the forensic process. There are many search tools that can assist the forensic analyst in his endeavor to locate damaging evidence. Some are designed specifically for computer forensic work. Some of these tools are commercial off-the-shelf (COTS) applications that were created for some other reason, other than forensics. It just so happens that these applications work well in a forensic environment. Remember that if the data is not on the hard disk, it may be on backup hard drives, thumb drives, or other form of backup media. Even if the data was recently deleted from a computer system, there may be a backup that has all of the original data.

Legal Proceedings

A brief description of the legal proceedings that occur subsequent to the investigation are necessary so the victim and the investigators understand the full impact of their decision to prosecute. Discovery is the process whereby the prosecution provides all investigative reports, information on evidence, list of potential witnesses, any criminal history of witnesses, and any other information except how they are going to present the case to the defense. Any property or data recovered by law enforcement will be subject to discovery if a person is charged with a crime. However, a protective order can limit who has access, who can copy, and the disposition of certain protected documents. These protective orders allow the victim to protect proprietary or trade secret documents related to a case.

If the defendant is held to answer in a preliminary hearing or the grand jury returns an indictment, a trial will be scheduled. If the case goes to trial, interviews with any witnesses will be necessary. The trial may not be scheduled for some time based upon the backlog of the court that has jurisdiction in the case. Additionally, the civil trial and criminal trial will occur at different times, although much of the investigation can be run in parallel.

Summary

As you probably gleaned from this chapter, computer crime investigation is more an art than a science. It is a rapidly changing field that requires knowledge in many disciplines. Although some of the concepts may be difficult to grasp, as with most investigations, computer investigations are still based on sound and traditional investigative procedures. Planning is integral to a successful investigation. The investigator may have the added responsibility of building a team of specialists, and, again, examination of digital evidence from devices may coincide with more traditional police detective work and investigations.

With knowledge of the law and forensics, the investigative team may be able to piece together who committed a crime, and how and why the crime was committed. Finally, to be successful, the computer crime investigator must, at a minimum, have a thorough understanding of the law, the rules of evidence as they relate to computer crime, and computer forensics. With this knowledge, the investigator should be able to adapt to any number of situations involving crimes perpetrated using computers and wireless devices. Likewise, the investigation can uncover data on those crimes where evidence is stored on devices, in GPS or user logs, or in the cloud. Social media can likewise be used to prove or disprove the perpetration of crimes in the physical world.

Test Yourself

Multiple Choice

1. Which of the following devices is not generally used in committing computer crime?
   a. Laptop
   b. GPS
   c. PDA
   d. Cell phone
   e. Tablet computer
2. Which of the following is generally not a type of data that is sought in investigating computer crime?
   a. Mailed letters
   b. Digital data
   c. Audio data
   d. Video data
   e. Emails
3. Which type of crime is not generally associated with modern computer crime?
   a. Malicious destruction of property
   b. Sexual predation
   c. Identity theft
   d. Breaking and entering of a business
   e. Disruption of utilities such as power grids

4. Which of the following is not common to physical and virtual crimes?
    a. Discovery of evidence
    b. Processing of dead bodies
    c. Chain of custody maintenance
    d. Retrieval of evidence
    e. Documentation of the crime scene
5. Which of the following is not necessary for the digital forensic investigator to have knowledge of?
    a. Computer hardware systems
    b. Computer software systems
    c. Relevant legal rules
    d. Procedures for seizing evidence
    e. All of the above are necessary
6. Which of the following is not a recognized computer crime?
    a. Denial of service
    b. Sabotage
    c. Child Pornography
    d. Assault
    e. Embezzlement
7. Which of the following is not a federal law that impacts computer crime?
    a. Computer Fraud and Abuse Act
    b. Wire Fraud Act
    c. Frye Act
    d. Sarbanes–Oxley Act
    e. Computer Security Act
8. Which is not part of a proper computer crime investigation?
    a. Determination of whether a crime has occurred
    b. Immediately turning off a computer that is on when discovered
    c. Examination of surrounding physical evidence
    d. Determination of the need to obtain search and seizure warrants
    e. Examination of the computer operating system
9. A detailed computer crime investigation plan contains which of the following:
    a. Identify potential witnesses and suspects
    b. Identify the digital devices that are to be seized and examined
    c. Obtain needed warrants
    d. Determine the risks of a suspect destroying digital evidence
    e. All of the above
10. All of the following data should be obtained about a digital device prior to seizure except:
    a. What is the probable cause?
    b. What laws may have been violated
    c. What computer security systems are in place?
    d. Whether the suspect can afford to hire an attorney
    e. Are passwords being used to access data

True/False

11. Over the past three decades the frequency of computer-related crimes has remained fairly steady.
12. Computer forensics is the study of computer technology as it relates to the law.

13. The contents of social media has become a major source of data for forensic investigators.
14. When a cell phone is discovered as evidence of a computer crime, it should immediately be turned off to prevent remote erasing of its data.
15. A Faraday container is a type of packaging that is used for digital evidence to prevent anyone but the investigator from gaining access to the contents.
16. As in physical crime investigation, the first order of business at a cyber crime scene is to secure and protect the scene.
17. The fifth amendment of the U.S. Constitution controls how and when a cyber crime scene can be searched.

Matching—Match Each Definition with the Term

18. Commercial off-the-shelf
19. Any criminal or civil violation dealing with computers
20. A type of social media
21. The act of preventing use of a utility or corporation by disrupting its computer controlled systems
22. A container that prevents a cell phone inside from receiving external cell signals

a. Blog
b. Denial of service
c. COS
d. Faraday bag
e. Cyber crime

Short Essay

23. What is the difference between computer crime and computer forensics? Give examples of each.
24. What are the major considerations when investigating a cyber crime when a cell phone is involved?
25. Discuss the role that social media have in the investigation of cyber crime?

Further Reading

Ciaramitaro, B. (2013). Social media forensics, In *Digital Forensics Explained*, G. Goglin, ed. Auerbach Publications, Boca Raton, FL.
Goglin, G. (ed.). (2013). *Digital Forensics Explained*. Auerbach Publications, Boca Raton, FL.
Marcella, A. Jr. and D. Menendez. (2008). *Cyber Forensics: A Field Manual for Collecting, Examining, and Preserving Evidence of Computer Crimes*, 2nd edn. Auerbach Publications, Boca Raton, FL.
Welch, T. (2007). Section 10-2, In *Information Security Management Handbook*, 6th edn., H.F. Tipton and M. Krause, eds. Auerbach Publications, Boca Raton, FL.

On the Web

http://www.fbi.gov/about-us/investigate/cyber—The FBI cyber crime website.
http://criminal.findlaw.com/criminal-charges/cyber-crimes.html—Some legal aspects of cyber crime.
http://www.interpol.int/Crime-areas/Cybercrime/Cybercrime—Cyber crime website of Interpol, an international umbrella organization for policing worldwide.

9

Forensic Engineering*

* The authors would like to thank Christopher Puckett who provided photos and reviewed the accident reconstruction portion of this chapter.

Learning Objectives

1. To understand the role of a forensic engineer in failure analysis cases
2. To be able to give examples of types of cases that a forensic engineer would investigate
3. To describe the function of a forensic investigator in a forensic engineering case
4. To understand the role of a collision reconstructionist in a motor vehicle collision
5. To describe the type of investigative work involved in an automobile accident
6. To appreciate the role of physics and mathematics in forensic engineering type of investigations

Chapter 9
Forensic Engineering

Chapter Outline

Mini Glossary

Accident reconstruction: The application of the principles of physics and engineering to vehicular collisions in order to recreate or explain how the incident occurred.

Drag factor: A numeric ratio that gives an indication of the frictional properties between the road surface and tires of a vehicle.

Engineer: An individual who applies knowledge of science to the design and construction of various types of machines to improve society.

Engineering: The application of the principles and mathematics of science to produce products that make life easier and/or more efficient.

Forensic engineering: The application of the science and process of engineering to solve cases of a judiciary nature.

Hot shock: The deformation of a lightbulb filament in a vehicle lamp.

Liability: A state of being legally responsibility for something.

Physics: The study of matter and energy and how they interact in nature.

Primary defects: Structural defects that arise due to design flaws, manufacture flaws, construction mistakes. or faulty materials used in construction.

Scientist: An individual who studies the laws of nature.

Secondary defects: Product defects due to design problems, but not identified until the material has been used by the public.

Skid mark: A black mark on a road surface left by the heating of tire rubber due to braking and sliding the tire on the road.

Yaw: A pattern of skid marks caused by the side slipping of the rotating tire in a nonbraking turn of a vehicle.

Acronyms

DUI: Driving under the influence
ETWS: Electronic total work station
FWA: Federal Works Administration
GPS: Global positioning device
NAFE: National Academy of Forensic Engineers
NASA: National Aeronautics and Space Administration
NHTSA: National Highway Traffic Safety Administration

Introduction

A walkway collapses, the temporary stage at a State Fair falls to the ground, a nuclear power plant has a meltdown, a space shuttle explodes in midair, two cars collide at an intersection, or a pickup truck flies through the glass window of a restaurant. Every one of these events would involve a forensic investigator who specializes in either engineering or motor vehicle collisions. A common thread is that both types of investigators apply the concepts of physics and the language of mathematics to interpret the events at the accident scene (Figure 9.1).

When an accident occurs, it changes the circumstances. There may be damage to property. This damage could be minimal or extensive. Individuals may be injured. The injuries could be minor, serious, or fatal. Structures could be damaged that subsequently could affect the daily lives of other individuals. In any accident, minor or substantial, it is important to ascertain what events occurred to cause the accident. An accident is called such because it is something that is not supposed to happen. If it does, then the reason for it must be determined.

If the accident is due to a part or machine malfunction, then that fault must be discovered so that further accidents can be avoided. If the accident is due to the careless actions of an operator, then that person might need to be arrested and prosecuted. It is the role of the investigators in this area of forensic science to reconstruct events to determine failure, be it human or nonhuman in causality (Figure 9.2).

This chapter will explore the types of investigations that are rooted in engineering and physics. An overview of the types of investigations, the basic procedures followed in the various types of investigations, and some engineering and accident cases will be included as examples.

Terminology

An *engineer* is someone who applies knowledge of science to the design and construction of various types of machines to improve society. A *scientist* concentrates

Figure 9.1 The aftermath of a structure collapse. (Photo courtesy of Gary Chambers, Wolf Technical Services, Inc., Indianapolis, IN.)

Figure 9.2 Starting the forensic engineering investigation. (Photo courtesy of Gary Chambers, Wolf Technical Services, Inc.)

on understanding the laws of nature and our physical world, whereas the engineer uses that same body of knowledge to design practical objects that make living in the physical world more productive, safer, and pleasant.

The engineer is a scientific problem solver. In designing systems, an engineer not only must design a device that solves a problem, but also passes restrictions due to government regulations, and space limitations by the contracting company. The new design must be more efficient and take less time than the previous device. Oh, and of course, it should do all that in a cost-effective manner. By the very nature of their training, the engineer is a good forensic investigator, being able to look at more than one aspect of a situation. According to the National Academy of Forensic Engineers (NAFE), *forensic engineering* is "the application of the art and science of engineering in matters which are in, or may possibly relate to, the jurisprudence system, inclusive of alternative dispute resolution." By knowing how to design a good system, the forensic engineer also has a practical knowledge of inefficient and poorly designed systems, which is key to reconstructing an industrial or civil accident.

Some forensic engineers are trained to investigate motor vehicle accidents. If a forensic engineer is hired to investigate a car accident, most likely they are investigating the collision for a private insurance company. The majority of motor vehicle accidents are investigated by local or state police agencies. Each year in the United States, over two million people are injured in car crashes, another 32,000 people die in a crash, and countless other collisions only suffer injury to the vehicles involved. Because there are so many motor vehicle accidents every day, it would be very ineffective and costly to have a forensic engineer investigate all vehicle crashes. This area of investigation is best done by police officers trained in *accident reconstruction* or collision reconstruction. Accident reconstruction is the area of forensic science that uses the physical evidence at the scene to determine how and why the vehicular accident occurred.

Engineering Profession

History of Engineering

If you think about the earliest feats of structural engineering, the Pyramids in Egypt most likely come to mind. To build monuments of such magnificence without the assistance of modern tools and devices is mind boggling to most. Construction had to be planned and coordinated by individuals whom today we would call engineers. It has been said that one of the first engineers was the Egyptian architect and physician, Imhotep, the designer of the pharaoh's tomb, the Step Pyramid in the 2600s BC. This is an engineering marvel that has lasted through time.

In addition to the marvels of Egyptian design and construction, the Romans also mastered the mathematics and science of structural engineering with building feats such as the Colosseum, Roman theatres, Roman baths, aqueducts, and roads. The Romans were builders and material designers. Around the second-century BC, they crafted a concrete mixture used to construct the Pantheon, which has withstood the sands of time.

Architects and engineers continued to design great structures thorough history; however, the materials changed as our knowledge of science changed. In the thirteenth century, metal working was incorporated into engineered structures. More diversity and sophistication in structural design arose in the eighteenth century with the development of schools of engineering. Academia was now awarding degrees in the areas of civil and mechanical engineering. This was followed by the Industrial Revolution and the discovery of electricity. In addition to electric lighting, engineers could now design convenience devices that operate using electric current, stoves, televisions, vacuum cleaners, etc. A new branch of engineering, electrical engineering, was born.

Other engineering professions were developed as our world's industrial knowledge grew. Chemical engineering grew out of our more industrialized society. Our need for knowledge in metallurgy, production of processed foods, development and production of drugs and medicine, and production of fibers for the textile industry increased our need for chemical engineers. Paper engineering and nuclear engineering are twentieth-century products of our society's need for products and energy. The need for advanced medical treatments and artificial body parts gave rise to biomedical engineering. Computer engineers are an integral part of our digital age. Today, there are so many various fields of engineering that almost any student who enjoys science and mathematics could find a field that would be of interest as a profession.

What Does an Engineer Do?

Engineers are problem solvers. Our quality of life over the years has been enhanced by the work of engineers. They design systems that make life easier, safer, and/or more efficient. They need to have an understanding of science and be able to apply that knowledge to solve a challenge. Engineers must be creative. They need also to be flexible, as sometimes their designs may need to change due to parameters of which they have no control.

Basically, all engineers employ similar approaches to problem solving, no matter the specialty or complexity of the issue. First, they must isolate the problem using scientific analysis methods. Then, a plan of attack or design of a solution is developed. Within this development are hours of research and consultation. Construction of a working model or prototype to test follows the design process. Extensive testing is done. This can then lead to redesign, possibly more research and consulting, and more testing. Once the final product is produced, additional testing is done to certify that the product is safe and follows whatever protocols that may be in place, many times involving the environment. Product testing also involves examination for any defects post operation. Additionally, the design engineer may be involved in training operators on proper safety, handling, and maintenance of equipment.

In this profession, the individual must have a working knowledge of scientific principles applicable to the type of engineering work being done as well as mathematical skills. The engineer spends a great deal of time on the computer and is skilled in the use of graphic design software to construct prototypes. Presentation and communication skills are necessary to effectively share ideas and engage in discourse.

Besides civil and mechanical engineers, the industry recognizes almost 25 different engineering specialties. Those include biomedical, nuclear, chemical, and environmental engineers. In addition, there are computer, electronic, and aeronautical engineers, as well as agricultural and industrial engineers. These are just a few of the many various engineering specialties. It is interesting to note that some of these specialties can apply their training to other fields as well. For example, a chemical engineer may be able to use their skills in a medical field and an electronic or electrical engineer may apply their engineering expertise to an occupation involving computers. This chapter focuses on the application of various fields of engineering to the areas of forensic science and the legal profession.

Forensic Engineer

Engineers versus Forensic Engineers

The forensic engineer is also a problem solver. However, unlike the regular engineer, the forensic engineer is not involved in birth of a new product or structure, but in the aftermath of product or structural failure. This could include collapse of buildings, bridges, or homes. It could involve accidents in aerospace or the automotive industry. Basically, the forensic engineer is called upon to investigate why an engineered product failed in its operation in any way. Forensic investigations can be criminal in nature or civil, involving *liability* in personal or property damage.

Failure of products, structures, or parts of structures can be due to aging, lack of maintenance, faulty materials or design. The investigator uses engineering skills to determine which of these might apply to the failure in each case. Depending on the outcome of the investigation, penalties may be dispensed. Quite often in these cases, the forensic engineer works for insurance companies who provide property coverage for the structures and liability coverage for the owners. In other instances, a worker might sue his boss for injuries, claiming the employer had faulty equipment; in this case, a civil lawsuit.

Sometimes, an accident is due to tampering with a product. In this case the investigation becomes more criminal in nature. Intentionally causing failure that leads to damage, injury, or possibly death pairs the forensic engineer with law enforcement. Detectives and engineers work together to determine what happened, how it happened, and who might have the knowledge and expertise to intentionally compromise the item.

What Does a Forensic Engineer Do?

Forensic engineers inspect failures and reconstruct, if necessary, the conditions prior to the accident to determine any improprieties. Accidental events are diverse. Events could be caused by structural failure, malfunction of machines, or operator error. Most of the time the engineer is called in long after the event occurred. The investigator must examine equipment, hopefully undisturbed, to determine the point and cause of failure. Once cause is determined, then the investigator must establish who was liable for the accident. The outcome of the liability investigation will determine if the case will end up in either a civil or criminal court. If the determination is criminal (intentional tampering), the investigation will look very similar to any other crime scene investigation. Evidence is collected from the scene, extensive photographs are taken, witnesses are interviewed, and forensic testing is done in the crime lab. Forensic engineers can work for law firms, government agencies, and private consulting companies or be employed by a large industrial manufacturer.

There are two areas of defect that are investigated when failure occurs. *Primary defects* are those that arise due to design flaws, manufacture flaws, construction mistakes, or faulty materials used in construction. Defects that are considered as secondary are those that are the result of operation or use. *Secondary defects* can be due to design problems, but unfortunately are not identified until the material has been used by the public. Good examples of these are product recalls issued by manufacturers as a result of various degrees of product failure or safety issues in the marketplace. Many child care products or toys are recalled due to safety concerns that may not have been anticipated by the engineer and manufacturer.

In these types of accident cases, it is common for the forensic engineer to be called to court to testify as an expert witness. There are many forensic engineers in private practice, working for their own agency or as part of a team. In a criminal case, the independent forensic engineer can be hired by the prosecution or by the defense. In a liability case, an insurance company may hire the engineer to determine fault or no fault.

Experience is vital to be an expert forensic engineer. Most forensic engineers have years of experience in their chosen field of engineering. Some of the engineering specialties that contribute greatly to forensic investigations include civil, mechanical, and materials engineering. Engineers who expand their work to include forensic investigations in most cases have over 25 years of work experience past their advanced degree (usually a PhD). This is not a beginning job, but more likely the last one before retirement.

Forensic Engineering Case Studies

Space Shuttle Challenger Disaster

In 1986, the nation watched as the first teacher was embarking on her inaugural journey into space from Kennedy Space Center in Florida. Christa McAuliffe did not fulfill her dream. The January 28th mission was cut horribly short when, less than 2 minutes after liftoff, the *Challenger Space Shuttle* exploded in midair. All seven crew members, Michael J. Smith, Ronald McNair, Dick Scobee, Gregory Jarvis, Ellison Onizuka, Judith Resnik, and Ms. McAuliffe, perished in this disaster. Following the disaster, President Reagan commissioned a group to investigate the explosion and to determine the cause. The group was called the Rogers Commission, after the head of the investigation, William P. Rogers, former secretary of state. Members of the commission included Neil Armstrong and Sally Ride, former astronauts, pilot Chuck Yeager, and Richard Feynman, a physicist, among the list of credentialed commission members (Figures 9.3 and 9.4).

After an extensive investigation that included looking at frame-by-frame camera footage of the launching and flight of the space shuttle, interviews of NASA personnel and administrators and engineers for Morton Thiokol (the firm that built the *Challenger* shuttle), the Rogers Commission made their report to Congress. History recounts that it was physicist Richard Feynman who went straight to the Thiokol engineers for background information on the design and operation of the shuttle. Feynman is credited for finding the problem with the O-rings, a sealing mechanism on the solid rocket fuel tank joints. These seals were to prevent hot gases from escaping the rocket fuel tanks as the tanks heat up and expand. It was discovered, however, that these seals do not work effectively in cold temperatures. At launch time on the 28th, the temperature was in the mid-30 degrees Fahrenheit. Cold temperatures limit the expansion of the seals that prevent the hot gas from escaping. *Challenger*'s O-rings did not seal and allowed the release of hot gas from the solid rock fuel tanks. These hot gases caused the fittings to expand and impinge on the external fuel tank. The fitting expansion resulted in structural failure and led to the release of hydrogen gas and the explosion of the shuttle.

Once the commission identified the cause of the accident, the investigation turned to the company who designed the shuttle, Morton Thiokol. It was determined that the Morton Thiokol engineers knew that the O-rings did not respond well in cold

Figure 9.3 Explosion of the *Challenger* Space Shuttle January 28, 1986. (From http://grin.hq.nasa.gov/IMAGES/SMALL/GPN-2000-001423.jpg.)

Figure 9.4 Richard Feynman testifying for the Rogers Commission in 1986. (AP photo, Dennis Cook/Associated Press.)

temperatures; however, Thiokol management and NASA officials did not respond appropriately to these design flaws in the O-rings of the solid rocket fuel tanks. As a result of the disaster, NASA's shuttle program was grounded for more than 2 years in order to complete a restructuring of protocols and a redesign of the solid rocket fuel tanks.

Tacoma Narrows Bridge Collapse

The Tacoma Narrows Bridge was built in 1940 to span the Tacoma Narrows in the state of Washington. Claiming to be one of the lightest bridges of its kind and one of the most modern suspension bridges of that period, it was to be an engineering marvel.

Figure 9.5 Tacoma Narrows Bridge, November 1940, breaking apart after winds caused it to oscillate like waves on a spring.

From the time of its completion, people noticed that the bridge had a sway to it and affectionately gave the bridge the nickname, "Galloping Gertie." One day in November of that same year, the winds were howling at 40–45 mph. The sway of the bridge was severely affected by the winds. Gertie began undulating in a wave-like motion as if the bridge was made of flexible rubber instead of concrete. The wave motion seemed to increase in amplitude until finally the structure could not withstand the swaying and broke apart in the center of the bridge. Concrete, wire supports, and one lone abandoned automobile tumbled into the Narrows (Figure 9.5).

Postcollapse inspection showed the cables were twisted by the violent wave motion of the bridge. Even the huge metal towers at either end of the suspension bridge suffered irreparable damage. The metal was bent and buckled due to the twisting torsional wave of the roadway.

What caused this disaster? When designing the Tacoma Narrows Bridge, engineers were striving for a lighter, less bulky suspension bridge. However, less weight also meant less inertia and the bridge was more susceptible to motion by the force of winds. The higher winds caused the bridge to resonate and create standing waves that only amplified the crests and toughs of the wave motion. It has been estimated that the amplitude of the swaying bridge was over 20 ft. At some point, the displacement of the undulating road was too much for the supports and concrete road and it began to crumble in the middle, tearing the bridge apart.

The Federal Works Administration (FWA) organized a group of three prominent engineers to investigate why this structure was adversely affected by wind. Their findings were not surprising; the cause of failure was the "random action of turbulent wind." The more important question that followed was why designers of the Tacoma Narrows Bridge did not know that the lightweight design would rise and fall dangerously in the wind. An interesting finding by the engineer panel was that the deck and girding performed like an airfoil, causing lift and drag like an airplane. Clearly, more research in aerodynamics needed to be conducted before more suspension bridges of similar design could be built. It is unfortunate, but the collapse of the Tacoma Narrows Bridge acted as a wakeup call for engineers involved in designing large suspension bridges. The effects of aerodynamic forces on such structures needed to be studied and tested thoroughly before any new construction commenced.

Hyatt Regency Walkway Collapse

On July 17, 1981, disaster struck at the Hyatt Regency Hotel in Kansas City, Missouri. A suspended walkway connecting one half of the hotel to the other above an open atrium collapsed, killing 114 people and injuring upward of 200 more. Unlike the Tacoma Narrows Bridge incident, this tragedy was not due to design flaws in the walkway, but rather mistakes in manufacturing and changes made to the design during construction.

There were three suspended walkways above the first floor atrium. The bridge connecting the second floor sections and the one connecting the fourth floor sections were stacked one above the other, leaving the third floor walkway slightly offset and free from the other two. The original design had one large connecting ceiling rod for support of the two walkways. Due to issues with threading during manufacture and transport of such a large rod, the design was changed from one rod to two, smaller in size. Additionally, there were changes to placement of the rods and what walkways they would support. Unfortunately, one of the beams carried the load of two beams and the nuts at the attachment were not designed to hold against the increased weight.

On the day of the collapse, there was a dance party in the atrium on the first floor and it was very crowded. Spectators lined the second, third, and fourth floor walkways for a great view of the show from above. People were both standing and dancing on the suspended hotel bridges. Unfortunately, the changed support rods were barely strong enough to support the weight of the walkway itself, let alone 30–40 people, some jumping up and down while dancing. Soon the fourth floor walkway gave way and tumbled down on to the second floor bridge below it, causing both structures to crash into the crowded atrium below. The third floor walkway, given its offset placement, was not affected.

Forensic investigation found various issues, mostly with the construction of the walkway. First, there was a flaw in the design of the walkways in that the weight-bearing load of people was not correctly taken into consideration when planning the connections. The bigger issue revolved around the changes made to original plans. The design engineer should have consulted with the manufacturer regarding the size and design of the support rods. When the changes were made, substituting the two rods for the single, there was no consultation among parties involved. The fabricator did not discuss changes with the design engineers, no testing was done to ensure that the change would not adversely affect the support of the walkways, and no final checks were completed to be sure the specs matched the final product. This disaster could have been avoided if communication between design engineers, fabricators in the manufacturing sector, civil engineers, and construction personnel would have continued throughout the entire build from its inception to completion.

Stage Collapse at the Indiana State Fairgrounds

Sugarland was due to take the stage at the Indiana State Fairgrounds and play to a packed crowd of fans. It was near dusk on a summer day in Indianapolis, Indiana, on August 13, 2011. There were severe storms predicted in the Midwest. The stage

Figure 9.6 Photo sequence of the Indiana State Fair Hoosier Grandstand stage collapse August 13, 2011: (a) the daytime photo prior to collapse, (b) the stage beginning to fall in the evening, and (c) the aftermath and the beginning of the investigation. (Photos courtesy of Gary Chambers, Wolf Technical Services, Inc., Indianapolis, IN.)

was a temporary grandstand assembled for performances during the state fair. The country music duo was due to take the stage at approximately 8:45 pm. Officials monitoring the conditions and the management of Sugarland conversed back and forth about whether to cancel the concert or continue after the opening act finished. They decided to continue with the concert, and take the stage at 8:50. The stage collapsed at approximately 8:46 pm. Seven people perished and 58 were injured (Figure 9.6).

The Indiana State Fair Commission called an investigation by two firms, Thornton Tomasetti and Witt Associates. The Chicago-based Tomasetti Firm was assisted by Wolf Technical Services, a forensic engineering group in Indianapolis. The methodology used to investigate this disaster was site surveying and extensive documentation, onsite testing of the support structures, wind tunnel testing of mock stage models, metallurgical evaluation, computer modeling of the structure, and data analysis including calculations. It was determined that there were two major factors in the tragedy; failure to meet industry safety standards for the stage rigging and lack of an organized emergency plan and policy in case of inclement weather. Structurally, the stage rigging and supports were inadequate and not up to industry code. Additionally, there were no inspections of the temporary structure prior to the concert. Industry safety standards dictate that these structures must be able to withstand winds up to 68 mph. The Indiana stage and roof were held in

Figure 9.7 Evidence from Hoosier Grandstand collapse: (a) one bent metal leg of a tower column, (b) a ratchet strap tear, and (c, d) evidence that the concrete barrier braces for the guy wires slid out of position. (Photos courtesy of Gary Chambers, Wolf Technical Services, Inc., Indianapolis, IN.)

place by support wires fastened to concrete barriers. Upon inspection it was determined that the rigging built for the stage would only maintain support in winds of 25, maybe up to 43 mph, much lower than the required 68 mph. Figure 9.7 shows evidence that the concrete barriers that were anchoring the guy wires moved a substantial distance prior to collapse. Evidence post collapse showed the webbing on the ratchet straps failed and the metal columns supported by the guy wires bent at the footing when they fell.

Records show the stage began to fail when the winds reached 33 mph. Total collapse occurred after a 3 second wind gust of approximately 59 mph. Once the rigging gave way, the remaining supports and roof began to lean to the right. Once the supports failed, gravity pulled the entire structure to the right and slightly forward, down onto the stage platform and the crowd at the front of the stage.

The cancellation or not decision-making process behind the scenes prior to the concert was faulty and disorganized. Backstage, there was confusion between the band management and the state fair event coordinators. Fair officials were unsure about whether to call off the concert. They monitored the weather but failed to get the severe thunderstorm warning issued by the National Weather Service at 8:39 pm. By the time the decision was made to cancel the performance, the stage was already compromised and collapsing. There was no formal protocol in place for decision-making in case of emergency. The murky chain of command only contributed to the tragedy that may have been averted given supports up to code and protocol for weather emergencies. In the end, the Indiana Occupational Health and Safety Administration issued fines up to $80,000 citing incompetence in building and inspecting a safe temporary structure and failure to have a proper procedure in place in case of weather emergencies.

Accident Reconstruction

Vehicular Collisions and Physics

Physics is the study of how matter and energy interact in nature. When one automobile unintentionally comes in contact with another vehicle or with any other object, their matter and energy interact, unfortunately with a less than positive outcome. Accident investigation is the application of the principles of physics and engineering to vehicular collisions in order to recreate or explain how the incident might have transpired (Figure 9.8).

Clues at the accident site direct the investigation. Experienced accident investigators look for evidence at the scene that might give insight as to why the collision occurred. Classical physics principles such as Isaac Newton's laws of motion and the laws of conservation of linear momentum and mechanical energy apply whenever two objects in nature collide. The laws studied in the classroom play out in real life during an accident investigation when such things as speed of the vehicle, stopping distance, forces of impact, and path of the vehicles prior to and during the accident must be determined. Not only must the condition of the vehicle and occupants be analyzed, but consideration of the road conditions and environment prior to the incident is important and needs to be assessed. It is also important to establish the circumstances inside the vehicle prior to the accident such as the location of the occupants, whether they were using seatbelts or in car seats, and possibly what they were doing in the car prior the accident. These questions and many more must be addressed in the physical reconstruction of the incident.

Figure 9.8 Vehicle involved in a fatal crash. (Photo courtesy of Forensic Science Educational Consulting, LLC, Portage, MI.)

Education and Training

According to the National Highway Traffic Safety Administration (NHTSA), in 2013 over 32,000 individuals in the United States died in motor vehicle crashes. Many, many more US citizens were injured, an astounding 2.3 million. Given the frequency of car crashes and the types of violations involved, most accident investigations are done by local police agencies.

Due to the complexity of investigating an automobile accident, specialized training is necessary for the law enforcement officer in charge of collision reconstruction. Accident investigation institutes conduct courses for police officers to learn how to apply physics and mathematics in a practical way. Many of these courses involve up to 10 weeks of intense classroom and laboratory experience. Various types of collisions are recreated and investigated in the laboratory, giving students experience in using specialized data collection equipment and mathematical equations that are essential tools of the trade.

Investigative Procedures

There are two types of individuals who have the expertise to investigate a motor vehicle accident, the law enforcement officer trained in collision reconstruction and the forensic engineer who specializes in automobile crashes. A forensic engineer would be involved if hired by an insurance company to determine liability or by an attorney for an injured party in cases of financial responsibility. Both parties will use similar techniques and data analysis methodologies in their investigation. However, it is the law enforcement examiner who responds at the outset and the forensic engineer who joins the investigation days, weeks, or even months after the incident. Therefore, the procedures discussed here will follow the protocol of a law enforcement accident reconstructionist, rather than the engineer, since it the reconstructionist who takes all the data at the actual scene of the crash.

At the Scene

When an accident occurs, someone dials 911 and law enforcement responds. Usually, that first responder is a trooper or patrol officer, and it is their job to secure the scene, administer aid, call for backup, and make it safe for other vehicles and pedestrians. When the accident investigator arrives, the first task is to talk with that first responder to ascertain what was found upon arrival. Perhaps, some pertinent details have been determined by that officer and the investigation can proceed efficiently. The accident investigator walks the path of the collision to get a visual of what has occurred.

From that visual, the investigator determines what evidence might be sensitive and should be attended to first. Sensitive evidence is evidence that could be lost due to weather conditions or manipulation of the mangled vehicles. Extensive photography and videography is performed. After photography of the undisturbed scene is complete, the measurement process begins. This includes measuring *skid marks*, tire marks, and position of vehicles or anything else that was involved in the collision. A detailed drawing of the scene must be completed for the report and placement of every piece of evidence in the scene is important. The combination of good measurements and excellent photography make this task easier. In order to take accurate measurements, the vehicles should remain at the scene as long as possible before being driven or towed away. Depending on the severity of the crash,

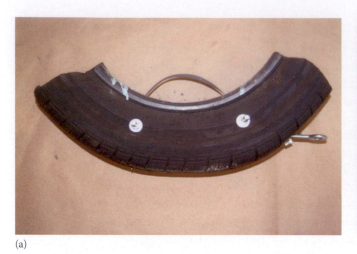

(a)

(b)

Figure 9.9 Police drag sled (a: side view and b: top view) used at the accident site to help determine the frictional properties of the highway surface. (Photo courtesy of Forensic Science Educational Consulting, LLC, Portage, MI.)

documenting the scene could take a long time. This is why roads are closed or partially closed during an accident and traffic gets snarled. Accuracy takes time.

The types of evidence explored on the road surface are skid marks, yaw marks, and any scratches or gouges in the road. When a vehicle skids to a stop, it can be determined how fast the car was going when it began the skid. In order to complete this calculation, test skids are done at the scene using police vehicles if it is safe to do so. It is important to run the test skids at the site of the crash under similar road conditions. The braking is done as close to the actual skid marks as possible and in the same direction of motion. The data collected will then determine the minimum speed of the driver prior to hitting the brakes. If road conditions are such that it is not safe to run skid tests, a drag sled (1/3 of a tire filled with cement) is pulled across the road surface near and in the direction of the skid (see Figure 9.9). This will aid in the establishing the frictional properties between the tire and the road, a quantity called the drag factor in accident investigation.

Once the drag factor and the length of the skid marks are determined, the investigator then uses a specific mathematical formula derived from a series of physics equations to calculate the speed. Figure 9.10 shows accident vehicle skid marks (longer skids) and two sets of test skids at a crash site.

There are essential tools used by law enforcement to take pertinent data at the scene that than can be analyzed later in the office. One is called the Vericom VC3000 Brake Test Computer, mounted in the test skid vehicle. This device measures the acceleration of the vehicle while it is moving and braking. The braking data produced are crucial for the investigator doing skid mark analysis. The VC3000 details the speed of the test run, the skidding distance, the total time the car was skidding, and data about the drag factor (a ratio that indicates the frictional properties between the tires and the road) (Figure 9.11).

Another useful tool is the Sokkia Electronic Total Work Station (ETWS). This device looks similar to a surveying tripod that you may see out on the roadways. This tool is used by the accident investigator to get a precise location of any physical evidence at the crash location as well as the location of all involved parties and vehicles. It also records various characteristics of the roadway, from slope of the road to lane markings and width. Once all the data is retrieved from the scene, the investigator takes the information back to the station and downloads the data directly into a drawing program that produces a scale drawing of the crash site.

Figure 9.10 Skid mark analysis at an accident site. The longer skid marks are from the vehicle involved in the crash. The shorter sets of skid marks are from two test skids done by the state police at the crash site. (Photo courtesy of Forensic Science Educational Consulting, LLC, Portage, MI.)

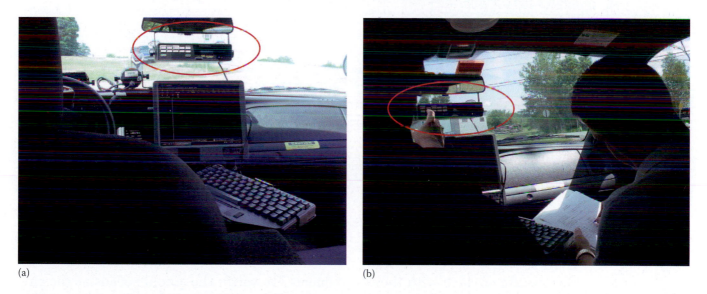

(a)   (b)

Figure 9.11 (a) Vericom VC3000 in police car. (b) VC3000 in use during test skid. (Photo courtesy of Forensic Science Educational Consulting, LLC, Portage, MI.)

This eliminates having to use tape measures and collect data by hand, an extremely time-consuming task. The total work station is a far more accurate way to take data and a real-time saver in the investigation (Figure 9.12).

Postscene Analysis

In addition to completing the scale drawing of the crash site, the accident reconstructionist has additional detail work postscene investigation. Interviews of parties involved as well as witnesses are analyzed. Evidence processed will either

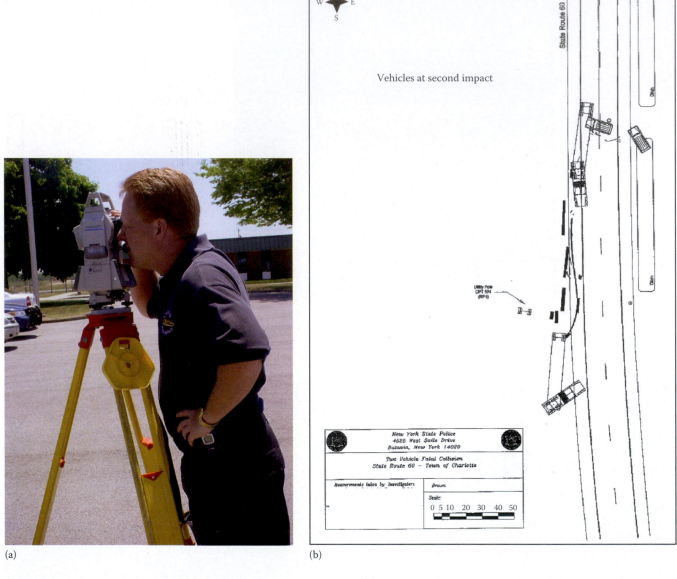

(a)   (b)

Figure 9.12 (a) The Sokkia Electronic Total Work Station. (b) Accident scale drawing. (Photo courtesy of Forensic Science Educational Consulting, LLC, Portage, MI.)

corroborate or clash with these statements. To verify the actual speeds at the site, skid mark data are inputted into formulas to determine speeds of the vehicles. *Yaw marks* are sometimes present at the accident scene. Yaw marks are special types of skid marks that are produced when a vehicle makes a sharp turn without braking, almost to the point of flipping the vehicle. The tire marks are made as the wheels are still turning, but the vehicle is moving laterally, trying to slide to the outside of the circle. Under normal driving conditions, the rear tires will track inside the front tires during turns. For example, during a left-hand turn, the rear tires will appear to the left or inside the front tires. However, if a vehicle enters a turn too quickly or an operator over corrects, the rear tires will travel outside the front tires. It is during this time a vehicle is said to be in a *yaw*. This is evidenced by striations in the tire marks that are perpendicular to the direction of travel. In contrast, a regular skid mark has striations parallel to the direction of travel. If the vehicle continues

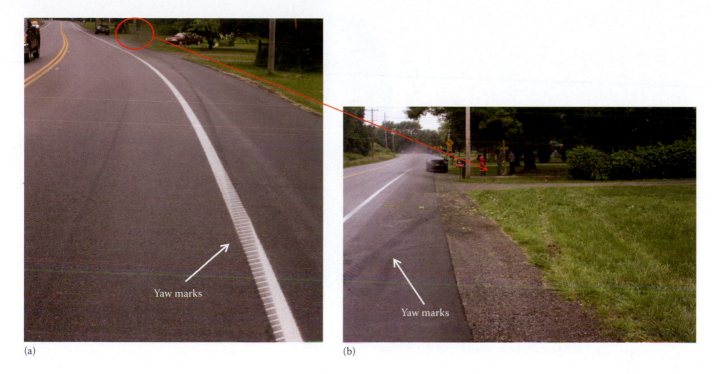

(a)   (b)

Figure 9.13 (a) Shows the truck yaw marks as the vehicle begins to slide off the road, failing to negotiate the curve. (b) Shows the yaw marks continuing off the road prior to impact into a tree. (Photo courtesy of Christopher A. Puckett.)

to rotate, it is no longer said to be in a yaw, but now is a side skid. The tire marks deposited during a side skid must be calculated differently.

Figure 9.13 shows yaw marks made by a pickup truck traveling at approximately 100 mph on a winding road and losing control, sliding in one direction to one side of the road and then correcting and swerving to the opposite side of the road. The truck ended up flipping and hitting a tree. The driver and passenger did not survive.

To determine the speed of the truck during the yaw maneuver, the accident investigator measures a chord line of the circle and then finds the length of the middle ordinate of the chord. This data is then inputted into a few formulas, which will calculate the absolute speed during the yaw (Figure 9.14).

Other aspects of the accident are explored. The make, model, and year of the automobiles involved in the accident are researched looking for possible safety issues or recalls, and whether or not the owner serviced those recalls.

Towed vehicles are examined at the police garage for further evidence. There are a myriad of pieces to the accident puzzle, but a few of the things that are examined more closely in the garage are the restraint and safety systems (seat belt, shoulder harness, air bags), the braking system of the vehicle, and the headlights and taillights of the car. Evidence pertinent to not wearing a seatbelt are extensive damage to the dashboard and steering wheel of the vehicle as well as a seat belt/shoulder harness with no burn mark or puckering that would show stress on the

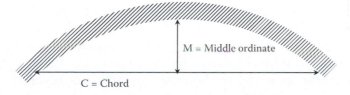

Figure 9.14 Measuring a yaw skid mark.

Figure 9.15 This photo shows damage to the dashboard of an automobile caused by an unrestrained driver. (Photo courtesy of Christopher A. Puckett.)

webbing of the straps. Figure 9.15 shows the front section of a small car that hit a pickup truck broadside. The occupant was not using the seatbelt/shoulder harness restraint mechanism and did not survive. The entire front interior of the car is pushed forward by the occupant's continuing forward motion after the vehicle itself had stopped.

The shoulder harness pictured in Figure 9.16a is from the same automobile. There are no indications of puckering or stress; therefore, the investigator concluded that the victim was not wearing a seatbelt. Figure 9.16b illustrates how a shoulder harness would look in a crash in which the driver was using the seatbelt mechanism. The signs of stress are indicated in the photo.

When the wheels of the towed crash vehicles are dismantled, investigators can ascertain the conditions of the braking mechanisms. Mechanical failure can often contribute to or exacerbate a motor vehicle collision. If mechanical failure is found to be the fault of the owner due to lack of proper maintenance and driving an unsafe vehicle, possible criminal charges due to such negligence could be filed. Figures 9.17 and 9.18 show defective braking systems in vehicles that were involved in accidents. In Photo 9.17, the car's rear disc brakes had a defective brake rotor; the outer friction surface of the rotor is missing. As a result, the overall effectiveness of braking is reduced by approximately 20% for this particular vehicle. The percentage is determined by the amount of vehicle weight on each axle. In this case, the rear axle was responsible for 40% of the total vehicle weight; 20% for each brake. This has been present for some time based on the amount of brake dust and rust present on the rim. Interestingly, the vehicle passed a safety inspection about one and a half months prior to the crash. Either the brake failed very quickly or the inspection was shoddy.

Figure 9.18 illustrates defective rear drum brakes on an automobile that was involved in an accident. When the rear drum of one of the wheels was removed, the investigator discovered that the brake shoe surface was covered with brake fluid and debris. Throughout the entire braking mechanism, there was a heavy amount of brake fluid loss. Inspection of the other rear wheel of the same vehicle yielded less

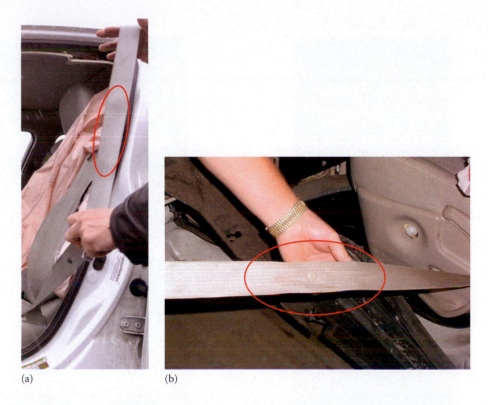

(a)   (b)

Figure 9.16 (a) The shoulder harness has no discoloration due to stress or any puckering of the webbing material, indicating the driver was not wearing the restraint. The shoulder harness in (b) has discoloration of the material due to stress caused by restraining the driver.

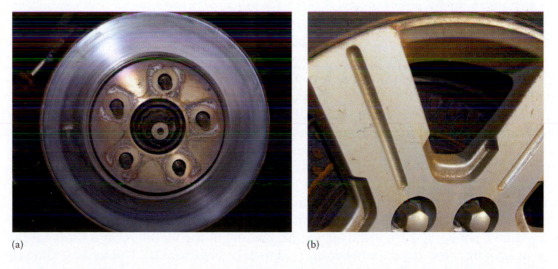

(a)   (b)

Figure 9.17 The picture (a) shows a disc brake rotor that is in good condition. The friction surface is intact and without rust and wear. The picture (b) is from an accident vehicle with defective rear disc brakes. The outer friction surface of the rotor is missing. (Photo courtesy of Christopher A. Puckett.)

damage, but that brake also had a minor leak on one end and the friction surface was covered with rust and debris. This was deemed an underperforming brake as well due to the severe fluid loss on the other side of the axle. Damage to the braking system had been present for some time based on the amount of brake fluid covering every component, especially the friction surface of the drum and the friction surface of the brake shoes.

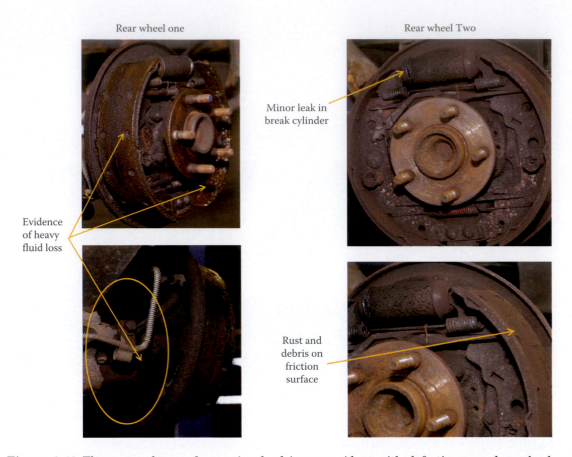

Rear wheel one

Rear wheel Two

Minor leak in break cylinder

Evidence of heavy fluid loss

Rust and debris on friction surface

Figure 9.18 These are photos of a car involved in an accident with defective rear drum brakes. The pictures on the left show extensive damage due to excessive loss of brake fluid and buildup of debris from the braking mechanism. The other wheel had less damage, but also was defective. (Photo courtesy of Christopher A. Puckett.)

Working headlights, taillights, brake lights, and turn signals are essential for safe operation of a vehicle. If the lights are not in working order or the driver does not use them, an accident can result. There are times in an investigation when it is important to determine whether the driver was using proper lighting when an accident occurred. What might be called in question is whether or not turn signals were used, and/or did the driver use high or low beam headlights at the time of the crash. An investigator can tell if the lights are on in a car or truck by closely examining the filament of the lightbulb. If the light was in use at the time of the collision, the filament will stretch and deform as a result of the rapid change in motion while the metal filament is hot. This is called *hot shock*. If the light is not on during a collision, the filament will be unchanged, showing the normal spring like coiling of the metal. A dual filament bulb of a headlight (high beam, low beam) is shown in Figure 9.19. One of the filaments exhibits hot shock and the other is unaffected. This gives evidence that the low beam headlight was in operation at the time of the crash and the high beam was not.

Additional Postscene Analysis

One of the newer aides to accident investigation is the addition of the "black box" to later model automobiles. In 2012, the U.S. Senate mandated that by 2015 all vehicles must be equipped with a Crash Data Retrieval device. The addition of the black box has aided investigations by making data gathering easier. Rather than relying solely on the driver's recollection of what happened during an accident,

Figure 9.19 Dual filament bulb with the filament on the right showing hot shock and the filament on the left unaffected. This tells the investigator that the right filament was on at the time of the crash. (Photo courtesy of Forensic Science Educational Consulting, LLC, Portage, MI.)

the unbiased data retrieval device collects data such as decreases in velocity, deployment of airbags, and braking of the vehicle as well as seat belt usage. Other new technologies that give an accident reconstructionist a picture of what was happening at the time of a collision are global positioning devices (GPS) and cell phones. GPS gives a picture of the general path of the vehicle and cell phone inspection can alert the investigator of any texting or manipulation of the phone while operating the motor vehicle leading to distracted driving.

Other aspects of an investigation might be related to intoxication. In 2013, greater than 10,000 individuals were killed in alcohol impaired motor vehicle accidents. Of the total number of motor vehicle traffic fatalities in the United States, alcohol-related driving accounted for approximately 31%. Driving under the influence leading to death or serious injury can lead to criminal charges against a driver. Some states have expanded the DUI laws to include driving under the influence of drugs, leading to impaired ability while operating a vehicle. Determination of DUI is usually done at the scene with various field tests of sobriety done by the trained police officer. Blood tests usually confirm whether or not the individual was driving over the legal limit of alcohol in their system.

Road and weather conditions can be major factors in motor vehicle accidents. Drivers need to react with caution when the weather turns detrimental to driving. Slowing down and keeping distance between other vehicles are always suggested by state police who patrol the highways. Sometimes, a combination of weather and road conditions can precipitate a chain reaction multiple vehicle pileup, as evidenced by the 193 vehicle calamity on Interstate 94 near Kalamazoo, Michigan, in January 2015. Miraculously, there was only one fatality. Trucks caught fire including one semi truck loaded with fireworks that erupted at the scene (see Figure 9.20).

Something for You to Do

How long does it take a human to react if they are aware of a possible collision? How long does it take to react to something seen by an individual? There is much to be processed when an event happens. First, the body physiologically must process seeing the event, and then the brain alerts the body to make the proper response. This takes time. A very simple experiment can be done to ascertain the approximate reaction time of an individual to a very simple event. You will

Figure 9.20 Multivehicle chain reaction incident on Interstate 94 in Michigan.

need a partner, a 30 cm (12 in.) ruler, and a calculator. Have your partner hold the ruler vertically at the 30 cm end. Place your thumb and index finger on either side of the ruler on the opposite end, at the 1 cm mark. Your partner should drop the ruler without warning and you catch it with your fingers, noting the *centimeter* distance on the ruler. Subtract 1 from this distance (you started at 1), and record the dropping distance (*y*). Repeat four more times and find the average dropping distance from the five trials. Convert the distance in centimeters to meters by dividing by 100. Using your dropping distance (*y*) in *meters* and the derived physics formula in the following, calculate *t* or your *reaction time* to seeing and catching the falling object.

Use "*g*" (acceleration due to gravity) = 9.8 m/s² $t = \sqrt{\dfrac{2(y)}{g}}$

Summary

Forensic engineering is a broad area of forensic investigation. It can be subdivided into two more specific areas, structural forensic engineering and accident reconstruction. The common thread in both areas is that they both extensively employ physics principles and mathematics in analyzing an event to ascertain causality. Both the forensic engineer and the accident reconstructionist need specialized training to determine how the incident occurred in addition to how it could have been prevented. Liability and criminal negligence determination are common to both areas.

Test Yourself

Multiple Choice

1. A person who examines structural evidence from an accident looking for defects in design or construction would be called a(n)
   a. Accident reconstructionist
   b. Scientist
   c. Engineer
   d. Forensic engineer
2. Secondary defects in products are those that
   a. Occur during design
   b. Occur during construction
   c. Occur after use
   d. Occur during manufacturing
3. Primary defects in products are due to
   a. Wear and tear of normal use
   b. Poor design or manufacture
   c. Misuse of the product by the consumer
   d. Poor construction only
4. The primary difference between a scientist and an engineer is
   a. The scientist makes the design and the engineer builds it
   b. The scientist explains the laws nature and the engineer applies the laws of nature
   c. The scientist does experiments and the engineer checks them for accuracy
   d. The scientist designs models of nature and the engineer tests those models
5. Which of the following investigations would not normally be done by a forensic engineer?
   a. Multicar collision
   b. Collapse of the roof of a grocery store
   c. Explosion on a manufacturing line
   d. Roadway bridge failure
6. Which of the following investigations would be done by an accident reconstructionist?
   a. Multicar collision
   b. Collapse of the roof of a grocery store
   c. Explosion on a manufacturing line
   d. Roadway bridge failure
7. By analyzing the skid marks in a skid to stop accident, the investigator can determine the
   a. Defects in braking system
   b. Weight of the vehicle
   c. Speed at the beginning of the skid
   d. Average speed during the skid
8. During a yaw, the driver is not using
   a. The gas pedal
   b. The brakes
   c. The steering wheel
   d. The seat belt

9. Seat belt negligence (not wearing one) in an accident is evidenced by
    a. Absence of burn marks, puckering, or stress on the seatbelt
    b. Absence of line marks on the seatbelt
    c. The spring mechanism no longer works
    d. The seatbelt not extended, it is in the resting position
10. Hot shock affects the
    a. Brake rotors in the rear wheels
    b. Radiator of the car engine
    c. Filament of lightbulbs in use
    d. Filament of lightbulbs not in use

True-False

11. On average, the forensic engineer has 5–10 years of engineering field experience.
12. Liability is an issue in building collapse, but never in motor vehicle accidents.
13. The Tacoma Narrows Bridge collapse was brought on by winds that caused it to resonate.
14. Vehicular accidents can be caused by negligence in maintenance.
15. Black box data retrieval systems were mandated for all vehicles in the year 2010.
16. Over 50,000 fatal accidents per year in the United States are caused by alcohol-impaired drivers.
17. Global positioning devices are of no use in accident investigations.
18. The space shuttle *Challenger* accident was due design flaws in the O-ring mechanism.
19. The Hyatt Regency Walkway's original design was flawed from the start.
20. Most vehicle accidents are investigated by specially trained forensic engineers.

Short Essay

21. Briefly describe the difference between the duties of a scientist and those of an engineer.
22. Detail the basic protocol for the accident reconstructionist at the scene.
23. Under what circumstances would a forensic engineer be asked to investigate a motor vehicle accident?
24. What types of physical laws of nature apply to forensic engineering (including accident investigations). Give examples for each.
25. Describe how are normal skid marks different from yaw marks? Include a sketch of each type.

Matching

26. A person who constructs a viable explanation to a phenomena   a. Drag factor
27. A person who designs devices used for the betterment of society   b. Engineer
28. A number that gives an indication of the roughness of a surface   c. Physics
29. The side slipping of a tire as it makes a tight turn without braking   d. Scientist
30. The study of matter and energy in the universe   e. Yaw

Further Reading

Rivers, R. W. (2004). *Basic Physics, Notes for Traffic Crash and Investigators and Reconstructionists.* Charles C Thomas, Publisher LTD, Springfield, IL.

Van Kirk, D. J. (2001). *Vehicular Accident Investigation and Reconstruction.* CRC Press, Boca Raton, FL.

On the Web

Hyatt Regency Hotel NIST Report: http://www.fire.nist.gov/bfrlpubs/build82/PDF/b82002.pdf.

Indiana State Fair Stage Collapse Report: http://www.wittobriens.com/external/content/document/2000/1883990/1/Witt-Associates-Indiana-State-Fair-Report_April2012.pdf.

National Academy of Forensic Engineers: http://www.nafe.org/.

National Highway Traffic Safety Administration: http://www.nhtsa.gov/.

Space Shuttle Challenger Accident—Rogers Commission Report: http://science.ksc.nasa.gov/shuttle/missions/51-l/docs/rogers-commission/table-of-contents.html.

Space Shuttle Challenger Report Appendix by Richard P. Feynman: http://www.ralentz.com/old/space/feynman-report.html.

Tacoma Narrows Bridge Collapse Video: https://www.youtube.com/watch?v=j-zczJXSxnw.

PART III

Patterns and Impressions

10
Fingerprints and Other Impressions

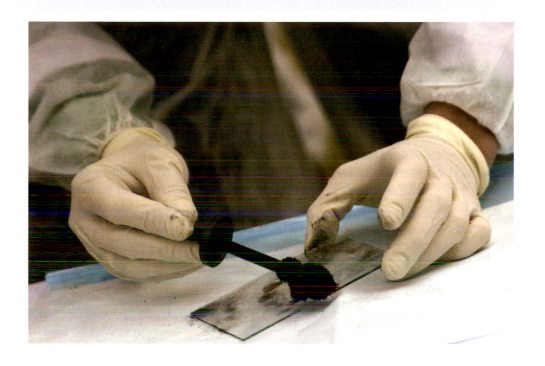

Learning Objectives

1. To be able to define dactyloscopy and ridgegology
2. To be able to describe the main events in the history of fingerprint science
3. To be able to name and describe the underlying principles that govern fingerprint examination
4. To be able to recognize the different types of fingerprint patterns
5. To be able to describe the three levels of data derived from fingerprint examination
6. To be able to name and describe the common methods for physical and chemical detection of fingerprints
7. To be able to describe cyanoacrylate fuming and the use of lasers in fingerprint development
8. To be able to describe how IAFIS works
9. To be able to describe some of the latest digital methods of fingerprint comparison and identification

a fingerprint on the butt of a rifle. The rifle is fumed with Super Glue and then Rhodamine 6G added. A laser is aimed at the print and a picture is taken of the fluoresced print using a special filter on the camera that blocks out the laser light.

Since laser fingerprint development was pioneered by the argon laser and Rhodamine 6G, lasers have been replaced by alternate light sources. These are powerful lamps that use filters to shine one wavelength of light on a fingerprint. Rhodamine 6G remains the laser dye of choice in examining fluoresced prints. This has now become one of the most popular methods of fingerprint development in forensic science laboratories today.

Comparison of Fingerprints

The purpose of developing or visualizing latent fingerprints is to be able to compare them to fingerprint images taken from an individual who is a suspect in a criminal investigation. Known fingerprints are collected from a subject on a 10-print card. This card is used universally to gather known fingerprints. A 10-print card is shown in Figure 10.11. It has space for information about the subject. There is a block for the rolled print of each finger. To collect the print, each finger is rolled in printer's ink from cuticle to cuticle and then rolled out into the proper box on the card. The 10 blocks start with the right thumb and proceed to the right little finger in the top row and then the left thumb through the left little finger on the bottom row. Below these 10 blocks are spaces for tap prints. The four fingers of each hand are tapped in the printer's ink and then tapped into the proper block on the card. Tap prints are also made of each thumb.

Beginning in the 1990s, many law enforcement agencies began replacing the inked 10-print card with computer images of fingerprints. The digital method called Live Scan compiles images of the friction ridges in a manner similar to the inking procedure, except that the fingerprints are "rolled" onto a scanning bed linked to a computer and a digital 10-print card is instantly compiled and downloaded to a fingerprint database. Obvious advantages of this modern method for storing fingerprint records are the virtually instantaneous recording of the fingerprints into the database and the absence of smudging and damaging of fingerprints rolled in printer's ink (see Figure 10.12).

Classification of Sets of Fingerprints

There are two types of fingerprint comparisons. The first is used when the goal is to identify a particular person from his or her fingerprints. In this case, a complete set of inked fingerprints is taken and sent to a database such as the one at the FBI, which maintains many millions of sets of prints. It would be impossible to manually compare the submitted set of prints to so many sets in the database. The way this is handled is by using a classification system. The one adopted and developed by the FBI is widely used by fingerprint laboratories in the United States today. It is based on the original Henry system. The Henry system used several methods of classifying prints (Table 10.2). Each one was based on a different set of characteristics. Letter and number symbols were used to describe the type of each classification and the end result looked like a fraction containing a series of numbers and letters in the numerator and denominator. A description of the complete system is beyond the

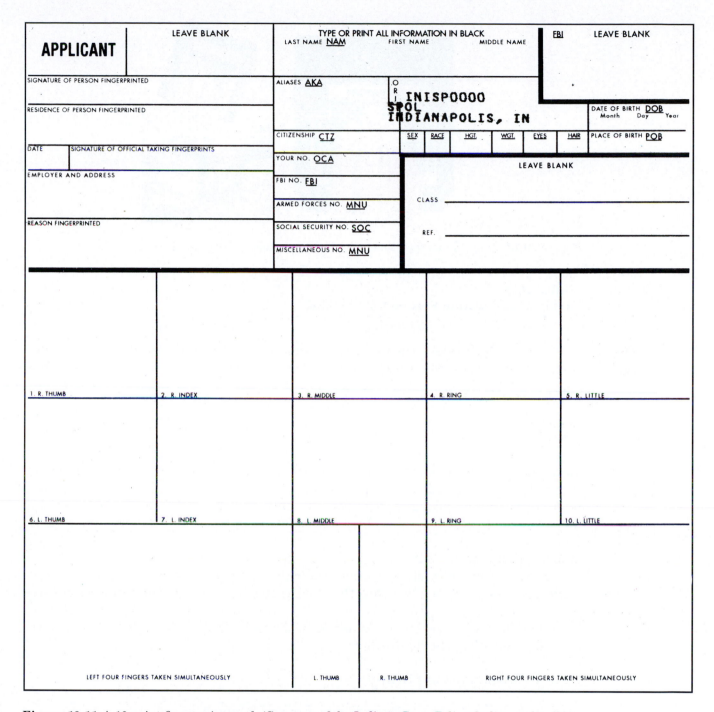

Figure 10.11 A 10-print fingerprint card. (Courtesy of the Indiana State Police, Indianapolis, IN.)

scope of this book, but the primary classification will be described to illustrate how the Henry system (and the FBI system) operates.

Primary Classification

Take another look at the 10-print fingerprint card in Figure 10.11. Each of the 10 boxes at the top is assigned a number. The boxes across the top containing the right-hand fingerprints is given the numbers 1 through 5 and the ones below containing the left-hand prints are numbered 6 through 10. Each finger is examined and its type

Figure 10.12 Digital Fingerprinting using Live Scan fingerprint scanner.

TABLE 10.2
Henry Classification System Using Whorls

Finger	Right Hand					Left Hand				
	Thumb	Index Finger	Middle Finger	Ring Finger	Little Finger	Thumb	Index Finger	Middle Finger	Ring Finger	Little Finger
Digit number	1	2	3	4	5	6	7	8	9	10
Henry value	16		8		4		2		1	

(arch, loop, or whorl) is determined. For the purpose of this classification, any print that is a plain whorl, double loop, central pocket loop, or accidental is considered to be a whorl. In the primary classification, only whorls are counted. Each box that has a whorl print gets a value. If there is a whorl in boxes 1 or 2, the value is 16; in 3 or 4, the value is 8; in 5 or 6, the value is 4; in 7 or 8, the value is 2; in 9 or 10, the value is 1 (see Table 10.2).

To get the primary classification, the values of all of the even-numbered boxes containing whorls are added together and then 1 is added to the total. This is the numerator of the fraction. The values of the odd-numbered fingers containing whorls are added together and then 1 is added to the total. This is the denominator of the classification. Note the following formula:.

Henry Classification Formula

$$\frac{\text{Even Digits Henry Value}+1}{\text{Odd Digits Henry Value}+1}$$

OR

$$\frac{\text{R Index}+\text{R Ring}+\text{L Thumb}+\text{L Middle}+\text{L Little}+1}{\text{R Thumb}+\text{R Middle}+\text{R Little}+\text{L Index}+\text{L Ring}+1}$$

Example Problem:

   Right thumb = radial loop
   Right index = radial loop
   Right middle = plain whorl

Right ring = tented arch
Right little = double loop
Left thumb = plain whorl
Left index = ulnar loop
Left middle = accidental
Left ring = ulnar loop
Left little = plain whorl

Whorl prints are on finger numbers 3, 5, 6, 8, 10. The even-numbered fingers containing whorls receive the following values:

6 = 4
8 = 2
10 = 1

The numerator of the fraction would be: 4 + 2 + 1 + 1 = 8
The odd-number fingers containing whorls get the following values:

3 = 8
5 = 4

The denominator of the fraction would be 8 + 4 + 1 = 13

$$\textbf{OR} \quad \frac{0+0+4+2+1+1=8}{0+8+4+0+0+1=13}$$

The primary classification would then be

$$\frac{8}{13}$$

Careful examination of the Henry primary classification scheme shows that there are 1024 possible fractions. A 1 is added to both the numerator and denominator so that the computers that store and classify sets of prints do not have to deal with 0. Approximately 25% of all sets of fingerprints have a classification of 1 over 1; that is, they have no whorls.

The other classifications within the FBI system also create hundreds or thousands of classes of prints. Using all of the classifications, there are many thousands of classes. When a set of 10 prints is classified and the database is searched, there may be a few hundred sets that match that classification. It is a lot easier for a fingerprint technician to scan these relatively few sets of prints to see if there is a match.

Comparison of Single Fingerprints

Unfortunately, few crime scenes contain complete sets of fingerprints. More likely there are one or two and they may be partial prints; that is, part of the pattern is missing. Partial prints can be matched to a known print if enough ridges are present.

When the fingerprint examiner determines that there are sufficient points (friction ridge details) present in the unknown scene print and a known print, then a decision of identification of the unknown is made. Until a few years ago, many states and many countries had standards that set forth the number of points that a fingerprint examiner must find in a known and unknown print in order to declare that identification had been made. In some places, the minimum number of points was 10, while in others it was 12 or 16, etc. When there are many standards for the same identification, there is no standard. In 1990, the membership of the International Association for Identification, an umbrella group for experts including fingerprint examiners, declared that henceforth there would be no standard minimum number of points for identification. Instead, each examiner would determine how many points would be necessary.

There are three levels of friction ridge details:

Level 1 details include the general features and pattern (e.g., ulnar loop) of the fingerprint. These cannot be used for individualization but can be used to exclude a print from comparison.

Level 2 details include particular ridges such as endings or bifurcations. These minutiae (characteristics) enable individualization of an unknown print. What is important here is not that the known and unknown prints contain the same number of each type of ridge, but that each detail is in the same position relative to other ridges in each print. In that sense, it is like comparing two samples of handwriting. The individual characteristics lie not in the fact that the known and unknown contain the same number of *a* and *e* letters, but that the specific shapes and sizes of each letter are the same in each exhibit. Recall that Figure 10.4 shows how a known and an unknown fingerprint are compared using levels 1 and 2 minutiae. This is the most familiar way of displaying fingerprint identifications in a court.

Level 3 details require a low-power microscope to uncover. These are the minute imperfections in a print such as cuts, scars, edge shapes, ridge contours, and even sweat gland pores. These minutiae are so unique that their presence in the known and unknown print virtually insures individuality. It should be noted, however, that the presence of many of these features depends on how good the image of the print is. Some methods of fingerprint visualization show level 3 details better than others, and this must be taken into account when comparing prints. In Figure 10.13, sweat pores can be seen as tiny white holes in the ridges of the print.

Figure 10.13 An inked fingerprint that shows the pores on the friction ridges. The pores appear as the white uninked circles on the fingerprint.

Automated Fingerprint Identification Systems (AFIS and IAFIS)

The development of high-powered, easy-to-use, and readily available computers has had a profound effect on forensic science. One of the most dramatic advances facilitated by computers is the automated search process for fingerprints. Prior to the development of computerized searching systems, it was impossible for law enforcement agencies to search vast data sets of 10-print fingerprint cards. In the beginning, law enforcement agencies proceeded very slowly in using computers for this task. This was because computers with enough memory capacity to hold large databases of fingerprints were available only at great expense. In addition, the technology for faithfully capturing fingerprint images was rudimentary. When AFIS systems first came out, single fingerprints from crime scenes had to be enlarged and then the major ridges traced so they would be of high enough quality for the computers to scan them for searching.

A standard format for storing fingerprint data was developed by the FBI with the help of the National Institute of Standards and Technology (NIST) and the National Crime Information Center (NCIC). Unfortunately, the companies that developed the hardware and software for conducting the searches did not use standard protocols and it was difficult to share data among users of different systems. In 1999, the FBI implemented a new automated system called the *Integrated Automated Fingerprint Identification System (IAFIS)*. This is an entirely digital system that compares a person's set of 10 fingerprints against a database of millions of sets of prints in a matter of a few minutes. In addition, it can search the database for a single, latent print developed from a crime scene.

All scanned fingerprints can now be digitally enhanced to improve clarity. The problem of incompatibility among different searching systems is being solved by the development of a new generation of workstations that are able to input fingerprints from all the systems commercially available today. When these workstations are fully developed, law enforcement agents can search local, state, and national databases simultaneously.

AFIS systems operate by anchoring the position of a fingerprint and searching the database using two types of ridges: bifurcations and ridge endings. The database is queried to find prints with the same number of these ridges in the same relative positions. The most likely candidates can be displayed for direct comparison. Unlike what is seen in the media, AFIS rarely matches a suspect fingerprint to one individual. The computer system generates a list of possible matches for the fingerprint examiner to analyze and determine a probable match. The human element is still an integral part of fingerprint identification.

Common Questions about Fingerprints

1. Can you sand off your fingerprints?

   Yes, it is possible, but it will leave scars on your hands that will be permanent and unique, creating more individuality to your fingerprints. This would ultimately make your fingerprints *easier* to identify.

2. Can you surgically alter your fingerprints by cutting them off all the down to the dermal papillae?

Yes, it is possible, but no documented successful cases have been noted.

3. Can you graft someone else's surgically removed fingerprints onto yours?

Yes, it is possible, but again no documented successful cases in a criminal arena have been noted. A plastic impression of someone else's fingerprint can be made and then that piece of plastic can be laid over your fingerprint. This has been depicted on TV and the movies, and it does work. One of the episodes of the *Mythbusters* TV program shows the casting and testing of fingerprints, with a positive outcome.

4. Can fingerprints wear down with use or age?

Yes. Alkaline substances such as lime can wear down fingerprints. Construction workers who work mainly with cement or concrete have been shown to have almost invisible ridge patterns after years of work, owing to the presence of lime and other alkaline materials.

Other Impressions: Footwear and Tire Treads

When one object makes physical contact with another, it may leave some of its physical characteristics on the recipient in the form of an *impression*. If the recipient object is soft or pliable such as putty, mud, concrete, or soft dirt, the impression will be three-dimensional. If the recipient material is hard and the donor object has some material such as dirt, dust, blood, or ink on its surface, the impression will be left on the surface of the recipient and will be two-dimensional.

There are many examples of impression evidence. Fingerprints are the most familiar example. Oils and other materials on the surfaces of the fingers are deposited on surfaces as two-dimensional impressions. These are discussed in detail in this chapter. Firing pin impressions are made by guns on the backs of cartridges. These are discussed in Chapter 12. Automobile tires and footwear can leave tread or sole impressions in dirt. These types of impressions are the subject of this section.

Footwear Impressions

Many types of shoes have soles with distinctive tread patterns whereas others are smooth. Footwear evidence can be extremely valuable in associating perpetrators of crimes with the crime scenes. There may be footwear impressions at and near the entry points to a crime scene, at the scene, and at and near the exits. In fact, there are many footwear impressions at and around crime scenes that are never discovered or collected. It is reasonable to conclude that there are more potential footwear impressions at crime scenes than there are fingerprint impressions.

There are a number of reasons why footwear evidence is overlooked in crime scene investigations. The impressions are generally on the ground, which may be uneven or not conducive to holding impressions. They may be invisible or nearly so. They may have been tramped on by paramedics or other personnel before they can be preserved. Many crime scene investigators lack the necessary training to discover, preserve, and process footwear impressions. Police, detectives, judges, and juries often misunderstand or undervalue footwear evidence. They are often surprised to find that a footwear impression can be associated to the exact shoe from which it arose. This, in turn, discourages police investigators from collecting this potentially important evidence.

Some people believe that footwear impressions are very fragile and do not last very long. In fact, many impressions can last permanently. Those that cannot can be permanently recorded by a combination of photography and casting. There is no way to know, however, how much time has passed since an impression was made. Inferences may be made from circumstances surrounding the incident, but the impression itself contains no time markers. Impressions made in sand or snow may start to deteriorate very soon after being formed, and the rate of deterioration is dependent on many environmental factors.

Individual or Class Evidence

As with other impression evidence, the conclusion that can be reached from a comparison of known and unknown footwear evidence depends on the number of unique details in the impression. When shoes are brand new, impressions of their soles will be pretty much the same as the impressions of all other shoes of the same type and size. Wear over time produces random markings and imperfections that begin to alter the impression, making it more unique as time passes (see Figure 10.14). Eventually, there will be enough unique details present in an impression to permit a competent examiner to conclude that the impression arose from one particular shoe (or other type of footwear). There are no definitive standards that dictate how many points of identification must be present or the type and quality of the points.

Figure 10.14 The bottom of this athletic shoe shows wear patterns that are unique to this shoe. The wear patterns, imbedded materials, and imperfections make this shoe individual evidence.

It is a matter of the experience and comfort level of the particular examiner that determines whether a conclusion of individuality will be made.

More than 1.5 billion shoes are sold annually in the United States. Given the large variety of types and sizes of shoes available, any one type and size of shoe will be worn by a very small fraction of people at any one time. The very fact that a footwear impression is the same type and size as a shoe worn by the suspect will eliminate a large portion of the population from consideration, irrespective of any unique wear patterns in the impression. The presence of some wear marks and manufacturing imperfections will add discrimination to the comparison even if they fall short of permitting individualization. This is an important concept that should not be ignored by investigators.

Aside from the probable wearer of the shoe, other information can be determined from a footwear comparison. It can indicate the type and make of shoe and the approximate or exact size. From the number and types of impressions, the number of perpetrators as well as their entry and exit paths from the crime scene may be determined.

How Footwear Impressions Are Formed

Footwear impressions can occur in one of two ways. One impression could be three-dimensional (having length, width, and depth) and another could be two-dimensional, showing only length and width. If the surface is soft enough to hold the impression, the shoe can deform the surface, leaving a permanent or temporary impression. Traces of material may be transferred from the shoe to the surface (positive impression) or from the surface to the shoe (negative impression). The transfer of material to and from the shoe can be aided by the buildup of static electricity that takes place when a shoe makes contact with the ground. Positive impressions are much more common than negative impressions because the latter requires that the shoe be clean and that is not a very common condition. Positive and negative impressions are most often two-dimensional. Figure 10.15 shows a two-dimensional footwear impression, and Figure 10.16 shows a three-dimensional impression that was made in soil.

Figure 10.15 A two-dimensional inked footwear impression. (Reprinted from Bodziac, W.T., *Footwear Impression Evidence*, 2nd edn., Taylor & Francis, Boca Raton, FL, 1996.)

Figure 10.16 A three-dimensional footwear impression made in soil. (Reprinted from Bodziac, W.T., *Footwear Impression Evidence*, 2nd edn., Taylor & Francis, Boca Raton, FL, 1996.)

How Footwear Impressions Are Preserved

All footwear impressions must be photographed at the scene. Today digital photography is widely used for this purpose. In all cases, a ruler or other measuring tool must be inserted in the photograph if it is to be used in court. A reference object such as a coin is not acceptable. In the case of two-dimensional impressions, the photograph will be used for comparison with the known footwear so it must be of the highest quality. The camera should be mounted on a tripod for the best results.

Three-dimensional footwear impressions can be preserved by *casting*. Casting is a process by which a three-dimensional impression is filled with a material that hardens and captures an image of the impression. Unlike a photograph, a casting captures virtually every important characteristic of the impression including surface texture, unevenness of the depth, and even microscopic details that differentiate one footwear impression from another. Castings do not have the perceptual or focus or lighting problems that sometimes accompany photography, and they form a positive image so that raised ridges on the cast are the same as the raised ridges of the footwear and a direct comparison can be made.

Over the years, many casting materials have been used. Some of the most popular were various types of plaster including Plaster of Paris. None of these were really suitable for footwear casts because they were too soft. Attempts to remove debris such as soil from the cast resulted in the loss of significant detail from the cast. Today the universal product for making footwear casts is dental stone. This is a gypsum cement adapted for use by the dental industry to make high-quality teeth impressions. It is harder than plaster and captures detail to a much greater extent. Figure 10.17 shows a cast of a footwear impression made in soil. The upper half of the cast is made with Plaster of Paris, and the lower half is made with dental stone. The upper arrow points to the dividing line between the two materials the lower arrow points to minutae in the impression, and it can be seen that the level of detail is greater in the detail stone.

Tire Tread Impressions

A tire tread is the part of an automobile tire that makes contact with the road. Today's tire treads have complicated designs in them that serve several functions. In some ways, tire treads are similar to footwear soles. They both serve to increase friction at the point of contact, and this helps to minimize slippage. These functions

Figure 10.17 A plaster cast of a footwear impression using dental stone (lower half) and plaster (upper half) casting methods. The upper arrow points to the line of separation between the two materials. The lower arrow shows the greater detail due to using dental stone in the lower half. (Reprinted from Bodziac, W.T., *Footwear Impression Evidence*, 2nd edn., Taylor & Francis, Boca Raton, FL, 1996.)

are more important in tires than shoes because tires travel at much higher speeds in all sorts of weather on a variety of surfaces. They also must be able to start and stop rapidly while maintaining control. Tires also support more weight than footwear so they must be made of durable materials. Like footwear, tires are mass produced and brand new ones bear few, if any, unique characteristics. With time and use, however, tire treads pick up increasing numbers of details that set them apart from all other tires. In such cases, a tire tread can be individualized to a particular tire.

Development of Tire Treads

The first air-filled (pneumatic) tire was developed by John Dunlop in 1888. His tires, manufactured by Dunlop Tires, were bald—they had no tread. At first, this was not a problem because there were no roads and cars traveled very slowly, so the need for traction was not pronounced. By the beginning of the twentieth century, roads were developed and the need for friction-producing surfaces on tires became evident. In 1907, Harvey Firestone designed the first traction design for tire treads. The tread pattern was not scientifically designed. It consisted of the words "Firestone and nonskid" carved into the tread. Every time a Firestone tire left a tread print, it advertised the company. Today, computers are used to help design tire treads that not only provide gripping power, but also channel away water to prevent hydroplaning. Some tread elements also reduce road noise.

Identification Markings on Tire Sidewalls

Take a look at the tires on your car. The sidewalls have several groups of numbers that have been stamped into the tire. A tire sidewall is shown in Figure 10.18.

Some of the markings indicate the make and model of the tire. Others are not so easy to interpret. Consider the following set of numbers and letters on a tire sidewall:

LT225/65 R 14

The "LT" indicates that the tire is made for a light truck such as a pickup truck or some SUVs. If the vehicle were a passenger car, the first letter would be a "P." The "225" is the cross section of the tire measured in millimeters. The cross section is measured from sidewall to sidewall. A tire can be mounted on several different wheel rims and this would affect the measured cross section. The designated cross

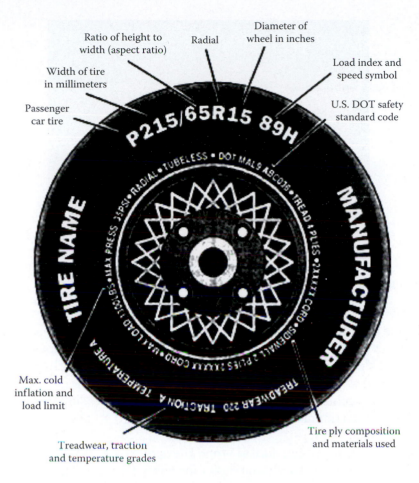

Ratio of height to width (aspect ratio)

Radial

Diameter of wheel in inches

Width of tire in millimeters

Load index and speed symbol

Passenger car tire

U.S. DOT safety standard code

TIRE NAME

MANUFACTURER

Max. cold inflation and load limit

Tire ply composition and materials used

Treadwear, traction and temperature grades

Figure 10.18 A tire sidewall. (Tire Guides, Inc., Boca Raton, FL, www.tireguides.com.)

section is obtained when the tire is mounted on the wheel rim for which it was made. The "65" is called the aspect ratio and is measured from where the tire is sealed to the rim (the bead) to the top of the tread. The aspect ratio is actually the percentage of the height to the width. In this case, the height is 65% of the width and should measure 146 mm. The final R designates the type of tire. The most common type is radial although there are also diagonal bias (D) and belted (B). The last number is the diameter of the wheel rim for which the tire was developed in inches.

Evidential Value of Tire Impressions

Even though an estimated two-thirds of major crimes in the United States involve automobiles, it is unfortunate that many crime scene investigators overlook this potentially important evidence. In some cases, the only way a vehicle may be identified is from tire impressions left at the scene. A properly prepared record (photograph or casting) of a tire impression can be associated with the exact tire that made it and can thus be individual evidence.

Capturing Tire Impressions

Tire impressions are similar to footwear impressions in some respects. They may both be two-dimensional or three-dimensional and two-dimensional impressions

Figure 10.19 A plaster cast of a part of a tire impression.

may be positive or negative, depending on how they are produced. However, tire impressions are usually much larger than footwear impressions, making them more difficult to collect and match to the tire. As is the case with all types of impressions, tire tread impressions should be photographed at the scene whether or not a casting will be made. In the case of three-dimensional tire impressions, castings must be made at the scene because the object containing the impression cannot be taken to the laboratory for casting or further analysis. Figure 10.19 shows a plaster cast of a tire tread impression.

With footwear impressions, dental stone casts of three-dimensional impressions are nearly always superior to photographs for comparison with known shoes. This is not always the case with tire tread impressions. Sometimes there are difficulties with making a good cast and the investigator is better served by photographs. For example, making a cast on a steep incline can be difficult because the casting material may flow downhill. The upper part of the cast may be too thin and will fall apart when the cast is lifted. In other cases, the tire impression may be several feet long resulting in very heavy and bulky casts. In such situations, a series of overlapping photographs may be a better way to record the impression. Finally, all three-dimensional casts of tires make negative impressions. It is never good practice to compare a negative impression with a positive tread surface or photograph. Instead, the tire is photographed and the negative of the picture is used for the comparison.

As with footwear impressions, dental stone is the preferred casting material for most surfaces. For tire impressions in snow, casting wax is used. In all cases, as with footwear, a suitable measuring instrument must be included in photographs of casts or impressions.

In addition to tread patterns and wear details, tire tread impressions can be used to derive other information about the tire and vehicle. For example, the Michigan State Police Forensic Science Division maintains a database containing measurements of wheelbase and stance. The wheelbase of a vehicle is the distance from the center of the front wheel hub to the center of the real wheel hub. The stance is the distance from the centerline of the right tire to the centerline of the left tire. Combining the wheelbase and stance data with the tread pattern of the tires (if original equipment), the make and model of a car or truck may be determined.

Summary

Fingerprints are among the oldest methods of personal identification. There is anecdotal evidence that the Chinese used fingerprints to help identify people thousands of years ago. Only within the past 150 years has fingerprint science been used with some degree of reliability for personal identification. Fingerprints are created during gestation and, once formed, do not change throughout life, except in size. It is believed that all fingerprints are unique, and this is the underlying principle that allows fingerprints to be used for identification of a person.

All fingerprints form patterns. There are eight patterns in all. The major types are loops, arches, and whorls. Within these types are subtypes. There are radial and ulnar loops, tented and plain arches, plain whorls, central pocket loops, accidentals, and double loop whorls. These patterns are made up of fingerprint ridges. There are several types of ridge characteristics including dots, ridge endings, bifurcations, trifurcations, and enclosures. For comparison purposes, there are three levels of data. Level 1 includes the overall pattern of the print and general ridge characteristics. Level 2 includes the arrangements of various ridge types relative to each other. Level 3 includes the details of the ridge characteristics including edges and sweat pores.

When a finger touches an object, it leaves an image of the ridge characteristics. The image is made up of sweat, skin cells, proteins, fats, and other materials. A *latent fingerprint* is one that must be visualized or developed using chemical or physical methods. Patent prints are those that are already visible because they have been made in fresh blood, paint, etc. Plastic prints are impressions made in a pliant material such as putty. One of the major breakthroughs in fingerprint visualization technology is Super Glue (cyanoacrylate) fuming, which forms a hard image of a fingerprint. This image can be treated with a fluorescent dye and then a strong light source can cause the dye to fluoresce, thus clarifying the image further.

There are several methods for classifying sets of 10 fingerprints. The method used in the United States and Europe was developed by Sir Edward Henry, and today bears his name. It actually has five different classifications, each of which focuses on a different set of fingerprint characteristics. Together the system creates thousands of classes in which a set of prints can be placed. This makes searching for the right set out of millions fairly easy.

The development of computers and electronic imaging has made automated searching of fingerprint databases possible. These AFIS systems are being standardized so that local, state, and federal law enforcement agents can search the same databases and share information.

Footwear and tire impressions can be two- or three-dimensional. Impression evidence can be individualized to one particular object if there are sufficient unique characteristics present. These characteristics arise from the random wearing of the shoeprint or tire tread.

Preserving impressions is very important because they often cannot be transported intact to the forensic science lab. Proper, high-resolution photography is commonly done, with digital photography becoming more popular. A suitable measuring instrument must be in the picture to facilitate scale determination. The measuring instrument must be a ruler or other device that actually measures distance. Dental stone has become the casting material of choice for many impressions because of its ease of use and high definition.

Test Yourself

Multiple Choice

1. Which of the following types of ridges are "counted" in the primary Henry classification of a set of prints?
   a. Loops
   b. Arches
   c. Whorls
   d. All of these

2. The police official who developed a fingerprint classification system still used in Central and South America is
   a. Henry Fauld
   b. Will West
   c. Juan Vucetich
   d. Juan Valdez

3. A radial loop
   a. Always opens toward the left
   b. Is a type of whorl pattern
   c. Comprises 50% of all fingerprints
   d. Opens toward the thumb side of the hand

4. IAFIS is
   a. The International Association that sets standards for fingerprint analysis
   b. A type of automated searching system for fingerprints
   c. An abbreviation for a type of chemical that is used to cause fingerprints to fluoresce
   d. A federal agency that sets standards for forensic evidence analysis

5. Level 3 fingerprint data include
   a. The positions of sweat pores along fingerprint ridges
   b. The general pattern type of a fingerprint
   c. Only bifurcations and ridge endings
   d. Only ridges that can be seen with Super Glue fuming

6. Ruhemann's purple is
   a. Formed from the reaction of cyanoacrylate with fingerprint residues
   b. Formed from the reaction of ninhydrin with fingerprint residues
   c. Formed from the reaction of silver nitrate and fingerprint residues
   d. The color that Rhodamine 6G emits when an argon laser is shined on it

7. Which of the following is *not* a type of whorl pattern:
   a. Tented arch
   b. Double loop
   c. Accidental
   d. Central pocket loop

8. If the primary Henry classification of a set of fingerprints is 1/1, which 2 fingers have whorls?
   a. Left index/right middle
   b. Left and right thumbs
   c. Left and right little fingers
   d. No fingers have whorls

9. If the primary Henry classification of a set of fingerprints is 17/1, which finger has a whorl?
   a. Right thumb
   b. Right index
   c. Right middle
   d. Left thumb
10. Alphonse Bertillion was famous for
   a. Recognizing that fingerprints were individual
   b. Discovering Super Glue fuming
   c. Developing a system of body measurements to identify people
   d. Discovering ninhydrin
11. When AFIS searches its database of fingerprints, it searches for which types of patterns:
   a. Arches and loops
   b. Ridge endings and enclosures
   c. Whorls and loops
   d. Ridge endings and bifurcations
12. Iodine fumes adhere to what type of fingerprint residue:
   a. Water
   b. Amino acids
   c. Lipids and fats
   d. Salts
13. Ninhydrin reacts with what type of fingerprint residue:
   a. Water
   b. Amino acids
   c. Lipids and fats
   d. Salts
14. Three-dimensional footwear evidence can be preserved by
   a. Fuming
   b. Dusting
   c. Casting
   d. Photography
15. Tire impressions are important because
   a. They show direction
   b. They can be matched to a specific tire
   c. They match the type of vehicle
   d. They are permanent

True/False

16. An arch has two deltas.
17. Attempts to alter existing fingerprints make them easier to identify.
18. Footwear impressions in soil leave a three dimensional image.
19. Tire treads impressions are considered as class evidence, not individual.
20. The pores on friction ridges exude sweat that leaves residue on a surface.

Short Answer

21. Look carefully at the footwear impression casts A–C. Match the inked shoeprints (P1–P6) to the footwear casts. Identify individual points of match on the impression and the print.

Footwear cast A   Footwear cast B   Footwear cast C

P1   P2   P3

P4   P5   P6

22. Look carefully at the tire impression casts A and B. Match the inked tire tread prints to the tire casts (T1–T6). Identify individual points of match on the impression and the inked tread.

Tire impression cast A   Tire impression cast B

23. Look carefully at the inked fingerprint. Which of the eight types of finger-
    prints does it represent?

24. For the fingerprint shown in Question 23, identify the parts labeled a through e.

Short Essay

25. Construct a flow chart showing the development of the human classification
    system from the first attempts to differentiate individuals to modern day
    methods.

Matching

26. Arch	a. One type of fingerprint that has two deltas
27. Loop	b. A fingerprint invisible to the naked eye
28. Whorl	c. The active ingredient in Super Glue that reacts with fingerprint residue forming a white precipitate
29. Plastic fingerprint	d. A visible fingerprint left behind due to residue on the finger such as blood, grease, or paint
30. Patent fingerprint	e. One type of fingerprint that has no deltas
31. Latent fingerprint	f. Change of phase from a solid directly to a gas
32. Rhodamine 6G	g. One of the oldest chemical methods of fingerprint visualization
33. Cyanoacrylate	h. One type of fingerprint that has one delta
34. Silver nitrate	i. A liquid fluorescent dye used to enhance fingerprints
35. Sublimation	j. A visible fingerprint impression in a soft solid

Further Reading

Lee, H. C. and R. E. Gaensslen (eds.). (2001). *Advances in Fingerprint Technology*, 2nd edn.
    CRC Press, Boca Raton, FL.
Cowger, J. E. (1992). *Friction Ridge Skin*. CRC Press, Boca Raton, FL.

On the Web

www.ccs.neu.edu/home/feneric/cyanoacrylate.html.
www.crime-scene-investigator.net/footwear.html.
www.fbi.gov/hq/cjisd/iafis.htm.
www.fbi.gov/hq/cjisd/takingfps.html.
www.forensic-evidence.com/site/ID/ID00004_2.html.
www.forensicmag.com/articles.asp?pid=114.
www.galton.org.
http://galton.org/fingerprints/books/henry/henry-classification.pdf.
http://query.nytimes.com/mem/archive-free/pdf?_r=1&res=980CE5D81E3BEE3ABC4151D
    FB0668382609EDE.
www.sciencedaily.com/releases/2005/03/050322135157.htm.
www.sciencedaily.com/releases/2008/09/080915210509.htm.
www.youtube.com/watch?v=9_6WyZXTaBo.

11
Questioned Documents

1. To be able to define a questioned document
2. To be able to describe the training that a questioned document examiner must undergo
3. To be able to describe how handwriting is developed over time
4. To be able to describe the methods for analyzing and comparing handwriting
5. To be able to describe the proper methods for collection of handwriting exemplars
6. To be able to describe methods for uncovering erasures and other obliterations
7. To be able to describe ESDA and how it is used in questioned document analysis
8. To be able to describe the methods used for analysis and comparison of inks and papers
9. To be able to describe the methods of analysis of copier toners
10. To be able to describe how forgeries and tracings are detected

Chapter 11
Questioned Documents

Chapter Outline

Mini Glossary

Best evidence rule: Rule that governs the admissibility of document evidence. Generally, only the original document is admissible.

Exemplar: A sample of handwriting whose source is known. Used for comparison with questioned document.

Graphology (graphoanalysis): Determination of personality or certain personality characteristics by examination of someone's handwriting.

Nonrequested exemplar: Already-existing documents that are part of the suspect's everyday correspondence.

Palmer: A method of teaching hand printing and writing by copying letters. See Zaner–Bloser.

Pattern evidence: Consists of markings that are believed to be individual to each person.

Questioned document: Any written or printed communication between individuals whose source or authenticity is in doubt.

Requested exemplar: Samples of handwriting that the author is asked to provide.
Zaner-Bloser: A method of teaching hand printing and writing by copying letters. Related to Palmer method.

Acronyms

ABFDE: American Board of Forensic Document Examiners
ASQDE: American Society of Questioned Document Examiners
ESDA: Electrostatic Detection Apparatus

Introduction

This chapter is all about questioned documents. This is a broad term that encompasses many types of evidence. Most people think of questioned document examinations as having to do with comparing handwriting samples, and many forensic cases still involve handwriting analysis, but this is rapidly changing as many documents are now being created by digital means. As we shall see, questioned document analysis involves so much more than just handwriting: charred and indented writing, paper and ink analysis, forgeries, watermarks, etc. Handwritten documents are a type of *pattern evidence* that consists of markings that are believed to be individual to each person. Like other types of pattern evidence such as fingerprints and firearms, questioned document examiners are largely trained by classical apprenticeship methods, where the trainee spends 2–3 years learning from a professional document examiner, mostly one on one.

Of all of the disciplines of forensic science, questioned document analysis is one that is most commonly involved in civil cases. Many questioned document examiners spend as much time on civil cases as they do on crimes. Some of these civil cases are very famous and have helped give questioned document analysis much (but not always favorable) publicity. An interesting example of handwriting examination in a famous case is given below.

On April 5, 1976, the reclusive billionaire industrialist Howard Hughes died on a plane that was bringing him back from Acapulco, Mexico, to Houston. He had been in a coma when he was put on the plane. At the time he died, Hughes was estimated to control a financial empire worth nearly $3 billion. In today's dollars, that would easily be twice as much. His empire included casinos, real estate, and a helicopter company. He had no wife, no children, no siblings, and no living parents. The last few years of his life, Hughes was a recluse and was rarely seen in public and for that matter, rarely seen even by his closest aides. Questions were raised about who would inherit his vast estate and where the estate would be probated. He had interests in Texas, California, and Nevada. Each of these states would receive inheritance taxes worth millions when the estate was probated.

There was a great deal of speculation in the media about the possible existence of a will, but none surfaced right away. Then on April 27, officials of the Mormon Church in Salt Lake City, Utah, discovered what was purported to be a will of Howard Hughes. The will was *holographic* (entirely handwritten) and three pages long. The papers had been left in an office of the Church. Besides the will, there were two envelopes and a note requesting that the will be delivered to the Clerk of Clark County (Las Vegas), Nevada. The note was in the same handwriting as the will. Two other handwritten items were included, but they appeared to be written in a different handwriting.

A questioned document examiner made a preliminary determination that the will was authentic, and the will was filed in Clark County. A battle then ensued, resulting in a 6-month trial over the authenticity of the will. This challenge to authenticity was triggered by a provision in the will that part of the estate, more than $150 M, was to go to Melvin Dummars. Dummars indicates that he met Howard Hughes in the Southwestern desert during a trip to Los Angeles. Hughes had been injured in a motorcycle accident when Dummars came across him on the highway. He picked up Hughes and dropped him off at a casino in Las Vegas. The bequest in Hughes will was a reward for Dummars' kind behavior.

During the trial, Dummars' story changed a number of times and several questioned document examiners from the United States and Europe pored over the will. Ultimately, the jury found that the will was forged by Dummars. One of the most prominent of the examiners, John J. Harris, was sure from the start of his examination that the will was probably a fraud. After his work, he had no doubt. He gave a number of reasons for the surety of his conclusions. These included that there was ample writing in the will and known samples of Hughes writing to make comparisons, that the writing in the will was forced and labored (unlike Hughes normal flowing writing style), and that the writing in the will lacked natural variation that is usually found in long passages of writing.

In this chapter, both handwriting and digital media will be considered as sources of questioned documents. Although there are still typewriters being used to create documents, their use has dropped drastically and they will not be covered in detail in this chapter.

What Is a Questioned Document?

A *questioned document* is any written or printed communication whose source or authenticity is in doubt. The document does not have to be written on paper. Questioned documents have been written on the sides of houses, on mirrors, and on tables. They can be written in ink, blood, paint, or even lipstick. Questioned documents include forged passports, wills, currency, draft cards, and driver's licenses. Anytime there is commerce between people that involves a document, there is the potential for fraud, forgery, alteration, counterfeiting, or theft. Questioned document examiners must know a great deal about writing, printing, typewriting, inks, papers, and methods of altering or obliterating writing. Documents are unique in that they are subject to the *best evidence rule*. This means that the original document must be examined and admitted into court. With few exceptions, copies of documents are not permitted for identification and court purposes. This rule has even been extended to movies before they were made digitally.

Questioned Document Examiner

Document Examiners compare unknown handwriting, typewriting, and other documentary evidence with known standards in an attempt to establish the origin or authenticity of the unknown materials. They also attempt to restore obliterated or damaged writings and analyze paper and inks. This field has, over time, become more dependent upon chemical methods for the analysis of writing instruments and inks and obliterated or altered writing. The educational trend among examiners is to require a college degree. There are few college level and continuing education courses on questioned document examination. The path to the profession is generally through an apprenticeship. This is similar to the way that people become fingerprint examiners or firearms examiners. In questioned document examination, the apprenticeship lasts 2–4 years. The training program consists of literature readings and research, lectures, examinations, and practical problems. There are also mock trials toward the end of the training period. When a document examiner has completed the apprenticeship, (s)he becomes a *journeyman examiner*. Then there is a voluntary certification process through the American Board of Forensic Document Examiners, ABFDE, http://www.abfde.org/. This certification is a tremendous advantage to the questioned document examiner because it adds greatly to one's qualifications as an expert, especially in court. The professional organization of questioned document examiners is the American Society of Questioned Document Examiners, ASQDE, http://www.asqde.org/. A bachelor's degree in a natural science or a related field is highly desirable as is ABFDE certification.

Sometimes, questioned document examination is confused with *graphology (graphoanalysis)*. Graphologists claim to be able to discern certain personality characteristics by examination of someone's handwriting. For example, around the time that President Nixon was impeached, at least one graphologist published an article analyzing Noxon's handwriting and purporting to show that his handwriting indicated that he was dishonest. There is no scientific basis for linking personality traits to handwriting characteristics. Unfortunately, some judges have confused graphology with questioned document analysis and have permitted graphologists to testify in court concerning matters of questioned document identification and authenticity. Graphologists are not permitted to become certified by the ABFDE. Some attorneys, facing the selection of a jury for a trial, will enlist the help of graphologists to aid in uncovering hidden biases in potential jurors that could help or hinder the attorney's case.

Handwriting Analysis

Handwriting and hand printing evidence is the most common and most challenging of all of the examinations that document examiners are called upon to perform. Even though computer printing is replacing handwriting in many applications, there are still many types of documents that are handwritten or which contain handwritten signatures that must be compared. Handwriting comparisons have been admissible in U.S. courts for more than 100 years. The basis for handwriting comparisons and conclusions is that a person's handwriting contains a number of unique, reproducible characteristics that can be individualized to that person. There are no standards for the amount of handwriting sample that must be present in order to make a comparison or the number of unique features that must be found in the known and unknown specimens. There is also no hard and fast definition of what constitutes a unique feature. Little has been reported in the scientific literature that would conclusively establish the basis for individualization of handwriting. In recent years, these issues have been brought up in courts during challenges to the identification of a writer from their handwriting. Increasingly, judges have ruled that there is not a sufficient scientific basis for the individuality of handwriting. The National Academy of Sciences Forensic Science Committee also questioned the validity of handwriting comparisons as it did for other types of pattern evidence, based upon the lack of scientific validation of the techniques used.

How Handwriting Develops

The methods used in schools to teach people to print and then write have changed little over the past century or more. Most schools use a variation of either the *Palmer* method or the *Zaner-Bloser* method of teaching handwriting. Each method uses a set of printing and writing fonts. Figure 11.1 shows a sample of some Palmer fonts. The capital and lower case letters are written out on a large, lined piece of paper mounted atop the blackboard in front of the room, and each student spends many hours copying the letters and eventually making words. The students are initially evaluated by the teacher on the degree to which they are able to exactly copy the letters and words. A more recent system of handwriting called cursive is a sort of bridge between printing and writing. This is sometimes used after printing is taught or on its own. In recent years, the trend is to teach only cursive and some states are opting to stop teaching beyond print altogether. Once the student has achieved a measure of penmanship and dexterity so that someone else can read their hand printing or writing, the lessons shift towards what is being written rather than how it looks. At this point, students pay less attention to the appearance of their handwriting and the writing process becomes internalized and "automatic." Each person brings embellishments to their writing to make it their own. It becomes such a habit that people do not even think about how their writing looks. They are generally not concerned about the characteristics that make up their handwriting. Ironically, this makes it more difficult for someone to deliberately disguise their handwriting because they are not aware of its nuances and traits. As we will see later, this can be exploited when collecting known specimens of someone's handwriting.

ABCDEFGHIJKLMN OPQRSTUVWXYZ

Figure 11.1 Palmer fonts. These letter shapes are commonly used to teach young children to print.

Even though handwriting becomes internalized with time, it is not static and unchanging like fingerprints. Handwriting changes as a person ages. This may be due to a matter of personal preference or to changes in dexterity brought on by advancing age or to infirmity or disease. Handwriting can also change, although less markedly, as the purpose of the writing changes. Depending upon the circumstances, a person's signature may be very neat or practically illegible. A long, languid love letter will have different handwriting characteristics (it is usually readable) than notes scribbled during a physics lecture. In spite of these circumstantial changes, a person's handwriting maintains its essential unique features regardless of the circumstances surrounding the writing. Other factors can also affect handwriting on a short- or long-term basis. One of the most profound influences is health. Diseases can cause temporary or permanent weakness of muscles that control writing. Sometimes, changes happen gradually over time and sometimes they may be quite abrupt such as the case of a hand injury or arthritis. Tremors caused by advancing age or diseases such as Parkinson's disease may cause major changes in handwriting. Alcohol and drugs may cause temporary changes to writing. If the subject suffers from chronic alcoholism or drug abuse, these changes may become permanent.

Handwriting Comparisons

Handwriting comparisons depend upon two major factors; the presence of sufficient unique characteristics in the questioned specimen of writing and the proper collection of *exemplars*, which are the specimens of writing from the suspected author. Handwriting has a natural variation and some of the characteristics of a person's handwriting depend upon the writing instrument, paper, physical condition, and mental condition of the author at the time the document was written. Thus, the general rule of handwriting exemplars is that the exemplars should be as similar in all controllable aspects as the unknown. If the unknown is printed rather than cursive, the known must be printed. If the writing instrument used in the questioned document is pencil then the exemplars must also be collected in pencil. Because handwriting changes with time, known and unknown specimens must be of approximately the same age.

Exemplars can be *requested* or *nonrequested*. Requested exemplars are samples of handwriting that the author is asked to provide. These samples are taken under conditions that are established by the document examiner. They are usually the preferred method of getting known handwriting specimens because of the high degree of control that the examiner has over their collection. Nonrequested exemplars are already-existing documents that are part of the suspect's everyday correspondence. These are collected instead of requested specimens when the suspect is uncooperative, unavailable, incapacitated, or deceased. They may also be collected along with requested samples for additional comparison purposes when it is suspected that the suspect may be purposefully altering his handwriting. There are rules and guidelines for the collection of requested and nonrequested writings. They are given as follows.

Requested Exemplars

Requested exemplars are sought by an investigator or may be ordered by a court. There is no question of authenticity in these circumstances so admissibility in court is usually not an issue. When exemplars are requested, the circumstances of the session are arranged so that the conditions are as similar to those of the unknown sample as possible. These include, but are not limited to, the following:

- Unless it is known for certain that the questioned document was made when the writer was in an uncomfortable position, the subject should be made as comfortable as possible. The chair, table, and lighting should be optimal.
- The same type and color of writing instrument should be used. This means that, if the questioned document were written with a blue gel pen, for example, so should the exemplar.
- The paper should be the same type (lined or unlined) for both exemplar and unknown.
- The exemplar should always be taken by dictation. The subject is usually not shown the questioned document and is not allowed to copy it. Dictation reduces opportunities to alter handwriting. Remember that the act of handwriting is subconscious. Altering one's handwriting on purpose takes conscious effort. If a passage is dictated, the subject must listen to the words and write them down. This makes it harder to concentrate on disguising the handwriting.
- Sufficient exemplars should be taken. Requesting long passages of handwriting will ensure that a representative sample is being gathered. It also helps to uncover attempts to disguise handwriting. As the length of the passage increases, it becomes increasingly difficult to maintain deliberately altered writing. Eventually, most people will lapse back into their habitual ways of writing.
- Although document examiners recommend that the subject should not see the actual questioned document, it is often helpful to dictate some phrases and sentences from the document. This is especially important where there are misspellings or mistakes in grammar in the questioned document. The subject may repeat these same mistakes in the exemplar.
- Exemplars should be taken in context. If the questioned document is a check, then the subject should be asked to fill out a number of checks (10–20) for various amounts. If the questioned document is a signature on a document, then the subject should be asked to write his or her signature many times on documents similar to the questioned document.

There are inherent disadvantages to requested writings. Foremost is that it calls attention to the fact that the subject's handwriting is at issue and the subject may then be tempted to alter their handwriting. This may also cause the subject to be apprehensive or nervous. These conditions may cause unintended alterations in handwriting. There are also times when it is pretty obvious that the suspect is attempting to disguise handwriting. In order to minimize this activity, there are a number of strategies that can be used. These include taking frequent breaks and even taking the requested writings over several days, challenging the suspect on the abnormal appearance of his handwriting, and using other requested and nonrequested specimens.

Nonrequested Exemplars

Nonrequested writing consists of documents written by the subject for purposes other than the questioned document case. They may be written in the normal course of business or correspondence or documents such as diaries. They are likely to represent the writer's true handwriting. The writer did not write the document with the idea that it may be used as an exemplar or that it was to be part of a criminal or civil action. No emphasis or attention is directed at the writing. Even though nonrequested writings represent the writer's true penmanship, there are also disadvantages to this type of exemplar. First, unless these writings clearly identify the author, it may be difficult to have them introduced as evidence in court. Also, the nonrequested writing will likely not bear any resemblance to the questioned document and may not contain a sufficient number of letter combinations, words or phrases from the questioned document, making comparison more difficult. It is also important that the exemplar and the questioned document be about the same age. Many questioned document examiners prefer that the exemplars consist of a combination of requested and nonrequested samples.

Characteristics Used for Comparison of Handwriting

Handwriting comparisons can be complex and difficult depending upon the characteristics of the unknown specimen and the circumstances surrounding the case. Nonetheless, there are a few basic rules that guide examiners in their analyses. They should be kept in mind at all times:

- No two people have identical handwriting.
- There is a natural variation in a person's writing and that he or she will not write the same letter or number exactly the same way twice. This is one reason why large samples of writings are needed for the examiner to learn the individual's range of variation in his or her writing.
- There is no one single writing characteristic that is so unique by itself, that it will individualize handwriting.
- There is no set number of characteristics that must be present for an examiner to identify the author of a questioned document. As with any type of evidence comparison: There must be sufficient number of similarities between the known and unknown and no unexplainable differences.
- As with other types of pattern evidence, the scientific validity of handwriting comparisons to establish authorship is in dispute as discussed by the NAS Forensic Science Committee.

As with many types of evidence, handwriting contains class characteristics and those that can potentially be used in individualization. Document examiners must make sure that their conclusions about the authenticity or authorship of a questioned document are based on individual characteristics. For example, the *slant* of writing is generally a class characteristic, whereas *unusual flourishes* at the end of words or *ornate capital letters* are individual characteristics. When a questioned document examiner focuses on particular letters or letter combinations, he will generally create a chart that shows several instances of these letters in the known and unknown writing samples to demonstrate the natural variation in the writer's style and the similarity of the characteristic in both documents to the jury at a trial. This type of exhibit is shown in Figure 11.2.

Signatures can be especially problematic for a questioned document examiner. The questioned document may consist entirely of one signature. For example, a fraudulent check may have only the payee, the amount, and the signature on it. Although all of this writing can be used for identification, the key is the signature. The characteristics of one's signature are very sensitive to context and the

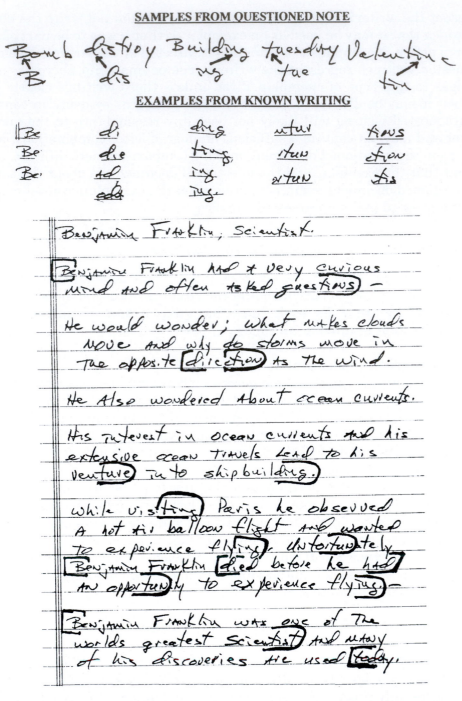

Figure 11.2 A court document prepared by a questioned document examiner showing the comparison of handwriting characteristics from the questioned document and a known sample of the subject's handwriting. (Courtesy of Robert Kullman, Speckin Labs, Okemos, MI.)

exemplars must be taken under conditions that approximate those under which the questioned document was made. Figure 11.3 shows how signatures are compared in a questioned document analysis. For example, if the questioned document is a check, then the requested exemplars would normally consist of a series of blank checks that the suspect would fill out to various payees for various amounts.

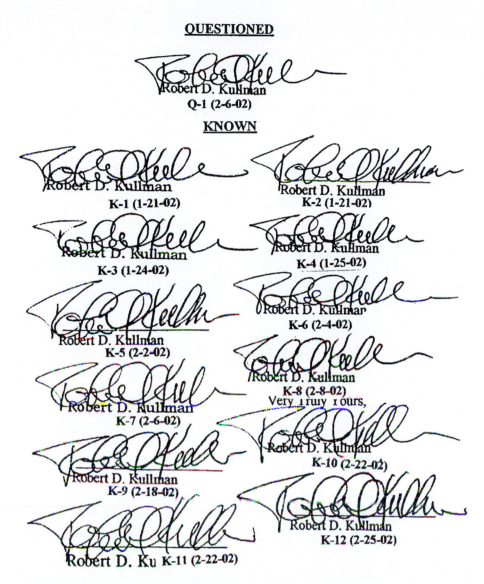

QUESTIONED

KNOWN

Figure 11.3 Comparison of a questioned signature with known signatures. Note that several specimens of the known signature are taken to allow for natural variation in the signature. (Courtesy of Robert Kullman, Speckin Labs, Okemos, MI.)

Fraud and Forgery

There are numerous cases where a forger attempts to mimic or forge another person's handwriting. Forgers will obtain authentic samples of handwriting from an author and then practice writing in the same style until they are proficient. Very often, this will occur with signatures. Unless the forger is an expert, attempts at forgery can usually be uncovered by careful examination of the writing by a questioned document examiner. Of course, when a document such as a check is forged, the merchant who takes the check does not have authentic samples of the real author's handwriting and even if he did, he would most probably not be able to tell that the check was a forgery. Some of the signs of forgery include differences in line quality (e.g., thickness, smoothness), connecting strokes, pen lifts, starts and stops and retouching. Figure 11.4 shows an analysis of a fraudulent document.

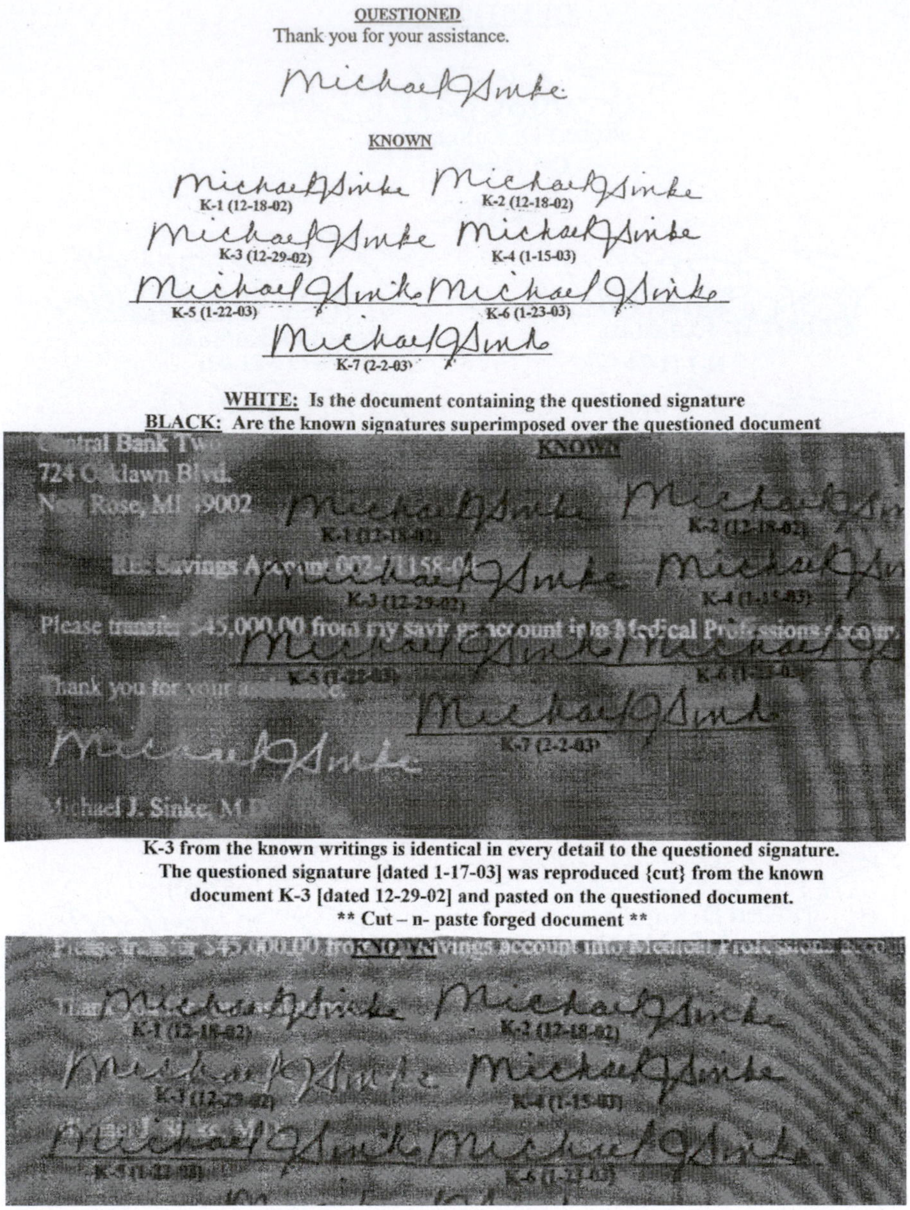

Figure 11.4 This shows how a forged signature can be cut and pasted onto a document, in this case, a letter to a bank. (Courtesy of Robert Kullman, Speckin Labs, Okemos, MI.)

Sometimes, a document forger will resort to *tracing* a sample of someone else's handwriting. This may be accomplished in any of several ways. For example, the forger may put a piece of tracing paper over the document and trace the writing using a sharp object. This will be used as a template for the forged writing. Sometimes, a new document will be placed over the original and the writing directly traced onto the new document.

Something for You to Do—Try Your Hand at Forgery

Take a document with your signature and then place a thin piece of paper over it and trace your signature on the top sheet. Then compare the signatures. When you trace handwriting like this, you invariably do it slowly so that you can capture as many of the handwriting characteristics as possible. Unless you have an extremely steady hand, the line quality of the tracing will be uneven and will look like it has been drawn. These characteristics are very common and questioned document examiners usually have little problem in detecting tracings.

The third and least elegant type of forgery occurs when the forger forgoes any pretense of copying or tracing someone else's handwriting. Instead, he will use his own handwriting, usually disguised, to write the document. Since the merchant receiver of the document will not have ready access to the authentic handwriting of the victim of the forgery, he will not be able to tell that this is a forgery until after the document has been passed.

Erasures, Obliterations, and Alterations

A large number of questioned document cases involve alteration of a document. There are several types of alterations. These include erasures, obliterations, additions, and charring. In addition, a questioned document may be written on the top sheet of a pad of paper and then that sheet is removed and is unavailable to the document examiner. In these cases, it may be possible to determine what was written by visualizing the indented writing that appears on the sheets below the top sheet. See the section on "Indented Writing" below.

Erasures

Erasure involves actually removing writing from a document through mechanical or chemical means. Mechanical erasures are accomplished by rubbing an abrasive material over the writing. If this is done thoroughly, it will be impossible to determine what writing was erased. It is not difficult, however, to determine that an erasure has occurred. Mechanical erasures invariably disturb some of the fibers in the paper and this can be seen with a stereomicroscope. Figure 11.5a shows a mechanical erasure, and Figure 11.5b shows the confirmation of the erasure using ESDA.

Chemical erasers are usually some type of bleaching agent that destroys the dyes in the ink so they are no longer visible. The paper will often be discolored or bleached where the chemical has been applied. Sometimes, the erased area will show up as a different color from the rest of the paper when exposed to infrared or ultraviolet light. Figure 11.6 shows a chemical erasure.

Obliterations

Besides erasure, there are other ways to render handwriting unreadable. It can be crossed out with another writing instrument or completely written over by another writing instrument such as a marking pen. In two cases examined by one of the authors of this book, a questioned document examiner brought some pages of computer printed contracts that had parts obliterated by a black marker. In both cases, his clients wanted to be able to see what was under the obliteration. In one of the cases, the writing was visualized by immersing the document in methyl alcohol. This dissolved enough of the marker to show the writing underneath. The marker on the other document case was resistant to solvents. Instead, some mineral oil was

John Anderson agrees to pay Betsy Wilson
$300.⁰⁰ per month for A LOAN. Payments
start October 1, 2003 And The LOAN will be
PAID in full on March 1, 2006 . LOAN MAy be
PAID off early . —   John Anderson 9/10/03
*   Betsy Wilson 9/10/03.*

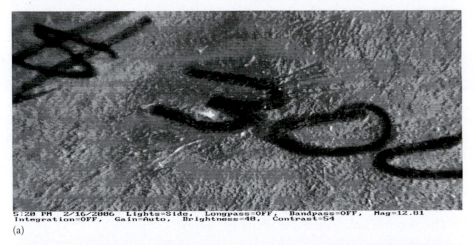

5:20 PM 2/16/2006 Lights=Side, Longpass=OFF, Bandpass=OFF, Mag=12.81
Integration=OFF, Gain=Auto, Brightness=40, Contrast=54

(a)

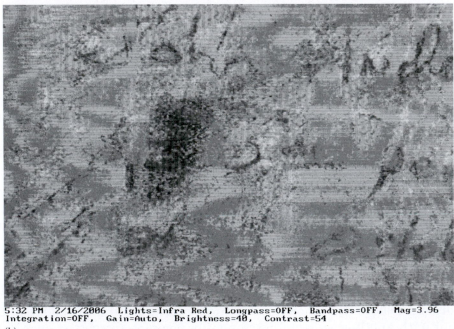

5:32 PM 2/16/2006 Lights=Infra Red, Longpass=OFF, Bandpass=OFF, Mag=3.96
Integration=OFF, Gain=Auto, Brightness=40, Contrast=54

(b)

Figure 11.5 (a) The top part of the figure is a questioned document concerning the payment of $300 per month on a loan. A close-up of the $300 indicates that the area where the "3" is has been altered by erasure. This is confirmed with an electrostatic detection test (ESDA) shown in (b) that clearly shows the area where the "3" is has been erased. (Courtesy of Robert Kullman, Speckin Labs, Okemos, MI.)

Laboratory report: Direct light   Laboratory report: Ultra-violet light

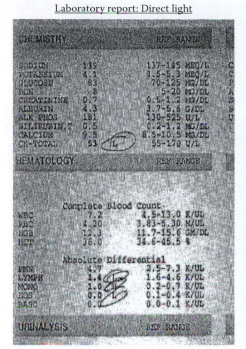 

Figure 11.6 This is an altered medical laboratory report. On the right side of the report, shown under ultraviolet light, there are two chemical erasure spots. The small one was a "3" and the larger one was a "H" with a circle around it. (Courtesy of Robert Kullman, Speckin Labs, Okemos, MI.)

added to wet the document and then a strong light was shined through the marker. The obliterated printing could be seen (backwards) on the back side of the document. This was held up to a mirror and photographed. In some cases, writing that has been crossed out with another writing instrument can be successfully recovered using infrared or ultraviolet light. If the ink used to cross out the document is transparent to the light, one can "see" through it to the writing below. This is shown in Figure 11.7, which is a draft card with the signature altered. The altered signature is transparent in the infrared light so that the real signature can be seen.

Another type of obliteration occurs when an attempt is made to destroy a document by burning. This can be done purposefully or accidentally as in cases of a house fire where documents are damaged. If the document is not completely burned up, it may be charred. This blackens the paper making it difficult to see the writing. Fortunately, some inks and pencil leads will burn more slowly than paper and the writing may be preserved and viewed under a strong or oblique light. Some charred writing is shown in Figure 11.8.

Indented Writing

Indented writing occurs when someone writes a document on the top sheet of a pad of paper. If the pressure of the writing instrument on the paper is great enough, an image of the writing can be seen in the sheets underneath the top page. Sometimes, TV shows or movies depict the restoration of indented writing by having someone lightly rub the indented writing with the side of a pencil lead. Not only does this not work, but it also destroys the evidence so that tests that do work cannot be used. One way that sometimes works is to shine a desk lamp on the indented writing at an oblique angle. Then the writing can be photographed. Oblique lighting is shown in Figure 11.9.

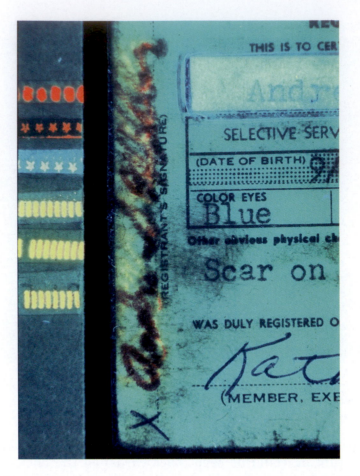

Figure 11.7 The altered signature in this draft card can be seen using ultraviolet light.

Figure 11.8 The lettering on this document can be clearly seen even though an attempt was made to burn the paper.

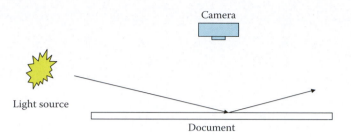

Figure 11.9 This shows how oblique lighting can be used to examine indented writing in a document.

Something for You to Do—Amaze Your Friends!

Get a pad of notebook paper (lined or unlined). Have someone else (it's not fair to do it yourself) write a message in pen or pencil on the top page. Do not tell them the purpose of doing this. Tell them to tear off the top page and hide it from you. Take a goose neck lamp or desk lamp if you have one or a large flashlight and hold it at a steep, oblique angle to the next sheet on the pad as shown in Figure 11.9. You should be able to read the indented writing on this page. It may help to turn out all of the lights in the room except for the one you are shining on the paper. You can then tell the writer what the message said. If the pen or pencil pressure was hard enough, you may be able to read the writing on the third page in the pad. Do not use heavy weight stationary or computer paper for this as the indentation may be too slight to read.

A great improvement in the detection of indented writing is the *electrostatic detection apparatus* (ESDA). This instrument is capable of recovering indented writing several pages under the original. ESDA takes advantage of the fact that a document that is charged with static electricity will build up greater charge within the furrows of the indentations in the paper, even microscopic ones. In practice, the document is laid on a flat platen on the ESDA. It is covered with a clear plastic sheet to protect it. The plastic is made to adhere tightly to the document by a vacuum applied from below. Next, a wand charged with high-voltage electricity is passed over the plastic sheet, imparting a high static charge to the plastic sheet and the document. Then a fine mist of toner, similar to copier toner, is applied to the charged plastic sheet. Particles of the toner are attracted to the sheet in general, but more so to the furrows of the indented writing. Thus, the toner forms an image of the indented writing. This can be photographed or a sticky sheet of plastic laid on top of the toner to capture it permanently. Figure 11.10a shows a note given to a bank teller during a robbery. Figure 11.10b shows indented writing recovered by ESDA from the sheet underneath the extortion letter.

ESDA also has other uses besides reading indented writing. Sometimes, a questioned document examiner may be confronted with a document that has two overlapping strokes usually made by two different writing instruments. The question here is which stroke was made first. One of the authors of this book has been asked to examine several such cases in connection with student cheating on exams. In a typical case, students would be called upon to do problems in a space provided underneath the question on an exam. If the student left the answer space blank, then the grader was instructed to put a red ink slash through the empty space. The exam would be returned to the student who would then fill in an answer in that space and then question the instructor about why their answer

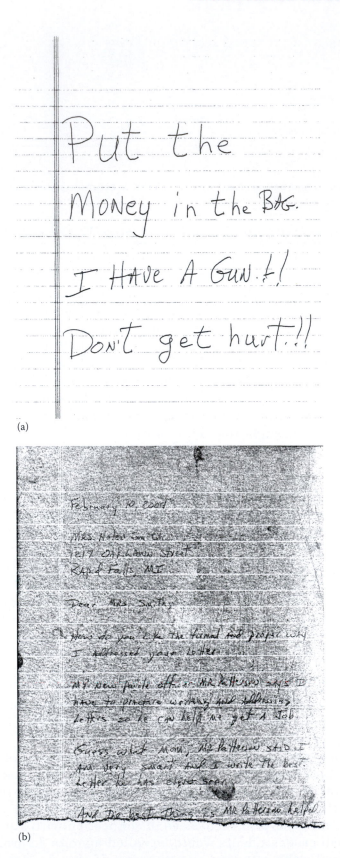

Figure 11.10 (a) A much better way to examine indented writing is by ESDA. This note was given to a bank teller during a robbery. (b) This is what was recovered on the paper that the note was written on. This writing was made on the sheet above this one in the pad and the writing was indented into the page containing the robbery note. An ESDA machine. (Courtesy of Robert Kullman, Speckin Labs, Okemos, MI.)

Figure 11.12 Characteristics of typewriter type. The flaws in the "E" from this typewriter can be clearly seen and are common to the document and the typewriter ribbon. (Courtesy of Robert Kullman, Speckin Labs, Okemos, MI.)

and held in those regions where there is a static charge. The rest of the toner falls away. The paper is then passed over the drum. The toner is transferred to the paper and then heat is applied to fuse the toner to the paper. Under normal circumstances, it is not possible to individualize a document to a particular printer. There may be circumstances where individual markings are deposited on paper when copies are made. For example, the device that feeds the paper into the machine leaves *grabber marks* on the paper. These may yield information about the make and perhaps the model of the copier. As the copier is used, toner may build up in areas of the cylinder or in some cases, there may be toner gaps. These can then leave unique markings on each copy made by that machine. Once the machine is cleaned, these will usually go away. There may also develop mechanical defects in the cylinder or camera that cause permanent unique markings to be deposited on copies.

Computer printers come in a variety of types. The first ones were of the *dot-matrix* type that deposited letters on paper in a similar fashion to typewriters except much faster. Today, computer printers are chiefly of two types: *laser printers* and *ink jet printers*. Laser printers work very much like photocopiers. They use similar toners and lasers to help with the deposition and fusing processes. They are very fast printers. Ink jet printers literally spray ink on the paper in the form of letters, numbers, and symbols. The solvent in the ink evaporates rapidly, leaving the dyes behind. Modern technology has resulted in the development of very reliable printers that seldom have defects and thus, do not exhibit individual characteristics very often.

Paper Examination

There are some questioned document cases where the issue is whether a multipage document has had pages added to it after the original document was written. A will or contract falls into this category. If the document is handwritten, then there may be differences in the characteristics of the writing or writing instrument. If the document is printed, there may not be any obvious differences in the printing but there may be differences in the paper. Even though papers may all look the same, there are chemical and physical differences between them. Some papers contain fillers that help improve color and appearance. Some papers are coated to facilitate printing. Sizing agents are added to help keep ink from penetrating into the paper. Chemical tests can be performed on paper to identify these additives, but they are mostly destructive and therefore cannot be done on questioned documents.

Nondestructive physical examinations may also be done on paper. Even though different papers may be nominally 8.5 × 11 in., there may be slight, but consistent differences from paper to paper that careful measurements can reveal. Likewise, the thickness of papers may be slightly different, although these differences are in the thousandths of inches and measurements must be made with a special paper micrometer.

Ink Examinations

Ink examinations may be used to help identify the writing instrument or even to help determine how old a document or part of a document is. Identification of the writing instrument may be accomplished by analysis of the dyes in the ink. The United States Secret Service maintains a library of more than 5000 ink samples that can be compared to a sample from a questioned document.

The questioned document examiner must not deface the document when taking ink samples. There are tools available that can punch out a hole in a document that is smaller in diameter than the width of a pen stroke. This way samples can be taken of the ink in a document without ruining the writing or unduly defacing the document. One of the more popular methods for analyzing ink samples is thin layer chromatography. Ink plugs from the questioned document can be compared against those from the writing instrument in question. A thin layer chromatogram of ink samples is shown in Figure 11.13.

Document dating using the characteristics of ink writing is becoming more common as methods of analysis have improved. There are basically two types of cases where this comes into play. The first involves a series of dated writings made on the same document at different times. An example of this is patient's medical chart where the doctor makes entries each time the patient is examined. In medical

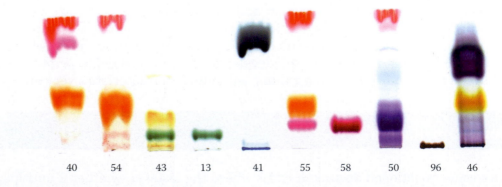

40   54   43   13   41   55   58   50   96   46

Figure 11.13 This TLC plate shows 10 pens. All off the dyes in the pens are different and the pens can be easily distinguished.

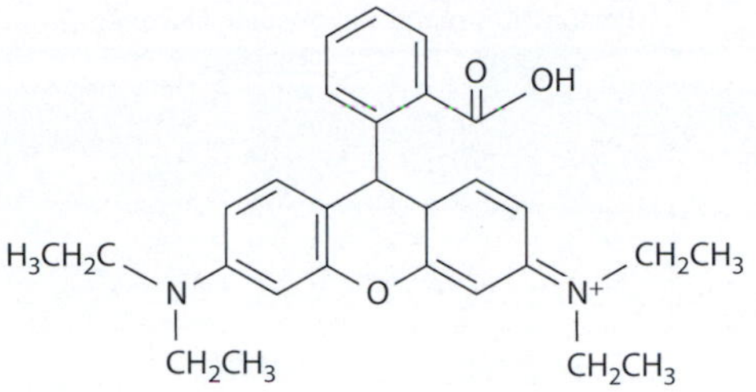

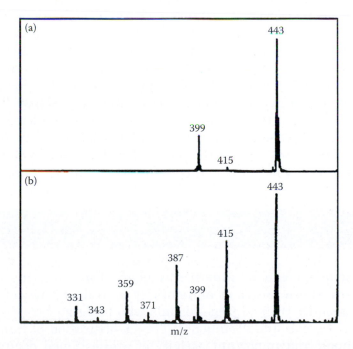

Figure 11.14 The structure of rhodamine B, a common dye in pens.

malpractice cases, the issue of when a particular entry was made in the record can be important evidence. The entry may have a date on it and the examiner would want to know if this entry was made after the one before it in the record and before the one after it. In other cases, the age of the entire document may be at issue. This may be a matter of determining whether the dyes used in the writing ink existed at the time that the document was purported to have been written. For example, the dye *crystal violet* was introduced into blue ballpoint pens in about 1956. If a document was written with this dye and purports to be written in 1940, this is clearly fraud. The United States Secret Service ink database contains starting and ending dates of manufacture for all of the inks in its library.

Recently, new methods have been developed for determining the age of an ink sample by tracking the degradation of certain dyes as the ink ages. One method for doing this is *laser desorption mass spectrometry* (LDMS). In this technique, a laser is used to drive molecules of ink off the surface of a document. The molecules are ionized and separated in a mass spectrometer. As the dye ages due to light and oxygen, it degrades into smaller molecules. This process can be roughly correlated with time. One common example of this is the LDMS of rhodamine B in ballpoint pens. The structure of this dye is shown in Figure 11.14. Note that there are four ethyl

Figure 11.15 Mass spectra of partially aged rhodamine B: (a) a relatively new sample of ink and (b) a sample that has aged for many months or years. Each of the major, lower weight peaks represents the replacement of successive ethyl groups (MW = 29) with a hydrogen (AW = 1). (Courtesy of John Allison.)

Perforation match on postage stamps

Figure 11.16 Physical match with stamps. The way that the torn perforations in the stamps line up can be seen clearly. This is a very old case as can be seen by the postage (10 cents) on the stamps!

(–CH$_2$–CH$_3$) groups on this molecule. As it ages, the dye successively loses these groups and they are replaced by hydrogen atoms (–H). The mass spectrum loses 28 mass units each time a methyl group is lost. Figure 11.15 shows the mass spectrum of this dye. The mass spectrum shows how this dye degrades.

Physical Matches on Torn Paper

In a questioned document analysis, torn paper is evidence in a surprising number of cases. For example, a piece of paper may be torn in half and a document may be written on one of the halves. A piece of paper may be torn out of a spiral notebook, leaving jagged edges on the torn paper and on the remnants that are often left enmeshed within the metal spirals. Papers such as rolls of stamps may contain perforations that have irregular edges where the stamps have been torn off. One such case occurred many years ago when someone sent a series of threatening letters to a U.S. Senator, who saved the letters and envelopes and turned them over to the FBI. The stamps on the letters were collected. When a suspect was identified, a search warrant was executed for his home and a roll of stamps was seized. The perforations on the stamp at the end of the roll and on the stamps on the letters were all compared and it was determined that the stamps on the letters came off of that roll of stamps. Figure 11.16 shows some of the physical matches made on the stamps. You can see that this is a very old case as the stamps cost only 10 cents!

Summary

A questioned document can be almost any object that contains handwritten or printed characters whose source or authenticity is in doubt. Questioned document examiners are specially trained professionals who undergo a 2–3 year apprenticeship to learn how to examine documents. The identification of handwriting is the single most common and important activity of a questioned document examiner. The key to being able to successfully compare handwriting is to have sufficient, high-quality known samples (exemplars). These can be requested from the subject or be nonrequested samples taken from the subject's correspondence.

Handwriting is learned at an early age and quickly becomes an internalized, subconscious activity. At this point, people develop their own, unique style of handwriting. If a sufficient number of these characteristics are present in a questioned document and exemplar, then the document examiner may conclude that the handwriting was written by the subject.

In addition to the comparison of handwritings, document examiners compare type writings, photocopier copies, and computer printed documents. They also examine erasures and obliterations as well as indented writings. Besides writing and printing, questioned document examiners are called upon to compare samples of paper and ink.

Test Yourself

Multiple Choice

1. Which of the following is not a good practice in taking requested handwriting exemplars?
   a. Collect a lot of writing samples
   b. Have the subject copy the questioned document
   c. Use the same type of writing implement and paper as the questioned document
   d. Dictate the requested exemplar
2. Which of the following is not an example of a questioned document?
   a. A forged passport
   b. A stolen traveler's check
   c. A copy of a 10 dollar bill made in a photocopier
   d. A threatening message written in spray paint on the side of someone's house
   e. All of the above are examples of a questioned document
3. Which of the following is not true of a questioned document examiner?
   a. They can learn their craft solely by getting a college degree in questioned document examination
   b. They usually perform a 2–3 year apprenticeship with a practicing questioned document examiner
   c. There is an opportunity for a questioned document examiner to achieve certification after training
   d. Questioned document examiners do not have to have a college degree to become certified.
4. Which of the following is not an acceptable method for revealing indented writing?
   a. Oblique lighting
   b. Intense lighting
   c. Rubbing with a pencil lead
   d. ESDA
5. Which of the following method is used for the comparison of ink samples?
   a. Gas chromatography
   b. Thin-layer chromatography
   c. Infrared spectrophotometry
   d. Fluorescence spectroscopy

6. In the Mormon will case, discussed at the beginning of the chapter, one of the characteristics of the will that indicated that it was not Howard Hughes writing was
   a. Written in a forced, halting manner
   b. Written in pencil
   c. Entirely handwritten
   d. Not signed

7. Which of the following is not true of handwriting?
   a. It changes throughout life
   b. It is not affected by drugs or alcohol
   c. It is a subconscious behavior
   d. It can change with the context of the writing

8. Which of the following practices of collecting exemplars will help to minimize the chance of the writer deliberately altering his writing?
   a. Have the subject stand up while writing
   b. Always use lined paper to make sure that the subject writes in straight lines
   c. Dictate long passages
   d. Show the subject the questioned document

9. ESDA is used mainly for
   a. Identifying ink
   b. Determining that a document is a photocopy
   c. Determining the age of a handwritten document
   d. Reading indented writing

10. Which of the following is most likely to develop individual characteristics when it is used a lot?
    a. Typewriting
    b. Photocopying
    c. Dot-matrix printing
    d. Laser-jet printing

True or False

11. Over writing can always be detected by oblique lighting.
12. Identification of the writing on a charred document depends upon the observation that ink and lead burn slower than paper.
13. The age of a document can be estimated by determining the degree of chemical degradation of the ink used to write it.
14. It is not possible to determine if writing has been mechanically erased.
15. Specialized lighting such as infrared or ultraviolet can be used to uncover attempts to alter a document by addition of extra numbers or letters.
16. A nonrequest exemplar is one that already exists at the time of the questioned document case.

Short Essay

17. Explain the difference between request and nonrequest exemplars. When would one want to use nonrequest exemplars?
18. What is indented writing? How is it analyzed?
19. Under what conditions, if any, can a document made by a typewriter be individualized to a particular machine?

Matching: Match Each Term with its Definition

20. ESDA   a. Method of teaching printing
21. Chemical erasure   b. A type of angular lighting
22. Palmer method   c. A method for uncovering indented writing
23. Oblique lighting   d. A device that prints documents using mechanically
                                            struck keys
24. Grabber marks   e. Obliterates writing by bleaching ink
25. Typewriter   f. Made on paper by copier

Further Reading

Brunelle, R. L. (2002). Questioned document examination, in *Forensic Science Handbook*, vol. 1, 2nd edn., R. Saferstein, ed. Prentice Hall, Upper Saddle River, NJ.

Hilton, O. (1982). *Scientific Examination of Questioned Documents*, 2nd ed. Elsevier, New York.

Osborne, A. S. (1929). *Questioned Documents*, 2nd edn. Boyd Printing Company, Albany, NY.

On the Web

A great site for viewing classic typewriters: http://staff.xu.edu/~polt/typewriters/index.html.

Newspaper account of how the CIA used questioned documents in a case linking Iraq to uranium ore: http://www.commondreams.org/headlines03/0322-04.htm.

Use of stereomicroscopy and specialized lighting to detect overwriting: http://www.youtube.com/watch?v=qSF4ENiQeek.

Website of the American Society of Questioned Document Examiners: http://www.asqde.org/.

12
Firearms and Toolmarks

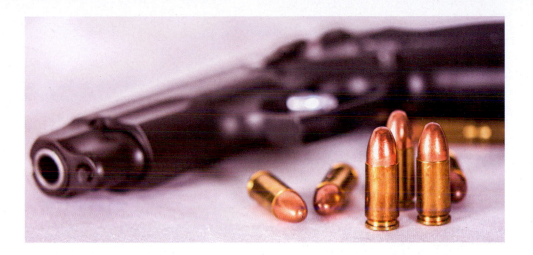

Learning Objectives

1. To be able to define toolmark analysis and toolmarks
2. To be able to define firearms analysis
3. To be able to define rifling and how it arises in weapons
4. To be able to list the various types of weapons
5. To be able to define and give examples of stria
6. To be able to describe the various types of markings left on bullets and cartridges by weapons
7. To be able to describe how bullets and cartridges are matched to particular weapons
8. To be able to describe the various types of propellants and primers used in weapons
9. To be able to describe how distance-of-firing determinations are made with weapons
10. To be able to describe other types of toolmarks
11. To be able to describe how serial number restorations are accomplished and the principle behind them.

Chapter 12
Firearms and Toolmarks

Mini Glossary

Ballistics: The study of projectiles in motion.

Caliber: The bore diameter of a rifled gun barrel.

DRUGFIRE: A database of fired cartridge cases developed by the FBI in 2002.

Firearms identification: A category of toolmark identification in which the examiner matches fired bullets, cartridge cases, or other ammunition components to a specific firearm.

Gauge: A way of measuring the bore diameter of a shotgun based on the number of solid spheres of a diameter equal to the inside diameter of the barrel that could be made from a pound of lead.

Groove: The curved track machined into the barrel of a firearm that causes the bullet to spin upon exit from the barrel.

GSR: An acronym for gunshot residue, which is the burned and unburned gunpowder that exits the firearm after the bullet.

IBIS: An acronym for Integrated Ballistics Identification System, a database developed by the Bureau of Alcohol, Tobacco, Firearms and Explosives to compare markings on fired bullets.

Land: The part of a gun barrel that is untouched by the machining process that cuts the grooves into the barrel.

NIBIN: An acronym for National Integrated Ballistic Information Network, a database that combined the FBI's DRUGFIRE database of cartridge casings and the ATF's IBIS database of fired bullets.

Rifling: The cutting of curved grooves in a firearm barrel during the manufacturing process. Rifled barrels impart spin on fired bullets that increases stability and accuracy in flight.

Stippling: Small, dry, reddish orange abrasions on skin or small, black specks on objects caused by unburned powder and small metal fragments from a discharged firearm.

Toolmark: A scratch or other microscopic marking left by the action of a tool on an object when the two come into contact.

Twist: A term used in bullet identification that refers to the direction of the grooves impressed into the fired bullet by the lands in the gun barrel.

Acronyms

ATF: Bureau of Alcohol, Tobacco, Firearms and Explosives
GSR: Gunshot residue
IBIS: Integrated Ballistics Identification System
NIBIN: National Integrated Ballistic Information Network

Case Study

Bartolomeo Vanzetti and Nicola Sacco handcuffed in 1923

On Friday, April 15, 1920, in South Braintree, Massachusetts, two men robbed two security guards who were delivering payroll money to the Slater and Morrill Shoe Factory. During the robbery, both guards were fatally wounded by gunshots from the robbers. The robbers then drove off in a black car with the payroll boxes containing $16,000. Later, police recovered the stolen getaway car and recovered six cartridges from the crime scene. These were later traced back to three ammunition manufacturers: Remington, Peters, and Winchester. Because the same car was implicated in an earlier robbery, the investigation focused on a known thug named Mike Boda. However, he had already fled to Italy by the time the payroll robbery took place. Police then arrested two of Boda's known associates, Italian laborers Nicola Sacco and Bartolomeo Vanzetti. At the time of their arrest, both were carrying guns and Sacco's was the same caliber, .32 Colt automatic, as the murder weapon. Sacco was also carrying ammunition made by the same three manufacturers.

Sacco and Vanzetti were tried for the payroll robbery and the murder of one of the security guards. Four bullets had been recovered from the dead guards and experts for the prosecution and defense were retained to determine whether Sacco's .32 Colt pistol was the murder weapon. Not surprisingly, the prosecution experts, though somewhat in disagreement, testified on the whole that Sacco's gun was the murder weapon. The defense experts testified that it was not. It is noteworthy that none of the experts based their opinions on any scientific analysis. None had any formal training in firearms examinations. Ultimately, the jury found Sacco and Vanzetti guilty. They based their opinion in large part on the fact that the bullets that killed the guard were so old and outdated that no one could locate any others except in the possession of Sacco. During the trial, the jurors were furnished with magnifying glasses so that they could view the markings on the bullets.

There was an immediate cry to have the verdict overturned and to set a new trial. The defense hired Albert Hamilton who stated that the murder weapon was definitely not Sacco's, but Hamilton had no real experience or expertise from which to draw these conclusions. Hamilton was a controversial character who had a reputation as someone who would testify to anything he was paid for: a hired gun. The prosecution's expert, Charles Van Amburgh, re-examined the bullet evidence and stuck to his opinion that Sacco's gun fired the fatal bullets. At a hearing to determine whether a retrial was needed, Hamilton brought another gun into court that was the same make and model as Sacco's and tried to exchange the barrels of the two weapons! He was caught by the judge who subsequently denied the motion for a retrial. In 1927, a committee of expert firearms examiners examined the bullet and cartridge evidence and concurred with the prosecution. Even the defense's new expert agreed. Sacco and Vanzetti were executed for the murder. The evidence was re-examined in 1961 and again in 1983 and both supported the conclusions of the 1927 panel. In 1977, however, the governor of Massachusetts issued a proclamation that Sacco and Vanzetti were innocent! The case remains controversial today.

Protests over the guilty verdict and
death sentence for Sacco and Venzetti.

Introduction

This chapter is about toolmarks. A *toolmark* is a scratch or other microscopic marking left by the action of a tool on an object. Toolmarks are created when a metal tool comes in contact with another hard surface. Examples of toolmarks include the microscopic impressions left by the blade of a wire cutter on the end of a cut wire and the scrapings of the edge of a screwdriver left on a door jamb during an attempted break-in. A major part of the science of *firearms identification* also involves the analysis of toolmarks. In many guns, a tool is used to ream out the barrel. These toolmarks are then transferred to the surface of any bullet fired through the barrel. Other markings are left on cartridge cases as a bullet is fired. Tools that made the parts of the weapon that come into contact with the cartridge originally made these markings. Each time the object comes in contact with the tool, the microscopic markings on the tool surface change and becomes more unique. It may develop more scratches, nicks, or other wear patterns. These individual characteristics are then transferred to the subsequent metal object the tool contacts.

The reader should keep in mind the conclusions of the Forensic Science Committee of the National Academy of Sciences in its 2009 report. The Committee cautioned that the underlying principle of individuality ascribed to such evidence types as firearms and toolmarks, as well as fingerprints, handwriting, shoeprints, and tire treads, has not been scientifically validated. Since the report came out, new research is being done to establish this validity. More information on the NAS report can be found in Chapters 1 and 3.

Firearms Identification

Trafficking of illegal firearms and the commission of crimes using firearms remain two of the most serious problems in American society today. In 2002, the Bureau of Alcohol, Tobacco, Firearms and Explosives reported that over 80,000 weapons were sold illegally in the United States and nearly 2,000 people were charged with selling guns illegally. As the population ages in the United States, the number of crimes has stabilized or been reduced and this is reflected in the stability in recent years in the number of offenses in which a firearm was used. It is currently about 350,000 per year.

The science of firearms identification covers a number of related disciplines. Most people are aware that bullets and cartridges can be traced back to a particular weapon under certain circumstances and this is a major part of the firearms examiner's job. Examiners also determine whether a particular firearm can be fired. This comes into play when a firearm has been deliberately disabled or modified or when a gun is fished out of a creek or lake. Firearms examiners may also be called upon to estimate the distance from which a bullet or shotgun pellet(s) was fired. *Serial number restorations* on firearms and other objects are often the jobs of a firearms examiner. Some firearms examiners also analyze gunshot residue (GSR) from hands or other objects to determine whether that person recently fired a weapon. In many crime labs, the trace evidence section of the lab carries out this activity. In recent years, most forensic science laboratories have ceased to perform GSR analysis because of difficulties in interpreting a positive result.

Ballistics is often used as a synonym for firearms examination. This is a misnomer because *ballistics* is defined as the study of projectiles in motion. These projectiles can range from bullets to baseballs to rocket ships. Firearms examiners are interested in ballistics as part of their knowledge because they must understand the characteristics of bullets and shot gun pellets as they are fired by a weapon and reach their target. But a firearm examiner additionally studies the toolmarks left behind on fired ammunition to match a weapon to a crime. Firearms examiners also work with forensic pathologists in the area of *wound ballistics*, the study of patterns of injury caused by firearm projectiles.

Types of Firearms

There are a bewildering variety of firearms on the market today and precise definitions are often elusive. Firearms examiners generally characterize weapons into one of five categories:

1. *Pistols*: These are also sometimes called *handguns* because they were originally designed to be operated with one hand. Pistols are in turn divided into two subcategories:
   a. *Revolvers*: These are pistols that contain revolving cylinders with chambers that hold individual *live rounds* (bullets plus cartridge cases). As the weapon is cocked, the next chamber comes into line with the *firing pin* and barrel. After the bullet is fired, the cartridge case remains in the cylinder and must be manually removed.
   b. *Self-loading*: These pistols are usually loaded with a *magazine* that contains a number of bullets. The magazine is loaded into the grip of the gun and the bullets are fed into the firing chamber by a spring load. The cartridge casings are extracted and ejected from the chamber automatically after firing.
2. *Rifles*: Rifles are similar to pistols but are made to be operated with two hands. There are a large number of different types that range from single shot to automatic rifles.
3. *Machine guns*: These are fully automatic weapons that obtain their ammunition from magazines or belts. These weapons produce heavy recoil when fired and cannot be safely fired by holding with two hands. They must have a fixed mounting.
4. *Submachine guns*: These weapons are like machine guns but are meant to be hand held.
5. *Shotguns*: Shotguns differ from the other four types of weapons in that they do not fire bullets. Instead, they fire a range of ammunition, such as shotgun shells or single slugs. Shotgun shell ammunition, such as buckshot and birdshot, consists of plastic cartridges which contain small, usually round, pellets. Because shotguns do not fire bullets, they are not rifled.

Rifling

When a quarterback throws a football to a receiver, he lets the ball fall from his fingertips as he throws. This imparts a spin to the ball along its long axis. This spinning motion imparts angular momentum to the ball, which keeps the ball on its intended trajectory. The consequences of the failure to impart spin to a projectile are put to good advantage by a knuckleball pitcher in baseball. The pitcher throws the ball purposefully without spin using his knuckles to grip the ball. Without the spin, the ball is subject to air resistance and will travel toward the batter with an unpredictable trajectory. This makes the ball much harder to hit because the batter does not know where the ball is going. Neither does the catcher who often will be unable to catch a knuckleball.

When someone fires a weapon at a target, he would like to ensure that the bullet has the best chance to hit where it is aimed. This means that the bullet must be made to spin on its long axis as it emerges from the barrel of the weapon. This is accomplished by manufacturing the barrel of the weapon so that rifling is incorporated. The rifling process bores the inside of a gun barrel from one end to the other, producing a series of *lands* and *grooves*. When the barrel is manufactured, a tool such as a rifling button or gang broach is used to dig grooves into the inner surface of the barrel. Figure 12.1 is a diagram of the barrel of a weapon showing the lands and grooves. Figure 12.2 shows one of the metal tools used by a gun manufacturer to make the grooves in a gun barrel.

The grooves are dug in a spiral fashion. Each groove spirals as it travels through the barrel. Between each groove is a raised area called a land. *Rifling* is similar to a series of hills and valleys. The valleys are grooves in the earth and between each valley is a hill (land). There may be an odd or even number of lands and grooves. The numbers range from two to nine of each.

The *number* of lands and grooves, the *direction* of their *twist* through the barrel and the *angle* of twist are all class characteristics that can give valuable information to the firearms examiner about the manufacturer and model of the weapon. The twist of the lands and grooves is noted as a right twist (clockwise) or left

Figure 12.1 Lands and grooves in a rifled barrel. This view looks through the barrel toward the trigger. Note the spiral shapes of the lands and grooves. (Courtesy of David Brundage, Indiana Forensic Services Agency, Marion, IN.)

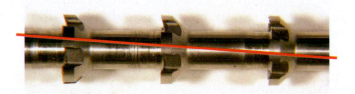

Figure 12.2 Rifling broach for gun barrel. Note the downward path to the notches that carve the grooves in the barrel. This imparts the twist in the bullet. (Photo courtesy of www.precisionforensictesting.com.)

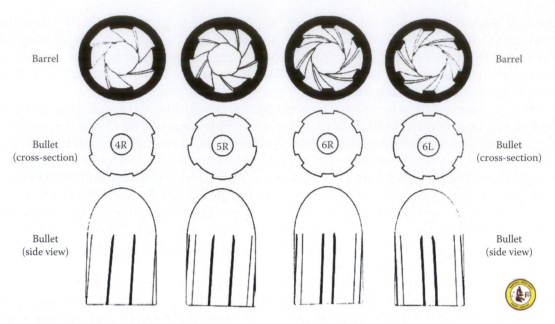

Figure 12.3 Some class characteristics of firearms. The barrel imparts lands and grooves to the sides of the bullets. The number of lands and grooves as well as the angle and direction of twist are class characteristics. (Courtesy of David Brundage, Indiana Forensic Services Agency, Marion, IN.)

twist (counterclockwise). Figure 12.3 shows some of these class characteristics. Note that the *groove* in the barrel makes a *land* in the bullet and a *land* in the barrel makes a *groove* in the bullet. Also note that the number and letter in the bullet drawing represent the number of lands or grooves and the direction of twist. For example, 4R means 4 lands or grooves with a right twist.

The broach or button that makes the lands and grooves is a tool. Its cutting surfaces contain microscopic imperfections made by the tools used to manufacture them. These microscopic markings are transferred to the surfaces of the lands and grooves during the manufacture of the barrel. When the bullet is fired, it will pick up not only the lands and grooves but the microscopic imperfections. These usually appear as tiny striations or stria in the lands and grooves and are shown in Figures 12.4 and 12.5, which is a comparison of the stria in two bullets under a comparison microscope. Striations impart individuality (individual characteristics) to the bullet and aid in the identification of a match between a test-fired bullet and one taken from the crime scene.

If the proper size ammunition is used in a rifled weapon, the bullet expands due to the heat of the gunpowder being ignited. The bullet expands into the grooves and follows them like tracks as it exits the barrel. Because the grooves spiral through the barrel, the bullet spins as it leaves the barrel. Each land in the barrel will dig a groove in the side of the bullet. Each groove in the barrel will become a land in the bullet. Thus, the number of lands and grooves, the angle, and direction of twist can all be determined by examining the fired bullet. The lands and grooves of the bullet contain the stria that are present in the barrel's lands and grooves.

Size of Ammunition and Barrels

The size of rifled firearms is described by their *caliber* or bore diameter. To find the bore diameter of a rifled barrel, the distance from opposing lands is measured.

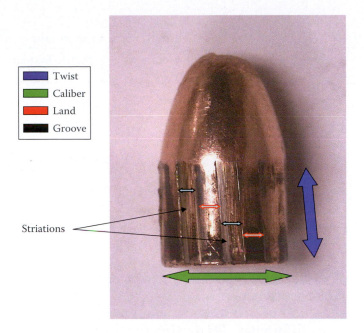

Figure 12.4 Class and individual characteristics of a fired bullet. (Courtesy of www.precisionforensic testing.com.)

Figure 12.5 A photomicrograph showing comparison of bullet stria. The vertical line near the left side of the picture is the dividing line between the two bullets. (Courtesy of David Brundage, Indiana Forensic Services Agency, Marion, IN.)

If there is an odd number of lands and they do not oppose each other, the bore diameter is the diameter of a circle that touches the tops of the lands. Caliber is no longer used to describe the size of a barrel. It is now used to describe the size of a particular cartridge case or the base of a fired bullet. In the United States, this is the diameter of the base of the cartridge case or bullet measured in hundreds or thousandths of

TABLE 12.1
Common Calibers of Guns with the Bore Diameters in Inches and in Millimeters

Gun Barrel Caliber	English System Measurement (in.)	Metric System Measurement (mm)
22 caliber	0.22	5.56
25 caliber	0.25	6.35
30 caliber	0.30	7.62
32 caliber	0.32	7.65
38 caliber	0.38	9.00
9 mm caliber	0.38	9.00
40 caliber	0.40	10.0
45 caliber	0.45	11.25

inches (millimeters in Europe). Table 12.1 shows typical gun calibers in both metric and English system measurements.

Because shotguns do not use bullets, the size of the barrel and the ammunition are measured differently. Many shotgun barrels are constricted by the maker to produce a choke. This narrows the barrel so that the pellets are kept in a tight grouping as they leave the barrel. As they travel toward the target, the pellets will naturally tend to spread out in a cone pattern. The choke reduces the diameter of the cone at any given distance so that the pellets will form a smaller pattern at the target. The diameter of the shotgun barrel is called its *gauge*. The gauge is a measure of the number of pellets weighing 1 lb that would have the same diameter as the barrel if they were grouped in a circular pattern. For example, 12 lead pellets that together weigh 1 lb would have the same diameter as a 12-gauge shotgun. Figure 12.6 shows a typical shotgun cartridge with lead pellets.

Figure 12.6 Shotgun ammunition. (Courtesy of www.precisionforensictesting.com.)

Anatomy of a Live Round (Cartridge)

Figure 12.7 is a diagram of a live round or cartridge. A cartridge is made up of a bullet that fits into the top of a cartridge case. It is held in place by a series of small grooves that circle the bullet near the base. These are called cannelures. Bullets come in three types:

1. *Lead (or lead alloy)*: Originally, all bullets were made of nearly pure lead. When the technology of propellants improved to increase velocity, bullets became hotter and the soft lead had a tendency to foul the inside of the barrel, so antimony is usually added as an alloy to harden the lead.
2. *Fully jacketed bullets*: These bullets have a layer of copper, brass, or steel that completely girdles the base. This hardens the bullet but reduces its expansion upon firing. Jacketed bullets will also usually not pick up as much detail in the lands and grooves as lead bullets.
3. *Half-jacketed bullets*: These bullets have a jacket around only half the bullet. Usually this is the base of the bullet. The nose is exposed.

Figure 12.8 shows some common types of bullets for comparison.

There are many variations of the types of bullets, including hollow points, Teflon-coated (armor piercing), and exploding bullets. Cartridge cases are made of brass, nickel-plated brass, or aluminum. They come in a variety of shapes to accommodate different types of firearms. Like bullets, cartridge cases may have cannelures impressed into their surfaces. These keep the bullet from being pushed too far down into the casing. Figure 12.9 shows the three types of cartridge cases.

The heads of some cartridge cases contain markings stamped into the surface. These can reveal the manufacturer and/or the caliber. Other markings on cartridge cases can be imparted by extractors and ejectors in the case of self-loading pistols as well as firing pin impressions and breech face markings. Some of these markings on a cartridge cases are shown in Figure 12.10a and b.

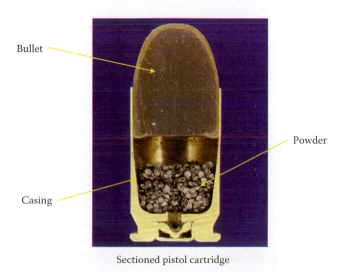

Sectioned pistol cartridge

Figure 12.7 A diagram of a live round, also called a cartridge. (Courtesy of David Brundage, Indiana Forensic Services Agency, Marion, IN.)

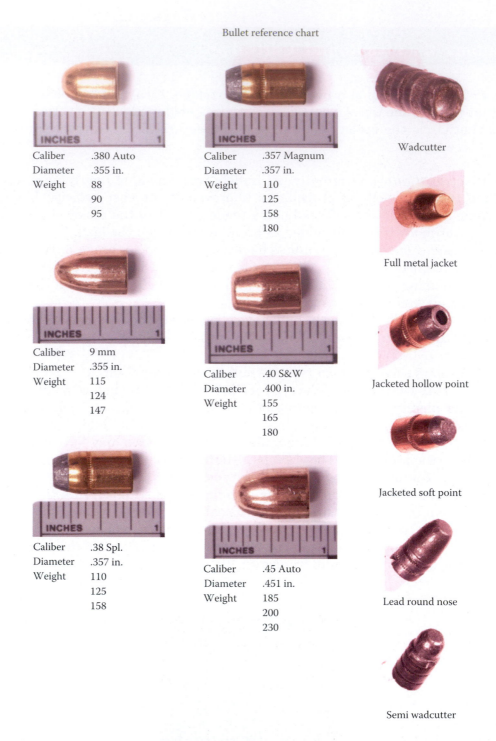

Figure 12.8 Common types of bullets for comparison. (Courtesy of www.precisionforensictesting.com.)

Propellants

The oldest recorded propellant is black powder, invented by the Chinese around the tenth century. It was used for signals and fireworks. Black powder is a physical mixture of finely divided particles of charcoal (C), sulfur (S), and saltpeter (KNO_3 or potassium nitrate). Formulations vary, but saltpeter is always the major component. Saltpeter furnishes the oxygen while the charcoal and sulfur are the fuels

Figure 12.9 Types of cartridge case materials: (L–R) aluminum, brass, and nickel-plated brass. (Photo courtesy of www.precisionforensictesting.com.)

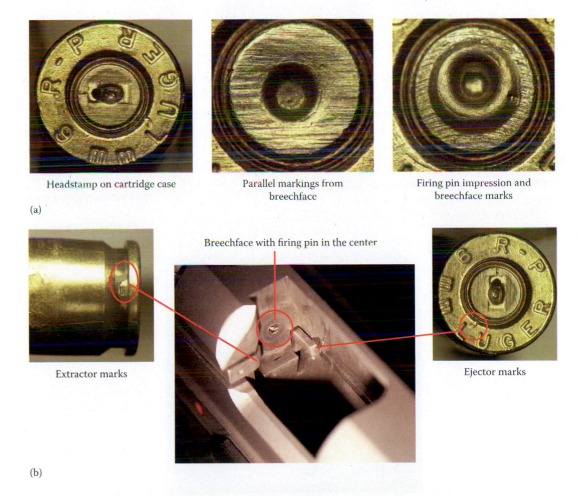

Headstamp on cartridge case

Parallel markings from breechface

Firing pin impression and breechface marks

(a)

Breechface with firing pin in the center

Extractor marks

Ejector marks

(b)

Figure 12.10 Diagrams showing some of the markings made on cartridges by firing a weapon. (a) Three cartridge case markings after a gun is fired. (b) Chamber of a gun showing the breechface, firing pin, extractor, and ejector, as well as where the marks can be found on the cartridge. (Photo courtesy of www.precisionforensictesting.com.)

that react with the oxygen. See Chapter 23 for a discussion of how explosives work. Even though black powder has been entirely replaced as a commercial propellant by smokeless powders, it is still used by battle re-enactors and fans of old weapons.

Smokeless powder was developed in the late nineteenth century to replace black powder as a propellant in weapons. Black powder produces a great amount of smoke that could easily reveal the position of the shooter. Smokeless powder emits much less smoke. Smokeless powders come in two varieties: single base and double base. Single-base smokeless powder consists of cotton lint or wood pulp that has been titrated by a nitric acid/sulfuric acid mixture. The nitrate ions combine with the hydroxyl groups on the cellulose. This is a chemical mixture of the oxygen and fuel that produces a potent propellant. Double-base smokeless powders consist of about 70% ± 10% cellulose nitrate, and about 30% ± 10% nitroglycerine. These make for more energetic propellants per unit weight, in part because the nitroglycerine lowers the amount of water present in the mixture from about 2% to less than 1%. Water adversely affects the power of the propellant by acting as a heat sink. It is important to note that smokeless powders do not explode inside a cartridge; but instead, they combust. Since the combustion occurs in a closed space, it can have the force of an explosion.

Primers

In 1807, a Scottish clergyman named James Forsythe discovered the shock-sensitive explosive called mercury fulminate [$Hg(ONC_2)$]. This type of explosive detonates if it is struck or shocked. A spark will also set it off. By 1850, cartridges were being manufactured that contained mercury fulminate inside the head of the cartridge as the primer. At the beginning, the primer was inserted inside the rim of the cartridge. A small pin protruded from the back of the rim. When this pin was struck by the hammer, it struck the primer and detonated it. The detonation caused the powder inside the cartridge to ignite. By 1850, this system was replaced by a simpler one in which the primer was inserted into a tiny cup inside the center of the cartridge head. This portion of the cartridge is commonly referred to as the primer cup (Figure 12.11).

Figure 12.11 The nickel center of this cartridge case is the primer cup (shown circled). The firing pin strikes this part of the cartridge in the gun chamber to initiate the explosion. (Photo courtesy of www.precisionforensictesting.com.)

The firing pin was mounted on the end of the hammer. When it struck the primer cup, it compressed the primer and detonated it. The flame produced by the detonation escaped through a hole in the cup and ignited the propellant. Over time, the composition of primers has changed, first by potassium chlorate ($KClO_3$) and today, by a mixture of lead styphnate, antimony sulfide, barium nitrate, and tetracene. When a gun is fired, not all of the gunpowder is burned completely and that powder exits the barrel as smoke and soot. The material that leaves the gun with the bullet is called gunshot residue. When GSR is analyzed from the hands of a shooter, the examiner looks for particles of antimony, lead, and barium from the primer.

Examination of Firearms Evidence

Crime Scene Processing

As with all crime scenes, those that contain firearms evidence must be clearly documented and photographed. Because bullets and cartridge casings are small, they must be identified in photographs with labels or markers of some type. Often, bullets or shotgun pellets may be found in walls or ceilings. The preferred collection method in such cases is to remove the section of the wall or ceiling and send it to the lab where the bullet or pellets can be safely removed. If this is not possible, rubberized tools must be used to remove the bullets.

Bullets and cartridge casings must never be marked for identification anywhere on their surfaces where there might be forensically significant markings. Many crime scene investigators do not mark them at all but put them in small vials or boxes and then mark the containers. Likewise, weapons should never be marked in places were there might be evidence. Sometimes, tags can be used. Guns should never be handled by inserting a pencil or anything else in the barrel. This could change the markings in the barrel and render test firings useless. Figure 12.12 shows one way that a weapon can be packaged for shipment to the laboratory.

In many cases, firearms are coated with a thin layer of lubricating oil. This makes them unsuitable surfaces for retaining fingerprint images. Nonetheless, weapons should always be packaged in such a way that fingerprints could be collected if present.

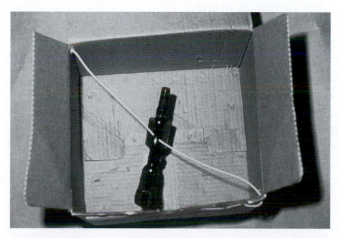

Figure 12.12 A proper method for packaging a weapon for shipment to the crime lab. The gun is suspended in the box by the trigger guard.

Preliminary Examination

Firearms examiners should always keep in mind that weapons may be sources of significant trace evidence and the examination of the weapon may have to be put off until trace evidence is processed. As previously mentioned, fingerprints are unlikely but not impossible to recover. Blood, fibers, or paint flecks may be on the weapon. Bits of tissue from a close-in or contact shot may be present on the weapon or inside the barrel. If the weapon were in the owner's pocket, it may have picked up trace evidence such as lint, fibers, dirt, etc.

Once recovered, as much information as possible should be gathered from the weapon in hopes of identifying the owner or user. The serial number is especially important. Criminals also know this and in many cases they will grind down or file off the serial number. As we see at the end of this chapter, there are methods for restoring obliterated serial numbers.

Bullet and Cartridge Case Comparison

Bullets

At the heart of bullet and cartridge case identification is the need to correctly collect known samples for comparison. For bullets, this means test firing the weapon into a trap. The same type of ammunition must be used as the questioned type. All test firings must be done into the same type of trap. Cotton or other cloth wadding has been used as a trap, but it may cause abrasions on the bullet from the cloth or may partially obliterate markings from the barrel. A better solution is a large water tank. These tanks are made of stainless steel and are long, narrow, and deep. The weapon is usually fired through a short pipe into the water. The bottom of the tank is in the shape of a cone in the middle so that all fired bullets will fall into the cone where a small basket is used to retrieve them.

Once the bullets are recovered, their *class* characteristics should first be determined. These include caliber, the number of lands and grooves, and their angles and directions of twist. If these all match the crime scene bullets, the examiner can proceed with the comparison of *individual* characteristics. This is always done with a comparison microscope as described in Chapter 6. If matching stria are found in a pair of land or groove impressions, the bullets should be rotated together to the next land or groove. If the bullets were fired from the same weapon, stria from all of the intact lands and grooves should match.

Just because two bullets were fired from the same weapon does not mean that the stria will always match. For example, rust may build up inside the barrel of a weapon and the stria in a bullet may be due mainly to rust. As bullets are fired through such a gun, rust particles are removed and the stria change. Even if rust is not a problem, repeated firings of a weapon will cause changes in the stria pattern, especially with metal-jacketed bullets. Imperfections in the surface of the jacket can impart stria to the barrel of the gun and remove some that are already there. After 50 firings or so, the stria of the 50th bullet may not match the first. Some weapons have interchangeable barrels. This will clearly cause problems if the barrel has been changed between the time the crime scene bullet was fired and the time that the weapon was test-fired.

Cartridge Cases

Cartridges cases can yield the same types of information as bullets. The examiner will attempt to determine the type of weapon used. If a suspect weapon is present,

Figure 12.13 Comparison microscope photograph matching stria created by a firing pin impressed on two cartridge cases. The line dividing the two cartridges is just to the left of the center of the picture. (Courtesy of David Brundage, Indiana Forensic Services Agency, Marion, IN.)

it can be determined whether the cartridge case was fired by that weapon. There are a number of markings on cartridge cases that help make these associations. Stria are present in firing pin impressions, extractor and ejector markings (except in revolvers), breech face markings, and sometimes chamber markings. Figure 12.13 shows the firing pin impression on two cartridge cases. The pin on the end of the hammer strikes the head of the cartridge case, detonating the primer. There are a few stria on the surface of the firing pin that are then transferred to the casing.

When a bullet is fired, the cartridge case recoils in the chamber towards the back of the gun. A block of metal, called the breech, stops the cartridge case from hitting the shooter. This block contains stria that are transferred to the surface of the head of the casing. A comparison of breech face markings on two cartridge casings is shown in Figure 12.14.

Figure 12.14 Stria created by the action of the cartridge slamming up against the breech as the bullet is ejected. Two cartridges shown here were fired by the same weapon. (Courtesy of David Brundage, Indiana Forensic Services Agency, Marion, IN.)

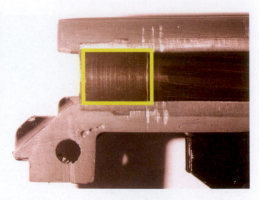

Figure 12.15 Chamber marks on a fired cartridge case and the gun barrel chamber. These fine striations can aid in identification. (Photo courtesy of www.precisionforensictesting.com.)

After the bullet is fired from the cartridge, the casing must be removed so that another round can be loaded into the gun. The metal extractor grabs the cartridge so that it can be expelled from the chamber by the metal ejector. Extractor marks can be found on the lip of the cartridge case and extractor marks on the headstamp. Examples of both markings are shown in Figure 12.10b.

Striations on the sides of the cartridge case called chamber marks aid in identification. Chamber marks are produced by the expansion of gases and heat when the cartridge is fired. The casing is pressed tightly against the gun chamber and marks are impressed as it expands and moves. Figure 12.15 shows chamber marks on a cartridge case and the portion of the gun barrel that made the marks.

Digital Imaging Systems for Ammunition

In 1993, the FBI began the *DRUGFIRE* system. This system is a database of firing pin and primer impressions on spent cartridge cases recovered from crime scenes. A computer network was set up so that firearms examiners could search the database for impressions. The examiner determined whether a crime scene cartridge casing or one test-fired from a seized weapon matched any of the impressions in the database. If a match was found, then arrangements were be made to procure the actual cartridge casing so that a physical, microscopic comparison could be completed.

At the same time that the FBI was developing DRUGFIRE, the Bureau of Alcohol, Tobacco, Firearms and Explosives (ATF) developed the Integrated Ballistics Identification System (IBIS) to capture and rapidly compare bullet stria. Unfortunately, IBIS and DRUGFIRE were not compatible. In order to be able to search both databases, an examiner had to have two different computer workstations. As a result, in 1997, the FBI and ATF established the National Integrated Ballistic Information Network (NIBIN) that permits searching of bullets or cartridge cases using the same computer system.

The development of the bullet and cartridge case databases led to the concept of ballistic fingerprinting. Under this program, each new weapon is test fired at the factory and the cartridge case is recovered. Breechface marks and firing pin impressions are stored in a computer database. If cartridge cases are recovered at a crime scene and no weapon is found, the breechface markings and firing pin impressions can be compared to those in the database. Although this may seem like an effective program, it has been fraught with problems. First, it is expensive to implement.

Second, it is often hard to substantiate a paper trail of a gun purchase. False identification documents may be used. Sales may be made illegally. Weapons can be stolen from original owners. Finally, if many rounds are fired between the time the gun is manufactured and the time it is used in a crime, firing pin impressions and breechface markings, like bullet stria, may change enough so that they can no longer be matched to a test-fired sample. Presently, only two states require ballistic fingerprinting of handguns sold.

Distance-of-Fire Determinations

Gunshots

When a bullet is fired from a gun, hot gases containing residue from the primer and smokeless powder will be expelled from the barrel and will travel for short distances in a roughly conical pattern. This residue is composed of soot from the burned powder and *stippling*, which is unburned gunpowder and barrel residue. Depending on the distance from the weapon to the target, some of this residue may be deposited on the target. The size of the GSR pattern can be used to determine the approximate distance between the weapon and the target when the bullet was fired. There are a number of limitations to this test that must be kept in mind when distance-of-firing measurements are made.

GSRs do not travel far before being dispersed. It is rare to find GSR on a target that is more than 18 in. from the weapon. If no residues are found on the target, the range is called a distance shot. If GSRs are found on the target, the range is called a close range shot. In a contact shot, the muzzle of the barrel is in direct contact with the target and no GSR will be found on the target. If the target is a human head, GSR may be injected into the soft tissues of the head and will be found inside the wound.

A distance shot produces a bullet hole that is roughly round. The edges of the hole may be burned or singed due to friction from the bullet as it passes through the target. This contusion ring may be partially or totally obscured by a ring of dirt made up of lubricant, dirt and dust, and metal shavings. The size, shape, and other characteristics of the bullet hole do not change with distance so these characteristics cannot be used to estimate the distance of firing.

GSR will be deposited in a close range shot. The residue consists of large and small particles of burned or unburned propellant and some primer particles. The largest are easily seen as discrete particles and are called stippling or tattooing. The smaller particles appear as soot.

Distance-of-firing determinations are done by test firing the same weapon and ammunition at various distances and then comparing the size of the stippling and soot pattern on the target. Not even another weapon of the same exact type will reproduce gunshot patterns and serious errors can occur in interpretation if the exact same weapon is not used. Figure 12.16 shows the various characteristics of a bullet hole in a target.

Shotgun Shots

As a shot leaves the barrel of the shotgun, it tends to spread in a conical pattern. When the shot strikes the target, the pellets form a roughly circular pattern.

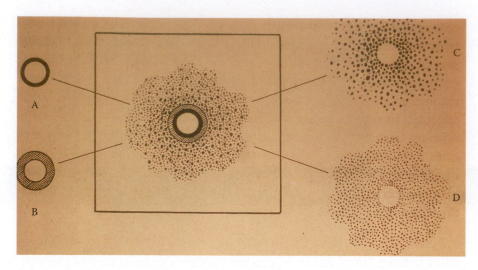

Figure 12.16 The anatomy of a bullet hole in a target: (A) A contusion ring caused by friction. (B) A ring of dirt that is deposited on the target by the bullet. (C) Stippling, or unburned and partially burned particles of gunshot residue. (D) Soot from the gunpowder.

The size of the pattern increases as the distance of firing increases. Although this sounds straightforward, a number of problems can arise in determining the distance of firing.

Humans are usually the targets of shotgun firings. The human body is a relatively small target and unless the target is fairly close to the firing, some of the pellets will miss the body altogether. This means that it may be difficult or impossible to establish an accurate pellet pattern.

If there is an intermediate target such as a window screen, the pattern on the final target may be distorted because the leading pellets will be slowed by the intermediate target and may be hit from behind by the trailing pellets, thus causing scattering. This is not predictable and not reproducible.

As with gunshot distance-of-firing determinations, test firings of shotguns must be done with the same weapon and ammunition in order to make proper interpretations

Normally, distance-of-firing determinations of shotgun patterns are performed by comparing the size of the pattern of the known and unknown shots.

Toolmarks

At the beginning of this chapter, a toolmark was defined as a scratch or other microscopic marking left by the action of a tool on an object. The discussion of firearms analysis showed that the markings left on bullets and cartridges from a fired weapon are all the results of toolmarks. The analysis of toolmarks takes advantage of the observation that no two toolmarks, even those left by the same type of tool, are identical. This implies that, in general, toolmarks should be individualizable. This is borne out in part by the observation that even consecutively manufactured guns whose parts are machined by the same tool will be distinguishable by their toolmarks. There has been almost no research, however, into the toolmark characteristics left by brand new tools, such as wire cutters, that were consecutively manufactured. Thus, care must be taken when extending the observations about bullets to all tools. The criterion of a match of known and unknown toolmarks: *that there be a sufficient number of similarities and no unexplainable differences* must be applied cautiously since there have not been sufficient studies to determine a *standard* number of similarities in toolmark identification.

Virtually any tool can leave markings and these markings may be used to help determine the source of the evidence. Take, for example, the evidence shown in Figure 12.17. This case involved a breaking and entering into a remote country house. The perpetrator cut the telephone lines with a wire cutter so the occupants could not call for help. When he was arrested, the wire cutters were still in his possession with his fingerprints all over the handles. Test cuts were made on a metal sheet to get the entire cutting blade surface. The photo shows how the some of the toolmarks in the cut wires match the test cuts in the metal sheet. These matches are shown as photomicrographs taken with a comparison microscope.

Figure 12.18 shows a fairly common toolmark examination. Here, a screwdriver was used to attempt to pry open a door. The blade left markings on the doorjamb. Test scrapings were made into sheet metal. Once again, the stria in the knowns and unknowns can be seen to match.

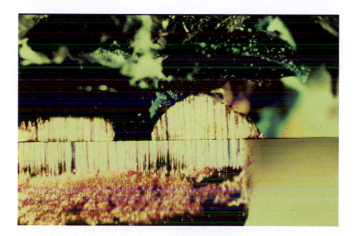

Figure 12.17 A match and nonmatch. A comparison of two cut wires with a piece of sheet metal, all cut by the same wire cutter. The two wires are in the top photo and the piece of sheet metal is in the bottom photo. Note that the striations on the *right* wire line up perfectly with the striations on the sheet metal, whereas the striations on the *left* wire do not match. This is because the wire on the left was cut by a *different* part of the wire cutter.

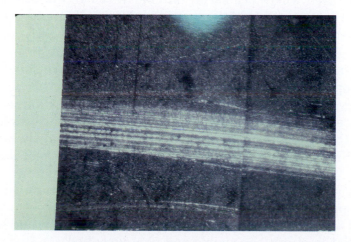

Figure 12.18 Stria made by a screwdriver on a piece of metal. Two scrapings were made by the same tool. The stria are virtually the same with each scraping.

Figure 12.19 Toolmark comparison. This is a comparison microscope photo of toolmarks made by the same metal tool. Notice how the individual striations line up left to right. (Photo courtesy of www. precisionforensictesting.com.)

Figure 12.19 shows a comparison microscope photo of a tip of a screwdriver on the left scraping across a surface. The photo on the right shows a scrape by the same screwdriver tip along a similar surface. Notice how the abrasion lines match left to right.

Serial Number Restoration

One of the more interesting toolmarks is a serial number that is stamped into an object, usually metal. When the machine stamps the serial number into the metal, the area below the stamped letter becomes strained. The metal bonds are weakened. Often, a thief will attempt to remove the serial number from a stolen object such as a gun by filing or grinding off the serial numbers. He will usually stop when the number disappears, that is, when he has filed off the metal that surrounds the stamped serial number until the whole surface is level. What he does not realize is that the strained metal below the serial numbers is a sort of "memory" of the numbers. If a solution that dissolves the metal is swabbed on the filed surface, the area where the serial number was will dissolve much faster and the number will reappear, at least temporarily. The swabbing process must be done with camera at the ready to record the serial numbers as they appear. Once they disappear again, they will be gone forever. Figure 12.20 is a series of diagrams of a serial number stamped into a metal surface. The first figure shows the top view of the letter 1 stamped into a piece of metal. Figure (a) shows this as viewed from the side as a cutaway. The shaded area is where the number is stamped into the metal. In (b), the surface has been ground down until it is level and the serial number disappears. In (c), the dissolving solution has been applied and the area beneath the serial number dissolves much faster than the surrounding metal and the number reappears.

Figure 12.21 shows the restoration of an actual serial number obliteration. In (a), the sanding process to smooth the surface for chemical treatment is illustrated. In (b), the serial number begins to appear when chemicals are added to the prepped surface and in (c) the number is visible and photographed.

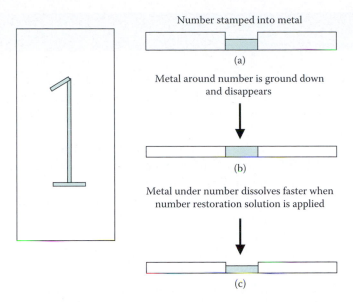

Number stamped into metal

(a)

Metal around number is ground down
and disappears

(b)

Metal under number dissolves faster when
number restoration solution is applied

(c)

Figure 12.20 A diagram showing how a serial number that is stamped into metal can be restored: (a) The indentation of the number 1 in a piece of metal. (b) The metal around the number being scraped off using a grinder. Although the number is no longer visible, the metal is deformed where the number was stamped. (c) The diagram shows how the metal under the number dissolves more rapidly than the surrounding metal. The number reappears for a short time and can be read.

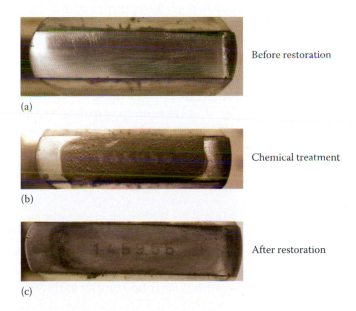

Before restoration

(a)

Chemical treatment

(b)

After restoration

(c)

Figure 12.21 Serial number restoration: The surface that contains the obliterated serial numbers is (a) first sanded smooth, (b) then treated with chemicals, and (c) then wiped clean to reveal the numbers. Recovered serial numbers are then photographed before they fade from view. (Photos courtesy of www.precisionforensictesting.com.)

There are a number of recipes for solutions suitable for recovering serial numbers. These solutions are specific for different types of metals. Most serial numbers are applied to an iron or steel surface. One of the more popular solutions consists of 100 mL each of concentrated hydrochloric acid and water and 90 g of cupric chloride ($CuCl_2$). This solution acts as a reducing agent that dissolves iron and deposits copper.

Summary

Toolmarks are scratches made by tools that are used to fabricate objects such as guns and wire cutters. The tools leave microscopic markings on the surface of the object. These markings are unique to each tool and can be used to individualize the object. Firearms analysis is a major area of toolmarks. Tools are used to put the grooves and lands in rifled barrels that make bullets spin as they leave the barrel. The tools that dig the grooves leave microscopic markings called stria or striations on the inside of the barrel. These are transferred to the surface of the bullet as it passes through the barrel. Other parts of the weapon, also manufactured by tools, leave markings on cartridge cases. These include extractor and ejector markings and chamber marks as well as breech face and firing pin impressions. All of these are potentially individual markings. The number of lands and grooves in a bullet as well as the angle and direction of twist are class characteristics. The striations within a groove in a bullet are individual characteristics. There is no set number of individual characteristics that must be present in order to declare that a bullet or cartridge casing was fired from a particular weapon.

Shotguns fire pellets rather than bullets and the barrels of these guns are not rifled. The pellets cannot be traced back to the individual weapon, but markings on the cartridge such as firing pin and breech face impressions can individualize the cartridge.

Distance-of-firing determinations can be estimated if the same weapon and ammunition are available. For bullets, the distance of firing is determined by the pattern left by propellant and primer that follows the bullet out of the barrel. The stippling and soot are only deposited on the target for a short distance. Beyond that, there is no reliable way of making distance of firing determinations. With shotguns, the diameter of the pellet pattern on the target can be used to determine the distance-of-firing if the same weapon and ammunition are used.

Other tools such as screwdrivers and wire cutters also leave stria or striations on the surface of objects. These markings may also be traceable back to the particular tool.

Serial number restoration is related to toolmark analysis except the goal is to identify the serial number that was ground off the metal surface of an object such as a gun. The metal bonds beneath the stamped serial number are weakened. When a dissolving or etching solution is used, this weakened metal dissolves faster than the surrounding metal and the serial number will be temporarily visualized.

Test Yourself

Multiple Choice

1. Rifling of a barrel refers to
   a. The grooves made in the barrel
   b. The stria in the barrel
   c. The lands and grooves in the barrel
   d. The firing pin impression

2. Which markings will not be found on a cartridge casing fired from a revolver?
   a. Lands
   b. Extractor markings
   c. Firing pin impressions
   d. Breechface markings

3. Which of the following is a class characteristic of a fired bullet or cartridge casing?
   a. Number of lands and grooves
   b. Ejector markings
   c. Breechface markings
   d. Bullet striations

4. Which of the following is true of distance-of-firing determinations of shotguns?
   a. Distance of firing cannot be determined with shotguns
   b. When a human being is the target, distance-of-firing determinations are easy because all of the pellets usually hit the target
   c. Intermediate targets have no effect on distance-of-firing determinations
   d. The same weapon and ammunition must be used to determine the distance of firing

5. Which of the following is true about the stria in a barrel of a gun?
   a. They are present in all weapons
   b. They are class characteristics
   c. They never change as the weapon is fired repeatedly
   d. They are initially made by the tool that makes the barrel

6. The major propellant used in firearms today is
   a. Smokeless powder
   b. Sodium azide
   c. Black powder
   d. Mercury fulminate

7. Which of the following is not a rifled weapon?
   a. Pistol
   b. Shotgun
   c. Machine gun
   d. Submachine gun

8. Today, "caliber" is defined in the United States as
   a. The diameter of the base of the cartridge in thousandths of inches
   b. The distance from the top of opposite lands in the barrel
   c. The distance from the bottom of opposite grooves in the barrel
   d. The length of the bullet in inches

9. Which of the following is true about serial number restoration?
   a. Serial numbers can be restored on any surface
   b. The metal below a stamped serial number is more dense than the surrounding metal, making it slower to dissolve in an etching solution
   c. The metal below a stamped serial number is strained, making it faster to dissolve in an etching solution than the surrounding metal
   d. Once restored, serial numbers remain visible permanently

10. In the Sacco–Vanzetti case discussed at the beginning of the chapter, the jury based its guilty finding mainly on
    a. The matching striations on the bullets to Sacco's gun as determined by a firearms examiner
    b. The fact that the type of ammunition used in the killings was very rare and only the defendants had any of it

c. The fact that all of the firearms examiners for the defense and prosecution agreed that the bullets taken from the dead guard matched Sacco's weapon

d. Sacco's admission of guilt on the stand in his trial

11. Determining the path of a bullet is considered to be part of the study of

a. Trajectories

b. Firearms identification

c. Ballistics

d. Toolmark identification

12. Which of the following weapons does *not* have rifling in the barrel?

a. Revolver

b. Shotgun

c. Pistol

d. Handgun

True or False

13. When a manufacturer rifles a barrel of a gun, it uses a broach tool to cut grooves into the metal barrel.

14. Once a toolmark has been impressed upon a surface, the tool making the mark never changes.

15. If a perpetrator sands down a serial number to the point where it is no longer visible, it is beyond the point of restoration.

16. Chamber marks on cartridge cases are considered individual characteristics.

17. Stippling on a surface is caused by metal shavings exiting a gun barrel.

18. Chemicals dissolve the unstamped area of a metal more rapidly than the stamped area, causing obliterated serial numbers to appear.

19. Extractor marks, breechface marks, striations, and serial numbers are all examples of toolmarks.

Short Answer

20. Bullet diagram. Name the labeled parts. Is the twist left or right?

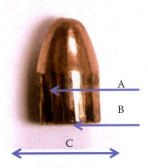

21. When a bullet is found at a crime scene imbedded into a material, the crime scene technician should use rubberized tools to extract the bullet. What is the reasoning behind this?

22. A weapon is recovered from a crime scene. What types of evidence might the firearms examiner retrieve from the weapon and in what order, if any, should the evidence be processed?

23. List the class characteristics of a fired bullet. How can a fired bullet become individualized to a weapon?

24. Describe an instance when a fired bullet would *not* match the weapon from which it was fired?
25. If ballistic fingerprinting can create a database of manufactured weapons, why do more states not enlist such a program?

Matching

26. The powder that leaves the barrel of the gun   a. Breech
27. A metal block that holds a cartridge case in place   b. Ejector
28. A metal device that grips a cartridge after firing   c. Extractor
29. A metal device that ousts the cartridge after firing d. Gunshot residue
30. A pressure activated explosive mixture in a gun   e. Primer

Further Reading

Davis, J. E. (1958). *An Introduction to Toolmarks, Firearms, and the Striagraph*. Charles C Thomas, Springfield, IL.

Heard, B. J. (1997). *Handbook of Firearms and Ballistics*. Wiley & Sons, Chichester, U.K.

Rowe, W. F. (1988). Firearms identification, in *Forensic Science Handbook*, vol. 2, R. Saferstein, ed. Prentice Hall, Upper Saddle River, NJ.

On the Web

Case solved using firearms database: www.saf.org/USAtoday102799.html.

Firearms: www.ct.gov/dps/cwp/view.asp?a=2155&q=315176.

http://library.med.utah.edu/WebPath/TUTORIAL/GUNS/GUNINTRO.html.

National Integrated Ballistic Information Network (NIBIN): http://dci.sd.gov/lab/nibin.htm.

Sacco & Vanzetti: www.youtube.com/watch?v=C3SuTTcj2u8.

Stippling: www.fbi.gov/hq/lab/fsc/backissu/april2004/research/2004_02_research02.htm.

Toolmarks: www.fbi.gov/hq/lab/fsc/backissu/april2000/schehl2.htm#Toolmark.

www.fbi.gov/hq/lab/fsc/backissu/april2000/schehl1.htm#Introduction.

www.firearmsid.com.

www.nibin.gov/.

PART IV

Forensic Biology

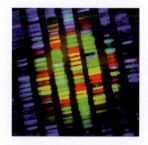

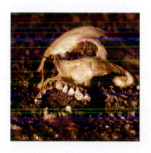

13
Forensic Pathology

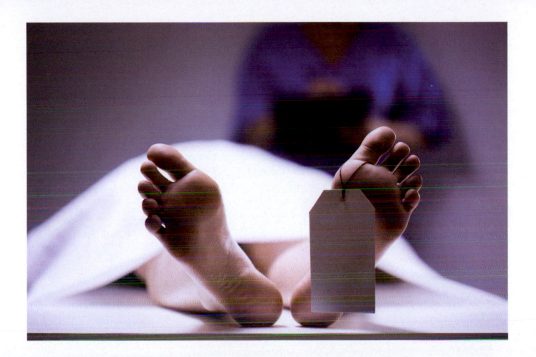

Learning Objectives

1. To be able to define pathology and forensic pathology and explain the differences
2. To be able to describe the coroner and medical examiner systems and describe their differences and similarities
3. To be able to define and distinguish between the cause of death and the manner of death
4. To be able to define and describe the medicolegal autopsy and explain when a coroner or medical examiner must perform an autopsy
5. To be able to describe the patterns of injury and characteristics of mechanical, electrical, thermal, and chemical types of death
6. To be able to define the postmortem interval and explain how short- and long-term PMIs are estimated

Chapter 13
Forensic Pathology

Mini Glossary

Algor mortis: Cooling of the body after death.

Anatomic pathology: Study of the structural and morphological changes to the body as the result of a disease state.

Autopsy: Internal and external investigation of a body to determine cause and manner of death.

Autopsy: Internal and external medical investigation of a body to determine cause and manner of death.

Cause of death: Trauma or injury or the disease (or combination of both) that resulted in cessation of life.

Clinical pathology: Analysis of various materials removed from the body including blood, saliva, spinal fluid, urine, etc., for the purpose of determining the presence of drugs and/or poisons and their role in illness or death.

Coroner: Elected official whose function is to determine the cause and manner of death in cases that are statutorily mandated.

Crowner: Chief tax collector in medieval England. Functions included determining cause and manner of death.

Embalming: Addition of a preservative chemical to the body shortly after death.

Exhumation: Removal of a body after burial.

Hyperthermia: Extreme heat.

Hypothermia: Extreme cold.

Livor mortis: Tendency of the blood to pool at the lowest part of the body under the influence of gravity after death.

Manner of death: Set of circumstances that existed at the time the death was caused. There are only four manners of death: *homicide*, natural causes, accidental, or suicide.

Mechanism of death: The actual physical, physiological, or chemical event that brings on cessation of life.

Medical examiner: Appointed official whose function is to determine the cause and manner of death in cases that are statutorily mandated. Must be a physician.

Medicolegal autopsy: Part of postmortem investigation of the body. Same as autopsy.

Pathology: The medical specialty concerned with the determination of the causes and manners of disease and death.

Postmortem interval (PMI): Time since death.

Rief of the shire: Local official appointed by the Crowner to help with the determination of cause and manner of death.

Rigor mortis: Stiffening of the joints within hours after death.

Stippling: Particles of burned and unburned gunshot residue that is deposited on the surface of the target of a gunshot.

Acronyms

PMI: Postmortem interval

Introduction

Forensic pathology is one of the most important of the forensic applications of biology. Although *pathology* is a medical specialty that involves both the living and the dead, *forensic pathology* is involved only with the dead. Pathology originally involved the study of the structural and morphological changes to the body as the result of a disease state. Today, this is called *anatomic pathology*. In modern times, pathology has been expanded to include the study of disease by analytical laboratory methods. This includes the analysis of various materials removed from the body including blood, saliva, spinal fluid, urine, etc., for the purpose of determining the presence of drugs and/or poisons and their role in illness or death. Today, this branch is called *clinical pathology*. The difference is the purpose for which the pathology is being carried out. Most clinical pathology today is done by forensic toxicologists who work with forensic pathologists in helping determine the cause and manner of death in postmortem cases. Forensic toxicology is discussed in detail in Chapter 20. Both anatomic and clinical pathology are used in the practice of forensic pathology. Forensic pathology is the determination of the cause and manner of death in cases of suspicious or unexplained death. In this chapter, we will study the role of the forensic pathologist in the investigation of death and will learn a bit about how the cause and manner of death can be determined and who has the responsibility for making these determinations.

How to Become a Forensic Pathologist

After high school, it takes approximately 14 years to become a fully trained, board certified forensic pathologist. First, one must obtain a college degree (at least 4 years) and apply to medical school, since pathology is a medical specialty and practitioners must first obtain a medical degree. Medical school generally takes four more years after obtaining a college degree. After completing medical school, many physicians desire to become specialists in a specific type of medicine such as pediatrics, internal medicine, or pathology. This requires a residency in a specialty. This generally takes 3–4 additional years after medical school. After a 4-year residency in pathology, the physician can become board certified as a pathologist. However, to obtain certification in forensic pathology, the pathologist must spend an additional year or two in a residency and can then apply for certification from the American Board of Forensic Pathology.

The major duties of a forensic pathologist are

- To determine the apparent cause of death
- To determine (estimate) the *postmortem interval (PMI)* or *time of death*
- To ascertain the manner of death
- To determine the identity of the deceased

Investigation of Death: Coroners and Medical Examiners

Every country and, in the United States, each state, has a system in place to investigate deaths. This system includes one or more officials who are in charge of the death investigation process and one or more pathologists who assist in the investigation by conducting a *medicolegal autopsy* or *post-mortem investigation* of the body. Today, in the United States and some other countries, there are two systems of death investigation; the *Coroner* and the *Medical Examiner*. Before explaining these, a bit of history is necessary.

The first system for the investigation of death in the Western world was developed around 1000 BC in England. Officials called *Crowners* were named by the King to collect taxes from around the country. At some point, landholders would die and a decision had to be made as to the disposition of his land holdings. This was a very important function to the King because much of his wealth derived from goods and taxes that were given by the landholders as a condition of continuing in possession of the land. Thus, if a landholder committed suicide, his land and wealth would be forfeited to the Crown because by the act of taking his own life he had in a way, deprived the King of a taxpayer. By the same token, someone who killed a landholder would likewise be removing a taxpayer from the roles and would forfeit his land as part of his punishment. The process of determining how and why someone died fell to the Crowner because of the goods and taxes implications of the death. In a far flung empire, this was a complicated system and the Crowner would enlist help by appointing local officials in each county (shire), the *Rief of the Shire* (or Shire Rief) to help with death investigations. The Shire Rief would investigate the crime, often by enlisting the help of local upstanding citizens who would view the body and the evidence from witnesses and help reach a conclusion as to the cause and manner of death. There were no physicians, let alone pathologists at the time who could provide expertise to this process. That would not happen until much later.

When the American Colonies were founded, citizens imported much of the English legal system including the system of death investigation. The Crowner became the *Coroner* who is responsible for the determination of cause and manner of death. Most states had a coroner for each county and in some cases, for major cities. The Shire Rief became, of course, the Sheriff whose job became one of law enforcement and jail management rather than having a specific role in the investigation of death. As time passed, it became evident that there are some problems with the coroner system. First, for the most part, coroners did not have to be pathologists or even physicians. They did not have to have any medical training whatsoever. Some coroners were, and are today, funeral home directors. This means that the coroner could steer business to his own funeral home after completing examination of a body. This has led to some abuse of the system. As medical education developed in the United States and pathology became a recognized medical specialty, coroners began to enlist their help in investigating deaths. In recognition of these problems, a *Medical Examiner* system was developed. Under this system, the official who is responsible for the determination of the cause and manner of death must be a physician (although usually not a pathologist) and is appointed by the government of the county or state. If the medical examiner is not a pathologist, he or she will enlist the aid of one or more of them to help with death investigations. Massachusetts was the first state to have a medical examiner, in 1877. Today, about half of the states use the medical examiner system and the other half use a form of the coroner system. Some have mixed systems with both medical examiners and coroners.

The NAS Forensic Science Committee devoted a separate recommendation to the medico-legal death investigation system is the U.S. Recognizing the problems described above with the coroner system and addressing the shortage of forensically trained pathologists, the Committee recommended that the coroner system be abolished and replaced by a medical examiner. In addition, the Committee recommended that incentives be given to medical students to learn and practice forensic pathology. Since coroner or medical examiner systems are under the control of each state and sometimes each county, the Committee recognized that the federal government had no supervisory role to play and could only provide monetary incentives to adopt a medical examiner system in a given jurisdiction.

Death Investigation Process

Once a body is found under suspicious or unexplained circumstances, a medical examiner or coroner (or deputy) is called to the death scene. At that time, the official determines that the person is, in fact, dead and makes some preliminary observations about the cause and manner of death by noting the position of the body and the surroundings of the death, as well as obvious wounds or trauma. In addition, data is collected that can be used to estimate the *post-mortem interval* (PMI) or *time since death*. This is often a critical piece of information in solving a homicide. When the pathologist is finished with this examination, the body is often turned over to a special death investigation scene team, which is specially trained to examine a body so as to be able to spot, document, and collect important trace and other evidence before moving the body to the morgue. Improper handling of a body at a death scene can cause the loss or compromise of critical evidence of the cause and manner of death. Only after this careful search for evidence and documentation of the scene is the body removed.

Death Certificate

Every state requires that a *death certificate* be executed for every death that occurs within each jurisdiction. State law provides for what the death certificate must contain and whom may fill it out and sign it. The law also describes those situations where a death must be investigated by the coroner or medical examiner and signed by him or her. Although these laws vary somewhat, they require that suspicious or unexplained deaths and those of people who have not recently been under the care of a physician must be investigated by the medical examiner or coroner. Typically, this will involve about one-third of all deaths. These deaths will usually, but not always, involve a medicolegal autopsy as part of the death investigation process. The two critical pieces of information on the death certificate are the cause and manner of death. Figure 13.1 shows a portion of a typical death certificate.

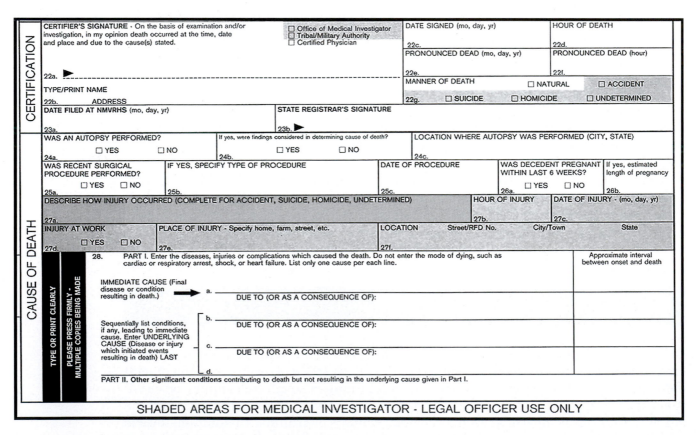

Figure 13.1 A portion of a death certificate showing the possible manners of death. The medical examiner or coroner must choose one of these for each death. Note that the area under "cause of death" permits several entries.

Cause of Death

There are many causes of death. The trauma or injury or the disease (or combination of both) that resulted in cessation of life is the *cause of death*. Normally, a pathologist will determine the *primary or immediate cause of death* and, if present, *secondary or contributing cause(s) of death*. For example, consider the case of a man who is driving his car on a highway. He suddenly has a stroke, which causes the loss of sight in his eyes and loss of motor control of his arms and legs. He loses control of his car and crashes into a tree. The impact forces the steering column into his chest, causing fatal trauma to his heart. The primary cause of death is the injuries sustained in the crash. The stroke would be a contributing cause of death. If the man had high blood pressure, it may have contributed to causing the stroke and could be viewed as a contributing cause of death. In other cases, the injury or disease itself causes death quickly and there are no other secondary causes. An especially lethal snakebite would be an example of this.

Some pathologists also speak of the *mechanism of death*. This is the actual physical, physiological, or chemical event that brings on cessation of life. Here, the pathologist must carefully examine the organ or system that failed due to the application of the cause of death and describe exactly what changes occurred that were incompatible with life.

Occasionally, determination of the cause of death can be tricky. For example, suppose that someone suffered a nonlethal gunshot wound when he was being robbed at gun point. The bullet became lodged in an inoperable location in the man's head, but does not cause him to die or even be ill. Years later, he gets into a fight with another man in a barroom brawl. The other man hits him in the head with a chair, but not hard enough to kill him. The blow dislodges the bullet from its location and its movement causes trauma to the brain that causes uncontrollable bleeding that causes death. What was the actual cause of death? It can be difficult to determine years after the first contributing factor.

Manner of Death

The *manner of death* is the set of circumstances that existed at the time the death was caused. There are only four manners of death and thus, all deaths must be attributed to one of them. These are *homicide, natural causes, accidental,* or *suicide*. There is a space on the death certificate that requires the coroner or medical examiner to list the manner of death. See Figure 13.2. In some states, the official must put one of the four, even if he or she has to make an educated guess. In most states, however, the official can put "undetermined" if there is not enough information to reach a definite conclusion about the manner of death.

In many cases, the manner of death is evident. If someone dies after a massive heart attack in his home, the manner of death will be listed as *natural causes*. If a person is driving a car while talking on a cell phone and accidentally drops the

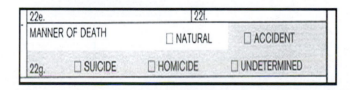

Figure 13.2 A close up of the manner of death portion of a death certificate. This certificate permits a conclusion of "undetermined." In some states, this is not permitted.

phone and then loses control of the car while trying to retrieve the phone, and then has a fatal crash, the manner of death will be *accidental*. About 30 years ago, there was a poisoning case in Michigan where a housekeeper, angry at not getting a raise in salary, set out to kill her employer by putting ant syrup (a combination of honey and arsenic used to attract and poison ants) in her coffee. Instead, the employer's visiting sister drank the coffee by mistake and died. The manner of death was a *homicide* even though the housekeeper did not mean to kill the sister.

Medicolegal Autopsy

One of the most critical parts of the investigation of death is the autopsy. In medicolegal cases, it is hard to imagine how one could accurately determine the cause and manner of death without probing the exterior and interior of the body. The term *autopsy* means to "see with one's own eyes." This does not seem like an appropriate term to describe the examination of a dead body. The term *necropsy* or "looking at the dead" is a better descriptor. Many religions throughout the world forbid or limit autopsies. Certain mid-eastern religions forbid them. The religions of Judaism, Christianity, and Islam put limitations on when autopsies can be performed. Under English Common Law, the kin of the deceased must give their permission for an autopsy to be done. This has carried over to the United States and is the policy in most states today. The exceptions occur when the law states that the medical examiner or coroner must perform an autopsy. The number of autopsies that are performed in this country has declined greatly since World War II. Today, hospital autopsies are performed in less than 5% of deaths. There are several reasons for this. First, autopsies can be expensive and the cost must be borne by the hospital. Second, a hospital autopsy is usually only done with the consent of the family and there may be personal or increasingly, religious reasons for the family objecting. This trend is unfortunate because autopsies present a great learning opportunity for pathologists. Many of the most important advances in medicine have occurred as the result of knowledge gained by autopsies. As shown in Figure 13.3, medicolegal autopsies make up about one-third of all autopsies.

Autopsy Process

Any type of autopsy, medicolegal, or a routine examination performed in a hospital proceeds in a logical manner from the outside in. In many cases, the pathologist will

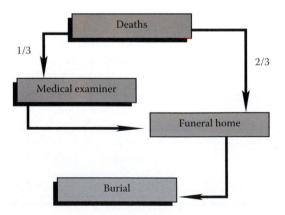

Figure 13.3 This chart shows the distribution of deaths and the fraction that are sent to a medical examiner or coroner for autopsy. (Courtesy of Meredith Haddon.)

dictate her findings during the autopsy. These will later be reduced to written notes. Sometimes, sketches will be made of wounds or injuries but photography is more commonly used. One of the most important characteristics of a medicolegal autopsy is that it involves not only an examination of the body to determine the cause and manner of death, but also requires a search of the body for physical evidence that can yield clues to the identity of the deceased if it is not known, or perhaps the identity of the perpetrator in the case of a homicide. Pathologists who are not trained in forensic pathology often overlook or compromise significant physical evidence. Types of evidence that are often overlooked by nonforensically trained pathologists include trace evidence such as hairs and fibers, dirt and skin under nails, gunshot residues, and other small wounds that might have forensic significance. Also, forensic pathologists are specially trained to recognize patterns of injury and associate them with particular causes.

External Examination

The external examination of the body can be very important. It can yield clues about the cause and manner of death, provide identifying markings such as tattoos or unusual clothing and can, of course, provide trace evidence that can help associate the deceased with the crime scene and/or perpetrator. A detailed examination of the entire body is made. The body is extensively photographed clothed and unclothed. Wounds and trauma are noted such as entry and exit gunshot wounds or defensive wounds.

Internal Examination

After the external examination is made and properly documented, standard incisions are made in the torso and the internal examinations are done. Body fluid samples including blood, urine, and other fluids are usually removed and sent to a forensic toxicologist for examination to determine if there are drugs or poisons in the body that could have caused or contributed to death. All of the major organs are removed, weighed, and measured. They will also be examined to determine if there are characteristic wounds or injuries that can give clues as to the cause and manner of death. Wounds or injuries that appeared on the outside of the body and travel inside are traced. These would include gunshot wounds and knife wounds. If there are bullets or shotgun pellets still in the body, they will be located and removed. The body may be x-rayed so that this can be compared to ante mortem x-rays in case the identity of the deceased is an issue.

Patterns of Injury and Classification of Violent Deaths

The major purpose of the autopsy is to determine the cause and manner of death, especially in the case of violent death. The most important evidence of the deceased is the pattern of injury that is evidenced by certain types of violent deaths. Forensic pathologists are trained to recognize these patterns and relate them to the cause of death. A pathologist who is not forensically trained may not spot the patterns or may misinterpret them. Patterns of injury in violent deaths can be put into one of four classes; *mechanical, thermal, electrical, or chemical*. Some types of death may overlap two or more of the classes. For example, *asphyxiation* (oxygen deprivation to the brain that causes death) can be mechanical, chemical, or electrical in nature.

Deaths due to Mechanical Causes

The most common mechanical types of violent death are gunshot and stabbing. Other types include motor vehicle incidents and falls. *Sharp force injuries* include knives and other implements. The type of wound produced by a sharp implement is called in *incised wound*. It has relatively sharp edges. A *blunt force injury*, on the other hand, causes *lacerations*. These have rougher edges than incisions. Figure 13.4a is a drawing of an incision and Figure 13.4b is a laceration. Forensic pathologists can examine a wound and generally tell the type of weapon used. If a knife has serrations in it, these can show up in the margins of the wound. If the knife strikes bone, the serrations can be detected on the surface of the bone. It is generally not possible to determine the exact size of the weapon that causes a laceration or incision. In order for a sharp implement to cause death, it must damage a major artery or the heart or brain or spinal cord. Blunt force injuries can cause death by a variety of means.

Firearm injuries are a type of blunt force injury. Different injury patterns arise from bullet wounds than shotgun pellet wounds. High-speed bullets from hunting and military rifles cause more damage to a body than do lower speed bullets from hand guns. Some gunshots penetrate the body but do not exit. They become lodged in bone or an organ. Gunshots that enter and exit the body are called *perforating wounds*.

In the case of gunshot wounds, pathologists often attempt to determine how far away from the victim the gun was when it was shot. Gunshots can be divided into three types: contact, intermediate, and distant. In a *contact shot*, the gun is pressed up against the body and discharged. The entry wound will show blackening

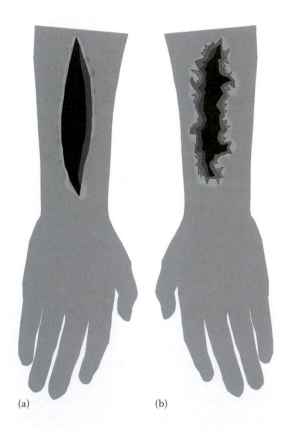

(a)   (b)

Figure 13.4 (a) An incision and (b) a laceration. Note the ragged edges on a laceration. (Courtesy of Meredith Haddon.)

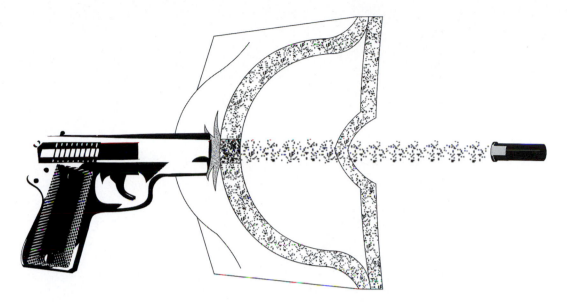

Figure 13.5 Diagram of a contact shot. Hot escaping gases from the muzzle of the gun are injected into and underneath the skin, causing it to bulge out. If there is any stippling it is confined to a narrow circular area. There will usually be burns at the point of contact with the skin. (Courtesy of Meredith Haddon.)

and swelling. The swelling is due to the injection of hot, escaping gases from the barrel of the gun (see Chapter 12 for a discussion of firearms) under the skin. This swelling often causes lacerations in the skin. Figure 13.5 is a drawing of a contact shot.

In an *intermediate shot*, particles of unburned and partially burned propellant (usually smokeless powder) lodge in the skin. This effect is called *stippling*. The diameter of the ring of stippling around the wound is proportional to the distance of firing. For most weapons, stippling appears only when the gun is discharged within a few feet of the target. Beyond that distance, the stippling either does not reach the target or falls off when it hits. These are called *distance shots*. Figure 13.6 shows stippling on a target.

Deaths due to Chemical Causes

The fate of drugs and alcohol in the body is discussed in detail in Chapter 20. Drugs and alcohol are contributory factors in death far more often than they are the cause of death. This is because it generally takes a good deal of a drug to cause a fatal overdose and many people will pass out before they can ingest a fatal dose. Also, certain drugs and alcohol cause detrimental changes in motor coordination and functions that can lead to death if the victim takes part in activities that require these functions. Drunk or drugged driving is an example of a situation where death may occur because the driver is intoxicated and loses control of the car and dies.

Drugs that cause death are most commonly depressants. A high overdose of alcohol, for example, can cause the person to lapse into a coma and respiration will slow so much that the victim ceases to breathe and dies. The cause of death is lack of oxygen owing to the slow breathing rate. In many cases, a person who has taken a large quantity of alcohol over time will start to vomit. This will bring up the alcohol in the stomach and it no more will be absorbed. If the overdose occurs rapidly, the vomiting reflex may be depressed and the person will not vomit and death will ensue.

The amount of a drug or alcohol that can cause death depends in part on the person's history of taking the drug. With most drugs, a tolerance builds up that

Figure 13.6 Stippling around a bullet hole in cloth. This consists of partially burned and unburned particles of gunshot residue They can be enhanced by chemical treatment.

allows the person to tolerate increased levels before death ensues. As discussed in Chapter 20, synergism is also a factor in the role of drugs in causing death. Alcohol and barbiturates are both depressants. They do not work in exactly the same way but they do magnify each other's effects so that a person can die from a combination even though the dose of either one by itself would not be lethal. Entertainers such as Janice Joplin and Jimi Hendrix died from an accidental overdose of alcohol and barbiturates. Besides the barbiturates, opiates and diazepam (e.g., Valium) overdoses cause death by the same mechanism. There have been no known death overdoses of marijuana. Cocaine has been reported to cause overdose deaths but by a different mechanism than for depressants. Cocaine is a stimulant. At very high doses, it causes seizures and uncontrolled heart beating, both of which can cause death.

Carbon monoxide (CO) is a product of incomplete combustion of hydrocarbon fuels such as natural gas and gasoline. (Complete combustion results in the formation of carbon dioxide). CO is a colorless, odorless, tasteless gas. When ingested, it attaches to *hemoglobin* in the blood. Hemoglobin is the substance in blood that carries molecules of oxygen to each cell in the body. Carbon monoxide ties up the hemoglobin, forming *carboxyhemoglobin* so there is less of it for oxygen to attach to. As a result, the victim dies of asphyxiation. Carboxyhemoglobin is bright red and victims of CO poisoning have a characteristic red coloration. Blood levels of CO as low as 20% can kill. Levels as high as 90% are common among people trapped in fires.

Hydrogen Cyanide (HCN) can also cause death. It is highly poisonous and has the characteristic odor of almonds. It acts by interfering with oxygen delivery to the brain, causing asphyxiation. It has been used as an instrument of carrying out executions of felons sentenced to death in the *gas chamber*. In such cases, potassium cyanide tablets or powder is mixed with a strong acid. This forms HCN, which the prisoner then inhales, causing death. Swallowing potassium cyanide has the same effect because it is converted to HCN by stomach acid.

Deaths due to Electrical Causes

Electrical deaths can occur in any of several ways depending upon the type and magnitude of the electrical current that the victim is exposed to. Alternating current of moderate voltage (less than about 1000 V) causes the heart to quiver uncontrollably. This is called *ventricular fibrillation*, and can cause death within just a few minutes. The person may not even be burned by the electrical energy at these levels. At higher levels of voltage, the heart stops beating because the electrical current disrupts the nervous impulses that keep the heart in rhythm. Also, voltages of this magnitude can cause severe burns in seconds and destruction of cellular material in the body.

Deaths due to Burns or Extreme Cold

Extreme heat is called *hyperthermia*. Extreme cold is called *hypothermia*. In order for the body to function normally, it must maintain a temperature very close to 37°C (99°F). Significant deviations from this temperature for even a few minutes can cause injury and can lead to death. Because of this, a person who dies from hyperthermia or hypothermia may not show outward signs of the cause of death unless there are visible burns or signs of frostbite on the body. The determination of the cause of death is often made by noting the environment where the body was found. Alcohol can be especially dangerous when a person is exposed to low temperatures. Alcohol dilates (expands) blood vessels that can increase heat loss and, as a person's intoxication level increases, sensitivity to heat and cold decreases so that the person may not perceive the presence of dangerous temperature levels.

Postmortem Interval: Time of Death

Determination of the PMI is very important in death investigation. It can help establish or refute the alibi of a suspect. It can be a key piece of evidence in determining the manner of death. Unfortunately, the PMI cannot be determined exactly because the modern methods of determination do not result in sufficiently accurate data. In addition, the environment surrounding a corpse can greatly affect changes in the body that are used to determine PMI. For example, if someone dies and the body is left outside in cold weather, the rate of body cooling slows markedly. Because of this uncertainty, pathologists always express the PMI as a range of hours or even days, reflecting the uncertainty of measurement of the relevant factors. The investigation of the PMI begins at the death scene. The temperature and physical environment is noted. The amount of clothing or other covering of the deceased is also important. The attending pathologist will usually take the core temperature of the deceased to develop a preliminary estimation of *algor mortis*, the tendency of a body to cool after death. Preliminary observations of the pooling of blood at the lowest part of the body caused by gravity (*livor mortis*) are also made. The degree of stiffening of the body (*rigor mortis*) is also estimated. All of these factors help the pathologist estimate an early PMI, up to 48 h. If the deceased has been dead for several days, or weeks, or sometimes longer, then the above factors are no longer present and other methods must be used to estimate the PMI. These include the degree of decomposition of the body and the activities of insects on the body. The latter is covered in Chapter 15.

Early Postmortem Interval

Rigor, livor, and algor mortis all take place during the first 48 h after death has occurred. There are well-established guidelines of the time intervals for each of these actions. These must be tempered, however, by the temperature and environment where the deceased died. High or low temperatures and/or humidity can affect the rates at which these activities take place as will the degree of protection (clothing, indoors v. outdoors, land or water) of the body.

Algor Mortis

A good rule of thumb for the cooling of a body after death is that, under moderate conditions of temperature, an adult clothed appropriately for that temperature will cool 1°C each hour after death. It will thus take the better part of a day for a body to cool from its normal temperature of 37°C to a room temperature of 20°C (70°F). The ambient temperature can have a great effect upon this assumption. If the body is found in the desert in the summer where the temperature can be over 40°C, the body may actually warm up after death! If the temperature is very cold, the body will cool faster than 1°C per hour. There are numerous diseases that cause a fever so that the body temperature is higher than 37°C at death and this will affect PMI determinations. Generally speaking, pathologists will only use algor mortis as a method of estimating PMI if the death took place within 12 h of being discovered.

Rigor Mortis

When a person dies, his or her joints and muscles are relaxed. After 2–5 h, the muscles begin to contract causing stiffening of the joints. The process is complete between 12 and 24 h after death. Then, over the next 2 or 3 days, the rigor mortis disappears. These times are subject to the same variations that affect algor mortis. Rigor mortis is accelerated by heat and by strenuous physical activity shortly before death.

Livor Mortis

When a person dies, blood stops circulating. When this occurs, the blood tends to pool at the lowest part of the body under the influence of gravity. If, for example, the deceased is lying on his back at death, the blood will pool toward the floor. This area of the body will become pinkish to purple. The upper parts of the body will become pale. The surface that is in contact with the body may leave an impression on the skin as livor proceeds. This may indicate if a body has been moved since livor mortis began. The livor mortis pattern may be disrupted where the body is resting on a floor or other surface because the pressure exerted by the body's weight prevents blood pooling in that area. Livor mortis onset is fairly rapid, appearing as soon as 30 min after death. After a few hours, the livor mortis becomes fixed; the blood pressure has ruptured the vessels and the blood starts to permeate the surrounding tissues. Once this happens, the area where livor mortis has taken place changes from reddish to greenish and then to brown. Sometimes, livor mortis can be confused

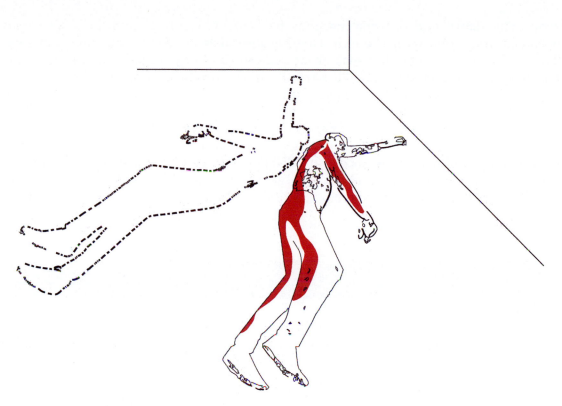

Figure 13.7 Diagram showing *livor mortis*. In this drawing, the body is found on its right side in the area where the outline is drawn. The body is turned over to show how the blood collects on the parts that are in contact with the floor. The dark area is the *livor mortis*. (Courtesy of Meredith Haddon.)

with bruises or contusions, especially after several hours have elapsed. Figure 13.7 is a drawing of how livor mortis looks.

Other Methods of Estimating PMI

Some chemical levels may be related to the PMI. These include potassium levels in eye fluids and certain chemicals in the brain. The appearance of a film over the eye is also related to PMI. Cardiac pH, ultrasound tests in muscles, electrical activity of skeletal muscles and the appearance of wounds are all methods that have been evaluated as contributors to the estimate of PMI. Examination of stomach contents has been a standard part of an autopsy for many years because the presence of chemicals or undigested drugs can be important evidence in determining the cause and manner of death. Stomach contents may also be used to help estimate PMI. It takes about 2–4 h for the stomach to digest a meal. If there is evidence of food in the stomach at death, then a presumption is that the person must have died no more than 2–4 h earlier. Stomach emptying may only be used as a corroborative test however, because there is great variation in the time of digestion owing to the condition of the deceased at the time of death. Some digestion also takes place after death and during putrefaction.

Late PMI

After 1 or 2 days have passed, other activities take place on and in the body that can help in establishing the PMI. For example, decomposition of a corpse begins soon after death and putrefaction may be evident within 2 or 3 days. The body becomes discolored with the skin turning greenish near the abdomen and hips. The action of anaerobic bacteria from outside the body and the intestinal tract begin to cause decomposition. This results in the production of copious quantities of gas that cause the body to bloat. If a person has drowned and sunk to the bottom of the water, the gas formation can actually cause the body to rise and float. The decomposition of the body depends upon the availability of oxygen. If the body is submerged in water or is buried, the decomposition process takes place much slower. High temperatures accelerate decomposition. When a body is discovered several days or weeks after death, the action of insects on and in the body can provide valuable information about the PMI. This subject is discussed in detail in Chapter 15.

Exhumations

Throughout history, human beings have developed a myriad of ways of dealing with death and especially the body after death. In some cultures, there have been attempts to preserve bodies for as long as possible. Mummification is an example of this and it is very effective at long-term preservation of bodies. One of the most common burial traditions in the United States is *embalming* of the dead before burial in a vault or casket. Embalming is a chemical treatment process whereby a chemical such as formaldehyde is added to preserve the body tissues and retard decomposition so that the body will be in a presentable condition for viewing prior to the funeral. Unlike mummification, embalming is a temporary preservation process whose effects wear off in a matter of months. From a forensic death investigation viewpoint, embalming presents serious problems that arise if and when a body must be removed from the vault or casket after burial because of questions concerning cause or manner of death. If there is a drug or poison in the body at the time of death, embalming will usually dilute it, replace it in the body or react chemically with it to alter or destroy it. It is sometimes possible to detect the presence of certain drugs or poisons even if they have been exposed to embalming agents.

Teamwork Approach

Death investigation can be very complex and usually requires the talents and skills of a number of individuals to be successfully concluded. The Medical Examiner's Office or Chief Coroner's Office is often the epicenter for these investigations. Sometimes the local crime laboratory is located within the ME's Office or the Coroner's Office. These laboratories may have a forensic anthropologist, entomologist, or odontologist on staff or under a consulting arrangement to assist with death investigations. This arrangement is common in large metropolitan areas or in jurisdictions that span a large geographical area. We will discuss the role of forensic anthropology and odontology in more detail in Chapter 14, and forensic entomology in Chapter 15.

Summary

Pathology is the medical subspecialty that studies the changes that a body undergoes as the result of injury or disease. There are two major branches to pathology; anatomic and clinical. Anatomic pathology involves the study of the body and its organ and tissue systems, whereas clinical pathology involves the analysis of blood and body fluids for drugs and poisons and their role in the cause of death. Forensic pathology involves both anatomic and clinical pathology in the determination of the cause and manner of death in cases of suspicious or unexplained death.

Each state has a system for the practice of forensic pathology. Approximately half of the states use the medical examiner system whereby the administrator is an appointed physician, although not necessarily a pathologist. The other states use the coroner system, whereby the administrator is elected on a county wide or statewide basis. In most states, the coroner does not have to be a physician. Each state has laws that determine the types of cases that must go to the medical examiner or coroner. They generally fall under the categories of unexplained or violent deaths or those where the deceased was under the care of a physician.

The medicolegal postmortem examination or autopsy involves a careful exterior and interior examination of the body for injuries, wounds or disease, as well as any trace or other evidence that might link the death to a perpetrator. The autopsy should be done by a forensically trained pathologist. The pathologist must determine the cause and manner of death as well as an estimate of the postmortem interval (PMI) or time since death. The PMI can be estimated in a number of ways including core temperature, livor mortis or rigor mortis, and other changes to the body. Longer term PMI can be estimated by observing decomposition or insect activity on the body.

The manner of death can be by accident, suicide, homicide, or natural causes. The cause of death refers to the actual incident or condition that is incompatible with sustaining life. There are certain patterns of injury that are usually present in various types of death.

Test Yourself

Multiple Choice

1. Which of the following is *not* a manner of death?
   a. Accidental
   b. Homicide
   c. Heart attack
   d. Suicide
   e. Natural causes
2. The original function of the coroner in medieval England was
   a. Surgeon
   b. Tax collector
   c. Legal advisor to the King
   d. Pathologist
   e. Town crier

3. Today, the medical examiner
    a. Must be a physician
    b. Determines cause and manner of death
    c. Signs the death certificate
    d. Is appointed
    e. All of the above
4. If a body has been discovered several days after death, the PMI may be determined by
    a. Insect activity
    b. Bloating
    c. Livor mortis
    d. Rigor mortis
    e. None of the above
5. Settling of the blood to the lower parts of the body after death is called
    a. Rigor mortis
    b. Algor mortis
    c. Livor mortis
    d. Bloating
    e. None of the above
6. Analysis of blood and body fluids to determine if drugs or poisons contributed to the death is part of
    a. Anatomic pathology
    b. Clinical pathology
    c. Systemic pathology
    d. Coroner's responsibility
    e. None of the above
7. Which of the following is not a duty of a pathologist who attends a crime scene when a body is discovered?
    a. Make sure that the person is dead
    b. Collect data concerning the PMI
    c. Supervise the search for trace evidence around the body
    d. Begin the autopsy
    e. Authorize transport of the body to the morgue
8. When someone has been poisoned by carbon monoxide, the main pattern of injury is
    a. Red coloration of the skin
    b. Blue coloration around the eyes
    c. Hemorrhaging in the eyes
    d. Bleeding around the mouth
    e. Accelerated rigor mortis
9. When someone has been killed by a contact shot, the area around the wound shows
    a. Lots of stippling
    b. A large entry wound
    c. Blackening and swelling
    d. Little if any bleeding
    e. A wound the size of the caliber of the bullet
10. Which of the following circumstances surrounding a death would be least likely to be investigated by the medical examiner or coroner
    a. A death in a two car auto crash
    b. A heart attack in an elderly woman while at home

    c. A body hidden under some brush in the woods

    d. A boy killed while deer hunting

    e. A death in a hospital during major surgery

True or False

11. All accidental deaths are investigated by the coroner or medical examiner
12. The only difference between a coroner and a medical examiner is that the coroner is elected
13. Autopsies consist of both external and internal examinations of the body
14. Death by a gunshot through the heart is an example of a manner of death
15. It takes at least 12 years of education beyond high school to become board certified as a pathologist

Matching—Match Each Term with Its Definition

16. Livor mortis
17. Rigor mortis
18. Algor mortis
19. PMI
20. Examination of the body after death

a. Stiffening of the joints after death
b. Autopsy
c. Cooling of the body after death
d. Time since death
e. Pooling of blood into lower body parts after death

Short Essay

21. What is the difference between the cause of death and the manner of death?
22. Briefly explain the history of the coroner system.
23. What are some of the ways that a pathologist can estimate the PMI? What are their advantages and disadvantages?
24. Briefly describe how a forensic pathologist is educated and trained.
25. Under what conditions would a medical examiner or coroner be required to receive a body for autopsy?

Further Reading

DiMaio, J. M. and M. D. DiMaio. (1989). *Forensic Pathology*. Elsevier, Boston, MA.

Fisher, R. S. and C. S. Petty. (1977). *A Handbook of Forensic Pathology for Non-Forensic Pathologists*. National Institute of Law Enforcement and Criminal Justice, US Department of Justice, Washington, DC.

Spitz, W. (ed.). (1993). *Medicolegal Investigation of Death*. Charles C Thomas, Springfield, IL.

On the Web

Forensic pathology on the famous Shroud of Turin : http://www.shroudofturin4journalists.com/pathology.htm.

Frequently asked questions about forensic pathology careers: http://web2.airmail.net/uthman/forensic_career.html.

Home page of the National Association of Medical Examiners: http://thename.org/.

John Ydstie talks with Dr. Ryan Parr, an anthropologist at Ontario's Lakehead University, about a 4-year effort to determine the identity of a 13-month-old child who died in the Titanic disaster. The child was buried in Halifax, Nova Scotia. Parr coordinated the work of over 50 scientists, genealogists and Titanic researchers, using DNA to trace the child to living family members: http://www.npr.org/templates/story/story.php?storyId=835398.

This resource consists of exercises and materials for a game in which students analyze forensic evidence from a fictitious murder. The evidence is used to formulate hypotheses and open up avenues of i…: http://www.ableweb.org/volumes/vol-22/minor/index.htm.

14
Anthropology and Odontology

Learning Objectives

1. To be able to define anthropology and forensic anthropology and give examples of each
2. To be able to describe the functions of the forensic anthropologist
3. To be able to describe the development and structure of bones
4. To be able to describe the various components of the biological profile
5. To be able to describe how bones are individualized
6. To be able to describe the various anthropological tests that can be done on skulls to help identify them
7. To be able to define forensic odontology and describe the functions of the forensic odontologist

Chapter 14
Anthropology and Odontology

Chapter Outline

Mini Glossary

Antemortem: Term is used to describe an occurrence prior to death.
Anthropology: Study of the human race, including lifestyle, culture, and physical traits, throughout time.
Deciduous teeth: The first set of teeth, commonly called the "baby teeth."
Diaphysis: A term that is used to identify the mid-section of a bone, or the shaft of the bone.
Epiphyseal line: Line toward the ends of the long bones marks the location of the childhood epiphyseal plate and is found between the diaphysis and the epiphysis in adult bones.
Epiphyseal plate: Found in the metaphysis, this part of a long bone is a hyaline cartilage plate in children who are growing, but matures into bone in adults and is replaced by the epiphyseal line.

Epiphysis: A term that is used to identify the rounded ends of a long bone.

Forensic anthropology: A specialty area within physical anthropology that uses characteristics of bone structure (osteology) to determine the identity of human remains and present findings in a court of law.

Forensic odontology: Forensic odontology uses human dentition for forensic purposes, such as determining identity of human remains, approximating the age of a person, analyzing bite marks, and examining dental structure of a person suspected to be the victim of abuse.

Greater sciatic notch: Located on the posterior portion pelvic bone between the ilium and the ischium, this notch is an important trait used by forensic anthropologists in the determination of the gender of the decedent.

Metaphysis: The part of a long bone that lies between the diaphysis and epiphysis, and is the growth area of the bone that produces an increase in stature in children.

Odontology: The scientific study of human dentition.

Osteology: The scientific study of bones.

Permanent teeth: These teeth are the second set of human teeth that replace the deciduous teeth.

Physical anthropology: The study of the biological traits and evolution of those traits in humans throughout time.

Postmortem interval (PMI): A term used to describe the amount of time since death occurred.

Pubic symphysis: The right and left pubic bones of the pelvis come together at this cartilaginous joint called the pubic symphysis.

Acronyms

PMI: Postmortem interval

Introduction

Anthropology is the study of the human race, and encompasses the cultural study of humans as well as the biological study of humans. The latter is usually called *physical anthropology*, although the term *bioanthropology* is more accurate. *Forensic anthropology* is a specialty within physical anthropology. It involves applications of *osteology* and *skeletal identification* to matters involving the law and the public. Osteology is the study of bone. Forensic anthropologists work with skeletal remains and try to determine the identity of the deceased. They often work with forensic pathologists and forensic odontologists (dentists) to help determine the cause and manner of death and the *postmortem interval (PMI)* or length of time since death.

The underlying principle of skeletal identification is that the human skeleton is unique in some ways. Most bones have unique characteristics that arise from genetics, growth, use, injury, or trauma. A forensic anthropologist identifies these characteristics in skeletal remains and compares them to *antemortem* (before death) evidence. If enough of these unique characteristics exist in an unknown skeleton and a suspected person, then an identification can be made and possibly a determination of the cause and manner of death.

Forensic anthropologists not only identify skeletal remains but are the principal investigators that collect the remains once they are discovered. This process is akin to an archeological dig, where artifacts (often skeletal remains) are discovered. The proper collection of skeletal remains is crucial to a successful identification and must always be done under the watchful eye of an experienced forensic anthropologist.

In recent years, the role of the forensic anthropologist has extended beyond the identification of skeletal remains. In mass disasters such as the destruction of the World Trade Center or plane crashes, forensic anthropologists are routinely called upon to help recover bodies. Some forensic anthropologists are experts in constructing facial features over a skull in the hope that someone will be able to identify the person. In other cases, forensic anthropologists can superimpose a face on a skull using a computer or digital camera in order to determine whether a skull belonged to a particular person. Forensic anthropologists help with facial and body recognition of people in crowds and even analyze characteristics such as *gait* (the visual characteristics of walking or running) as a means of identification.

Human Skeleton

The central focus of the work of forensic anthropologists is the human skeleton. Before describing how the skeleton is used in this work, it is important to understand some features of the skeletal system. A photograph of a human skeleton is shown in Figure 14.1, identifying some of the major bones of the human body.

The basic unit of the skeleton is the bone. There are 206 bones in the normal human skeleton. Bones are living functioning entities and the skeleton is considered to be an organ system. Bones grow and change over time, altering and repairing themselves as needed. The interior of many larger bones contains *marrow*, which, among other

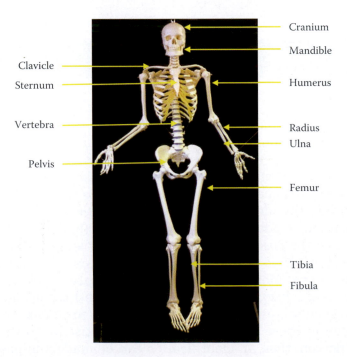

Figure 14.1 Anterior view of the human skeleton. (Courtesy of Norman Sauer.)

things, is responsible for the production of red blood cells. Bones have a number of functions in the body. First, they provide support for the other organs and tissues. Muscles attach at bones and their contractions make motion possible. Bones also serve a protective function for some of the more delicate soft tissues. The rib cage protects the heart and lungs. The skull protects the brain from shock. Bones are also the center for growth. Growth of bones begins at birth and continues until early adulthood.

Bone Structure

Bone is a complex material with several layers. Figure 14.2 shows the structure of bone. The outermost layer is called *compact bone*. It is hard and smooth. In long bones, there is an internal layer called *trabecullar bone*, which is light and spongy. It adds strength to bone without adding much weight. The bone marrow is contained in long bones in the center in a *medullary cavity*.

In many forensic anthropology cases, there are only fragments of bone present and the macrostructure described earlier may not be present in sufficient quantity or quality to identify the bone. It may be necessary to identify the material as bone using its microstructure. A thin cross section of a bone sample is prepared and would look similar to Figure 14.3. There are special growth units in bone called *osteons*. They are deposited in layers and eventually form chambers. The chambers have canals where blood vessels travel to reach each cell in the bone. This network of canals is called the *Haversian System*. The individual cells in the bone are called *osteocytes* and make up most of the compact bone. Osteocytes are connected by a microscopic canal system called the *canaliculi*. Even if bone is burned, it can usually be identified by the presence of Haversian canals.

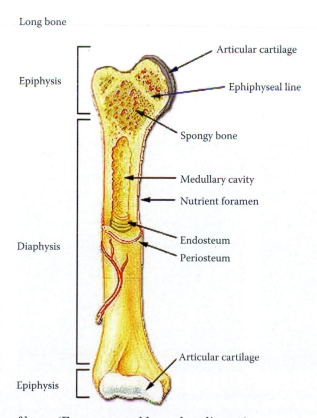

Figure 14.2 Structure of bone. (From newworldencyclopedia.org.)

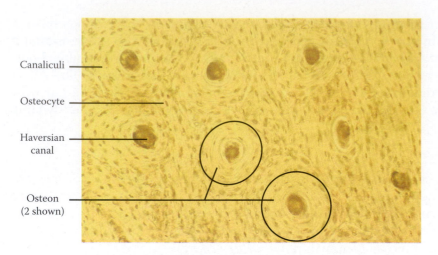

Figure 14.3 The Haversian system in long bones. (Courtesy of Norman Sauer.)

Identification of Skeletal Remains

On a leisurely stroll through the woods in early spring enjoying the sunshine and budding spring flora, someone stumbles on some miscellaneous bones. They look human. Authorities are called, the scene is documented, bone specimens collected, and the investigation begins (Figure 14.4).

The ultimate goal of the identification of skeletal remains is to determine the identity of the bones. Whose are they? This process requires that there be some individual features of the bones that aid in identification. Individual features include antemortem (before death) injuries or trauma to the bone and any unusual shapes or features in the bone. Absolute identification is often not possible, and in such cases, the forensic anthropologist will resort to class or general feature identification to determine age, gender, race, stature, cause of death, and other factors. In doing this, the forensic anthropologist will develop a *biological profile* of the remains.

Figure 14.4 Human skeletal remains found in a wooded setting. The skull (photo one) and parts of the pelvis (photo two) are shown undisturbed. The last photo shows some of the long bones collected. (Photo courtesy of Forensic Science Educational Consulting, LLC.)

Before the biological profile and individual characteristics are determined, three questions must be answered regarding the submitted specimen:

1. Is the material bone?
2. If so, is it human?
3. Does the age of the bone make it useful for forensic purposes?

Is the Specimen Bone?

In cases where there are whole bones or large pieces of bone present, identification is usually straightforward. In those cases where there are only fragments of bone or it has been burned or bleached or otherwise damaged, then microscopic analysis must be used. In these cases, the presence of Haversian canals is proof that the material is bone.

Is the Specimen Human Bone?

Depending upon the size and condition of the bone, the species may be determined macroscopically by comparing its features to those of various animal species. This sometimes presents a challenge because some pig and sheep bones and some bear paws can appear very similar to human bones. Sometimes there will be tissue and/or hairs clinging to the bone and these can be observed and analyzed to determine their species. If the bones are too small or too damaged to be examined macroscopically, then microscopic analysis can be undertaken. In such cases, the exact species may not be determined but human bone may be ruled out. A type of bone not found in humans, but present in many animals is called *plexiform*. In plexiform bone, the Haversian canals are arranged in geometric patterns and packed tightly together with little or no bone between them. In human bone, the Haversian canals are even spaced and there is bone between them. Even so, it is not always possible to make a definitive determination that tiny fragments of bone are human in origin.

Significance of Age

Other than radiocarbon dating (measuring the remnants of the isotope carbon-14), there are no reliable methods for dating skeletal remains. There may be other clues as to the age of skeletal remains making an estimation of age possible. There are practical, criminal justice considerations about the age of bone. If the skeletal remains are determined to be more than 50 years old, then its value forensically is limited. Suppose someone was murdered and the body buried and then discovered 50 years later. The chances are that the murderer is also dead or at least so elderly that prosecution would be useless.

Biological Profile

After it has been determined that the bone is human and of fairly recent origin, the process of identification begins. First, class characteristics are established as part of a biological profile. Then, if possible, individual characteristics are determined that could lead to absolute identification. The class characteristics will enable the anthropologist to put the skeletal remains in a subgroup such as males or as part of a particular race. Other factors such as stature, socioeconomic status, and time since death may also be determined. Because there is variation in skeletal characteristics among individuals within the same subgroup, it is sometimes necessary to consult databases or collections of skeletons that belong to a particular subgroup so that the range of variation within a subgroup can be known. The more common *class characteristics* that are determined as part of a biological profile are *age, gender, race,* and *stature*.

Determination of Age

Although bones change throughout life in response to activity or inactivity, aging, disease, and injury, there are definite intervals during which bones are actively growing. Once they have reached maturity, the bones will not grow except for repairs and reactions to aging. Thus, the mechanisms by which the age at death is estimated are different for people who die while their bones are still growing (sub-adults) compared with those whose bones have stopped growing (adults).

Using Dentition to Determine Age

One of the most reliable ways of determining the age of a sub-adult is by assessing the formation of teeth and their eruption through the gums. In most cases, temporary teeth (deciduous teeth) are formed and then permanent teeth form and erupt in a fairly predictable time period. There are many available charts that list the timetables for the formation of temporary and permanent teeth for various populations. Males and females have significant differences in the rates at which certain teeth mature and the charts reflect these differences.

Using Bone Development to Determine Age

Bones also have definite phases of growth that are age dependent. When the long bones start to grow, they consist of the shaft or *diaphysis* and the end(s) or *epiphysis*. As the individual develops, these two fuse together at the growth area, called the *metaphysis*. Within the metaphysis is the *epiphyseal plate* or growth plate, which lengthens as the immature bones grow. When the union is complete, growth ceases, and what remains is a thin line where the growth area was located called the *epiphyseal line*. The union is not an event; it takes place over years. Figure 14.5 shows the three stages of union of the diaphysis and the epiphysis. In general, union of individual bones takes place earlier for females than males. For example, the clavicle in the shoulder has an epiphysis that fuses in women between the ages of 17 and 21 but in males the union takes place between the ages of 18 and 22.

Using Pubic and Rib Bones to Determine Age

After a person has reached adulthood, bones have stopped growing (approximately 25–30 years). Changes to the bones are more subtle, and there are fewer places on the skeleton where changes can be directly related to age. The main areas in the body where age determinations are made in adults are the *pubic bones* and *rib bones*. Many researchers have spent years of careful measurement to refine the data that can be derived from changes in these bones and improve the accuracy of age at death determinations.

Pubic Symphysis   In adults, there are several ways of determining age at death. One of the most common methods is the macroscopic observation of the condition of the

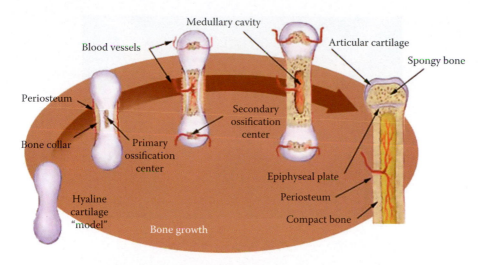

Figure 14.5 Bone growth. (National Cancer Institute.)

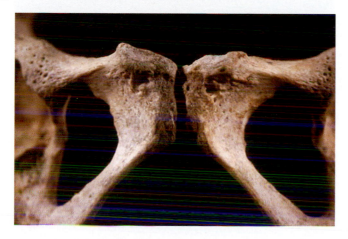

Figure 14.6 Female pubis. (Courtesy of Norman Sauer.)

pubic symphysis. The left and right hip (pelvic) bones join at the *pelvis.* Where these join, there is a symphysis or space that has a small amount of cartilage. When the cartilage is removed and the bones are separated, the shape and surface texture on the medial (inner) surfaces can be examined. These portions of the pelvic bone change in a predictable way as a person ages. The surface is rough and billowed in younger adults, but by age 35 the surface becomes increasingly smoother and develops a rim. After age 35, the symphysis steadily degenerates and the surface begins to erode.

Figure 14.6 shows a female human pubis. Figure 14.7 shows a male pubis. The space in the middle of the bone photo is where the pubic symphysis would be located and the inside edge of the exposed area in the middle is what is examined to help determine approximate age.

Although male and female pubic symphyses undergo similar changes with age, the age ranges are different for each phase of change.

Changes in the Ends of the Ribs

In addition to the pubic symphysis, the ends of the ribs that meet in the front of the body (the *sternal ends*) also change as a person gets older. The rib ends change in several ways. These include the shape of the surface and the amount of pitting, the type and quality of bone, and the presence of projections from the bone. Figure 14.8 shows the sternal rib area of an older adult.

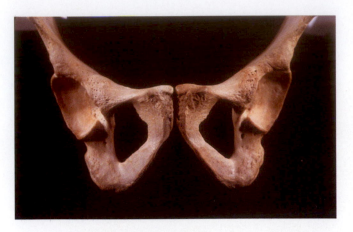

Figure 14.7 Male pubis. (Courtesy of Norman Sauer.)

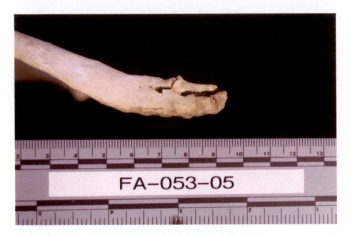

Figure 14.8 Sternal rib in older person. (Courtesy of Norman Sauer.)

Determination of Gender

In general, human males are larger than females, but this is more obvious when the person is alive. Skeletal remains show more subtle differences in size. In many cases there is little difference between the male and female skeletal size, so anthropologists focus on structural difference in certain regions of the skeleton to determine gender. It must be noted, however, that the regions used to determine gender develop throughout childhood and into puberty. Therefore, it may be hazardous to try and determine the sex of a skeleton that is younger than about 18. Most commonly the skull and the pelvis are the areas that are most diagnostic of gender.

The pelvis is the most obvious place to determine gender. This is largely due to the pelvis having different functions in males and females. In females, the pelvic region must support a fetus throughout development and delivery. The male pelvis is generally larger than the female while the female pelvis is broader. The most obvious locations on the pelvis where gender differences can be seen is the *greater sciatic notch* and the area below the pubic symphysis that forms the *sub pubic angle.* Figures 14.6 and 14.7 show the location of the sub pubic angle on a male and female pelvis, with Figure 14.9 showing the angle in more detail. Generally, the angle is less than 90° in males.

The greater sciatic notch is located in the posterior end of the pelvis, one on either side of the coccyx or tail bone (see Figure 14.10). In females, the notch is quite broad with an angle greater than 60°, whereas in males, the angle is much smaller. This is a very reliable test for determining the gender of skeletal remains.

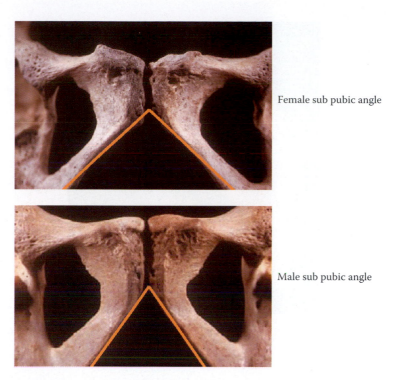

Figure 14.9 The sub pubic angle is much greater for females (top photo) than in males (bottom photo). (Original photo courtesy of Norman Sauer.)

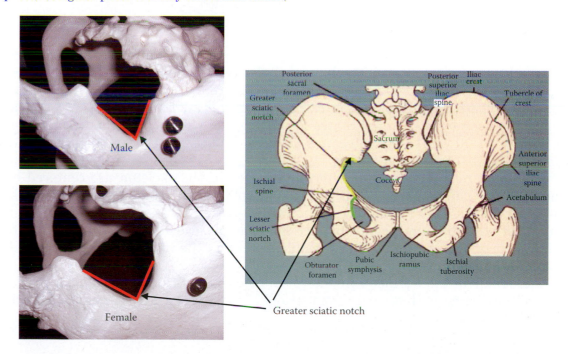

Figure 14.10 The greater sciatic notch is larger in females, generally greater than approximately 60°. The top photo shows the notch in a male pelvis whereas the bottom photo illustrates the notch in a female pelvis.

In the absence of pubic bones, there are features of the skull that are good indicators of sex. A number of bones in the skull have traits that differ between males and females. These include the prominence of *brow ridges*, the shape of the *mastoid process of the temporal bone*, the absence or presence of the *external occipital protuberance*, and the shape of the forehead. Figure 14.11 shows a male skull with a large mastoid process,

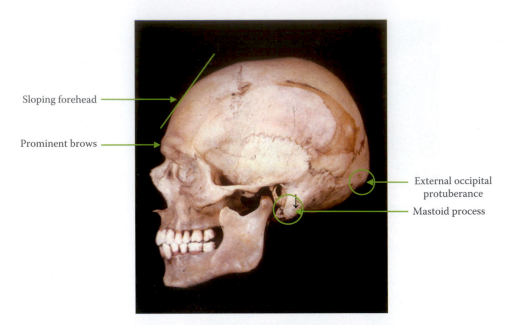

Figure 14.11 Some of the skull traits that help determine the sex of the remains. (Photo courtesy of Norman Sauer.)

prominent brow ridges, an external occipital protuberance, and a gently sloping forehead; all generally male characteristics.

Determination of Race

The determination of a person's race or ancestry can be difficult. The skeleton does not contain many obvious characteristics that define racial characteristics. Certainly today there are no pure ethnic or racial groups, and there may never have been any. There are also a number of different ways of defining ancestry. A typical scheme is used by the United States Department of Commerce in its census that is done every 10 years. The categories used are Caucasian, Blacks, Asians, Native Americans, Hispanics, and others.

The most reliable means of determining race in the skeleton are centered on the skull and can be based on either gross morphological examination or by mathematical analysis of various morphological features. There are a number of skull characteristics that are racially distinct. For example, eye orbits vary from round to triangular or rectangular. Other variations occur in the nasal apertures, the palate, and the mouth region.

The femur in the leg also exhibits racial characteristics, specifically the curvature of the diaphysis that varies from straight in Black people to curved in persons with Caucasian ancestry.

Determination of Stature

Attempts at stature determination have been made since the beginning of the twentieth century. Today the most practical method for determining stature uses measurements of long bones. Sometimes, a large fragment of a long bone may be used. The long bones are the humerus, radius, and ulna of the arm and the femur, tibia, and fibula of the leg. There is a linear relationship between the lengths of these bones and the overall stature of the individual. When estimating stature, the more long bone measurements that can be obtained, the better. Table 14.1 shows the

TABLE 14.1
Stature for Males and Females, Various Ethnic Groups

Race/Sex	Formula (cm)	Standard Deviation
Caucasian male	2.89 * humerus + 78.10	±4.57
	3.79 * radius + 79.42	±4.66
	3.76 * ulna + 75.55	±4.72
	2.32 * femur + 65.53	±3.94
	2.42 * tibia + 81.93	±4.00
	2.60 * fibula + 3.86	±3.86
Caucasian female	3.36 * humerus + 57.97	±4.45
	4.74 * radius + 54.93	±4.24
	4.27 * ulna + 57.76	±4.30
	2.47 * femur + 54.10	±3.72
	2.90 * tibia + 61.53	±3.66
	2.93 * fibula + 59.61	±3.57
African male	2.88 * humerus + 75.48	±4.23
	3.32 * radius + 85.43	±4.57
	3.20 * ulna + 80.77	±4.74
	2.10 * femur + 72.22	±3.91
	2.19 * tibia + 85.36	±3.96
	2.34 * fibula + 80.07	±4.02
African female	3.08 * humerus + 64.47	±4.25
	3.67 * radius + 71.79	±4.59
	3.31 * ulna + 75.38	±4.83
	2.28 * femur + 59.76	±3.41
	2.45 * tibia + 72.65	±3.70
	2.49 * fibula + 70.90	±3.80
Asian male	2.68 * humerus + 83.19	±4.16
	3.54 * radius + 82.00	±4.60
	3.48 * ulna + 77.45	±4.66
	2.15 * femur + 72.57	±3.80
	2.39 * tibia + 81.45	±3.27
	2.40 * fibula + 80.56	±3.24

Source: Burns, K.R., *Forensic Anthropology Training Manual*, 2nd edn., Pearson-Prentice Hall, Upper Saddle River, NJ, 2007.

mathematical formulas used to estimate stature for males and females of various ethnic groups. The stature is measured in centimeters.

To use the table one must know the gender and ethnic origin of the bone. An example calculation follows.

Suppose a femur of length 54 cm has been recovered from an excavation of skeletal remains. The biological profile indicates that the skeleton is a male and is most likely Caucasian. The proper formula from the table is

$$2.32 * \text{Femur} + 65.53 \pm 3.94$$

Inserting "54 cm" for the femur length into the formula gives the result of 194.75–186.87 cm or 76.67–73.57 in. (remember: 2.54 cm = 1 in.). This translates to a height range of 6 ft 4 in. to 6 ft 1 in. tall.

Individualization of Human Bone

The elements of the biological profile described earlier are all class characteristics of bone. It would be useful to be able to individualize bones or a skull to a particular individual. In the case of bones, this can only be done by comparing unique features of the bone with one from a known source. Typically, this would involve taking postmortem and antemortem x-rays of the bone. In the case of a skull, superimposition of the face on the skull using computer or camera-based techniques can lead to a more positive identification.

Bone Trauma and Individual Features

Most people receive some injuries to bones during life. If a bone is broken, then it will show signs of the break as it heals. These signs will usually remain throughout life and will show up in x-rays. A postmortem x-ray can be compared with the antemortem x-ray, and this may provide positive evidence of the identity of the person.

Even if a bone is not injured during life, there are many instances where a bone exhibits enough variation among individuals that x-rays of these bones can be used for identification. There are several bones in the skull including the frontal sinuses and places where arteries and veins enter and leave the skull that can be individualized. In cases where these bones are to be used for identification, comparisons are made between postmortem and antemortem x-rays and also with x-rays of the same bones of other individuals of the same sex and race to ensure that the features are in fact unique.

Analysis of Skulls

If all or most of a skull is recovered, there are at least two ways that identifications may be made. The most reliable method is *photographic superimposition*. This involves the comparison of the skull with a photograph of the suspected owner. One of the newer methods of accomplishing the comparison is to use video cameras to capture the image of the skull and of the actual photo and then superimpose the two. Videography has the advantage of permitting manipulations of the images including fading and using various sizes and angles. Computers can also be used to superimpose images and analyze them to determine if they came from the same individual. Figure 14.12 shows a drawing of superimposition of a face on a skull.

When a skull is recovered and no identification made, investigators can use a sculpture technique to recreate a face. A three-dimensional reconstruction of the soft tissues of a face are built up onto the skull. Compilations of tissue thicknesses for various parts of the face have been compiled for various races of males and females. A proper reconstruction requires that the race and sex of the skull be known. Using the measurement tables, the anthropologist uses pegs and clay to build up the face (see Figure 14.13).

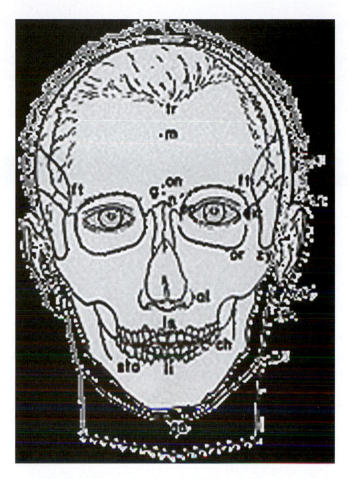

Figure 14.12 Drawing of superimposition of a face on a skull.

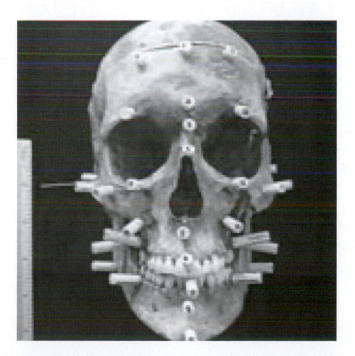

Figure 14.13 Facial reconstruction using a recovered skull. The pegs determine the depth of the tissue. Clay will then be added to the peg depth creating the final facial image.

Some guesswork is involved in choosing lips, the nose, eyebrows, etc. Prosthetic eyes and wigs are also used. This method is not used for identification of a particular individual. Sometimes facial reconstructions are prepared and photographed. The picture is distributed to the news media and broadcast in the hopes that the family of a missing person will recognize it.

Collection of Bones

Most physical evidence at crime scenes is discovered and collected by crime scene technicians or investigators. On the other hand, skeletal remains are seldom discovered this way. Most often bones are happened upon by hikers, hunters, or other people who are in a wooded or remote area, often near a lake or stream. Because such scenes are unbounded and unsecured when discovered, it is especially important for law enforcement agents to seal off and protect these scenes. The search for and collection of skeletal evidence in outdoor scenes must be left to professional anthropologists who are trained in recognition and collection of material above ground and buried. If the remains retain decomposing flesh, the search may be aided by the presence of flies or other arthropods (see Chapter 15) or by specially trained dogs (see Chapter 7). In some cases where bodies may be buried in shallow graves, military planes with ground-penetrating radar may be used to help locate the remains.

Something Extra: An Australian "Body Farm"

In Western Australia, the Departments of Anthropology and Entomology of the University of Western Australia maintain a sort of Body Farm. Unlike the United States Body Farm in Tennessee, Australian researchers are prohibited from using human cadavers for the study of decomposition and insect activity. Instead, they use very large pigs (up to 300 lb). The decomposition of pigs proceeds in a similar manner to humans. The pigs are euthanized and then placed in various locations in a remote plot of ground near the University. Some are dressed in clothes, some are covered by brush or branches, and some are buried in shallow graves. The pigs spend about 40 days in this field and are visited daily by researchers. The Australian Air Force also uses the Body Farm to train their pilots in the use of ground penetrating radar. The pilots perform regular flyovers to see if they can find the buried pigs with their radar.

Collection of bone evidence from an outdoor crime scene is somewhat like an archaeological dig. The perimeters of the scene are located and marked. Depending upon its size, the scene may be divided into quadrants to organize the search. The entire scene is carefully photographed before any search takes place. Each piece of bone is carefully marked with a flag or other marker and documented. After the surface bones have been collected, then excavation will be employed to discover buried bones.

Forensic Odontology

Forensic odontology (dentistry) is a part of forensic medicine. It deals with the examination of dental evidence including teeth, mouth, and jaws, and the presentation of expert evidence in a court of law. There are a number of aspects of forensic odontology. They include

- Identification of human remains in crimes and mass disasters
- Estimation of the age of a person living or dead
- Analysis of bite marks found on victims of an attack and in objects such as foods or other substances including wood and leather
- Examination of the dentition and face of a person suspected to be the victim of abuse

Structure and Development of Teeth

Teeth are unique in the human anatomy for a number of reasons. First, the outer part of a tooth is made of a substance called *enamel*. This is the hardest substance that is produced by the human body. Because of this, it can leave impressions in a wide variety of materials from wood to flesh. These impressions can, under certain conditions, provide a means of identification. When a person dies and is interred, the teeth are among the longest surviving structures and may provide a means of identification long after all of the soft tissues have decayed away. Teeth also interact directly with a person's environment and thus their condition may reflect elements of that individual's lifestyle and experiences.

Dentists describe teeth using a numbering system. This is shown in Figure 14.14. Each time an individual visits a dentist a chart will be kept of the condition and treatment of each tooth by number. When a skull is recovered from a crime scene or disaster scene, this chart can be extremely helpful in identifying the dental remains.

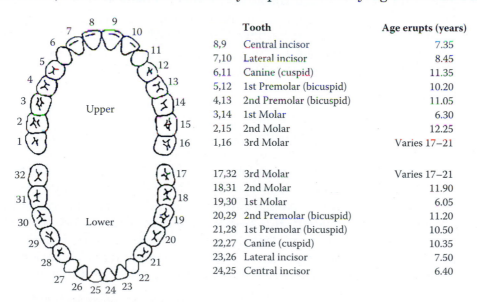

	Tooth	Age erupts (years)
8,9	Central incisor	7.35
7,10	Lateral incisor	8.45
6,11	Canine (cuspid)	11.35
5,12	1st Premolar (bicuspid)	10.20
4,13	2nd Premolar (bicuspid)	11.05
3,14	1st Molar	6.30
2,15	2nd Molar	12.25
1,16	3rd Molar	Varies 17–21
17,32	3rd Molar	Varies 17–21
18,31	2nd Molar	11.90
19,30	1st Molar	6.05
20,29	2nd Premolar (bicuspid)	11.20
21,28	1st Premolar (bicuspid)	10.50
22,27	Canine (cuspid)	10.35
23,26	Lateral incisor	7.50
24,25	Central incisor	6.40

Figure 14.14 A dentist's chart showing the tooth numbering system with a chart of the tooth names and average age that the tooth is visible.

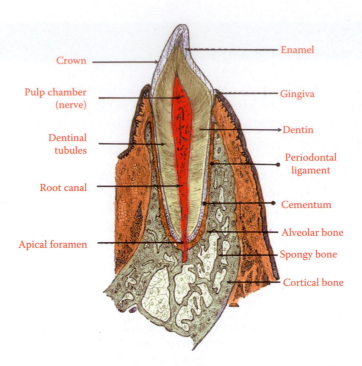

Figure 14.15 The anatomy of a tooth. (Courtesy of Martin S. Spiller, D.M.D., www.doctorspiller.com.)

Each tooth is made up of three parts: the *crown, the body,* and *the root*. The anatomy of a tooth is shown in Figure 14.15.

Teeth are also oriented by their sides. The chewing surface of the tooth is the *occlusal* surface.

Humans develop two sets of teeth as they grow. The first set is the "baby" teeth. Dentists refer to this set as the *deciduous* teeth. They are gradually replaced by the *permanent* teeth. Different teeth develop at different rates. Dentists can estimate the age of a person by the development of various teeth. For example, the first *deciduous* incisor tooth erupts through the gums at about 9 months of age. The first *permanent* tooth is a molar that erupts at about 6 years. The third molar or "wisdom" tooth erupts between 17 and 21 years. The wisdom teeth often erupt irregularly and have to be removed by the dentist.

Identification of Dental Remains

Although there is usually sufficient evidence to identify a dead body, sometimes dentition is the only way of achieving a positive identification. Cases aided by dental record checks include burning, drowning, fire or explosion and decomposition. All mouths and dentition are different, and a trained forensic odontologist may be able to provide enough information for a positive identification. This is normally done by charting the teeth of the deceased and comparing this with dental records of persons who may have been involved in the incident. If a suspected person is identified, then comparison of postmortem and antemortem dental x-rays can be used to confirm the identity. Even if a person has no teeth, there may be enough identifying information from the analysis of dentures and the structure of the jaw and skull as revealed by x-rays.

Bite Marks

There have been a number of cases in recent years where a bite mark impression made on a person's body by an attacker has been compared with a cast of the

Problem solving

21. Measure your height in feet and inches. Determine the length range of each of your long bones using Table 14.1 for your gender and race.

True or False

22. The development of the teeth has no bearing on the age of a person past 10 years old.
23. The biological profile includes the age, gender, race, and occupation of an individual.
24. In order to determine height from the femur, you must measure the width of the bone.
25. Forensic anthropology is the study of bones and their characteristics.

Matching

For each trait given, match it with the biological information it will determine from this list: (A—age, G—gender, R—race, S—stature)

26. Epiphyseal lines
27. Length of humerus
28. Shape of eye orbit
29. Greater occipital protuberance
30. Greater sciatic notch

Further Reading

Burns, K. R. (2007). *Forensic Anthropology Training Manual*, 2nd edn. Pearson-Prentice Hall, Upper Saddle River, NJ.

Sauer, N. (1984). Manner of death, in *Human Identification: Case Studies in Forensic Anthropology*, T. Rathbun and J. Buikstra (eds.). Charles C Thomas Publishers, Springfield, IL, pp. 176–184.

Ubelaker, D. (2000). *Human Skeletal Remains*. Taraxacum, Washington, DC.

Ubelaker, D. H. and H. Scammell. (1992). *Bones: A Forensic Detective's Casebook*. Edward Burlingame Books, New York.

White, T. D. (2000). *Human Osteology*. Academic Press, London, U.K.

Helpful Websites

Forensic Anthropology
http://www.pbs.org/saf/1203/teaching/teaching2.htm.
http://biology.clc.uc.edu/courses/bio105/bone.htm.
http://scienceblogs.com/afarensis/2006/06/17/lessons_from_kennewick_fitting/.
http://www.anthro4n6.net/forensics/.
http://www.forensicanthro.com/.
http://whyfiles.org/192forensic_anthro/.
http://facstaff.unca.edu/cnicolay/BIO223-F08/HO-forensic.pdf.
http://www.forensicanthro.com/resources.html.
http://www.mnsu.edu/emuseum/biology/humananatomy/skeletal/terms.html.

http://www.mnsu.edu/emuseum/biology/forensics/.
Case report, example of an investigation and the application of mathematics: http://www.
    anthro4n6.net/forensics/report.html#Inventory.

Forensic Odontology
http://www.3dmouth.org/6/6_1.cfm.
http://en.wikipedia.org/wiki/Tooth_development.

Facial Reconstruction
http://www.forensicartist.com/reconstruction.html.
http://www.karenttaylor.com/.
Tennessee Body Farm: University of Tennessee Forensic Anthropology Center: http://web.
    utk.edu/~fac/.

15
Forensic Entomology

Learning Objectives

1. To be able to define entomology and forensic entomology and give examples
2. To be able to describe the contributions that forensic entomology can make in solving death cases
3. To be able to describe the ways that forensic entomology can help determine the postmortem interval
4. To be able to list and describe the various types of arthropods that invade a body after death
5. To be able to describe the contributions of forensic entomology to the determination of the presence of drugs and poisons in a body
6. To be able to describe the five stages of decomposition of a body after death

351

Chapter 15
Forensic Entomology

Chapter Outline

Mini Glossary

Entomology: Generalized study of insects and related arthropods (crustaceans, spiders, etc.)

Forensic entomology: The application of entomology to civil and criminal incidents

Instar: Developmental stages of the larva of a fly

Medicolegal forensic entomology: This type of forensic entomology is used in the investigation of death, abuse, and neglect cases

Necrophage: Insects that feed on the tissue of the corpse

Omnivore: Arthropods that feed not only on the body but on other insects that have been attracted to the corpse. Omnivores include mainly wasps and beetles

Postmortem interval (PMI): Time since death. In the context of forensic entomology, it is the time interval between when the body is first exposed to insects and when it is discovered

Urban forensic entomology: The analysis of the presence of arthropods in homes, businesses, gardens, and farms

Acronyms

ABFE: American Board of Forensic Entomology
ARPE: American Registry of Professional Entomologists
PMI: Postmortem Interval

Introduction

The earliest record of the use of entomology in a criminal investigation is described in a book published in China in the thirteenth century. The book, called *Hsi Yuan Lu*, (which can be translated as *The Washing Away of Wrongs*) contains a description of a murder investigation in a rice paddy. The incident involved a homicide committed by one of the workers. The investigator lined up the workers and told them to lay their sickles on the ground. One of the implements contained very faint traces of blood. Although this could not have been identified as blood scientifically at that time, it almost immediately attracted flies. Since the only implement that could have caused the murder was a sickle, and the murderer had to be one of the workers, the flies "identified" the guilty worker's sickle as having blood on it. The perpetrator of the crime was, in effect, caught red-handed and he confessed. This incident is a textbook example of the use of insects in solving crimes and is the subject of this chapter. We will see that forensic entomology not only is a useful science in crime investigation, but can also be helpful in civil incidents in rural areas and cities alike.

Entomology is the generalized study of insects and related arthropods (crustaceans, spiders, etc.). *Forensic entomology* is the application of entomology to civil and criminal incidents. The most important and noteworthy applications of forensic entomology involve its use in criminal cases, but it has very important applications in the civil area. For example, *urban forensic entomology* involves the analysis of the presence of arthropods in homes, businesses, gardens, and farms. There have been a number of cases where the indiscriminate use of pesticides has killed many arthropods. The location and quantity of these dead animals provide strong evidence that the pesticides were used improperly or without proper cautions being taken against their spread. There are also cases where insects invade food and other consumer products such as soft drinks, salad dressings, and even candy. These situations often lead to litigation because of improper storage of food materials. Forensic entomologists are often called into such cases to provide testimony about how and why these insects were able to invade food storage containers and facilities.

Medicolegal forensic entomology is the most visible and common application of entomology. This type of forensic entomology is used in the investigation of death, abuse, and neglect cases. Although most noteworthy for its contribution to estimation of the postmortem interval (PMI) or time since death, there are many other types of information that can be gleaned from the study of arthropods at crime scenes. These include the climatic and temperature conditions at death, the location of a body and determination of whether the body had been moved shortly after death, how the body was stored, the location of antemortem (before death) injuries, whether the body had been buried or submerged in water, and sometimes the presence of drugs and poisons in the body. Suspects have been linked to a scene by the presence of arthropods. The extent of abuse or neglect of infants and elderly persons can be established by insect activity. Considering all of these situations, the role of the forensic entomologist in a crime investigation can be a major one. His or her principle role is to collect and identify arthropod specimens and then interpret these findings in relation to environmental variables. Arguably the most important contribution of medicolegal forensic entomology to crime investigation is in the estimation of the PMI in cases where a body is discovered days after death. The contribution of forensic entomology in late PMI determination is discussed in detail in Chapter 13. The basis for estimation of the PMI by forensic entomologists is that many different types of insects will invade a corpse at predictable intervals after death, some very soon after the body has deposited. These arthropods have predictable developmental stages and parts of the body that they will inhabit. Forensic entomologists examine the insects on and in a body when it is discovered. From the types of insects present, their developmental stages and the degree of activity on the body, they can sometimes make remarkably accurate and precise determinations of the PMI, even days after death. Insect behavior may also yield information about how or even if, a crime occurred.

With all of these valuable uses of entomology, it is interesting to note that this type of evidence is badly underused in homicide investigations. Insects are often ignored as evidence and are treated as a gross nuisance by investigators at crime scenes and by pathology personnel at autopsies. There are several reasons for this. Crime scene technicians who collect evidence are seldom trained to recognize the significance of the presence of arthropods on a body. They do not realize the importance of this evidence and are not trained in the proper methods of collection of insects. Investigators are told that this evidence is unreliable and that entomologists can only give an estimate of the PMI, not an exact determination. In fact there are no methods that can give an exact PMI at any time after death. Finally, there are only a few dozen forensically trained entomologists in the whole United States. If untrained entomologists are called in to crime scenes, mistakes are often made and the value of the evidence is diminished or lost, further contributing to the lack of regard for this science.

Becoming a Forensic Entomologist

To become certified as a Diplomate in the American Board of Forensic Entomology (ABFE/ http://research.missouri.edu/entomology/), one must first obtain a PhD in entomology. There are a number of universities nationwide that offer this degree. Some universities also offer bachelor's or master's degrees in forensic entomology. There is a formal organization of professional entomologists who are Board Certified. This is the American Registry of Professional Entomologists (ARPE).

PMI: The Life Cycle of the Blowfly

As was discussed earlier, the key evidence presented by arthropods in determining the PMI is the determination of what types are present in and around a body and what stages of life are exhibited. Many species of arthropod invade a body, and they normally arrive at predictable intervals in particular order. Of course, all of this is highly dependent upon the environmental conditions surrounding the corpse. Like most life activities, cold conditions slow down insect activity. If a body is heavily clothed or partially or totally buried, it will take insects longer to reach the body. Many insects are inactive at night so, if a body is left at an outdoor sight at night, there may be no activity until dawn. It generally takes insects longer to get to a body that is indoors or under water. Even with all of these environmental variables, there are a remarkable number of constants and consistencies about insect behavior at the site of a dead body. It is also important to note that, with respect to forensic entomology, the PMI is not the same as the time since death, but is the time interval since the body was put into an environment where interaction with insects is possible. For example, if someone is killed and the body is put into the trunk of a car, which is then driven for 8 h to a location where the body is dumped, insect activity can only begin at that time and determination of the PMI will not reflect the time that the body spent in the car.

In many situations the common blowfly is the first insect to reach a dead body. Flies are able to find and invade a corpse long before the police or crime scene unit arrives. They can squeeze into the tightest of spaces to get to a body. In cases where bodies are buried in the rubble of a fire or explosion, it is sometimes possible to "follow the flies" to the bodies in the rubble. This method was used to help locate bodies in the rubble of the Murrah building in the Oklahoma City bombing. Once female flies find the body, they will immediately lay eggs and the life cycle of the fly begins as described in the following text.

Egg laying begins in naturally moist areas of the body such as the mouth, eyes, nose, and around open wounds. Generally egg laying takes place only in daylight so if a death occurs at night, egg laying will be delayed. One female blowfly can lay hundreds of eggs in a short period. Another common carrion fly, the flesh fly, deposits live larvae in the same areas as blowfly eggs. Figure 15.1 is a picture of a blowfly. Figure 15.2 is a picture of an adult flesh fly.

Fly larvae go through three developmental stages called "instars." During each instar, the maggot increases in size dramatically. By the time a maggot reaches the third instar, most of the flesh of the body has been consumed. Under moderate dry conditions the first instar of the blowfly forms from the egg about 8 h after the egg is oviposited. The second instar forms around 20 h later and the third about 20 h after that. After about 5 days, the larva stops feeding and rests. After a few more days the larva becomes a pupa. The adult fly emerges about 3 weeks after the eggs are laid. Figure 15.3 shows blowfly maggots and Figure 15.4 shows pupae of a number of species of flies.

Using the time intervals given earlier, an entomologist can begin to develop clues that will help determine the PMI. Again, it must be stressed that the time intervals of some of the stages given earlier depend somewhat upon the environmental conditions present. There are also other artifactual situations that can affect the entomologist's

Figure 15.1 An adult blowfly. (Courtesy of Dr. Richard Merritt.)

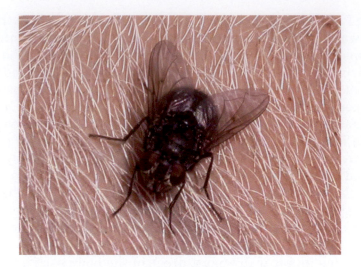

Figure 15.2 An adult flesh fly. (Courtesy of Dr. Richard Merritt.)

Figure 15.3 Blowfly maggots. (Courtesy of Dr. Richard Merritt.)

Figure 15.4 Pupae of several species of flies. (Courtesy of Dr. Richard Merritt.)

estimation of the PMI. One forensic entomologist (Richard Merritt, private communication) tells of a case where an entomologist encountered unusually large maggots in a body. His conclusion was that the maggots had been feeding at the body for some time, and his determination of the PMI was based on this long interval. However, other measurements of insect activity were at odds with the PMI determination based on the data from the maggots. Forensic toxicology of the remains of the body showed that the victim had ingested cocaine shortly before death. Some of this was transferred to the maggots as they fed on the body tissues. The stimulant effect of the cocaine caused the maggots to eat much more rapidly than normal, accelerating their growth greatly and leading to the incorrect data. This raises two interesting points: First, if possible, the entomologist must not rely on only one piece of life cycle or insect data in reaching conclusions about PMI. Corroborating evidence should always be obtained where possible. Second, if there is insufficient tissue remaining on a dead body for drug screening, maggots can be collected and tested for the presence of drugs. Another important point about making observations from insect activity is that the act of eating and digesting tissues by insects releases a great deal of energy. Temperatures around a body that is being consumed by insects can reach nearly 150°F at times. This, in turn, accelerates decomposition of the body and insect activity.

The life cycle of the fly described earlier is only one example of the use of arthropod life cycles to estimate PMI. Other types of insects invade bodies and lay eggs on a predictable schedule. Still others will attack and eat the eggs and larvae of other insects, also on a predictable schedule. This way, entomologists usually have several data points from which to draw conclusions concerning the PMI.

Decomposition of a Body after Death

When a person dies, decomposition of the tissues and organs begins to take place almost immediately although outward evidence may not be seen for hours depending upon the temperature and moisture conditions. Much of this decomposition is carried out by bacteria inside and outside the body but when they are available arthropods can speed up this process remarkably. Catts and Goff (1992) describe four roles that arthropods play in decomposition of bodies:

1. *Necrophages*: These are insects that actually feed on the tissue of the corpse. Many of them are flies. Entomologists study the life cycles of these insects on the body to help determine PMI.
2. *Omnivores*: Some arthropods feed not only on the body but on other insects that have been attracted to the corpse. Omnivores include mainly wasps and beetles. It is interesting to note that if omnivores are present in large quantities, they may deplete the population of necrophages thus retarding decomposition.
3. *Predators and Parasites*: Some categories of arthropods including some flies and mites, act as parasites on other insects and some may start out as necrophages and then end up becoming predators of other insects at a later stage.
4. *Incidentals*: These are arthropods including some spiders, centipedes, mites, and others that use the corpse as part of their normal habitat. They move into the corpse and make it their home, at least for a time.

Figure 15.5 shows a picture of carrion beetles.

Figure 15.5 Carrion beetles. (Courtesy of Dr. Richard Merritt.)

Stages of Decomposition

There is great variability in the time it takes for a body to decompose. The major determinate is temperature. Warm temperatures will accelerate the decomposition process and cold weather will depress it. A level of decomposition that might take 18–24 h in cool weather can take only a few hours in tropical weather. Another factor is the amount of protection that the body has. Clothing slows down decomposition as does burial or immersion in water. A forensic entomologist who uses the life cycles of various arthropods to help determine the postmortem interval must take these variables into consideration.

Even with this great variability, there are common patterns to the decomposition process. There are several distinct stages to decomposition, and they will occur in the same order each time. The environment of the body will determine the duration of each stage and the local arthropod population will also have some effect. Forensic entomologists generally identify five stages of decomposition. The first three comprise one phase where the arthropods feed on the body and their life cycle proceeds increasing the biomass greatly. Maggots are the major arthropods in this phase. Under moderate environmental conditions, this phase takes about 10 days. The three stages in this phase are listed as follows along with their average durations and some of the insects that are commonly found on the carcass during each stage:

- *Fresh* (1–2 days): Adult blowflies, flesh flies, yellow jackets
- *Bloated* (2–6 days): Blowflies and other flies, some beetles, yellow jackets
- *Decay* (5–11 days): Some flies and beetles, cockroaches

When this phase is complete, the maggots leave the body and the decomposition fluids have mostly seeped away. At this point, there has been a drastic decrease in biomass at the scene. The second phase of decomposition has two stages and takes on the order of 2 weeks or more. The stages are as follows:

- *Post-decay* (10–24 days): Some beetles, fruit flies, gnats, some flies
- *Dry stage* (24+ days): Some beetles, ants, and flies

Factors that Affect PMI

During this chapter, we have briefly mentioned some of the factors that can affect the determination of the PMI. This section organizes these factors, and they are discussed in a bit more detail.

Physical Factors

A body buried in a vault or casket will be much more resistant to attack by insects than one that is dumped into a hole, which is then filled with dirt. Even burying a body in soil will affect the rate of attack by arthropods. The temperature a few feet underground will generally be more constant than on the surface. It will be dark that inhibits egg laying by insects. It may be difficult for many insects including flies to reach the body. There is also generally less air if the body is tightly compacted by soil. Anaerobic bacteria are much more active in deep soil, and this may affect decomposition of the body. There is also generally more moisture in soil a few feet below ground. If a body is submerged in water, especially if it is trapped in a car or other container, decomposition due to insects is very different than on land. The temperature is usually more constant, there may be less light depending upon how deep the body is and the variety and types of arthropods available to feed on the body will be very different than on land. All of these factors make determination of the PMI more difficult for the forensic entomologist.

Chemical Factors

In Chapter 13, the role of embalming on the determination of the presence of drugs or poisons in a body was discussed when a body was exhumed. Embalming chemicals also affect insect attack on dead bodies. These agents are generally poisonous to most arthropods, so their activity will be greatly retarded by the presence of embalming fluids. As the body decomposes, the embalming agents may leak out or evaporate and some insect activity can then take place, but it is retarded. If a body is placed or buried on land where insecticides are used to control pests that attack crops, these poisons will also affect arthropods that feed on bodies. Again, the usual effect is to greatly retard insect activity and reproduction, thus making the normal entomological data suspect. It was also previously mentioned that drugs which are present in a body at death may be consumed by arthropods. The drugs will, in turn, affect these animals. Stimulants, such as cocaine will accelerate insect activity whereas depressants can retard activity. There has been little attention paid to the effects of hallucinogens such as LSD or marijuana on insect activity.

Climate

It was previously mentioned that high temperatures accelerate virtually all biological activity. Likewise, cold weather will have the opposite effect, so it is not surprising that temperatures will affect the rate of activity and reproduction of insects that have invaded a body. In addition, high winds may cover or uncover a body with debris and make it harder for flying insects to find and land on a body. Heavy rains can wash insects off of a body, and if the body becomes partially submerged, it can dramatically affect insect activity.

8. Which of the following is *not* a factor that affects decomposition of a body and insect activity?
   a. Cold
   b. Wind
   c. Rain
   d. Embalming fluid
   e. All the above are factors

True or False

9. The only application of forensic entomology is determination of the PMI.
10. Urban entomology involves the analysis of the presence of arthropods in homes and businesses.
11. Forensic anthropology can be used to link a suspect to a crime scene.
12. The life cycle of a fly will slow down in very cold weather.
13. The blowfly is usually the first insect that will discover a dead body.
14. Insect evidence is often treated as a nuisance by investigators and pathologists.
15. If temperatures are moderate, a forensic entomologist can determine a PMI to within 1 h of death.
16. Fly larvae go through four instars before becoming an adult.
17. Some arthropods such as spiders will actually move into a corpse for a time and make it their home.

Matching—Match Each Term with Its Definition

18. Instar	a. Fly larva
19. Omnivore insect	b. Chemical that retards insect activity
20. Insecticide	c. Eats other insects as well as flesh
21. Bloated stage	d. Developmental stage of a fly
22. Maggot	e. A stage of decomposition

Short Essay

23. What contributions can forensic entomology make in the investigation of death?
24. How do forensic entomologists determine the postmortem interval? What time frames are involved?
25. How does insect behavior help pinpoint the locations of wounds on a body?

Further Reading

Byrd, J. H. and J. L. Castner (eds.). (2001). *Forensic Entomology: The Utility of Arthropods in Legal Investigations*. CRC Press, Boca Raton, FL.

Catts, E. P. and M. L. Goff. (1992). Forensic entomology in criminal investigations. *Annual Review of Entomology* 37:253–272 (Annual Reviews, Palo Alto, CA).

Goff, M. L. (2001). *A Fly for the Prosecution: How Insect Evidence Helps Solve Crimes*. Harvard University Press, Cambridge, MA.

On the Web

A comprehensive bibliography on forensic entomology: http://www.forensicentomology.com/literature.htm.

Case studies in forensic entomology: http://research.missouri.edu/entomology/casestudies.html.

Excellent introductory site for forensic entomology: http://www.forensicentomology.com/.

Homepage of the American Board of Forensic Entomology: http://research.missouri.edu/entomology/.

Many images of insects: http://entomology.unl.edu/images/.

Video showing decomposition of a pig: http://lubbock.tamu.edu/ipm/AgWeb/videos/Forensic/Forensicvideos.html.

16
Serology

Learning Objectives

1. To be able to define and describe the components of blood
2. To be able to describe preliminary tests for blood
3. To be able to describe confirmatory tests for blood
4. To be able to define semen and describe its components
5. To be able to describe the preliminary and confirmatory tests for semen
6. To be able to describe the common tests for vaginal secretions
7. To be able to describe the common tests for saliva
8. To be able to describe the role of bloodstain pattern analysis in crime scene reconstruction
9. To be able to describe the physical properties of blood and how they contribute to the various types of bloodstains
10. To be able to describe the various types of bloodstains

Chapter 16
Serology

Chapter Outline

Mini Glossary

Agglutination: The coming together or clumping of antigen bearing red blood cells and the antibodies specific to that antigen.

Altered bloodstains: Shed blood that has been changed physically or physiologically.

Antibody: Antibodies are found in the blood serum and are specific to a blood type. They serve as protection from noncompatible blood types.

Antigen: Antigens in blood are inherited substances on the erythrocyte (red blood cell) that are responsible for eliciting a blood group reaction to specific antibodies.

Blood: A solution of various materials important for sustaining life.

Bloodstain pattern analysis (BSPA): An area of forensic science that interprets the patterns seen in deposited blood and relates them to the actions that could have caused the pattern.

Confirmatory test: A test that used to identify the *specific* fluid or material present.

Erythrocytes: A component of the solid part of the blood responsible for carrying oxygen and removing carbon dioxide from the cells, commonly called red blood cells.

Forensic serology: The examination and identification of body fluids as they relate to a crime scene.

Leucocytes: A component of the solid part of the blood responsible for fighting infection, commonly called white blood cells.

Passive bloodstains: Blood that is shed and travels under the influence of gravity only.

Plasma: The liquid portion of the blood, which has, in suspension, blood cells and platelets along with water, glucose, proteins, and other chemical compounds.

Spatter bloodstains: Blood that moves due to a force in addition to gravity which exhibits directionality and specific distribution patterns.

Screening (presumptive) test: A test that establishes the *possibility* that a specific type of fluid or substance is present in the sample.

Serology: The examination and identification of body fluids.

Thrombobocytes: A component of the solid part of the blood that assists in the clotting process. They are commonly called platelets.

Viscous: A term used to describe a liquid that has a resistance to flow.

Acronyms

BSPA: Bloodstain pattern analysis
CSC: Criminal sexual conduct
DNA: Deoxyribonucleic acid
PIC: Picroindigocarmine (dye)
PSA: Prostate-specific antigen
SAP: Seminal acid phosphatase

Introduction

One of the first blood spatter cases in the United States took place in Utah. The case involved the admissibility of blood spatter evidence. A man was seen entering the home of his girlfriend and then, a few minutes later, exited carrying the girl in his arms. He put her in the back seat of his car and drove off. A neighbor witnessed this and called the police, who located his car and stopped him. He claimed that he had found the girl lying on the floor and picked her up to take her to the hospital. The police were suspicious and arrested him. The girl died as the result of stab wounds. As part of the investigation, the accused's blood-stained clothes were sent to the crime laboratory for analysis. The serologist examined his shirt and pants and determined that the blood stains were the result of blood spurting out under pressure from a source in front of him which then landed on his clothing. At his trial for murder, the defendant sought to exclude the blood spatter evidence on the grounds that its underlying basis had not been proven. The court rejected the argument and admitted the blood spatter evidence. The defendant was convicted. He appealed to the Utah Supreme Court, which upheld the admissibility of the evidence.

In recent times, DNA testing has received a great deal of attention. The pulse of this attention has been quickened by media publicity. The public has learned of DNA's ability to identify someone from traces of biological material left at crime scenes and of cases where wrongly imprisoned people have been set free by postconviction DNA typing. Many people, including some law enforcement personnel, believe that the only test necessary for blood analysis is DNA typing. The public is unaware of how blood was analyzed in a crime lab before DNA typing and what tests are still necessary to fully characterize blood and other body fluids. Many of these tests are still used in modern crime labs. These older techniques are still valuable in cases where DNA typing cannot be done or is of limited use for one reason or another. In those cases where DNA typing has caused the reversal of a conviction, it means that pre-DNA serological testing was done at the time of the crime. In most cases, this testing was done properly and proper interpretations were made concerning the likelihood that the evidence came from the suspect or victim. The problem is that the serological evidence is not as powerful as DNA evidence and cannot *individualize* blood to a particular person. If a case is reopened because of DNA typing, testimony may be required concerning the serological analysis that was done before the original trial. Thus, a good working knowledge of forensic serology can be very important to a forensic biologist.

This chapter has three parts: the analysis of blood, the identification of other biological fluids and stains, and the analysis of bloodstain patterns. All of these areas of inquiry make up the science of *forensic serology*. Serology is defined as the examination of body fluids. These include blood, saliva, seminal fluid, vaginal secretions, urine, feces and even tissues and organs. The majority of serological evidence consists of blood and the body fluids that are generated by sexual assault cases: semen, saliva, and vaginal secretions. Bloodstain pattern analysis is an emerging forensic science that has become quite popular in the past 30 years or so. Figure 16.1 shows an example of an impact pattern bloodstain due to gunshot.

Figure 16.1 Bloodstains produced by a bullet traveling through a blood-soaked sponge. (Photo courtesy Forensic Science Educational Consulting, LLC, Portage, Michigan.)

Blood

Before discussing the analysis of blood, it is important to understand the basics of blood. Blood is a solution of various materials in water. It is also a suspension whereby insoluble materials are carried through the body by the water. The liquid portion of blood is called *plasma*. It comprises about 55% of the total volume of blood. The substances dissolved in the plasma include proteins, carbohydrates, fats, salts, and minerals and antibodies. In addition, plasma contains materials that are responsible for blood clotting.

The suspended materials in blood make up the other 45% and include red blood cells, white blood cells and platelets. Red blood cells (*erythrocytes*) are formed in bone marrow and are primarily responsible for transporting oxygen to cells and carrying away carbon dioxide as waste. They have no nucleus, so therefore they do not possess nuclear DNA. White blood cells (*leukocytes*) are normally formed in the lymph nodes and are primarily involved in the body's immune system. Leukocytes do have a nucleus and can therefore contain nuclear DNA. Platelets (*thrombocytes*) are a major part of the blood clotting process. Figure 16.2 is an electron micrograph of these three blood components.

Analysis of Blood

The purpose of analyzing blood at a crime scene is to determine its source. The blood may be on the floor, wall, or an object at the scene. It may be on clothing worn by the victim or the suspect of the crime. It may be wet or dry. Blood may be partially degraded or putrefied. Depending upon the conditions of the scene, there may be a very small amount of blood present, limiting the types of analysis that can be done or, in some cases, may not permit any analysis. Blood is a perishable biological material and failure to properly collect and preserve it may result in spoilage, inability to analyze it, or inadmissibility of the analytical results in court.

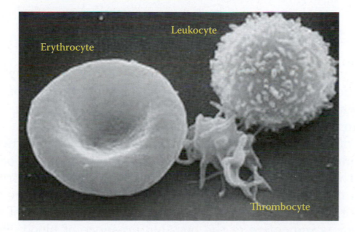

Figure 16.2 These are single examples of the solid parts of the blood as seen under an electron microscope. The red blood cell (erythrocyte) is on the left, the white blood cell (leukocyte) is on the right, and the platelet (thrombocyte) is in the middle. As a group, these solid materials constitute 45% of human blood. (Produced by Electron Microscopy Facility at the National Cancer Institute, Bethesda, Maryland.)

Preliminary Considerations

Most people think that a bloodstain is easy to spot. Nothing else could look like wet or dried blood. Many believe that visual identification should be enough. The fact is, however, that scientific and legal requirements make a positive identification of the blood through scientific means a necessity. Good laboratory practice requires that properly validated protocols be employed for the positive identification of blood. Varying the protocol is permissible as long as there are sound reasons for doing so. The protocols for the chemical analysis of blood follow the same protocols as any other types of evidence and have at least the following elements:

1. Careful preliminary physical examination of the item to spot potential evidence
2. Careful recording of the evidence (photos and videotaping) and its exact location
3. Preliminary or *screening tests* that permit a *presumption* of the presence of certain types of evidence
4. Sensitive and specific *confirmatory tests* of the chemical identity of the evidence

In the case of serological evidence, additional tests are done after there has been confirmation that the evidence is or contains blood or another body fluid. These include the determination of the species of the blood and analysis of the markers in the blood that serve to limit the number of people from whom the blood could have arisen. Today that test is usually DNA typing.

Locating Blood on Objects

The fact that a stain is dark red or blackish brown may mean that it is blood. Sometimes, these stains are very small or are on dark surfaces that mask their presence. In some cases, blood has been washed off the surface. There are some tests that are used to help locate bloodstains. These also serve as preliminary tests for blood. Two major testing solutions used for this purpose are *luminol* and *fluorescein*. Both of these tests use luminescence to locate faint or small bloodstains on objects at a crime scene.

Luminol

Luminol is a very sensitive reagent that undergoes oxidation by hydrogen peroxide in alkaline solution in the presence of the *heme* part of *hemoglobin*, a molecule in red blood cells that carries oxygen to and carbon dioxide from cells. The structure of heme is shown in Figure 16.3.

The reaction of luminol with hydrogen peroxide is shown in Figure 16.4. It is catalyzed by heme but heme does not take part in the reaction. The product of the reaction, 3-aminophthalate, undergoes *chemiluminescence*. When the product is formed, it emits light on its own. No additional light is needed. At a crime scene, the area is darkened and the luminol reagent is applied. The appearance of a bright blue to yellow-green color is indicative of the possible presence of blood. The color should appear immediately and last for at least 30 seconds before another application of reagent is needed.

Some research has been done to answer the question of whether luminol can contaminate a blood sample and render it unusable for further analysis. For the most

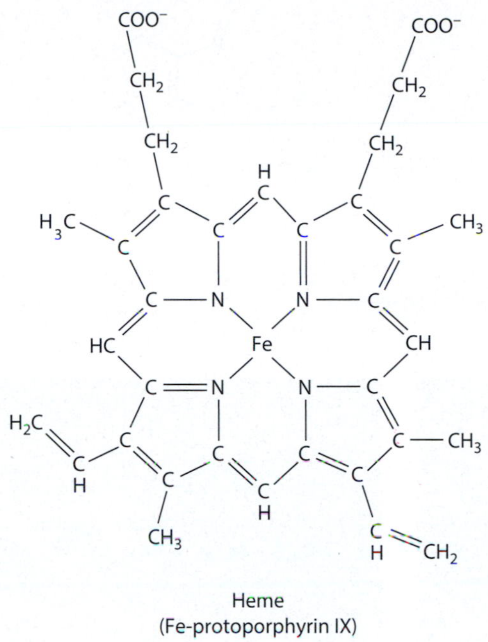

Heme
(Fe-protoporphyrin IX)

Figure 16.3 The structure of heme.

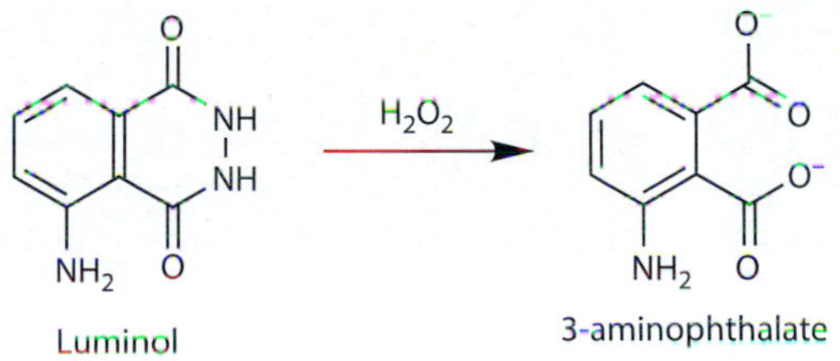

Luminol   3-aminophthalate

Figure 16.4 The luminol reaction.

part, luminol does not affect blood, at least as far as DNA testing goes. In any case, luminol, like other reagents, should only be used when necessary to avoid possible contamination of the blood sample.

Fluorescein

Fluorescein, like luminol, emits light when exposed to an oxidant and heme. Unlike luminol, however, fluorescein undergoes fluorescence rather than chemiluminescence. It is applied to a suspected bloodstain along with hydrogen peroxide. A strong, short wave light is then used to induce fluorescence. The structure of fluorescein is shown in Figure 16.5.

Commercial fluorescein preparations contain a thickening agent that allows it to be used on vertical surfaces. Luminol solutions do not. Research has shown that fluorescein does not interfere with DNA typing. The luminous effect of both reagents is shown in Figure 16.6.

Confirmatory Tests for Blood

Luminol and fluorescein are very useful for locating blood on large surfaces but they are not specific for blood. Other substances including certain vegetable extracts can give false positive tests for blood. At times it may be useful or necessary to confirm

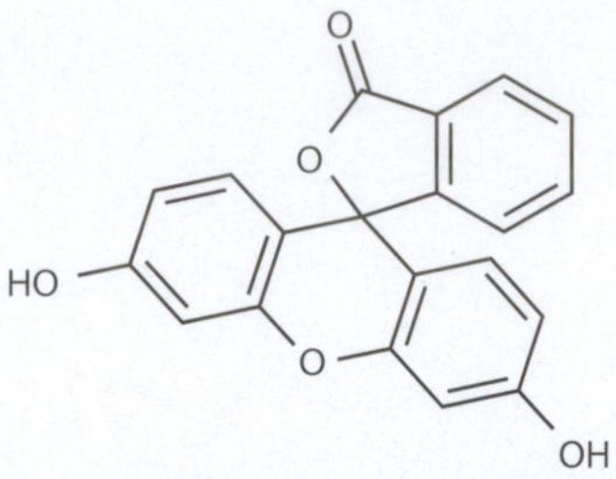

Figure 16.5 The structure of fluorescein.

(a)   (b)

Figure 16.6 Chemical enhancement of blood to visualize the bloodstain: (a) shows the addition of luminal to show the presence of blood and (b) shows the addition of fluorescein showing a bloodstained handprint.

the presence for blood. The two most popular chemical tests for the confirmation of blood are the *Teichmann* and *Takayama* tests. Both are *microcrystal* tests. A crystallizing reagent is added to suspected blood. The presence of characteristic shaped crystals formed by the reaction of the reagent and heme is confirmatory for blood. Figure 16.7 shows the results of the two microcrystal tests—a photomicrograph of Teichmann crystals and a photomicrograph of Takayama crystals.

Species Determination

After determining that a stain is blood, the next step is to determine if it is human or not, what type of animal that it comes from. Most of the common tests that determine the species of origin of blood are of the *immunoprecipitation* type. A test animal, usually a rabbit, is injected with human blood serum that contains proteins called *antigens*, which define the blood as being human. The rabbit's immune system will determine that this is foreign (not rabbit) material and will produce a substance known as an *antibody*. The function of an antibody is to attack the foreign materials so they cannot harm the host. The rabbit blood is now an *antiserum* for human antigens and can be used to test for their presence. Some of the rabbit antiserum is added to a suspected sample of human blood, either in a test tube (*precipitin ring test*) in solution or in a gel (*Ouchterlony double diffusion test*). If the blood is

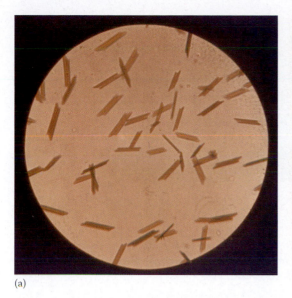

(a)   (b)

Figure 16.7 (a) shows Teichmann crystals obtained from the reaction with blood, while (b) shows Takayama crystals obtained from the reaction with blood. (Reprinted courtesy of Nordby, J.J. and James, S.H., *Forensic Science, An Introduction to Scientific and Investigative Techniques*, CRC Press, Boca Raton, FL, 2003.)

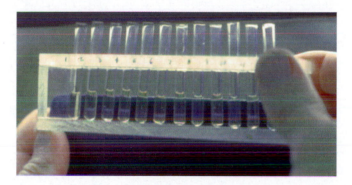

Figure 16.8 The precipitin ring reaction. Note the whitish ring in many of the culture tubes indicating a positive reaction. (Reprinted courtesy of Nordby, J.J. and James, S.H., *Forensic Science, An Introduction to Scientific and Investigative Techniques*, CRC Press, Boca Raton, FL, 2003.)

human, then there will be a reaction between the antihuman antibodies in the rabbit antiserum and the human antigens in the blood. The reaction will be seen as a *precipitate*. In the precipitin ring test, a ring is seen where the antiserum and blood meet (see Figure 16.8).

In the Ouchterlony test, the antigens and antibodies diffuse through the gel toward each other. They form a precipitate where they meet. This is shown via a diagram in Figure 16.9a. If the bloodstain is not human, no precipitation will take place. In the Figure 16.9a, there is precipitate formation in front of stains 2, 3, and 5, but not in front of stains 1 and 4. Therefore, it can be deduced that the human blood is only in samples 2, 3, and 5.

Figure 16.9b shows an actual Ouchterlony precipitate test, with positive test results shown in 3 of the four samples. The only negative result is the sample in the lower-left-hand portion on the plate in the photo.

In the field there are portable tests for blood that investigators can perform. The presumptive or screening test to determine if the reddish brown substance found at the scene is blood is called the Kastle–Meyer test. This test can be packaged for field use or done in the lab. The major compounds used in the test are phenolphthalein, a

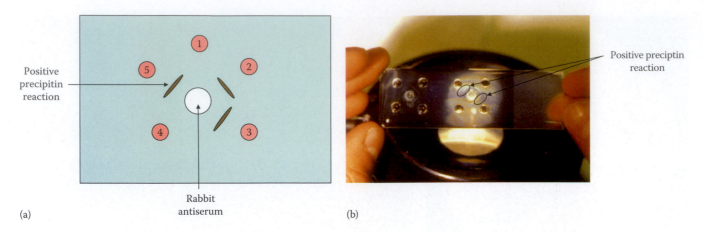

(a)   (b)

Figure 16.9 (a) shows how the Ouchterlony test works and (b) is an actual Ouchterlony test. Note the whitish streaks in all but the lower left corner around the center well. (Reprinted courtesy of Nordby, J.J. and James, S.H., *Forensic Science, An Introduction to Scientific and Investigative Techniques*, CRC Press, Boca Raton, FL, 2003.)

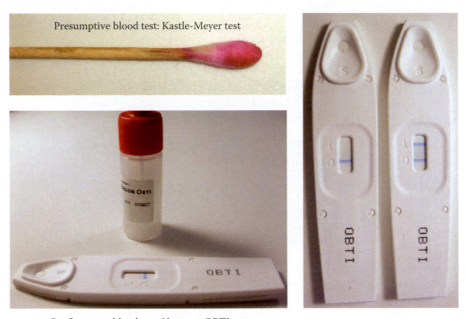

Figure 16.10 Presumptive and confirmatory blood tests that can be done in the field. Top photo is a positive result for blood with the Kastle–Meyer test. The other photos show the Hexagon OBTI test. A positive result for human blood is the strip with two blue lines; the top line is positive for human, and the bottom is the positive control for the test. The left strip is a negative result, and the right is positive. (Photo courtesy Forensic Science Educational Consulting, LLC, Portage, Michigan.)

color indicator, and hydrogen peroxide, which reacts by combining with the *heme* in hemoglobin. If blood is present in the sample, the reaction produces a vivid fuchsia or pink color. This, however, only indicates that the stain contains hemoglobin, and hemoglobin is present in both human and animal blood. See the cotton swab on the left in Figure 16.10, showing a positive presumptive test for blood.

The confirmatory test for human blood done in the field is the called the Hexagon OBTI test. This testing device looks similar to that used in a home pregnancy test and works in a similar manner, with blue lines as indicators of positive results. In the absorbent strip are blue particles and monoclonal antihuman Hb antibodies. When the sample blood mixed with the OBTI reagent (in the bottle) and dropped into the well on the end, the solution migrates up the strip to the position that contains the antihuman antibodies and forms a thin blue line, indicating a positive result for human blood. The second blue line is a control and must register as a blue line in every test or the strip is deemed defective and the test invalid. Figure 16.10 shows the Hexagon OBTI kit components and a positive human test result (blue line at "T") alongside a negative for human blood test (notice the "C" or control is positive, indicating a valid test).

Genetic Markers in Blood

Red Blood Cell Antigens

Not all human blood is the same. Red blood cells contain various genetically inherited antigens that comprise a number of blood groups. There are many different types of blood groups, but only a few have been used to characterize blood forensically. The antigens in a blood group are all formed at a single locus in a single gene and are formed independently of other genes. The most familiar of the blood groups is the *ABO group*. There are four subgroups or types of blood in the ABO system, A, B, AB, and O. Figure 16.11 is a model of the four blood types showing the antigens on the red blood cells and the antibodies in the serum for each type.

Each is characterized by the presence of certain antigens on the surface of the red blood cells and by the presence of certain antibodies in the serum. Table 16.1 shows the properties of each of the subgroups of the ABO group and information on donating and receiving blood according to blood type.

When antibodies and antigens of the same type (e.g., anti-A and A) come together, *agglutination* takes place. This is a process where the antigens and antibodies attach together. The antigens are on the red blood cell surfaces and the antibodies come from a foreign serum or other source. To the naked eye or under a microscope,

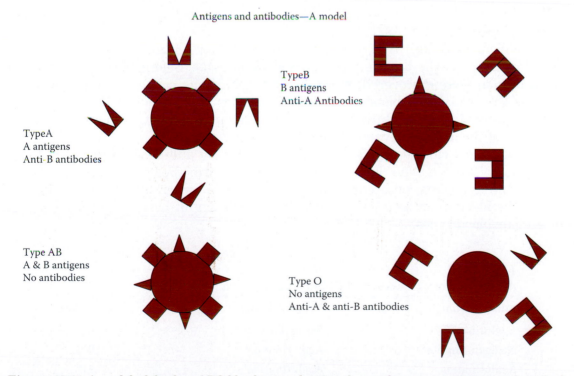

Figure 16.11 A model of the four ABO blood types showing the erythrocytes, antigens, and antibodies. (Courtesy Forensic Science Educational Consulting, LLC, Portage, Michigan.)

TABLE 16.1
Properties of Blood Types of the ABO Group

Type	Antigens	Antibody	Can Give Blood To	Can Receive Blood From	Population Percentage
A	A	Anti-B	A, AB	O, A	42
B	B	Anti-A	B, AB	O, B	12
AB	A, B	None	AB	A, B, AB, O	3
O	None	Anti-A and Anti B	A, B, AB, O	O	43

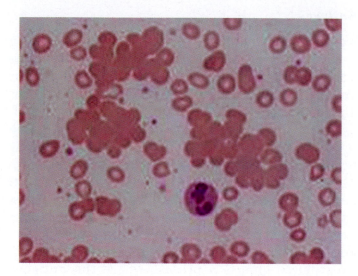

Figure 16.12 Agglutination of red blood cells.

it appears as if the red blood cells have become stuck together. This is shown in the slide in Figure 16.12.

Note from Table 16.1 that a person's blood does not contain antibodies that are the same type as the antigens on the red blood cells. Before blood systems and agglutination were discovered, many blood transfusions caused injury and death because the transfused blood contained antibodies that attacked the host's antigens, causing massive agglutination. Karl Landsteiner won the Nobel Prize for his discovery of the different types of blood in the ABO system.

Human blood can be typed in the ABO system by adding a serum containing antibodies of known type. For example, if anti-A antibodies are added to a blood sample and agglutination occurs but it does not occur when anti-B antibodies are added, the blood must be type A. Table 16.2 shows agglutination and blood typing for all four blood types.

TABLE 16.2
Agglutination Reaction of Blood Typing Sera

Anti-A Serum	Anti-B Serum	Blood Type
Agglutination	No agglutination	A
No agglutination	Agglutination	B
Agglutination	Agglutination	AB
No agglutination	No agglutination	O

Another blood group system inherited genetically is the *Rh factor*, which is also expressed as an antigen on the red blood cell. A human will either be Rh positive (Rh$^+$) or Rh negative (Rh$^-$), depending on whether they possess the antigen or not. The Rh factor is usually written along with the blood type, for example, A$^+$ or A$^-$, the former has a gene for the Rh factor and the latter does not have the Rh gene.

There are other blood group systems in human blood that have different antigens and antibodies associated with them. Examples of these are *Lewis and MN* blood systems.

Blood Enzyme Markers

As seen in Table 16.1, the ABO blood type is not very discriminating. Even the rarest blood type still includes 3% of the human population. Therefore, blood type is considered to be *class* evidence, and blood typing of crime scene evidence is used to exclude suspects. During the 1970s and early 1980s, scientists searched for tests that included fewer people in a given classification. One of the important constraints on markers was that they had to survive the drying process. In many, if not most, of the cases where blood was found, it was dried. Most of the blood antigen systems except for ABO could not be used when the blood dried because the antigens were destroyed. One viable solution was so-called *polymorphic enzymes*. These are enzymes found in human blood. They have the property of polymorphism; they exist in several forms. Each person has one of the forms of each enzyme. Databases were built that determined the population frequency of each form of each enzyme. If several enzymes are analyzed, then the odds of a person having a particular set of enzyme forms would be quite rare. Many of these enzymes also survive the drying process and are thus forensically useful where dried stains are found as evidence. This type of analysis is seldom being used any more, having been replaced by DNA typing that is much more specific.

Other Biological Fluids and Stains

A number of other biological fluids besides blood occur as evidence in crimes. Three of the most important are *seminal fluid, vaginal secretions*, and *saliva*. All may be prominent evidence in *criminal sexual conduct* (CSC) crimes. Saliva may be found on or in evidence in many other types of crimes. These can be very important types of evidence in cases where the perpetrator is a stranger to the victim. In most cases, there are no witnesses to CSC crimes. It may be crucial to be able to associate physical evidence with the suspect. In some cases, locating biological evidence may be important so that it can be DNA typed. In other cases, confirmation of the type of evidence may be necessary to establish that CSC has taken place.

Seminal Fluid

Seminal fluid or semen is a mixture of cells, sperm, and a variety of organic and inorganic materials. It is a gelatinous material produced in males by the seminal vesicles, prostate, and Cowper's glands. In a normal male, about 5 mL of semen is ejaculated and contains about 100 million sperm. Some males have low sperm counts (*oligospermic*) or may have no sperm in their semen (*aspermic*). Sperm consist of a head that contains the DNA from the male and a flagellated tail that helps it move.

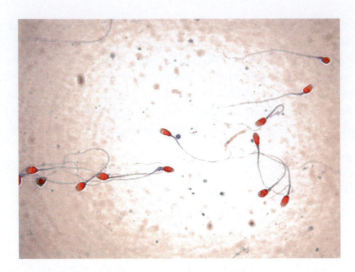

Figure 16.13 Sperm stained with Christmas tree stain. (Reprinted courtesy of Nordby, J.J. and James, S.H., *Forensic Science, An Introduction to Scientific and Investigative Techniques*, CRC Press, Boca Raton, FL, 2003.)

Preliminary Tests for Semen

Seminal fluid contains large concentrations of an enzyme known as *seminal acid phosphatase* (SAP). There are other forms of acid phosphatase in some body fluids and the presence of SAP is considered to be *presumptive*. Over the years, the SAP test has emerged as the only acceptable presumptive test for seminal fluid throughout the world. The *Brentamine Fast Blue B* reagent is the major test for seminal fluid. An intense purple color that appears within 2 min is considered to be positive for SAP. The reagent is carcinogenic and must be handled with care.

Confirmatory Tests for Semen

Identification of Sperm

The only unambiguous test for seminal fluid is the identification of sperm cells. In most cases, the sperm analyzed in a crime lab are no longer motile and a stain is used to identify the sperm in the presence of other cellular material in the stain. A pair of dyes, *picroindigocarmine* (PIC) and *Nuclear Fast Red*, collectively called Christmas tree stain, have been developed for the specific purpose of visualizing sperm cells (see Figure 16.13).

Prostate-Specific Antigen

As mentioned previously, some males are oligospermic or aspermic and sperm may not be present in a suspected semen stain. In 1978, George Sensabaugh demonstrated that seminal fluid may be confirmed if the stain reacts positively for the presence of seminal acid phosphatase and if *prostate-specific antigen* (PSA or p30) is identified. P30 is secreted into semen by the prostate gland and is found mainly in semen. P30 may be found in some other body fluids, but the concentrations are below the limits of detection of the test. A special antibody-antigen test kit for PSA was developed in 1999 and is used in crime labs today.

Vaginal Secretions

The analysis of vaginal secretions can be important when a foreign object has been inserted into the vagina. The major test for vaginal secretions is to identify *glycogenated epithelial cells.* These cell types are formed during menstruation and their quantity depends on what stage of the menstrual cycle the female is in, with ovulation producing the highest concentrations of glycogenated cells. The test consists of staining the glycogen using *periodic acid–Schiff reagent* (PAS). It stains glycogen a bright magenta color. It is not a specific test since glycogenated epithelial cells may be found in other parts of males and females, although in lower concentrations.

Saliva

Saliva is produced in the mouth for the preliminary digestion of food. More than one liter of saliva is produced each day in normal humans. It consists of water, proteins, enzymes, and salts. There are no specific tests for saliva. The generally accepted test for saliva is the *alpha-amylase* test. Alpha-amylase is an enzyme that is used to help break down starches in foods. Although it is found in many other body fluids, its concentration in saliva is many times higher than in any other fluid. The *starch-iodide* test is commonly used to identify alpha-amylase.

Bloodstain Pattern Analysis

Bloodstain pattern analysis (BSPA) is a growing field of crime scene analysis and forensic technology. It has become an important tool in helping the forensic investigator determine what happened in a violent incident where blood has been shed. It can be used to provide evidence against a suspect or to exonerate an accused person. It can also be an invaluable tool in crime scene reconstruction.

Physical Properties of Blood

In order to understand how blood spatter patterns are formed and how to interpret their characteristics, it is necessary to know something about the physical properties of blood. Although the majority of blood is water, blood does not act like water when it is dripped or projected. Blood has a fairly high surface tension that tends to cause a decrease in its surface area and makes it difficult to penetrate. This means that blood droplets tend to adhere to an external surface. Blood will only separate and spatter when there are sufficient external forces to overcome surface tension. When a droplet of blood separates from a larger quantity and falls toward the earth, it will form a *spherical drop*, not a teardrop as is commonly depicted. Figure 16.14 shows the shape of a blood droplet as it falls from a blood soaked article. A blood drop in flight will oscillate from this oval or elliptical shape to a circular shape and back again until it contacts a surface and collapses.

The size of the spherical blood droplet will depend upon the size of the surface from which it falls. A larger surface will produce a larger blood droplet. Blood is also very *viscous.* This means that it will flow more slowly than water. It has also been shown that the longer the distance that a blood droplet falls, the larger the diameter of the stain on the floor or other surface, although there is a physical limit to the size that a falling droplet will achieve. Blood falling under the influence of gravity will accelerate like any other falling object under the influence of gravity. At some point,

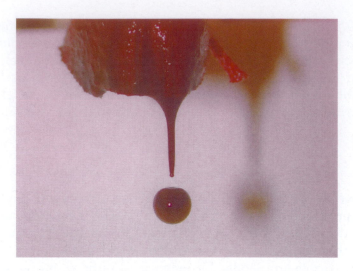

Figure 16.14 A blood droplet dripping from blood-soaked cloth. Note the spherical shape. (Reprinted courtesy of Nordby, J.J. and James, S.H., *Forensic Science, An Introduction to Scientific and Investigative Techniques*, CRC Press, Boca Raton, FL, 2003.)

the force of gravity will equal the frictional force of the air on the droplet. When this happens, the falling blood drop will no longer accelerate, but reach a stable velocity, called *terminal velocity*. The terminal velocity of blood is dependent on the volume of the drop, but generally the average terminal velocity is approximately 25 ft/s for a blood drop of 0.05 mL volume. At heights greater than the height where terminal velocity is reached, the diameter of the blood drop will not increase. Studies have shown that the averaged sized blood drop will reach terminal velocity at a height of approximately 7 feet.

When water falls to the floor, it tends to *spatter* or break up into smaller droplets. This is due to surface tension and viscosity. In contrast to water, blood droplets will not break up into smaller droplets if they hit a hard, smooth surface such as tile. Blood molecules have cohesive properties that hold the blood molecules together and increase the surface tension in the blood. If the surface is rough like concrete, then the jagged edges will break up the surface tension of the blood and cause it to spatter, creating *satellite spatter* and *spines*. Figure 16.15 shows blood dropped at right angles or 90° onto various surfaces from a height of 36 inches. The circled projections in the first photograph designate the *spines* (projections of blood that extend beyond the parent drop of blood) and *satellite spatter* (small droplets that leave the parent blood drop and land near it).

Geometry of Bloodstains

When blood is thrown or cast onto a surface at an angle, the leading edge of the droplets will be elongated relative to the back or trailing edge. The shape of the droplet can be used to determine the direction from which it came as well as the approximate angle relative to the surface it strikes. If there are a number of bloodstains, the *area of convergence* can be determined by drawing lines from the leading edge of the stains through the long axis. These lines will come together in a general area which is the approximate area where the blood originated. This can be seen in Figure 16.16.

The angle of impact can be determined by measuring the length and width of the stain in millimeters as shown in Figure 16.17, being careful only to measure the *original* shape of the stain and not the projections (spines and tails). The arcsin

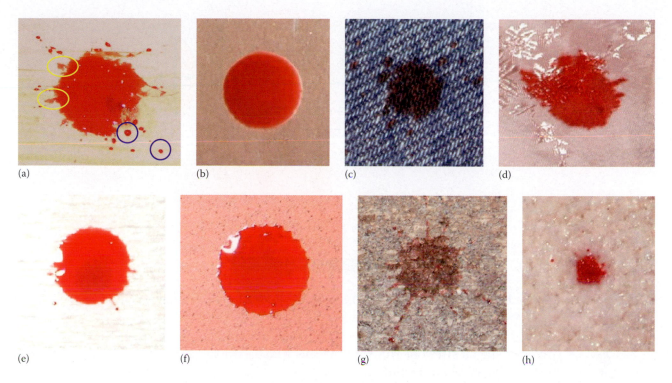

(a)   (b)   (c)   (d)

(e)   (f)   (g)   (h)

Figure 16.15 These photos show one blood drop released from a height of 36 in. onto various target surfaces at 90°. Notice the difference in size and shape and the absence or presence of *spines* and *satellite spatter*. The yellow ovals in photo a designate spines and the blue circles show satellite spatter. The target surfaces are as follows: (a) raw wood, (b) smooth plastic, (c) cotton jean, (d) polyester, (e) painted wood, (f) tile, (g) cement, and (h) carpet. (Photos courtesy Forensic Science Educational Consulting, LLC, Portage, Michigan.)

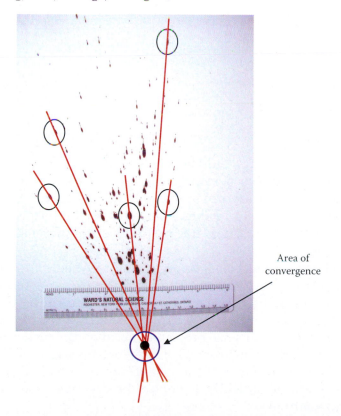

Area of convergence

Figure 16.16 Diagram showing how the area of convergence of an impact blood spatter pattern is determined. (Courtesy Forensic Science Educational Consulting, LLC, Portage, Michigan.)

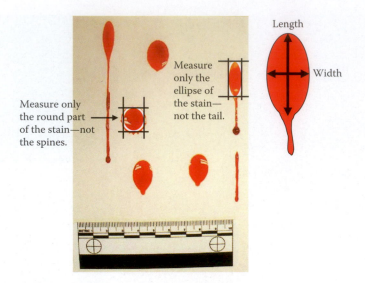

Figure 16.17 Measuring width and length of bloodstains to determine impact angle. (Courtesy Forensic Science Educational Consulting, LLC, Portage, Michigan.)

(inverse sin or sin^{-1}) of the ratio of the width (W) to the length (L) is equal to the angle of impact (see Equation 16.1).

$$\Theta = \arcsin \frac{\text{Width (mm)}}{\text{Length (mm)}} \qquad (16.1)$$

where Θ is the angle of impact.

For example, if the width of a bloodstain is 1.3 mm and the length is 2 mm, then

$$\Theta = (\arcsin) \frac{1.3 \text{ mm}}{2.0 \text{ mm}} = (\arcsin)0.65 = 40.54°$$

Therefore: The angle of impact would be about 41°.

The shape of the angled bloodstains gives the investigator a general idea of the point of origin. The "tail" of the stain and any spines visible are clues to the original direction of the blood. Figure 16.18 shows blood dripped multiple times at 10° angle increments. Notice how the elliptical nature of the stain increases with the angle of impact to the surface.

Figure 16.19 shows actual bloodstains being analyzed. Step one is to measure the bloodstain length and width, and then use the formula to determine impact angle. Lines are drawn lightly through the stain to determine the area of convergence on the target surface (or strings can be used in place of pencil lines to preserve the stains). Lastly, strings are projected based on the measured impact angles out into space to determine the area of convergence or origin of the blood. Another method that can be used in place of the last stringing step is to use another trigonometry formula to mathematically calculate the distance from the target surface (see graphic in Appendix A).

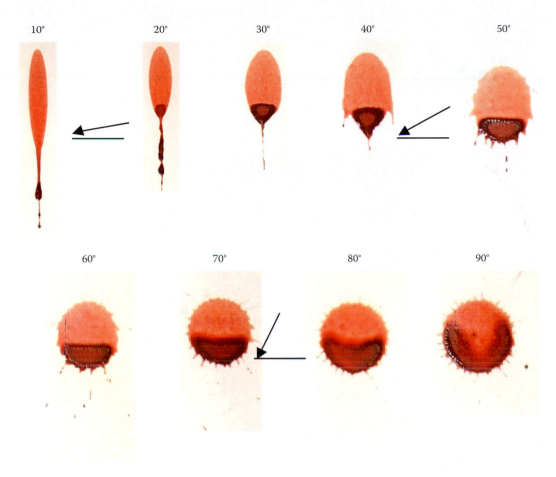

Figure 16.18 Blood drops at various angles of impact. (Photos courtesy Forensic Science Educational Consulting, LLC.)

Bloodstain Patterns

There are many types of bloodstain patterns. Bloodstains can be divided into three basic categories: *passive*, *spatter*, and *altered*. *Passive* stains are created due to the force of gravity acting on the blood. Examples of passive bloodstains are *vertical* blood drops (blood dripping at 90° to the surface), *transfer* stains (blood on an object that contacts another object and leaves a bloody pattern—swipes, footprints, etc.), *large volume* bloodstains (blood exiting in mass from a person or object), and *flow* (large pool of blow moving down a wall or incline). Examples of passive bloodstains can be seen in Figures 16.20 and 16.21.

Spatter stains involve a force in addition to gravity, and bloodstains in this category show directionality and distribution to the blood. Included in this group of bloodstains are *impact spatter due to blunt force* that are the result of a bloodied object or person receiving a blow. This stain must first have blood on its surface to create this type of pattern. In most cases, the first blow will not produce an impact stain. Subsequent blows will result in impact spatter. Impact stains due to blunt force range in length from 1 to 4 mm in size and are usually the stains are "strung" by law enforcement. *Impact stains due to gunshot* are smaller in size, usually less than 1 mm in length, and have a misty appearance. Spattered stains also include those *projected* away from the body. One of these patterns is called a *cast-off*, which is a pattern produced from a bloodied object such as a knife, baseball bat, or hand.

Figure 16.19 Locating an area of convergence in space using impact angles of a bloodstain: (a) measuring length and width of small bloodstains, (b) drawing the area of convergence on the contact surface, and (c) "stringing" the angles of impact into three-dimensional space to locate the origin of the blood. The red circle shows the area of convergence in that third dimension. (Photos courtesy Forensic Science Educational Consulting, LLC, Portage, Michigan.)

These stains form a linear pattern, often on the ceiling. Figure 16.22a shows examples of spatter stains.

Other spatter-type blood stains are *arterial spurts* and *expirated* blood. Arterial spurts easily recognized by an arc pattern that is due to the rise and fall of blood pressure and indicates that a major artery (carotid, femoral) has been compromised in the victim. This is shown in Figure 16.22b. Expiratory blood is ejected with force from the mouth or the nose. Individuals with injuries to the face or chest will commonly cough or sneeze blood, a natural reaction to fluid in the breathing passages. The pattern from expiratory blood looks similar to impact spatter, but sometimes air bubbles can be seen in the blood drops.

Bloodstains that have been physically or physiologically changed are placed in the *altered* category (examples shown in Figure 16.23). Physiologically altered stains arise when insects interact with the blood, when blood clots, or when water or other

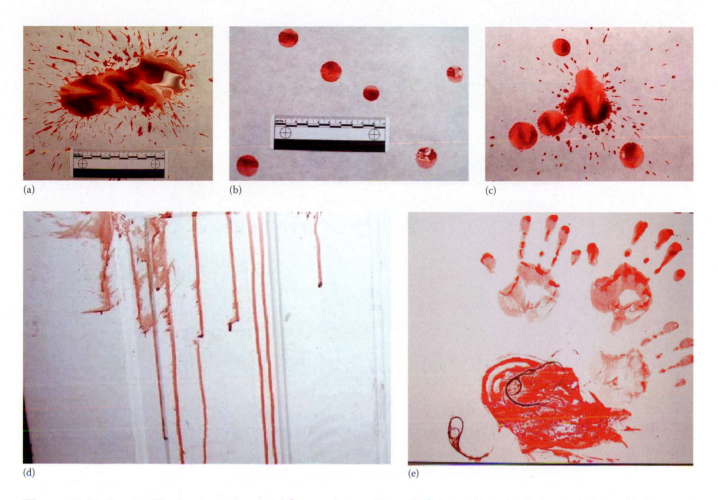

Figure 16.20 Passive bloodstain patterns: (a) large volume, (b) vertical drips, (c) multiple vertical drips, (d) flow, and (e) transfer.

Figure 16.21 A swiped bloodstain pattern in which a bloodied object contacted the surface and deposited blood in a sweeping motion. (Reprinted courtesy of Bevel, T. and Gardner, R.M., *Bloodstain Pattern Analysis: With an Introduction to Crime Scene Reconstruction*, 2 edn., CRC Press, Boca Raton, FL.)

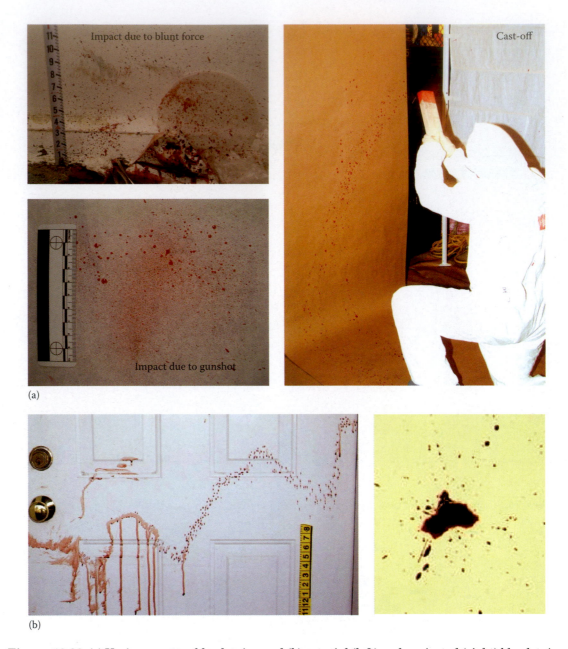

Figure 16.22 (a) Various spatter bloodstains and (b) arterial (left) and expired (right) bloodstains. (Photos courtesy Forensic Science Educational Consulting, LLC, Portage, Michigan.)

foreign materials mix with the existing blood. Physically altered blood examples are *voids* (blood should be present, but it is not) and *wipes* (blood was present, but a person or object moved through it and changed its appearance). A wipe can be distinguished from *swipe* (passive stain) by noting the evidence that the blood was deposited prior to the motion through the blood, such as the dried outside boundaries of the stain (see Figure 16.23).

The three bloodstain categories and types of patterns in each category are summarized in Table 16.3.

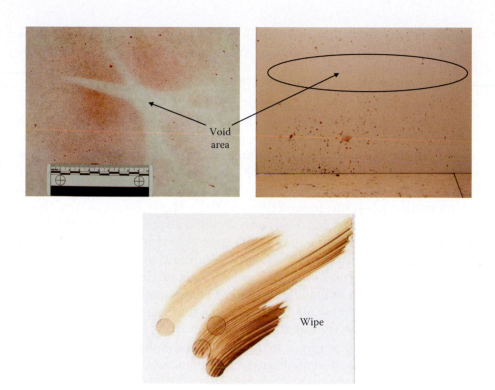

Figure 16.23 Altered bloodstains.

TABLE 16.3
Bloodstain Patterns and Their Classification

Passive	Spatter	Altered
Vertical drips	Impact spatter blunt force	Insect activity
Prints (shoe, hand, hair, etc.)	Impact spatter gunshot	Addition of foreign material
Large volume	Cast-off	Void
Flow	Arterial	Wipe
Swipe	Expirated	

Summary

Blood is a suspension of solid, mostly cellular material in a fluid that consists of water with many dissolved materials in it. It is often necessary to determine if a reddish stain found at a crime scene is blood. There are several preliminary and confirmatory tests for the presence of blood. Most of these tests involve the heme molecule as a catalyst in a chemical reaction or series of reactions. After a stain is identified as blood, it is necessary to determine if it is human. This is done using immunological tests. Rabbit antiserum is used to determine if human blood is present by demonstrating that the human antibodies in the rabbit's blood will agglutinate red blood cells in the blood. Field testing can be done on suspected stains to determine if they are blood or not. The Kastle–Meyer test and Hexagon OBTI are tests that can be packaged for field testing.

Other body fluids such as saliva, vaginal swabs or secretions, and semen must also be identified at crime scenes. There are also screening and confirmatory tests for these substances.

Before DNA typing, there was blood typing. Blood contains proteins such as antigens as well as certain enzymes that are polymorphic; they exist in more than one form. These substances can be used to subdivide a human population according to which forms of these materials are present. Groups of associated antigens (proteins on the surface of red blood cells) provide one means of differentiating blood samples. These antigens form blood groups such as ABO or Rh. In addition to blood groups, there are enzymes associated with red blood cells and white blood cells that are also polymorphic. Electrophoresis is used to separate and identify these enzymes in a blood sample. Several blood groups and enzymes used to be typed in a typical blood case. Even though these substances are all independent of each other, the cumulative population frequencies were not as discriminating as DNA typing. In addition, many of these substances do not survive the drying process and cannot be typed on dried stains.

The physical properties of blood give rise to blood spatter patterns that occur by several mechanisms. It is possible to determine the angle and direction of a blood spatter by measuring the size and shape of the spatter. It is also possible to determine the point of origin of a series of related blood spatters using triangulation. Different types of blood spatter mechanisms give rise to characteristic blood spatter patterns. Three general categories of bloodstain patterns are passive, spatter, and altered. Bloodstains found at crime scenes can be classified into one of these groups.

Appendix A: Trigonometry Calculation for Locating a Bloodstain

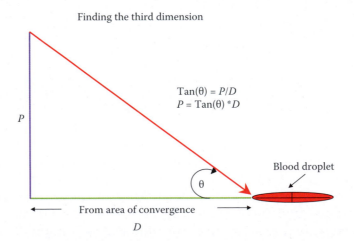

Finding the third dimension

$Tan(\theta) = P/D$

$P = Tan(\theta) * D$

P

θ

Blood droplet

From area of convergence

D

Try It Yourself: The Genetics of Blood Typing

A child's blood type is inherited from the parents. One allele (code for blood type on the chromosome) comes from the mother and one allele comes from the father. The possible

17. A person w
   a. Another
   b. A perso
   c. An A
   d. Any blo
18. A person w
   a. Another
   b. A perso
   c. An A
   d. An AB
19. Type B blo
   a. AB
   b. A
   c. B
   d. None
20. One paren
   offspring is
   a. AB
   b. OO
   c. AO
   d. all of th
21. Which is th
   a. AB
   b. O
   c. A
   d. B
22. Which is th
   a. AB
   b. O
   c. A
   d. B

True or False

23. The major
   materials.
24. The platele
25. The Teichn
   is blood or
26. The most c
27. PSA is the

Matching

28. Liquid port
29. Part of the
   ates the cel
30. Part of the
   infection

combinations of alleles (genotype) and resulting blood type (phenotype) are listed later. The allele for type O is recessive and the alleles for A and B are codominant.

Blood Type A	Blood Type B	Blood Type AB	Blood Type O
A, A	B, B	A, B	O, O
A, O	B, O	B, A	

Using a Punnet Square allows one to see the possible prodigy of a genetic cross (parents). The GENOTYPE of each parent is entered into the top and side of the square. The combinations of alleles give the GENOTYPE of the offspring. For example,

Parent Genotype	A	O
A	A, A	A, O
B	A, B	B, O

The PHENOTYPE (what trait is expressed) of the parents are blood types A and AB. The PHENOTYPE of the offspring are blood types: A, AB, and B. The chances are approximately 50% that their children will be type A, 25% will be type B, and 25% will be type AB.

Your turn:

1. Complete the following crosses of parents using the Punnet Square method.
2. Predict the genotype and phenotype of the offspring.
3. What are the percent chances for each type?

Group 1: Dad is AB, Mom is AB
Group 2: Dad is OO, Mom is AB
Group 3: Dad is AA, Mom is BO
Group 4: Dad is BO, Mom is AO

Extension: The Rh factor can also be added to the crosses. Rh$^+$ is dominant and Rh$^-$ is recessive.

Test Yourself

Short Essay

1. What are the two major components of blood?
2. What parts of blood are important forensically for typing?
3. Name two preliminary and two confirmatory tests for blood?
4. What is the most common test for identifying saliva?
5. What is the only test that is absolutely confirmatory for semen?
6. Describe briefly how a blood sample is determined to be human?
7. What are the two major mechanisms that give rise to blood spatter patterns?
8. Give an example of a type of spatter bloodstain.
9. Give an example of a type of altered bloodstain.
10. Give an example of a type of passive bloodstain.

Chapter 17
DNA Typing

Chapter Outline

Mini Glossary

Allele: One of the forms of a gene.
Amelogenin: A piece of DNA found in the X and Y chromosomes that determine gender.
Annealing: Addition of DNA primers in PCR to begin the replication process.
Denaturation: Unzipping double-stranded DNA to single strands under the influence of high temperature.
DNA: A large, polymeric molecule found in virtually every cell in the body.
DNA polymerase: An enzyme used in PCR to add bases one at a time.
DNA primers: Short strands of DNA used to begin the replication process of PCR.
Elimination samples: Samples of DNA from someone who might have handled biological evidence during collection and analysis.
Extension: Addition of individual bases to a single strand of DNA to replicate it in PCR.
Gene: Part of a chromosome consisting of a sequence of base pairs. These sequences ultimately tell the cell what proteins to manufacture that result in expression of characteristics such as eye color, gender, and height.
Hypervariable region: A locus of DNA that is highly polymorphic.
Length polymorphism: A type of polymorphism whose forms differ in the length of a repeating segment of DNA.
Mitochondria: Structures present in every cell in the body without exception. They are in the cytoplasm, outside the nucleus. Mitochondria are responsible

for energy production in the cell and they contain DNA, which helps in this function.

Polymerase chain reaction (PCR): A method for replicating DNA using temperature and bases under the influence of an enzyme.

Polymorphic: A gene or other part of DNA that exists in more than one form.

Population frequency: How often a particular type of DNA occurs in a given population.

Restriction enzyme: An enzyme that cuts DNA strands at predetermined loci.

Restriction fragment length polymorphism (RFLP): DNA typing that uses long length polymorphs to characterize DNA.

Sequence polymorphism: A type of polymorphism whose forms differ in one or more base pairs.

Short tandem repeats: A method of DNA typing using short length polymorphs.

Substrate control: A piece of a material on which biological evidence has been deposited; a form of negative control.

Y-STR: A short tandem repeat found only on the Y chromosome.

Acronyms

CODIS: Combined DNA Index System
DNA: Deoxyribonucleic acid
PCR: Polymerase chain reaction
RFLP: Restriction fragment length polymorphism
STR: Short tandem repeat

Introduction

In March of 2013, Johnny Williams, 38, was released from prison in California after having served 14 years in prison for raping a 9-year-old girl. His conviction was overturned after new evidence discovered by the Northern California Innocence Project (IP) proved he was not guilty of the rape. The evidence was a DNA sample on a shirt that the girl was wearing at the time of the assault. The IP attorneys arranged for the DNA to be tested. It did not match Williams' DNA type, resulting in the overturning of his conviction and subsequent release from prison.

The assaults took place over 2 days against the girl as she was going to school. At the time, police investigators did not find any biological evidence on the girl's clothing. She identified Johnny Williams as her attacker because he lived in the neighborhood and the attacker told her that his name was Johnny. At Williams' trial, the prosecutor had only the girl's identification as evidence. Her shirt was never admitted into evidence. The defense admitted the shirt and argued that the lack of biological evidence on it was proof that Williams was innocent. Subsequent further analysis of the shirt by officials of the IP uncovered trace evidence. This was typed for DNA and run through local, state, and national databases, but no hit came up. The DNA type was different from that of Williams.

In 1992, attorneys Barry Scheck and Peter Neufeld founded the IP. It is affiliated with the Benjamin N. Cardozo School of Law at Yeshiva University in New York.

The IP was set up to provide assistance to persons who had been convicted of a serious crime where postconviction DNA typing could be used to prove claims of innocence. Several types of cases are examined by the IP. These include challenges based on a claim of ineffective counsel, mistakes by crime laboratory scientists, or cases where the conviction was based in part on pre-DNA typing blood analysis that falsely associated the accused with the victim or put him at the crime scene. These situations often occurred because blood typing, as it was practiced before DNA typing, could not associate someone to biological evidence with the level of certainty that DNA typing does today. In several cases investigated by the IP, the accused was included in a population of possible owners of biological evidence (e.g., blood, hair, semen) by blood typing procedures and convicted partly because of this. Postconviction DNA typing proved conclusively that the accused and convicted person could not have been the source of the incriminating biological evidence. To date, more than 310 falsely convicted people have been exonerated by postconviction DNA testing. Of these, more than a dozen were sentenced to death!

The IP has not only obtained the release of many innocent people but has served to illustrate that wrongful convictions are not isolated, once-in-a-lifetime occurrences in the United States. Because of the high numbers of wrongful convictions discovered by the IP, at least one state has suspended its death penalty until more safeguards are put into place to ensure that all death penalty convictions have been arrived at properly. There are now IPs in practically every state in the United States.

In the previous chapter, on serology, we learned the concept of polymorphism. Some biological evidence such as blood contains substances that occur in several forms distributed throughout the human population. Many of these factors have been extensively studied and population frequencies have been determined for them. This gives forensic scientists hard data on which to base conclusions concerning the degree of association of biological evidence to a victim or suspect. This approach, although helpful in determining whether a person left biological evidence at a crime scene, suffers from three major deficiencies. First, many polymorphic enzymes and antigens do not survive the drying process and cannot be measured in dried blood stains, which are more commonly encountered at crime scenes than fresh blood. Second, even if many of them are measured in a particular person, there is not enough total variation from one person to the next to be able to use these blood groupings to definitively associate a person with biological evidence. Finally, these polymorphic substances are present mainly in blood. If the perpetrator or victim of a crime left other biological materials such as skin, saliva, or hair, these substances wouldn't be of any help.

In the early 1980s, a revolution in forensic biology occurred. Scientists demonstrated that certain parts of the DNA structure were different enough to divide human populations into many groups. Using DNA has enhanced the potential for matching a suspect or victim to biological evidence from the crime scene. It has also been shown that DNA measurements can be achieved on almost any type of biological evidence from blood to hair to skin to saliva. DNA can be typed on fresh or old evidence, even on ancient preserved mummies! In this chapter, we will explore the chemical nature of DNA and how it varies from person to person. We will show how DNA can be typed, how databases of DNA types can be constructed and searched, and how databasing can help solve old, cold cases.

What Is DNA?

Deoxyribonucleic acid (DNA) is a large, polymeric molecule that is found in virtually every cell in the body. Two significant exceptions are red blood cells and nerve cells. Red cells are produced in bone marrow and have no need of DNA for replication, and nerve cells do not generally regenerate. DNA can be found in two regions of a cell: the nucleus and the mitochondria. Mitochondrial DNA has a different structure than nuclear DNA, is inherited differently, and will be discussed later in this chapter.

Nuclear DNA is a unique type of molecule. Its shape is called a "double helix" (see Figure 17.1). Consider a very long ladder. This ladder has two poles connected by many rungs. Each rung consists of two complementary pieces that are joined together. Now take the ladder and twist it many times throughout its length until it resembles a spiral staircase. This is the geometry of the DNA molecule. The poles of the DNA molecule (called the backbone) are not significant forensically. They are exactly the same in all people. The rungs are special, however. Each rung is made up of two *bases* or *nucleotides* that are joined together in the middle as well as to the poles, so each rung is made up of a base pair. These base pairs are comprised of two of the following:

Adenine (A)
Thymine (T)
Guanine (G)
Cytosine (C)

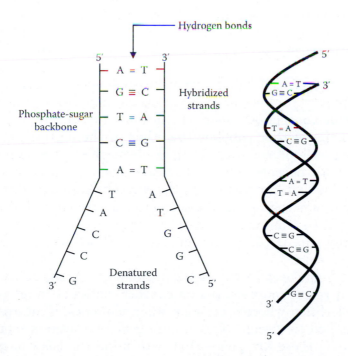

Figure 17.1 Base pairing of DNA strands to form a double-helix structure. The four bases are adenine, thymine, guanine, and cytosine. (Contribution of the National Institute of Standards and Technology, Gaithersburg, MD, 2010.)

Figure 17.2 A base pair sequence. Only "A" can pair with "T" and only "C" can pair with "G."

Because of the complex chemical structure of the bases, only certain pairs can join together. The rule is that adenine can only bond to thymine and guanine can only bond to cytosine. No base can join with itself. A strand of DNA has millions of base pairs and the rules can never be violated. Figure 17.2 shows a portion of a DNA strand with some representative base pairs.

Notice that base pairs will often repeat themselves. The T-A pair repeating three times in the DNA strand in Figure 17.2 illustrates this. The order of the base pairs seems to be random. In most cases it is not. The repeats are important and the overall order of the base pairs throughout the DNA is very significant. It comprises a genetic code that directs the body to ultimately build proteins that are the building blocks for all human organs and tissues. This code literally makes us who and what we are. Since the DNA comes equally from our mother and father, we inherit their characteristics according to certain rules of inheritance or laws of genetics.

Cellular DNA

Nuclear DNA is arranged in structures called "chromosomes," which are dense packages of DNA. In human beings, there are 22 matched pairs of *autosomes* that are responsible for the genetic makeup of the individual and one pair of sex-determining chromosomes. A male contains one X and one Y sex-determining chromosome and a female contains two X chromosomes. Thus, human cells each contain 23 pairs of chromosomes. Figure 17.3 shows the human genome with the chromosomes.

Chromosomes in each cell, except for sperm and egg cells, are in a *diploid* state. They contain a pair of chromosomes. Each parent supplies one member of each of the 23 pairs during conception, where the father's sperm cells supply one member of each pair and the mother supplies the other in the egg cell. It is through the chromosomes that each person inherits their physical, mental, and emotional characteristics from both parents. These characteristics are defined within a *genetic code* that is contained within portions of the chromosomes called "genes." A gene is a part of a chromosome consisting of a sequence of base pairs. Genes make up less than 5% of the DNA in humans. The other 95% of DNA between the genes was once thought of as being *junk* DNA, but recently, it has come to light that this DNA may have other functions.

The base pair sequences in the genes ultimately tell the cell what proteins to manufacture that result in expression of characteristics such as eye color, gender, and height. The location where a gene (or other sequence of interest) is found on a chromosome is called its "locus." The human *genome* contains more than 100,000 genes. For example, there are genes that determine the color of one's hair. Since different people have different hair colors, there must be some variations within the hair color genes that result in the different hair colors in a population. These variations in characteristics are due to differences in the genetic code caused by differences in the order of the base pair sequences. A gene that exists in more than

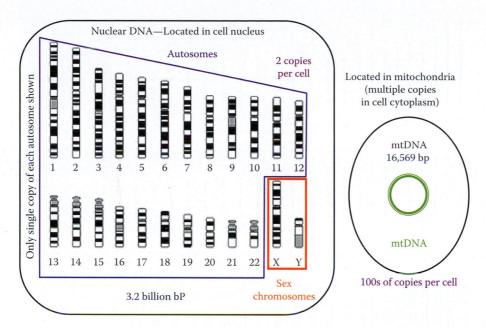

Figure 17.3 The human genome contained in every cell consists of 23 pairs of chromosomes and a small circular genome known as mitochondrial DNA. Chromosomes 1–22 are numbered according to their relative size and occur in single copy pairs within a cell's nucleus with one copy being inherited from one's mother and the other copy coming from one's father. Sex chromosomes are either X, Y for males or X, X for females. Mitochondrial DNA is inherited only from one's mother and is located in the mitochondria with hundreds of copies per cell. Together the nuclear DNA material amounts to over three billion base pairs (bp) while mitochondrial DNA is only about 16,569 bp in length. (Contribution of the National Institute of Standards and Technology, Gaithersburg, MD, 2010.)

one form is referred to as "polymorphic." The different forms of genes are called "alleles." Thus, there is an allele for brown hair, red hair, etc. Some hair colors are intermediate between pure colors because a person inherits different alleles from each parent. If an individual inherits the same allele for a particular characteristic from both parents, he or she is said to be *homozygous* with respect to that gene. If he or she receives a different allele from each parent, then he or she is *heterozygous* with respect to that gene. Figure 17.4 shows how both parents contribute one chromosome of each of the 23 pairs to the offspring.

If a person inherits genes from a parent that codes for brown hair and genes from the other parent that code for blond hair, he or she will usually have brown hair. This is because the allele for brown hair is *dominant* and the allele for blond hair is *recessive*.

DNA Polymorphisms and Population Genetics

There are two types of polymorphism in genes. The first is called "sequence polymorphism." This occurs when there is a difference in one or more base pairs within a gene. Examine the base pair sequence in the short strand of DNA shown here. Note the difference in the base pair at the position marked by the arrow. The two sequences are identical except for that single base pair.

```
C T C G A T T A A G G       C T C G T T T A A G G
: : : : ▲ : : : : : :  and  : : : : ▲ : : : : : :
G A G C T A A T T C C       G A G C A A A T T C C
```

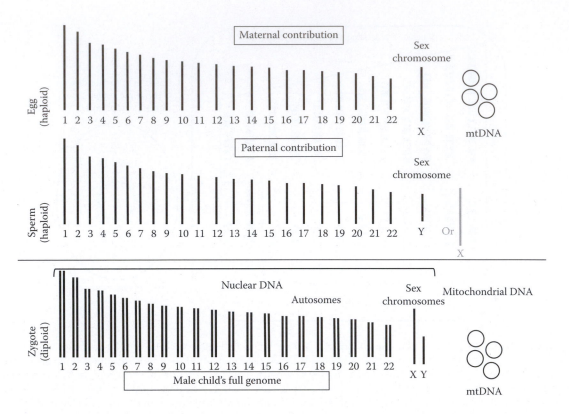

Figure 17.4 Human genome and inheritance. The haploid complement of chromosomes from a female's egg combines with the haploid chromosomal complement of a male's sperm to create a fully diploid zygote, which eventually develops into a child whose nongamete cells each contain the same genome. Half of the 22 autosomes come from each parent while mtDNA is only inherited from the mother. The father's contribution of either an X or a Y chromosome determines the child's sex. (Contribution of the National Institute of Standards and Technology, Gaithersburg, MD, 2010.)

The other type of polymorphism is called "length polymorphism." This occurs in strands of DNA where repeating sequences of base pairs are encountered. Examine the following DNA strands:

```
C A T G T A C – C A T G T A C
: : : : : : : : : : : : : :
G T A C A T G – G T A C A T G


C A T G T A C – C A T G T A C – C A T G T A C – C A T G T A C
: : : : : : : : : : : : : : : : : : : : : : : : : : : :
G T A C A T G – G T A C A T G – G T A C A T G – G T A C A T G


C A T G T A C – C A T G T A C – C A T G T A C – C A T G T A C – C A T G T A C
: : : : : : : : : : : : : : : : : : : : : : : : : : : : : : : : : : : : : :
G T A C A T G – G T A C A T G – G T A C A T G – G T A C A T G – G T A C A T G
```

All three of the strands contain the base pair sequence:

```
C A T G T A C
: : : : : : :
G T A C A T G
```

In the first strand, the sequence repeats twice. In the second strand, the same sequence repeats four times, and in the third strand, six times. Because the repeats occur right next to each other, without any intervening base pairs, they are referred to as "tandem" repeats. Length and sequence polymorphism are very important in distinguishing one person's DNA from another because certain strands of DNA might differ from one person to the next only by a small sequence or length polymorphism. Modern methods of DNA typing take advantage of length polymorphisms. In these methods a locus is examined to determine if the repeats are the same or different. The frequency of these repeats in the human population can then be estimated. Other loci can then be examined to determine the repeating sequences there and their population frequency. These frequencies are expressed as the probability that this pair of frequencies would occur. The loci that are examined in DNA typing today are all independently derived, and thus the probability that an overall DNA type would occur is the product of the probabilities of occurrence at each individual locus. If DNA from an evidentiary sample has the same alleles at each locus as does the DNA from a suspect, the probability that the DNA belongs to someone else (a chance occurrence) is extremely small. If the DNA sequences at even one locus do not match, then that suspect could not be the source of the DNA. There are vast databases of DNA types at each of the loci that are used in modern DNA typing. These databases can be searched digitally to determine if an individual has the same DNA type as that of evidence derived from a crime.

The product rule can be illustrated by the process of repeated flipping of a coin. There are two possible outcomes from flipping a coin: heads (H) or tails (T). Since they are equally likely of occurring, the probability of getting heads is 1/2 or 0.5. Suppose a coin is flipped twice. What are the odds that it will come up heads both times? There are four possible outcomes from flipping a coin twice: H–H, H–T, T–H, and T–T. Each of these possibilities has an equal likelihood of occurring since a coin has no memory of how it lands on each flip. Thus, the probability that it will come up heads both times (H-H) is 1/4 or 0.25. This number can be arrived at using the *product rule*. This rule states that the probability of two or more independent events occurring is the product of the probabilities of each event. Thus, the probability of two coin flips coming up heads is 1/2 × 1/2 = 1/4 because the probability of heads coming up on one flip is 1/2 and on the other flip, 1/2. Likewise, the probability of getting heads three times in a row is 1/8 or 0.125. This is because there are eight possibilities that can occur when a coin is flipped three times: H–H–H, H–H–T, H–T–H, T–T–H, H–T–T, T–H–T, T–H–H, and T–T–T. Only one of these possibilities (H–H–H) results in getting heads all three times. The more times a coin is flipped, the less chance that any particular outcome will occur. It is very important that each event be independent of the others or the rule will not apply.

Something for You to Do

Take a deck of 52 cards. How many different cards are there and how many of each card are there in a full deck? What is the probability that a card drawn at random will be an ace? Now what is the probability that the next card you draw will also be an ace? Remember how many cards are left and how many aces are left in the deck if you draw an ace on the first try. Using probabilities, you can calculate the chances of getting dealt any poker or blackjack hand. The proprietors of casinos at gambling establishments determine their payouts on various games of chance by the probabilities of your drawing each kind of hand and the chances that you will beat the house on each type of game. For example, a roulette wheel contains the numbers 1 through 36 plus a 0 and 00. If you bet $1 on any number and the payoff for hitting that number is $36, you will eventually lose your money because the probability of hitting a given number on a spin of the wheel is 38 to 1. If you bet $1 on the number 7 every time, it should come up once on the average of every 38 spins. If it comes up on the 38th spin, you have bet $38 and you finally get back $36 for hitting the number. Over time, you have to lose.

Going back to the coin flip, what are the odds of getting a tail 10 times in a row? It is more than a 1000 to 1. One way to visualize this is that you would have to make more than 1000 tries at flipping a coin 10 times to ensure on the average that one of those tries would give 10 straight heads.

Collection and Preservation of DNA Evidence

It has been said many times that forensic evidence is only as good as the skills of the people who collect it. Some people describe this as "garbage in, garbage out." This is especially true with biological evidence that can be highly perishable. Even though DNA is an amazingly hearty substance, its degradation can be a problem. Improperly preserved DNA can be rendered useless in a short time. Today, traces of DNA are sufficient to obtain a complete profile. Stamps and envelopes that have been licked with saliva contain enough cells to be DNA typed. Toothbrushes, pillows, the inside of a hat, and discarded chewing gum are all potential sources for DNA.

Special care must be taken in collecting biological evidence. It should always be assumed to be infectious; it could be a carrier for diseases such as hepatitis or AIDS. There should be minimal contact with the evidence. Contamination of biological evidence is a real problem, especially since so little DNA is necessary to type. All precautions against contamination must be taken. These include wearing protective clothing that minimizes the loss of hair or dandruff or other biological material from the person collecting the evidence, wearing gloves and changing them every time new evidence is to be collected, using tools such as tweezers to collect evidence, and making sure that positive and negative controls are collected as well as *elimination samples*. These are known samples of DNA collected from all personnel at the scene who could possibly have contributed DNA.

Biological evidence must never be packaged in airtight containers because moisture can build up, which promotes the growth of bacteria that can degrade DNA. Paper bags or other *breathable* containers should be used. Wherever possible, if a garment or other material is suspected to contain blood, the whole article should be submitted. If that is not possible, then samples can be removed and sent to the lab. These must always be accompanied by a sample of the article that doesn't contain any biological material. This is called a "substrate control," a type of negative control. See Chapter 3 for a discussion of positive and negative controls and their importance in chemical analysis of evidence. Although most cellular material in humans contains DNA, known samples are usually collected from gently scraping the inside of the cheek. These *buccal samples* contain more than enough DNA for typing and are obtained easily and with a minimum of invasion of the person's body. If blood samples are taken, they should be put in tubes that already contain a preservative such as *ethylenediamine tetraacetic acid*.

History of DNA Typing

The DNA typing community settled on a technique of DNA analysis known as *STRs* in the late 1990s, and this technique is still being used, albeit with refinements. But STRs did not arise from a vacuum. They are the result of many years of research and trial and error into the best ways to incorporate validated DNA typing methods to the unique circumstances of evidence development from humans (or perhaps other animals). Before discussing current methods of DNA typing, it is useful to look at how typing methods developed.

Prior to about 1985, DNA typing had not been adapted for evidentiary purposes. Virtually all work in isolating and characterizing DNA was done for medical purposes.

Prior to DNA, typing blood was analyzed for components that differed among segments of the human population. The first breakthrough occurred in 1900, when Dr. Karl Landsteiner, an Austrian researcher, discovered that there were four different types of blood types that differed by the presence or absence of certain antigens on the surface of red blood cells. This gave rise to the ABO blood typing system, described in the chapter on forensic serology. Later, the MNSs and Rh blood typing systems were discovered. Each of these systems divides or *bins* the human population into various groups by which of the blood types they have in each system. Their use spread all over the world over the next few decades, including use in forensic blood typing. Today, more than 30 different blood typing systems have been recognized. This method of blood typing for forensic purposes was replaced by DNA typing, in part because the blood types are not nearly as discriminating as DNA typing. Some blood types, principally, the ABO antigens, also show up in body fluids such as semen, saliva, and sperm. This made it possible to type these body fluids in the same way that blood could be typed.

As the 1900s proceed, polymorphic red and white blood cell enzymes were developed and characterized. These systems turned out to be more discriminating than antigen-based blood types, and, for a time, blood cell enzymes were used both in criminal cases on blood evidence and in paternity cases, where it was necessary to establish if a particular male was the father of a child born out of wedlock.

Restriction Fragment Length Polymorphism

DNA typing (or DNA fingerprinting as it was then known) was first developed by Sir Alec Jeffries, a British geneticist. In 1985, Dr. Jeffries discovered that certain sequences of DNA repeated themselves like pearls in a necklace and, further, that there was variation in the number of these repeats within a human population. He developed a technique to determine the length of the repeating fragments in a sample of blood or any other tissue that contained DNA. He called the repeating sequences "variable number of tandem repeats" (VNTRs), and the technique for analyzing them became known as "restriction fragment length polymorphism" (RFLP). This name described in part the process used to determine the VNTRs. The DNA was separated from other cellular materials and then the double-stranded DNA was denatured, unzipped into a single-strand DNA. Special enzymes called "restriction enzymes" were created that could seek out and identify the ends of the repeating DNA sequences in the VNTRs wherever they appeared in a cell's DNA and snip the DNA strands at these ends, thus

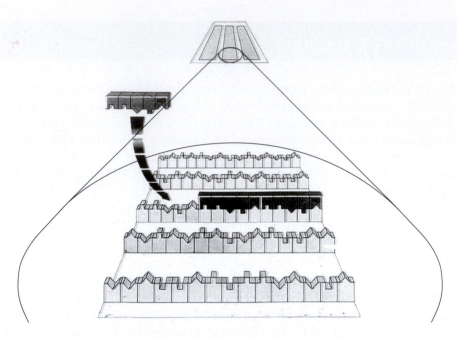

Figure 17.5 Probe hybridization. The black pieces are radioactive or fluorescent probes that are engineered to be complementary to the variable number of tandem repeats (VNTRs). The result is that the VNTRs become radioactively or fluorescently labeled.

isolating the VNTRs. Once the restriction enzymes had done their work, the cut DNA strands were subjected to a form of gel electrophoresis that separated the strands by length. Of course, all of the pieces of DNA were separated and were present somewhere on the plate where the electrophoresis was carried out. The VNTRs were then *hybridized*; complementary strands of DNA, called "probes," were introduced that bound themselves to the VNTRs only. Figure 17.5 shows how hybridization works.

These probes of DNA were originally radioactively labeled so that an image of the gel electrophoresis plate would expose a photographic plate only where the radioactivity occurred, thus visualizing the parts of the plate containing the VNTRs. Later, the probes were labeled with phosphors that glowed when exposed to ultraviolet light. Some of the difficulties with RFLP included the need to have a relatively large amount of material (compared to more modern methods) to get a successful analysis, the need for high-molecular-weight DNA molecules (mainly nondegraded DNA), and long analysis time frames. Figure 17.6 is a summary of the RFLP process.

PCR

At about the same time that Dr. Jeffries was developing his *DNA fingerprinting* methods using RFLP, work was going on in the United States to develop another method of DNA typing. Dr. Kary Mullis had invented a technique for making exact copies of pieces of DNA. This technique could be used to make millions of copies of any desired strand of DNA, large or small in a relatively short time, using extremely small amounts of material. He called this technique "polymerase chain reaction (PCR)." As with most other methods for the manipulation of DNA, PCR was not originally developed for forensic purposes, so it took several years for the forensic community to develop genetic marker systems that could take advantage of the speed and sensitivity of PCR.

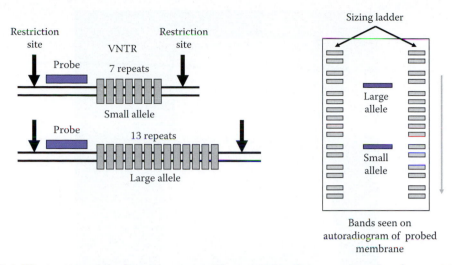

Figure 17.6 Illustration of the key processes with restriction fragment length polymorphism analysis. DNA from an individual, possessing two different size alleles at a single variable number of tandem repeat (VNTR) locus, is digested with a restriction enzyme. Arrows indicate restriction sites around a small and a large VNTR allele that varies in size due to the number of repeat units. The digested DNA is separated in terms of size via gel electrophoresis and transferred to a nylon membrane via Southern blotting. The membrane is washed with a radioactive or chemiluminescent probe that binds at a single probe site on each allele. A sizing ladder is run in adjacent lanes on the gel in order to estimate the VNTR allele sizes. The DNA fragments are placed into bins based on their size and then compared to other samples. The first probe is then removed and another probe is hybridized to the membrane and the process repeated to obtain results from typically four to six probes. (Contribution of the National Institute of Standards and Technology, Gaithersburg, MD, 2010.)

DNA Amplification by PCR

DNA is amplified through the action of *DNA polymerase*, an enzyme that is present in all living organisms. As a cell divides, DNA is replicated so the exact same type and amount is present in the new cell. During cell division the DNA first denatures, becoming single stranded. DNA polymerase catalyzes the addition of complimentary base pairs to the DNA, thus forming new double-helix strands. Dr. Mullis developed a *thermal cycler*, an instrument that can be heated to various temperatures under controlled conditions. Figure 17.7 shows a picture of a thermal cycler.

The PCR process takes place in the thermal cycler. The DNA that is to be replicated is mixed with a solvent, the DNA polymerase, as well as short pieces of DNA called "primers," and a supply of the four bases (C, T, A, G) that will be added to the DNA one by one to replicate it. The amplification process takes place in three steps. The process is shown in Figure 17.8.

1. *Denaturation*: The mixture is heated close to boiling causing the strands of DNA to denature and become single stranded. Each piece of complimentary single-stranded DNA will become the template for the formation of a new strand.
2. *Annealing*: The temperature of the mixture is lowered. The primers then add to one end of each of the single-stranded DNA. These will be the starting points for the formation of new double-stranded DNA.
3. *Extension*: In the presence of DNA polymerase as a catalyst, a base (nucleotide) adds to the first open position next to the primer according to the base that is already on the single strand. This process repeats until the new strand is complete. The same thing is happening to both of the single strands, so when the process is complete, there are now two complete double strands of DNA.

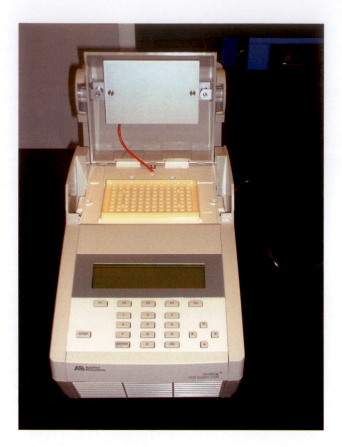

Figure 17.7 A thermocycler. (Courtesy of Richard Li.)

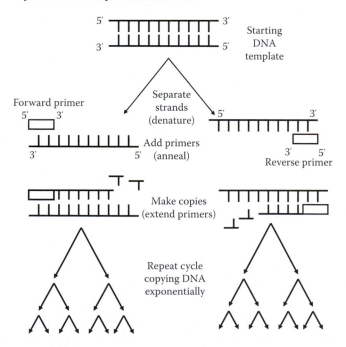

Figure 17.8 7.2 DNA amplification process with the polymerase chain reaction (PCR). In each cycle, the two DNA template strands are first separated (denatured) by heat. The sample is then cooled to an appropriate temperature to bind (anneal) the oligonucleotide primers. Finally, the temperature of the sample is raised to the optimal temperature for the DNA polymerase and it extends the primers to produce a copy of each DNA template strand. For each cycle, the number of DNA molecular fragments (with the sequence between the two PCR primers) doubles. (Contribution of the National Institute of Standards and Technology, Gaithersburg, MD, 2010.)

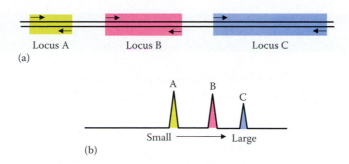

(a)

(b)

Figure 17.9 Schematic of multiplex polymerase chain reaction (PCR). A multiplex PCR makes use of two or more primer sets within the same reaction mix. Three sets of primers, represented by arrows, are shown here to amplify three different loci on a DNA template (a). The primers were designed so that the PCR products for locus A, locus B, and locus C would be different sizes and therefore resolvable with a size-based separation system (b). (Contribution of the National Institute of Standards and Technology, Gaithersburg, MD, 2010.)

The mixture is now reheated and the two strands denature and the process repeats. The second time the process is completed there are now four strands. Each cycle doubles the previous amount of DNA. In most cases, 25–30 cycles are completed. In theory, if 30 cycles are completed, there should be 2^{30} strands of DNA or about 1 trillion pieces of DNA! Thirty cycles of PCR can be carried out in a matter of a few hours. It is also possible to simultaneously amplify several locations on DNA using PCR. This is shown in Figure 17.9.

First PCR-Based DNA Typing Methods

Over the years since the PCR was developed and adapted to forensic purposes, a number of methods for DNA typing have been developed that can narrow down the possible source of biological evidence.

The first method was used to detect sequence polymorphisms in a gene that expressed a white cell blood enzyme called HLA DQ alpha/DQA1. The first form of this test detected six different alleles of this DNA fragment, resulting in 21 different DNA types at this locus. A later development resulted in the detection of an additional allele and 28 different DNA types.

Later, the developer of the DQ alpha system, the Perkin-Elmer Corporation, developed a more robust PCR-based system called PolyMarker. In this method, the DQ alpha gene was amplified and detected along with five additional DNA fragments. These had only two or three different alleles each, and thus its discrimination power, although improved, still could only narrow down the source of a DNA sample to about one in 10,000.

In order to increase the discrimination power of PCR-based DNA typing, the forensic biology community led by the FBI explored possible length polymorphic loci that could be exploited. Collectively, these were called "amplified fragment length polymorphisms" (AMP-FLPs). The first one that gained widespread acceptance in the early 1990s was called DS180. This consisted of a 16 bp repeating unit. The repeats occurred between 14 and 41 times. The DNA segments were amplified by PCR and then separated on a gel by capillary electrophoresis. Silver staining was used to visualize the bands. The DS180 system suffered from several drawbacks; the analysis was time consuming and required a good deal of user intervention, which precluded the ability to automate the analysis. In addition, it employed a large fragment of DNA that limited its use on degraded samples, and the large size of the fragment precluded simultaneous analysis with other shorter AMP-FLPs.

Current Method of DNA Typing: STRs

At about the same time that these PCR methods were being developed, some scientists began evaluating shorter length polymorphisms. These so-called microsatellites had repeating sequences that were 2–7 bp long, in contrast to DS180 and other *minisatellites*, which had repeats that were generally between 10 and 100 bp. As will be demonstrated in the next section, the use of these *STRs* provided significant advantages over minisatellite methods, and ultimately, STRs became the method of choice worldwide. When STRs were first developed, the DNA fragments were separated and displayed using gel electrophoresis. This is shown in Figure 17.10.

Later, capillary electrophoresis was developed for use with STR analysis. It is modified to group the loci and display them in different colors by using several filters. A schematic of a capillary electrophoresis apparatus is shown in Figure 17.11.

Figure 17.12 shows an electropherogram containing 16 loci including amelogenin (to determine sex). Notice that for most of the loci, there are two peaks indicating that two alleles were present. Remember that this is because we inherit one allele from each parent and they are often different forms.

Table 17.1 lists the known population frequencies for 13 common loci to illustrate how statistics are used in interpreting DNA types. When the population frequency of each allele at each locus is known, the product rule will yield probabilities of an overall frequency in the population that are staggeringly small as can be seen in Table 17.1 for a hypothetical African-American male.

The first column is the locus where the STR is found. The second column (genotype) is the particular alleles that this individual possesses. Note that he is heterozygous at 10 loci and homozygous at D13S317, D8S1179, and FGA. The third column (allele frequencies) contains the allele frequencies for each allele. For example, in CSF1P0, the 10 allele is found in 271 out of every thousand people in the black population. The fourth column (match statistic) is two times the product of the allele frequencies when the locus is heterozygous and the square of the allele frequency

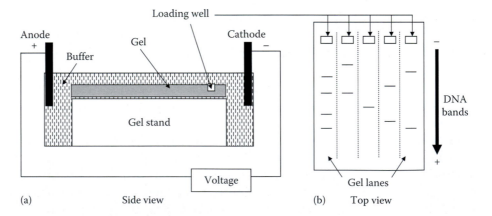

Figure 17.10 Schematic of a gel electrophoresis system. (a) The horizontal gel is submerged in a tank full of electrophoresis buffer. DNA samples are loaded into wells across the top of the gel. These wells are created by a "comb" placed in the gel while it is forming. When the voltage is applied across the two electrodes, the DNA molecules move toward the anode and separate by size. (b) The number of lanes available on a gel is dependent on the number of teeth in the comb used to define the loading wells. At least one lane on each gel is taken up by a relative molecular mass size standard that is used to estimate the sizes of the sample bands in the other lanes. (Contribution of the National Institute of Standards and Technology, Gaithersburg, MD, 2010.)

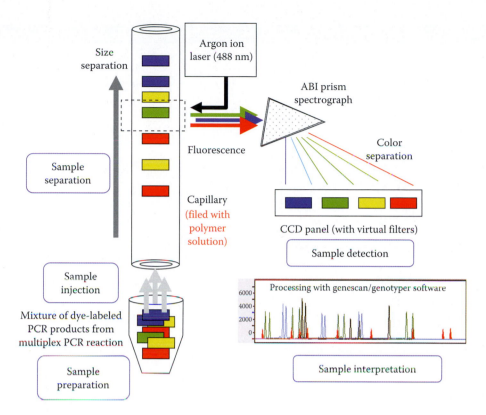

Figure 17.11 Schematic illustration of the separation and detection of STR alleles with an ABI Prism 310 Genetic Analyzer. (Contribution of the National Institute of Standards and Technology, Gaithersburg, MD, 2010.)

in homozygous cases. To find the random match statistic, all 13 match statistics are multiplied (rule of multiplication). The final number, 7 septillion, is astronomic. As a point of reference, it is estimated that there have been no more than 100 billion (100,000,000,000) people that have ever lived on earth.

How does one interpret this final number? It is sometimes called "the odds of a chance occurrence." Suppose that the evidence at a crime scene has DNA of the exact type shown in Table 17.1. Further, suppose that a suspect in the case has the exact same DNA type. A very important question for the trier of fact at a trial would be: "What are the chances that the owner of the DNA could be someone else other than the suspect?" If the trier of fact is going to assume that the suspect is the owner of the DNA, it would be very disturbing to find out later that someone else coincidentally had the same DNA. The huge final match statistic, 5.422×10^{-19}, shows that the chance of a coincidental match is extremely remote. The statistic indicates that only 1 out of every 1,837,000,000,000,000,000 people in the black population should have this same DNA type. This doesn't mean that no two black people have this same DNA type. These population frequencies for each allele are drawn from a sample of the black population, not the entire population. It would never be possible to conclude that no one else has this same DNA type without testing the entire population, a practical impossibility. Thus, the idea of individualizing even DNA evidence is controversial. It is not possible to prove individuality and it shouldn't be inferred from statistical arguments. One must be very careful about making inferences from so-called rare events, such as a particular DNA type. Consider birthdays; there are 365 possible birthdays. One would suppose that in a room containing 100 people, the odds of two of them having the same birthday would be small. In fact, it is nearly a 50% chance! Nonetheless, consider that people who become suspects in crimes are

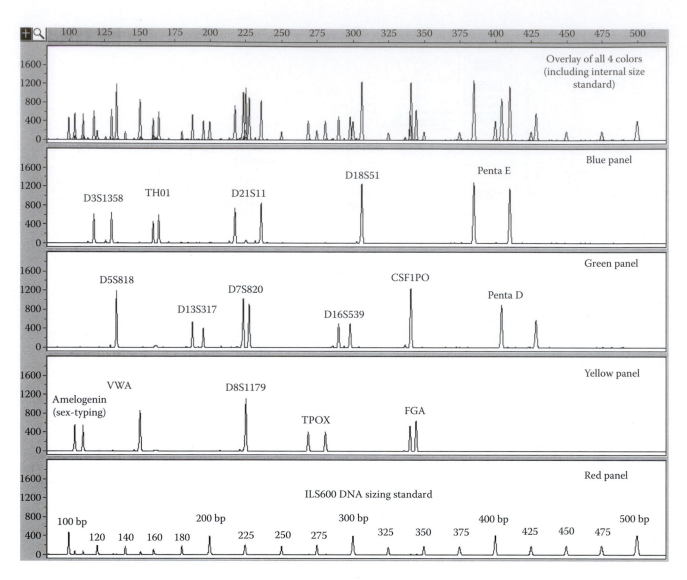

Figure 17.12 PowerPlex 16 result from 1 ng genomic DNA. (Contribution of the National Institute of Standards and Technology, Gaithersburg, MD, 2010.)

there for a reason or usually multiple reasons. There will always be multiple types of evidence that makes that person a suspect. The DNA type is only one of those pieces of evidence. The conclusion that the DNA type in question is very rare and the chances of a coincidental match between evidentiary DNA and a suspect is very small should be sufficient in a criminal trial.

Determination of Gender

In many cases, especially those involving sexual assault, it is important to know if the biological sample belongs to a male or a female. There are two approaches taken in gender determination. The first involves analysis of the locus called "amelogenin." Amelogenin is found in one region of the chromosomes that determine gender. These are the *X* and *Y* chromosomes. Amelogenin is not an STR but is commonly analyzed along with STRs by capillary electrophoresis. At one region of the amelogenin locus males have six more base pairs than do females. Females always receive an X chromosome from each parent whereas males have one X chromosome and one

TABLE 17.1
Population Statistics for 13 Loci in Hypothetical African-American Male

Locus	Genotype	Allele Frequencies	Match Statistic
CSF1PO	10, 12	0.257; 0.298	0.153
D13S317	11, 11	0.306	0.09036
D16S539	11, 12	0.318; 0.096	0.125
D18S51	14, 18	0.072; 0.123	0.0177
D21S11	27, 37	0.078; 0.002	0.000831
D3S1358	15, 17	0.302; 0.205	0.123
D5S818	8, 12	0.048; 0.353	0.0338
D7S820	8, 10	0.236; 0.331	0.156
D8S1179	12, 12	0.141	0.0199
FGA	22, 22	0.196	0.0384
THO1	6, 9	0.124; 0.151	0.0374
TPOX	10, 11	0.089; 0.219	0.0389
vWA	15, 16	0.236; 0.269	0.127

Source: Courtesy of Orchid Genescreen, East Lansing, MI.
Note: Random Match Statistic: 2.327×10^{-18} or 1 person in 427,800,000,000,000,000 chosen at random from the black population would be expected to match by chance.

Y chromosome. Females will thus show only one band for amelogenin whereas males will have two bands, one of which is six base pairs longer than the other. Even if the stain is mixed with a male fraction and a female fraction, it will be possible to determine that both are present using amelogenin.

The other method of gender determination is to analyze the STRs that are present only on the Y chromosome. These are called "Y-STRs." This type of analysis is also useful in mixed stains, even those that are badly degraded or contain a large female fraction, as would be expected in vaginal swabs in a sexual assault case.

Mitochondrial DNA

Sometimes it is not possible to obtain nuclear DNA for analysis or it may be so degraded that analysis is not possible. This is sometimes the case with skeletal remains. Fortunately there is another kind of DNA present in the body, although it makes up only about 1% of the DNA. This DNA is located in the *mitochondria*. Mitochondria are structures present in every cell in the body without exception. They are in the cytoplasm, outside the nucleus. Mitochondria are responsible for energy production in the cell and they contain DNA that helps in this function. There are thousands of mitochondria in each cell and thus thousands of copies of DNA whereas there are only a few copies of nuclear DNA in each cell.

Mitochondrial DNA differs from nuclear DNA in important ways. First, it is not arranged in a double helix but instead is circular. This is shown in Figure 17.13. There are 37 genes in human mitochondrial DNA that direct energy production, but the forensically important part consists of about 1100 base pairs within two regions that do not have a genetic code function. These regions are highly variable (*hypervariable*) and are quite useful in DNA comparisons. The two regions are called "HV1" and "HV2."

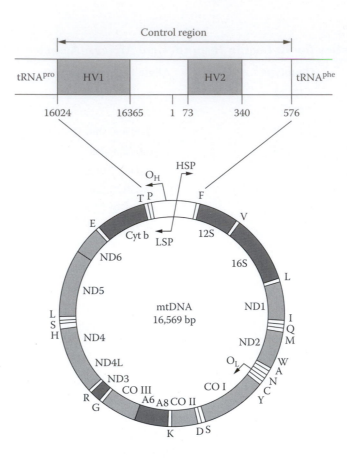

Figure 17.13 There are 37 genes in human mitochondrial DNA that direct energy production, but the forensically important part consists of about 1100 base pairs within two regions that do not have a genetic code function. These regions are highly variable (*hypervariable*) and are quite useful in DNA comparisons. The two regions are called "HV1" and "HV2."

Mitochondrial DNA is inherited only from the mother. There is no contribution to mitochondrial DNA from the father. This makes mitochondrial DNA typing a useful vehicle for tracing one's parentage back through the maternal line. Every sibling in a family has the same mitochondrial DNA as each other and their mother and maternal grandmother, etc. Although there is a great deal of variability in mitochondrial DNA among unrelated people, there are only two regions that exhibit this variability so that the match probabilities in mitochondrial DNA typing are much lower than with cellular DNA.

CODIS

One of the most important advances in DNA typing has been the development of local, state, and national databases that contain DNA types of many people who have been involved in crimes. When DNA from an unknown suspect is found at a crime scene, it can be typed and the type sent to a database that contains thousands of DNA types from people who have been convicted of a felony or, in some cases, arrested for felony crimes. There have been many cases where blind hits have been made even in cases where the perpetrator committed crimes in a different state. The set of DNA databases is called "CODIS" or *Combined DNA Index System*. CODIS was begun in 1990 and is arranged in three layers. The first is the local level where

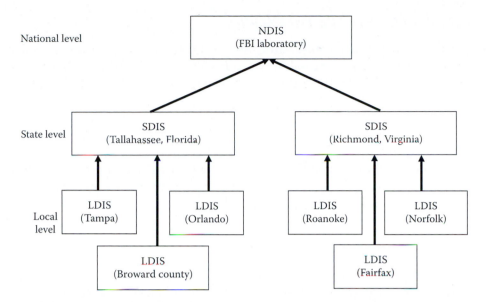

Figure 17.14 Schematic of the three tiers in the Combined DNA Index System (CODIS). DNA profile information begins at the local level, or Local DNA Index System (LDIS), and then can be uploaded to the state level, or State DNA Index System (SDIS), and finally to the national level, or National DNA Index System (NDIS). Each local or state laboratory maintains its portion of CODIS while the FBI Laboratory maintains the national portion (NDIS). (Contribution of the National Institute of Standards and Technology, Gaithersburg, MD, 2010.)

all of the DNA profiles are first entered. These local databases feed into a statewide database. The 50 state databases then feed into a national CODIS database. This system allows crime laboratories to search a particular case at the appropriate level for that case. This saves time and resources. Every state in the United States participates in the CODIS and each state has passed legislation that mandates which offenders must contribute samples of DNA for inclusion in the database. The only thing that has held back the development of CODIS is a lack of funding to crime laboratories for processing the samples. Active cases are the top priority of every crime lab, and samples that are collected just for entry into CODIS must take a back seat. As a result, there are hundreds of thousands of cases backlogged in crime labs nationwide. It is important to get this data entered into CODIS because law enforcement agencies are now going back to old cases where they have biological evidence but no suspect and are now processing the evidence and entering the data into CODIS for search purposes. There have been hundreds of hits nationwide in these so-called cold cases. There are three levels of CODIS that can be used to search for a hit. They are *local*, *state*, and *national*. This is illustrated in Figure 17.14.

In order to make CODIS work, all of the data that is entered for each case must be of the same type. The 13 loci that are described in Table 17.1 are the standard loci for CODIS and each sample must have a DNA type at those 13 loci. According to the FBI, more than 27,000 investigations have been aided in 49 states, in federal labs and in Puerto Rico as of August 2005. An investigation in this context is a case where a match for DNA was produced by CODIS that would not have otherwise occurred (see http://www.fbi.gov/hq/lab/codis/aidedmap.htm).

CODIS Success Stories

The FBI periodically describes CODIS success stories on their website. Three examples are given in the following (see http://www.fbi.gov/success.htm).

Solving a Double Murder in the Deep South

In the summer of 1992, Rita Baldo and her daughter Lisa were murdered in their Florida apartment. Both had gunshot wounds to the head and Lisa had been raped. Investigators found DNA in the saliva of three cigarette butts at the scene (neither of the women smoked). The DNA profile was compared with those taken from various suspects in the case, but none matched. The profile was uploaded to CODIS in 1998. Three years later, a Wisconsin forensic scientist matched a profile from that state's convicted offenders' database with the DNA from the Florida case. The profile came from convicted felon James A. Frederick, who was serving time in Wisconsin. A later, more sophisticated test of hairs in the apartment also matched Frederick's DNA. Frederick was indicted in May 2003.

Putting a Rapist on Parole behind Bars for Good

In September 2000, Carol Shields was found suffocated and murdered in a friend's apartment in North Kansas City. Her clothes were missing, and the scene had been meticulously cleaned by the killer. Still, investigators managed to find DNA underneath the victim's fingernails. The following June, that DNA was linked to a profile in the National DNA Index System (NDIS) from paroled Arkansas rapist Wayne DuMond, who had not been a suspect in the case. DuMond was arrested, tried, and convicted—largely on the strength of the DNA evidence. He was given a life sentence without parole.

Cracking a 1968 Murder Case

In 1968, a 14-year-old girl named Linda Harmon was raped and murdered in San Francisco while babysitting for a neighbor. A semen sample from the autopsy was collected and stored by the San Francisco medical examiner. The case went unsolved, but last year the sample was tested for DNA. It matched that of William Speer, a convicted rapist who had been confined to an Arizona mental hospital. It is believed to be the oldest "cold" case solved by CODIS. Speer was arrested and pled not guilty to Harmon's murder. He was ultimately convicted of murder.

Summary

DNA is the building block of life. It directs all cellular functions. More than 99% of human DNA is identical in all people. Less than 1% makes us different. Parts of this DNA are polymorphic; they exist in more than one form. By typing this DNA, or describing the forms that are present in biological evidence and in suspects or victims, such evidence can be associated with one particular person in some cases.

There are several ways that DNA typing can be done. RFLP was the first type developed. It separated and identified long chains that contain shorter repeating units of DNA that have different numbers of repeats in different people. RFLP requires a relatively large amount of DNA that has not been significantly degraded. PCR was developed to replicate DNA through a heat-controlled process that duplicates single-stranded DNA and makes more double strands. Each cycle doubles the amount of DNA present. Today, DNA is typed using STRs, which combine the advantages of RFLP and PCR. STRs are short strands of DNA with many repeats.

They are highly variable in the human population and there are many of them in the human genome. PCR is used to amplify them and capillary electrophoresis is used to separate them by size. Currently, 16 loci are used in STR DNA typing. The same 13 loci are used to compile the CODIS database, which contains DNA from offenders in all 50 states. The database can be searched for possible suspects in crimes where the perpetrator has left DNA but is unidentified.

Test Yourself

Multiple Choice

1. Which of the following is NOT a nucleotide used to make up DNA?
   a. Adenine
   b. Guanine
   c. Argenine
   d. Thymine
   e. Cytosine
2. Which of the following is NOT a step in PCR?
   a. Addition of primers to ends of DNA strands
   b. Denaturation
   c. Addition of individual nucleotides
   d. Southern blotting
   e. All the above are steps in PCR
3. Which of the following is true about RFLP?
   a. The repeat strands are very short
   b. It analyzes only mitochondrial DNA
   c. It involves amplifying DNA
   d. Restriction enzymes are used to cut the DNA at the ends of the repeat sites
   e. None of the above are true
4. Which of the following is true of mitochondrial DNA compared to nuclear DNA?
   a. There are many more variable regions in mitochondrial DNA
   b. There are longer repeats in mitochondrial DNA
   c. There are many more copies of mitochondrial DNA in cells
   d. Mitochondrial DNA comes only from the father
5. Which of the following is a method used to determine the gender of a biologic sample?
   a. Mitochondrial typing
   b. RFLP typing
   c. PCR
   d. Amelogenin typing
6. Two strands of DNA having the same repeating base pair sequence but different numbers of repeats of that sequence is an example of:
   a. Length polymorphism
   b. Sequence polymorphism
   c. Hypervariability
   d. Hyperventilation
   e. Number polymorphism

7. Which of the following is not a component of the CODIS system?
   a. Local database
   b. National database
   c. Convicted felon samples
   d. Convicted misdemeanor samples
   e. State database
8. Which of the following best describes a gene?
   a. A physical characteristic
   b. A repeating sequence of base pairs
   c. A part of a chromosome that gives rise to a particular characteristic of a human such as hair color
   d. A sequence polymorphism
   e. None of the above
9. STRs are
   a. Length polymorphisms
   b. Sequence polymorphism
   c. Genes
   d. PCR products
   e. Found only in mitochondria
10. In RFLP DNA typing
    a. DNA is fragmented by restriction genes
    b. Fragments are made up of length polymorphs
    c. The fragments are 4–7 base pairs long
    d. Capillary electrophoresis is used to visualize the fragments

True or False

11. Because random match probabilities for DNA typing by STRs are so low, DNA can be associated reliably with one and only one person in the world.
12. Biological evidence should be stored in breathable containers to prevent degradation.
13. RFLP fragments are more susceptible to degradation than STRs.
14. Mitochondrial DNA is passed from generation to generation by the father only.
15. Mitochondrial DNA has only two regions that are polymorphic.
16. There is only one CODIS database that covers the whole country.
17. There is no DNA in hairs.

Matching

18. PCR   a. Analyzes DNA by fragmentation of long length polymorphs
19. DNA   b. Short gender determining repeat
20. RFLP   c. Clones DNA
21. STR   d. Analyzes DNA at 13 loci
22. Y-STR   e. Deoxyribonucleic acid

Short Essay

23. Briefly describe how the PCR process works.
24. Briefly describe the precautions that must be considered when collecting potential DNA evidence.
25. Briefly describe the differences between STR and RFLP analysis.

Further Reading

Butler, J. M. (2010). *Fundamentals of Forensic DNA Typing*. Academic Press, Burlington, MA.

Inman, K. and Rudin, N. (2002). *An Introduction to Forensic DNA Analysis*, 2nd edn. CRC Press, Boca Raton, FL.

Li, R. (2008). *Forensic Biology*. CRC Press, Boca Raton, FL.

On the Web

A brief history of DNA typing. Good graphics: http://www.cstl.nist.gov/div831/strbase/ppt/intro.pdf.

A really good primer on DNA typing: http://www.ornl.gov/sci/techresources/Human_Genome/elsi/forensics.shtml.

http://video.google.com/videosearch?hl=en&q=dna+fingerprinting&revid=1171294260&ei=I5mtSbWLAouINbag_OUE&resnum=0&um=1&ie=UTF-8&ei=YJqtSfi_GciLngeClty5Bg&sa=X&oi=video_result_group&resnum=4&ct=title#: Some good videos that explain DNA typing.

18
Hair

Learning Objectives

1. To be able to define and describe hair
2. To be able to explain the origin and growth patterns of hair
3. To be able to describe the microscopic structure of human and nonhuman hairs
4. To be able to explain how to differentiate human from nonhuman hair
5. To be able to explain how hairs are compared
6. To be able to explain how known hair samples are collected
7. To be able to explain the role of mitochondrial DNA typing of hair in the analysis of hair from a crime scene

Chapter 18
Hair

Chapter Outline

Mini Glossary

Anagen growth phase: Active growing period of hair.
Catagen growth phase: Transition phase between growth and rest phases.
Cortex: Middle and thickest layer of hair in humans; contains color granules.
Cortical fusi: Small, bubble-like structures in the cortex of hair.
Cuticle: Outermost layer of hair; consists of overlapping scales of keratin.
Epidermis: Outer layer of skin.
Follicle: Structure from which hairs originate and grow.
Keratin: Substance that makes up the cuticle of the hair.
Medulla: Inner layer of hair.
Melanin: Pigment responsible for hair color.
Melanocyte: Cells that produce melanin; the pigment responsible for hair color.
Ovoid bodies: Structures in cortex; their function is unknown.
Telogen growth phase: Rest phase when hair stops growing completely.

Acronyms

DNA: Deoxyribonucleic acid
FBI: Federal Bureau of Investigation
THC: Tetrahydrocannabinol

Introduction

On March 20, 1987, an 8-year-old girl was attacked in her home in Billings, Montana, by an intruder who had broken in through a locked window. She was repeatedly raped and then the intruder left after stealing a purse and jacket that were in the girl's room. The victim was examined the same day. Police collected her underwear and the bed sheets upon which the rapes were committed. Several hairs were collected from the bed sheets and semen was identified on her underwear. After a description by the victim, police produced a sketch of the intruder. An officer who had seen the sketch thought it looked like Jimmy Ray Bromgard. Eventually the victim picked him out of a lineup but was unsure if he was the perpetrator. In court, she expressed some doubt of the identity of Bromgard but his assigned counsel didn't object to the identification.

At the trial, the entire case against Bromgard revolved around the hairs found in the bed sheets. The semen on the underwear could not be typed to determine what blood group it belonged to (this was before DNA typing was developed). The forensic expert testified that the head and pubic hairs found on the sheets were indistinguishable from Bromgard's hair samples. He then told the jury that the chances that the crime scene head hairs came from someone else where 100 to 1. He also reached the same conclusion concerning the pubic hairs. He then concluded that the chance that someone else was the owner of the hairs was 10,000 to 1, which is $1/100 \times 1/100$. The statistics used by the expert were not scientific. There are no credible data that would permit a hair examiner to determine the likelihood that a particular person was the owner of shed hairs. The 100 to 1 statistic had no scientific basis. In addition, had these statistics been valid, the only way that the overall odds of Bromgard being the perpetrator of 10,000 to 1 would be valid is if the head hair and pubic hair statistics were totally independent of each other. Clearly, this cannot be the case if the head and pubic hairs came from the same person. This testimony was extremely damning to Bromgard and yet went virtually unchallenged. He was convicted of rape and spent years in prison. His conviction was finally vacated when the New York Innocence Project had the semen reanalyzed years later against Bromgard's DNA and found no match. The semen could not have been deposited by Bromgard.

In 2007, an expert review panel condemned the forensic hair examiner's testimony as being without scientific foundation, and they concluded that there is no way that statistics can be applied to determine the likelihood that a crime scene hair matched a particular individual.

The same hair examiner who analyzed the hair in the Bromgard case also analyzed hair in many other cases and offered similar scientifically flawed conclusions. There have also been other hair examiners who have reached unsupportable conclusions concerning hair analysis. Some of these cases, like the Bromgard case, have been reversed owing to the work of the Innocence Project. This has called into question the practice and value of hair analysis. This is unfortunate because hair has a number of characteristics that make it valuable as a source of evidence. Hair is very stable. It can be found years after someone is buried in a casket. It is very inert to chemical attack. It contains DNA so it can be used for identification. It is easily lost from a person's body and transferred to another person or an object and thus can help track a person's location and movements. It is also a repository for anything from foods, minerals, drugs and poisons that a person has ingested.

The average head hair remains on the head for around 3 months so this repository characteristic can be very useful.

What was wrong with the conclusions reached by the hair examiner in the Bromgard case and in other, similar cases? Hair shares some of the same issues as fingerprints, bullets, shoe prints, etc. It is basically pattern evidence. As we will see, hair consists of a number of layers that can exist in any of a number of configurations. There is no classification system for hair structure, no way to classify it into a finite number of classes. Thus, there is no data that would reveal how rare or common a particular configuration of hair structure is. Because of this, there is no way that a hair examiner can calculate the probability that a hair came from a particular person. This is complicated by the fact that there is a good deal of variation in hair structure within a person's head or other area of the body. Sometimes this variation exceeds that which occurs between two different people. It is very important to be aware of these limitations of hair analysis. There are no circumstances where a hair can be matched to a particular individual by comparing the hairs visually, microscopically, and/or chemically. Thus, hair is class evidence. It is possible for a degree of association to be made between hairs from a crime scene and those taken from a suspect or victim. If there are sufficient physical and chemical characteristics common to both, then it is permissible to conclude that the crime scene hairs *could have come from* the suspect or victim. As stated earlier, there are no statistics available to determine the certainty with which the association can be made. It is of course, quite proper to reach a conclusion that crime scene hairs could not have come from a particular person. The National Academy of Sciences Forensic Science Committee reached similar conclusions concerning hair analysis that they did with respect to other pattern evidence. Many times forensic analysts overreach in their conclusions about hair comparisons. The Committee also cited a lack of scientific validation of the conclusions reached in hair analysis.

In recent years, DNA typing has added a great deal of information to the analysis of biological evidence because there are a finite number of DNA types and a DNA classification scheme has been developed that permits conclusions about how rare or common a particular DNA type is. The role of DNA in hair analysis will be discussed later in this chapter.

What Is Hair?

Hair is an outgrowth of the *epidermis*, or outer layer of the skin. It is found only in mammals. Figure 18.1 is a diagram of the cross section of human skin. It shows the layers of the skin and hair *follicles*. Follicles are the structures from which hairs originate and grow. When hair begins to grow, its outer covering is soft. When it reaches the top of the skin, the outer layer begins to harden into *keratin*. Keratin is made of proteins. It is the same material that makes up fingernails and toenails in humans and horns in other animals.

Inside the follicle, where the hair is growing, it is enervated by blood vessels that provide nourishment and which exchange materials between blood and the inside of the hair. Anything that is ingested by the person, such as food, drugs, or poisons, will eventually be incorporated into the growing region of the hair. When the hair reaches the surface of the skin and keratinizes, it is essentially dead. It is no longer in contact with blood vessels and doesn't exchange anything with its biologic environment. This means that whatever substances were absorbed by the growing part

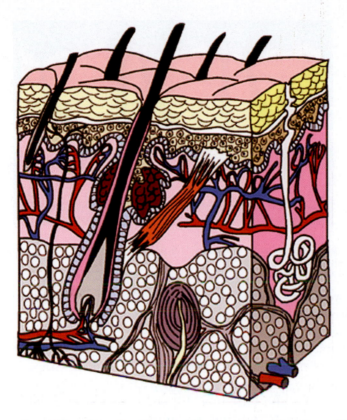

Figure 18.1 Cross section of dermis and epidermis of human skin. (Courtesy of Max Houck.)

of the hair will remain there. In this regard, the hair is a sort of "file cabinet" that files cannot be removed from. Thus, when hair grows, it is really being "pushed up" by the growing part of the hair in the follicle. It is analogous to the size of a stack of dinner plates growing taller by continuously adding more plates to the bottom of the stack. The plates on the top aren't getting bigger, they are being pushed out and up by the ones being added from below. If a person smokes marijuana, for example, some THC and other substances present in the plant will be absorbed into the growing region of the person's hair. As this section of the hair gets pushed up and out from the follicle, the THC remains in that segment of the hair until the hair is cut or falls out. This is why drug analysis is being performed increasingly on hair. The hair retains some of the drug each time the person uses it. Unlike urine analysis, which provides only a snapshot of the drugs in a person's body, hair analysis provides a history. Head hair grows approximately ½ in. per month. This can be used to estimate the time when a drug or other substance was ingested. The average head hair falls out after about 90 days.

Hair Growth

Most tissues grow in a smooth, regular fashion. Anyone who observes his or her hair growing out after cutting would assume that hair also grows like this, but such is not the case. In fact, there are three distinct stages of hair growth. These are depicted in Figure 18.2.

The active growing period of hair is called the *anagen* phase. The follicle produces new hair cells that are added to the shaft of the hair, thus pushing the hair

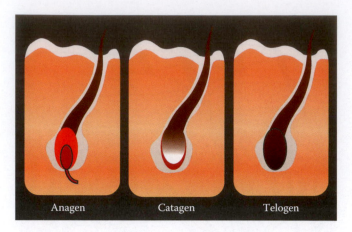

Figure 18.2 Growth stages of hair. They are the anagen, catagen, and telogen from left to right. (Courtesy of Meredith Haddon.)

up the follicle toward the surface of the skin. This is the most active phase of hair growth. At any given time, the majority of hairs are in the anagen phase.

After the anagen phase is complete, the next phase begins. This is the *catagen* phase. It is a transition between growth and rest. Cell production in the follicle declines and the root of the hair shrinks into a bulb-like shape. Figure 18.3 shows the bulbous root of human hair associated with the catagen phase of growth.

In the *telogen* phase, the hair has stopped growing completely. It will stay this way until the hair is lost by pulling (combing or brushing) or shedding. Hairs lost in one of these ways will contain the root. The loss of the hair triggers the end of the telogen phase and the resumption of the anagen phase and a new hair begins to grow. Normally, a person will naturally shed a few dozen hairs per day. This number can increase with frequent and vigorous brushing or combing. It takes about

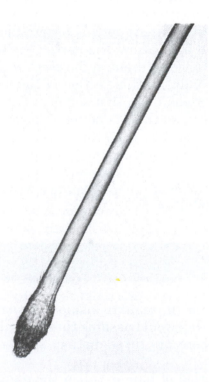

Figure 18.3 A human hair root in the telogen phase. (Courtesy of Max Houck.)

6 months to completely regrow a scalp hair. Some people believe that cutting or shaving hair can stimulate hair growth. There is no evidence that this happens. Cutting off a hair above the root does not stimulate the resumption of the anagen phase of growth. Hair will continue to grow at its normal rate if shaved or cut and if the hair is in the anagen phase at the time. At any given time, about 85% of human scalp hairs are actively growing.

Forcible Removal of Hair

Remember that humans are constantly shedding hair, especially from the scalp. This is one reason why hairs are found so often at even nonviolent crime scenes. Sometimes hairs are forcibly removed by yanking or tearing or by violent contact and are also left at scenes. It is often important to know whether a hair was shed or removed. Can it be determined if a hair has been forcibly removed? It is not as easy as it sounds. There are obvious cases. Some, but not all, forcibly removed hair will have follicle cells clinging to the hair. Some may actually have blood on the root. This would be especially true if the hair were still growing (anagen phase). If the hair was in the resting phase when pulled, it may not have any of the follicle sheaths on it because bulbous roots of the hair in this phase are not tightly held in the follicle. The amount of cellular material on the root depends on how fast the hair was pulled. If the hair is pulled quickly, the chances of finding cells from the follicle are increased.

Something for You to Do

Get a hairbrush and brush your hair as you normally do. Do not use any extra force. Brush until you have about a dozen hairs on the brush. Remove them and examine them with a magnifying glass or low-power microscope. Concentrate on the root of the hairs. Are the roots all the same shape? How would you describe the shape of the roots? Do you see cellular material clinging to any of the roots? (You may need a higher-power microscope to see this.) The presence of cellular material clinging to the root of a hair may indicate that the hair was forcibly removed as opposed to merely falling out. Now look at the hairs from someone else in your family or a friend. Are their roots the same shape as yours? You can also compare the color of your hairs and compare those to the others. Check out the average length of the hairs and the presence of damage such as split ends. Look for variation between the hairs from your head. Some people have significant differences in structure and appearance in hairs taken from the same head.

Hair Color

Look around you. There seems to be a wide variety of head hair colors, from very light to black. Of course, some of these colors are made from artificial coloring agents that grow out with the hair and fade with time, but naturally colored hair also comes in various shades that are under the control of our genetic inheritance. As hair grows, special cells called *melanocytes* produce granules of *melanin*. Melanin is the pigment that gives hair its color. There are two types of melanin. One is dark brown and the other is lighter, almost blond. Under the influence of genetic instructions, these two

Figure 18.7 A human head hair showing the cortex and the medulla. The hair is mounted in a liquid with the same refractive index as the cuticle, so it cannot be seen.

Something for You to Do

You can easily make a scale cast of a human hair. You need some clear nail polish, a microscope slide, and some hairs. Deposit a thin layer of nail polish on the surface of the slide and lay one or more hairs across the slide. Leave them there until the nail polish dries (about 10 min) and then pull them off. A cast of the scale patterns will be visible in the nail polish. You will need at least a low-power microscope to clearly see the pattern. Try this on some of your own scalp hair and some hair from your friends and family. Do all of the scale casts look similar? In a shingle roof, the shingles are arranged in a neat pattern. Is that the case with human hair cuticular scales? If you can get the hairs from animals such as a cat and/or dog, make scale casts of them. How are the scales arranged compared to human scales?

The middle layer of hair is the *cortex*. In humans, this is the most prominent and thickest layer. The cortex is made up of spindle-shaped cells and is also transparent. Pigment granules are dispersed throughout the cortex. These granules are generally not spaced in an even pattern but instead are often found in clumps. They vary from person to person in size and shape as well as distribution. The cortex also contains *cortical fusi*. These are small bubble-like structures. Their appearance may be related to the transition from anagen to catagen growth phase of hair. *Ovoid bodies*, which look like large pigment granules, may also be present in the cortex. Their function is not known. They do not exhibit a pattern but appear irregularly within the cortex.

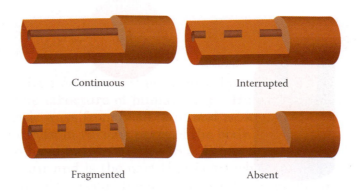

Figure 18.8 Four types of medullae found in human hair. (Courtesy of Meredith Haddon.)

The innermost layer of the hair is the *medulla*. It is made up of cells that form a shaft through the middle of the hair. In human head hair, the medulla may be totally absent, or it may be present in a few areas of the hair, or it may be mostly present except for a few gaps. In some cases, the entire shaft may be visible. This gives rise to a classification system for human hair medullae. Figure 18.8 shows a diagram of the four possible states of a human medulla.

Human versus Nonhuman Hairs

Human hairs differ from animal hairs in several important ways. This is due, at least in part, to the function of hair in many animals, which is protective and for camouflaging. In humans, hair has lost its protective function through evolution and is mostly decorative. In many animals, hair has evolved to perform different specialized functions. Many animals possess three different types of hair. The first are called *guard hairs*. These are firm hairs with a protective function. They have distinct features that make them useful for forensic purposes. They are most often used for microscopic comparison. The rest of the animal's coat is filled in with *fur hairs*. These are relatively featureless and do not provide much information about the type of animal. Finally, there are *whiskers*. Whiskers are sensitive to touch and are used by the animal for sensory purposes. Even though animal hairs differ from human, they still mostly contain the same three layers: cuticle, cortex, and medulla. There are, however, a number of microscopic characteristics that can be useful in distinguishing human from nonhuman hairs:

- The cuticular scales of human hairs tend to be unorganized and overlap like roof shingles. Other animals have more organized, patterned scales. The cuticle is usually thicker relative to the rest of the hair in other animals. You can observe this when you make scale casts of human and animal hairs as directed earlier.
- The medullae of other animal hairs tend to be thicker relative to the rest of the hair. In humans, the medulla is less than one-third of the hair diameter, whereas in other animals, it is more than half. Many animals have thick, continuous medullae. Animals do not have the same classification system for medullae, as do humans. Animal medullae are always continuous. Interrupted, fragmented and absent medullae are present only in humans. Some animals such as cats and mice have *ladder* or *stacked* medullae that resemble a stack of dinner plates or a string of pearls. Members of the deer family have medullae that look like fine latticework. Figure 18.9 shows the interior structure of some animal hairs.

Hair Treatment and Damage

Humans subject their hair to many types of treatments and these can help in the comparison of known and unknown hairs. For example, razor cutting of hairs leaves angled tips whereas scissor cut hair has straight tips. Bleaches oxidize the cortical hair pigment granules, thus removing their color. When hair is dyed, it has a painted appearance, and there is an abrupt color change between the natural color

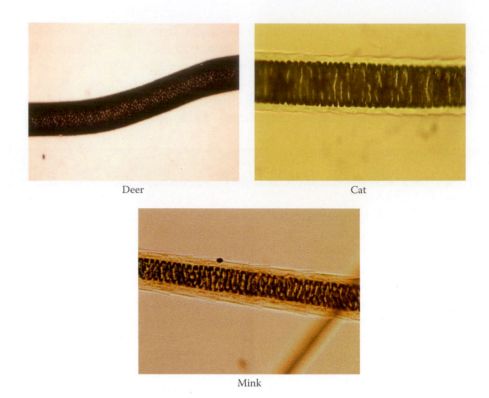

Deer   Cat

Mink

Figure 18.9 Hairs from a deer, a cat, and a mink. (Courtesy of Max Houck.)

and the dyed color. Hair is also subject to disease and degradation from drying out or chemical treatments. These conditions can have forensic value in hair comparisons because they are relatively unusual and they give the affected hairs a unique appearance. Figure 18.10 shows some hairs that have been damaged by treatment or disease.

Burned hair   Split ends

Crushed hair

Figure 18.10 Various types of damage to human hairs. (Courtesy of Max Houck.)

Comparison of Human Hairs

Hair evidence is found in a great variety of crimes. Most commonly, it is evidence at scenes of crimes of violence such as criminal sexual assault. In these types of crimes, pubic hairs from the victim and perpetrator will often be found on each other and on the surface where the attack took place as well as surrounding areas. This is especially powerful evidence since it demonstrates the transfer of two types of evidence between perpetrator and victim. This is often accompanied by the transfer of fibers making it even more probative evidence. Hairs are shed naturally and may be found at scenes. During a violent incident, hair may be pulled and found at the scene. In all of these incidents, hair is very good class evidence and can provide information about the identity of the perpetrator and the victim as well as the circumstances of the incident. Hair is easily transferred from one surface to another and may undergo several transfers after being shed. One of the authors of this book once did a study about the mass transfer of textile fibers to clothing at a large forensic science meeting. One of the findings was quite unexpected; a large number of dog and cat hairs from the owners' pets were found on clothing being worn at the meeting.

As with other types of evidence, the collection of known samples is important. In the majority of cases, either head or pubic (or both) hairs are left as evidence at crime scenes. It is important to get a sufficient number of known hairs and they must represent the head or pubic area as a whole. At least two dozen hairs are needed for comparisons. Fifty is better. They must be combed and (gently) pulled to ensure that hairs in all stages of growth are represented. The known sample must contain hairs from areas that have been treated. This includes dyeing, braiding, bleaching, and graying. There are natural variations of morphological characteristics of hairs within the same head or other area of the body. There must be enough known samples present so that the hair examiner is aware of the degree of variation. Hairs are mounted on microscope slides and immersed in a suitable liquid that enable the examiner to see through the cuticle into the inner layers of the hair. The cuticle has a refractive index of about 1.50. Suitable Cargille liquids can be used as can glycerin (RI = 1.475). The microscope should be able to provide magnification of 25–200 power. A comparison microscope is ideal so that known and unknown hairs can be viewed together. Scale casts should also be taken of some of the hairs from the crime scene as well as the samples from the suspect and/or victim. Various charts are used by hair examiners to record the data about the known and unknown hair. There is no standard set of data that must be collected. The examiner typically collects data about the hair as a whole including lengths, diameters, coloring, diseases, and treatments. In addition, specific information is noted for the root, shaft, and tip. Characteristics of the medulla are noted including its diameter, continuity, and color. The cortex is examined for the presence and distribution of color granules, ovoid bodies, and cortical fusi.

On the basis of the comparison of unknown hairs, there are three possible conclusions that a hair examiner can reach. If there are sufficient common characteristics between the knowns and unknowns and there are no unexplainable significant differences, then the hair examiner can conclude that the unknown hairs *could have originated* from the person who provided the known samples. Note carefully the wording here. The conclusion is *not* that known and unknown hairs definitely

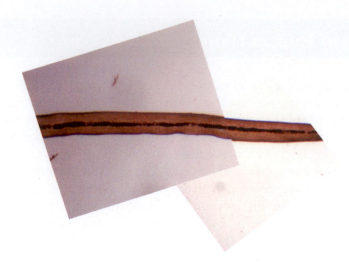

Figure 18.11 Hair comparison. This figure shows a comparison of two human, pubic hairs that came from the same body. Magnification is 250×. (Courtesy of Max Houck.)

came from the same source to the exclusion of all other sources. It merely states that the known could be the source of the unknown hairs. Lacking a proper database of how common different types of hair are, the analyst cannot ascribe a probability to the association of the known and unknown hairs. If the known and unknown samples exhibit significant differences that exceed the range of variation within a set of hairs, then the conclusion would be that the known donor could not have been the source of the unknown hairs. If there are some similarities between the known and unknown but there are also some slight variations, then no conclusion about the association can be given. Figure 18.11 shows a comparison of two hairs that came from the same source.

What Can Be Determined from the Structure of Hair?

As we have seen, a great deal can be determined from the structural analysis of hair. These include the following:

- *Human or animal*: It is easy to determine if a hair is human or animal, especially head hair. Recall that humans have fragmented or absent medullae in their head hair whereas animals have continuous medullae. The medulla in human hair is generally less than 1/3 of the diameter of the hair whereas in animals, it may be more than half. In humans, the cuticular scales are irregular, whereas in animals, they are arranged in a much more regular fashion.
- *Part of the body*: For human hair, it is usually not difficult to determine what part of the body hairs came from. Most crime scene hairs are either from the head or the pubis. Pubic hairs tend to be shorter, curlier, and stiffer and contain more pronounced medullae than head hairs.
- *Color*: Hair that has been colored has more of a painted look than hair with a natural color. The natural color is due to clusters of melanin whereas dyed hair has a coating on the surface. As hair grows, the line of demarcation

between the dye and the natural color becomes more pronounced. If hair is bleached, the melanin particles have a washed out appearance.
- *Disease, mistreatment*: Diseased or teased or artificially straightened or curled hair can usually be detected under a microscope.

There are also a number of characteristics that some people believe that hair can reveal. This, however, is generally not true. Some of these are listed as follows:

- *Age*: Age cannot be determined from the examination of hair. The fact that hair is gray doesn't mean that the person is old. The only hair that can be differentiated by age is the very fine hair called *lanugo* that newborns are born with.
- *Gender*: At one time, perhaps 50 years ago, people may have concluded that long hair was female. If hair spray was present, it must be female. One would be tempted to say that only females dyed their hair. None of these are true today, if they ever were. The only reliable determinate for gender in hair is a DNA analysis to see if the "Y" (male) chromosome is present.
- *Race*: There are some racial characteristics of hair that show up if the person has fairly pure racial ancestry. These include different hair diameters, cross-sectional shapes, thickness of cuticle, and distribution of pigments. As intermarriages take place, these characteristics tend to become less pronounced.

DNA Analysis of Hair

Except for the root, hair does not contain sufficient nucleated cells to perform genomic DNA analysis, but hair cells do contain mitochondria and mitochondrial DNA typing is now routinely done on hair samples. DNA typing is explained in Chapter 17. Mitochondrial DNA is inherited only through the maternal line. One's father does not contribute mitochondrial DNA. As a result, everyone has the same mitochondrial DNA as his or her mother. Because of this, mitochondrial DNA is not suitable for individualization. In cases where mitochondrial DNA typing narrows down the possible suspects to siblings, the microscopic analysis of the hair may distinguish among the hair of the siblings and perhaps the techniques taken together may provide better association. In other cases, there may be insufficient DNA to perform complete analysis. It is becoming clear that microscopic analysis and mitochondrial DNA analysis are complementary techniques that can both be valuable in the analysis of hair. Since the maturation of mitochondrial DNA analysis, many hair examiners including those of the FBI have developed a protocol for the analysis of hair that employs both structural analysis and mitochondrial DNA analysis. The hairs are first compared microscopically. If there are no unexplained differences and sufficient similarities to provide evidence of an association between the known and unknown hairs, then mitochondrial DNA analysis is done. If the DNA types are the same, then an association is made, but this is not individualization. It just narrows down the population that could have been the source of the hair and strengthens the association.

Hair as a Source of Drugs

Earlier in this chapter, it was noted that, as hair grows, it has a blood supply to nourish it. Anything that is in the blood will be in equilibrium with the growing part of the hair. This means that, if the person were taking a drug such as cocaine, some of it would end up in the hair. Remember also that when the hair stops growing, it ceases to exchange materials with the blood stream and becomes a repository for whatever substances were introduced into it during the growing phase. This has implications for testing someone for illicit drugs. When a person is to be tested for the presence of illicit drugs (controlled substances) as is the case in many workplaces or preemployment drug screens, the conventional sample is usually urine, although blood may also be used. The problems with urine drug screening include the ability to tamper with the sample, flushing the urine with diuretic drugs and the fact that the urine test yields only a snapshot of what drugs are present in the body, but provides no information about how often the person has taken the drug or for how long. Blood analysis also has the limitation of being a snapshot of the drugs that are in the person at the time when the blood was drawn. Hair testing for drugs overcomes all of these problems. The subject cannot tamper with the hair, diuretics have no effect on drugs in hair (in fact, the diuretic will show up in the hair), and the hair provides a kind of memory of drug use. Each time the drug is taken, it will show up in the hair, so for as long as the hair is on the head, it will provide a history of drug use. Drug testing in hair is also less invasive than taking a urine or blood sample—the hair is simply combed out or snipped off. Although drug testing in hair is a bit more expensive than urine testing, the cost has come way down and continues to decrease as more laboratories are doing this type of testing and there is more demand for it.

Summary

Hair is an appendage that grows out of the skin or dermis. It has three growth stages: anagen, catagen, and telogen. Hair consists of three layers. The outermost is the cuticle. The middle layer is the cortex. It contains the color granules that define the color of the hair. The inner layer is the medulla, a shaft that runs the length of the hair. The cuticle is made up of overlapping scales like shingles on a roof. Human and nonhuman hairs differ in all three layers. The scales in the cuticle of human hairs tend to be less organized than those of other animals. The medullae in human hairs are generally less continuous than those of animals and may be absent altogether. At least a couple of dozen known hairs are collected for comparison with unknowns because of the large amount of variation in the structure of hairs within a single subject. Hairs are compared by noting the microscopic characteristics of the hair as a whole and of the individual layers. If there are sufficient characteristics in known and unknown hairs that match, the donor of the known hairs could be the source of the unknowns. Hair is virtually always class evidence. Mitochondrial DNA typing can be performed on hairs. It is a complementary technique to microscopic analysis of hairs. Many laboratories now use both structural analysis and mitochondrial DNA analysis in tandem. Hair is also a good source of illicit drugs. There are no problems with tampering with the sample or flushing the drugs, and hair provides a memory of how often the subject took the drugs instead of just a one-time snapshot.

Test Yourself

Multiple Choice

1. Which of the following is not a type of medulla found in a human hair?
   a. Fragmented
   b. Continuous
   c. Stacked
   d. Interrupted
   e. Absent
2. Which of the following is not a layer of hair?
   a. Medulla
   b. Root
   c. Cortex
   d. Cuticle
   All the above are layers of hair.
3. Which of the following is not found in the cortex?
   a. Color granules
   b. Ovoid bodies
   c. Cortical fusi
   d. Scales
4. In which of the following growth stages of hair does active growing take place?
   a. Catagen
   b. Anagen
   c. Telogen
   d. Antigen
5. If a hair falls out on its own, without any combing or pulling, it is likely in which growth stage?
   a. Catagen
   b. Anagen
   c. Telogen
   d. Antigen
6. A hair with a thick cuticle and regular scales and a continuous medulla is
   a. Animal other than human
   b. Human
   c. Could be either one
   d. Neither human or other animal
7. If a known and unknown hairs have very similar microscopic characteristics and no unexplainable differences, then
   a. The unknown had to have come from the known source.
   b. The unknown could have come from the known source.
   c. The unknown could not have come from the known source.
   d. There is a 95% probability that the unknown came from the known source.
8. Which is true about DNA typing of hair?
   a. Genomic DNA typing can be done on the shaft of the hair.
   b. Only mitochondrial DNA typing is commonly done on human hair.
   c. No DNA typing can be done on human hair.
   d. Only hair in the anagen growing phase can be DNA typed.

9. Which of the following is an advantage of drug testing using hair rather than urine?
   a. It is cheaper.
   b. It gives a short term drug use history.
   c. It can detect more drugs.
   d. It doesn't require confirmation.
10. Hair is individualizable evidence when
    a. Mitochondrial DNA typing is done.
    b. When the known and unknown both have a continuous medulla.
    c. When all three layers of hair are similar in the known and unknown.
    d. Hair evidence is not individualizable.

True–False

11. True or false: Hair continuously grows all along its shaft.
12. True or false: In the case described at the beginning of the chapter, instead of multiplying the 100:1 odds for the head and pubic hairs, the hair examiner should have added the two together.
13. There are three stages of growth in hair.
14. The average lifetime of head hair on the head is about 3 months.
15. The chances of two individuals having a fragmented medulla in their hair is about 100 to 1.
16. Human head hairs seldom have a continuous medulla.
17. Cuticular scale patterns in human head hairs tend to be very regular.

Matching: Match each term with its definition.

18. Catagen stage   a. Middle layer of the hair
19. Continuous medulla   b. Transition stage in hair growth
20. Cortical fusi   c. Small cells located in cortex
21. Melanin   d. Rapid growth stage of hair
22. Cortex   e. Substance that makes up hair pigment
23. Anagen stage   f. Found mainly in animals

Short Essay

24. Describe how hair grows. What are the stages of growth?
25. Describe the major differences in the structure of hair in humans and animals.

Further Reading

Bisbing, R. (2002). The forensic identification and association of human hair, in *Forensic Science Handbook*, vol. 1, 2nd edn. Prentice Hall, Englewood Cliffs, NJ.

Hicks, J. W. (1977). *Microscopy of Hairs: A Practical Guide and Manual*, US Government Printing Office, Washington, DC.

Ogle, R. R. and M. J. Fox. (1996). *Atlas of Human Hair: Microscopic Characteristics*. Taylor & Francis, Boca Raton, FL.

Robertson, J. (ed.). (1999). *Forensic Examination of Hair*. Taylor & Francis, New York.

On the Web

http://www.fbi.gov/hq/lab/fsc/backissu/july2000/deedric1.htm—Good introduction to hair analysis by FBI.

http://www7.nationalacademies.org/stl/April%20Forensic%20Bisbing.pdf—Presentation to National Academy of Sciences on Hair Analysis by McCrone Associates.

a-s.clayton.edu/shornbuckle/CHEM4204/2008%20presentations%20and%20objectives/...—Good powerpoint presentation on hair analysis.

PART V

Forensic Chemistry

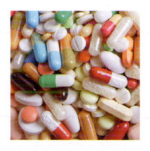

19
Illicit Drugs

Learning Objectives

1. To be able to define a drug and distinguish licit drugs from illicit ones
2. To be able to describe the characteristics of the federal schedules for controlled substances
3. To be able to describe the classification of drugs by major effect
4. To be able to put common illicit drugs in their proper classification
5. To be able to describe how an illicit drug is analyzed in by a forensic chemist

Chapter 19
Illicit Drugs

Chapter Outline

Mini Glossary

Confirmatory drug test: Test used to conclusively identify a pure drug substance.

Depressant: A drug that has been prescribed to relieve anxiety, nervousness, and restlessness.

Drug: A substance that is designed to have specific physical and/or emotional effects on people or, in some cases, animals.

Hallucinogen: Drugs that cause people to see and hear things that aren't there.

Illicit Drug: Illicit drugs, sometimes called *abused drugs* or *controlled substances* in the United States, are of two types. The first consists of licit drugs that are abused or taken for purposes other than those for which they were originally developed. The other type of illicit drug is a substance that has no recognized medical purpose.

Narcotic: Powerful sleep-inducing, central nervous system depressant.

Screening drug test: The most general tests for drugs, also sometimes called spot tests or field tests.

Separation drug test: Test used to separate a drug from a mixture of cutting agents and diluting agents.

Stimulant: Drugs that elevate a person's mood and cause euphoria.

Withdrawal: A syndrome of symptoms that occur in a drug addict when she stops taking the drug.

Acronyms

DEA: Drug Enforcement Administration
FDA: Food and Drug Administration

LSD: Lysergic acid diethylamide. The most powerful hallucinogen
MDMA: Methylenedioxymethamphetamine. A derivative of methamphetamine and a powerful hallucinogen
PCP: Phenylcyclohexylpiperidine. A powerful hallucinogen
SWGDRUG: Scientific working group on the analysis of illicit drugs

Introduction

In April 1976, one of the authors of this book was working as a drug chemist with what was then called the Virginia Bureau of Forensic Sciences. The Arlington County Virginia Police Department received a tip that some people were manufacturing drugs in a subdivision home in the county. The tip came from a neighbor who saw several suspicious looking people carting boxes and drums of what appeared to be chemicals into the house. The police department, in cooperation with U.S. Drug Enforcement Administration (DEA), staked out the house to see if further activity was taking place. They ascertained that the inhabitants were probably making phencyclidine (PCP; sometimes called "angel dust"). The police department narcotics agents contacted the Virginia lab and asked for a chemist to help them ascertain how far the PCP preparation had gone. It was proposed that one of the agents along with the chemist (the author of this book) would walk slowly by the house and sniff the air. The idea was that an odor of benzene and/or ethyl ether would indicate that the clandestine drug manufacturers would be in the last step of the synthesis of the PCP. In prosecuting drug manufacturers, it is much easier for the prosecution if the target drug is actually present. This is legally termed "manufacture." If there is no controlled substance present, but there is other evidence that a drug was being prepared, a charge of "attempted manufacture" can be leveled.

As a result of this reconnoiter, the police and DEA raided the house and uncovered a major clandestine PCP lab. The entire floor of the two-car garage was covered with 6 in. of parsley, and the PCP had been dissolved in camp stove fuel and had been poured on the parsley. Had the house not been raided, the fuel would have been allowed to evaporate, and the PCP-treated parsley (called "wobble weed" on the street) would have been bagged up and sold for smoking. The narcotics agents estimated the haul to be worth more than $1 M.

The recreational use of illicit drugs is one of the most serious societal problems in the United States. The use of illicit drugs costs many millions of dollars in lost productivity and medical expenses and many more millions in efforts by law enforcement agents to stem the flow of drugs into the country and arrest users and distributors of drugs. Crime laboratories are swamped with illicit drug cases, and American crime labs have a collective backlog of thousands of drug cases. Many drug cases go to court, and forensic drug chemists spend many hours testifying or waiting to, while new cases pile up back in the laboratory. Since the presidency of Ronald Reagan, beginning in 1980, the federal government has been waging a war on drugs. The thrust of the government's activities has been to try and interdict the drugs on their way into the United States. This has yielded generally unimpressive results, and this has not stemmed the flow of drugs into the United States or even slowed it down. This is, in large part, because U.S. borders are relatively open, and drugs come up from Mexico and South and Central America (cocaine, marijuana, MDMA—known as ecstasy, methamphetamine) and from Europe and Asia (heroin). In addition, there are many large and small laboratories that manufacture methamphetamine, MDMA, PCP, and lysergic acid diethylamide (LSD), and there are many recreational marijuana growers in the United States. The government has also spent money on treatment and drug prevention programs but not nearly as much as has been spent on interdiction. The issue of interdiction vs. prevention has raged in this and other countries for many years. There have been joint task forces involving U.S. personnel that attempt to destroy drug growing and lab operations in the countries of origin. Because illicit drugs can be such a major cash crop, local government cooperation has been mixed also. In this chapter, we will discuss the history of illicit drugs, how they are controlled by federal and state laws, and how they are used and abused.

Illicit Drugs

Most people think of the term "drug" as a substance prescribed to treat a disease or other illness. In fact, a drug is a substance that is designed to have specific physical and/or emotional effects on people or, in some cases, animals. The vast majority of drugs are produced by pharmaceutical companies for a particular disease or disorder. These are called *licit drugs*. Under this definition, ethyl alcohol, which is used in beer, wine, and spirits, is not a drug and the laws that control illicit drugs do not include alcohol. It may have some benefits in moderate quantities, but it is not prescribed for that purpose. Alcohol will be covered in Chapter 20. From a legal standpoint, all licit drugs in the United States must have a recognized medical use *as defined by the U.S. Food and Drug Administration (FDA)*. If the FDA doesn't recognize a drug as having a legitimate use, it isn't a licit drug.

Illicit drugs, sometimes called *abused drugs* or *controlled substances* in the United States, are of two types. The first consists of licit drugs that are abused or taken for purposes other than those for which they were originally developed. Methamphetamine is a good example of this. For many years, methamphetamine was legitimately marketed as a stimulant, to counter feelings of fatigue or depression and as an appetite suppressant. It even played a role in controlling hyperkinesia, which is a nerve disorder manifested by hyperactivity. Today, however, methamphetamine is hardly used for these purposes. Instead, tablets and capsules that have been diverted from legitimate channels (stolen) and powdered forms made in clandestine laboratories are ingested by people for the purpose of "getting high." It is also possible to use a licit drug for the purpose it was developed, but to use it fraudulently or inappropriately. An example of this would be the use of steroids and other performance-enhancing drugs by Olympic athletes as well as other amateur and professional athletes to give them an unfair competitive advantage.

The other type of illicit drug is a substance that has no approved medical purpose. It could be a synthetic substance, like PCP, or it could be derived from a plant, like cocaine and morphine (which is then made into heroin). In some cases, part of the plant itself is ingested, as in the case of marijuana or opium. These illicit drugs are far and away the most popular throughout the world. Because these drugs do not have any legitimate medical purpose, it is illegal to manufacture, possess, use, grow, or sell them. Why is this so? What harm is there in a person smoking marijuana, for example, in his own home, not bothering anyone else. Many people believe that this kind of behavior is a detriment to our society. It is wasteful, perhaps harmful behavior that does not advance society and may cost a good deal of money for treatment of drug disorders such as addiction. Others believe that it is hypocritical and irrational to control and penalize the use of such substances for recreational purposes when an additive substance such as ethyl alcohol is freely available and heavily abused by a large segment of the adult population. This argument has been waged for many years and for now comes down on the side of controlling illicit drugs and keeping alcohol more or less freely available.

Control of Illicit Drugs in the United States

The possession, use, and sale of illicit drugs have been the subject of governmental control since the early part of the twentieth century. During this time, the issue of drug control has been affected by research and popular culture, and as a result, the laws and regulations have been somewhat disjointed and uncoordinated. Prior to the beginning of the twentieth century, drugs like marijuana, opium, heroin, and cocaine were used in the United States, but there was little in the way of control over their use. In many cases, these drugs were mixed with flavorings and/or alcohol and sold as elixirs from the back of traveling wagons. They were marketed as medicinals that could cure practically every disease. Of course, they had little or no effect and represented fraudulent advertising. In the early twentieth century, the federal government began to exert some control over many of these drugs. In part the government intervention was prompted by public reaction to opium smoking among Chinese immigrants, the rise of cocaine use, and increased activity by purveyors of patent medicines. In 1906, the *Pure Food and Drugs Act*, which prohibited interstate commerce in mislabeled or adulterated food or drugs, was passed by Congress and signed into law. Among the substances targeted by the law were marijuana, cocaine, heroin, and opium. This act was administered by the Department of Agriculture.

In 1914, Congress passed a major tax and control bill, the Harrison Act, which is properly known as "An act to provide for the registration of, with collectors of internal revenue, and to impose a special tax upon all persons who produce, import, manufacture, compound, deal in, dispense or give away opium or coca leaves, their salts, derivatives, or preparations, and for other purposes." This law was enforced and administered by the Bureau of Internal Revenue in the Treasury Department. It gave the federal government broad control over cocaine and narcotics traffic in the United States. Much of the Harrison Act was aimed at controlling the rise of drug addiction. At first, the attitude of government officials was that it was best to permit addicts continued access to the addicting drugs while trying to remove the supply by putting the dealers out of business. A few years later, in the late 1920s, public sentiment had changed and it was now felt that addiction to drugs could be cured by abstinence: taking the supply of drugs away from the addicts. This meant cracking down on physicians who were supplying addicts with their drugs using prescriptions. Clearly, the emphasis on drug control was changing from viewing addiction as a medical problem to a law enforcement issue.

By 1930, law enforcement of drugs had become even more of a major issue, and Congress passed legislation that formed the Bureau of Narcotics within the Treasury Department. This removed control of drug abuse from the Agriculture Department to Treasury, again because of the tax issue. The Bureau of Narcotics stepped up law enforcement against illicit drugs, particularly opium, heroin, cocaine, and marijuana. At this time, anyone who wanted to buy or import or sell any of these drugs had to register and pay a tax. Because marijuana was included, it was labeled a narcotic in all relevant federal laws, a label that stuck until the early 1970s. In 1956, the Narcotic Drug Control Act was passed by the Congress in reaction to testimony that indicated that postwar drug use had exploded and that half of all crime in major cities in the United States was related to illegal drug use. Penalties for use and sales of drugs greatly increased. Stiff jail sentences went to all but first-time offenders and anyone who sold drugs to a minor faced the death penalty. This law also had another important feature. If a new drug came into the marketplace that had a potential for abuse, a recommendation to control it could be made by the FDA to the Secretary of Health, Education, and Welfare. Drugs such as amphetamines, barbiturates, and LSD were brought under control during this time. Rather than labeling them narcotics, they were referred to in the law as "dangerous drugs." The Bureau of Narcotics was changed to the Bureau of Narcotics and Dangerous Drugs (BNDD), and they became the chief enforcers of the new laws. In 1970, the Congress passed the Comprehensive Controlled Substances Act of 1970. This law put all controlled substances in the federal realm. This meant that the federal government could prosecute anyone for a drug offense regardless of whether interstate trafficking was involved and irrespective of state laws. *The Comprehensive Controlled Substances Act* resulted in a number of major changes in drug enforcement in the United States:

- Control of drugs became a direct law enforcement activity rather than through registration and taxation.
- Enforcement was moved from the Treasury Department to the Justice Department and the BNDD became the DEA.
- The decision on which drugs should be controlled rests with the Secretary of Health and Human Services, which delegates to the FDA the determination of which drugs should be controlled. In making decisions about whether a drug should be controlled, the FDA evaluates such factors as pharmacological effects, ability to induce psychological dependence or physical addiction, and whether there is any legitimate medical use for the substance (as defined and recognized by the FDA).
- Under this law, tobacco and alcohol products are excluded. Controlled drugs are put into five schedules. See Table 19.1 for a summary of the schedules and the drugs that are found in each one. More comprehensive information about the federal schedules can be found on the DEA website at http://www.dea.gov/concern/abuse/chap1/contents.htm.

Today, the federal laws that regulate illicit drugs are in the Federal Code, Title 21—Food and Drugs: Chapter 13—Drug Abuse Prevention and Control. http://www.deadiversion.usdoj.gov/21cfr/cfr/. Under these laws, many of the illicit drugs are termed controlled substances and are put in one of five schedules, or categories. Most of what we define as illicit drugs are in one of these schedules. With a few exceptions, all of the drugs that are in the same schedule have the same penalties for possession or distribution (sale). In some cases, penalties increase as the amount of illicit drug increases. So if someone possesses 50 g (about 2 ounces) of cocaine, they would get a stiffer penalty than someone who possesses only one gram.

Determination of a Drug Schedule

Since the 1970 law put the responsibility of controlling drugs in federal hands, it became the responsibility of the U.S. Congress to determine which drugs fall into

TABLE 19.1
Drug Schedules

Schedule I

- The drug or other substance has a high potential for abuse.
- The drug or other substance has no currently accepted medical use in treatment in the United States.
- Some Schedule I substances are heroin, LSD, and marijuana.

Schedule II

- The drug or other substance has a high potential for abuse.
- The drug or other substance has a currently accepted medical use in treatment in the United States or a currently accepted medical use with severe restrictions.
- Abuse of the drug or other substance may lead to severe psychological or physical dependence.
- Schedule II substances include cocaine and methamphetamine.

Schedule III

- The drug or other substance has a potential for abuse less than the drugs or other substances in Schedules I and II.
- The drug or other substance has a currently accepted medical use in treatment in the United States.
- Abuse of the drug or other substance may lead to moderate or low physical dependence or high psychological dependence.
- Anabolic steroids, and aspirin or Tylenol® containing codeine, are Schedule III substances.

Schedule IV

- The drug or other substance has a low potential for abuse relative to the drugs or other substances in Schedule III.
- The drug or other substance has a currently accepted medical use in treatment in the United States.
- Abuse of the drug or other substance may lead to limited physical dependence or psychological dependence relative to the drugs or other substances in Schedule III.
- Included in Schedule IV are Darvon, Equanil, and Valium.

Schedule V

- The drug or other substance has a low potential for abuse relative to the drugs or other substances in Schedule IV.
- The drug or other substance has a currently accepted medical use in treatment in the United States.
- Abuse of the drug or other substance may lead to limited physical dependence or psychological dependence relative to the drugs or other substances in Schedule IV.
- Some over-the-counter cough medicines with codeine are classified in Schedule V.

the five schedules and which schedule a particular drug will be in. In order to make these decisions, the Congress relies on experts to answer two questions:

1. Does the drug have a legitimate medical use in the United States?
2. What is its potential for abuse?

The first question is pretty easy to answer. Remember that the U.S. FDA decides if a drug has a legitimate medical use, so the Congress looks to that agency for guidance. The second question is a bit more difficult to answer. Several factors go into determining the potential for abuse of a particular drug. Is the drug addictive? Many drugs cause physical changes to take place in the body, and after a time, the person becomes physically dependent on the drug. Dependency is characterized by development over time of a constant craving that can only be satisfied by having the drug. After a while, *tolerance* builds up and it takes more and more of the drug to satisfy the craving. Heroin and a form of cocaine called *crack* are examples of physically addictive drugs. If you become addicted to a drug and then try and stop taking it, you will become sick. This sickness is called *withdrawal* and it can be very dangerous to the addict. Most people eventually recover from withdrawal, but the craving for the drug may last for years. Some illicit drugs don't cause addiction but instead cause psychological dependence. The craving for the drug is there, but there is no withdrawal if the person suddenly stops taking the drug. Drugs that cause either physical or intense psychological dependence are said to have a high potential for abuse. Please see Chapter 20 for a more detailed discussion of the issues of addiction, tolerance, and dependence of drugs. Other factors that contribute to the potential for abuse have to do with the availability of the drug. If a drug is relatively cheap and easy to get or manufacture with minimal risk of getting caught, this contributes to its having a high potential for abuse. The way these two factors come into play in putting illicit drugs in particular schedules is summarized in the following text.

As might be expected, drugs that are placed in schedules I and II carry the most severe penalties. Possession or sale of one of these drugs can result in several years in prison and heavy fines. Once an illicit drug is placed in a federal schedule, it generally stays there. Movement in and out of the schedules is very rare and Congress must consider each action separately. Moving a drug to a higher-numbered schedule is especially problematic as it invites charges that congressmen and senators have gone "soft on drugs." This has been especially contentious with marijuana, which has long been in Schedule I. As such, it has no legitimate medical use and a high potential for abuse. This flies in the face of many years of research that indicate that marijuana may play a role in arresting the progress of certain types of glaucoma (a progressive disease of the eyes that leads to blindness) and in mitigating some of the side effects of metabolic drugs that are taken for cancer treatment and which may cause crippling nausea.

State Modifications of Controlled Substance Laws

Part of the Comprehensive Drug Control Act of 1970 provided that federal laws supersede state laws when it comes to controlling drugs. Nonetheless, states are permitted some latitude in fashioning their own drug control laws. For example, there is variation in what schedule a particular drug may be put in. This is common with marijuana. In other cases, some states have more or fewer schedules. Penalties for possession, manufacture, and distribution can also vary from state to state. When states have tried to legalize certain drugs or decriminalize them, however, the federal government has stepped in to prevent it and the courts have sided with the federal government over the states. In just the past few years, there have been two dramatic changes that have pitted states against the federal government in enforcing the laws that control marijuana. First is the trend toward recognition of the medical benefits of marijuana in treatment of glaucoma and in mitigation of the side effects of anticancer drugs. At this writing, nearly 20 states have passed laws that permit people with glaucoma or cancer to obtain marijuana or an extract for treatment. These so-called "medical marijuana" laws are spreading quite rapidly. The federal government has chosen to not prosecute such enterprises that are tightly controlled by the states.

The other slow but unmistakable trend is toward legalization of possession of small quantities of marijuana. At this writing, two states, Colorado and Washington, have passed legislation that legalizes the possession of small quantities of marijuana. Colorado has gone the furthest, permitting the operation of shops that sell marijuana that is permissible to possess. Although this activity is in clear violation of the Comprehensive Controlled Substances Act of 1970, the U.S. Department of Justice has decided to permit these states to operate and enforce these laws. It is of course, possible that another federal government administration may have other ideas and may choose to prosecute under federal laws in the future.

Classification of Illicit Drugs

Besides putting drugs in federal schedules, there are other ways to classify them that are more organized and that put similar drugs in the same class. For example, drugs can be classified by their origin. In this system, all illicit drugs would fall into one of three classes:

1. Naturally occurring substances (e.g., marijuana, cocaine, morphine)
2. Derived from a naturally occurring substance (heroin, made from morphine; LSD (synthesized from lysergic acid)
3. Synthetic (methamphetamine, PCP)

The most common method of classifying illicit drugs is by their major effects on a human being. This is the system that will be used in this chapter. Under this scheme, there are five major classes of illicit drugs:

1. Stimulants
2. Depressants
3. Narcotics
4. Hallucinogens
5. Performance-enhancing drugs (e.g., steroids)

Performance-enhancing drug use is not being actively controlled in the same way that drugs in the other four classes are. Although use of these drugs is not limited to professional and amateur athletes, cases of abuse of these drugs by athletes have lead to high-profile publicity and actions by sports leagues and the Olympics to ban their use and punish abusers. As such, this topic will not be further covered in this chapter.

Stimulants

Central nervous system stimulants have the effects of elevating a person's mood, temporarily increasing energy levels, relieving some symptoms of depression, and stimulate people who are tired or lethargic. Their "street" or slang name is *uppers*. For the most part, stimulants are not physically addictive but there are some exceptions. Many of them have powerful effects and can cause strong, intense psychological dependence. Two of the best examples of illicit stimulants are cocaine and methamphetamine.

Cocaine

The stimulant properties of cocaine have been known for centuries. It is a naturally occurring substance, derived from the *Erythroxylum coca* plant. Note that this is not the same as the *cocoa* plant, from which chocolate is derived. The coca plant grows mainly in only one part of the world: the Amazon slopes of the Andes Mountains in South America. The epicenter of cocaine production in recent times has been Colombia. Figure 19.1 shows coca leaves.

Figure 19.1 Coca leaves. Cocaine can be extracted directly from the leaves by chewing. Bits of seashell will enhance the extraction. Chemical extractions are done on a commercial basis.

Medically, cocaine is a topical anesthetic. This means that it causes numbness of any area of the body that it comes in direct contact with. It is still used in some medical procedures as an anesthetic but has largely been replaced by other drugs. As a topical anesthetic cocaine is similar to other drugs such as procaine (novocaine), which is used to numb the teeth and gums in dental procedures, and benzocaine, which is used to treat the pain of sunburn. Clearly, people don't abuse cocaine because it numbs their skin. For thousands of years, the indigenous farmers of the mountainous regions of South America have known that they could increase their energy and endurance by chewing on the leaves of the coca plant. Their saliva served to extract some of the cocaine from the leaves, and this gave them a temporary stimulant high to enable them to do the arduous work of farming the hilly land. Later, many of these people chewed on bits of seashell with the coca leaves. This provided an alkaline environment in the mouth that made the extraction of the cocaine more efficient so the effects of the cocaine were increased and lasted longer. In the latter part of the nineteenth century and the early part of the twentieth century, cocaine became used more and more in the United States as a stimulant. It was used in many elixirs, which are liquids that contain various medicinal and flavoring ingredients that are sold for particular medical purposes. In the early part of the twentieth century, some people sold these concoctions out of the back of wagons and represented them as miracle cures. It is interesting to note that, when the federal government cracked down on elixirs containing cocaine and made the producers remove it, they substituted another, legal stimulant, caffeine. Today, most cola soft drinks have caffeine in them; some used to have cocaine.

Preparation and Ingestion of Cocaine

Since cocaine is a naturally occurring substance, all that is necessary to abuse it is to extract it from coca leaves. The leaves are chopped up and dissolved in hot, alkaline water or an organic solvent. The cocaine is extracted from the leaves. Then another solvent containing hydrochloric acid is added that precipitates the purified cocaine.

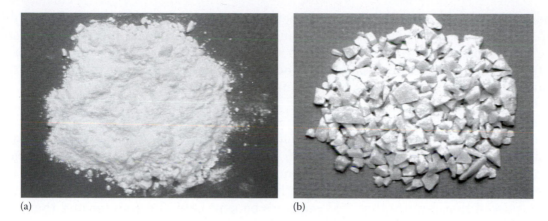

(a)   (b)

Figure 19.2 (a) Cocaine flake (hydrochloride) and (b) crack cocaine. Crack is made from cocaine flake by treatment with an alkaline substance such as sodium bicarbonate.

The powder that is produced is *cocaine hydrochloride*. This is a flaky white powder that is sometimes called *snow* because it is so white and fluffy. It is also called *flake* or *blow*. Cocaine is almost always diluted when sold to users. Typically, it is cut with an inert powder like sugar so that the final product is 20%–50% pure. The most common way of ingesting cocaine flake is by *snorting*. A line of cocaine is laid down on a flat surface such as a mirror. Then, using a tiny spoon or a straw, the cocaine is drawn up into the nose. The first sensation one gets from snorting coke is to get numb in the nose— remember that cocaine is a topical anesthetic. After that, the cocaine "high" will occur within about 30 min and last an hour or so, depending upon how much was snorted and one's experience with the drug. Because the cocaine has to pass through the nasal passages to the blood stream in order to be effective, some of it is blocked or chemically changed and never gets through, thus reducing the potency of the drug. In this form, cocaine is thought to not be addicting.

In the 1980s, a new form of cocaine, called *crack*, became popular. Crack can be made from cocaine flake using household chemicals such as lye and cleaning fluid. Unlike cocaine flake, which is a fluffy powder, crack comes in the form of small rocks that are easily cracked or broken (hence the name). Also, unlike cocaine flake, crack is smoked using a small pipe. In this form, cocaine can be physically addictive because so much more of it gets into the bloodstream through the lungs. For this reason, the federal government and many states attach more severe penalties for the possession of crack than they do for the same amount of flake. In the past couple of years, this practice of differential sentencing for crack and flake is being rethought, especially at the federal level, where it is no longer the standard policy. Interestingly, some people believe that the term "crack" comes from the Gaelic word "craic," which means "have a good time." Figure 19.2a shows cocaine flake and Figure 19.2b shows crack.

Methamphetamine

Methamphetamine and its cousin, amphetamine, have been popular illicit drugs for more than 40 years. Both drugs have had legitimate medical uses in the United States and continue to do so. They are legally marketed as stimulants to relieve lethargy, drowsiness, and depression. Both have also been prescribed for hyperkinesia (a type of overactivity) and both have been used as appetite suppressants. Because they are so frequently abused, they are hardly produced for licit purposes anymore. For many years, methamphetamine and amphetamine were obtained by theft from pharmacies and warehouses, but today, these sources are so tightly controlled that most of the drugs, especially methamphetamine, are produced in (clandestine) labs. In some places in the United States, "meth" labs have become practically an epidemic. Methamphetamine was nicknamed "speed" on the streets because of its powerful stimulant properties, especially when taken pure. High doses of this drug can cause death, and in the 1960s, the warning on the street was that "speed kills."

Preparation and Ingestion

The most popular method of preparation of methamphetamine uses an over-the-counter cold remedy called *pseudoephedrine*. This drug is a very popular decongestant. In some places, people buy huge quantities of cold remedies and extract the pseudoephedrine so they can make methamphetamine. In some states, laws have been passed that require that cold remedies be kept behind a counter and that only small amounts can be sold to a person and that everyone who buys any quantity would have to show identification and sign for the drug. A second major ingredient for this method of preparation of methamphetamine is ammonia. Many farmers use pure, liquid, anhydrous ammonia as an ingredient in fertilizer and they keep large tanks on their property. Reports of thefts of large quantities of ammonia are on the rise all over the country. The other chemical needed for the synthesis is lithium, which can be extracted from some batteries. Methamphetamine production is becoming so popular in some areas of the country that law enforcement agents are at a loss in trying to control it. The passage of state laws that severely restrict the availability of pseudoephedrine have helped a great deal. Some counties now report that the "mom and pop" meth labs have practically dried up. The methamphetamine is still coming in but increasingly it is being traced to large, well-financed laboratories in Mexico. This used to be the primary source of methamphetamine in the United States before the epidemic of locally made drug. Figure 19.3 shows a clandestine methamphetamine lab.

Depressants

In the 1960s and 1970s, depressants were much more popular illicit drugs than they are today. By far, the most popular depressants were the *barbiturates*. These are a whole family of drugs that have been prescribed to relieve anxiety, nervousness,

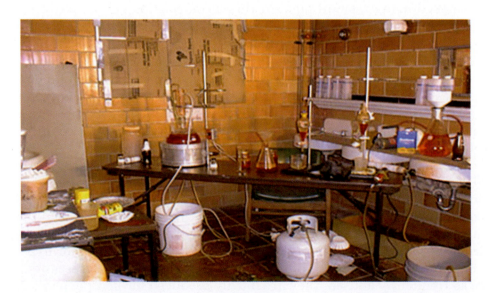

Figure 19.3 A clandestine methamphetamine laboratory. Such a laboratory is very dangerous because of open, toxic chemicals and flammable gases.

and restlessness. They range from the mild acting, such as phenobarbital, which was, at one time, an ingredient of some allergy medicines, to the very powerful types, such as pentobarbital and thiopentobarbital (sodium pentothal). The former is used to put very sick animals to sleep. Pentothiobarbital, or sodium pentothal, is used as a general anesthetic that puts people to sleep during major surgery. Both have been used as the "lethal injection" for some criminals who are sentenced to die. In recent years in the United States, controversy has arisen over the use of barbiturates in the execution of criminals. There are very few sources for these drugs worldwide and most of the laboratories are outside the United States. Most of them refuse to sell the drug in the United States if it is to be used as part of the "cocktail" of drugs that are employed for executions. This has caused a major shortage of these drugs, forcing states that have the death penalty to search for alternatives.

The barbiturates are highly addictive drugs and are unusual in that, sudden withdrawal, sometimes called "cold turkey withdrawal," can be fatal. Some people have gotten into vicious cycles with amphetamines and barbiturates where they take increasing doses of both to counteract the effects of the other. Some of the more potent barbiturates can cause death when taken with liquor. Accidental overdoses of alcohol and barbs caused the deaths of some celebrities including possibly Janis Joplin and Jimmy Hendrix. For the most part, barbiturates are not prescribed anymore because of their addictive nature and overdose danger. Other drugs such as Valium have replaced them. When Valium and its near neighbor, Librium, came out as part of the family of benzodiazepines, it was felt that they would be superior to the barbiturates because they would not be addictive and withdrawal would not be a problem. This has turned out to not be the case, although the addiction is not as severe or life threatening as it is with the barbiturates.

Hallucinogens

The most notorious of the illicit drugs are hallucinogens. These drugs cause audio and visual hallucinations, which mean that they cause people to see and hear things that aren't there. Some of the more popular hallucinogens are marijuana, LSD, mescaline, and psilocybin.

Marijuana

Marijuana has been called by many colorful names over the hundreds of years that it has been used. These include weed, hop, Mary Jane, toke, and many others. Marijuana is classified as a hallucinogen, mainly because it doesn't fit in the other categories. It doesn't cause hallucinations to the degree that the other members of this group including LSD and some mushrooms and some cactus extracts do. The effects are usually more of a mellowing out, but there can be a wide range of effects depending upon the person and how experienced he or she is with the drug. One of the more interesting effects of marijuana that has been widely reported is *the munchies*. Smoking marijuana apparently makes some users ravenously hungry.

Preparation and Ingestion

Marijuana is a plant belonging to the genus *cannabis*. It grows virtually anywhere although warm and sunny conditions are favored. The leaves and flowers of the plant contain a number of naturally occurring substances that cause its psychological effects. The most important member of this group of chemicals has the tongue-twisting name of *tetrahydrocannabinol* or *THC*. The leaves and flowering parts are usually separated from the plant and dried in an oven. Then they are chopped up and

Figure 19.4 Marijuana leaf. These leaves always have an odd number of fronds.

rolled into cigarettes and smoked. Marijuana can also be ingested by baking it into a number of foods. Marijuana brownies have been popular for more than 50 years. The higher the THC content, the more potent are the effects. Marijuana cigarettes may range from 1% THC on up. Genetically engineered marijuana with a THC content of nearly 40% has been reported! The stems, roots, and seeds do not contain any appreciable quantities of THC. Figure 19.4 shows some marijuana leaves.

A number of preparations of marijuana have been made. Sometimes the pure resin is harvested from the flowering parts of the plant. This thick, sticky liquid has the highest THC content of any part of the plant. It is called hashish oil or just "hash oil." This is smoked in small pipes designed for this purpose. It is also common to take chopped up marijuana and extract it with a solvent. When the solvent is evaporated, a semisolid, cake-like material called hashish is left. This is formed into bricks and sold. To use it, a small piece is broken off and smoked it in a hash pipe or a "bong." Figure 19.5 shows some of the various forms of marijuana and some

Figure 19.5 Marijuana exhibits. The chunks in the dish on the right are pieces of hashish. The pipes are mostly homemade and are used to smoke the hashish.

devices used for smoking hashish. The large, brown chunks in the dish on the right side of the figure are pieces of hashish. Sometimes marijuana leaves are mixed with or coated with another drug such as PCP. This is called "wobble weed." PCP is itself, a powerful hallucinogen. When mixed with marijuana and smoked, the effects are similar to very strong, high-quality marijuana. Many times marijuana buyers will pay for high-quality weed but get garden-variety marijuana laced with PCP.

Other Hallucinogens

LSD

LSD is probably the most potent hallucinogen. One small droplet (approximately 50 µg) can cause visual and auditory hallucinations that can last up to 12 h. Because of its potency, it is taken in some unusual dosage forms. A common form of LSD is called "blotter acid." LSD is diluted with a solvent and dripped onto blotter paper or other absorbent paper. The paper is cut into tiny squares that are then eaten. LSD has also been made into tiny tablets called "microdots" or other colorful names such as "orange sunshine" or "purple haze." It has even been mixed with gelatin and cut into small squares called "windowpanes." It has also been found on decals that kids lick and put on their bodies. LSD can be absorbed through skin, so law enforcement agents and forensic chemists must be careful when handling it. See Figure 19.6 for a picture of blotter acid LSD.

Figure 19.6 "Blotter acid" forms of LSD. The LSD is dissolved in a liquid and poured on the paper, which has been previously treated with the designs.

Peyote

The peyote cactus can be found in the southwestern part of the United States as well as parts of Mexico and other desert areas. For hundreds of years, some North American Native American tribes have used the buttons from this plant in their religious rites. The buttons contain a hallucinogenic drug called *mescaline*. The buttons are eaten and hallucinogenic symptoms start shortly thereafter. Because the buttons contain lots of plant material, they are often not well digested. One of the authors of this book was once involved in a clandestine drug lab raid where more than 300 buttons were found along with a blender and some cocoa powder. The perpetrator was apparently making mescaline milk shakes to try and avoid the nausea that comes from eating raw cactus buttons. Figure 19.7 shows some of peyote cactus buttons.

Psilocybin

Remember "Alice in Wonderland" where Alice eats some mushrooms and grows really, really big and some other ones make her really small? There are more than a dozen types of mushrooms that grow in the United States and can cause hallucinations. These mushrooms contain *psilocybin* and *psilocin*. These are relatively mild, short-acting hallucinogens. If one is not absolutely sure about what to look for, gathering and eating these mushrooms can be a bit like Russian roulette.

Figure 19.7 Peyote cactus buttons. These were seized in a raid in Virginia. More than 300 buttons were found in a house.

Figure 19.8 Psilocybin mushrooms. There are at least 15 varieties of mushrooms that contain psilocybin. There are many poisonous lookalikes.

Many mushrooms are very poisonous and attempts to get high could easily be fatal if the wrong ones are eaten. Figure 19.8 shows some varieties of psilocybin mushrooms.

Narcotics

The term *narcotic* is often associated with illicit drugs and generally has a bad connotation in the United States. The word comes from the root *narco*, which means "sleep." All narcotics are powerful sleep-inducing, central nervous system depressants. In legal circles, the term "narcotic" has referred to substances that are derived from the *opium poppy (Papaver somniferum)*. Remember "The Wizard of Oz"? On the way to Oz, Dorothy and her friends fall asleep while tramping through the poppy fields. This is because, at the top of the poppy plant, is a large pod that contains a gooey resin. For centuries people have been harvesting the dried resin and smoking it in opium dens. About 10% of this resin is made up of *morphine* (named for *Morpheus*, the God of sleep). Morphine is a powerful narcotic. In addition to causing sleep, it exhibits the other major characteristic of narcotics; it relieves pain. Morphine is sometimes used as a pain reliever for people who have had major surgery or trauma. Another naturally occurring narcotic found in opium is *codeine*. It is less powerful than morphine. It is used mainly in treating coughs by depressing the nerves that trigger coughing. It is also mixed with Tylenol® or other analgesics for treatment of pain after minor surgery and toothaches.

The most famous (or infamous) narcotic is *heroin*. Heroin is a semisynthetic substance made from morphine. Poppies grow mainly in the Far East, and the raw opium is shipped to France and other countries where the morphine is extracted and converted to heroin, which is distributed all over the world. The movie "The French Connection" told the story of the heroin trade in New York. Heroin is 10 times stronger than morphine for the same dose and is used in some countries for the same purpose as morphine. In this country, heroin has no accepted medical use and is in Schedule I. All of the narcotics are physically addictive, heroin especially so, and withdrawal symptoms can be quite severe but seldom fatal.

Preparation and Ingestion of Heroin

Heroin is sold on the street as a white or brown powder that is about 3%–10% pure. The rest is made up of cutting agents like sugars. Heroin is commonly ingested by injection with a syringe. This can cause problems beyond the heroin itself. Addicts have a habit of sharing needles and this is a good way to transmit blood-borne diseases such as AIDS and hepatitis. Typically, some of the powder is put in a small container such as a discarded bottle cap and some water is added. The mixture is heated to dissolve the heroin and then the liquid is pulled into the syringe, filtering it through a small wad of cotton or similar material. Heroin addicts will have telltale needle tracks on their arms and will often find other places on their bodies to inject the drug in order to avoid detection.

In addition to morphine and codeine, there are other narcotics in opium but they occur only in trace quantities. In recent years, many synthetic narcotics have been developed. These have similar properties to some of the naturally occurring ones but with fewer side effects. The best known of these is *methadone*, which is used as a substitute for heroin for people who are trying to "kick the habit." There are also a number of other synthetic narcotics that have been abused off and on for years but which have made a major comeback in just the past few years. The two most popular of these are *hydrocodone* and *oxycodone*. Hydrocodone is often mixed with an analgesic such as ibuprofen and sold with a prescription as a pain reliever. Oxycodone is sold as Oxycontin®, another pain reliever. This has been widely abused as part of "rave" parties, large gatherings of young people where drugs and alcohol are liberally imbibed. As the U.S. population ages and baby boomers approach advanced age, these drugs have become prescribed to an alarming degree for aches and pains. The FDA and DEA have moved to restrict the flow of these drugs by cracking down on overprescribing. The result is that heroin is making a major comeback because people are becoming addicted to the pain-killing drugs. Because of the restrictions on them, heroin is becoming more available and cheaper.

Analysis of Illicit Drugs

Agents of the U.S. DEA as well as state and local police have personnel that are dedicated to lessening the flow of drugs into the United States and arresting people who possess or sell them to others. When these drugs are seized, they are sent to a crime laboratory where forensic drug chemists analyze them. There are a number of considerations that determine how the drugs will be analyzed. These include the following:

- What the drug is and what form it is in?
- Is there a large amount of the drug in one package or in many packages?
- Is there a very small amount of the drug?
- Is the weight of the drug mixture a consideration?

Requirements for the Analysis of Drugs

Any conclusion given by a forensic scientist in a court or on a laboratory report must be scientifically reliable and defendable. This means that if a scientist identifies a white powder as containing cocaine, he or she must prove this *to a degree of reasonable scientific certainty*. This is the standard of proof in a court. There must be no reasonable alternative to the conclusion reached by the scientist. For this reason, most drug samples must have at least one confirmatory test performed. There are a number of protocols for the analysis of drugs. The one employed by a particular chemist depends on the lab, the caseload, and the instrumentation available. The international Scientific Working Group on Drug Analysis has developed standards and protocols for the analysis of common illicit drugs (www.swgdrug.org).

Schemes of Analysis for Drugs

In general, tests for drugs proceed from the general to the specific. Each test serves to give more information about the possible identity of the drug and either the scheme as a whole or a confirmatory test will positively identify the drug.

Screening Tests

The most general tests for drugs are called screening tests. These are also sometimes called spot tests or field tests. There are screening tests for most of the common illicit drugs. Most of these tests consist of adding one or more chemical reagents to a pinch of the suspected drug and then observing one or more color changes. For example, the common screening test for marijuana involves three chemicals and the final color is purple. For cocaine, the test uses three chemicals and the final color is turquoise. The purpose of these tests is to narrow down the possibilities for a drug sample. This can be especially important if the submitted sample is a white powder. This could be any of a number of things and screening tests can be very important in leading the chemist toward the actual drug. It is important to emphasize that screening tests are never used to confirm the presence of a specific drug. For each screening test, there may be many substances that could give a positive reaction.

Separation Tests

Very few illicit drug samples, especially powdered samples, are sold on the street in a pure form. Virtually all of them are diluted with one or more materials. This is done to maximize profits and minimize overdoses. Cocaine, for example, is often cut with sugars or other white powders. The same is true for heroin and methamphetamine. In order to eventually positively identify the drug, it must be separated from the cutting agents. This can be done on a large scale using liquid solvents to extract the drug away from cutting agents. On a small scale, where only a small amount of the drug may be present, gas chromatography is used. For some drugs liquid chromatography may be used. These techniques are discussed in Chapter 4. Figure 19.9 is a chromatogram of two drugs, caffeine and cocaine.

Confirmation Tests

As mentioned earlier, most drug samples must be confirmed by a single test so that there is no uncertainty in the identity of the drug. In most crime labs, the

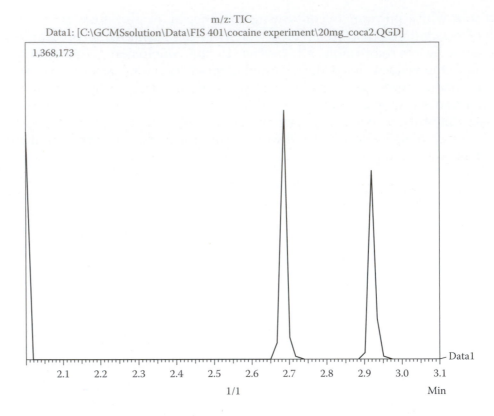

m/z: TIC
Data1: [C:\GCMSsolution\Data\FIS 401\cocaine experiment\20mg_coca2.QGD]

Figure 19.9 Gas chromatogram of caffeine (first peak) and cocaine (second peak). These are common stimulant drugs.

confirmatory test is mass spectrometry. This test is explained in Chapter 5. Figure 19.10 is a mass spectrum of cocaine.

One of the few drugs that didn't normally require a confirmatory test is marijuana. This is because it is a plant that is easily recognized. The visual recognition of parts of the plant under a microscope is part of the protocol. Other tests, such as a screening test and perhaps a separation test are usually done to isolate the THC and the protocol as a whole is considered to be confirmatory for marijuana. Sometimes it is not possible to confirm the presence of a drug when there is so little drug present that there is not enough to complete the analysis. Examples of this might be testing the residue in a syringe for heroin or the dust in a straw for cocaine. In such cases, nondestructive tests are done first. Other tests would only be performed if there were enough of the drug left to test further. Sometimes this partial scheme results in a report that gives only a qualified identification of the drug. Sometimes the opposite problem arises when there is a very large amount of the drug in many packages. Decisions must be made as to how the packages will be sampled and tested and how many packages will be opened and tested. One of the authors of this book once had a case that consisted of 16,000 lb of marijuana in 50 lb bricks. Samples of each of the 320 bricks were taken and tested. In another case, the author received 535 small packets containing suspected cocaine. All of them were opened and weighed and screened. All were about the same weight and responded the same to the screening test for cocaine. Portions of the packets were subjected to further testing to confirm the presence of the cocaine. This is permissible as long as representative samples are tested.

R.Time: 2.9(Scan#: 55)
MassPeaks: 11

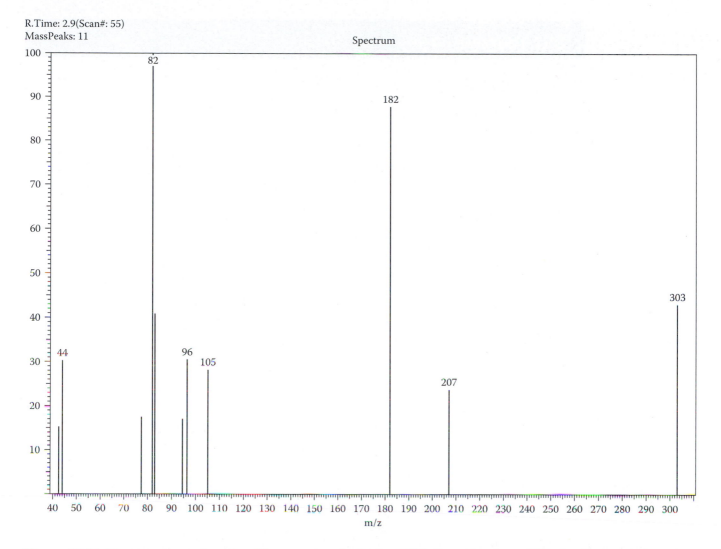

Figure 19.10 Mass spectrum of cocaine. The parent peak of *m/e* = 303 is the molecular weight of unfragmented cocaine. The base peak (most intense) is at *m/e* = 82.

Summary

Illicit drugs are those that are either legitimately manufactured drugs that are taken for purposes other than those they were made for or they are drugs that have no medical use and are taken solely for abuse purposes. Illicit drugs fall into four classes by major effects: stimulants, depressants, narcotics, and hallucinogens. The federal government controls many illicit drugs through a set of laws that create five schedules where drugs are put. These schedules regulate drugs by the presence or absence of a legitimate medical use and by their potential for abuse. Illicit drugs are analyzed by forensic chemists who develop protocols for analysis that take into account the form and quantity of the drug present as well as its purity. In most cases, a confirmatory test must be done on a drug sample to unequivocally identify it.

Test Yourself

Multiple Choice

1. Which of the following would not be an illicit drug?
   a. Aspirin
   b. Cocaine
   c. Heroin
   d. Tylenol with codeine
   e. LSD

2. A drug with a high potential for abuse and a legitimate medical use would most likely be put in federal schedule
   a. 1
   b. 2
   c. 3
   d. 4
   e. 5

3. Heroin is classified as a
   a. Stimulant
   b. Narcotic
   c. Steroid
   d. Hallucinogen
   e. Over-the-counter medicine

4. Marijuana
   a. Comes from a plant
   b. Is totally synthetic
   c. Is chemically made from another drug
   d. Is a plant
   e. Is usually injected with a syringe and needle

5. If a forensic chemist receives only a very small amount of a drug
   a. She won't analyze it at all.
   b. She will do nondestructive tests first.
   c. She will do only the confirmatory test.
   d. She will do just one test and then stop.
   e. She will analyze the drug but won't write a report of her findings.

6. SWGDRUG is
   a. A confirmatory test for illicit drugs
   b. A liquid form of cocaine
   c. An international committee that set standards for the analysis of drugs
   d. The federal agency with the responsibility for arresting drug traffickers

7. Which of the following is not classified as a hallucinogen?
   a. Marijuana
   b. Methadone
   c. Psilocybin
   d. LSD
   e. Mescaline

8. If a new drug were discovered that had a high potential for abuse and no accepted medical use, it would most likely be put in schedule
   a. 5
   b. 1

c. 2

d. 6

e. It wouldn't be in a schedule

9. If a chemist received a case that contained 1000 small baggies of a tan powder, all in the same type of packaging and with all about the same weight of powder, which scheme should he or she use to test these?

a. Run all tests on all 1000 packets.

b. Run a field test on all 1000 packets and then confirm the identity on one sample.

c. Combine the powders from all 1000 packets and run one set of tests.

d. Take a representative sample of the packets and run the tests on them.

e. Pick out one sample of the 1000 at random and run all tests on it.

10. Which of the following drugs does not require a confirmatory test?

a. Cocaine

b. Heroin

c. Marijuana

d. PCP

e. None of the above

True or False

11. Mass spectrometry is a confirmatory test for drugs (true or false).

12. Most street drugs are relatively pure and separation tests are seldom needed.

13. Prescription drugs are not put in any federal schedule.

14. States' drug laws must be exactly the same as the federal laws.

15. LSD is considered to be the most powerful of the hallucinogenic drugs.

16. Cocaine is a naturally occurring substance found in the poppy plant.

17. Marijuana analysis does not normally require a confirmatory test.

Matching. Match Each Term with Its Definition

18. Hash oil	a. Naturally occurring drug from poppy plant
19. Mescaline	b. Synthetic hallucinogen
20. Morphine	c. Synthetic narcotic
21. PCP	d. Preparation of marijuana
22. Methadone	e. Naturally occurring drug from cactus

Short Essay

23. Name and describe the two criteria that are used for the classification of drugs into a federal schedule. Who has the ultimate responsibility for putting drugs in a schedule?

Go to the following web site: http://www.dea.gov/pubs/abuse/index.htm.

Use the information in the publication "Drugs of Abuse" published by the DEA to find the following information:

24. What Schedule is marijuana in? _____

25. What Schedule is cocaine in? _____

Further Reading

Liu, R. H. and D. E. Gadzala. (1997). *Handbook of Drug Analysis: Applications in Forensic and Clinical Laboratories*. American Chemical Society, Washington, DC.
Siegel, J. (2004). Analysis of illicit drugs, in *Handbook of Forensic Science*, vol. II, 2nd edn., R. Saferstein, ed. Prentice-Hall, Upper Saddle River, NJ.
Smith, F. (2004). *Handbook of Forensic Drug Analysis*. Academic Press, San Diego, CA.

On the Web

Information on careers in forensic drug analysis: http://www.forensiccareers.com/index.php?option=com_content&task=view&id=27&Itemid=30.
Powerpoint presentation on forensic drug analysis: http://www7.nationalacademies.org/stl/April%20Forensic%20Bono.pdf.
The homepage of swgdrug, the scientific working group on drug analysis: www.swgdrug.org.

20
Forensic Toxicology

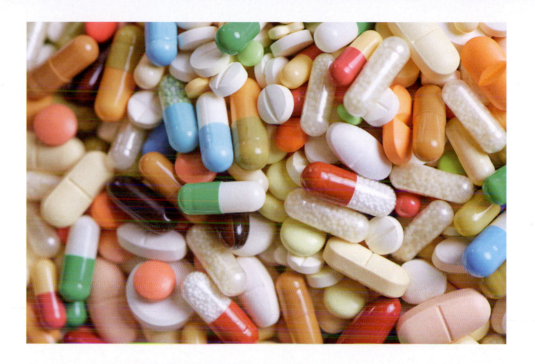

Learning Objectives

1. To be able to define forensic toxicology
2. To be able to define and give examples of absorption, metabolism, elimination, and metabolite
3. To be able to describe the major effects on the rate of absorption of alcohol from the stomach into the bloodstream
4. To be able to describe the major metabolites of alcohol
5. To be able to describe the major effects on the rate of elimination of alcohol from the bloodstream
6. To be able to draw and describe a Widmark curve
7. To be able to describe the major effects of alcohol on the body
8. To be able to describe the major methods of measuring blood and breath alcohol

Chapter 20
Forensic Toxicology

Chapter Outline

Mini Glossary

Addiction: Physical effects of a drug on a person, manifested by an extreme craving for the drug. If deprived of the drug, withdrawal will set in.

Deciliter: One-tenth of a liter. 100 mL.

Dependence: A psychological phenomenon. Any physical changes that may accompany regular use of a drug are insufficient to cause addiction. There may still be a powerful craving for the drug but failure to take the drug does not cause withdrawal.

Enteric dosage form: Form of a drug that is made to be released overtime in the bloodstream.

Forensic toxicology: The legal application of toxicology as well as other scientific disciplines such as analytical chemistry and clinical chemistry to criminal and civil cases including drug use, medicolegal investigation of death, and poisoning.

Half-life: The time it takes for the concentration of a drug in the body to be reduced by 50%.

Horizontal gaze nystagmus: Movement of the eyeball as an object is passed slowly in front of the eyes horizontally.

Implied consent: Permission to submit to a drunk driving alcohol test that you give when you sign your driver's license.

Metabolite: The action of the liver on a drug to change it into a different substance that is generally less harmful and easier to eliminate from the body.

Oxidation–reduction reaction: In this type of reaction, electrons are moved from one substance to another, changing the valence state of one or more atoms.

Pharmacology: The study of drugs and all of their harmful and beneficial effects on living things.

Proof: A measure of alcohol concentration in hard liquors. It is equal to twice the percentage of alcohol in the drink.

Synergism: Magnified effects from a combination of similarly acting drugs.

Tolerance: Occurs when increasing doses are required to maintain the same level of effects on the subject as the original dose.

Toxicology: The study of the harmful effects of drugs and poisons on living things.

Withdrawal: A syndrome; a set of reactions to the lack of the drug. The symptoms include sleeplessness, restlessness, nausea, hallucinations, headaches, and other pain. Withdrawal can last for days or even weeks.

Acronyms

BAC: Blood alcohol concentration
LSD: Lysergic acid diethylamide
Redox: Oxidation–reduction reaction

Introduction

Janice Joplin, a famous 1960s and 1970s rock star, died of an overdose of heroin, possibly complicated by alcohol. Jimi Hendrix, another famous rock star of the same era, died of an accidental overdose of barbiturates. The website http://www.av1611.org/rockdead.html lists forty rock stars who died from drug overdoses.

In some of these cases, drugs are sometimes combined with alcohol to cause death, often accidental. In Chapter 19, we learned that central nervous system depressants are one of the four major types of abused drugs. Alcohol is also a central nervous system depressant, although it works somewhat differently from the drugs. It is not too difficult to accidentally overdose on this combination, when someone takes depressants that, by themselves, wouldn't be lethal and drinking an amount of alcohol that, likewise, wouldn't be lethal by itself. As we shall see in this chapter, drugs can combine their effects to cause overall effects that are greater than the sum of the individual effects. This can result in an accidental (or deliberate) overdose.

Chapter 19 covered illicit drugs seized from drug users and sellers on the street. The major categories and effects of these substances were discussed. Of course, the effects that drugs have on a particular person depend upon the physical and emotional traits of the person as well as the amount and strength of the drug and the frequency that is taken by the user. This chapter is concerned with the fate of these drugs when they are ingested. First, the general principles of toxicology are covered. These include the methods of ingestion of drugs, how they get into the bloodstream and then to the various organs in the body, how they are treated chemically in the body, and how they are eliminated. Then, the particular example of ethyl alcohol (spirits) is used to illustrate these principles. Although alcohol is not classified as an illicit drug, its behavior in the human body provides an excellent example of how drugs in general are handled. In addition to the toxicology of alcohol, its chemical analysis for the purpose of drunk driving enforcement is also discussed. More than half of the cases that forensic toxicologists receive in public crime laboratories are concerned with drunk driving, so it is appropriate that we focus on alcohol.

Forensic Toxicology

Toxicology is the study of the harmful effects of drugs and poisons on living things. It includes study of symptoms, mechanisms, treatment, and detection of these drugs and poisons. Toxicology is part of the science of **pharmacology**, which is the study of drugs and all of their harmful and beneficial effects on living things. So when scientists use the principles of pharmacology to analyze the harmful effects of drugs and poisons on living things in cases involving the criminal justice system, they are practicing **forensic toxicology**; the legal application of toxicology as well as other scientific disciplines such as analytical chemistry and clinical chemistry to criminal and civil cases including drug use, medicolegal investigation of death, and poisoning. The relationships between toxicology, pharmacology, and forensic toxicology are illustrated in Figure 20.1.

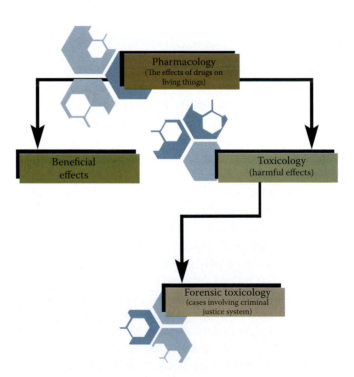

Figure 20.1 Relationships between pharmacology, toxicology and forensic toxicology.

Becoming a Forensic Toxicologist

One of the most important tasks of a forensic toxicologist is to measure the concentration of drugs and poisons in various body fluids and substances such as blood, urine, and breath. This is done in some cases on living humans as in drunk driving cases, but mostly on people who have died under circumstances where the coroner or medical examiner would have to determine the cause and manner of death. These measurements are a type of analytical chemistry, and so much of what forensic toxicologists have to know is chemistry. A good preparation for becoming a forensic toxicologist is a bachelor's degree in chemistry. Some universities also offer bachelor's degrees in clinical chemistry or in toxicology although these are more often offered at the graduate level. With a bachelor's degree, a scientist is qualified to make measurements of drug, poison, and alcohol levels in a body but would not be qualified to interpret these levels in terms of their contribution to a death. In order to make these determinations, a scientist must be educated in pharmacology and toxicology. This normally requires a PhD in one of those fields. A PhD in chemistry is normally not specific enough unless it is in clinical chemistry. A forensic toxicologist with a PhD may be certified by the American Board of Forensic Toxicology (www.abft.org). A bachelor's level toxicologist may be certified as a forensic toxicologist specialist.

Principles of Pharmacology

In Chapter 19, the term "drug" was defined as a substance that is designed to have specific physical and/or emotional effects on living things. Licit drugs are manufactured to have beneficial effects. Poisons, by definition, have harmful effects. Some drugs, if taken inappropriately or in combination with other drugs or in high doses, can have harmful effects and a person can therefore be poisoned by them. Pharmacologists study all sorts of drugs and poisons. They learn what happens to a drug when it is taken, and what effects it has on organisms and the effects of drugs taken in combination with other drugs or alcohol. This chapter is concerned mainly with what happens to a drug when it is taken. This branch of pharmacology is called "pharmacodynamics." It includes methods of ingestion of a drug, how it is absorbed into the bloodstream and other parts of the body, how it is distributed throughout the body, how it is changed (metabolized) into other substances, and how it is eliminated.

Drug Intake

Drugs can be administered in a number of ways. These include swallowing a powder, tablet, or capsule or dissolving a powder in water and then drinking it. Liquids and vapors may be inhaled through the nose. Sometimes drugs are taken via an intramuscular, subcutaneous, or intravenous injection with a syringe and needle. The best method of ingestion for a particular drug depends upon how it interacts with organs such as the stomach and how quickly the drug needs to be absorbed and distributed. If stomach acids destroy a drug, then this route of ingestion must be avoided. In order to prevent a drug from dissolving too quickly in the stomach or small intestine, it may be coated with a material that slows down solution of the drug or it may come in the form of tiny, coated particles that enter the bloodstream over a long period of time (timed release capsules). Drugs that are protected in this way are called "enteric dosage forms." The route of ingestion will also affect the rate that the drug enters the bloodstream. As will be shown later, this has a profound influence upon the effects of the drug. Intravenous injections directly into the bloodstream provide the fastest route, followed by intramuscular and subcutaneous injections. Oral administration is normally the slowest means of getting a drug into the bloodstream. Occasionally, drugs enter the body via unusual routes. One of the most popular ways of ingesting cocaine used to be by "snorting" or inhaling through the nose. Now the most popular method of taking cocaine and some other drugs such as marijuana is by smoking it in a pipe or, in the case of marijuana leaf, by rolling it into cigarettes. Some drugs that are designed to act on the digestive system or intestines are administered anally (suppositories).

Absorption

Once the drug has entered the body, it is absorbed into the bloodstream. If the drug is a vapor and is inhaled into the lungs, then it will eventually enter the blood through tiny capillaries that are in contact with the smallest sacs in the lungs, known as "alveoli." Figure 20.2 shows the structure of a human lung including the alveoli.

Drugs that are introduced via intramuscular or subcutaneous injection enter the bloodstream through capillaries that are present in muscle or skin tissue. If the drug is taken orally, it will first enter the stomach. It may then pass through the stomach through the "pylorus" (a valve that connects the stomach to the small intestine) and then into the small intestine. Some drugs are absorbed into the bloodstream from the stomach, some from the small intestine, and some drugs are absorbed in both places. Figure 20.3 shows the stomach, and small intestine.

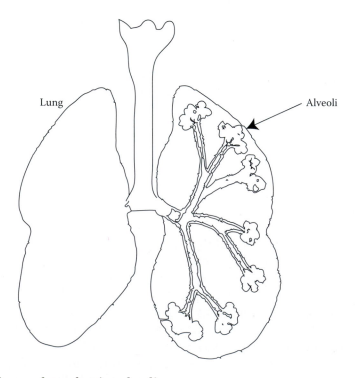

Figure 20.2 The human lung showing alveoli.

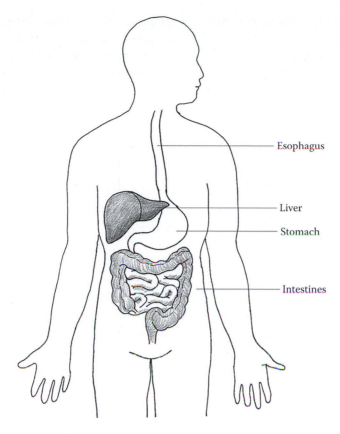

Esophagus

Liver

Stomach

Intestines

Figure 20.3 The stomach and small intestine. (Courtesy of Richard Li.)

With the exception of oral ingestion, the drug user has no control over the rate of absorption of a drug. When the drug is taken orally, then the rate of absorption depends upon what is in the stomach already. If the stomach is empty, then the drug will be absorbed rapidly. If there is already food in the stomach, then the drug will have to compete with the food already there for absorption into the bloodstream. This means that the drug will be absorbed more slowly and the ultimate concentration of the drug in the blood will be lower than if the stomach were empty. To some extent, the type of food in the stomach will affect the rate of absorption of the drug. Some foods are absorbed more slowly than others and so they will inhibit the absorption of a drug more or less depending upon the type of food. This concept is especially important to grasp in the study of drunk driving cases, where the ultimate concentration of alcohol in a person's body will be dependent upon what he or she has eaten prior to drinking.

Circulation of Drugs in the Bloodstream

Once drugs enter the bloodstream, they circulate throughout the body. Although some drugs are targeted for specific organs such as the heart, drugs have their most important effects in the brain. Pharmaceutical chemistry has advanced to the point where drugs can be manufactured to have a particular interaction with a single part of the brain resulting in a predictable effect. The higher the concentration of the drug in the bloodstream, the more pronounced the effects would be. In some cases, certain effects don't even appear at low drug concentrations. In theory, every drug should distribute itself more or less equally throughout the body because the bloodstream carries the drug to every tissue and every cell. In fact, some drugs have a tendency to collect in certain tissues or organs. For example, pesticides will collect and build up in fatty tissues. This makes them especially dangerous overtime. A pesticide may not cause too much harm at low concentrations; however, as it builds up in fatty tissues instead of being eliminated, its concentration can reach toxic levels overtime. Heavy metals such as mercury or lead will collect preferentially in teeth and gums, fingernails and toenails, and hair. LSD appears to collect and remain in certain parts of the brain. This may explain the so-called flashbacks that occur with LSD whereby a person can have a relapse effect from LSD taken years earlier.

Elimination of Drugs from the Body

As the drug is absorbed into the bloodstream, its concentration increases. As it circulates through the body, its concentration begins to decrease in the blood through mechanisms such as metabolism, the action of kidneys, a preference for certain types of tissue, etc. Pharmacologists describe the decrease in concentration of a drug in terms of its "half-life." This is the time interval it takes for the concentration of a drug to drop to half of its initial concentration. Half-lives can vary greatly. The hypnotic drug gamma-hydroxy butyric acid (GHB) has a half-life of about 30 min, whereas cocaine's half-life is 60–90 min. By contrast, heroin has a half-life of only 3 min. The decrease in concentration of a drug is caused mainly by two processes: metabolism and elimination.

Metabolism

As drugs circulate throughout the body in the bloodstream, sooner or later they will reach the liver. This is the body's chemical factory. The liver has the ability to change a drug into a different substance, forming what is called a "metabolite." This primary metabolite may itself be metabolized into another substance, forming a secondary metabolite. For example, the primary metabolite of heroin is morphine, another naturally occurring narcotic. Figure 20.4 shows the conversion of heroin to morphine.

Metabolism in the liver generally accomplishes one or more of the following: it changes the drug into a less harmful or toxic substance, it changes the drug into a form that cells can more easily convert to energy, or it changes the drug into a form that makes it easier to eliminate in the urine, usually by making it more water soluble. This is normally done by changing the drug into an ionic, salt form that is much more soluble in water, the main component of urine. With many drugs, metabolism takes place so quickly that toxicologists don't look for the parent drug in a blood sample. They look for known metabolites whose presence proves that the

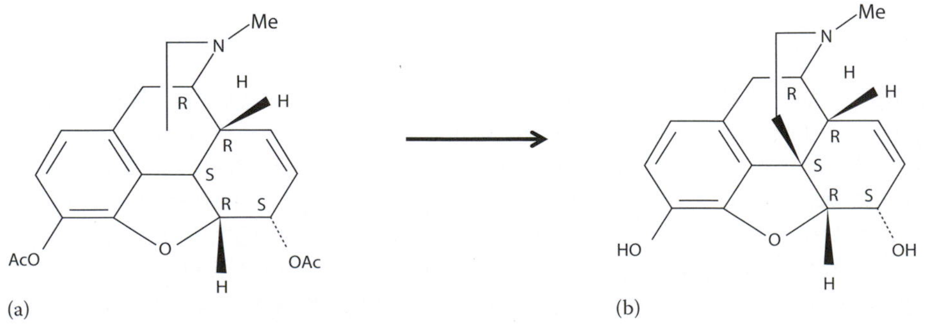

Figure 20.4 The metabolism of (a) heroin into (b) morphine.

parent drug was there previously. A person has no control over the rate of metabolism of a substance by the liver. This rate varies from person to person and depends upon the general health of the person at a given time and especially upon the condition of the liver.

Elimination

There are several ways that drugs can be eliminated from the body. If the drug is volatile (easily vaporized), it can be exhaled in the breath. If the drug is water soluble, it can be sweated out during vigorous exercise or exposure to hot, humid conditions. At best, these account for only a small percentage of the elimination of drugs. The majority of drugs are eliminated in urine, either as the drug itself or after metabolism by the liver. The person or animal has no control over the rate at which this happens. It cannot be speeded up or slowed down by intervention. This process is entirely under the control of the liver and kidneys.

Synergism

At the beginning of the chapter, the issue of how and whether accidental overdose of depressant drugs and alcohol can cause death was raised. A toxicologist might conclude that the victim did not take enough of either substance to cause death. It was the combination of the two that killed him. This phenomenon, whereby someone exhibits magnified effects from a combination of drugs, is called "synergism." It means that the whole is greater than the sum of the parts. In this particular overdose case, it means that the effects of the alcohol and barbiturates taken together are greater than the sum of their effects if taken separately. In this case, both alcohol and barbiturates are central nervous system depressants. The synergistic effects slow down the victim's respiration so much that he or she stops breathing and dies. Synergism can be very tricky. With so many new drugs coming on the market, it is very important for pharmaceutical companies to test new drugs against existing ones to uncover possible dangerous synergisms. Toxicologists and pathologists must be careful in assessing the role that drugs could have had in causing death. Synergism must be ruled out before the drug levels are taken into account in determination of cause and manner of death.

The term synergism is used in other fields besides pharmacology. It is often used in business to denote how different divisions of a company can work together to achieve results that go beyond what both divisions can achieve acting separately.

Tolerance

"Tolerance" to a drug occurs when increasing doses are required to maintain the same level of effects on the subject as the original dose. It shows up very often in people who continually abuse the same drug. For example, someone who abuses methamphetamine may get "high" initially from a 10 mg dose. After several days, he might find that he must take 20 mg at a time to get the same effects he was getting from 10 mg before. Then, it may go up to 30 mg and so on. This can become a serious problem when the person becomes addicted to a drug and then wants to quit. If he tries to quit, withdrawal symptoms will set in because the person has become biochemically dependent on the drug. In some cases, such as with barbiturates, sudden ("cold turkey") withdrawal can be fatal, so the person has to be taken off the drug very slowly. If a person becomes tolerant to a drug, that means he can take ever larger quantities without having catastrophic reactions. When a person dies and a high concentration of a drug is found in his bloodstream, the toxicologist must determine the drug history of that person before making a conclusion about the role that the drug played in the death. A high concentration does not necessarily mean that the drug caused death or even contributed to it.

With certain drugs, a type of "reverse tolerance" effect has been noted. This is sometimes reported by marijuana users, who indicate that they get more heightened effects overtime without taking more of the drug. One explanation for this observation is that the symptoms resulting from marijuana use are learned behavior. The more one smokes marijuana, the more that the effects will be expected and this is perceived as reverse tolerance. There is also evidence that tetrahydrocannabinol (THC), the active ingredient in marijuana, may remain in the body for months after ingestion and, with regular use, will increase in concentration, thus increasing its effects. LSD is another drug to which reverse tolerance has been reported. The reasons for this are not well understood.

Addiction v. Dependence

The term "drug addict" is familiar to everyone but what does it really mean? Why do some drugs cause addiction and some cause dependence and what is the difference? "Drug addiction" is a physical process. As a person takes a drug, it may, with time, cause biochemical changes in the body as a means of helping to tolerate the drug. After a period of time, the person may become addicted to the drug. Addiction is manifested by an extreme craving for the drug. One's entire life is centered on how to get the next dose. Personal hygiene and health may be neglected. A significant amount of crime committed today in this country is the result of addicts getting money to buy drugs. Failure to procure the drug will cause "withdrawal." This is a syndrome; a set of reactions to the lack of the drug. The symptoms include sleeplessness, restlessness, nausea, hallucinations, headaches, and other pain. Withdrawal can last for days or even weeks. Some drugs are not addictive. Instead users can become dependent on the drug. "Dependence" on a drug is a psychological phenomenon. Any physical changes that may accompany regular use of a drug are insufficient to cause addiction. There may still be a powerful craving for the drug but failure to take the drug does not cause withdrawal. For some, drug addiction or dependence depends upon the amount of the drug taken. Cocaine is a good example. Cocaine in its salt form is usually "snorted" through the nose. Once in the nasal passages, the cocaine is absorbed slowly into the bloodstream and usually will not reach concentrations that are high enough to result in addiction, even with repeated use. If cocaine is injected into a muscle or vein or if it is smoked (e.g., crack), it is absorbed more efficiently and can reach high enough concentrations to be addictive.

Pharmacology and Toxicology of Ethyl Alcohol

Ethyl alcohol, also called ethanol, can be distilled from a number of foodstuffs and is a product of fermentation. Its chemical structure is shown in Figure 20.5.

Ethanol is the active ingredient in all spirits, wine, and beer. In spirits, its concentration is measured in "proof," which is twice the volume percentage of ethanol. Thus, 100-proof whiskey contains 50% alcohol by volume. In beer and wine, ethanol is measured in volume percent. A typical wine contains 12–15% ethanol

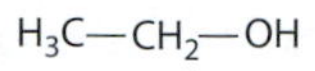

$$H_3C-CH_2-OH$$

Figure 20.5 Ethyl alcohol (ethanol).

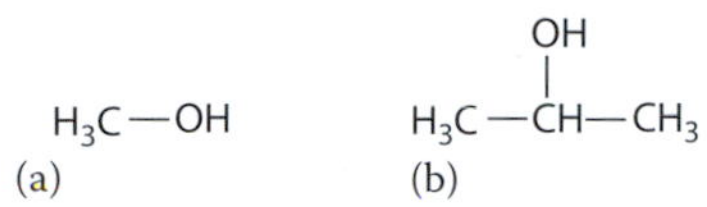

$$H_3C-OH \qquad H_3C-\overset{\overset{\displaystyle OH}{\displaystyle |}}{C}H-CH_3$$

(a)   (b)

Figure 20.6 (a) Methyl alcohol (methanol) and (b) isopropyl alcohol (isopropanol).

and a typical beer contains about 4–6% ethanol. Ethanol is a central nervous system depressant. It acts as a mild tranquilizer. It is also a "neurotoxin," which is a substance that kills nerve cells. It is estimated that 1 ounce of ethanol will kill about 10,000 nerve cells. Early in the twentieth century, the federal government attempted to prohibit the use of ethanol in drinks in the United States by enacting a constitutional amendment that prohibited alcohol use. This had disastrous results in that it promoted illegal "bootlegging" of liquor by organized crime and it caused many people to turn to substitutes such as methyl alcohol and isopropyl alcohol (rubbing alcohol) as substitutes. Both of these alcohols destroy optic nerves and cause blindness. Figure 20.6 shows the structures of methyl alcohol (methanol) and isopropyl alcohol (isopropanol). After a time, the amendment was repealed and the use of alcohol was mitigated by the passage of laws involving public intoxication, drunk driving, and the requirement that taxes had to be paid on each unit of alcohol sold.

Because of its depressant properties, ethanol can have a range of effects on a person depending upon its concentration in the body. For this reason, the federal government and every state have laws that regulate the amount of alcohol a person can drink before being legally drunk when operating a motor vehicle. To be rigorous and properly scientific, alcohol levels should be measured in the brain since that is where it has its effects; this is obviously not practical. Therefore, toxicologists use surrogates (substitutes) to infer relative levels of alcohol in the brain. The most common surrogate is breath. Next is blood. Urine is not a good surrogate because it does not give accurate measurements of alcohol in the body. Most states describe the level of alcohol in terms of its "BAC" or "blood alcohol concentration." In the United States, the concentration of alcohol in the blood is expressed as the number of grams of alcohol (weight) present in 0.1 L (100 mL or 1 dL) of blood (volume). Currently, a person is considered under the influence of alcohol when operating a motor vehicle when the BAC = 0.08 g/dL. When a driver is stopped for suspicion of drunk driving, the officer will usually determine the alcohol concentration by measuring the subject's breath rather than blood. There are instruments that measure breath alcohol and convert it to BAC by using an equivalent of 210 L of breath instead of 100 mL of blood. The instruments do an automatic conversion of breath alcohol to BAC. At least one state, Oklahoma, has a separate law that relates operating a vehicle under the influence of alcohol to breath alcohol level. Their breath testing instruments do not make the conversion to BAC. One reason for this is that the conversion factor to 210 L of breath may not be accurate for all people.

There has been a good deal of research into how most people react to a given BAC of ethanol. It should be pointed out that people react differently to the same quantity of alcohol. There are many factors at work here, including the person's weight, experience with alcohol, what is already in the stomach at the time of drinking, and the form of the alcohol being ingested (beer v. wine, v. hard liquor). Even so, there are some general findings about the effects of alcohol on people. Some of these findings are listed in the following:

- Most people will begin to feel some effect from alcohol when their BAC reaches as little as 0.02.
- At 0.04, there is a definite feeling of relaxation.
- At 0.06, most people will definitely be less able to make rational decisions about their own capabilities. Their driving will start to become impaired.
- At 0.08, there is definite impairment in motor coordination skills and the ability to drive safely is seriously compromised. This is now the level at which a driver is considered to be intoxicated in most states and under federal law.
- When the BAC reaches 0.12, vomiting may occur in people who are not experienced drinkers.
- At 0.15, balance is seriously compromised. This amount of alcohol is equivalent to half pint of liquor in the bloodstream.
- At 0.4, most people will lose consciousness and will die. This is called the LD_{50}—the dose that will cause death in 50% of the population.

Absorption of Ethanol

The ultimate concentration and therefore the effects that alcohol will have depend upon the rate at which it is absorbed. Ethanol is absorbed from both the stomach and small intestine. Two major factors affect the rate at which ethanol is absorbed. They are the concentration of alcohol in the drink and the contents of the stomach at the time of drinking. The more concentrated the drink, the faster it will be absorbed into the bloodstream and the higher the level that will be reached. If the stomach has food in it when the ethanol is ingested, then the rate of absorption will be slowed due to competing absorption of the food that is already in the stomach. This food will slow the passage of the alcohol into the small intestine and into the bloodstream and lower the ultimate BAC. Research has shown that the most effective foods at slowing alcohol absorption are carbohydrates because they are the slowest foods to be absorbed from the stomach into the small intestine. The implication of these influences on the rate of absorption of alcohol is that the same amount of alcohol taken on an empty stomach will result in a higher BAC than if the stomach had food in it at the time of drinking. In addition, the same amount of alcohol taken in highly concentrated drinks will result in a higher BAC than more dilute drinks.

Circulation of Ethanol in the Bloodstream

Once ethanol gets absorbed into the bloodstream through the stomach and small intestine, it circulates throughout the body, eventually reaching the brain. The alcohol will first act on the outer surfaces of the brain. These are the areas that affect motor coordination. If the concentration of the alcohol is high enough, it will penetrate into the inner parts of the brain overtime. These areas affect the ability to see and talk clearly, balance, judgment, and inhibitions. If the alcohol is able to penetrate more deeply into the brain, it will affect the autonomic nervous system where involuntary functions such as breathing are controlled. As a central nervous system depressant, alcohol will cause loss of consciousness and then slowing down and eventually cessation of breathing, thus causing death. Not only does alcohol reach the brain but it also penetrates other organs and parts of the body. If a person dies and there is not enough blood left to get an accurate measurement of BAC, other body fluids can be used because they will contain alcohol in proportion to the concentration in the blood. Forensic toxicologists will commonly use spinal fluid, vitreous humor (eye fluid), urine, and sometimes even brain tissue to obtain BAC equivalents.

Elimination of Ethanol

On its journey through the body, alcohol eventually reaches the liver. The liver acts on the alcohol by metabolizing it to substances that are less harmful and more easily eliminated from the body. One of the pathways of metabolism of alcohol is to change it to "acetaldehyde" and then to "acetic acid." Both of these are oxidation reactions and take place under the control of liver enzymes. This chemical path is shown in Figure 20.7.

As ethanol is metabolized, the metabolites are eliminated from the body by dissolving in urine and passing. Thus, as ethanol passes through the liver, its concentration decreases. In most people, the rate of metabolism of ethanol is about $0.015\%/h \pm 0.03$. This means that if a person has a BAC of 0.15%, it will take approximately 10 h to remove all of it. Ethanol can be eliminated in other ways besides metabolism. It can be exhaled through the breath. This is because ethanol is fairly volatile and will pass easily from the bloodstream through the alveoli in the lungs and be exhaled through the breath. This is the principle behind breath alcohol concentration instruments. Alcohol can also be eliminated through perspiration; however, elimination by breathing and perspiration together accounts for a maximum of about 5% of the total elimination.

Maximum Blood Alcohol Concentration

As soon as ethanol starts being absorbed into the bloodstream, the BAC starts to rise. As it reaches the liver, it starts to metabolize, which acts to reduce the BAC. As long as ethanol is being absorbed faster than it is being metabolized, the BAC will increase. At some point, the absorption will slow until it is occurring at the same rate as the elimination, and the BAC remains at a steady state. Then elimination will surpass absorption and the BAC will start to decline. When absorption ceases, only elimination is taking place (at an average rate of 0.015% per hour) until there is no more alcohol. Since 95% or more of ethanol is eliminated by metabolism and subsequent elimination in the urine, elimination is taking place at a nearly constant rate. Only the rate of absorption will alter the ultimate concentration in the blood. If drinking takes place rapidly on an empty stomach with high concentration drinks, then absorption will be rapid and the ultimate BAC will be high. If, on the other hand, there is food in the stomach, and/or drinking takes place slowly using beer or wine, the maximum BAC will be lower even if the same amount of alcohol is consumed.

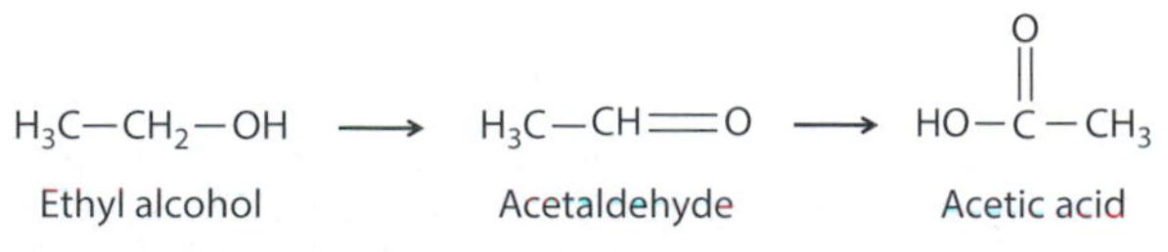

$$H_3C-CH_2-OH \longrightarrow H_3C-CH{=\!=}O \longrightarrow HO-\overset{\overset{\displaystyle O}{\|}}{C}-CH_3$$

Ethyl alcohol   Acetaldehyde   Acetic acid

Figure 20.7 Metabolism of ethanol into acetaldehyde and acetic acid.

Something for You to Do

You can illustrate the interplay between absorption and elimination of alcohol using a plastic bucket or similar container and water. Get a one-gallon disposable paint bucket and punch a few holes in the bottom about the thickness of a pencil. Put the bucket on some sort of stand so that the holes in the bottom are not obstructed. Start adding water to the bucket. The level of water at any time represents the BAC. Adding water to the bucket represents the absorption of alcohol into the bloodstream. Water escaping through the holes represents the elimination of alcohol by metabolism and excretion in the urine. If you add water rapidly to the bucket, the level will rise quickly. If you slow down the addition of water so that it is escaping as fast as you are adding it, the level will remain constant. If you slow down the amount of water you add and then stop adding it altogether, the level will drop because it is escaping faster than you are adding it. You can see the analogies to the principles of alcohol absorption and elimination explained earlier.

These concepts are embodied in the results of work by Professor Erik Widmark at the University of Lund in Sweden in the early 1930s. The BAC level overtime is illustrated with the "Widmark curve" as shown in Figure 20.8.

Figure 20.8 shows two curves, one for alcohol on an empty stomach and one where the subject has eaten a plate of French fries before drinking. French fries are mostly carbohydrates that impede absorption of alcohol most efficiently. In both cases, the same amount of alcohol has been ingested. Several features of the curve (which is not to scale) are important to note. First, region "a" is where essentially only absorption taking place. Note that the absorption is slower in the case where food is present. At region "b," elimination is starting to take place but absorption still dominates. In region "c," both processes are taking place approximately equally. Note here that the BAC is much higher where drinking has taken place on an empty stomach and that it has taken longer for the

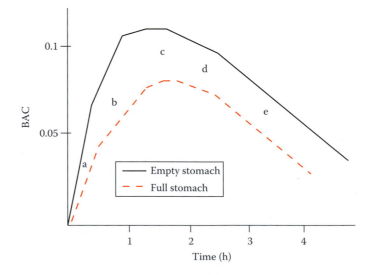

Figure 20.8 The Widmark curve. In region a, essentially only absorption of ethanol is taking place. In region b, some elimination by metabolism is beginning. In region c, the rates of absorption and elimination are approximately the same. In region d, absorption has slowed and elimination predominates. In region e, only elimination by metabolism and excretion by the urine is taking place at a constant rate.

maximum BAC to be reached. In region "d," elimination is starting to dominate, and in region "e," only elimination is taking place at the same constant rate in both cases.

How Much Drinking Does It Take to Get Drunk?

How much alcohol does it take to achieve a given BAC? Pharmacologists have worked out formulae that will give approximate numbers.

Given the following set of conditions, assume that

- Drinking is done on an empty stomach
- The drinks are 100-proof liquor and are taken in one swallow (volume is in ounces)
- Weight (wgt) is in pounds
- BAC is in g/dL

For a male:

$$\text{Volume} = \frac{\text{wgt} \times \text{BAC}}{3.78} \qquad (20.1)$$

For a female:

$$\text{Volume} = \frac{\text{wgt} \times \text{BAC}}{4.67} \qquad (20.2)$$

As an example, a 140 lb female wants to know how many ounces of liquor she can drink so that her BAC will just reach 0.08, the level at which she would be considered intoxicated in most states.

$$\text{Wgt} = 140, \text{BAC} = 0.08$$

$$\text{Volume} = \frac{140 \times 0.08}{4.67}$$

$$\text{Volume} = 2.4 \text{ oz}$$

One shot of whiskey contains about 1.25 oz, so this woman will be intoxicated after just two drinks. If she is drinking wine, then 10 oz would do the job, assuming that the wine contains 12% alcohol. If she is drinking beer, with an alcohol concentration of about 6%, then she could drink 20 oz of beer and her BAC would be 0.08. That is not even two beers!

Something for You to Do

Using the earlier equations, calculate how much 100-proof liquor, wine, and beer that a 140 lb man would have to drink in order to reach a level of 0.08 BAC. Then do the same calculation for yourself, using your own weight. You don't have to hand this in so be honest about your weight!

Drunk Driving Laws

Every state has a set of laws that seek to control drunk driving and punish people who drive while intoxicated. This starts when a person applies for a driver's license. When you sign your license, you are giving "implied consent" that you will submit to a blood or breath test if you are stopped for drunk driving. Refusal to submit to the test when requested by a law enforcement agent may result in your losing your license to drive whether or not you are subsequently found to be intoxicated. The action to take your license is done by the Bureau of Motor Vehicles or Secretary of State as an administrative procedure. The length of time you lose your license is usually between 90 and 180 days.

Testing Alcohol Levels

Most states use a breath testing instrument to obtain an alcohol level in the field. The venerable breathalyzer is still used in many places although it is being gradually replaced by portable breath testers. Breathalyzers work by a type of chemical reaction called "oxidation–reduction (redox)." In this type of reaction, electrons are moved from one substance to another, changing the valence state of one or more atoms. In the redox reaction that is the heart of the breathalyzer, alcohol participates in the reaction.

The major reaction is given as follows:

$$2K_2Cr_2O_7 + 3CH_3CH_2OH + 8H_2SO_4 \rightarrow 2Cr_2(SO_4)_3 + 2K_2SO_4 + 3CH_3COOH + 11H_2O$$

Potassium dichromate (orange) Ethanol Sulfuric acid Chromium sulfate (green) Potassium sulfate Acetic acid Water

(20.3)

The solution without alcohol starts out orange owing to the potassium dichromate. As alcohol is added, it changes the potassium dichromate to chromium sulfate, which is green. A spectrophotometer is used to measure the loss of the orange color. This loss is proportional to the amount of ethanol present. The subject introduces the alcohol into the instrument by breathing into a tube connected to the breathalyzer.

Newer breath testing instruments use fuel cell technology whereby the alcohol is part of a fuel cell that produces electricity. The more alcohol that is present, the more electricity is produced. Other instruments measure the amount of infrared light that is absorbed by alcohol. In most cases, the breath alcohol concentration measured by these instruments can be converted to BAC internally using the experimentally determined 210:1 ratio (210 L of breath contain the same amount of alcohol as one deciliter of blood).

Once a BAC level is determined in the field, how is it interpreted? How does the police officer or toxicologist know where on the Widmark curve the measurement is? This can be an important consideration in many drunk driving cases as can be seen in the following example:

A driver is stopped for operating a vehicle while intoxicated. The officer administers a breath test and determines that the BAC is 0.06. The driver was seen leaving a bar 2 h prior to the stop. If the toxicologist uses the rate of elimination figure of 0.015% per hour and back-calculates 2 h previously, then the

driver's BAC must have been 0.09 when he left the bar. (How did he arrive at
this number?) That means that the driver was intoxicated when he left the bar
and got behind the wheel because the law defines intoxication as a BAC of 0.08
or above.

Can the driver be prosecuted for operating a motor vehicle while intoxicated?
There are some prosecutors who will prosecute this as an intoxication case if they
can get a toxicologist to testify to this back-calculation. Most toxicologists are wary
of doing this because of the assumptions that have to be made. The most important
one is that the rate of elimination is exactly 0.015% in every person. This is known
to be not accurate. It could be higher or lower in a particular case. The only way to
find out would be to take a series of BAC or breath alcohol measurements overtime
on that particular person. In some states, there is a provision for charging a driver
with being *impaired* rather than intoxicated in cases where the BAC is over 0.05%
but less than 0.08% when the driver is stopped.

Field Sobriety Testing

Although drunk driving laws in most states require only that the driver's BAC be
over the limit in order to sustain a charge of operating a vehicle while intoxicated,
sometimes officers will want to document the impaired behavior of the driver when
the driver is stopped. Many states have adopted a field sobriety testing program
that was first developed in California. Officers who administer the suite of tests are
specially trained and certified. The suite includes three tests and all of them must
be done:

1. *Walk and turn*: The subject must walk in a straight line putting one foot
   directly in front of the other with the toe of one foot touching the heel of the
   other. People who are intoxicated will not be able to keep in a straight line
   and may lose their balance.
2. *Stand on one foot*: The subject must lift one foot and stand on the other for a
   period of time. People who are intoxicated will not be able to keep one foot off
   the ground or will lose their balance.
3. *Horizontal gaze nystagmus*: The officer holds a pencil or similar object about
   12″ in front of the subject's face at eye level. The officer then moves the pencil across the field of view of the subject, instructing the subject to keep the
   head still and follow the pencil only with the eyes. The eyes of a sober person
   will move smoothly as he follows the pencil back and forth. The eyes of an
   intoxicated person will travel with jerky movements when trying to follow
   the pencil.

In states that recognize the field sobriety testing program, the results of the tests
are admissible in court as evidence of impairment. Many illicit drugs will also elicit
similar responses to those of ethanol. If a person is driving erratically and stopped
for drunk driving and a breath testing instrument indicates that the subject wasn't
drinking, then the field sobriety testing program can show that the subject was
under the influence of an illicit drug.

Measurement of BAC

Drunk driving cases represent more than half of the caseload of forensic toxicologists nationwide. Even though the results of a breath test may be admissible in court as evidence of intoxication, many prosecutors require that a blood test be done to directly measure BAC. Some forensic science laboratories get dozens of blood samples each day that were taken from people suspected of driving while intoxicated. These people are taken to a hospital or clinic and have their blood drawn by a professional phlebotomist. The blood is then sent to the crime lab. The most popular method of BAC analysis in a forensic science lab is by gas chromatography using headspace analysis. The tube containing the blood is heated slightly and a gas tight syringe is inserted and a sample of the vapor above the blood is withdrawn and injected into a gas chromatograph. An internal standard is also put in the tube to help in the quantitative analysis of the alcohol in the blood. An automatic sampler is often used so that many blood samples can be run automatically overnight. A computer calculates the amount of ethanol present. The next day, the toxicologist interprets the findings and writes the reports.

Summary

Pharmacology is the study of the effects of drugs and poisons on living organisms. Forensic toxicologists determine the presence and amount of drugs and poisons in people and interpret their effects. They study the ingestion, absorption, and elimination of drugs from the body. They also have to be aware of synergistic effects and tolerance. In order to do proper interpretations of findings about drugs, the toxicologist must know the subject's drug history including any addictions or drug dependencies. The most commonly abused substance is ethyl alcohol, or ethanol. More than half of the caseload of forensic toxicologists is in drunk driving cases. The BAC is affected by the type of drinks, the amount of alcohol, how fast it is ingested, and what is in the stomach at the time of ingestion. Ethanol is a central nervous depressant and neurotoxin. It is eliminated from the body mainly by metabolism and excretion in the urine. The concentration of ethanol can be measured in either blood or breath. Field sobriety testing is also used as additional evidence of impairment.

Test Yourself

Multiple Choice

1. Which of the following is not a metabolite of ethanol?
   a. Acetaldehyde
   b. Acetone
   c. Acetic acid
   d. All of the above are metabolites of alcohol

2. Most drugs and ethanol are eliminated from the body mainly by
   a. Breathing
   b. Sweating
   c. Metabolism followed by excretion in the urine
   d. Decomposition by the kidneys
3. Synergism takes place when
   a. Someone becomes addicted to a drug
   b. A person has to take larger doses of a drug to get the same effects
   c. A drug is metabolized into two different substances
   d. Two drugs are taken at once and their effects magnify each other
4. When a person builds up tolerance to a drug, it means that
   a. He must take larger doses to continue to realize the same effects
   b. He will undergo withdrawal if he stops taking the drug
   c. He will no longer be affected by the drug
   d. He must stop taking the drug right away
5. Which of the following is not used in field sobriety testing?
   a. Walk and turn
   b. Count backwards from 100
   c. Horizontal gas nystagmus
   d. Stand on one foot
6. Which of the following would not affect the rate of absorption of ethanol into the bloodstream?
   a. How fast you drink
   b. The concentration of alcohol in the drink
   c. What is in the stomach at the time of drinking
   d. How soon before drinking you exercised
7. The Widmark curve displays
   a. The relationship between absorption and metabolism
   b. The blood alcohol level as a function of time
   c. The blood alcohol level as a function of metabolic rate
   d. The ratio between the amount of alcohol eliminated by metabolism to that eliminated by respiration
8. Synergism is
   a. A form of metabolism in the liver
   b. The buildup of drugs in fatty tissue
   c. The travel of drugs from the stomach to the small intestine
   d. The magnification of the effects of two or more drugs that have similar actions
9. Tolerance is
   a. The need for ever-increasing amounts of a drug the more it is taken
   b. The elimination of a drug directly through the urine without passing through the liver
   c. A measure of the activity of a drug on the brain
   d. Slowing down absorption of a drug into the bloodstream by the presence of food in the stomach
10. The most common surrogate for brain alcohol measurement in drunk driving cases is
   a. Blood
   b. Breath
   c. Urine
   d. Vitreous humor

True–False

11. Stopping taking an addictive drug will bring on symptoms of withdrawal.
12. If you are stopped for driving while intoxicated and you refuse to take a sobriety test, you can lose your driver's license.
13. The LD_{50} of alcohol is about 0.4 g/dL.
14. Marihuana is believed to exhibit a reverse tolerance effect at times.
15. The half-life of a drug is the time it takes to reduce its concentration in the blood by 50%.
16. The LD_{50} of a drug is the concentration of the drug that causes death in half the people who take that amount.
17. The amount of alcohol in the bloodstream that constitutes being under the influence in drunk driving cases is 1.0 g/dL.

Matching—Match each term with its definition

18. Toxicology
19. Pharmacology
20. Metabolism
21. Acetaldehyde
22. Half-life

a. Time it takes to decrease drug concentration by 50%
b. Substance that liver converts alcohol into
c. Study of harmful effects of drug and poisons
d. Study of all effects of drugs
e. Action of liver on drugs

Short Essay

23. What is the Widmark curve? What does it tell you about blood alcohol concentration?
24. What are the major methods for analyzing alcohol in the blood? Which one(s) can be used at the scene?
25. What is synergism? How does it work?

Further Reading

Garriott, J. C. (ed.). (1996). *Medicolegal Aspects of Alcohol*, 3rd edn. Lawyers and Judges Publishing Co., Tucson, AZ.
Levine, B. (ed.). (1999). *Principles of Forensic Toxicology*. AACC Press, Washington, DC.

On the Web

http://en.wikipedia.org/wiki/Forensic_toxicology—Good overview of forensic toxicology.
http://home.lightspeed.net/~abarbour/vlibft.html—Comprehensive list of forensic toxicology web sites.
http://www.soft-tox.org/—Homepage of Society of Forensic Toxicologists.
http://www.abft.org/—Homepage of American Board of Forensic Toxicologists, which offers certification of forensic toxicologists.

21
Fibers, Paints, and Other Polymers

Learning Objectives

1. To be able to define a monomer and polymer
2. To be able to describe the types of evidence that are polymer based
3. To be able to define paint
4. To be able to describe the different types of paint by end use
5. To be able to describe how paint evidence is encountered, collected, and preserved
6. To be able to describe the common methods of analysis of paint
7. To be able to describe the different types of fibers
8. To be able to describe the common types of natural fibers
9. To be able to describe the common types of synthetic fibers
10. To be able to describe how fiber evidence is encountered, collected, and preserved
11. To be able to describe the common methods of analysis of fibers
12. To be able to describe how other types of polymer-based evidence are analyzed

Chapter 21
Fibers, Paints, and Other Polymers

Chapter Outline

Mini Glossary

Clear coat: The final layer of paint applied to an automobile that adds durability and ultraviolet protection to the colored paint layer.

Dye: Generally organic substances that bind to fiber and absorb various wavelengths of light, producing a colored appearance.

Fracture match: Matching broken objects to the original source.

FTIR: Acronym for Fourier transform infrared spectrophotometry. FTIR microscopy is used to analyze the composition of small objects.

Metamerism: The quality of some colors that causes them to appear differently under different light sources. For instance, two color samples may look identical in natural light but not in artificial light.

Monomer: Single repeating units of molecules.

Natural fiber: A fiber that exists in nature. Natural fibers can come from animals, plants, or minerals.

Pigment: Mostly inorganic particles, small in size and insoluble; they suspend in the chemical mixture of a fiber and absorb different wavelengths of light.

Polymer: Long chains of repeating molecular units or long chains of monomers.

Primer: The primer layer is the coating layer applied to the unpainted automobile—the first layer applied after the bare metal has been treated for rust.

PyGC: An acronym for pyrolysis gas chromatography, an instrumental technique used to analyze the chemical compositions of small amounts of evidence.

Refractive index: A number that represents the ratio between the speed of light in air and the speed of light in the medium analyzed.

Semisynthetic fiber: A fiber that is sourced to a natural, nonfibrous material but undergoes chemical processing to produce a fiber.

Synthetic fiber: Fibers that are man-made chemical compounds formed into predetermined fiber shapes by extrusion from a machine.

Tear match: Two materials that have been ripped in pieces that can be shown to match based on examination (usually microscopically) of the patterns.

Topcoat: The coating layer for an automobile that imparts the color to the vehicle.

Acronyms

DNA: Deoxyribonucleic acid
FBI: Federal Bureau of Investigation
PyGC: Pyrolysis Gas Chromatography
THC: Tetrahydrocannabinol

Introduction

On July 28, 1979, a woman hunting for empty cans and bottles along an Atlanta, Georgia roadside stumbled upon a pair of dead African-American males. One had been shot and the coroner later determined that the other had been choked to death. Both had been reported missing for about a week. Thus, the investigation of a string of homicides of young, black males in the Atlanta area began. Ultimately, Wayne Bertram Williams was blamed for 23 of 30 homicides. He was convicted of the deaths of two of them, both adult ex-convicts. Williams became a suspect when officers starting staking out bridges over the Chattahoochee River because several of the victims had been dumped into the river. On May 22, 1981, an officer heard a splash in the water. At the same time, a car drove across the bridge near where the officer was stationed. He radioed to FBI and police nearby who stopped Williams and then interrogated him for over 2 hours and then released him. On June 21, Williams was arrested and charged with the murders of Nathaniel Carter and Jimmy Payne.

Since there were no witnesses to the killings, no fingerprints on the bodies, and DNA typing had not yet been developed, trace evidence became very important in this case. Dog hairs that matched Wayne Williams' dog and carpet fibers that matched known fibers from his car and office were found on a number of the victims. The FBI took great pains to research the fibers from Williams' office. They traced the fibers back to the manufacturer and followed the trail to carpet manufacturers who used the fibers to make carpets. They determined how many yards of carpeting were made from this type of fiber and estimated how many yards were sold in Atlanta. They also made estimates of the number of rooms in homes and apartments in the Atlanta area and, from that, estimated the likelihood that a room contained a carpet of the same type as Wayne Williams' office. They were able to testify that the fibers in Wayne Williams' office were rare and that the fibers of this type found on the victims were likely to have come from his office. Williams was subsequently convicted of the murders and is currently serving a life sentence in prison.

This chapter covers several types of forensic evidence. They may seem to be different from each other, but they share common characteristics. First, they are all *polymers*. This means that they have a special chemical structure that dictates how they will be analyzed. The major types of polymer evidence are paints, other coatings, and textile fibers. Other polymers are less frequently encountered and include plastics, rubber, and paint-like products such as varnishes, shellacs, stains, and even some types of inks. Human and animal hairs are also polymers, but they are different enough from the other types of polymer evidence that they will be covered in a separate chapter. Another aspect that these objects share is that they are examples of *trace evidence*. Trace evidence is evidence that occurs in small quantities or that is naturally small in size.

What Is a Polymer?

Most substances are arranged in relatively small, discrete molecules. They tend to have relatively low boiling and melting points (except for metals). There is a class of materials that exist as long chains of repeating molecular units. These chains are called polymers. The repeating units are called *monomers*. The general structure of polymers is shown in Figure 21.1.

Figure 21.2 shows a substance called styrene. When it polymerizes, it forms long, repeating units called polystyrene, also shown in Figure 21.2. The part of the molecule inside the parentheses is the repeating unit. Polystyrene is a common plastic and also a member of a subclass of polymers called *homopolymers*. These are polymers with only one repeating unit. Because of this, few modifications can easily be made to the polymer, and therefore, few subgroups are possible.

Monomer unit

Figure 21.1 General chemical structure of a polymer.

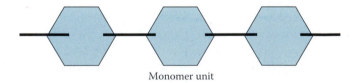

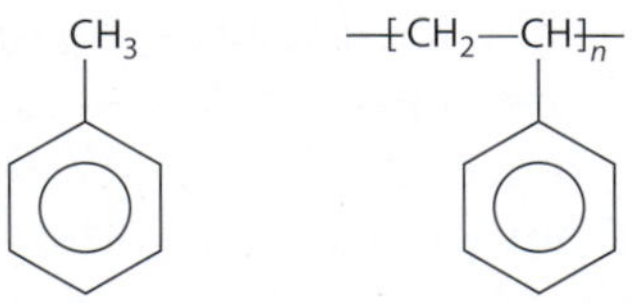

Figure 21.2 The chemical structure of styrene (left) and polystyrene (right).

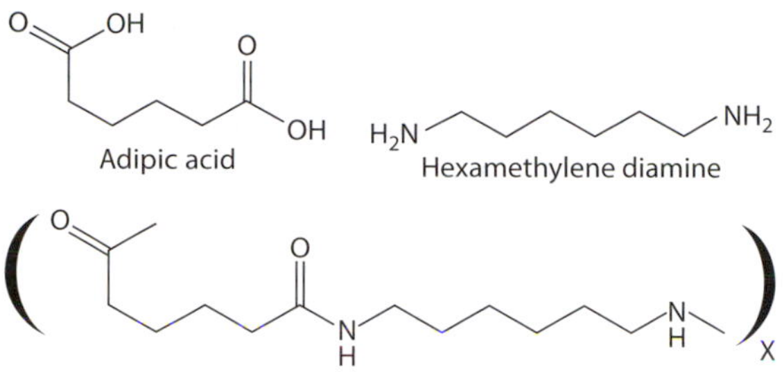

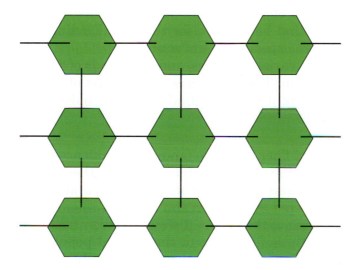

Figure 21.3 The chemical structure of one of the nylon polymers.

Figure 21.4 Cross-linking of polymers to form two-dimensional films.

Some polymers use two (or more) monomers to construct a polymer. These are called *copolymers*. An example of a copolymer is *nylon*. The term nylon actually refers to a family of polymers. There are currently more than 40 different types of nylon being commercially manufactured. One of the common types of nylon is nylon 66. This is made up of alternating monomers. One of them is *adipic acid*, a diacid containing six carbons. The other monomer is *hexamethylenediamine*, a diamine containing six carbons. The two monomers react by a process known as condensation. A molecule of adipic acid loses an OH group and the diamine loses an H. Water is formed and the two molecules combine to form an *amide*. This is shown in Figure 21.3.

Finally, there are *block polymers*. These contain blocks of similar monomers that repeat. Polymers form long chains of monomers and are fibrous in shape. They are ideal for use as textile fibers. If the polymer is to be used to make sheets as in plastics, rubber, or paints, the polymer strands are *cross-linked*. These cross-links are small molecules that attach two strands together as shown diagrammatically in Figure 21.4.

Textile Fibers

Textile fibers are very common in our environment. They are used in the manufacture of clothing, automobile seats and carpets, home furnishings, and a host of other items. Depending on the characteristics of the fabric, fibers may be easily shed.

Figure 21.6 T.I.S. identification key for dye stain testing of fabric.

types of fiber using microscopic methods and Figure 21.6 shows a comparison chart for dye matching.

Size: Fibers range in diameter from 10 to 50 μm (micrometers) or from 2×10^{-3} to 4×10^{-4} inches. Naturally occurring fibers are measured in micrometers (μm). Synthetic fibers are usually measured in denier. This is a measure of the weight of a bundle of fibers that is 9000 meters long. More dense fibers will have higher deniers.

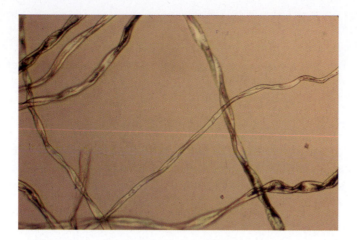

Figure 21.7 Photomicrograph of cotton fibers. Note the natural twist in the fibers.

Cross section: Not all fibers are round. Their cross sections may give a clue to their end use. For example, many carpet fibers are trilobal or bilobal. Synthetic fibers can have any of hundreds of cross-sectional shapes.

Color: Many natural fibers are white or some shade of brown. They are usually bleached before they are dyed. Fibers are colored by either dyeing them or printing a pattern directly onto the fabric. An individual fiber that has been dyed will usually have a uniform appearance under a microscope, whereas a fiber that has been printed may be uneven in color.

Crimp: Some fibers have a natural wave or twist. Cotton is one of these fibers and its twisting nature is shown in Figure 21.7. Synthetic fibers must have a wave mechanically applied. The crimp value is the number of crimps per unit length.

Analysis of Synthetic Fibers

There are a number of physical and chemical tests for individual fibers. No amount of testing will result in individualization of a fiber to a particular fabric. If the evidence consists of a piece of torn fabric and the possible source is also available, then it may be possible to individualize the torn piece by way of a *tear match*. This is illustrated in Figure 21.8. In such cases, it is helpful if the tear is irregular and/ or if there is a pattern to the fabric.

Figure 21.8 A fabric tear match.

Microscopy

A great deal can be discerned from microscopic analysis of fibers. General characteristics of the fiber such as color, length, diameter, and cross-sectional shape can be viewed.

Cross Section

Many fibers are manufactured with particular shapes optimized for end use. For example, many carpet fibers are trilobal because this shape helps to hide dirt and gives the carpet a desired feel and texture. Figure 21.9 shows some trilobal fibers in cross section.

Diameter

Measurement of the diameter of a round fiber is straightforward. However, many fibers are not round. They may be oval, elongated, bilobal, or trilobal. The method for determining the diameter of a fiber depends on the shape. For example, oval and elongated fibers have two diameters and both are recorded. Figure 21.10 shows some fibers and how their cross sections are measured.

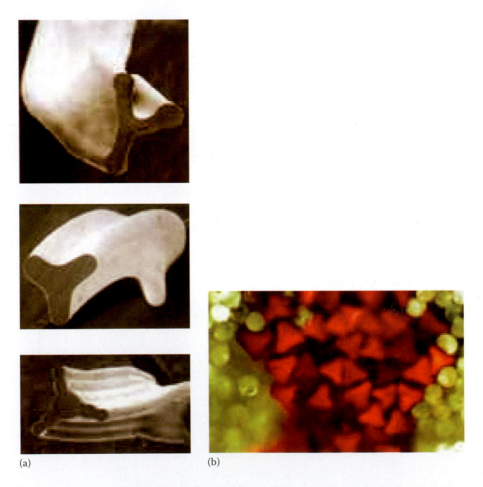

(a)   (b)

Figure 21.9 Cross section of trilobal synthetic fibers using a scanning electron microscope (a) and a regular microscope (b). (From Deedrick, D.W., *Forensic Sci. Commun.*, 2(3), July 2007. www.fbi. gov/hq/lab /fsc/backis su/july2000/deedric 3.htm#Index (Fibers).)

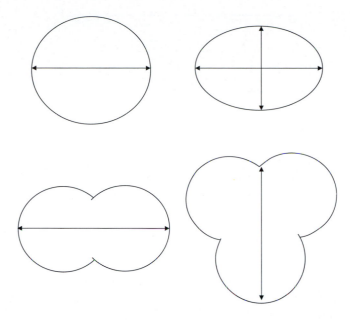

Figure 21.10 How diameters of various fiber shapes are measured.

Delusterants

Many synthetic fiber polymers are shiny when exposed to light. This may give an undesired sheen to the fabric. Delusterants are finely ground materials, usually titanium dioxide, introduced into the chemical mixture from which the fiber is made. They scatter light and reduce the luster of the fabric. Different manufacturers use different delusterants as well as different shapes, sizes, and distributions of delusterant particles. These characteristics help in determining the degree of association of known and unknown fibers.

Refractive Index

A discussion of how refractive indices are measured in liquids and solids is presented in Chapter 22. Like glass, fibers are transparent and also exhibit the property of *refractive index*. (Refractive index is a measure of the speed light travels through a transparent substance as compared its speed in air.) One difference, however, is that the shape of a fiber may cause it to have more than one refractive index. Many fibers have two refractive indices because light will travel at a different speed depending on whether it is traveling the length of the fiber or through the diameter of the fiber. This is shown in Figure 21.11. Even if a fiber is not round, there will not be enough of a difference in refractive indices between the various diameters of the fiber to be detected.

Color

A microscope isn't needed to examine the colors of fibers. The human eye is a remarkable instrument for discerning colors and shades of differences in color when known and unknown fibers are viewed under the same light conditions. There are two problems with this method in examining scientific evidence. First, examination by the eye is qualitative and subjective. There is no objective or numerical measurement that would confirm that two fibers are the same color. The other problem is called *metamerism*. It is possible for two fibers or other objects to appear to be exactly the

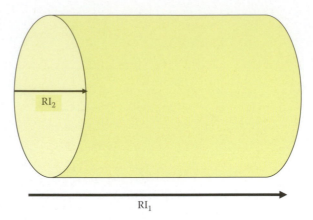

Figure 21.11 Two refractive indices of a round fiber.

same color to the eye under one set of light conditions but actually be different colors when measured under a different set of conditions. To guard against this, a visible microspectrophotometer should be used to obtain the visible spectrum of the fiber. This will objectively determine the exact color of the fiber and will prove that two fibers have or do not have the same color. Microspectrophotometry is discussed in Chapters 5 and 6.

Color is imparted to fibers using *dyes* and *pigments*. Dyes are generally organic substances that absorb visible light. They are soluble in the chemicals from which the fiber will be produced and are introduced during production. Pigments are generally, but not always, colored inorganic materials. They are finely divided into small particles that are generally insoluble. They can be suspended in the chemical mixture as the fiber is made or bonded to the surface of the fiber after manufacture. Coloring fibers can be a complex process. There are more than a dozen ways that dyes and pigments can be applied. Most fabrics are dyed with more than one dye and are dyed in batches rather than in a continuous process. Because of this, there will virtually always be slight differences in dye colors and concentrations from batch to batch of the same fabric. This can be a useful characteristic when comparing fibers.

Fibers may also be colored by printing colored patterns onto the surface of the fabric. This is more akin to painting than dyeing.

Chemical Analysis of Fibers

Fibers contain a polymer backbone and one or more dyes or pigments. There may also be delustering agents added during manufacturing. Some chemical examinations are performed on a fiber as a whole. It is also possible to extract dyes from the fibers and analyze them separately.

Analysis of Fibers as a Whole

There are two major methods for analyzing the chemical composition of fibers.

1. *Fourier transform infrared spectrophotometry (FTIR)* microscopy is widely used in crime labs. It is nondestructive and cannot only determine what broad class the fiber belongs to but can also identify the subclass. For example,

nylon 66 can be differentiated from nylon 6–12 by FTIR. The microscope permits the analysis of one single fiber. FTIR microscopy is discussed in Chapter 5.

2. *Pyrolysis gas chromatography* (*PyGC*) is also used to analyze fibers. A pyrogram can be generated from as little as $1/8$ in. of fiber, but it is a destructive technique. It is superior to FTIR in distinguishing closely related fibers because it is sensitive to small differences in chemical makeup of the fibers. PyGC is discussed in Chapter 4.

Examples of FTIR and PyGC testing results will be illustrated in the next section about paints.

In addition to the aforementioned analytical tests, other examinations may be employed on fibers. Different classes of fibers are soluble in different solvents. Although this test is destructive, *solubility* can be accomplished using very little fiber and can be a quick way of determining the class to which a fiber belongs.

Dye Analysis

Dyes can be extracted from fibers using organic solvents. The particular solvent used depends on the type of fiber and dye. Once extracted, dyes are usually analyzed by thin layer chromatography. The dyes are not identified. Dyes from known and unknown fibers can be compared by this method. More recently, liquid chromatography/mass spectrometry has been employed in the analysis of fiber dyes. This method can be used to both separate and identify the individual dyes.

Interpretation of Fiber Evidence

As mentioned previously, target fiber studies show that most fibers occur infrequently in the environment. The main exception would be indigo-dyed cotton (blue jeans). This means that, if known and unknown fibers are similar in all physical and chemical respects, the degree of association is likely to be high. This is not the same as individualizing the evidence. *Only a tear match can individualize fibers.*

Fiber evidence can also assist in piecing together a crime. Fibers are easily transferred from one fabric to another or from a fabric to another surface such as a chair seat. Once transferred, the fibers may persist on the recipient object or be easily transferred again (secondary transfer). Analyzing the journey of fibers from one place to another can help determine whether the wearer of the source of the fibers was at the scene of the crime. There have been a number of recent studies concerning primary and subsequent transfers of hairs and fibers as well as the ease of transfer and persistence of fibers.

Paints and Other Coatings

In 1996, a man was injured when driving his motorcycle through the downtown streets of Detroit, Michigan. He claimed that he was sideswiped by a white Detroit Police Department car. This caused him to lose control of his motorcycle and career into another police car that was parked on the street. The man was

Automotive paints are, by far, the most commonly encountered paints in forensic science. Automobiles are always painted with several layers of paint, each one of a different type. The layer structure of automotive paints presents some interesting analytical challenges and evidentiary opportunities that are not usually found with other types of paint. For this reason, the remainder of the chapter focuses on automotive paints, although the sections on collection and analysis could be generalized to the other types (structural and artistic).

How Cars Are Painted

Most cars have four coats within the paint finish when they are first manufactured. The exception would be some luxury cars that have more than one topcoat layer. Two coats of rustproofing are first applied to the car by bathing it in a pool of liquefied zinc and then an electroplate process is used. After this, the *primer* is applied. This is also done by electroplating. The pigments in this paint are designed to minimize corrosion of the body of the car. The color of the pigments is similar to that of the topcoat layers.

The next layer is the topcoat. This is the layer that imparts color to the car. It may contain metallic or pearlescent pigments that provide unique color effects. Traditionally, topcoats have been lacquers or more expensive enamel paints that use organic solvents. Today, water-based systems are more environmentally friendly. Topcoats usually dry by heat (thermosetting).

The final layer of paint is the *clear coat*. At one time, only the most expensive cars received clear coating, but today, all new cars have this top layer. The clear coat is acrylic or urethane based and has no pigments. It imparts extra durability and ultraviolet light resistance.

Each coat of paint imparts a layer to the overall paint job. A cross section of the paint on a car would show each layer. Many cars are repainted after an accident or simply because the owner wants to spruce up the car. Depending on the circumstances, different parts of the car may have different layer structures. This has implications on how paint evidence is collected from cars suspected of being involved in crashes or crimes.

Collection of Paint Evidence

Paint evidence comes in two types: *chips* (*flakes*) and *smears*. Paint chips contain most or all of the layers in the paint. Figure 21.13 shows paint chips from two different colored cars in a cross-sectional view. During a crash, paint chips may fall from the car and be transferred to a person or another object and even another car. Because the layer structure is intact, paint chips provide the most information in analysis. There are a number of methods used to remove chips of paint from a car surface. If the chips are loose, they can be pried off. If not, a sharp scalpel or knife is used to cut the chips out. The knife must cut all the way down to the surface on which the paint was applied to make sure that all the layers are collected.

Paint smears are much more difficult to handle. Paint smears usually consist of just the top layer of paint. When the top layer is a clear coat, it may be difficult to see the transferred paint. Smears are often transferred when an automobile sideswipes

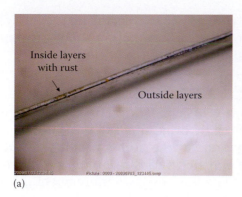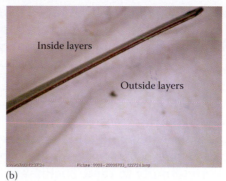

(a)   (b)

Figure 21.13 The photos are cross-sectional views of paint chips taken from a black car (a) and a red car (b). The black vehicle was an older car and showed evidence of rust on the inner coating of the paint chip.

Figure 21.14 The impact site of a two-car automobile crash. Known paint samples should be collected near this site but not along any portion of the crushed area.

another object. When the other object is a car, it is even more difficult to interpret a smear since it may be mixed in with other layers of paint.

Proper collection of known samples of paint from an automobile is critical to successful analysis. Like most forensic evidence, paint analysis is most valuable when the unknown can be compared with the known. It is important to collect all of the layers of paint in the known sample. Where the paint is collected from is just as important. In general, known paint samples should not be collected from the damaged area of the car, such as the driver's side of the car as shown in Figure 21.14. It is likely that foreign materials from the object that the car hit or that hit the car have gotten into the paint. Paint from the other object may have become intermixed with paint that is original to the car. The best practice is to gather known samples from *undamaged* areas as near as possible to the damaged area. Taking paint far away from the damaged area can be misleading. Parts of cars may have been repainted or even replaced and the characteristics of the paint in those parts may be very different from those in the damaged area.

Paint smears should not be removed from the surface of the object at the scene. The entire object or car part should be sent to the laboratory where the smear can be removed.

Paint chips should never be taped to a card or other object. The chip may be difficult to remove from the tape and the tape adhesive can contaminate the paint chip and perhaps rendering chemical testing ineffective.

Malcolm Fairley Case

In 1984, England was stricken with a series of crimes from an unknown assailant. The perpetrator began the crime spree by breaking and entering homes in quiet neighborhoods and stealing money and various items from the homeowners. As time passed, the criminal nature of his crimes escalated from robbery, to assault, and finally to rape. Nicknamed "The Fox" by law enforcement, Malcolm Fairley would break into homes, sometimes while the owners were away, watch videos under tents made from blankets and furniture, and eat food from the kitchen. Due to this type of behavior, the police coined his nickname. When the homeowners returned to their residence, he would tie them up and rob and/or assault them.

During one of his later robberies, Fairley recovered a shotgun from his victim. He used the gun to intimidate others during subsequent crimes. Although he claimed it was not loaded and he had no intent of shooting anyone, the possession of the gun was enough impetus to intensify the severity of his crimes from robbery to rape.

Fairley could not be identified by his victims because he wore masks during his crimes. One mask was a leg cut from a pair of trousers with two slits cut into the pant leg for the eyes. Although he did not kill anyone, Fairley assaulted the females, threatened the males with the gun in their faces, and then raped the female while the male watched. He would then leave with some of their possessions and money. This continued for almost a year, and at one point, the shotgun went off and hit a male victim in the leg. Fairley was shocked by this and decided to hide the gun, mask, and gloves in a wooded area. The burial was the beginning of his downfall. After hiding the items under some brush, The Fox's British Leyland car scraped a tree and left a paint trail. There were paint flecks on the branches.

Police found the mask, gloves, and gun, and then happened on the tire tracks that led them to the scraped tree. They took samples, analyzed them, and identified them as the Harvest Yellow color of a British Leyland vehicle. The task then was to question the thousands of owners of that class and color of car. Upon questioning various owners, one office located Malcolm Fairley washing his scraped Harvest Yellow vehicle. They searched his property and also found the trousers with a leg missing, the match to his mask. The Fox, Malcolm Fairley, was apprehended, put on trial, and sent to prison for this crime spree. He was sentenced in London to six life sentences but has been released under a new identity after serving 20 years.

Analysis of Paint

Paint possesses a number of physical and chemical properties that can be exploited in the analysis and comparison of paint. Some focus on the pigments, while others target the binders. Others are performed on the paint sample as a whole.

Physical Properties

The most important characteristic of paint as evidence is the *color layer sequence*. Automotive paints and some structural paints contain layers. In the case of automotive paints, each layer may have a different composition and color. If an unknown paint sample and a known sample have different color layer sequences, then the known can be eliminated as a source for the unknown. It is well known that the weakest bond in an automotive paint job is the bond between the bottom layer of paint and the bare metal. Even so, paint chips may break off between layers of paint and not all layers may be present. In this case, the known and unknown may still have a common source, even if all of the layers are not present. This is shown in Figure 21.15 where A is an unknown paint chip and B and C are knowns. Note that B can be the source of A even though it has extra layers. A could have sheared off between the top layer of rust proofing and the primer layer whereas B was collected all the way down to the metal.

The exact colors of each layer of the paint can be confirmed using visible microspectrophotometry. In this case, the layers will have to be analyzed separately. This can be done by making "peels," peeling each layer off using a sharp scalpel. A cross section of the paint can also be made using a microtome and each layer can then be analyzed separately. Figure 21.16 shows a cross section of a paint sample.

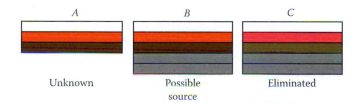

A — Unknown

B — Possible source

C — Eliminated

Figure 21.15 Color layer analysis of paint. Note that the only difference between the paint in A and B is that there are two more layers in B. In a real case, this could mean that a paint chip could have sheared off between the third and fourth layer, giving a chip such as A. Thus, the automobile painted with paint B could still be the source of the unknown A. The paint chip C cannot be the source of the unknown because the second layer (topcoat) is clearly a different color.

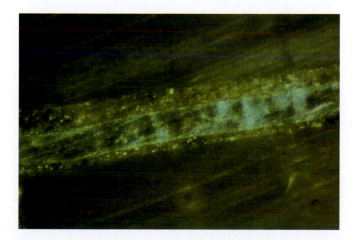

Figure 21.16 A cross section of a real paint chip showing three layers.

Chemical Properties

Solubility

Automobile paints may contain different binders. This can be a function of the man-ufacturer (General Motors used to employ only acrylic lacquers) or the cost of the car. Different binders may be soluble in different solvents or not soluble in any com-mon solvent. The acrylic lacquers used in GM cars were the only automobile paints soluble in acetone. A tiny paint chip is put in a white spot plate under a stereomi-croscope. A drop of solvent is added. The paint may be insoluble, soluble, or partially soluble. The pigments almost never dissolve.

Chromatography

Paints must be pyrolyzed if they are to be chromatographed. Typically a paint chip is analyzed intact and pyrolyzed at about 600°C–800°C. The resulting pyrogram will be a composite of all of the binders present in the paints. In general, the pigments will not appear in pyrolysis if they are inorganic. Figure 21.17 shows a pyrogram of an automobile paint sample. Figure 21.18 depicts sample pyrograms of two types of paint.

Infrared Microspectrophotometry

Infrared spectra of paints can be obtained in one of two ways. The entire paint chip can be ground up and mixed with potassium bromide and pressed into a pellet. The transmission spectrum of the paint as a whole can then be obtained. This spectrum will be a composite, which contains peaks for all of the binders and dyes, if any, that are present in the paint. This is useful for comparing one paint chip with another but is not used to determine the nature of a single binder. Another way to obtain a spectrum of paint is to make peels and run the transmission spectrum of each layer.

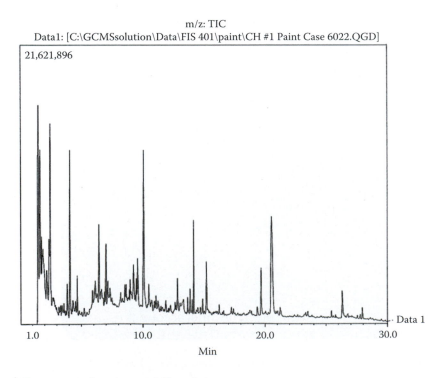

Figure 21.17 Pyrogram of an automobile paint.

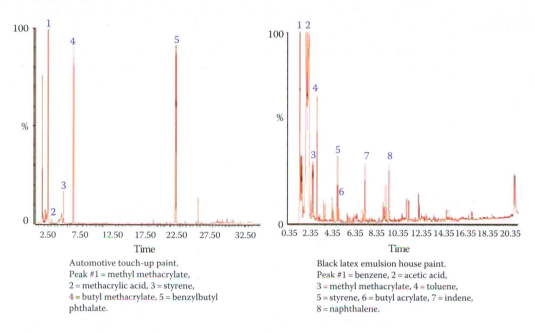

Automotive touch-up paint.
Peak #1 = methyl methacrylate,
2 = methacrylic acid, 3 = styrene,
4 = butyl methacrylate, 5 = benzylbutyl
phthalate.

Black latex emulsion house paint.
Peak #1 = benzene, 2 = acetic acid,
3 = methyl methacrylate, 4 = toluene,
5 = styrene, 6 = butyl acrylate, 7 = indene,
8 = naphthalene.

Figure 21.18 Sample pyrograms of vehicle touch-up paint and house paint.

Figure 21.19 Infrared spectrum of an automobile paint.

Finally, a cross section can be made of the paint chip, and each layer can be viewed and analyzed under the microscope attached to the FTIR. Figure 21.19 shows the infrared spectrum of a paint chip. The sample was prepared by pressing the chip into a pellet with potassium bromide (KBr).

Pigments

Most pigments are inorganic. Many are colored minerals. One of the best ways to analyze pigments is by scanning electron microscopy with energy-dispersive x-ray analysis (SEM/EDX). This will show what elements are present and in what relative concentrations. This method is quick and practically nondestructive. It is a good complement to color analysis. As mentioned previously, peels or cross sections of paint chips can be analyzed for color by visible microspectrophotometry.

Paint Smears

Paint smears can present significant problems. If they are transferred to another surface by impact, they may be practically fused to the paint on that surface. They can be very difficult to remove. In many cases, there is mostly pigment present in the smear, and SEM/EDX may be the best way to characterize the smear. If it can be removed, visible microspectrophotometry can be used to determine the colors. If there is sufficient binder present, then FTIR and PyGC can be utilized in the analysis.

Evidentiary Value of Paint

With few exceptions, paint is class evidence. Mass production of automobiles at a single factory using robots means that many car paint jobs will be chemically and physically too similar to distinguish. Thus, paint analysis can easily eliminate a car from consideration but cannot individualize it. There are rare cases when a large paint chip is broken off a car and it can be *fracture matched* back to the original spot, but these occurrences are extremely rare.

With structural paints, the situation is the same. Usually, homes or objects will have only one layer of paint, and the color layer sequence will be absent. Many structural paints are applied by brush or roller, and the layers tend to be thicker than with automobiles. This means that the chance of finding a large enough paint chip to fracture match is increased, although this situation is still relatively rare.

Summary

Paints and fibers are examples of polymers, which are long chain molecules made up of repeating links or monomers. Fibers can be natural or synthetic. Natural fibers can be of plant, mineral, or animal origin. There are many varieties of synthetic fibers. Fibers are normally class evidence, except when large pieces of fabric can be fit together in a tear match. Fibers are long molecules with a variety of cross-sectional shapes. These are often designed for particular end uses and knowing the cross-sectional shape can give a clue to the possible source of the fiber. Fibers are analyzed using microscopy to describe the cross section, diameter, color, and refractive indices. FTIR and PyGC are used to characterize the polymers in the fiber. Dyes can be extracted and chromatographed for comparing known and unknown fibers. Fibers are easily shed and transferred to other objects. This can help in showing that a particular garment may have been worn to a crime scene.

Paints are also polymers, but the strands are cross-linked so that the polymer forms sheets. Paints are made up of binders that hold the pigments on the surface. Pigments impart color to the paint. There are other additives in paint that give it desirable characteristics. Automotive paints are the most commonly found types of paint evidence. Each automobile is painted with several layers of different types of paints, including rustproofing layers, primer, topcoat, and clear coat. Physical properties of paint, including color layer sequence, are measured. The pigments in paint are analyzed using SEM. The binders are analyzed using FTIR, solubility, and PyGC. Paint is normally class evidence unless it can be fracture matched back to a source, a rare occurrence.

Test Yourself

Multiple Choice

1. Which of the following fibers does *not* have a natural origin?
   a. Wool
   b. Rayon
   c. Silk
   d. Nylon
2. Which of the following fibers is animal in origin?
   a. Cotton
   b. Silk
   c. Asbestos
   d. Linen
3. Which of the following fibers is partially natural and partially artificial?
   a. Wool
   b. Rayon
   c. Silk
   d. Nylon
4. Which of the following fibers is *not* animal in origin?
   a. Cashmere
   b. Silk
   c. Linen
   d. Wool
5. Which of the following tests can individualize fiber evidence?
   a. Burn testing
   b. Solvent testing
   c. Refractive index
   d. Tear matching
6. Which of the following tests can individualize paint evidence?
   a. SEM analysis
   b. FTIR analysis
   c. Fracture matching
   d. Color layering
7. A fiber is examined under the microscope and it has a twisted appearance. The class of this fiber could be
   a. Cotton
   b. Wool
   c. Polyester
   d. Rayon
8. A polymer constructed with two or more monomers is called
   a. Homopolymer
   b. Copolymer
   c. Cross-linked polymer
   d. Block polymer

True–False

9. Paints and fibers are similar because they are examples of trace evidence.
10. It is possible to define the trail of a perpetrator by due to multiple transfers of fiber.
11. It is not possible to individualize a suspect fabric piece to a crime scene sample.
12. Forensically, there are only two paints that are most commonly analyzed for evidence: automotive (in accidents) and artistic (in forgeries).
13. Automotive paint can have four or more layers of paint finish.

Short Answer

14. What is a polymer? A monomer?
15. Define and give an example of a homopolymer and a copolymer.
16. What is paint? What are the major ingredients?
17. What is a fiber? What are the major types?
18. Why do some fibers have more than one refractive index?
19. Name and briefly describe the different layers of automobile paint.
20. What is a paint "peel"? What purpose does it have in paint analysis?
21. What is denier? What does it measure?
22. What does thermosetting mean?
23. What is color layer sequence? Why is it important in paint analysis?

Short Essay

24. A red fiber is found interlaced in the hair of a victim. Describe what types of tests and procedures might be performed to identify and trace the origin of the fiber.
25. A three-vehicle accident occurs. The three vehicles involved are different colors: blue, silver, and red. The investigator wants to take evidence from the crash to substantiate victim's stories of what happened in the crash. It is noted by the investigator that all three cars have paint transfer marks on them, and the colors seem similar to the vehicles involved. Describe in detail the proper procedure that should be followed to obtain evidence from the scene.

Matching

Match the fiber with its correct category.

26. Cotton   a. Natural
27. Acetate   b. Synthetic
28. Rayon   c. Semisynthetic
29. Asbestos
30. Linen

Further Reading

Caddy, B. (ed.). (2001). *Forensic Examination of Glass and Paint*. Taylor & Francis, New York.
Robertson, J. and M. Grieve (eds.). (1999). *Forensic Examination of Fibres*, 2nd edn. Taylor & Francis, New York.
Thornton, J. L. (2002). Forensic paint examination, in *Forensic Science Handbook*, R. Saferstein, ed. vol. 1, 2nd edn. Prentice Hall, Upper Saddle River, NJ.

On the Web

http://science.howstuffworks.com/forensic-lab-technique3.htm.
http://pslc.ws/macrog/lab/lab01.htm.
www.enotes.com/forensic-science/paint-analysis.
www.fbi.gov/hq/lab/fsc/backissu/july2000/deedric3.htm#Index.
www.forensic.santoshraut.com/physics.htm.

22
Glass and Soil

Learning Objectives

1. To be able to define and classify glass
2. To be able to define soil
3. To be able to define fracture match
4. To be able to sequence multiple fractures
5. To be able to determine direction of force on a piece of glass
6. To be able to define refractive index
7. To be able to describe the Becke line method for determining refractive index
8. To be able to describe the common methods for the analysis of soil

Chapter 22
Glass and Soil

Chapter Outline

Mini Glossary

Amorphous: This means to have no definite shape, form, or structure.

Becke line: The white line or "halo" around a solid object (in this case, glass) that has been immersed in a liquid medium, visible when viewed under a polarized light microscope.

Concentric fracture: The lines of fracture that tend to form a circle around the point of impact on a piece of glass.

Conchoidal lines: Curved stress lines along the side of a fractured piece of glass.

Fracture match: Fitting a piece of evidence into the source, like fitting a puzzle piece into a jigsaw puzzle, individualizing that piece of evidence.

Hot stage microscope: A special type of microscope in which the stage or platform for the slide changes temperature, heating the slide mounted on the stage.

Humus: The organic material in soil comprised of decayed plant and animal material.

ICP/MS: Inductively coupled plasma mass spectrometer, an instrument used to analyze the chemical composition of a sample material.

Radial fracture: The lines of fracture that extend outward from the point of impact on a piece of glass.

Refraction: The bending of light due to a change in speed as it travels from one medium to another of different density.

Refractive index: A measure of how the speed of light is reduced as it travels through a medium as compared to its speed of light in a vacuum.

Soil: A mixture of crushed rock, minerals, and decayed plant and animal materials.

Acronym

ICP/MS: Inductively coupled plasma mass spectrometer
RI: Refractive index

Introduction

On February 9, 1960, Adolph Coors III, an heir to the Coors Brewing Company and fortune, is kidnapped and killed on a bridge near his home near Morrison, Colorado, in what was eventually determined to be a botched ransom demand. The kidnapper was Joseph Corbett, who had been working at the Coors brewery so he could stalk Coors and determine his habits. Prior to the kidnapping, Corbett bought a 1951 four-door Mercury car under the name of Walter Osborne. Residents near the sight of the kidnapping saw the car parked there several times before the incident took place. A few days before the kidnapping, Corbett quit his job at the Coors brewery.

Newspaper headlines after Coors' disappearance.

On February 9, Coors left his home for the brewery. On the way, he was kidnapped. Residents near the home heard shouting and a crack that sounded like a gun. Later, a witness saw Coors' truck parked with the engine running on a bridge at the kidnapping site. Coors had apparently resisted the kidnapping attempt and was killed at the scene and put in the trunk. Later that day, Corbett mailed a $500,000 ransom note to Coors' wife. The next day, he drove up into the Rocky Mountains near Pikes' Peak and dumped the body in a trash dump near a religious retreat. He then drove to New Jersey. The FBI traced the name Walter Osborne to Corbett and found that he had escaped from prison in Washington State in 1955. They tracked him to Atlantic City, New Jersey, where his car was spotted on fire. Corbett had fled to Canada, where he was captured a few months later.

Even though the truck had been burned, investigators were able to locate soil under the wheel wells. There were four layers in total under each well. From the innermost layer, the soils were as follows:

- Fourth contained material from around New Jersey dump where he burned the car.
- Third contained pink feldspars of Pike's Peak granite—near where the body was found.
- Second had materials from Morrison hogback formation—around Coors' ranch.
- First had pink feldspars of other Front Range granites—generally related to Rocky Mountain Front Range.

The soils told the story of where the car had been since Corbett purchased it. The innermost layer was soil picked up from his routine trips around his home in Denver and the Coors Brewery. The second indicated that his car was near the Coors Ranch. The third was similar to soil near the burial site and the fourth from the area near where the car was buried. Although soil is not individual evidence, the evidence was clearly convincing that this was the right car.

This chapter is about glass and soils and similar materials. Although they are distinct types of evidence, glass and soils have some common characteristics. Forensic analysis involves primarily the physical properties of glass and soil, although some chemical analysis is performed on this evidence. Another common characteristic is that most laboratories do not do much testing on this evidence. A large portion of crime labs do no testing on soils directly. Examiners concentrate on soil analysis when soil at a crime scene contains a shoe print or tire tread. In many glass cases, the only testing that is done is the refractive index test, which will be covered in some detail in this chapter.

Glass

In school, everyone is taught that there are three states of matter: solid, liquid, and gas. Later on, the concepts of plasma and fluid may be introduced. Glass is an example of yet another form of matter: the *amorphous solid*. Most solids have an ordered structure and many have a definite crystal habit. Table salt (sodium chloride) is made of cubic crystals, for example. Even metals have an ordered structure, described as *metal–metal bonding*. Glass has no ordered structure and no crystal habit, making it an amorphous solid. In its purest form,

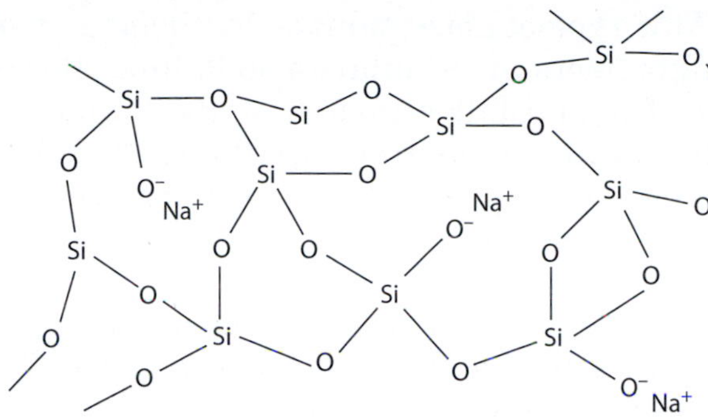

Figure 22.1 The chemical structure of glass.

glass is made up of silicon and oxygen molecules in the ratio of 2:1. All glass has, as a common base, the compound **silicon dioxide**. Its chemical formula could best be described as $(SiO_2)_n$. The chemical structure of glass is shown in Figure 22.1. Because of its properties, glass has also been referred to as a *super-cooled liquid*.

Glass has properties of a solid and some of a liquid. It has a high melting point, in excess of 2000°C, and is very hard and brittle like a solid. It is colorless and transparent and has no regular order to its chemical bonds like a liquid. There have been some reports that glass can flow, albeit very slowly. These have been the result of observations that glass windows that have been hung for many years seem to be thicker at the bottom than the top so that the glass sagged under the influence of gravity. There is no evidence that this happens and is likely due to poor-quality manufacturing of the glass.

Types of Glass

The basic ingredient in glass is silicon dioxide. It comes from very pure sand, which is heated until it melts and then allowed to cool. There are very few types of glass that are made of pure silicon dioxide. Most glass is made up of the base silicon dioxide with different chemical additives that give diversity to the properties of the glass and hence change its usage. Some types of glass may be similar in chemical content but differ in the way they are manufactured resulting in certain desirable properties. Some of the common types of glass are as follows:

- *Float glass or soda lime glass*: This is a type of glass that is used to make windows and other flat glass objects. There are three categories of chemicals that make up soda lime glass; the formers, the fluxes, and the stabilizers. The formers are the main ingredient common to all glass types; the silicon dioxide (SiO_2) or silica in the form of sand. Fluxes help lower the temperature of the mixture, making it easier to manufacture. Alkali ingredients are fluxes, and the float glass flux additive is sodium carbonate (Na_2CO_3) or soda. Calcium carbonate ($CaCO_3$) or calcined limestone is the third additive, the stabilizer, which adds strength and water resistance to the glass. It is easy to see from the list of ingredients how this type of glass came to be called "soda lime" glass. The ingredients are heated to 1500°C and then poured onto a bath of molten tin. The glass is very viscous, and the tin is very fluid so the two do not mix. As the glass cools, it forms a very flat surface because the surface of the molten tin bath is very flat.

- *Borosilicate glass*: This type of glass is made by "doping" molten glass with boron. The main ingredients are similar to soda lime. Borosilicate glass is composed of mostly silica, a smaller amount of alkali and boric oxide (B_2O_3, the source of the boron), and a smattering of aluminum oxide (Al_2O_3). The atoms of boron fit in holes in the glass structure and alter its properties. This type of glass has a high coefficient of thermal expansion. This means that it will not break easily when its temperature is rapidly increased or decreased. If you take a regular glass object and cool it down and then plunge it into hot water, it will break. Borosilicate glass (sometimes called Pyrex, which is a proprietary name) resists breaking due to a temperature change. It is used in cookware and other applications where stability in the presence of rapidly changing temperatures is needed.
- *Tempered glass*: This type of glass is used in automobile windows and plate glass windows in stores. Although it has the same chemical makeup as soda lime glass, it is specially treated so that it is up to four times stronger than regular glass. When it breaks, it forms small spheres that do not have sharp edges. It is made by taking regular glass and reheating it to about 700°C and then cooling rapidly. It can also be made using a chemical treatment.
- *Tinted glass*: This type of glass contains colorants. It is used for decoration or sometimes to reduce glare or heat penetration. The colorants in tinted glass are minerals of various colors. They are melted and mixed with the raw materials of the glass during the manufacturing process.
- *Leaded glass* (*crystal stemware*): This type of glass has become rare in today's society, due to the additive ingredient, lead oxide (PbO). Crystal wine glasses, figurines, and paperweights are examples in this category. The lead additive gives the glass a higher refractive index, causing light to bend more as it passes through, ultimately resulting in the sparkle of crystal glassware and figurines. A characteristic *ping* sound is produced when leaded glass is lightly tapped, a resonant property caused by the bonding of the additives.

Glass as Forensic Evidence

There are more than 700 types of glass but only about 70 are in common use today. Glass is widely used in consumer and commercial products and therefore is found just about everywhere. It isn't surprising that it shows up at many crime scenes, especially those that involve automobiles. On many city streets, there is broken glass left from some accident or left as debris from any action that could cause broken glass. This glass may be incidental to a crime or other some incident that might have happened at that location. It is very important to collect proper known samples so incidental glass can be eliminated from consideration.

Glass is forensically important because

- It is frequently found in most crime scenes due to its plentiful nature and due to actions commonly involved in a crime (broken windows and doors, bottles and drinking glasses, auto windows, etc.).
- It can be carried away undetected from the scene.
- It does not decay under normal circumstances; it is stable evidence.
- It can contribute as class evidence in the pool of evidence linking a suspect to a crime.

Fracture Match

Because glass is mass produced, there are few characteristics that are unique to a particular piece. For this reason, glass is generally considered to be *class* evidence, and a piece of glass cannot normally be matched to a particular source. There is one exception, however. This occurs when there are broken pieces of glass that are large enough to manipulate and they can be fitted together like pieces of a jigsaw puzzle. This is called a *fracture match* and is considered to be an *individual* characteristic. In some cases, there are a few pieces of glass, and the fracture match is fairly easy. Figure 22.2 is a broken Molotov cocktail, which is a device for starting fires. The glass container has been reassembled.

Other fracture matches are not so easy to interpret. Fortunately, there are microscopic characteristics that can help in making a decision about the suspected match. When glass breaks, the applied forces cause the glass to stretch first. Glass is not very malleable and it won't stretch very far, but microscopic stress marks will form in the glass at the break. Since the application of the breaking force is randomly applied (not easily reproducible), the pattern of stress marks on either side of the break are unique. This can be seen in Figure 22.3, which is a photomicrograph of the broken edges of a piece of glass. Note the numerous stress marks and how they all correspond to each other. It would be virtually impossible to break the same type of glass the same way and get the same pattern of stress marks. This means that if the two sets of stress marks match like the ones in Figure 22.3, this is an *individual* characteristic.

Figure 22.2 A Molotov cocktail.

Figure 22.3 Stress marks in glass. The two edges at a break in an eyeglass lens are shown. The white lines are stress marks in the glass caused by the break.

It is relatively rare to get pieces of glass from crime scenes that are large enough to fit back into a possible source. The majority of cases involve pieces of glass that are too small to fracture match and are thus *class* evidence.

Analyzing Broken Glass

Sequencing Glass Fractures

When a force is applied to a glass object, it will bend until it reaches its elastic limit. When the limit is reached, the glass splits in two. The portion of the glass that fails first will have a stress mark at right angles to the plane of the glass—whereas the remaining portion of the glass stresses to the breaking point. This results in a curved pattern of lines on the edge of a broken piece of glass, called "conchoidal lines." The edge of a broken piece of glass is shown in Figure 22.4 with visible conchoidal lines.

The point of impact is usually obvious and can also yield information to the glass examiner. The first task is to determine what type of object caused the damage to the glass. Examination of the hole (if there is one) or point of impact can help identify whether the object was a low-velocity or high-velocity projectile. A bullet or other projectile traveling at high velocity produces a hole on the entry side that is smooth and of similar diameter as the bullet. The exit side will be cratered around the hole, producing a much larger circle than the bullet. Figure 22.5 shows entry and exit holes in glass.

A low-velocity bullet hole will exhibit more shattering around the hole, and the hole may be irregular in shape. Sometimes, stones at high speed (coming off of a tire) may cause damage to glass that mimic bullet fracture patterns. Therefore, it

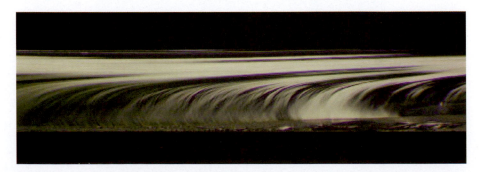

Figure 22.4 This is a photo of the edge of a broken piece of glass. The curved lines are called conchoidal lines. They are formed in this sample as a result of a force of impact from the top side of the glass to the bottom.

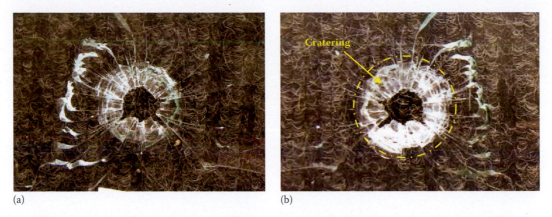

(a)   (b)

Figure 22.5 These two photos show the (a) entry and (b) exit holes produced by the same bullet going through a glass window. The hole on the left is entry, characterized by a smoother hole and no cratering on the entry side. The hole on the right is exit, characterized by the cratering around the entry hole (whiter areas around the hole highlighted by the dotted circle).

is important to carefully search the area of the crime scene for other evidence in order to determine what caused the breakage.

Two different lines of fracture are usually present near the impact site. These fracture lines can be helpful when determining the sequence of impacts when glass is impacted multiple times. For example, if a window has multiple gunshots, the shapes of the entry and exit holes will indicate the *direction* from which the shots were fired (from the inside or outside of the residence). Looking at the fracture lines, it is possible to determine the *order* of impacts. There are two types of fracture lines, *radial* and *concentric* (see Figure 22.6). *Radial fractures* extend outward in a line from the point of impact origin on the glass. *Concentric fractures* make relatively circular patterns around the point of origin of the force.

Radial fractures cause the glass to stress initially on the side *opposite* the force, causing the glass to break on that side first. The side of the glass where the force originated snaps after. The opposite is true of concentric fractures. The action of the radial break causes the side of impact to fail first and the opposite after. This is illustrated in Figure 22.7.

In the case of multiple impacts, the radial fracture lines give indication of which impact preceded another. No radial fracture can extend through an existing fracture line. If the glass has already been compromised, and the secondary fracture must end when it intersects a previous radial fracture. Therefore, it is possible to speculate on the order of a series of impacts. For example, in the succeeding sketch

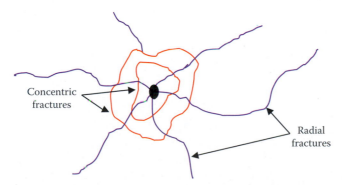

Concentric fractures

Radial fractures

Figure 22.6 The lines of fracture due to impact on glass. The fracture lines that originate at the point of impact and move outward are radial fractures. The circular lines of fracture around the impact point are concentric fractures.

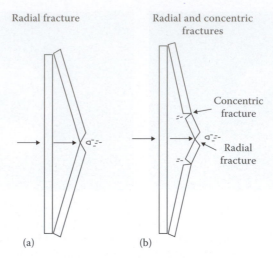

Radial fracture

Radial and concentric
fractures

Concentric
fracture

Radial
fracture

(a)   (b)

Figure 22.7 (a) Shows the path of a projectile through a window, first when it impacts the window from the left, and then upon exit, producing radial fractures. (b) Shows the path of a projectile upon entry (arrow at left) and then exit, producing radial and concentric fractures.

of a window with three impacts, A, B, and C, impact A had to have been first, because impact B's radial fractures terminate in impact A's. Impact C must have occurred after B, as its lines terminate in impact B's. Therefore, the sequence of impacts to the glass is A, then B, and lastly C.

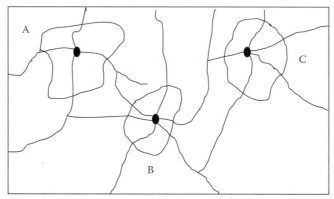

It is not always this easy. For instance, if the window had one more impact, impact D, nestled between A and B, the order is not as definite. Possible sequences could be A–B–C–D or A–B–D–C. The only statements that can be made for certain are that A was first and B came after A. The timing of C and D is unknown.

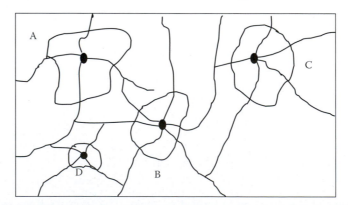

Sequencing fractures and analyzing holes in glass can be important contributions in reconstructing a crime.

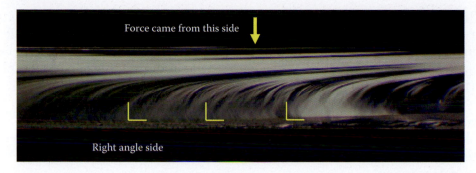

Figure 22.8 Direction of force using the *3R* rule for a radial fracture piece of glass. *Radial* fractures have a *right* angle on the *reverse* side of the force.

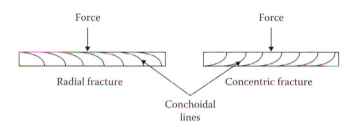

Figure 22.9 Using conchoidal lines on the edge of a piece of glass to determine direction of impact.

Direction of Force

The stress lines or *conchoidal lines*, formed as a result of impact and breakage as seen in Figure 22.4, are useful tools in the determination of the direction of impact (force) on the glass. This information may be viable to corroborate statements or reconstruct the incident. Remember that the radial fractures break first on the opposite side of impact and then stress until they fall apart on the side of impact. Conchoidal lines are the result of this two-step occurrence. The first side of the glass to fail forms a perpendicular (right angle) line to the surface as seen on the edge of the glass, and the side that fails last has lines that curve obliquely to its surface. The rule, commonly referred to as the *3R rule* is when looking at the side edge of a *radial* fracture line, there is a *right* angle on the *reverse* (opposite) side of the impact force. Figure 22.8 shows the same conchoidal lines with the right angles and direction of force labeled.

The opposite of the 3R rule applies to concentric fracture lines. In this case, the right angle is formed on the *same* side as the impact force. This again is because the concentric fractures break first on the side of impact and last on the opposite side. The graphic in Figure 22.9 illustrates how force is determined using these lines of fracture.

Class Characteristics of Glass

The number of class characteristics of glass is very limited because glass is so inert, resulting in its being difficult to dissolve in any common solvents. This limits the chemical properties that can be described. A few crime labs have access to an *inductively coupled plasma mass spectrometer*. This instrument is capable of digesting glass and performing elemental analysis to determine its chemical composition.

These instruments are expensive and require a good deal of skill to operate, and thus are not commonly used in local crime labs. As a result, most forensic scientists concentrate on the physical characteristics of the glass in making comparisons between glass of known and unknown sources. Some of the more common physical properties are as follows:

- Size, shape, dimensions, thickness
- Color
- Density
- Refractive index

Of these properties, the most discriminating is refractive index.

Refractive Index

Everyone learns in school that the speed of light is about 186,000 miles/s or about 3×10^8 m/s. This is only true when light travels through a vacuum. When light travels through any other transparent medium, it slows down. The effect that a particular medium has on the speed of light roughly correlates to its density. Just as you cannot walk as fast through water as you can through air (because water is denser than air and offers more resistance to your movement), so it is with light passing through water. The magnitude of the decrease in the velocity of light as it passes through a transparent medium is called the "refractive index," expressed as a ratio as shown in Equation 22.1

$$RI = \frac{\text{The velocity of light in a vacuum}}{\text{The velocity of light in the transparent medium of interest}} \quad (22.1)$$

The ratio or *refractive index* is a result of *refraction* of light passing through multiple media. The varying speed of light when it passes from one medium to another causes the light to refract, change its direction, or bend. This is shown in Figure 22.10. A straight straw is partially immersed in water. When viewed from the side, the straw appears to have been bent. This is an example of refraction.

Refraction has several interesting properties that are utilized in the analysis of glass.

- If two transparent materials, such as a liquid and a solid, have the same refractive index, then light beams that pass through them will be refracted the same amount, and light will not bend as it passes from one material to the other. The two materials will therefore look like one and cannot be distinguished. If the solid is immersed in the liquid, it will essentially disappear from human sight. Figure 22.11 is an example of a solid that has a refractive index similar to water. In the series of photographs, the transparent solid cube, a cross-linked polyacrylamide, is immersed into distilled water, and the cube seems to disappear.
- If a transparent material is heated, its refractive index will decrease. This is because, as a material is heated, it becomes less dense and more gas like. This means that light passing through it will encounter less resistance and

Figure 22.10 Refraction of a plastic straw partially immersed in water. The straw appears to bend due to refraction.

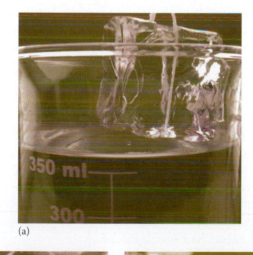

(a)

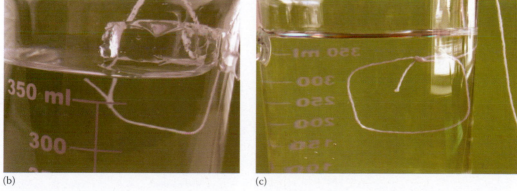

(b) (c)

Figure 22.11 These photos show the immersion of a solid, transparent material into a liquid of the same refractive index. (a) Shows the cube in air. In (b), the half of the cube still in air is visible, while the other half now in water is not. The solid is immersed and not visible in (c).

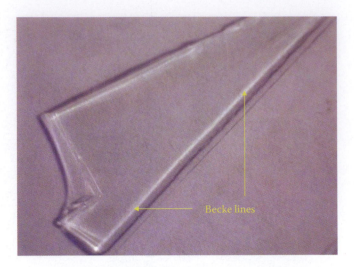

Figure 22.12 A Becke line. The white halo around the glass is the Becke line. It follows the exact contours of the glass.

bend to a lesser degree. This effect is much more dramatic on liquids than solids. Glass, being solid material, barely changes its refractive index as it is heated.

- The amount of refraction that light undergoes depends upon its wavelength. The longer the wavelength of light, the less it bends as it travels from one medium to the next. For example, red light, with a wavelength of approximately 700 nm, bends less than blue light, wavelength around 400 nm.

- If a transparent solid is immersed in a transparent liquid of different refractive index, a bright halo of light will be seen around the solid. This is called the *Becke line*. Since it is formed at the boundary between two different refractive indices, it will disappear if the solid and liquid have the same refractive index. Figure 22.12 shows the Becke line around a piece of glass immersed in a liquid at 100 times magnification.

- If a transparent solid is immersed in a transparent liquid of different refractive index and put under a microscope, the Becke line will move as the ocular to objective lens distance is increased. If the liquid has a higher refractive index than the solid, the Becke line will move away from the solid toward the liquid. This is illustrated in Figure 22.13.

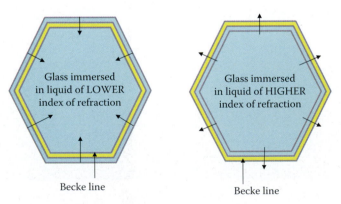

Figure 22.13 A diagram of how the Becke line moves as the focus of the microscope is changed. As the stage and objective are moved apart, the Becke line moves toward the medium of higher refractive index. If the glass has a higher refractive index than the liquid, the Becke line would move in toward the glass as the objective lens and stage are moved away from each other.

Refractive Index Determination of a Small Glass Fragment

In many cases, glass recovered as evidence is in the form of very small fragments. Figure 22.14 shows a very small piece of borosilicate (Pyrex©) glass being tested in two liquids of known indices of refraction. When the Pyrex is placed in water, which has an index of refraction of 1.33, the glass fragment is visible. When the Pyrex is placed in vegetable oil, which has an index of refraction of 1.47, it "disappears." This indicates that both the Pyrex glass and vegetable oil have the same refractive index. Figure 22.15a shows a laboratory beaker half filled with oil. Figure 22.15b shows a Pyrex test tube with nothing but air in it immersed in the oil. Figure 22.15c shows the same test tube with a small amount of the vegetable oil added. Notice that it looks like part of the tube has disappeared! Obviously vegetable oil and Pyrex refract light in the same manner.

In a similar fashion, the refractive index of such pieces of glass can be determined using a set of commercially available liquids whose refractive indices are known. Each liquid also has, printed on its label, the amount of refractive index change there is with each rise in temperature of one degree Celsius (1°C). Crime labs also use a *hot stage microscope*. This is a microfurnace that fits on top of the stage of a microscope. It can be heated under controlled conditions. A fragment of glass is immersed in a liquid whose refractive index is slightly higher than the glass and mounted on the hot stage. As the hot stage is heated, the temperature of

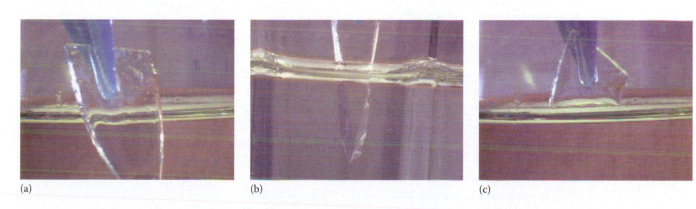

(a)   (b)   (c)

Figure 22.14 (a) Shows a small piece of Pyrex glass not immersed in a liquid. (b) Shows the same piece of glass immersed in water. (c) Shows the piece immersed in vegetable oil. Pyrex and vegetable oil have similar indices of refraction as evidenced by the disappearance of the glass in the oil.

(a)   (b)   (c)

Figure 22.15 The "disappearing" test tube. The Pyrex beaker in (a) is filled with vegetable oil. An empty test tube is placed in the oil in photo (b). The same test tube is partially filled with vegetable oil in photo (c).

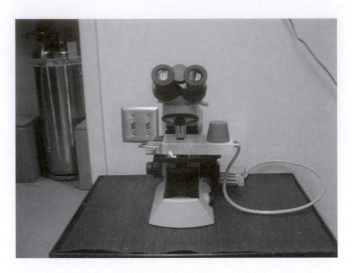

Figure 22.16 A compound microscope with a hot stage mounted on the stage.

the liquid and the glass will increase. The refractive index of the liquid will start to decrease. The refractive index of the glass will barely change because it is a solid. At some point, the refractive index of the liquid will drop until it is the same as the glass, and the Becke line will disappear. If the glass is thin enough, it too will disappear. The hot stage monitors the temperature and how much it increases. The increase is noted at the time the Becke line disappears. From the data on the decrease of the refractive index with each degree rise in temperature, the refractive index of the glass can be determined. Figure 22.16 is a microscope with a hot stage mounted on the stage.

The refractive index for known and unknown glass particles can be determined in this way. Some forensic scientists go a step further and use special filters on the microscope that select particular wavelengths of light that are shone on the glass. This way, several refractive indices can be determined. If two pieces of glass are similar, all their refractive indices taken at various wavelengths of light will have to agree. Remember that, even if two pieces of glass have the same physical properties such as refractive index, this is still *class* evidence.

Soil

Soil is found almost anywhere outdoors. It is very familiar to most people, who sometimes disparagingly call it "dirt." *Soil* is made up of crushed rocks and minerals mixed with decayed plant and animal material (*humus*). It can range from almost all crushed rock (beach sand) to almost all humus (peat bog). Except where there is water or man-made objects, soil covers the entire surface of the earth. Soil can be difficult to categorize, and it takes a good deal of skill to identify its components. For these reasons, most forensic science laboratories do not analyze soil evidence except to the extent that someone has left a shoe print or a car has left a tire tread in the soil. This is unfortunate because the presence of soil evidence can tell a good deal about where a person or object has been. A good example of how important soil can be in solving crimes is exemplified in the Coors kidnapping case presented at the beginning of this chapter.

Soil as Forensic Evidence

Soil evidence presents a number of challenges to forensic scientists. These may be the reason why few laboratories take the time to analyze it.

- Soil varies in its chemical and physical properties from place to place, even within the same plot of ground. Studies have shown that soil profiles may differ markedly within a few meters of each other horizontally and vertically.
- There is no forensic classification scheme for soils. This means that there are potentially an infinite number of soil types making it difficult to reach meaningful conclusions about associations among soil samples.
- It takes a good deal of skill to characterize the minerals present in soil. One must be familiar with crystal shapes and with polarizing light microscopy in order to analyze the inorganic fraction of soils.
- Soil is usually considered *class* evidence. There are few unique characteristics in soil that enable individualization.

Color Analysis of Soils

Sometimes, it is possible to characterize soils by their color. The color of a soil is due to its mineral distribution and moisture content. Many minerals have characteristic colors. For example, copper-based minerals are green or blue. Iron minerals tend to be red or brown. In the early 1900s, a professor named Albert Munsell developed a color chart of all the various color hues in soil. The Munsell color chart for soil, an offshoot of the master color chart, is used today by forensic geologists to analyze soil types. Soils can be examined visually for color, or sometimes, the minerals can be dissolved in water. If there are enough colored minerals in the soil, they will impart a tint to the water.

Physical Analysis of Soils

A soil sample's physical attributes can be analyzed microscopically. Equally sized samples of soil can be viewed under magnification, and the percent of humus versus mineral materials can be estimated. The color, size, and shape of rock and mineral grains can be compared.

The sample can then be filtered using a sieve, which separates the organic (plant and animal) material from the soil, leaving the inorganic, crushed rock, and mineral grains. The density of the sample can be determined using a density gradient, a column of various liquids of differing density. Soil components settle out in liquid layers of similar density, forming a visual column of soil density as seen in Figure 22.17.

Analysis of Humic Fractions of Soils

Some laboratories use high-performance liquid chromatography (HPLC) to separate and display some of the common humus components of soils. The soil is extracted with acetonitrile and filtered. The filtrate is analyzed by HPLC. Figure 22.18 shows the liquid chromatogram of a soil sample.

Figure 22.17 Soil density column.

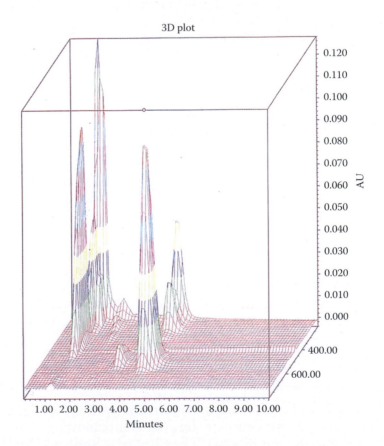

Figure 22.18 A liquid chromatogram of a soil sample. This is a pseudo-3D chromatogram. The *x*-axis is time in minutes. The *y*-axis is absorbance of light by the UV detector. The *z*-axis is the wavelength of light that exposes the soil sample. The wavelength range is 200–800 nm.

the liquid has a higher refractive index than the glass. The label on the bottle of the liquid indicates that the refractive index of the liquid at 25°C is 1.52. The hot stage is heated, and the Becke line disappears when the temperature of the liquid has reached 45°C. The label on the bottle of the liquid indicates that the refractive index of the liquid decreases 0.005 for each degree rise in temperature. From this data, determine the refractive index of the glass.

22. A beam of light passes from air through Plexiglas, which has an index of refraction of 1.43. By what amount does the speed of light change?

23. Light traveling into an aquarium slows to a speed of 2.26×10^8 m/s. Calculate the index of refraction of water.

24. Sequence the impacts for the glass fractures in Photos 1 and 2. Explain your reasoning.

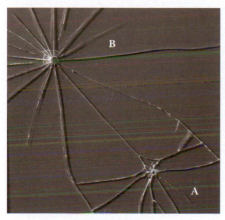
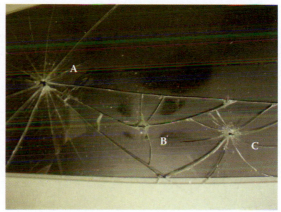

Glass photo 1   Glass photo 2

25. Photo A shows a piece of glass in water, index of refraction 1.33, and Photo B shows the same piece of glass in oil, index of refraction 1.47. Explain the results.

Photo A   Photo B

Further Reading

Caddy, B. (ed.). (2001). *Forensic Examination of Glass and Paint: Analysis and Interpretation*. Taylor & Francis, London, U.K.

Miller, E. T. (1982). Forensic glass comparisons, in *Forensic Science Handbook*, vol. 1, R. Saferstein, ed. Prentice Hall, Englewood Cliffs, NJ.

On the Web

Glass
http://micro.magnet.fsu.edu/optics/timeline/people/becke.html.
http://www.brocku.ca/earthsciences/people/gfinn/optical/becke4.htm.
http://www.edinformatics.com/inventions_inventors/glass.htm.

Soil Analysis
http://en.wikipedia.org/wiki/Munsell_color_system.
http://soil.gsfc.nasa.gov/forengeo/secret.htm.
http://soil.gsfc.nasa.gov/index.html.
http://soil.gsfc.nasa.gov/pvg/munsell.htm.

23

Fires and Explosions

Learning Objectives

1. To be able to define fire and explosion
2. To be able to define and give examples of arson and incendiary fires
3. To be able to define combustion and give examples of combustion reactions
4. To be able to describe how fire and explosion scenes are investigated and what evidence is sought
5. To be able to describe methods for the laboratory analysis of fire and explosion debris

Chapter 23
Fires and Explosions

Chapter Outline

Mini Glossary

Accelerant: A fuel that is used to start a fire that wouldn't start on its own or speed up a fire.

Adsorption/elution: A method of recovery of accelerant vapors from fire debris that employs a material that adsorbs the vapors that are then removed (eluted) and concentrated for analysis.

Black powder: A low explosive made from potassium nitrate, sulfur, and carbon.

Bomb seat: The point of origin of a bombing.

Combustion: A type of chemical reaction whereby a *fuel* reacts with oxygen to release energy.

Deflagration: A type of explosion whereby the oxygen is physically mixed with the fuel and is in a form where the O is bonded to other atoms that form weaker bonds than in O_2 and thus require less activation energy to break.

Detonation: An instantaneous explosion. It produces escaping gases that travel in excess of the speed of sound.

Dynamite: An explosive containing nitroglycerine that is impregnated in paper and other absorbent materials.

Exothermic: A chemical reaction that gives off heat.

Fire tetrahedron: A diagram that shows the four factors that must be present for a fire to start and maintain. These are fuel, oxygen, activation energy, and combustion.

Fire trail: This is when an accelerant is poured on a floor from room to room and then it is ignited. This is an efficient way to carry a fire from one place to another inside a building.

Griess test: A chemical test used in the analysis of explosive. It gives a positive reaction to all substances that contain nitrate or nitrite.

Headspace: The airspace above a closed container that contains debris from a fire.

Hydrocarbon: A substance made up of hydrogen and carbon atoms. Many are fuels used to accelerate fires.

Incendiary fire: A fire started deliberately with the intention of committing or hiding a crime.

Initiating (primary) explosive: A high explosive that is sensitive to detonation.

Low explosive: Explosions that produce escaping gases of velocities less than the speed of sound.

Molotov cocktail: A bottle or other breakable container that is filled with an accelerant such as gasoline. Then, a wick is inserted in the top. This is usually a length of rag. The wick is ignited and the bottle is thrown into the building or other place where the arsonist wants to start the fire.

Noninitiating (secondary) explosive: Explosives that require a booster charge.

Plastique: An explosive that is impregnated with a claylike material so it can be shaped.

Point of origin: The location where the fire started.

Solid-phase microextraction (SPME): A method of adsorption–elution where the adsorbing medium is a small, coated needle.

Spalling: Blistering of concrete by exposure to extreme heat.

Acronyms

Δ: The Greek letter "delta" that stands for heat or energy
ANFO: Ammonium nitrate and fuel oil
PETN: Pentaerythritol tetranitrate
TNT: Trinitrotoluene

Introduction

On November 28, 1942, one of the most destructive fires in the U.S. history occurred at the Cocoanut Grove Night Club in Boston. The club was supposed to have a capacity of 500 people but, on that night, had more than 1000. The club was formerly a speakeasy (an illegal bar that operated during Prohibition) during the 1920s. Some of the entrances and exits had been boarded up since then. The only working entrance was a revolving door in the front. The club also had flammable decorations such as cloth curtains and palm trees throughout. The refrigeration system used methyl chloride as the refrigerant. Methyl chloride is very flammable. It was a substitute for Freon, which was in short supply owing to World War II.

Fire scene investigators traced the point of origin of the fire to the Melody lounge in the basement. A lightbulb had burned out and a busboy was using a match for light while he changed the bulb. He apparently dropped the match. Within five minutes the entire lounge was engulfed in flame. Many people tried to escape through a stairway to the main floor but the door at the top was locked. Several people died in the stairwell from asphyxiation. The fire spread quickly to the main floor and engulfed it within another five minutes. Many people were trapped in the revolving door. Others were trampled to death and some died at their tables of asphyxiation from poisonous fumes. As a result of the fire, 490 people died and the owner was convicted of involuntary manslaughter and sentenced to 3½ years in prison.

This fire turned to be set by accident but the conditions in the night club were such that it should have been foreseen that any fire, deliberate or not, had the potential to kill and injure many people. Even as far back as 1942, there were fire codes in place that, had they been enforced, could have prevented many deaths. Surely that you can name a number of issues in this situation that caused the damage and loss of life. Many destructive fires occur by accidental causes and some by natural causes, such as lightning strikes. Still other fires are deliberate. There are two types of deliberate fires. The first does not involve any criminal activity or an attempt to cover a crime. In some communities, it is permissible to burn leaves or trash or other debris on one's own property although a license may be necessary. In other cases, however, a fire is set with the intent to commit a crime or cover up another crime. Such fires are called "incendiary," and the crime is "arson." For example, someone may burn down a failing business in an attempt to collect fire insurance money. In other cases, a murderer may burn a house where he has killed the owner in the hopes of destroying the body and any incriminating evidence. In still other cases, an accountant may destroy documents in a fire to hide evidence of embezzlement. As we will see later, the determination of whether a fire was incendiary may boil down to eliminating the other causes: natural or accidental.

What Is a Fire?

Fire is the evolution of energy in the form of light and heat and smoke as the result of *combustion*. Combustion is a type of chemical reaction whereby a *fuel* reacts with oxygen to release energy. Reactions that give off energy are termed "exothermic." When a fuel substance reacts with oxygen, the reaction is always exothermic. Equation 23.1 is the simplest combustion reaction. It is the reaction of natural gas (methane) with oxygen to form carbon dioxide and water and heat energy. This is the reaction that heats homes or stoves that use natural gas.

$$\underset{\text{methane}}{CH_4} + \underset{\text{oxygen}}{O_2} \xrightarrow{\Delta} \underset{\text{carbon dioxide}}{CO_2} + \underset{\text{water}}{2H_2O} + \Delta \qquad (23.1)$$

The symbol Δ (the Greek letter delta) is the symbol used for heat energy in chemistry and physics. Notice that the Δ also appears over the reaction arrow. In chemistry, a symbol put over the reaction arrow means "in the presence of." This means that heat is being put into the reaction. This heat is called the "activation energy." In order to get methane and oxygen to react, it is necessary to break up the oxygen molecule as shown in Equation 23.2. As long as the energy produced by the reaction is greater than the activation energy, the overall reaction is exothermic.

$$O_2 \xrightarrow{\Delta} 2O \qquad (23.2)$$

The atomic oxygen now reacts with the methane in the combustion. The amount of activation energy needed to get the reaction started is very little compared to the energy that is emitted by the reaction. The activation energy can be in the form of a spark or small flame. Exothermic reactions like methane and oxygen produce energy because the energy stored in C–H bonds is greater than that in C–O or O–H bonds. The excess energy is given off in the form of heat and flame and smoke.

Gasoline is a petroleum distillate that contains more than 300 substances. Most of them are *hydrocarbons*, which are substances made up of carbon and hydrogen. Methane is also a hydrocarbon. These are all potent fuels that will combust with oxygen. A very common combustion reaction takes place inside of the internal combustion engine. Here, gasoline is compressed into a small space and ignited with a spark plug. This provides the activation energy for the reaction. The gasoline combusts in the air present in the engine cylinders and the energy produced causes the pistons to move and propel the car. One of the compounds in gasoline is *octane*, C_8H_{18}. It combusts with oxygen as shown in Equation 23.3. The activation energy needed for this reaction serves two purposes. It breaks the oxygen molecule up into oxygen atoms (Equation 23.2) and it vaporizes the octane, which is a liquid at room temperature. In general, fuels must be in the vapor phase for them to undergo combustion. Activation energy is partly used to convert liquid and solid fuels to vapor.

$$2C_8H_{18} + 25O_2 \xrightarrow{\Delta} 16CO_2 + 18H_2O + \Delta \qquad (23.3)$$

Note: This equation is balanced. All chemical equations must have the same number of each type of atom on both sides of the equation.

There are many more bonds in this reaction than in the one involving methane, so there is much more energy given off by the combustion of octane. This reaction, along with many others in gasoline, can be put to work inside an internal combustion engine in a car. There are many other substances that can act as fuels in combustion reactions. Wood, plastic, natural and synthetic fibers and fabrics, carpeting, tile, drywall, and most building materials will undergo combustion as long as there is sufficient activation energy available to vaporize the fuel. Once sufficient activation energy is available and the combustion reaction gets going, it will produce enough energy to provide additional activation energy to vaporize more fuel so that the reaction can continue. The reaction will continue perpetually until the fuel or the oxygen is spent or the temperature falls below what is needed to continue to vaporize the fuel.

Extinguishing a Fire

Fire experts use the concept of the *fire tetrahedron* when describing the materials and conditions needed to sustain a fire. Figure 23.1 shows a diagram of a fire tetrahedron. At each apex of the tetrahedron is one of the elements that must be present for a fire to be sustained: fuel + oxygen + activation energy + combustion.

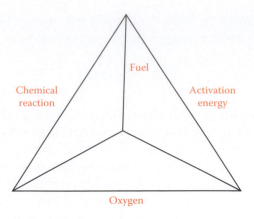

Figure 23.1 The fire tetrahedron.

All four of these elements must be present to have a fire. If any one of them is removed, the fire goes out. Fire extinguishers are based on this principle. They remove one or more of the elements of a fire. For example, water makes a good fire extinguisher for some fires. It cools the fire off so that there is insufficient activation energy to split oxygen molecules and/or vaporize the fuel. Fire blankets smother a fire by preventing oxygen from getting to the fuel. Foam extinguishers work like the blanket in that they prevent oxygen from reaching the fire. See Figure 23.2 for a picture of a foam extinguisher. Carbon dioxide extinguishers blow out the fire like blowing out a candle. The carbon dioxide is sprayed at the fire under pressure and it blows away the oxygen. Carbon dioxide will not support combustion so the fire goes out.

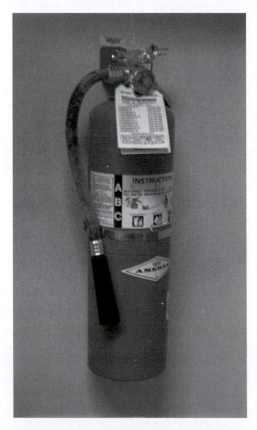

Figure 23.2 A chemical fire extinguisher. Different extinguishers are rated for different types of fires and are clearly marked with a lettering and symbol system as to which types of fires they are suitable for.

Go to various buildings such as your school, a department store, and a gas station and ask if there are any fire extinguishers. If so, look at the labels on them. The label will usually indicate what types of fires that the extinguisher is designed to put out. Particular types of extinguishers are designed for different types of fires. You can also see a variety of fire extinguishers at building supply stores. Fire extinguishers do not contain water since this is available at most homes and businesses in large quantities. Besides, water is not a good extinguisher for certain types of fires such as electrical or grease (why?).

Incendiary Fires

Fire experts and the legal system use two closely related terms to describe fires that are deliberately set. The term "incendiary fire" means a fire that is willfully and intentionally set. The National Fire Protection Association recently has changed from using the term "incendiary" to "intentionally," but *incendiary* is still widely used. When an incendiary fire is set in order to commit a crime or destroy evidence from a previous crime, the crime of *arson* has been committed. Arson is one of the most serious and costly crimes in the United States. Statistics from the U.S. Department of Homeland Security for the 10 years ending in 2003 and the costs of these fires are shown in Table 23.1.

This table shows that although the number of arson fires has been decreasing, there were still more than 37,000 arson fires in 2003 that cost almost $700 million.

TABLE 23.1
Arson Fire Statistics

Year	Fires	Deaths	Direct Dollar Loss in Millions
1994	86,000	550	$1,447
1995[a]	90,500	740	$1,647
1996	85,500	520	$1,405
1997	78,500	445	$1,309
1998	76,000	470	$1,249
1999	72,000	370	$1,281
2000	75,000	505	$1,340
2001[b]	45,500	330	$1,013
2001[c]	45,500	2451	$33,440
2002	44,500	350	$919
2003	37,500	305	$692

Source: National Fire Protection Association Fire Loss in the U.S. during 2003, www.nfpa.org.
[a] Includes 168 civilian deaths that occurred in the explosion and fire in the federal office building in Oklahoma City on April 19, 1995.
[b] Excludes the events of September 11, 2001.
[c] These estimates reflect the number of deaths, injuries, and dollar loss directly related to the events of September 11, 2001.

In 2001, the Federal Emergency Management Agency published the results of a research study on arson. A summary of their finding included the following:

- Arson is the leading cause of fires in the United States and the second leading cause of death.
- Fifty percent of arson fires occur outdoors, while 30% occur in buildings and 20% occur in vehicles.
- Half of all arson arrests are juveniles.
- Poorer neighborhoods experience 14 times the number of arson fires as do more well-off neighborhoods.
- Church arsons have increased since 1996.

There are a number of ways to start an incendiary fire. One could use a match or a lighter or a blow torch to get something burning and then just leave the premises. This may not be as easy as it sounds. Have you ever tried to start a fire in a fireplace by lighting a large log with a match? It usually doesn't work. You have to light small twigs or pieces of paper with the match and then gradually add larger pieces of wood until there is enough energy being put out by the fire to provide enough energy to vaporize parts of large pieces of wood. Generally, arsonists do not want to be at a fire scene any longer than necessary for fear of being seen. They want to start the fire as fast as possible and get out. In many cases, fires can be started remotely using a time delay to supply the activation energy. Figure 23.3 shows how matches can delay the start an incendiary fire.

For a moment, try and think of what an arsonist would want to accomplish if he or she were going to deliberately start a fire without being present when the fire started and without being caught. First, they would want to delay the start of the fire until they are out of the vicinity. Second, if complete destruction of the building is the goal, then fires need to be started in several places at once or there must be a method of causing the fire to spread rapidly. There must also be a continual source of air in the premises or the fire will extinguish after the oxygen present at the time of the fire is consumed. It is difficult to start a fire in several places in a building all at once remotely so arsonists often use *accelerants* to spread a fire rapidly throughout. An accelerant is a fuel that is used to start a fire that otherwise couldn't be easily started or to make a fire burn faster. Accelerants are generally liquids that require low activation energy so they can be readily combusted. They undergo highly exothermic reactions so there is plenty of energy around to keep the fire going and to

Figure 23.3 A fire was started in the carpeting in a car using a smoldering cigarette and a book of matches.

involve materials that are harder to burn. Accelerants can generally be obtained without calling attention to the purchaser. This is why gasoline, charcoal lighters, paint thinners, and other similar consumer products are widely used as accelerants. Gasoline is the accelerant of choice in more than half of all arson fires. Unfortunately for the arsonist and fortunately for forensic scientists, even burned accelerants leave residues behind that can be detected and identified as to type. In most cases, a forensic chemist can determine if an accelerant was used in a fire and if so, whether it was gasoline or some other type of product. If this evidence is located and collected by the fire scene investigator, a forensic chemist can usually determine what type of product (e.g., gasoline, kerosene) it is, but cannot determine if the accelerant came from a particular source such as a container found in the suspect's garage.

Investigation of a Fire

Trained fire scene investigators normally carry out investigation of fires. Most of these people are trained first as firefighters and come to fire scene investigation from a career as a firefighter. Some have college degrees. A few universities and community colleges offer classes and even degrees in fire science where students learn about the chemistry of fire and how fires start and spread, how they are suppressed, and how to investigate a fire and properly collect and preserve evidence. It is the responsibility of the fire scene investigator to determine the cause of the fire. This is done by a physical inspection of the fire scene, discussion with the firefighters and witnesses, support of the forensic science laboratory in the analysis of fire residues, and perhaps even the use of dogs that are specially trained to detect common accelerants. This process is made more difficult by what happens to the structure when a fire occurs and when the fire department responds to the fire. When a fire is discovered, the fire department will respond as quickly as possible. They have two major duties at a fire scene. The first is to remove everyone who may be trapped in the fire and the second is to extinguish the fire. The latter is normally accomplished with thousands of gallons of water. After the fire is put out, the electricity and gas are turned off if the fire didn't already knock them out. After the fire is out and the firefighters have left, the fire scene investigator takes over. Fire scene investigation can be very difficult. As aforementioned, there may be no light or heat or air conditioning. Everything will be very wet. The fire may have weakened the structure of the building and walking through it can be hazardous. There may be hazardous chemical fumes or residues present that were formed from burning materials. Figure 23.4 shows an indoor kitchen fire started by a defective coffee maker.

If a fire in a multistory building is severe enough, the upper floors may collapse on top of the lower floors. If the point of origin is on a lower floor, it may be buried in tons of material from upper floors. Heavy moving equipment may be needed to remove the debris layer by layer. This must be done carefully as important evidence may be found in any of the layers.

Causes of a Fire

From the standpoint of the fire scene investigator, there are three causes of fires:

- *Natural*: This could be a fire that is started by a lightning strike.
- *Accidental*: Someone accidentally drops a match in bed or an electrical circuit becomes overloaded.
- *Deliberate*: Arson.

Figure 23.4 A fire in a kitchen. Note the *V* pattern of burning on the wall on the left side. (Courtesy of James Novak.)

There are two ways that a fire scene investigator determines that a fire is arson. The first is to have compelling evidence at the scene. This could be the presence of a fire setting device such as a *Molotov cocktail*, a bottle, or other breakable container that is filled with an accelerant such as gasoline. Then, a wick is inserted in the top. This is usually a length of rag. The wick is ignited and the bottle is thrown into the building or other place where the arsonist wants to start the fire. The Molotov cocktail contains three of the legs of the fire tetrahedron: activation energy, fuel, and heat. Another piece of evidence that strongly suggests arson is a *fire trail*. This is when an accelerant is poured on a floor from room to room and then it is ignited. This is an efficient way to carry a fire from one place to another inside a building. A picture of a Molotov cocktail can be found in Figure 22.2 in Chapter 22 on Glass and Soil.

The other way that a fire scene investigator determines that a fire is arson is to eliminate all possible natural or accidental causes of the fire. If this is done then, the only type that is left is arson. Eliminating accidental causes of a fire can be difficult. Suppose, for example, that a furnace explodes during the course of a fire. This could have happened because it was rigged to explode and actually caused the fire or it could have gotten involved in a fire that started elsewhere in the building or it could have accidentally malfunctioned and caused the fire. Often, a fire scene investigator will call in a heating contractor to examine the remains of the furnace to try and determine what happened. Other appliances such as water heaters, dryers, toasters, and ovens may also be involved in fires or cause them. Electrical system overloads can also be hard to interpret. It is possible to create an electrical overload that causes overheating of wires and can cause a fire. Many fires are caused by accidental electrical overload, especially in older buildings.

Point of Origin of a Fire

By far, the most important piece of information that a fire scene investigator needs to determine the cause of a fire is the *point of origin*. This is the location where the fire started. If an accelerant was used to start a fire, its residue will be most likely found at the point of origin. If an appliance malfunction caused the fire, the point of origin will be near the appliance. In a multistory building, arson fires are generally started on the first floor so the arsonist can escape easily without getting trapped in the fire. As mentioned earlier, this means that locating the point of origin may mean moving tons of material that could have collapsed on it. The point of origin is

Figure 23.5 A fire trail in a mobile home. (Courtesy of Charles Hughes.)

generally where the most extensive burning takes place and where it often gets the hottest. Some of the characteristics that fire scene investigators look for in searching for the point of origin include V-patterns of burning, spalling (blistering) of concrete, the beginning of a fire trail, the presence of accelerants, and the apparent gathering or piling up of fuel materials.

It was mentioned before that arson fires are often characterized by fire trails and the presence of accelerants. Another clue that a fire may be arson is the presence of multiple points of origin. If an arsonist wants to make sure that an entire building becomes involved in the fire, then he will start fires at multiple points in the building. This can also be accomplished by the use of a fire trail. Here, an accelerant is poured in a trail from room to room. Then, the accelerant can be ignited at one point and the ensuing fire will travel along the trail. The result is that it appears as if multiple fires were started in each room. If the burning is not too severe, the fire scene investigator can see remnants of the fire trail. Figure 23.5 shows a fire trail.

Other Evidence at Fire Scenes

In their zeal to find the point of origin of a fire and determine its cause, fire scene investigators sometimes overlook other important evidence. Even though fires normally destroy much of the trace evidence that is found at other types of crime scenes, sometimes, the fire doesn't reach some of the evidence. Fingerprints, hairs and fibers, shoe prints, blood, and documents can survive a fire under the right circumstances. These should not be overlooked. It is normally not difficult to determine if a fire is arson but it can be very hard to determine who did it. Trace and other evidence can be crucial in making this determination.

Role of Accelerants

The presence of residues from a fuel such as gasoline can be strongly indicative of an arson fire. It should be kept in mind, however, that finding such residues doesn't necessarily mean that the fire was deliberate. Many people keep cans or bottles of gasoline, charcoal lighter, paint thinner, or other accelerants in their homes or businesses. Any fire could reach these stored liquids and they could easily become involved in the fire. It can sometimes be difficult to determine if these accelerants were used to start the fire or were innocently involved. Accelerants can also greatly increase the damage of a fire because they give off so much heat. Such increased damage can destroy evidence that would otherwise have survived the fire. An example of this was a fire aboard an aircraft carrier that was docked at the Norfolk, Virginia Navy Yard. The damage to some of the rooms below decks on the ship was horrific because the heat from the fire ruptured overhead lines that carried hydraulic fluid used in the elevators that moved the planes up to the flight deck. This hydraulic fluid emitted copious amounts of heat energy when it burned resulting in a great deal of damage. Metal beams that might otherwise have been weakened, deformed or twisted, actually melted, and collapsed.

Detection and Collection of Accelerants

Fire scene investigators are well trained to spot signs that accelerants were used in a fire. Evidence includes extreme heat and damage, sooty V-pattern burning, and fire trails. There are hydrocarbon *sniffer* instruments that can detect the presence of small quantities of common accelerants. In recent years, live sniffers—the so-called arson dogs—have become popular among fire scene investigators. These dogs are specially trained to detect minute quantities of common accelerants.

Some materials are better than others for trapping and holding accelerants. The best materials are those that can easily absorb liquids. These include bedding, furniture with cushions, carpeting, clothing, and soil. Substances like tile, wood, wall board, and other building materials do not absorb and trap liquids very well and are less suitable candidates for containing accelerant residues. The more absorbent a material is, the better it is for holding accelerants. If some of the accelerant can get into the material, it may be protected from the fire and some unburned liquid may be trapped. This is the best evidence for analysis by forensic chemists. Once evidence of an accelerant has been located, then the debris must be collected and packaged for delivery to the crime laboratory. Since accelerants are volatile and evaporate easily, they must be packaged in airtight containers. Forensic chemists strongly recommend employing unused paint cans for packaging fire scene evidence. They can be made airtight but at the same time, the top can be easily removed in case access to the debris is needed. They come in various sizes up to five gallons to accommodate various amounts of evidence. Some fire scene investigators use empty glass jars with screw caps. These are not as useful as paint cans because they are breakable and because they can crack or break if subjected to heat, which is sometimes used in the analysis of fire residues. If there are large pieces of fire debris, they can be packaged in plastic bags, but only the type that doesn't breathe (can be made airtight). Care must be taken to seal these bags tightly. From the analytical standpoint, it is better to use several paint cans than one large plastic bag because large bags are difficult to manipulate in the laboratory.

Analysis of Fire Scene Evidence

The biggest challenge facing forensic chemists in the analysis of fire scene evidence is separating and concentrating the accelerant residues from the fire debris. This can be a real challenge because of the amount of debris present (sometimes too much, sometimes too little), the way it is packaged, and the nature and concentration of the accelerant. Over the years, there have been a number of ways of separating and concentrating accelerant residues. The methods used today are designed so that once the concentration step has been accomplished, the identification of the accelerant type can be performed by gas chromatography (GC). This method is practically universal in crime laboratories. The concentration methods that are commonly used today are described here:

- *Passive headspace*: This is the most popular method of concentration of accelerant residues. This method is shown in Figure 23.6. The container is airtight. It is gently heated so that some of the accelerant will evaporate into the air space above the debris (*headspace*). Eventually, the amount of accelerant in the headspace will be in equilibrium with the amount in the debris. The higher the temperature, the more accelerant will be in the headspace. The container can only be heated a small amount because heating raises the pressure in the can and it could rupture. This is also why glass containers shouldn't be used. After the container is heated, the headspace can be sampled with a gastight syringe that can then be used to introduce the headspace vapor directly into a gas chromatograph.
- *Adsorption/elution*: This is a modification of the passive headspace method. Two small holes are punched in the top of the can and a tube containing *activated charcoal* (fine carbon powder) is put in each hole. A vacuum pump is then connected to one of the tubes. When the vacuum is turned on, it pulls the air out of the headspace of the can. The air is pulled through one of the tubes containing the charcoal. Instead of a vacuum, the accelerant can be removed by pumping an inert gas such as nitrogen through one of the tubes. This pushes the accelerant vapors out of the other tube. The charcoal traps the accelerant vapors. This apparatus can be seen in Figure 23.7. As the headspace becomes evacuated, air rushes in from the outside through the other tube. More of the accelerant will evaporate from the fire debris into the headspace to reestablish the equilibrium. But this air is continuously being pulled out of the can by the vacuum pump, and more air continually rushes in through the other tube. Eventually, practically all of the accelerant will be trapped (adsorbed) onto the charcoal. Then, the charcoal tubes are removed and a small amount of solvent is poured through the charcoal. This dissolves the accelerant and *elutes it* off the charcoal. The dissolved accelerant can then be injected into a gas chromatograph for analysis (Figure 23.9).

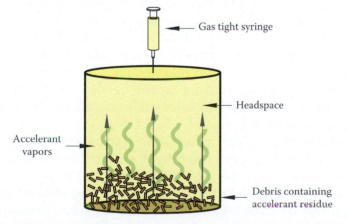

Figure 23.6 Diagram showing how the headspace in a sealed container of fire debris is sampled with a gastight syringe. The container is usually heated to drive more of the fire residue into the vapor phase. (Courtesy of Meredith Haddon.)

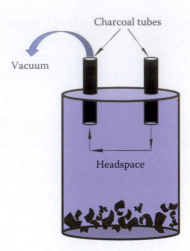

Figure 23.7 Absorption elution method of concentrating fire residue. The debris is heated, driving more of the residue into the vapor phase. A vacuum is drawn on the container that pulls the headspace vapors out, trapping them in the charcoal strip. Air rushes in through the other tube.

Think about "negative controls" (Chapter 3)

Figure 23.8 Answer to quiz question.

Something for You to Do

Why are there two holes in the top of the can? Why not simply put one hole in the can and insert a charcoal tube and then apply a vacuum to that tube? If you can figure out why there must be two holes in the can, then why is there a charcoal tube in each hole? If you cannot figure it out, then see the following hint (Figure 23.8):

- *Solid-phase microextraction (SPME)*: SPME is the newest technique in accelerant concentration. It takes advantage of the sensitivity of today's modern GC/MS instruments that require only a few micrograms of analyte. The SPME apparatus consists of a syringe whose needle is coated with charcoal or another polymer that is efficient at adsorbing accelerant molecules. The needle is inserted into the headspace in a container of fire residue. The residue is heated and the accelerant will adsorb onto the surface of the coated needle. After about 30 min, the needle is withdrawn and inserted directly into a gas chromatograph. The heat from the GC will elute the accelerant off the coating on the needle. SPME analysis removes the need for the concentrated accelerant to be eluted from whatever substrate it has been collected on.

- *Solvent extraction*: Solvent extraction is used to be a popular method of accelerant concentration. It is performed by opening the can of fire residue and adding a suitable solvent, usually pentane (C_5H_{12}) or a similar solvent and mixing well. Then, the mixture is filtered and the solvent evaporated to a small volume and injected into a gas chromatograph. The main drawback of solvent extraction is that many materials found in a home or business contain substances made from petroleum that will dissolve in the solvent and interfere with the GC used to analyze the accelerant.

Analysis of Accelerants

As aforementioned, the universal method for the analysis of accelerant residues is by GC, usually coupled to a mass spectrometer. The most common accelerants are gasoline and other consumer products such as charcoal lighter, paint thinners, and lamp oils. Fuels used in camping lanterns and stoves are also popular accelerants. Each of these products contains many components. Gasoline has more than 300 substances. The purpose of GC is not to identify each component, but to display the pattern of peaks obtained from a sample of fire debris. Figure 23.9 is a gas chromatogram of gasoline and Figure 23.10 is a gas chromatogram of charcoal lighter made from kerosene.

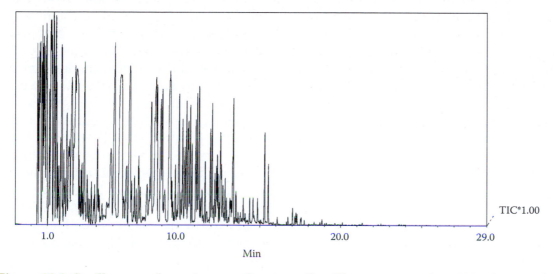

Figure 23.9 Capillary gas chromatogram of neat gasoline. There are more than 300 substances in gasoline. Most of them are displayed as discreet peaks.

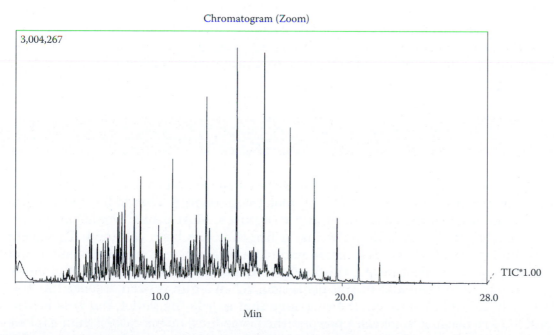

Figure 23.10 Gas chromatogram of a charcoal lighter fluid. This one is based on kerosene and the peak pattern is similar to that of any produce that is predominantly kerosene.

Interpretation of gas chromatograms of accelerants can be difficult. The chromatograms of gasoline and kerosene shown in Figures 23.9 and 23.10 are obtained from pristine materials, right out of the can. Accelerants that have been subjected to the heat from a fire undergo physical and chemical changes that will affect their chromatograms. Some of the components of all accelerants are volatile and will evaporate if exposed to heat. In the chromatograms in the figures, the most volatile substances are shown first (on the left). If they have evaporated, their peaks will be reduced and the chromatograms will be distorted. In extreme cases, an accelerant will evaporate or combust significantly and the associated chromatogram will look very different than the ones in Figures 23.9 and 23.10. Forensic chemists who analyze fire residues will prepare chromatographic libraries of common accelerants that have undergone various amounts of degradation due to partial combustion and/or evaporation. These can be used to compare against casework samples from a fire.

On the basis of the laboratory analysis of fire residues, a forensic chemist can reasonably conclude that accelerant residues are present in fire debris. If there is enough present, the chemist may be able to determine the type of product it is. One must be careful here. There are a number of commercial products made from the same material. For example, kerosene is used not only as a fuel itself for heating homes and businesses but also the main ingredient in many charcoal lighters and paint thinners. Thus, a finding of a kerosene pattern in a chromatogram of a fire residue does not itself justify naming what type of product it is, and of course, there are no circumstances where a chemist would be justified in reaching a conclusion that fire residue came from a particular container. There is nothing unique about a gas chromatogram of one sample of gasoline compared to another. No matter what conclusion the forensic scientist reaches about the presence and type of accelerant in fire residues, this information is only advisory to the fire scene investigator. The absence of an accelerant in fire residues does not mean that the fire was not deliberately set. The wrong evidence may have been collected or there may have been insufficient accelerant present in the evidence owing to its having been consumed by the fire. Likewise, the presence of an accelerant in fire residues doesn't mean that the fire was deliberately set. As was previously mentioned, it is not unusual for there to be accelerant materials such as gasoline stored in homes or businesses that may be innocently involved in a fire. It may be possible to determine the role of such materials in a fire if they are found some distance from the point of origin or are, in fact, used to make fire trail.

Explosions

If a fuel such as gasoline is confined to a closed space and then set on fire, gaseous products are produced (CO_2, H_2O, etc.) along with energy. This will cause the pressure to build up in the container until it ruptures. Most people would refer to this as an explosion, but it is actually just a fire that has been confined. To someone standing nearby, this is a distinction without a difference. It sure looks and sounds like an explosion. Most people think of an explosion as a violent release of energy, but a confined fire can also fit this definition. When a gun is fired, it looks like there has been an explosion inside the cartridge that expels the bullet, but this is also a confined fire because smokeless powder (the propellant) burns rather than explodes. To a forensic chemist, however, there are important differences between a confined fire and an explosion. The major difference between an explosion and a fire is the amount of energy released and how fast the products of the explosion travel as they move away from the point of origin. Chemical explosions are combustions just like fires. (Nuclear explosions operate on different principles and are not included in this discussion.) The difference between an explosion and a combustion lies in how much energy is emitted by a given amount of fuel and how intimate the oxygen is mixed with the fuel. There are two types of explosions: *deflagrations* and *detonations*.

Deflagration

Recall that the source of oxygen in a fire is in the air that surrounds the fuel in the form of O_2 and that activation energy is needed to break the oxygen bonds before the fire can take place. This is partly responsible for the relatively slow speed of the combustion in a fire relative to that in an explosion. In a deflagration, the oxygen is physically mixed with the fuel and is in a form where the O is bonded to other atoms that form weaker bonds than in O_2 and thus require less activation energy to break. An example of an explosive that deflagrates when activated is *black powder*. Black powder is one of the oldest known explosives. It is composed of potassium nitrate (KNO_3), charcoal (a form of carbon), and sulfur in a weight ratio of 15:3:2. The ingredients are all powders and are finely divided and mixed together. The activation energy to begin the combustion is supplied by a match or a spark. When ignited, the reaction will produce gases that escape at velocities up to the speed of sound (740 mph or about 1100 fps). The bonds between the nitrogen and oxygen atoms in potassium nitrate are broken by the activation energy, and these atoms then react with the carbon and sulfur forming many products. A great deal of energy is produced by these reactions. Explosions that produce escaping gases of velocities less than the speed of sound are referred to as "low explosives." Another low explosive that has been used in terrorist attacks such as the Murrah Federal Building in Oklahoma City (see Figure 23.11) is *ammonium nitrate and fuel oil (ANFO)*, which

Figure 23.13 T
Haddon.)

These genera
the consisten
can be direct
demolitions, e
minimum del
detonate at p
gallery of the
seattlepi.nwso

One of the n
The fuel in
its pure, liqu
ate (kieselgu
more stable
needs a blas
earthmover
explosive.
    The inve
and rose to
man, he was
chemistry. F
travels. In tl
owned by hi
handle and
settled on k
mite." He so
ued his chei

Figure 23.11 The Murrah Federal Building in Oklahoma City shortly after the 1996 bombing. (Courtesy of Oklahoma Bombing Investigation Committee, www.okbombing.org; Reprinted by Associated Press.)

to the development of artificial rubber and silk. As he grew older, Alfred Nobel became more interested in fostering the works of other inventors, especially those whose inventions or work benefited humanity. By the time he died in 1896, he had endowed a fund to make awards to people who exhibited great examples of human ingenuity. His first prize was awarded in 1901. Today, the most famous prize is the *Nobel Peace Prize*.

Ironically, Alfred Nobel thought that his invention of dynamite would banish war forever as man could see what terrible destruction it could wreak. He expressed this sentiment in a statement he made after receiving the patent on dynamite:

> My dynamite will sooner lead to peace than a thousand world conventions. As soon as men will find that in one instant, whole armies can be utterly destroyed, they surely will abide by golden peace.

One may reflect upon this statement and note that the same sentiments were expressed when the atomic bomb was developed by the United States. The real irony, of course is that the Noble Prize for Peace is given to a person or organization that promotes the cause of peace and this prize is endowed with profits from the manufacture and sale of an explosive used in war.

Investigation of Bombing Scenes

The investigation of the scene of a bombing can be one of the most difficult types of crime scenes. The majority of criminal or terrorist bombings take place outdoors and debris (and evidence) can be scattered over a wide area. Access to the scene after a bombing may be relatively uncontrolled and very difficult to seal off. People may enter the scene or leave it bringing in extraneous materials or carrying off evidence. There may be human remains and dead bodies that could present problems and health hazards. If buildings are involved, there could be secondary effects such as further collapse, dust, and hazardous debris. In some ways, investigation of bomb scenes is similar to that of fire scenes; the most important aspect is to locate the point of origin. In bombing scenes, the term "bomb seat" is often used but it means the same thing. The bomb seat will most likely be the best spot for locating and recovering unexploded residues of the explosive and/or parts of the bomb device. If the bombing takes place in the lower levels of a building, then the upper floors of the building may collapse onto the bomb seat, making its detection and recovery more difficult. In the first attempt to destroy the Twin Towers of the World Trade Center in New York in 2001, a truck loaded with explosives was parked in the parking garage under the center on the fourth level below the ground. Although the buildings didn't collapse, there was a great deal of damage to the parking garage. Upper levels of the garage including many cars crashed down onto the bomb seat. It took many weeks and heavy equipment to remove the rubble and expose the bomb seat where parts of the truck, bomb parts, and the unexploded and partially consumed explosive, urea nitrate, were found. In the Oklahoma City bombing, a truck filled with ANFO was parked in front of the Murrah building and the explosive was detonated remotely. There is evidence that the fasteners holding up wall of the truck that faced the building were loosened, so that the escaping energy and gases would be directed toward the building. The truck was not entirely destroyed and evidence of its identity was an important clue in this case.

amount of energy released and how fast the products of the explosion travel as they move away from the point of origin. Chemical explosions are combustions just like fires. (Nuclear explosions operate on different principles and are not included in this discussion.) The difference between an explosion and a combustion lies in how much energy is emitted by a given amount of fuel and how intimate the oxygen is mixed with the fuel. There are two types of explosions: *deflagrations* and *detonations*.

Deflagration

Recall that the source of oxygen in a fire is in the air that surrounds the fuel in the form of O_2 and that activation energy is needed to break the oxygen bonds before the fire can take place. This is partly responsible for the relatively slow speed of the combustion in a fire relative to that in an explosion. In a deflagration, the oxygen is physically mixed with the fuel and is in a form where the O is bonded to other atoms that form weaker bonds than in O_2 and thus require less activation energy to break. An example of an explosive that deflagrates when activated is *black powder*. Black powder is one of the oldest known explosives. It is composed of potassium nitrate (KNO_3), charcoal (a form of carbon), and sulfur in a weight ratio of 15:3:2. The ingredients are all powders and are finely divided and mixed together. The activation energy to begin the combustion is supplied by a match or a spark. When ignited, the reaction will produce gases that escape at velocities up to the speed of sound (740 mph or about 1100 fps). The bonds between the nitrogen and oxygen atoms in potassium nitrate are broken by the activation energy, and these atoms then react with the carbon and sulfur forming many products. A great deal of energy is produced by these reactions. Explosions that produce escaping gases of velocities less than the speed of sound are referred to as "low explosives." Another low explosive that has been used in terrorist attacks such as the Murrah Federal Building in Oklahoma City (see Figure 23.11) is *ammonium nitrate and fuel oil (ANFO)*, which

Figure 23.11 The Murrah Federal Building in Oklahoma City shortly after the 1996 bombing. (Courtesy of Oklahoma Bombing Investigation Committee, www.okbombing.org; Reprinted by Associated Press.)

is ammonium nitrate (NH_4NO_3) and fuel oil, a hydrocarbon fuel used to heat buildings. Ammonium nitrate is a pelleted fertilizer widely used by farmers. To make ANFO, these pellets are soaked in the fuel oil. This provides an intimate physical mixture of the fuel and the oxygen, but the velocities of the gases produced by the reaction are still slower than the speed of sound. Low explosives produce much more energetic products than fires but are still slow relative to high explosives, which are discussed next.

Detonation

A detonation is essentially an instantaneous explosion. It is so powerful that escaping gases travel at speeds greater than the speed of sound. Explosives that detonate are termed "high explosives." The tremendous forces produced by high explosives push the surrounding air with such power that it can collapse buildings and move huge amounts of earth. In a high explosive, the oxygen is actually incorporated into the fuel molecules. When the activation energy is applied, the bonds connecting the oxygen atoms to the explosive molecule break as do all of the other bonds, and then, recombination takes place forming lower energy products. Since the oxygen is so intimately combined with the fuel, the combustion reaction is essentially instantaneous. Examples of some high explosives are given in Figure 23.12.

Notice that all of these explosives have oxygen incorporated as NO_2 or COH. Oxygen in this form is readily available to react with the other atoms in the fuel to release large amounts of energy very quickly. Some high explosives have very low activation energy and can detonate when only with only a small disturbance. Others are very stable and need another explosive to cause detonation.

Initiating and Noninitiating High Explosives

There are two types of high explosives: *initiating and noninitiating*. These are also called *primary* and *secondary* high explosives. The relationships between these types of high explosives and some examples are given in Figure 23.13.

Initiating explosives are relatively sensitive to detonation. The extreme example of this is nitroglycerine, a syrupy liquid that is so sensitive that a small shock such as shaking or dropping can cause detonation. Noninitiating explosives such as dynamite or trinitrotoluene (TNT) require a *booster charge* such as pentaerythritol tetranitrate (PETN). See Figure 23.13. There have been a number of modern modifications of explosives so they can be adapted to specialized uses. One of the more important of these advances has been the development of *plastique* explosives.

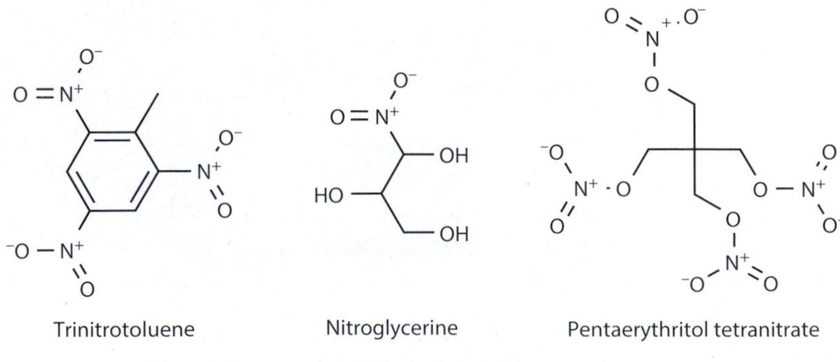

Trinitrotoluene   Nitroglycerine   Pentaerythritol tetranitrate

Figure 23.12 Chemical structures of some high explosives.

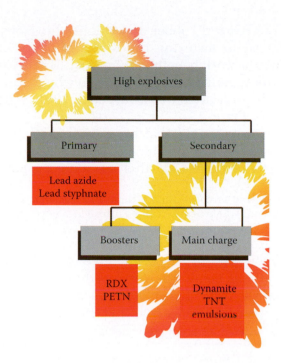

Figure 23.13 The relationships among different types of high explosives. (Courtesy of Meredith Haddon.)

These generally contain PETN and/or RDX mixed with a polymer plastic that has the consistency of clay. These explosives can be shaped or molded so their blast can be directed in particular directions. These explosives are highly popular in demolitions, especially of the type where a large building is to be destroyed with a minimum debris scattering. The charges are set in various locations and timed to detonate at particular intervals so that the building seems to implode. A picture gallery of the stadium Kingdome in Seattle, Washington, can be seen at http://seattlepi.nwsource.com/kingdome/gallery.asp.

Did You Know: Dynamite and the Nobel Prize?

One of the most potent and popular of all chemical high explosives is dynamite. The fuel in dynamite is nitroglycerine (Figure 23.12), but this is too unstable in its pure, liquid form, so it is mixed with *diatomaceous earth* and calcium carbonate (kieselguhr) and then rolled into a cylindrical shape. In this form, it is much more stable and easy to handle and is considered to be a secondary explosive. It needs a blasting cap or primer cord to detonate it. Dynamite is widely used as an earthmover because of its high pushing force. It has also been used as a military explosive.

The inventor of dynamite was *Alfred Nobel*. He was born in Sweden in 1833 and rose to be one of the most influential industrialists in the world. As a young man, he was fluent in five languages and was more interested in literature than chemistry. He wrote plays, poetry, and novels in his spare time on his extensive travels. In the 1860s, Nobel began experimenting with nitroglycerine in a factory owned by his father. He concentrated on making the sensitive explosive easier to handle and more stable. He mixed it with many different substrates and finally settled on kieselguhr. He obtained a patent on the mixture and called it "dynamite." He sold dynamite all over the world and became very wealthy. He continued his chemical research throughout his life, ultimately making contributions to the development of artificial rubber and silk. As he grew older, Alfred Nobel became more interested in fostering the works of other inventors, especially those whose inventions or work benefited humanity. By the time he died in 1896, he had endowed a fund to make awards to people who exhibited great examples of human ingenuity. His first prize was awarded in 1901. Today, the most famous prize is the *Nobel Peace Prize*.

Ironically, Alfred Nobel thought that his invention of dynamite would banish war forever as man could see what terrible destruction it could wreak. He expressed this sentiment in a statement he made after receiving the patent on dynamite:

> My dynamite will sooner lead to peace than a thousand world conventions. As soon as men will find that in one instant, whole armies can be utterly destroyed, they surely will abide by golden peace.

One may reflect upon this statement and note that the same sentiments were expressed when the atomic bomb was developed by the United States. The real irony, of course is that the Noble Prize for Peace is given to a person or organization that promotes the cause of peace and this prize is endowed with profits from the manufacture and sale of an explosive used in war.

Investigation of Bombing Scenes

The investigation of the scene of a bombing can be one of the most difficult types of crime scenes. The majority of criminal or terrorist bombings take place outdoors and debris (and evidence) can be scattered over a wide area. Access to the scene after a bombing may be relatively uncontrolled and very difficult to seal off. People may enter the scene or leave it bringing in extraneous materials or carrying off evidence. There may be human remains and dead bodies that could present problems and health hazards. If buildings are involved, there could be secondary effects such as further collapse, dust, and hazardous debris. In some ways, investigation of bomb scenes is similar to that of fire scenes; the most important aspect is to locate the point of origin. In bombing scenes, the term "bomb seat" is often used but it means the same thing. The bomb seat will most likely be the best spot for locating and recovering unexploded residues of the explosive and/or parts of the bomb device. If the bombing takes place in the lower levels of a building, then the upper floors of the building may collapse onto the bomb seat, making its detection and recovery more difficult. In the first attempt to destroy the Twin Towers of the World Trade Center in New York in 2001, a truck loaded with explosives was parked in the parking garage under the center on the fourth level below the ground. Although the buildings didn't collapse, there was a great deal of damage to the parking garage. Upper levels of the garage including many cars crashed down onto the bomb seat. It took many weeks and heavy equipment to remove the rubble and expose the bomb seat where parts of the truck, bomb parts, and the unexploded and partially consumed explosive, urea nitrate, were found. In the Oklahoma City bombing, a truck filled with ANFO was parked in front of the Murrah building and the explosive was detonated remotely. There is evidence that the fasteners holding up wall of the truck that faced the building were loosened, so that the escaping energy and gases would be directed toward the building. The truck was not entirely destroyed and evidence of its identity was an important clue in this case.

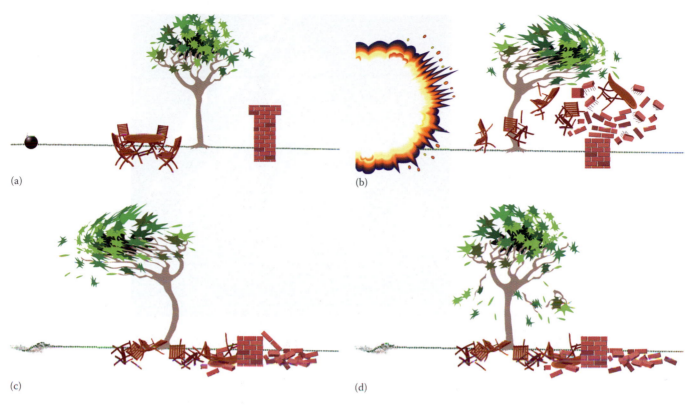

Figure 23.14 The progression of an explosion. (a) The condition of the scene before the explosion. (b) The positive pressure phase. (c) The damage after the negative pressure phase. (d) The condition of the scene after the explosion is over. (Courtesy of Meredith Haddon.)

Consider what happens when a bomb goes off. When the detonation takes place, very hot gases are formed, which race away from the bomb seat at high velocities, creating a *blast pressure* front and carrying debris and explosive residues along. The air around the explosion is pushed away, creating a partial vacuum at the site. As the blast pressure subsides, air rushes back toward the bomb seat to fill the vacuum, carrying debris with it and causing more destruction in the vicinity of the bomb seat. The actual location of the blast may be buried under tons of rubble. The progression of an explosion is depicted in Figure 23.14.

Finding parts of the explosive device can be very important, especially in terrorist bombings. The vast majority of terrorist bombs employ homemade devices and terrorist groups tend to use the same technology each time. Even small pieces of the device that set off the bomb can yield important clues about who made it or how it was made and detonated. Finding pieces of the device in large amounts of rubble can involve painstaking searching and sifting. Figure 23.15 shows a typical homemade bomb device.

Locating unburned explosive material can also be very important. This material can be directly analyzed by instrumental and other methods, and the exact explosive can then be identified easily. Exploded material will leave behind ions such as nitrite or nitrate, but these are generally components of soil anyway, and finding them is not certain evidence of the presence of an explosive. Explosive-sniffing dogs can help here.

It is very important to locate people in the wreckage of an explosion. Of course, finding survivors and getting them treated is the first responsibility of bomb scene responders. It is also important to locate dead bodies and remove them as early in the investigation as possible. The so-called cadaver dogs can be used here. See Chapter 7.

3. Which of the following is *not* a method of removing accelerant residues from fire debris?
   a. Gas chromatography
   b. Heated headspace
   c. Solvent extraction
   d. Absorption–elution
   e. SPME

4. In a low explosive, oxygen is
   a. Physically mixed with the fuel
   b. Chemically part of the fuel
   c. In the air surrounding the fuel
   d. Not needed

5. Secondary explosives
   a. Are a type of low explosive
   b. Are noninitiating
   c. Require a booster
   d. Always contain oxygen in the form of O_2 molecules

6. ANFO is
   a. A high explosive
   b. A mixture of a fertilizer and a commercial heating oil
   c. Burned rather than exploded when ignited
   d. Is very sensitive to detonation

7. Dynamite
   a. Is an initiating explosive
   b. Is a mixture containing nitroglycerine
   c. Deflagrates when ignited
   d. Produces escaping gases whose velocities are less than the speed of light

8. SPME
   a. Is a method for detecting explosive residues
   b. Is the same thing as absorption–elution but on a microscale
   c. Uses a coated wire inserted into the headspace of a container of fire debris, to adsorb accelerant residues
   d. Is a method for the identification of fire residues

9. The Griess test
   a. Is used in the analysis of accelerants
   b. Detects the presence of oxygen in any form
   c. Reacts with nitrates and nitrates
   d. Reacts with all explosives

10. The activation energy that is needed to get a fire started is used to
    a. Break up molecular oxygen into atoms
    b. Decompose the fuel into carbon dioxide and water
    c. Extract accelerant residues from fire debris in a closed can
    d. Convert liquid oxygen to a vapor

True–False

11. The bomb seat is the same thing as the point of origin.
12. If a fire scene investigator can eliminate natural and accidental causes of a fire, then the fire must be arson.
13. A low explosive creates gases that escape at velocities up to the speed of sound.

14. Nitroglycerine is an initiating high explosive.
15. The presence of a fire trail always means that the fire was arson.
16. The presence of an accelerant in fire residues always means that the fire is arson.
17. The most important evidence of the cause of a fire can usually be found at the point of origin.

Matching: Match Each Term with Its Definition

18. Detonation	a. Requires initiation by another high explosive
19. Incendiary	b. Damage to concrete by fire
20. Accelerant	c. Instantaneous combustion
21. Secondary high explosive	d. Deliberate fire
22. Spalling	e. Starts or speeds up a fire that otherwise wouldn't start on its own

Short Essay

23. Briefly describe and give an example of the three causes of a fire.
24. What is the fire tetrahedron? What are its parts? What relation does this have to putting out a fire?
25. What are the types of high explosive? How do they differ?

Further Reading

DeHaan, J. (1991). *Kirk's Fire Investigation*, 3rd edn. Prentice Hall, Englewood Cliffs, NJ.

Redsiker, D. and J. O'Connor. (1997). *Practical Fire and Arson Investigation*, 2nd edn. CRC Press, Boca Raton, FL.

Siegel, J. (ed.). (2000). Fire investigation, in *Encyclopedia of Forensic Science*. Academic Press, London, U.K.

Urbanski, T. (1964). *Chemistry and Technology of Explosives*, vols. 1–3. Pergamon Press, Oxford, U.K.

Yinon, J. and S. Zitrin. (1991). *The Analysis of Explosives*. Pergamon Press, Oxford, U.K.

Yinon, J. and S. Zitrin. (1993). *Modern Methods and Applications in Analysis of Explosives*. John Wiley, New York.

On the Web

Story and pictures of London, England bombing: http://en.wikipedia.org/wiki/7_July_2005_London_bombings.

Story and pictures of Madrid bombing: http://news.bbc.co.uk/1/hi/in_depth/europe/2004/madrid_train_attacks/default.stm.

Story and pictures of Oklahoma City Bombing: http://en.wikipedia.org/wiki/Oklahoma_City_bombing.

Very good website on fire and arson investigations: http://www.interfire.org/.

You Tube arson fire videos: http://www.mashget.com/topic/arson-fires/.

PART VI

Legal Aspects of Forensic Science

24
Presentation of Forensic Evidence in Court

1. To be able to define admissibility of evidence
2. To be able to define and give examples of relevance of evidence
3. To be able to define and give examples of competence of evidence
4. To be able to describe the contributions of *Frye v. United States* to the admissibility of scientific evidence
5. To be able to describe the contributions of *Daubert v. Merrell Dow* to the admissibility of scientific evidence
6. To be able to describe the main features of a good forensic science laboratory report
7. To be able to define expert witness and distinguish an expert witness from a lay witness
8. To be able to describe the procedure of offering expert testimony
9. To be able to define *voir dire* discuss its importance in expert testimony

Chapter 24

Presentation of Forensic Evidence in Court

Chapter Outline

Mini Glossary

Bench trial: A trial where the trier of fact is the judge.

Competence: A condition of admissibility of evidence. A set of legal constraints on the admissibility of evidence.

Expert witness: A witness who is qualified by knowledge, skills or education to offer expert testimony and inferences or opinions that the average person could not.

General acceptance: A standard for the admissibility of scientific evidence. It means that the underlying scientific principle of the evidence is agreed upon as true by the scientific community that would be most informed about the evidence.

Hearsay: A statement made outside of a court by someone who is not under oath that is being used in court to assert the truth of the statement.

Jury trial: A trial where the trier of fact is the jury.

Lay witness: A witness who is not an expert and can only testify what he or she experienced with their five senses.

Materiality: The evidence has something to do with the case being tried here and now.

Peer review: A process whereby a research manuscript is reviewed by experts in the scientific field of the manuscript subject.

Probative: Tendency to prove a fact.

Relevance: A condition of admissibility of evidence. It is made up of materiality and probativeness.

Statistically significant: A statistical test that determines whether differences between two measurements are real or a product of the sample or other issue.

Subpoena: A command to appear in court for a hearing or trial at a set date.

Subpoena duces tecum: A command to appear in court that includes all reports and records concerning the case.

Trier of fact: The party that makes the decision of guilty or not guilty in a trial.

Acronyms

AFIS: Automated Fingerprint Identification System
FRE: Federal Rules of Evidence
NAS: National Academy of Sciences

Introduction

In 1923, James Alphonso Frye was convicted of murder in Washington, D.C., in the Supreme Court of the District of Columbia. During his trial, he sought to have the results of a systolic blood pressure deception test admitted to help prove that he was not guilty of the crime. This test was a forerunner of today's modern polygraph test. The test measured changes in the subject's systolic blood pressure. The underlying principle of the test was that when someone spoke the truth, he did so without any conscious effort, but that telling a deliberate lie requires conscious effort and is stressful and results in an involuntary change in systolic blood pressure. The prosecutor objected to the admission of this test claiming that it was controversial and that scientists didn't agree whether the test was reliable, and therefore, the jury shouldn't have to speculate about its reliability and whether to put any weight on the results. The judge agreed with the prosecutor and Fry appealed to the U.S. Court of Appeals. The judges in the Court of Appeals affirmed the lower court ruling and sustained the guilty verdict. In their written opinion, the justices claimed that the systolic blood pressure deception test was not generally accepted by the relevant scientific community and was, therefore, not admissible.

The *Frye* decision is one of the most important in U.S. law and in its application to forensic science and scientific evidence. It set out the standard for admissibility of scientific evidence in most state and federal courts for more than a half century. Although it was overturned as the standard for admissibility of scientific evidence in federal court in the 1970s, it is still the standard for admissibility in close to half the states in the United States.

This chapter is about the relationship and interface between law and science. The reason that forensic science exists is because it helps provide evidence and answer legal questions such as who committed a crime, who is responsible for illegal acts that can harm society, and who should be blamed when a person is harmed. This book is mostly about the criminal justice system but it is important to know that there is a parallel civil justice system. This system is for when people or institutions are the victims of harmful or illegal acts that do not amount to a crime, but for which damages may be paid. Although there are significant differences in how justice is carried out in these two systems, the way that forensic science is viewed and employed is the same. The United States and many other countries employ an *adversary* system of justice. It is important to know that many other countries treat forensic evidence in court very differently than we do in the United States. They use an *inquisitorial* justice system.

Where does forensic science fit into the criminal justice system? Once a crime is reported or discovered, the police will launch an investigation. In large police departments, detectives perform criminal investigations. They take overall charge of the investigation. Part of the investigation will be a search of the crime scene. This is a critical phase because much or all of the physical evidence of the crime will be found at the scene. As explained in Chapter 2, most of the search of the crime scene is carried out by crime scene investigators. They collect, preserve, and package the evidence and have it sent to the forensic science lab for analysis. As the investigation proceeds, this is a continuing process. Before a trial, witnesses may be *deposed*, although this process is much more common in civil than criminal cases. This is an evidence gathering process for the attorneys who question witnesses outside the courtroom. In this setting, witnesses are under oath and the questions and answers are recorded. If there is a preliminary hearing and/or trial, forensic scientists may be called to testify as expert witnesses. In some cases, reports written by forensic scientists that set out their findings may be admitted in lieu of actual testimony. This process gives rise to three important considerations that affect the use of forensic science in the criminal justice system:

- The admissibility of scientific evidence
- Forensic science laboratory reports and their legal status
- The role of the expert witness in court

Of these, the most important and most studied is the admissibility of scientific evidence. Our adjudicative system operates by a series of rules. Some of these rules govern the admissibility of evidence in general and still others the admissibility of scientific evidence in particular.

Admissibility of Evidence

In the U.S. adjudicative system, the party that determines guilt or innocence of the accused is called the "trier of fact." In a *bench trial,* the trier of fact is the judge. In such cases, the judge presides over the trial and makes the final decision as to guilt or innocence. In a *jury trial,* the trier of fact is the jury. The jury can be as few as 6 people and as many as 12 (plus alternates). They listen to the evidence presented during the trial and are instructed by the judge as to the applicable law that governs the case. They apply the law to the facts and evidence of the case and reach a decision of guilt or innocence. In some cases, the jury may have a role in the punishment although this is usually the purview of the judge. During the trial, either or both parties (prosecutor or defendant) will present evidence that supports that side's theory of what happened in the incident. This evidence can take a variety of forms including testimony from eyewitness, police, or experts, as well as physical evidence such as drugs, blood, or bullets. All evidence must comport to rules governing its admissibility and it is up to the judge to make determinations of admissibility even in a jury trial. The judge always makes decisions that are legal in nature at a trial even if the trier of fact is a jury.

Admissibility of evidence is the determination of what matters may come before the trier of fact. There are many rules of evidence that seek to protect the jury from hearing evidence that is contaminated in one way or another. Examples include evidence that is prejudicial, irrelevant, time wasting, unconstitutional, or unreliable. The major rule that applies to ALL evidence, scientific or not, is that evidence must be *relevant* and *competent* in order to be admitted at trial. Evidence that is relevant may still be inadmissible if it is not competent. Each of these concepts will be discussed in turn. Please keep in mind that there are many exceptions to the rules that follow. The explanations of the rules are generalities that apply in the majority of basic situations. Also, keep in mind that legal terminology such as competence may have different meanings than it would otherwise have in a nonlegal setting.

Relevance

Relevance is made up of two components: *materiality and probativeness.* In order for evidence to be relevant, it must be both material and probative. *Material* means that the evidence has something to do with the case being tried here and now. It cannot refer back to evidence that arose from some previous incident. For example, assume that a person is on trial for sexual assault. The fact that he or she may have committed previous sexual assaults is not material to this trial and is generally not admissible. Juries are not permitted to hear of a defendant's previous criminal record because it is not material and may also be prejudicial. *Probativeness* means that the evidence must prove something. In legal parlance, it means that the evidence must make a proposition more or less likely than it would be without the evidence. Probative evidence can help prove or disprove a proposition or accusation or set of facts. For example, suppose a person is accused of killing another person by shooting him. When arrested, the suspect is found to be carrying a large knife. As the death was by shooting, the knife is not probative. It doesn't help prove or disprove that the defendant shot the victim.

To summarize, if evidence tends to prove or disprove a proposition about the case being tried here and now, it is probative and material and, therefore, relevant.

Competence

Competence doesn't mean the same thing in the context of admissibility of evidence as it does in other situations. Here, competence can mean a number of things having to do with the law:

- *Prejudice*: Evidence cannot unduly prejudice the trier of fact for or against the accused. Highly inflammatory, gory color pictures of an autopsy of the dead victim may be inadmissible because their probativeness is outweighed by prejudice. The jury may become so horrified by the pictures that they can no longer be objective about the guilt or innocence of the defendant. Prior criminal activity and evidence of bad character are also generally inadmissible on the grounds of prejudice (and perhaps relevance).

- *Constitutional constraints*: The fourth amendment of the constitution prohibits unreasonable searches of people and places and usually requires that a judge or magistrate issue a search warrant before a search can take place. The warrant and supporting affidavit (statement) must specify the location and persons to be searched and the items being sought. If evidence is seized in violation of these requirements, then it may be inadmissible no matter how relevant it is. Other constitutional amendments such as the Miranda rights, the right to a speedy trial, and the right to confront witnesses may also play into considerations of competency.
- *Statutory constraints*: The common law provides for a number of *privileges*. These are protected types of speech between doctor–patient, lawyer–client, marital partners, cleric–penitent, etc. For example, if one spouse makes potentially incriminating statements to his spouse in the course of private communication, the spouse cannot be compelled to testify against her husband, and the husband can prevent the testimony even if the spouse wants to testify. These are the marital privileges. All of these privileges are designed to foster communications that are deemed necessary without placing the speaker in danger of prosecution. You can see, for example, how you would want private communications with your attorney to remain private. Many people would not go to a doctor for treatment if they thought that information about their medical condition could show up in a workplace or court.
- *Hearsay*: Hearsay refers to a statement made outside of a court by someone who is not under oath that is being used in court to assert the truth of the statement. Hearsay evidence can be unreliable because the person who repeats the statement in court can only testify as to what he or she heard or saw and not the truth of the statement. For example, if Person A overhears a conversation between two people where Person B tells the other one that he or she robbed a bank, Person A's retelling of what he or she overheard in a courtroom would be inadmissible hearsay. Person A could only testify that he or she heard the statement but could not answer questions about its truth. Even written documents can be considered statements and may be inadmissible. For example, a laboratory report by a forensic scientist is a form of hearsay but still may be admissible in court as an exception to the hearsay rule. There are many exceptions to the hearsay rule in modern jurisprudence. The hearsay rule was originally developed in medieval England as a way of keeping unreliable statements out of court.

Remember that in order for any evidence to be admissible in court, it must pass both the relevance and competence tests. Sometimes, it is hard for the public to understand this. Have you ever heard of a situation where someone is found not guilty of a crime even though there existed incriminating evidence that couldn't be admitted because it was obtained illegally by a police officer who was executing an improper search warrant? Such cases are said to be decided unfairly because the defendant *got off on a technicality*. The fact is that the rules of evidence are all technicalities: hurdles that must be surmounted if the evidence is to be admitted into court. These rules of evidence apply to ALL evidence including testimony and physical evidence. In general, once evidence has been deemed to be relevant and competent, the trier of fact is presumed to possess enough knowledge to make judgments about the truth of the evidence and how much weight to give it.

Admissibility of Scientific Evidence

Have you ever seen a TV commercial for a product such as a new medicine? The spokesperson sometimes wears a white lab coat and perhaps even a stethoscope. The idea here is that the viewer is supposed to believe that the speaker is a doctor or other type of scientist and as such should be believed. This is the aura of truth that accompanies scientific matters simply because they are scientific. The problem is that much of the scientific and technical evidence presented in court is complex and often beyond the ability of jurors and judges who are not trained in science to understand. This opens the door for unreliable, unvalidated testimony that masquerades as science to be offered in court to unsuspecting judges and juries. There must be legal safeguards in place to ensure that the evidence that the trier of fact hears is reliable and scientifically valid. Therefore, in addition to all of the other rules of evidence discussed earlier, there are some special rules that apply only to the admissibility of scientific and technical evidence.

Development of the Rules for Scientific Evidence

Prior to 1923 in the United States, scientific evidence was treated like any other evidence. If there was a witness who could vouch for and explain the evidence and it was otherwise relevant and competent, it was admissible and the trier of fact could put whatever weight on it that they wanted. This is called the "relevance" standard for the admissibility of evidence. The *Frye* case described in the introduction to this chapter changed all that. A new standard for admissibility of scientific evidence arose from this case. It is called the "general acceptance" standard. It means that whenever a party seeks to introduce a new scientific test or technique, the relevant scientific community must first generally accept it. In the case of the systolic blood pressure deception test mentioned in the *Frye* case, the relevant scientific community would be psychologists and neurophysiologists. One of the problems with the *Frye* decision was that the Court of Appeals never defined what it meant by *general acceptance*. During the intervening years since *Frye*, general acceptance has grown to mean that the technique has been published in a *peer-reviewed* book or journal.

Did You Know: The Peer-Review Process

When a scientist makes a discovery, he or she will seek to publish it in a reputable book or journal so that he or she can claim credit for the discovery and so that other scientists can use his or her technique and build upon it and make other discoveries. That is how science progresses. How does a reader of the journal know that the articles are reliable? One way is to engage in a peer-review process. Before the publisher and editor of the book or journal will accept the manuscript, they will send it out to experts in the same field as the author (peers). They will read the manuscript carefully and may even try to replicate some of the methodologies to make sure that they work properly. If they agree, then the article is published. Although the peer-review process is very helpful in determining whether new methods and techniques are reliable and scientifically valid, it is not perfect. Very often the peers only read the manuscript and do not attempt to replicate the experiments or procedures because of lack of resources and time. Another problem is that a group of people who advocate the use of a scientifically questionable or invalid technique might set up their own journal and accept manuscripts from like-minded people. The manuscripts undergo a kind of peer review and the article gets published in the journal but its methods are still suspect. This type of practice is a form of *junk science*. Sometimes, it is difficult to discredit or stamp out this practice.

Once the *Frye* decision was announced, it became the rule for federal courts in the United States. Federal court decisions generally do not apply to individual state court systems, but about half of the states eventually adopted the *Frye* standard, while the other half continued to use the old relevancy standard. For the next 50+ years, new scientific techniques were subjected to a *Frye* test in court in an effort to insure that they were scientifically sound. Even DNA typing survived a number of *Frye* challenges in several states before being accepted nationwide.

Federal Rules of Evidence

It is the responsibility of the Congress to make rules that govern court procedures. This is done by enacting a set of rules called the "Federal Rules of Evidence" (FREs). Many of these rules arose from the common law that came down from medieval England when the United States was founded. Others have developed over time out of court decisions. Some of these rules refer to scientific evidence. In 1975, the Congress decided after many hearings, to overhaul and modernize the rules of evidence. These changes included the rules that applied to scientific and technical evidence. An extensive discussion of these changes is beyond the scope of this book but one new rule, FRE 702, warrants discussion. It reads as follows:

> If scientific, technical, or other specialized knowledge will assist the trier of fact to understand the evidence or to determine a fact in issue, a witness qualified as an expert by knowledge, skill, experience, training, or education, may testify thereto in the form of an opinion or otherwise, if (1) the testimony is based upon sufficient facts or data, (2) the testimony is the product of reliable principles and methods, and (3) the witness has applied the principles and methods reliably to the facts of the case.

Essentially, this rule hearkens back to the old relevancy standard. The judge decides if the proposed scientific testimony will help the jury understand the evidence. Then, the judge will permit an expert witness to testify about the scientific issue if the testimony is based on reliable scientific methods and principles. Note that the concept of general acceptance by a relevant scientific community is not mentioned.

Once the Congress passed these new rules, they became the law for all federal courts. Although they did not apply to state judicial systems, most states adopted many of these rules in whole or in part for their own courts. It is interesting to note that many federal courts ignored the FREs when making decisions about the admissibility of novel scientific evidence, instead continuing to rely on the *Frye* standard. This lasted until 1993 when the *Daubert* case was decided.

Daubert v. Merrell Dow

The *Daubert* case is an example of a *toxic tort*. A tort is a type of civil infraction. It is harm to a person or group by another person, group or organization, or company. A toxic tort is a harm that is alleged to have been caused by a dangerous or poisonous substance. The movie *Erin Brockovich* depicted a toxic tort caused by a company that dumped toxic substances into a water supply, leading to many illnesses and deaths. In the Daubert case, Mrs. Daubert was a pregnant woman whose doctor prescribed *Bendectin*, a drug that was commonly prescribed to relieve nausea among women in their first trimester of pregnancy. Mrs. Daubert took Bendectin during two successive pregnancies resulting in two babies that had birth defects. She sued the manufacturer of Bendectin, Merrell Dow, in federal court, claiming that the drug was the cause of the birth defects in her children. (The case was heard in federal court rather than state court because Merrell Dow engages in interstate commerce and federal courts have jurisdiction in such situations). Merrell Dow denied that their drug caused the birth defects and a trial ensued.

The biochemical mechanisms that result in birth defects are not well-known, and there was no way at that time to prove medically that Bendectin caused birth defects. As a result, the plaintiff, Mrs. Daubert, had to use *epidemiology*, the study of disease that occurs in a large population, to prove her case. This is the same type of strategy that is used in court to allege that cigarettes cause cancer. Essentially, her epidemiologists had to gather data about the number of women who gave birth to babies with birth defects, the number of women who took Bendectin while pregnant, and the number of women who took Bendectin while pregnant and gave birth to babies with birth defects. They then took these data and used statistics to determine whether there was a *statistically significant* increase in the number of birth defects in babies from women who took Bendectin over the number in women who did not. The statistically significant requirement is very important in statistics. It is a test that determines whether a difference between two measurements is a real difference or a trivial one. For example, statistics may show an increase in birth defects with Bendectin, but that increase may be due to the type and size of the sample of cases studied and may not be a true difference. Mrs. Daubert's statisticians determined that there was an increase and that it was statistically significant. Merrell Dow's statisticians determined from approximately the same data that there was no statistically significant difference in birth defects with Bendectin.

When Mrs. Daubert's epidemiologists were going to offer their testimony, the defense objected on the grounds that her scientists did not use *generally accepted* methods of statistics in order to reach their conclusions and because of that, their testimony should not be admitted. In raising this objection, the defense was invoking the *Frye* rule. The judge agreed with the defense and disallowed the plaintiff's testimony. As her statisticians could not testify about their data, the defense had no case and the judge directed the jury to return a verdict for Merrell Dow (this outcome of a case is called a "directed verdict"). Mrs. Daubert's lawyers appealed the decision on the grounds that the trial judge used the wrong standard of admissibility of the scientific evidence and should have allowed the statisticians for the plaintiff to testify. They claimed that the judge should have used the standards set out in FRE 702 and not the *Frye* standard.

The U.S. Supreme Court agreed to hear the appeal and ultimately agreed with Mrs. Daubert. They remanded the case back to the trial court for a rehearing and directed the judge to use the FREs to make his determination on the admissibility of the plaintiff's statistical evidence. The Supreme Court decision stated that the *Frye* standard no longer applied to the Federal Courts and that it was too restrictive. They determined that FRE 702 put the responsibility on the judge to act as a *gatekeeper* and determine the admissibility of scientific evidence on broader grounds. The justices indicated that there were many possible tests of scientific validity beyond general acceptance and, in their decision in the *Daubert* case, listed a few:

- *Falsifiability*: This concept refers to testing a new theory or method. When a new scientific theory is proposed, it is subjected to rigorous experimentation that attempts to prove that the theory is false or doesn't work. If repeated attempts to prove it false fail, this provides evidence that the theory is valid. An example would be the theory that gravity on earth pulls all objects toward the center of the earth. If someone drops a hammer on earth, it should fall.

Repeated tests of this theory show that a dropped hammer will always fall down and not up. As no examples of the theory being false have been shown, it must be true.

- *Known error rates*: During the development of a new technique or method, a scientist will determine or estimate the frequency of errors and their types when the method is used. All scientific tests and methods are subject to errors. Knowing the frequency of these errors will help the trier of fact determine the validity of the method.
- *Peer review*: The Supreme Court recognized the value of publishing and peer review of scientific methods and techniques, and they included it in their suggested means of assessing scientific validity.
- *General acceptance*: The Supreme Court didn't say that the *Frye* standard wasn't a valid means of assessing scientific validity, only that it cannot be the sole means of doing so. They recognized that scientific consensus has significant value in evaluating a new scientific technique.

Since the Supreme Court ruling in *Daubert*, most states have adopted the decision in whole or in part. There are still a few *Frye* states and a few that rely on the old relevance standard, but *Daubert* has essentially become the law of the land. There have been further court decisions that have clarified and extended Daubert since 1993, and there are still test cases being prepared to determine whether *Daubert* should be extended to *soft* sciences such as psychology and whether it can be applied to old scientific techniques that have already been accepted in court. For example, there have been challenges recently to fingerprint and handwriting testimony on the grounds that they have not been proven to be scientifically valid. These challenges would not have been possible under the *Frye* standard because that decision referred only to new or novel scientific evidence and did not apply to evidence such as fingerprints, which had been accepted in courts for more than one-hundred years.

Laboratory Reports

All scientific examinations, especially those that are meant for public consumption, culminate in a scientific report. This is always true in forensic science. Every case examined in a crime laboratory must have a written report that goes to the attorneys and to the court. The forensic scientist may be called to court to authenticate, substantiate, and explain the report to the trier of fact. The report is based on notes taken by the scientist during the evidence examination. These notes may also be required to be produced in court along with the report. There is no standard reporting system for forensic science in the United States. Some laboratories use a brief report format, reporting only the evidence received, demographic data, and the results of the tests. Other labs use formal scientific reports that include a description of the examinations, their limitations, and error rates. Figure 24.1 is a specimen of a brief laboratory report issued by a crime laboratory.

Recall the discussion of the Report of the Forensic Science Committee of the National Academy of Sciences (NAS), in Chapters 1 and 3. Recommendation 2 of the report is concerned in part with laboratory reports in forensic science. Testimony given to the committee indicated that laboratory reports in forensic science are often little more than certificates of analysis that lacked data and explanations of how conclusions are reached as well as detailed procedures for the analyses that are

---

REPORT OF LABORATORY EXAMINATION
IUPUI Forensic and Investigative Sciences

Date: 24 January 2005   **IUPUI case number:** 41-960

Contributing agency: Police Department   **County:**

Agency case number: PD.05.932   **Submitting official:** Police Officer

Item # Description of items received

One sealed plastic bag containing two plastic ziplock bags each containing green-brown plant material. Weight, item 1 = 23.3g
item 2 = 64.7g

Results of Examination

The green-brown plant material in items 1 and 2 were subjected to microscopic analysis, the modified Duquenois Levine test and thin layer chromatography, and were identified as marijuana, a schedule I controlled substance.

Figure 24.1 This is a specimen of a brief laboratory report issued by a forensic science laboratory. Note that the only information presented about the evidence is a description, weight, and the identity of the controlled substance. There is no information about what tests were done and their results.

being reported. Such reports are not considered to be scientific in nature. The recommendation calls for the establishment of model and scientific report formats that would have to be used by all accredited forensic science laboratories.

A recent study conducted by one of the authors of this book looked at 421 redacted forensic science laboratory reports from more than 40 laboratories nationwide. The study showed that the testimony before the Forensic Science Committee was very often borne out and that reports from forensic science laboratories were often inadequate from the standpoint of completeness and comprehensiveness, inclusion of data generated by the scientific analyses, and a discussion of how conclusions about the evidence were reached. This study also examined recommendations made by more than 30 organizations in forensic science and the legal and criminal justice systems. It was found that most of these organizations recommended that forensic science reports contain data and explanations and generally be scientific in nature.

Laboratory reports are an example of hearsay. They contain statements that are made outside of court by a person (the forensic scientist) who is not under oath at the time they wrote the report. Clearly, the opposing attorney cannot cross-examine the report, so unless the scientist who wrote it is present in court, the report would have to stand on its own. Many states have provisions in their laws that permit the admission of lab reports if both sides stipulate (agree). Other states require the author of the report to be present in court if the report is to be admitted as evidence. In some states, lab reports are admissible as a *business records* exception to the hearsay rule. This exception provides for the admission of records that are made in the regular course of business. They are deemed to be reliable because accurate records are essential to the functioning of a business. The U.S. Supreme Court has recently taken up some cases to decide under what circumstances a laboratory report may be admissible on its own, without supporting testimony by its author.

Sometimes, a laboratory report can play a crucial role in a trial. Over the course of a year, a forensic scientist may perform thousands of examinations on hundreds or thousands of cases. It is not unusual for a drug chemist to analyze more than 100 cases per month. Many of them are routine cases containing cocaine, marihuana, heroin, etc. Most of these cases will never be called to court and those that do may not be tried for 1–2 years later. When an old case does come to trial, the scientist may not remember working on that specific case. The only evidence that he or she analyzed the case is his or her notes and the laboratory report. In such situations, the best evidence of the analysis of the evidence is not the scientist, but the lab report! This situation is illustrated below.

Past Recollection Refreshed

Consider the case where a forensic scientist is in court to testify about a case involving the possession of cocaine. He or she analyzed this evidence 18 months ago and has since analyzed hundreds of other cocaine cases and other types of drug cases. He or she wrote a report detailing her findings in this case and has the notes he or she took at the time he or she did her analysis. During direct examination, the prosecutor shows her a bag containing the drug evidence and he asks her if he or she can remember analyzing this evidence. He or she answers that she cannot remember working on this specific bag of white powder. The prosecutor then shows her the lab report that she wrote that details her work on the case, and he asks her if she can now remember working on this case. If the lab report triggers her memory, then she can testify about the case. This is called "past recollection refreshed." The report and notes trigger her memory of the particular case, and then, she can remember analyzing it. Sometimes, having the report and notes is still not enough to refresh the scientist's memory. This gives rise to another possible remedy.

Past Recollection Recorded

If the scientist cannot remember doing the case even after looking at his or her report and his or her notes, then he or she cannot testify about the case but his or her lab report and notes can be admitted as a proof of the facts therein. The report is clearly the most reliable evidence about the case. This is called "past recollection recorded." This means that at the time of the analysis, the scientist took notes and wrote the report. As long as the notes and report can be linked unequivocally to the evidence in court, the report can be used as evidence that the evidence was analyzed even if the scientist cannot remember doing that analysis.

Expert Testimony

So far in this chapter, you have learned that there are two types of real evidence: scientific and nonscientific. There are also two types of witnesses that can offer testimony in court: *expert* and *nonexpert (lay)* witnesses. Different rules govern the types of testimony these witnesses are permitted to offer. A lay witness can only testify to matters that he or she witnessed. In this sense, the term "witnessed" means that a person can testify to what they experienced with their five senses (as long as the evidence is relevant and competent). In general, lay witnesses are not permitted to offer opinions except those that any juror would understand and agree with. For example, a lay witness is permitted to testify that it was cold outside when he or she saw the suspect leave the bank. He or she could not, however, testify that a man who was driving erratically was drunk because that would require an expert opinion.

Federal Rule 702, which is reproduced earlier, defines an expert witness as "a witness qualified as an expert by knowledge, skill, experience, training, or education."

This statement has several implications. First, the witness must be *qualified as an expert*. This is the judge's responsibility. In a trial, either party can decide that it wants to offer testimony by an expert. The witness is brought into court and the party offering him or her as an expert will ask questions about his or her qualifications to be an expert and the areas of his or her expertise. The other party will then have the opportunity to *voir dire* or challenge the witness. This is a French term that means "to speak the truth." After this, the judge will accept or reject the witness as an expert and indicate the areas of expertise. Note that FRE 702 doesn't require an expert to be a PhD or to be qualified solely by education. Consider the following scenario:

A man is killed in an automobile crash when he loses control of his car on a steep mountain road. A witness who was following the victim's car noticed that its brake lights were on most of the time but the car did not appear to be slowing down. After the crash, the car is taken to a repair facility for inspection.

Suppose an acquaintance of the victim were accused of tampering with the brakes so that the man would be killed. If there were a trial, then an important issue would be what caused the brakes to fail. How would this be determined? It would do little good to have the jury inspect its brakes because the average juror does not possess the knowledge needed to determine if and how the brakes failed. An expert would be needed to examine the brakes and *offer an expert opinion* about the condition of the brakes. This expert would be a brake mechanic who may have a high school education but who has many years of experience repairing brakes and may have taken classes that specifically addressed issues in how to diagnose and repair malfunctioning brakes. Experience can be just as important as formal education in qualifying an expert. Notice that the expert's testimony in this case consists of opinions about the condition of the brakes. The expert examines the brakes and then draws inferences (conclusions) about what caused them to fail. These inferences are beyond the knowledge of the average person. Therein lies another way of defining an expert witness: a person who is qualified to draw inferences from facts that the average person cannot.

This discussion has highlighted two important differences between an expert witness and a lay witness:

1. An expert witness must be qualified as an expert every time he or she testifies in court.
2. An expert witness is permitted to offer opinions, whereas a lay witness generally cannot.

Sometimes, an expert witness is required to offer an opinion even if he or she would rather not. This is often accomplished in the form of a *hypothetical question*. This tactic is used when an attorney wishes to ask a question that would ordinarily not be permitted. Consider the following situation:

A forensic pathologist is testifying about the death of a young child. The father has been charged with homicide, specifically for beating the child. The father claims that the child accidentally fell down the stairs. The prosecutor would like to ask the pathologist if the father beat the child, but that question is for the jury to decide and would not be permitted. Instead, the prosecutor will ask the witness to assume (hypothetically) certain facts, in this case, the exact pattern of injuries that the child sustained. Then, the prosecutor would ask for an opinion about whether these injuries are consistent with the child being beaten by a strong adult or they did likely arise from the child falling down the stairs. The prosecutor is counting on the jury to make the connection between the hypothetical set of circumstances and the real circumstances of the case.

Expert Witness in Court

Being an effective witness in court requires that one follows certain guidelines about behavior and comportment in court. A few of the more important rules are given here. Some of them apply to all witnesses, whereas others are for expert witnesses:

- All witnesses are called to a trial with a *subpoena*. This is an order to appear in court for a specific matter on a specific date. A judge signs it. Ignoring a subpoena can put one in contempt of court and result in a jail sentence. For an expert witness, a *subpoena duces tecum* is usually issued. This commands the witness to produce all documents that are relevant to the case. This would include all reports, charts, graphs, and notes produced by the witness during the analysis of the evidence.
- When not testifying, all witnesses are usually sequestered and are not permitted in the court room until they are called to testify. This is accomplished by one party or the other, invoking the *rule on witnesses*. Witnesses are instructed not to discuss the case or their testimony while in the waiting room.
- Court testimony by any witness consists of *direct examination* conducted by the party who has requested the witness and *cross-examination* conducted by the other party. This may be followed up by redirect and then recross and so on until both parties have finished asking questions.
- Expert witnesses may consult their notes or reports during testimony, but either attorney may inspect any documents they refer to in court.
- In a jury trial, it is good practice to look at the attorney when being asked a question, but one should focus on the jury when answering the question. If it is a bench trial, then the witness should look at the judge when answering. This is especially important for expert witnesses. Their testimony is most effective when they have established a rapport with the trier of fact.
- Expert witnesses are often called upon to explain complicated scientific or technical matters. It is easy to slip into the language or jargon of the trade. This language would be understood by other experts in the field but not by the average person. It is very important that an expert witness explain difficult concepts using language that the average person would understand.
- All witnesses would do well to remember that a jury or judge is free to give whatever weight they choose to witnesses' testimony. Just because someone is qualified by the judge to be an expert doesn't mean that the jury is required to believe what the witness says.

Bias in the Presentation of Forensic Evidence in Court

In 2004, a train station in Madrid, Spain, was bombed. Many people were killed. The Madrid Police immediately considered this to be an act of terrorism and began to seek out possible suspects. As part of the investigation, they recovered a partial fingerprint from the station and submitted a photograph of the print to the U.S. FBI and asked the bureau to conduct a search of its Automated Fingerprint Identification System (AFIS) to see whether any known terrorists came up on the database (see the chapter on fingerprints for more information on AFIS). An AFIS search normally returns the top 10 or so hits in its database; the closest matches to the submitted fingerprint. A search of the AFIS system yielded one Brandon Mayfield as the fourth best match. Mr. Mayfield was an attorney in the Portland, Oregon, area who had recently converted to Islam and whose wife was Egyptian born. These facts along with the similarities of Mayfield's prints to the print recovered in the bombing led to his being a person of interest in the investigation. An FBI examiner conducted an examination of his prints against the lifted print. No other known fingerprints of any other suspect were examined during this time. The FBI examiner concluded that the print lifted from the scene in Madrid matched one of Mr. Mayfield's prints, and he was subsequently arrested for the bombing. He protested his innocence and hired an attorney to help him. Wanting to protect against an error, the FBI had another examiner compare the prints in question. He was given the case file *including the report of the first examiner.* He supported the conclusion of the first examiner. Then, the file and prints were given to a third FBI examiner. The file included the reports of the first two examiners. The third examiner confirmed the conclusions of the first two.

Mr. Mayfield's attorney then retained the services of an independent expert fingerprint examiner to reexamine the print evidence. He was given access to all of the FBI files on the fingerprint examinations including the conclusions of the three Bureau examiners. Not surprisingly, he confirmed the conclusions of those examiners that Mayfield left the print at the Madrid bombing.

While these examinations were taking place in the United States, the Madrid and Spanish Police were continuing their investigation of the bombing. They were very skeptical of Mayfield's involvement and ultimately arrested a known terrorist suspect for the crime. His fingerprint was a spot on match for the print lifted from the scene. When informed of this development, the FBI sent a fingerprint team to Madrid to examine the fingerprint evidence. They concurred with the conclusions reached by the Spanish Police. Mayfield was released from custody. He was ultimately successful in a wrongful arrest lawsuit filed against the FBI, collecting millions of dollars in damages. Figure 24.2 shows the partial fingerprint lifted from the scene by the Madrid Police as well as the fingerprints from Mayfield and the suspect that the Madrid Police had arrested, which were used for comparison.

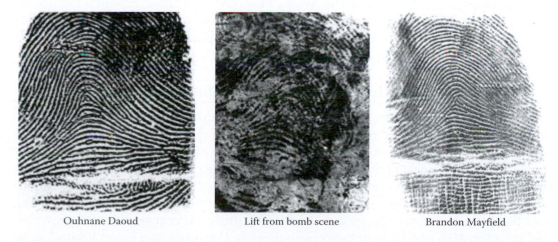

Ouhnane Daoud   Lift from bomb scene   Brandon Mayfield

Figure 24.2 Fingerprints from the Madrid bombing case. The print in the middle is a photograph of the partial fingerprint lifted from the bombing scene. The others are exemplars taken from Mayfield and Daoud.

The aforementioned case (and others like it) is an example of a *confirmational bias*. This arises from cases where one investigator or examiner confirms the conclusions of another, and it can be shown that part of the reason for the confirmation was the second examiner's knowledge of the conclusions reached by the first examiner. Confirmational bias is just one type of bias that has been shown to have sometimes severe repercussions in forensic analysis and many other types of scientific examinations. Another important type that occurs more frequently and can be more insidious is the so-called cognitive bias. This type of bias occurs when an examiner is in possession of knowledge about the case or investigation that may cause him or her to bias his or her analysis or conclusions toward or against this knowledge. An example of this in forensic science was reported by Dr. Itiel Dror in the United Kingdom. Five volunteer fingerprint examiners were each given different known and unknown fingerprints for comparison. Along with the prints, they received made-up case scenarios that described the circumstances under which the prints were obtained. Using this information, the examiners each reached conclusions about the associations of the unknowns to the knowns. Unbeknownst to the examiners, each of them had received the same evidence in previous casework along with information about the real circumstances that generated the print evidence. The circumstances given them by the researchers were purposely at odds with the original information. The result was that three of the five examiners changed their conclusions to comport to the new information. One did not change his conclusions and the fifth changed his conclusion from a match to inconclusive.

This research illustrates the damaging effects that knowing too much about a case can bias the conclusions reached by the examiner. Cognitive bias is well-known by the scientific community at large. The U.S. Food and Drug Administration, for example, requires *double-blind* testing of all proposed new pharmaceuticals before they will agree to permit them to be dispensed to the public. Double-blind testing refers to a methodology whereby a group of people who suffer from the disease or disorder that a new drug is supposed to affect is divided into two groups; one will get the new drug and the other will get a placebo (a fake dosage that looks like the authentic drug). Neither the participants in the study nor the scientists who are administering the drug or placebo know which participants are getting which. This will minimize the chance of cognitive bias influencing the results of the trial. The NAS Forensic Science Committee heard from Dr. Dror and others about cognitive and confirmational bias and felt that this was an area that needed study. Recommendation 5 calls for research on the general topic of human observer bias.

Something for You to Do: A Mock Trial

A mock trial is an excellent class project. The class can be divided into teams. The project may begin with a mock crime scene where members of the team collect evidence and perhaps even analyze it. Then, the team is divided up for the trial. There will be a prosecutor, a defense attorney, one or more government expert witnesses, and one or more defense expert witnesses. The prosecution team will prepare expert testimony about the evidence that was collected and analyzed, and the defense team will prepare to cross-examine the government's expert(s) and counter with expert testimony of their own. Someone can be appointed to be the judge and other members of the class can be the jury. At the end of the trial, the jury can vote to determine whether the defendant is guilty.

Summary

Scientific and technical evidence is treated differently than nontechnical evidence in our courts because it is difficult to understand by laypersons and because it has an aura of reliability by its very nature. The rules of evidence determine how and when evidence shall be admitted into court. Scientific evidence must obey all of these rules plus additional ones that have been developed by court cases such as *Daubert* and *Frye* as well as the federal and state rules of evidence. Laboratory reports of forensic scientific analysis can be important evidence in criminal and civil cases. They are the written record, along with the scientist's notes, of how a case was analyzed. If a scientist cannot remember doing the case, the report may be the best evidence.

Expert witnesses are treated differently in court than are nonexpert or lay witnesses. An expert must be qualified every time he or she testifies by reciting his or her qualifications. He or she is then subject to cross-examination on those qualifications (*voir dire*). The judge decides if that person can testify as an expert in that case. A person can be an expert by any appropriate combination of knowledge, skills, experience, and education.

Test Yourself

Multiple Choice

1. *Voir dire* is
    a. A French court
    b. A type of cross-examination about witnesses' qualifications
    c. A set of expert witness qualifications
    d. A famous case that helped shaped the rules for the admissibility of scientific evidence
2. A person can be qualified as an expert on the basis of
    a. Experience
    b. Education
    c. Knowledge
    d. Skills
    e. All of the above
3. In *Daubert v. Merrell Dow*, the U.S. Supreme Court set out some criteria for testing the scientific validity of a scientific method or technique. Which of the following is *not* one of those criteria?
    a. Peer review
    b. Whether anyone has ever offered testimony in a federal court on this topic
    c. General acceptance of the scientific principle
    d. Error rates of the technique
    e. Falsifiability of the underlying theory
4. Which of the following applies to all types of testimony?
    a. Relevance
    b. *Frye v. United States*
    c. *Daubert v. Merrell Dow*
    d. FRE 702

5. Relevance consists of
   a. Competence + admissibility
   b. Materiality + probativeness
   c. Materiality + competence
   d. Hearsay + constitutional constrains

6. Which of the following is not a type of competence (criterion for admissibility of evidence)?
   a. Relevance
   b. Obeys fourth amendment of the Constitution
   c. Prejudice
   d. Privileges

7. In *Daubert v. Merrell Dow*
   a. Mrs. Daubert prevailed because Merrell Dow's experts failed to prove that Bendectin doesn't cause birth defects.
   b. Merrell Dow prevailed because Daubert's epidemiologists didn't use scientifically valid methods for applying statistics to their data about Bendectin.
   c. The U.S. Supreme Court refused to hear the appeal of the trial court.
   d. The U.S. Supreme Court reversed the trial court's decision and awarded Mrs. Daubert damages for Bendectin's harm to her baby.

8. In *Frye v. United States*
   a. The trial court judge admitted the results of the systolic blood pressure deception test but he was reversed by the Court of Appeals.
   b. Frye was found not guilty of murder.
   c. The Court of Appeals set a standard of "general acceptance by the relevant scientific community" for the admissibility of scientific evidence.
   d. The U.S. Supreme Court ruled that the results of the deception test were inadmissible because of the decision in *Daubert v. Merrell Dow*.

9. Scientific laboratory reports
   a. Are never admissible in court
   b. May be admissible in some states if both sides agree
   c. Cannot be the included in a subpoena of a witness
   d. Cannot be viewed in court by anyone other than the scientist who wrote it
   e. Are always admissible in court as a *business records exception* to the hearsay rule

10. There are extra rules that govern the admissibility of scientific and technical evidence because
    a. Juries must be protected from junk science and unreliable or invalid science
    b. Only PhDs can offer expert testimony
    c. The U.S. Supreme Court ruled in *Frye v. United States* that scientific evidence must have extra rules
    d. Courts ruled as far back as medieval times in England that scientific evidence must be accorded special treatment

True–False

11. If evidence is probative, it is always admissible.
12. Properly signed laboratory reports are always admissible in court with our without the author's presence.
13. If a client makes a guilty admission to his or her attorney in private, the attorney cannot be compelled to testify against the client.

14. *Daubert v. Merrell Dow* is an example of a toxic tort case.
15. The *general acceptance* rule was developed in the *Frye* case.
16. An expert witness must have a college degree to be qualified to testify in court.
17. A judge can never be the trier of fact.

Matching

18. Federal Rule 702   a. Legal constraint on admissibility of evidence
19. *Daubert v. Merrell Dow*   b. Congressional rule concerning scientific evidence
20. *Frye v.* United States   c. Probativeness + materiality
21. Competence   d. Set out general acceptance rule
22. Relevance   e. Set out scientific validity standard for evidence

Short Essay

23. What are the two major criteria for the admissibility of evidence? Give an example of each.
24. How does an expert witness differ from a lay witness?
25. Why are there special rules for the admissibility of scientific or technical evidence?

Further Reading

Giannelli, P. C. (1996). *Snyder Rules of Evidence Handbook: Ohio Practice 1996*. West Information Pub Group, New York.

Kiely, T. F. (2001). *Forensic Evidence: Science and the Criminal Law*. CRC Press, Boca Raton, FL.

Moessens, A. A., Starrs, J. E., Henderson, C. E., and F. E. Inbau. (1995). *Scientific Evidence in Civil and Criminal Cases*, 4th edn. Foundation Press, New York.

On the Web

A brief analysis of the *Frye* case: http://www.daubertontheweb.com/frye_opinion.htm.

Complete Federal Rules of Evidence: http://www.law.cornell.edu/rules/fre/.

Excellent explanation of expert qualifications and testimony by Paul C. Giannelli: http://www.scientific.org/distribution/law-review/giannelli.pdf.

The complete U.S. Supreme Court opinion in *Daubert v. Merrell Dow*: http://supct.law.cornell.edu/supct/html/92-102.ZO.html.

Index

A

AAFS, *see* American Academy of Forensic Sciences (AAFS)
Absorption
  of drugs, 470–471
  of ethanol
    bloodstream, circulation in, 476–477
    elimination, 477
    maximum BAC, 477–479
  of infrared energy, 114
Absorption elution method, 545–546
Abused drugs, *see* Illicit drugs
Accelerant detector dog (ADD), 160
Accelerants, 540–541, 543–544
  analysis of, 547–548
  detection and collection, 544
Accidental death, 313–314
Accident reconstruction, 189
  accident scale drawing, 201–202
  drag factor, 200
  education and training, 199
  ETWS, 200–202
  law enforcement accident reconstructionist, 199
  motor vehicle accident, 199
  police drag sled, 200
  postscene analysis
    "black box," 206
    car's rear disc brakes, 204–205
    defective rear drum brakes, 204, 206
    DUI determination, 207
    GPS, 207
    hot shock, 206–207
    intoxication, 207
    multivehicle chain reaction incident, 207–208
    road and weather conditions, 207
    seatbelt/shoulder harness restraint mechanism, 204–205
    tire marks, 202–203
    yaw marks, 202–203
  sensitive evidence, 199
  skid mark analysis, 200–201
  vehicular collisions and physics, 198
  Vericom VC3000 Brake Test Computer, 200–201
Acetaldehyde, 477
Acetic acid, 477
Addiction, drugs, 445, 448, 474
Adobe Photoshop®, 46
AFIS, *see* Automated Fingerprint Identification System (AFIS)

Agglutination, 375–376
Air-filled (pneumatic) tire, 238
Air scenting, 157
Alcohol, 317–318
  BAC (*see* Blood alcohol concentration (BAC))
  in beer and wine, 475–476
  bloodstream, circulation in, 476–477
  bootlegging, 475
  chemical structure, 475
  drunk driving laws (*see* Drunk driving)
  elimination of, 477
  isopropyl alcohol, 475
  methyl alcohol, 475
  neurotoxin, 475
  proof, 474
  in spirits, 475
Algor mortis, 319–320
Alpha-amylase test, 379
Altered bloodstain patterns, 384, 386–387
Alveoli, 470
American Academy of Forensic Sciences (AAFS), 14, 18
American Heritage Dictionary, 170
American Journal of Police Science, 14
American Registry of Professional Entomologists (ARPE), 354
American Society of Crime Laboratory Directors (ASCLD), 18
Ammonium nitrate and fuel oil (ANFO), 549–550
Ammunition
  digital imaging systems, 294–295
  shotgun, 286
Amphetamine, 115, 452
Amplified fragment length polymorphisms (AMP-FLPs), 408
Anatomic pathology, 309
Angel dust, *see* Phencyclidine (PCP)
Anthropologists, 329–330
Anthropology, forensic, 8–9
  anthropologists, role of, 329–330
  bone evidence, collection of, 342
  bone trauma, 340
  definition, 329
  facial reconstructions, 340–342
  human skeleton
    anterior view of, 330
    bone structure, 331–332
    marrow, 331–332
  photographic superimposition, 340–341, 346
  skeletal remains, identification of age, 333–336

  biological profile, 333–334
  gender, 336–338
  individual characteristics, 332
  race, 338
  stature, 338–340
  in wooded setting, 332
Anthropometry, 219
Artistic paints, 499
ASCLD, *see* American Society of Crime Laboratory Directors (ASCLD)
Automated Fingerprint Identification System (AFIS), 233, 574–575
Autopsy
  chemical cause deaths, 317–319
  definition of, 314
  distribution of deaths, 314
  electrical deaths, 319
  external examination, 315
  hyperthermia, 319
  hypothermia, 319
  injury patterns, 315
  internal examination, 315
  mechanical cause deaths, 316–318
  physical evidence, search for, 315
  religious limitations, 314

B

BAC, *see* Blood alcohol concentration (BAC)
Backscattered electrons, 141
Ballistics, 282
Barbiturates, 318, 452–453
BATF, *see* Bureau of Alcohol, Tobacco, Firearms and Explosives (BATF)
Becke line, 524–525
Behavioral forensic sciences, 11–12
Bench trial, 564
Best evidence rule, 252–253
Bioanthropology, 329
Black powder, 288, 290, 549
Block polymers, 489
Blood alcohol concentration (BAC), 475–476
  absorption, 477
  breath testing instruments, 475
  elimination, 477
  gas chromatography, 482
  volume, 479
  Widmark curve, 478–479
Blood evidence, 387–388
  antibodies, 372, 375
  antigens, 372, 375